S0-AHK-125

Corporate Financial Decisions

James C. T. Mao
University of British Columbia

Corporate Financial Decisions

Pavan Publishers
Palo Alto, California

658.15
M 296

166935

Pavan

Copyright © 1976 by James C. T. Mao

All rights reserved. No part of this publication may be reproduced, stored in a retrieval system, or transmitted, in any form or by any means, electronic, mechanical, photocopying, recording, or otherwise, without the prior written permission of the publisher.

Library of Congress Catalog Card No. 75–18149
ISBN 0–915944–00–6

PAVAN PUBLISHERS
P. O. BOX 1661
PALO ALTO, CALIFORNIA 94302

Printed in the United States of America
10 9 8 7 6 5 4 3 2 1

Preface

This in an introductory textbook on corporation finance, written in the belief that many of the skills characterizing the successful executive can be learned in the classroom. Like other business managers, the financial executive is above all a decision-maker. For this reason, the major emphasis in the book is on a clear definition of the problems facing the financial executive, and on development of analytical tools for solving these problems. Decisions, however, are not made in a vacuum; a knowledge of financial institutions and practices is necessary to help formulate ideas and solutions. Therefore, both theory and practice are stressed, in order to aid the student in developing his talents toward practical decision-making.

In this book, I take up a wide range of problems a financial executive might encounter. In each case, I try to define the problem from the financial executive's viewpoint, and then present the most feasible method for solving it. A sophisticated theoretical model may fail the test of feasibility if it is too difficult or too time-consuming to apply, or if it requires more data than a businessman would have available. Very often, some adaptation is necessary to make such a model readily applicable. My approach here is to present those theories that can be most directly applied to actual problems of financial management.

With this in mind, I make a special effort to integrate theory and practice. For the last few years, I have been interviewing financial executives at all levels and in many different industries. My objective was to discover how they viewed their problems, what data they had available, and what tools they used to solve the problems. My interviews covered not only the areas of fixed and current asset management, but also the problems of capital structure and financing methods, as well as many other aspects of corporate policy. At several places in the book, the information I gathered is presented quite explicitly, while in others it guides the approaches I have adopted.

Because this is a textbook, I have included certain pedagogical features to make the book more useful as a learning device. These include numerical examples illustrating basic principles; case materials showing the relevance of theory; avoidance of complicated mathematics; and review questions and problems for the student to check his own understanding. Included also, in a separate appendix, is a set of computer programs as an aid to decision-making (e.g., forecasting financial statements, calculating rates of return, and leasing vs. borrowing). These programs have all been pre-tested for easy application.

As in any book of this kind, I am indebted to all writers who have contributed to the literature of finance. I am grateful as well to the many business executives whom I interviewed or corresponded with, for their willingness and patience in sharing their knowledge and experience with me. Also, I wish to thank those companies which provided me directly with data, or gave permission to reproduce materials from their publications. In addition, the editors of several journals gave me similar permission to use quotations and data from their publications.

I have used the material in this book in both undergraduate and graduate classes and have asked my students for ideas on possible improvements, many of which have been incorporated into the book. I am also indebted to my research assistants who helped in various ways. David Inhofe provided valuable assistance in preparing the computer programs. Julie Kaufman, my editor, greatly improved the clarity and style of the manuscript. Finally, I would like to express my appreciation for the facilities and assistance provided me by Stanford University, where much of this book was written.

James C. T. Mao

Contents

Part One

Introduction

1 The Finance Function

Corporations are turning increasingly toward financial executives to fill their top positions. In a recent study, *Forbes* discovered that of 774 chief executives surveyed, 41 percent had earlier experience principally in finance and administration, more than twice the number drawn from any other area.[1] General Motors, General Electric, and Sun Oil are all companies with former financial men at the top. The rise of the financial executive in the corporate hierarchy is a reflection of the growing importance of the function he performs. In the early 1970's, corporations experienced tight and costly capital, which caused increased pressure to manage existing assets more efficiently and to ration new capital more carefully. This is not to say that corporations were not previously concerned with optimizing financing and investment decisions; the difference is that money in the seventies is no longer as cheap and easy as it was in the sixties and that new theories of financial management developed by academicians have now been, for the most part, assimilated by business management. Tight money and new financial theories have forced the financial executive to play a greater role in corporate decision-making.

The finance function, like any other business function, is in a continuous state of evolution. The aspiring financial executive needs to know not only the present duties and responsibilities of a financial executive, but also what his duties and responsibilities are likely to be in the future. Because financial management is undergoing changes brought about by the application of economic theory, statistical analysis, management science, and the

[1] "Chief Executive Roster," *Forbes* (May 15, 1972), pp. 205–236.

computer, forecasting the role of tomorrow's financial executive is not easy. Fortunately, this problem has already received attention from financial theorists and top business executives. Therefore, although we cannot predict the future of financial management with certainty, we can at least indicate the probable trends. Let us consider the views of the businessman first, then those of the academician, and finally compare the two.

THE NEW FINANCE FUNCTION

The Business View

In recent articles, several top-level executives have identified planning and control as the critical aspects of the financial executive's function.[2] In the past, the basic duties of the financial executive were limited: insure sufficient available cash to meet bills and maturing obligations; keep accounts of the activities of the company; and protect the firm's assets by means of internal control and auditing. In the future, the financial executive will still have these responsibilities, but he must also participate in the formulation, execution, and control of top-level policy decisions. His judgment is now sought on such matters as product development, pricing policy, capital budgeting, financial structure, dividend policy, mergers and acquisitions, and recapitalization and reorganization. This wider involvement requires that in addition to his expertise in finance, he must be aware of the marketing and product implications of his decisions.

This view of the finance function stresses the financial executive's analytical objectivity. Since he is not involved directly in production or marketing, he is able to assess all aspects of the firm's operations from the perspective of the whole. His position makes him ideally suited to evaluate alternative courses of action and to develop the necessary systems of control. This planning and control is the primary concern of the executives referred to.

The Academic View

The business view of the new finance function has a counterpart in the writings of the theorists. During the 1950's, the traditionally vocational orientation of business education gave way to a more scientific professional curriculum incorporating aspects of the social sciences, modern mathematics, and statistics. At the same time, the emphasis in teaching shifted from description to analysis; and basic research on business theory and prac-

---

[2] See the articles by Ray W. Macdonald, A. Carl Kotchian, and Alfredo Amescua R. in the *Financial Executive,* cited in the chapter-end references.

tice assumed new importance. Professor Ezra Solomon was asked by the Ford Foundation to document these changes in order to accelerate the dissemination of this material among the teachers and students of finance. The result of that study is *The Theory of Financial Management* (1963) in which Solomon defines the finance function as the study of the problems involved in the use and acquisition of funds by a business.[3] His main concern is to provide a rational basis for answering these three questions:

1. What is the total volume of funds that should be invested in the business; i.e., what size and growth rate should the firm aim to achieve?
2. What specific assets should the company acquire, i.e., in what form should assets be held?
3. How should the required funds be financed; i.e., how should the liability side of the balance sheet be composed?

Do They Differ?

Solomon's definition is in basic agreement with the business view as we have described it. He stresses capital-expenditures decisions which involve the commitment of large sums of money over long periods of time and are therefore obviously crucial in setting the future course of the firm. Moreover, in order to answer each of the three questions Solomon asks, the financial executive must look into the future, forecast costs and benefits, and, taking cognizance of uncertainty, compare the relative merits of alternative courses of action against the overall goals of the firm. In other words, planning and control, which the business view stresses, are inherent in Solomon's concept.

Although both views are concerned with the future, there are two differences between Solomon's concept and that of the business executives. First, in their discussions of the planning and control function, business executives have in mind both short- and long-term planning: the day-to-day operations as well as the major capital-expenditures and financing decisions that usually arise less frequently. This short-term planning, sometimes known as "profit planning," encompasses the pricing, volume-of-output, and product-mix decisions. Since these decisions affect the firm's income, expenses, and cash flow, they must necessarily be an integral part of any short-term planning and control. Solomon, however, does not explicitly discuss short-term planning, although we may assume that he recognizes the importance of such planning.

---

[3] Ezra Solomon, *The Theory of Financial Management* (New York: Columbia University Press, 1963), p. 8.

The second area mentioned by business executives, but not by Solomon, is asset and liability management. Asset management refers to the control and utilization of the firm's existing resources: cash and marketable securities, accounts receivable, inventory, and plant and equipment. Given a firm's investments, its profitability depends on how efficiently its assets are utilized. Similarly, liability management refers to the control and adjustment of the firm's outstanding liabilities: accounts payable, commercial paper, bank loans, long-term bonds, and financial leases. Given the firm's indebtedness, management can often reduce the cost of borrowing by being alert to market opportunities and through improved internal procedures. A body of knowledge now exists about improved methods of asset and liability management. Because of its importance, asset and liability management deserves to be identified as a separate area of the finance function.

For the purposes of this book, we shall enlarge Solomon's definition of the finance function to incorporate profit planning and asset and liability management. By financial management, then, we mean solving the problems involved in asset and liability management, planning day-to-day operations, as well as making the firm's financing and investment decisions. All this is done with the aim of attaining the optimal size and growth rate of the firm, the most suitable combination of assets, and the best method of financing the required funds.

THE TRADITIONAL VIEW OF FINANCE

Whereas the new view of finance stresses the optimization of financial decisions, the traditional approach focused on the description of institutions, techniques, and instruments. This difference is reflected in the predominantly analytical and theoretical content of the new finance as compared with the generally descriptive and institutional aspects of the traditional approach.

In order to see the traditional view in its proper perspective, let us briefly trace the development of the study of financial management as an academic discipline. Financial management, or corporate finance, was originally studied as a minor aspect of the economics of a firm. By the turn of the century, however, as John A. Griswold points out, the complexity of American business brought about a need for systematic study of detailed financial problems and processes.[4] Finance was one of the first specialties to be differentiated from economics, and this happened when the first business schools were established. Still, corporation finance was not conceived in the terms it is today. Since the central concern of economics at

[4] John A. Griswold, "Finance," in Frank C. Pierson and others, *The Education of American Businessmen* (New York: McGraw-Hill Book Company, Inc., 1959), p, 393.

the time was with institutions and institutional arrangements, it is not surprising that the study of corporation finance took a legalistic, descriptive, and institutional flavor, focusing on instruments and practices. Thus, Edward S. Mead, the author of one of the earliest textbooks on corporation finance, states his purpose as:

> . . . to explain and illustrate the methods employed in the promotion, capitalization, financial management, consolidation and reorganization of business corporations.[5]

This trend toward an emphasis on institutions and practices was reinforced in a second popular text when Hastings Lyon stated that it was:

> . . . the duty of anyone undertaking a presentation of any aspect of the subject to steer a course between the legal and the accounting sides of corporate business.[6]

Although the initial emphasis that economics placed on institutions explains why corporation finance started out as institutional and descriptive, it does not explain why corporation finance remained so, while economics moved increasingly toward theory and analysis. Solomon offers a plausible reason: the publication in 1920 of Arthur S. Dewing's *The Financial Policy of Corporations*.[7] Using a descriptive-legalistic-institutional approach, this book firmly established the position of the traditional approach that was to last until the early 1950's. This definitive and scholarly text provided a structure for courses and remained the major text in the field for decades.

An examination of Dewing's book shows that approximately one third of it is concerned with the types of corporate securities and their marketing, one fourth with corporate bankruptcy and reorganization, often in legal terms, another quarter with the episodic events of corporate mergers, consolidations, and combinations; and the remainder with the accounting of depreciation and its implications for dividend policy. Even though there were five editions, the latest in 1953, Dewing's revisions did not affect his basic approach.

Although his work remains an excellent statement of the traditional approach to finance, Dewing's discussion is inadequate in terms of current concepts; he does not discuss several issues which are central to contemporary theory. He does not, for example, consider how much capital

---

[5] Edward S. Mead, *Corporation Finance* (New York: D. Appleton and Company, Inc., 1910), p. viii.

[6] Hastings Lyon, *Corporation Finance* (Boston: Houghton Mifflin Company, 1916), p. iii.

[7] Solomon, *op. cit.*, p. 5. Arthur S. Dewing was a professor of finance at Harvard University from 1911 to 1933. The following discussion is based on Dewing's first edition of *The Financial Policy of Corporations* (New York: The Ronald Press Company, 1920).

should be invested in a firm or how it should be allocated among various assets, nor does he explicitly treat the effect of an increased proportion of debt financing on both the value of the firm and the cost of capital to the firm. Moreover, he fails to consider the possible effect of dividend policy on the firm's value; instead, his discussion concentrates on the accounting and legal aspects of dividend policy. In general, the traditional approach, as exemplified by Dewing, focuses rather narrowly on the acquisition of funds, accepting the investment decisions as given, whereas the new approach also considers the optimal level and composition of investment.

THE TRANSITION TO THE NEW FINANCE

Although the traditional approach was generally accepted for many years, there was some dissatisfaction among financial writers. Criticism centered on the underemphasis on working capital management and the overly descriptive, rather than analytic, content. But there were no major changes until the mid-1950's.

At that time, several important new contributions to the literature of finance appeared, initiating a period of change and determining the course to be taken in the study of finance for the next twenty years. There may be some controversy as to which works were the most important in initiating the change, but we shall consider two publications: the famous 1958 article by Franco Modigliani and Merton H. Miller on the relationship between a firm's debt-to-equity ratio (capital structure) and the price it must pay to attract funds (cost of capital);[8] and Harry M. Markowitz's 1959 book on portfolio selection, which attempted to explain why and how investors diversify their security portfolios.[9] The development of the new finance also derived considerable impetus from the application of management science, but it would be difficult to single out any one of the many articles on the subject.

The significance of Modigliani and Miller's article is that it touched off the cost-of-capital controversy: whether or not the cost of capital is affected by the firm's capital structure. According to Modigliani and Miller, the cost of capital depends only on the business risk of the firm—for example, whether the firm is an aircraft manufacturer or a public utility. The overall cost does not depend on the relative proportion of debt and equity financing since the lower nominal cost of debt financing tends to be offset by the increasing cost of equity financing. The traditional theorists, however, disagree with Modigliani and Miller. They contend that debt financing can

---

[8] Franco Modigliani and Merton H. Miller, "The Cost of Capital, Corporation Finance and the Theory of Investment," *American Economic Review* 48 (June, 1958), pp. 261–297.

[9] Harry M. Markowitz, *Portfolio Selection: Efficient Diversification of Investments* (New York: John Wiley and Sons, Inc., 1959).

reduce the overall cost of capital to a firm, provided that total borrowing is held to a reasonable amount. As we shall see, Modigliani and Miller reached their conclusion by assuming a perfect capital market where there is unlimited competition, no taxes and no risk of bankruptcy. When these simplifying assumptions are dropped, it is now generally agreed that the debt-to-equity ratio in capital structure does affect a firm's cost of capital.

Markowitz's book is significant because of its relevance to capital budgeting within a firm and, in a broader context, its implications for the valuation of securities under uncertainty. Markowitz was originally concerned with how an individual investor faced with different securities with uncertain returns should allocate his money in order to maximize the rate of return at any given level of risk. His contribution was to formulate this investment decision as a problem in portfolio selection. The implications of such a model for business finance are obvious: a firm, like an individual, is faced with different investments with uncertain returns and wants to pick a portfolio that will maximize return at a given level of risk. Markowitz's model has also provided the theoretical basis on which other writers have constructed their theories of security valuation under uncertainty.[10] These theories explain what the demand for each stock will be, assuming all investors act in accordance with Markowitz's model. These theories are then able to relate the price of each stock to the investors' probabilistic assessment of it and to their aversion to risk.

A MODEL OF INVESTMENT DECISION-MAKING

So far, we have discussed the nature of the finance function in a very general way. In order to provide a better view, we shall now illustrate the discussion with a financial problem involving a capital-budgeting decision. Such a realistic example can help us understand the type of decision facing a financial executive, the point of view he must assume in order to make decisions, the analytical tools he employs, his position in a business organization, and his relation to other executives. An example will highlight these points more effectively than discussion.

The Problem

Our example is a capital-budgeting problem constructed by Alexander A. Robichek, Donald G. Ogilvie, and John D. C. Roach.[11] This particular problem is especially helpful since, as we shall see, capital budgeting

---

[10] See, for example, William F. Sharpe, *Portfolio Theory and Capital Markets* (New York: McGraw-Hill Book Company, 1970), especially Chapters 5 and 6.

[11] Alexander A. Robichek, Donald G. Ogilvie, and John D. C. Roach, "Capital Budgeting: A Pragmatic Approach," *Financial Executive* 37 (April, 1969), pp. 26–38.

is one of the most important decisions facing the financial executive; the example clearly illustrates how modern analytical tools can be used to help optimize financial decisions; and this problem illustrates conflicting goals and shows how they can be reconciled.

Imagine that you are the chief financial executive of Menlo, Inc. You need to know the following facts about your company:

1. It earned $500,000 after taxes for the year just ended.
2. The company is all-equity financed with 100,000 shares of common stock outstanding, so the earnings were $5 per share.
3. Management estimates that earnings for the current year before new investments will be $470,000, or $4.70 per share.
4. Total cash balance now is $1.2 million.
5. Total cash flow for the current year from existing projects is $1.13 million.

The firm now has an opportunity to invest in five projects. The cost, economic life, revenue, expenses, operating income, taxes, net income, and cash flow of each project are summarized in Table 1-1. Thus, Project A costs $100,000 now; it will generate total revenues of $140,000, $175,000, $175,000, and $175,000 at the end of the first, second, third, and fourth years respectively; and it will have total expenses of $110,000, $125,000, $125,000, and $125,000 during these years, so that the corresponding operating incomes will be $30,000, $50,000, $50,000, and $50,000. Since the tax rate is assumed to be 50 percent, the project will contribute $15,000 to the net income the first year, $25,000 the second year, $25,000 the third year, and $25,000 the fourth year. The expense figures include a $25,000 annual depreciation, which is a non-cash expense in each year. Therefore, the total cash inflow for the project is $40,000 the first year, and $50,000 in each of the following years. The figures for the other four projects should be interpreted in the same way. Table 1-2 summarizes the initial investment, first-year net income, and first-year cash flow for each of the five projects.

Table 1-2 also shows the "internal rate of return" for each project. Basically, the internal rate of return is the return the investor earns on the money put into a project calculated in an actuarial way. More technically, it is the annual rate of discount which equates the present value of the future cash flows of an investment with the cost of the investment. (We shall return to this and related concepts in Chapters 5 and 6.) For Project A, this rate is 30.4 percent, for B 45.6 percent, for C 13.5 percent, for D 24.2 percent, and for E 22.2 percent.

The financial executive must now decide which combination of these five projects the firm should invest in. As in most cases which the financial

Table 1-1 Investment Opportunities (in thousands of dollars)

Period	Investment	Total Revenues	Cash Expenses	Depreciation	Operating Income*	Taxes (50%)	Net Income	Cash Flow**
				Project A				
1	$100	$ 140	$ 85	$ 25	$ 30	$ 15	$ 15	$ 40
2		175	100	25	50	25	25	50
3		175	100	25	50	25	25	50
4		175	100	25	50	25	25	50
				Project B				
1	300	100	80	60	(40)	(20)	(20)	40
2		400	200	60	140	70	70	130
3		1,100	600	60	440	220	220	280
4		900	300	60	440	220	220	280
5		1,500	800	60	640	320	320	380
				Project C				
1	200	300	140	100	60	30	30	130
2		200	80	100	20	10	10	110
				Project D				
1	300	230	105	75	50	25	25	100
2		300	125	75	100	50	50	125
3		350	145	75	130	65	65	140
4		400	165	75	160	80	80	155
				Project E				
1	200	200	110	40	50	25	25	65
2		200	110	40	50	25	25	65
3		220	120	40	60	30	30	70
4		240	130	40	70	35	35	75
5		270	140	40	90	45	45	85

* Operating income = revenues − expenses − depreciation.
** Cash flow = net income + depreciation.
Source: Robichek, et al., *op. cit.*, p. 37.

executive will encounter, the optimal decision must be reached under constraints. That is, the projects in which the firm is to invest must be selected so that they satisfy certain conditions. For this problem, we shall assume that management has set the following goals and requirements for

Table 1-2 Summary of Investment Opportunities

	A	B	C	D	E
Initial investment (in $1,000's)	100	300	200	300	200
First year's net income (in $1,000's)	15	−20	30	25	25
First year's cash flow (in $1,000's)	40	40	130	100	65
Internal rate of return	30.4%	45.6%	13.5%	24.2%	22.2%

Source: Robichek, et al., *op. cit.*, p. 37.

the current year (we shall speak of one-year goals for simplicity; usually the goals and requirements cover a longer period of time):

1. The company would like to earn $5.30 per share, or a total of $530,000 during the current year. The new investment, therefore, must contribute at least $60,000 in first-year net income to what the company would otherwise earn.
2. The company would like to follow a 40 percent payout policy—i.e., $200,000 in dividends on last year's earnings.
3. $300,000 is needed for research and development projects.
4. Other necessary projects (e.g., safety devices, cafeteria) will require $60,000. (Note that since total cash balance is $1.2 million, $640,000 is left over for investment.)
5. The company wants a minimum cash flow of $1.3 million for the current year. We know that existing projects generate $1.13 million, so the new projects must generate $170,000 in cash flow during the current year.

Subject to these constraints, the financial executive must now decide in which projects the company should invest to maximize the overall internal rate of return.

The Solution

Robichek, Ogilvie, and Roach solved this problem by the linear programming method. Linear programming is a mathematical technique that provides optimal solutions to problems which can be put in a particular structural form. Since we shall not explain the essentials of linear programming until Chapter 4, here we shall merely report the results obtained by Robichek, Ogilvie, and Roach:

Project	A	B	C	D	E
Optimal amount	$100,000	$55,500	$0	$284,500	$200,000

(This solution assumes the projects are divisible, so that the firm can invest in each project fractionally.) If this program is adopted, the average internal rate of return will be 26.4 percent. The first-year incremental earnings will be $60,007 and the first-year cash flow generated by the program $207,230.

We should note that an internal rate of return of 26.4 percent is not the maximum which could be attained if the firm chose its projects ignoring the constraints. We know that Project B has an internal rate of return of 45.6 percent. So, if the firm were to invest only in Project B, it would earn a return of 45.6 percent on its funds. But that alternative is ruled out because, even if there were no other constraints, the current earnings and cash flow of such a program are unacceptably low.

Why would the management of Menlo, Inc., restrict their own freedom of choice by imposing constraints on the firm's capital-expenditures decisions? A simple and plausible explanation is that the firm may expect new financing. It wants its stock to sell at an attractive price and may feel that earnings growth and a liquid cash position are essential for this. In fact, some companies do use linear programming to select investment programs which will stabilize the growth rate of per-share earnings. In other situations, constraints may be imposed because of the limits of physical capacity and human resources. Other reasons for introducing constraints may also occur to the reader.

OTHER ASPECTS OF THE MODEL

In the above example, we were able to reach a reasonably clear-cut solution to the investment problem because of certain simplifying assumptions that we made. By assuming that the company had a fixed sum of money available for investment, we bypassed the important and difficult problem of how best to finance the investment. By assuming that the costs, revenues, expenses, and cash flows of the projects were all known with certainty, we avoided the complications created by uncertainty in decision-making. We shall now examine the additional problems that the financial executive faces when these simplifying assumptions are removed.

Financing and Dividend Policy

Suppose that instead of having $640,000 available, the financial executive must raise the funds to pay for the investments. In that case, as we shall see later in greater detail, the investment decision becomes more complicated because it is interdependent with the financing decision. The question of how much to invest now requires knowledge of the cost of capital to the firm, which may depend on the proportions of debt and equity financing employed by the firm. The optimal mix of debt and equity may, in turn, depend on the risk characteristics of the projects accepted.

Once the percentage of debt and the percentage of equity financing are set, there are still other problems. Is the debt to be long-term or short-term? If short-term, should the source be a bank loan, trade credit, or the issuance of commercial paper (open-market promissory notes)? If long-term, should the source be an insurance-company loan, a financial lease, or the issuance of bonds? The sale of bonds raises questions of maturity, collateral, interest rate, callability (whether or not the firm can call in its bonds for redemption before maturity) and convertibility (whether or not the bondholders have the option of converting their bonds into stock). In the case of equity, are the funds to be raised by selling preferred or common stock? If preferred stock is to be sold, the questions of contractual terms are similar to those just mentioned in connection with bond financing. If the funds are to be raised through common equity, is it to be through retained earnings or common stock? If common stock, the financial executive faces problems of marketing the issue similar to those in bond financing; he must determine the terms on which the issue is to be offered and make the necessary marketing arrangements with the investment banker.

The possibility of earnings retention raises the question of the best dividend policy for the firm to follow. If the company needs funds to finance its current operation or permanent investments, retention of earnings may be one method of financing. By paying lower dividends, the firm increases the amount of funds made available internally. An alternative course is to pay out the dividend to the stockholders and then raise funds externally by floating new stock or bonds. Which is the better policy? Our example bypassed this question by assuming that the firm was to follow 40 percent payout ratio; but in actual decisions, the dividend question is never so simple.

The Coordinating Function of Finance

Next, instead of assuming certainty, suppose that the cash flows, revenues, expenses, and income streams are random variables (i.e., variables whose values are known only probabilistically). Since the basic data pertaining to the investments are usually supplied by the various operating divisions, this uncertainty means that the financial executive must learn enough about the different aspects of the business to enable him to make an objective appraisal of the reliability of the figures he receives. For instance, in the case of a proposal to install a cost-saving device in a manufacturing division, the forecasts of revenue and expenses will usually be made by the engineering staff of that division. In the case of a new product, the sales estimates will generally be made by the marketing personnel and the cost estimates by the production personnel. Since these estimates are influenced by the pessimism or optimism of the forecasters, it is up to the financial executive to judge their reliability. In order to do this objectively, he must have a thorough understanding of all the different aspects of his firm's operation.

Capital budgeting is not, of course, the only situation in which such a comprehensive understanding is essential. A central aspect of the financial executive's job, you will remember, is planning and control. In many large firms, division executives and their staffs annually prepare detailed three- to five-year plans, taking into account such factors as revenues, operating costs, backlog of orders, rate of inflation, and changing product mix. The financial executive must consolidate the data furnished by the various division heads into a budget for the firm as a whole. After approval by corporate management, this overall budget serves as a guide for action as well as a yardstick for measuring performance. The usefulness of such a budget depends greatly on the reliability of the forecasts and on the coordination of the component plans. To judge reliability, the financial executive must know not only the various aspects of the business in great detail but also the biases and optimism or pessimism of the other executives. To insure smooth operation, he must coordinate the various division plans in order to eliminate conflicts among them and inconsistencies between them and the overall program. To achieve these objectives, he needs the close cooperation of the executives in the various operating divisions.

THE METHOD OF THIS BOOK

Broadly speaking, we shall attempt to present a body of knowledge useful for the optimization of financial decisions in modern corporations. We shall identify the major financial decisions made by the financial executives of corporations and present theories which explain the best way to solve problems. Because of this orientation, we must necessarily discuss a fair amount of theoretical material, but this does not mean that we shall ignore institutions, instruments, and practices. Financial decisions, like all business decisions, are made and executed in an institutional setting; any theoretical discussion that ignores this fact runs the risk of producing irrelevant conclusions. Therefore, we shall call attention to relevant information on institutions and practices at the same time that we present theory.

By financial theory we mean hypotheses which show the relationships within a set of financial variables and which enable us to say how changes in the values of some variables affect the values of the others. In any decision-making situation, there is certain information which the decision-maker simply takes as given. In addition to the givens, there are target variables, whose values the decision-maker is trying to influence, and policy variables, which he manipulates to affect the target variables. Financial theory tells us how changing policy variables affects target variables. In our example of a capital-budgeting problem, the cash flows, the revenues and expenses of the various projects, and the total resources available for investment were given. The policy variables were the amounts to be invested in each of the projects, and the target variables were the internal rate of return of the investment portfolio and the earnings per share of the firm. Our theory, the linear-programming formulation, tells us what values for earnings per share and internal rate of return will result from different combinations of projects.

The function of theory, then, is to help the financial executive to choose the course of action that will maximize the attainment of the firm's goals. To be useful, theory should describe the problem situation in sufficient detail to enable us to draw legitimate inferences about the results of different courses of action, but at the same time be sufficiently simple to enable us to understand and manipulate the available tools. The theory of finance has benefited in recent years from the application of analytical tools such as economic theory, statistics, and management science. We can now ask and solve questions which earlier financial theorists were unequipped to answer or even unable to see. But there is also a danger. With the emergence of all these powerful new techniques, there is the peril of manufacturing financial "problems" to fit the tools. We may safeguard ourselves by avoiding theories based on implausible assumptions. William J. Baumol is right in saying that:

> . . . one of the most convenient instruments for judging the appropriateness of our necessarily imperfectly realistic models is the examination of the plausibility of their assumptions. While ridiculous premises may sometimes yield correct conclusions, we have no confidence that they will do so.[12]

The need to examine the plausibility of assumptions does not mean that we shall revert to the narrow traditional focus on facts about institutions, practices, and instruments; we need to be selective. We need facts for three reasons. First, we need facts to help us identify the important financial decisions. For example, we need to know the standard contractual features in bond indentures in order to know what kinds of decisions and choices the financial decision-maker is faced with when he plans a bond issue with his investment banker. We need to know the seasonal nature of business if we are to define the problems of working capital management correctly. Second, we need facts to justify our assumptions. Behind our assumptions must be a knowledge of business institutions, practices, and psychology. For instance, standard finance theory assumes that the typical investor measures the risk of an investment by the variance of its return. Variance is a convenient concept since it is easy to manipulate algebraically; but do investors really think of variance as their risk measure? Only acquaintance with the realities of financial decision-making enable us to ask this kind of useful question about theory. Third, Milton Friedman has pointed out the need for factual evidence against which to test theory.[13] Realistic assumptions alone do not guarantee valid conclusions. For example, theorists disagree on the effect of dividend policy on share value. The controversy can be resolved only by statistically isolating the dividend effect from all the other forces affecting share prices.

---

[12] William J. Baumol, *Business Behavior, Value and Growth* (New York: Harcourt, Brace and World, Inc., 1967), p. 5.

[13] Milton Friedman, "The Methodology of Positive Economics," *Essays in Positive Economics* (Chicago: University of Chicago Press, 1953), p. 40.

AN OUTLINE OF THIS BOOK

The emphasis in this book on the optimization of financial decisions assumes that there is an objective against which we can measure the results of alternative policies or courses of action. We shall argue that the objective of financial management is to maximize the value of the company's shares; consequently, Chapter 2, the other chapter in this introductory section, will present a theory of share valuation. The second section of this book will deal with the analytical tools of financial measurement, planning, and control. The financial executive must convert the plans of the operating divisions into budgets so that they can be evaluated in terms of the firm's financial goals. Once these budgets have been drawn up, they will serve as an operational guide and as a standard of performance. This section will also take up certain accounting tools for measuring the liquidity, profitability, and solvency of a firm and certain management science techniques for use in planning decisions. The remainder of the text deals with the other areas of financial decisions: capital expenditure, management of fixed and working capital, financial leverage, dividend policy and valuation, long-term financing, short-term and intermediate financing, and corporate restructuring.

REVIEW QUESTIONS

1. Describe the traditional concept of finance and explain how it differs from the new concept.
2. Trace the transition from traditional finance to the new finance. How did the two seminal works, Modigliani and Miller's 1958 article and Markowitz's 1959 book, contribute to this transition?
3. "To be successful, the financial executive should become thoroughly familiar with his company's products, markets, engineering and research activities." Do you agrèe? Why or why not?
4. In Robichek, Ogilvie and Roach's capital-budgeting problem, how would the financial decision be complicated if we dropped the assumption of a fixed amount available for investment (e.g., by considering dividend policy as flexible, or by allowing external financing)? You may not be able to give a complete answer at this point, but at least try to list the new issues that would arise.
5. The internal rate of return was defined as the annual rate of discount which equates the present value of the cash flow of an investment with its cost. How is this different from or similar to the definition of the "marginal efficiency of investment" which you learned in your basic economics course?
6. In the following listings the names of financial writers and their theoretical contributions have been mismatched. Rearrange the names in the correct order.

William F. Sharpe	traditional theory of finance
F. Modigliani and M. H. Miller	model of portfolio selection
H. M. Markowitz	theory of capital structure
A. S. Dewing	theory of security pricing

7. What reasons are given in this chapter for the necessity for a financial theorist being familiar with financial institutions and practices? How does a knowledge of these facts help in the construction and application of financial theory? Give examples.
8. Milton Friedman has stated that "a hypothesis [theory] can be tested only by the conformity of its implications or predictions with observable phenomena." William J. Baumol has countered:

   > It seems to me that one of the most convenient instruments for judging the appropriateness of our necessarily imperfectly realistic models is the examination of the plausibility of their assumptions. While ridiculous premises may sometimes yield correct conclusions, we have no confidence that they will do so.

   With which opinion do you agree? Why?

REFERENCES

AMESCUA R., ALFREDO, "The Future and the Financial Executive," *Financial Executive* 41 (February, 1973), pp. 20–23.

BAUMOL, WILLIAM J., *Business Behavior, Value and Growth* (New York: Harcourt, Brace and World, Inc., 1967), Ch. 1.

CALDWELL, G. T., and J. R. LEVESQUE, *The Chief Financial Officer and His Functions in Canadian Business* (Ottawa: The Conference Board in Canada, 1973).

"Chief Executive Roster," *Forbes* 109 (May 15, 1972), pp. 205–236.

DEWING, A. S., *The Financial Policy of Corporations* (New York: The Ronald Press Company, 1920).

FRIEDMAN, MILTON, "The Methodology of Positive Economics," in *Essays in Positive Economics* (Chicago: University of Chicago Press, 1953).

FRIEND, IRWIN, "Mythodology in Finance," *Journal of Finance* 28 (May, 1973), pp. 257–272.

GRISWOLD, JOHN A., "Finance," in Frank C. Pierson and others, *The Education of American Businessmen* (New York: McGraw-Hill Book Company, Inc., 1959).

KOTCHIAN, A. CARL, "A President's View of a Chief Financial Officer," *Financial Executive* 36 (May, 1968), pp. 18–24.

LYON, HASTINGS, *Corporation Finance* (Boston: Houghton Mifflin Company, 1916).

MACDONALD, RAY W., "The Financial Executive and Senior Management," *Financial Executive* 37 (March, 1969), pp. 15–19.

MAISEL, SHERMAN J., "The Economic and Finance Literature and Decision Making," *Journal of Finance* 29 (May, 1974), pp. 313–322.

MAO, JAMES C. T., *Quantitative Analysis of Financial Decisions* (New York: The Macmillan Company, 1969), Ch. 1.

MARKOWITZ, HARRY M., *Portfolio Selection: Efficient Diversification of Investments* (New York: John Wiley and Sons, Inc., 1959).

MEAD, EDWARD S., *Corporation Finance* (New York: D. Appleton and Company, Inc., 1910).

MODIGLIANI, FRANCO, and MERTON H. MILLER., "The Cost of Capital, Corporation Finance, and the Theory of Investment," *American Economic Review* 48 (June, 1958), pp. 261–297.

ROBICHEK, ALEXANDER A., DONALD G. OGILVIE, and JOHN D. C. ROACH, "Capital Budgeting: A Pragmatic Approach," *Financial Executive* 37 (April, 1969), pp. 26–38.

SHARPE, WILLIAM F., *Portfolio Theory and Capital Markets* (New York: McGraw-Hill Book Company, 1970).

SOLOMON, EZRA, *The Theory of Financial Management* (New York: Columbia University Press, 1963), Ch. 1.

WESTON, J. FRED, "New Themes in Finance," *Journal of Finance* 24 (March, 1974), pp. 237–243.

2 The Objective of Financial Management

A financial decision can be judged only in terms of the objective it is intended to achieve. In this chapter, we shall first look at the objective of share-value maximization, proceed to the theory of security pricing and some empirical evidence, and conclude with what financial executives say about their firms' objectives. We shall place special emphasis on the relationship between the risk and the price of a security.

THE OBJECTIVE OF SHARE-VALUE MAXIMIZATION

Meaning and Logic

Our basic premise is that the objective of financial management is to enhance the wealth of the present common stockholders of a company; this is generally done by maximizing the value of the firm's currently outstanding common shares. There are at least two reasons for accepting wealth maximization as the objective of financial management. As a practical matter, stockholders tend to prefer financial executives who manage company affairs in a way that increases the value of their investments; financial managers who operate otherwise are likely to be replaced by the stockholders sooner or later. There is also a philosophical, or theoretical, basis: since the financial executive is an employee of the stockholders, it is his duty to manage the affairs of the firm to their best advantage, and the best interest of the stockholders is generally served when the value of their investments increases.

This focus on share value is more relevant than either the maximization of total profits or of the firm's earnings per share. Increasing total profits does not guarantee an increase in the market value of the currently outstanding common shares. If the number of shares should rise more than the total profits, earnings per share will drop; and even if earnings per share should increase, share price may not necessarily rise if investors believe there has been a deterioration in the quality of earnings. Therefore, maximization of share value is the most comprehensive objective, because it takes all factors into account.

Some readers who have heard of the random-walk theory of stock prices may ask how financial decisions can influence share prices at all, since statistical tests have shown that these prices fluctuate "randomly."[1] This question reflects a misunderstanding of what the random-walk theory actually hypothesizes. According to this theory, the stock market is so efficiently organized that a news item on any stock is instantaneously and fully reflected in the current price of the stock. Since successive news items are by definition statistically independent, the successive changes in the price of any stock must also be independent. So randomness here refers to the independence of successive stock price changes, not the average size of these changes. Therefore, random walk is not inconsistent with a rising trend of stock prices. In an uncertain but efficient market, stock prices will fluctuate randomly in the short run around their intrinsic values. Share-value maximization seeks by sound financial management to raise the company's stock prices in the long run.

Implementation

Although many financial writers have accepted share-value maximization as the goal of financial management, few have discussed the practical problems of its implementation.[2] The meaning of the maximization of share value at a given point in time is clear; the objective of maximization becomes ambiguous, however, when share price is interpreted as the pattern of share price over a period of time. If the financial executive is confronted with two time patterns of share price that criss-cross within his planning horizon, which of the two is to be preferred, according to the criterion of maximization? Current theory does not provide an answer.

Of course, this complication would not arise in a world of complete certainty, in which all securities would yield the same rate of return, which would equal the risk-free interest rate. The share price of a company at any

---

[1] For an explanation of the random-walk theory and related evidence, see James H. Lorie and Mary T. Hamilton, *The Stock Market: Theories and Evidence* (Homewood: Richard D. Irwin, Inc., 1973), Ch. 4.

[2] The following material is based on my article, "Survey of Capital Budgeting: Theory and Practice," *Journal of Finance* 25 (May, 1970), pp. 349–352.

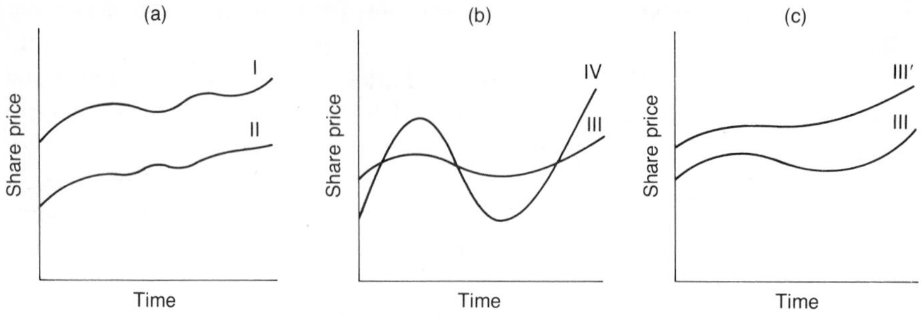

Figure 2-1 Time Pattern of Share Price

time t in the future would equal the current price of the share, compounded at the risk-free interest rate for t time periods.[3] Conversely, given the share price at time t, the current share price would be the value of this future price, discounted at the risk-free rate for t time periods. The financial decision which would maximize share value at any point on a firm's horizon would also maximize it at any other point on that horizon. This property would guarantee that the share-price patterns would not criss-cross. Thus, in Figure 2-1(a), curve I describes the time pattern of share price resulting from action I; and curve II, the pattern resulting from action II. In this case, the objective of maximizing share value is clear-cut; curve I dominates curve II and is therefore preferable.

However, under conditions of uncertainty, the prices of a share at two points in time are no longer related only through the risk-free interest rate. Hence, the relative share prices at the end of the horizon do not necessarily indicate the relationships among the prices during the time span. Two alternative courses of action by management could easily result in time patterns of share prices possibly intersecting at one or more points (see Figure 2-1[b]). In that case, the objective of maximizing share value has no operational meaning until there are criteria for choosing among criss-crossing price patterns.

In order to choose, we should consider the duration of the period for which one pattern exceeds the other, as well as the size of the difference. Thus, if the company is thinking of acquiring another firm by issuing stock in the immediate future, curve III may be more desirable than curve IV, since the market price of the company's shares is higher in the immediate future under III than under IV. Or, if the firm is taking a long-range view, it may prefer IV since IV results in a higher share price than III at the end of

[3] The company is assumed to pay no dividends between now and time t. This assumption will be removed in the next subsection.

the horizon. Analytical tools are of little use here, since the choice of criterion is necessarily subjective.

Let us suppose that price-pattern in curve III is preferred. How would it be possible to improve it further so that the share price would be raised at every point (see Figure 2-1[c])? That is, if there is an earnings-per-share series that corresponds to curve III, how could it be modified to raise the share prices of curve III to the level of those of curve III′? The answer lies in the theory of share valuation discussed in the next major section. As we shall see, an earnings-per-share series with a higher trend and with less risk usually results in a uniformly higher price.

Qualifications of the Objective

So far, we have assumed that the objective of maximizing shareholders wealth is equivalent to the objective of maximization of share value. Now we must qualify that, since there are certain financial decisions for which this is not true. As an example, let us consider the issue of dividend policy. The question here is how large the cash dividend should be. For this decision, the stockholders' wealth is measured not only by the value of their shares but also by the amount of cash received in dividends. Thus, the maximization of a firm's net present value may not result in the maximization of the shareholders' wealth. For instance, a company could retain all its earnings, thereby increasing share value (i.e., net present value) but precluding the payment of dividends. Such a policy, as we shall see later in this book, could in fact reduce the stockholders' wealth if the retained earnings were invested in projects which returned a rate not as high as that which the shareholders could have obtained by reinvesting the dividend proceeds themselves. Share repurchase (in which the company buys back some of the outstanding stock) and rights offering (in which the company sells new shares to its current stockholders) are other areas in which the objective of maximizing share value needs qualification.

To restate: the objective of maximizing share value is a valid guide for transactions which do not involve the transfer of assets between the corporate entity and the stockholders. For external transactions which do involve such a transfer, corporate decisions should be guided by the effect on share value—adjusted in accordance with cash or assets which the stockholders receive or give up as a result.

FUTURITY AND UNCERTAINTY IN SHARE VALUATION

Since the value of a share derives from benefits which are received over time and under conditions of uncertainty, we need analytical concepts for quantifying futurity and uncertainty in the valuation process. For convenience, we shall group these concepts under the general headings of "present value" and "probability distribution."

Present Value and Related Concepts

We all know that, even aside from inflation, a dollar now is worth more than a dollar in the future, since the dollar that we have now can be lent out to earn interest, whereas a dollar of the future can earn nothing until it is received. Under conditions of certainty, a dollar invested now at an interest rate of, say 10 percent, compounded annually, will have future values of $\$1(1 + .1)$ at the end of year 1, $\$1(1 + .1)^2$ at the end of year 2, . . . , and $\$1(1 + .1)^t$ at the end of year *t*. The future value grows with time, because the amount of interest earned increases with time. On the other hand, a dollar due *t* years from now earns no interest for the prospective recipient during the next *t* years; therefore, a dollar in the future is less valuable than a dollar now.

How much less valuable is a dollar five years from now than a dollar today? If one is offered a dollar payable in *t* years, how much in today's money should one be willing to accept in exchange for the future dollar? That is, what is the "present value" of a dollar payable in *t* years? To answer this question, we must consider the process of discounting, which is the reverse of compounding; i.e., instead of asking how much a one-dollar investment will grow in *t* years, we must ask how much one would have to invest now in order to have an investment value of \$1 at the end of year *t*. The answer is given by the equation:

$$\text{Present value of \$1 payable at the end of } t \text{ years} = \frac{\$1}{(1 + i)^t} \qquad (2\text{-}1)$$

where i is the annual rate of interest at which the money could be lent, and t is the number of years at the end of which the dollar is due. Given an interest rate of i, an investor will regard equally a dollar t years hence and a present value of $\$1/(1 + i)^t$.

Figure 2-2 shows the present value of a dollar for selected values of i and t. (A more complete set of data is tabulated in Table A-1 of Appendix A.) As we can see, the present value of a future dollar decreases exponentially with time, the decrease being especially rapid when i is high. Thus, at an interest rate of 10 percent, the present value of \$1 would be 90.9¢, 62.1¢, or 38.6¢, if the dollar were received at the end of the first, fifth, or tenth year, respectively. At an interest rate of 25 percent, the corresponding present values would be only 80.0¢, 32.8¢, and 10.7¢, respectively. The concept of present value can also be applied, of course, to a series of future payments; in this case, the present value of the series is obtained by simply adding the component present values, calculated term by term. Thus, at an interest rate of 10 percent, a series of three payments of \$4, \$5, and \$6, received at the

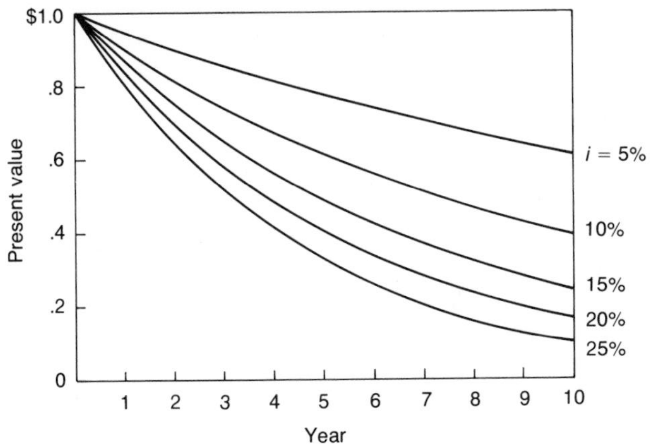

Figure 2-2 Present Value of $1

end of the first, fifth, and tenth years, respectively, has a present value of $9.06—i.e., $4(.909) + $5(.621) + $6(.386). This operation is sometimes referred to as "capitalizing" a payment stream.

The calculation of the present value of a series is simplified if each payment is the same amount and equally spaced. Let us consider, for instance, a uniform payment series (known as an annuity) of $1 per year for t years. If we apply the present-value formula term by term, we find that the present value of this annuity is:

$$\frac{\$1}{(1+i)^1} + \frac{\$1}{(1+i)^2} + \cdots + \frac{\$1}{(1+i)^t}$$

where i is again the annual rate of interest and t is the number of annuity installments. Summing the series of terms we get the simplified expression:[4]

$$\text{Present value of an annuity} = \$1\left[\frac{1-(1+i)^{-t}}{i}\right] \qquad (2\text{-}2)$$

Note that as t approaches infinity, Eq. (2-2) approaches $\$1/i$. Thus, to calculate the present value of a perpetuity of $1 per period, simply divide the constant payment of $1 by the interest rate.

Figure 2-3 gives the present value of an annuity for various values of i and t. (A more complete set of data is tabulated in Table A-2 of Appendix

[4] The sum of a geometric progression with n terms is given by the formula $\frac{a(q^n-1)}{(q-1)}$, where a is the first term and q the common factor. If $|q| < 1$, this formula becomes $a/(1-q)$ as n approaches infinity.

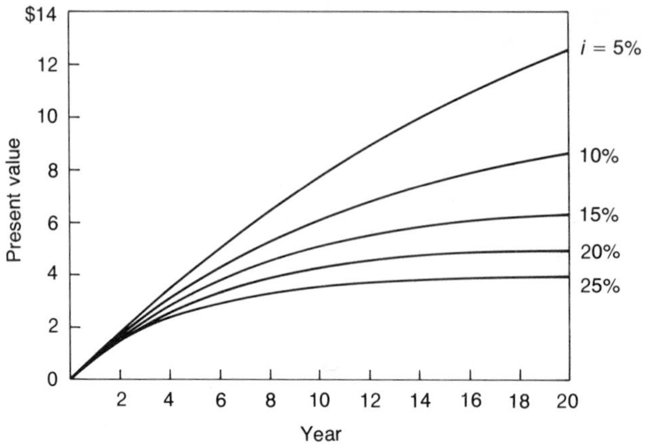

Figure 2-3 Present Value of an Annuity of $1 Per Year

A.) The present value of an annuity, like the present value of a dollar, varies inversely with i; but it varies directly with t because the larger the value of t, the more installments in the series. Thus, for $t = 10$, the present value of an annuity of $1 per period is $6.14 if $i = .1$ and $4.19 if $i = .2$. Similarly, given $i = .1$, the present value of an annuity is $6.14 if $t = 10$ and $8.51 if $t = 20$. We should note also that, given $i = .1$, the present value of the annuity increases by only $2.37 when t is doubled from 10 to 20. This is explained by the fact that the present value of a dollar decreases exponentially with time, so that the present value of an annuity is influenced much more by the early installments than by the late ones. In this example, 72 percent of the present value of the annuity is accounted for by the first ten terms and only 28 percent by the last ten terms. The percentage represented by the latter terms would have been even smaller at a higher discount rate.

Finally, the relationship between the present value and future value should be explained. The future value of $1 invested now at an interest rate of i for t periods is given by the formula:

$$\text{Future value of \$1 invested now} = \$1(1+i)^t \tag{2-3}$$

The future value of an annuity of $1 per period for t periods at an interest rate of i is given by the formula:

$$\text{Future value of an annuity} = \$1(1+i)^{t-1} + \$1(1+i)^{t-2} + \cdots + \$1(1+i)^0$$

$$= \$1\left[\frac{(1+i)^t - 1}{i}\right] \tag{2-4}$$

These future values are tabulated in Tables A-3 and A-4 of Appendix A for selected values of i and t. By comparing (2-3) with (2-1) and (2-4) with (2-2), we observe that in both cases the future value of a dollar equals the corresponding present value multiplied by the factor $(1 + i)^t$. This relation enables us to calculate the present value of a payment (or a series of payments) if we know its future value at time t.

Probability Distribution

Security price is affected not only by the futurity but also by the uncertainty of the return on the security. Probability distribution is a method of quantifying uncertainty when more than one outcome is possible and the actual outcome is uncertain. A variable whose value is known only probabilistically is called a random variable. When a marketing manager forecasts that sales will total \$3, \$4, or \$5 each with a probability of one-third, he is using a probability distribution to describe a random variable: the demand for his product. And when an investor predicts that the earnings per share for the coming year of Company XYZ will be \$1.20 with probability .25, \$1.50 with probability .50, or \$1.80 with probability .25, he is also describing a random variable: the firm's profits for the coming year.

A probability distribution, then, may be thought of as a table which relates the possible outcomes of an uncertain event to the probabilities of their occurrence. Figure 2-4 depicts graphically an investor's probability distribution of the per-share earnings for the coming year of Company XYZ. Two statistics can be calculated to summarize any given probability distribution: the expected value and the variance of the distribution. The expected value, which measures the central tendency of the distribution, is defined as the average of all possible outcomes of the distribution, weighted

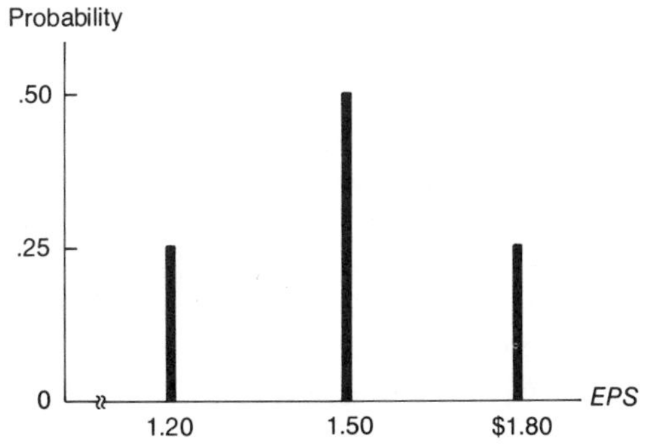

Figure 2-4 Forecast of XYZ's Per-Share Earnings

by their respective probabilities. If the possible outcomes are denoted by $x_1, x_2, \ldots, x_n$ and their respective probabilities by $p_1, p_2, \ldots, p_n$, then the expected value (μ) is given by the formula:

$$\mu = p_1x_1 + p_2x_2 + \cdots + p_nx_n$$

Thus, for Figure 2-4, $\mu = .25(\$1.20) + .50(\$1.50) + .25(\$1.80) = \$1.50$, which is the average earnings per share as forecast by the investor.

Given that the expected earnings per share is \$1.50, will the investor actually appraise the security as if next year's earnings per share is actually \$1.50? The answer depends on the investor's attitude toward risk and uncertainty: if he is neutral toward risk, he will. But studies show that the typical investor is averse to risk in that, given a choice between a lottery ticket with a 50–50 chance of winning \$10,000 or \$30,000 and a cash offer of \$20,000, he will play safe and take the \$20,000. For our purposes, this means that the risk-averse investor is likely to appraise a security on the basis of an earnings-per-share figure somewhat lower than the expected value. How much less depends on the intensity of his aversion to risk and on the amount of risk he envisages in the probability distribution.

This brings us to the variance of a probability distribution, the second summary statistic, which many writers have used to quantify the degree of uncertainty in a risky situation. Variance is defined as the average of the squared deviations of the possible outcomes from the mean of the distribution, weighted by their respective probabilities. It is an analytical concept designed to measure the dispersion of the distribution around its mean. If we define $x_1, x_2, \ldots, x_n$ and $p_1, p_2, \ldots, p_n$ as before, then the variance (σ^2) is given by the formula:

$$\sigma^2 = p_1(x_1 - \mu)^2 + p_2(x_2 - \mu)^2 + \cdots + p_n(x_n - \mu)^2$$

The larger the variance, the more dispersed is the distribution around its mean. The positive square root of the variance (σ) is known as the standard deviation of the probability distribution. As a measure of dispersion, standard deviation has the advantage of being expressed in the same unit as the mean of the distribution. When we apply this formula, we find that the probability distribution in Figure 2-4 has a variance of .045, which implies a standard deviation of 21.2 cents.

We should note that although financial writers have generally accepted variance as a measure of risk and have constructed their valuation theories on the basis of it, this concept does have some analytical shortcomings. Later in the chapter, we shall discuss these shortcomings and suggest ways to correct them.

FORMULAS FOR SHARE VALUATION

We shall now explain the three major approaches to share valuation: the dividend approach, the earnings approach, and the investment opportunities approach.

The Dividend Approach

To understand the dividend approach, let us consider the financial benefits of stock ownership. The owner of a share of stock is entitled to receive any cash dividend declared and paid by the company during the period of his ownership, as well as the price of the stock at the time that he sells it. The price he is willing to pay for these two privileges depends on the size and timing of these future benefits and also on the rate of the return he wishes to earn on his investment. More precisely, the price he will pay is determined by the present value of the expected future benefits, discounted at an appropriate rate k. Thus, if we let $D_1, D_2, \ldots, D_t$ denote the per-share dividend which the investor expects to receive at the end of years $1, 2, \ldots, t$, and let P_t stand for the expected price of the share at the end of the investor's planning horizon (year t), then P_0, the theoretical price of the share now, is given by the dividend-capitalization formula:

$$P_0 = \frac{D_1}{(1+k)^1} + \frac{D_2}{(1+k)^2} + \cdots + \frac{D_t}{(1+k)^t} + \frac{P_t}{(1+k)^t}$$

The discount rate k, known also as the investor's required rate of return, must be high enough to compensate the investor not only for the time value of his money but also for the risk he perceives in his forecast of future benefits.

This equation explains P_0 in terms of both the expected dividend payments $D_1, D_2, \ldots, D_t$ and the expected future share price P_t. But what determines the value of P_t? According to the dividend approach, share price at time t depends on future dividends and future share price; if we carry this line of reasoning far enough, we find that the current price of a share should equal the present value of an infinite series of future dividend payments:

$$P_0 = \frac{D_1}{(1+k)^1} + \frac{D_2}{(1+k)^2} + \cdots + \frac{D_t}{(1+k)^t} + \cdots \qquad (2\text{-}5)$$

P_0 is the theoretical value of the share in that if the investor pays this price now and actually receives the expected dividend payments, then he will realize the rate of return k which he desires on his investment.

In Eq. (2-5), if the annual dividends remain fixed at D_1, the right-hand side is a geometric series; the equation therefore can be reduced to $P_0 = D_1/k$. If the annual dividends increase at a constant percentage rate g each successive year, the right-hand side is still a geometric series; and the equation becomes: $P_0 = D_1/(k - g)$.

The Earnings Approach

While dividend payments constitute the ultimate benefit of stock ownership, a firm's ability to pay dividends depends largely on its earning power. According to the earnings approach, the theoretical price of a share is equal to the present value of its "adjusted" future earnings.

To understand what is meant by "adjusted," let us consider two companies, A and B, which are expected to report identical per-share earnings from now on. In order to attain this assumed pattern of earnings per share, A needs no further net investments and is therefore able to pay out all of its annual earnings in dividends. B, on the other hand, must invest half of its earnings each year in order to achieve the same pattern and is therefore able to pay out only half of its annual earnings in dividends. Shares of B are obviously less valuable because of B's need to commit additional funds each year merely to keep up with A in earnings per share. This suggests that, in calculating share value by the earnings approach, when additional investments are necessary to sustain the earnings stream which is being discounted, the annual earnings must be reduced by the amount needed for investment each year. Thus, if the per-share earnings of a company are $E_1, E_2, \ldots, E_t$ in years $1, 2, \ldots, t$, and the corresponding annual investments are $N_1, N_2, \ldots, N_t$, then the theoretical price of a share now is:

$$P_0 = \frac{E_1 - N_1}{(1+k)^1} + \frac{E_2 - N_2}{(1+k)^2} + \cdots + \frac{E_t - N_t}{(1+k)^t} + \cdots \qquad (2\text{-}6)$$

where $E_1 - N_1, E_2 - N_2, \ldots, E_t - N_t$ are the "adjusted" earnings, and the discount rate k, as before, is the investor's required rate of return.

The Investment-Opportunities Approach

This is a variant of the earnings approach in that it too calculates the value of a share on the basis of the company's earning power. But whereas the earnings approach makes no distinction between earnings generated by existing assets and those generated by assets which the company is to acquire in the future, the investment-opportunities approach does.

According to this approach, the value of a firm derives from two sources: existing assets and future growth opportunities. The value of the existing assets is simply the present value of the earnings that these assets are expected to generate. The value of future growth opportunities depends partly on the size of future investments and partly on the return that these investments are expected to earn beyond the rate required by investors to compensate for futurity and uncertainty. If the expected returns on future investments are equal to or lower than this required rate, their effect on share value is zero or negative. Future investments will increase the value of a firm's shares only if their expected return exceeds the investors' required rate of return.

Let us suppose that there is a firm which is expected to generate E dollars of earnings per share perpetually with existing assets alone. The riskiness of the business is such that if an investor undertakes a project of similar risk, he can get a return of k; that is, k measures the investor's required rate of return. Suppose also that this firm has the opportunity to invest N dollars (per share basis) each year at a perpetual annual return of r, where r is greater than k. According to the investment-opportunities approach, the theoretical current price P_0 of the company's share is given by the equation:

$$P_0 = \frac{E}{k} + \frac{N}{k}\,\frac{(r-k)}{k} \tag{2-7}$$

In this formula E/k is simply the present value of earnings generated by existing assets. $\frac{N}{k}\frac{(r-k)}{k}$ is the present value of future investment opportunities, derived in Table 2-1 as the difference between the present-value costs and benefits of all future investments. Note that this expression is the product of N/k and $(r - k)/k$, both of which have economic meanings: N/k is the present value of the costs of future investments, and $(r - k)/k$ is an index which measures the excess profitability of future investments over the investor's required return k.

The above formula assumes that the amount that the company can invest at a return of r is a constant, equal to N dollars each year. If we assume instead that the amount that can be so invested is equal to b percent of each year's earnings, then the present value of the costs of future investments is given by the expression $(bE)/(k - br)$, where bE is the amount of investment in the base year and br measures the annual rate at which earnings and hence investment will grow.[5] If we replace N/k by this new ex-

[5] In this situation, the present value of the costs of future investments is the sum of an infinite geometric series:

$$\frac{bE}{(1+k)^1} + \frac{bE(1+br)}{(1+k)^2} + \frac{bE(1+br)^2}{(1+k)^3} + \cdots$$

Applying the formula given in footnote 4, we obtain the expression $(bE)/(k - br)$.

Table 2-1 Deriving the Present Value of Future Investment Opportunities

Period	1	2	3	4	5	6	. . .	Present Value of Each Row
Costs of investments	$-N$	$-N$	$-N$	$-N$	$-N$	$-N$	. . .	$-\frac{N}{k}$
		Nr	Nr	Nr	Nr	Nr	. . .	$+\frac{Nr}{k}$
Benefits of investments			Nr	Nr	Nr	Nr	. . .	$+\frac{Nr}{k(1+k)}$
				Nr	Nr	Nr	. . .	$+\frac{Nr}{k(1+k)^2}$
					Nr	Nr	. . .	$\vdots$
Sum = Present value of future investment opportunities								$\frac{N}{k}\frac{(r-k)}{k}$

pression in Eq. (2-7), the theoretical price of a share will be given by the following formula:

$$P_0 = \frac{E}{k} + \left(\frac{bE}{k - br}\right)\left(\frac{r-k}{k}\right) \tag{2-8}$$

P_0 is still determined by existing assets and future investment opportunities.

Equivalence of Alternative Approaches

Franco Modigliani and Merton H. Miller have demonstrated that these three valuation formulas are mathematically equivalent, *provided* that the value of k is the same in each.[6] This is an important qualification, which lies at the source of a great deal of controversy on dividend policy. Given two companies with the same earning power, would the earnings be discounted by investors at different rates, depending on the dividend policy that the firm chooses to follow? We shall consider this issue later, in Chapter 15; at the moment, our problem is the valuation of a firm *given* its dividend policy. The investor's required rate of return k already includes the effect (if any) of dividend policy, so we shall get the same values regardless of which formula we use.

---

[6] See Merton H. Miller and Franco Modigliani, "Dividend Policy, Growth, and the Valuation of Shares," *Journal of Business* 34 (October, 1961), pp. 411–433.

To illustrate the equivalence of the three formulas for a given rate k, let us consider a company whose all-equity financing consists of 25,000 outstanding shares of common stock. The investing public estimates that with existing assets alone, the firm should be able to generate perpetual annual net earnings of \$50,000; i.e., \$2 per share. The company follows a policy of paying out 60 percent of each year's earnings in dividends and reinvesting the balance; reinvestments are expected to yield perpetual returns of 15 percent per annum. Given these facts, at what price will the investors appraise the shares of this company if they require a 12 percent return on their investment?

Let us begin by ascertaining the earnings and dividends expectations connected with ownership of this stock. Since the company earns \$2 per share and the payout ratio is 60 percent, current dividends are \$1.20. In the second year, the firm's earning will be enhanced by the return from the reinvestment made in the first year; since the company reinvested \$0.80 in the first year at a return of 15 percent per annum, share earnings are increased by $\$2(.4 \times .15) = \$0.12$, so per-share earnings in the second year total $\$2(1 + .4 \times .15) = \$2.12$. Similarly, in the third year, per-share earnings are $\$2(1+.4\times.15)^2 = \$2.24$, and the per-share dividend is $\$1.2(1+.4\times.15)^2 = \$1.34$. To generalize: in any year t, the per-share earnings are $\$2(1 + .4 \times .15)^t$, and the per-share dividend is $\$1.2(1 + .4 \times .15)^t$. Substituting the appropriate terms for $D_1, D_2, \ldots, D_t$ in the dividend-capitalization formula (2-5), we get:

$$P_0 = \frac{\$1.2}{(1+.12)^1} + \frac{\$1.2(1+.06)}{(1+.12)^2} + \cdots + \frac{\$1.2(1+.06)^t}{(1+.12)^{t+1}} + \cdots$$

Since annual dividends grow at a constant rate of 6 percent each successive year, the right-hand side of this equation is given by the expression $\$1.2/(.12 - .06)$; the stock consequently has a value of \$20.

To apply the earnings-capitalization formula, we need to ascertain the annual reinvestment necessary for the projected per-share earnings. In year 1, the reinvestments total \$0.80; in year 2, $\$0.8(1 + .06)$; in year 3, $\$0.8(1 + .06)^2$; and, in general, in year t, $\$0.8(1 + .06)^{t-1}$. Subtracting these reinvestments from the appropriate per-share earnings, and discounting, we get:

$$P_0 = \frac{\$1.2}{(1+.12)^1} + \frac{\$1.2(1+.06)}{(1+.12)^2} + \cdots + \frac{\$1.2(1+.06)^t}{(1+.12)^{t+1}} + \cdots$$

which is the same expression we got when we used the dividend-capitalization formula. As an exercise, the reader can verify the fact that the investment-opportunities formula will also yield the same result.

THE RISK OF A SECURITY

In the above valuation formulas, investment risk reduces security prices by raising the investors' required rate of return. An understanding of this risk variable is essential to the financial executive if he is to control it properly. In this section, we shall discuss the nature and sources of risk, and the method of its quantification.

The Nature and Sources of Risk

In defining risk, let us note that whether an investor is oriented toward current income or capital gains, his ultimate object is to earn a satisfactory rate of return. When he buys a share of stock, he is well aware that his actual return may turn out to be greater than, equal to, or less than his target return. If the return is the same as his target rate of return, his expectations are fulfilled; if it is greater than his target rate, he will be pleasantly surprised; and if it is lower, he will obviously be disappointed. The risk associated with an investment is, then, simply the prospect that the actual return may fall short of the target return. This definition of investment risk, as we shall see shortly, differs from the generally accepted concept, which defines risk as the variance of return.

Although financial writers may differ in their definitions of risk, they are in agreement as to the four sources of risk: business risk, financial risk, interest-rate risk, and purchasing-power risk. Business risk refers to any development that exerts an adverse effect on the operating income of the firm. For instance, changing consumer tastes, increased foreign competition, and a shortage of raw materials can all result in a smaller operating profit. Financial risk refers to the introduction of fixed charges, such as interest expense and preferred dividends, into the cost structure of a firm. The presence of these fixed costs, as Chapter 4 will show, tends to destabilize the after-tax net profits. Interest-rate risk refers to the possibility that the general level of interest rates may rise. When the interest-rate level rises, the investing public's required rate of return rises with it, causing share prices to fall. Finally, purchasing-power risk refers to the possibility that the general level of commodity prices may rise, causing a decline in the purchasing-power of money. Since World War II, common stock has provided a reasonable hedge against inflation, but there is no guarantee that this will hold true in the future.

The financial executive has direct control over only two of the four sources of risk affecting his firm: business risk and financial risk. The general levels of interest rates and commodity prices are determined by broad economic forces which an individual firm can view only as givens.

The Portfolio Approach to Risk Measurement

Earlier in this chapter, we used the variance of return to quantify risk, but we did not ask whether investors view individual stocks as elements with which to build diversified portfolios or simply as isolated investment opportunities. The answer determines whether we should use the portfolio approach or the specific-security approach to risk measurement. We shall start with the portfolio approach, based primarily on the contributions of Harry M. Markowitz, John Lintner, and William F. Sharpe.[7]

Markowitz. Markowitz's measure of investment risk is the variance of portfolio return. He argues that individual stocks should not be purchased for their own sake, but for their impact on the risk-return features of the overall portfolio. This portfolio approach to security appraisal means that the risk of a security is measured not only by the variance of its own return, but also by the "covariances" between its return and the returns of all other securities in the same portfolio. (Covariance is a statistical concept which expresses whether the returns of two securities are positively or negatively correlated with each other.) A security with a high variance may be judged risky when considered by itself. But if the security is negatively correlated with other securities, including it in a portfolio will stabilize overall return. Investors will deem the security as not risky in a portfolio context.

Markowitz formulated his portfolio-selection problem as follows: consider an investor who wishes to allocate a certain sum among a given number of securities. He has estimated the expected value and the variance of return on the individual securities and also the covariance between any pair of securities. He would like the expected return from his portfolio to be high and the variance of return to be low. How should he choose the optimal portfolio? Markowitz's solution consists of two steps. First, the investor should make a list of all of the possible portfolios that his resources permit, and single out those which are "efficient." (A portfolio is efficient when it has the smallest variance for a given expected return and the highest expected return for a given variance.) Then, from the list of efficient portfolios, he should choose the portfolio with the combination of risk and return that suits him best.

Lintner and Sharpe. Markowitz's model tells us how an investor should decide how much of any security to include in his portfolio. By assuming that all investors act in accordance with Markowitz's model, one can derive

---

[7] The original journal articles are cited in the references at the end of this chapter. A useful summary can be found in Charles W. Haley and Lawrence D. Schall, *The Theory of Financial Decisions* (New York: McGraw-Hill Book Company, 1973), Chs. 6 and 7.

the aggregate demand for any security. Since the supply of any security is fixed at any moment, one can then determine the equilibrium price of any security. Work along this line was first done independently by Lintner and Sharpe. For simplicity, Lintner and Sharpe assumed a capital market in which there is a riskless investment, and in which there are no taxes or transactions costs. Investors are assumed to have homogeneous expectations with respect to all future security prices. In this ideal situation, the portfolios held by all investors are similar in that they include every security in the exact proportion of its relative total value in the securities market. The portfolios may differ in size, but not in composition. Based on this fact, they separately derived a formula which expresses the risk of a security as an average of its own variance of return and all of its covariances with other securities in the market.

The Specific-Security Approach to Risk Measurement

According to the specific-security approach, investors typically view individual stocks as isolated investments. They appraise each stock not in a portfolio context, but solely in terms of its own risk and return. The risk of a security, then, is simply the variance of its rate of return. In the section on probability distribution, we presented an example which illustrates how this variance of return is calculated for a particular stock. That example is based on the specific-security approach to risk measurement.

No doubt some investors employ the portfolio approach to security appraisal and some employ the specific-security approach. But which approach dominates the actual behavior of investors? A survey conducted by the New York Stock Exchange revealed that the typical investor in the United States holds an average of less than four stocks in his portfolio.[8] This finding seems to suggest that individual investors typically follow the specific-security approach to stock appraisal. The institutional investors are more likely to employ the portfolio approach, but even here there is the question whether they actually do practice the portfolio approach. Thus, if a fund manager suffers a sizeable loss on any one security, would he justify the loss as an inevitable consequence of portfolio diversification, or would he view the stock as an isolated purchase and consider that he had made a bad buy? We do not yet have enough evidence to answer this question, but we do have some data to show that institutional investors tend to limit their investing to a handful of stocks. One investment banker, John C. Whitehead, recounts the case of a large pension fund with over $1 billion in new money to invest in one recent year.[9] It invested 65 percent of the sum in seven

---

[8] Cited in John Lintner, "Expectations, Mergers and Equilibrium in Purely Competitive Securities Markets," *American Economic Review* 61 (May, 1971), p. 108.

[9] "Are the Institutions Wrecking Wall Street?" *Business Week* (June 2, 1973), p. 59.

stocks, another 20 percent in eight others, and the balance in just fifteen more. It seems that the portfolio approach, even when practical, applies at most to a limited number of stocks. For the great majority of stocks, we are inclined therefore to accept the specific-security approach to risk measurement.

What Investors Perceive as Risk

As a working hypothesis, we shall accept the specific-security approach as the dominant investor behavior. But whether one accepts it or the portfolio approach, the question arises: what statistical measure best reflects the investor's perception of risk? To equate risk with variance is to assume that an investor uses the expected rate of return as a point of reference and perceives as risk the possibility that the actual return may be either above or below it. Is this assumption about investor psychology reasonable? It seems more reasonable to assume that an investor has a target return in mind, which may or may not be the expected return for the stock. He will be pleasantly surprised if the actual return is greater than his target and disappointed if it is lower. What the typical investor perceives as risk is the possibility of not earning the target rate.

It would seem, then, that a better way to measure risk would be to use the target rate of return as the point of reference and to measure risk by the possible downward deviations from this target. These two ideas are incorporated in the concept of semi-variance, which is calculated in the same way as ordinary variance, except that we choose the reference point for calculating deviations subjectively and we ignore positive deviations by assigning them values of zero. Thus, for the forecast of XYZ's per-share earnings in Figure 2-4, if the investor's target figure is \$1.00 per share, then his investment risk, as measured by semi-variance, is zero, since all possible deviations from this target return are positive. But, if this target return is \$1.60 per share, then his investment risk is equal to $.25(\$1.20 - \$1.60)^2 + .50(\$1.50 - \$1.60)^2 + .25(0)$, or .045. The investor, therefore, views the XYZ stock as more risky if he has a high earnings expectation for the company than if he has a low expectation.

In addition to the psychological argument in favor of semi-variance, there is also some empirical reason for viewing investment risk as downward deviations from the target rate of return. Using regression analysis, Burton G. Malkiel and John G. Cragg tested a theory which explains the price-earnings ratio (the price of a stock per dollar of earnings) in terms of three variables: the growth rate of earnings per share, the dividend-payout ratio, and an instability index of the earnings stream (i.e., the downward deviations of earnings from its trend line).[10] Using data on 178 companies, they found

---

[10] Burton G. Malkiel and John G. Cragg, "Expectations and the Structures of Share Prices," *American Economic Review* 60 (September, 1970), pp. 601–619.

that for a five-year period, their regression equation explained up to three quarters of the variations in price-earnings ratio. Moreover, the coefficient of the instability index had the expected negative sign (meaning that risk depressed share price) for each of the five years tested. Although facts cannot actually prove a theory, Malkiel and Cragg's results support our choice of semi-variance as a measure of investment risk.

When we apply semi-variance in a dynamic setting, we see that the financial executive would be wise to set a target rate of growth for the firm's earning power and follow a course which will minimize downward deviations from this growth pattern. This is the policy most likely to enhance the market price of the company's shares in the long run.

WHAT FINANCIAL MANAGERS SAY ABOUT THEIR OBJECTIVES

A number of financial executives were interviewed to find out what they regarded as the objective of financial management.[11] Specifically, they were asked whether or not they chose among alternative courses of action in order to maximize the value of the firm. This sampling is representative of their answers:

> Our objective is to finance the high growth rate of this company. Since we do not use debt, we have to make sure that we earn enough profit to finance the growth. It may be that share value is maximized as well, but we don't think about that.
>
> We have a goal of earnings per share which we manage astutely every quarter. Because this is a young, growing company, it is important in terms of future financing that we do not disappoint the investing public.
>
> The thing that means the most to the stockholder is the value of his stock. In determining the value of stock, the most critical factor is probably the earnings per share, but it also involves the fact that you are not static but moving forward and increasing your earnings per share. To increase earnings, you have to have sales growth which is the lifeblood of any business.
>
> The goal of the financial manager is to have his company produce a record that will enable it to raise capital at the lowest possible cost. To accomplish this goal, he needs a proper concept of stability and a proper concept of growth. In this company, we try to achieve a growth rate of 15 to 18 percent, compounded annually, in both sales and earnings.

Three things should be noted. First, although not always stated explicitly, maximization of the value of the firm is an implicit goal in each answer. Since management is operationally oriented, the goal of maximizing

[11] The eight companies which I interviewed included representative firms from the following industries: electronics, aerospace, petroleum, household equipment, office equipment, and electric utilities. Other aspects of this study will be referred to later in the text.

share value is expressed in terms of operating targets of growth and stability in the earnings stream. Second, the executives interviewed tend to view the value of their company independently of the effect of diversification by the investing public. Practically, this approach has the advantage of simplicity; theoretically, it is an adequate approach to valuation if investors predominantly view individual stocks not as elements for building portfolios, but as isolated investments. And third, if maximization of share value depends on consistent growth, then it is vital that executives have a constant flow of new ideas.

REVIEW QUESTIONS

1. What is the justification for viewing share-value maximization as the goal of financial management? What difficulties arise in implementation when share price is interpreted as a pattern over time rather than as the price at a given point in time?
2. Give examples of "external transactions." How must the objective of share-value maximization be modified in appraising the optimality of these transactions?
3. What is the random-walk theory of stock market prices? If stock prices are random, does it not make the objective of share-value maximization and the study of financial management fruitless? Why or why not?
4. Define and explain the present value and the future value of an annuity of $1 per period for t periods. How are these two values related if we assume the interest rate to be given?
5. At a given rate of interest, why does the present value of an annuity not increase at a constant absolute rate as the length of the annuity period, t, increases? Given the period t, why does the present value of an annuity vary inversely with the rate of interest?
6. Define and explain: random variable, probability distribution, expected value, variance, standard deviation, and semi-variance.
7. How are the dividend approach and earnings approach to share valuation similar or dissimilar? In what way is the investment-opportunities approach a variant of the earnings approach to share valuation?
8. Look up the definition of investment risk in standard textbooks on security analysis and compare it with the definition proposed in this chapter. Which concept of risk do you prefer, and why? (If the author of your security-analysis text does not provide an explicit definition of risk, infer the definition from his discussion of sources of risk.)
9. Outline the essentials of Harry M. Markowitz's model of portfolio selection. What role does this model play in John Lintner's and William F. Sharpe's theories of security pricing?
10. Distinguish between the portfolio approach and the specific-security approach to share valuation. How does this distinction affect how a firm should manage its risk profile so as to maximize share value?

PROBLEMS

1. Plot the present value of a dollar as a function of time, using an interest rate of 12 percent. Observe the negative slope of the function. Make a similar time-graph of the present value of an annuity of one dollar per period, using the same interest rate, and observe the diminishing rate of increase over time. Is there any connection between the negative slope and the diminishing rate of increase in the two graphs?

2. If the interest rate is 10 percent per period, an annuity of $1 per period for 10 periods has a present value of $6.14. Calculate the percentage of this total value of $6.14 that is attributable to the first five terms in the annuity formula. Repeat the calculation for an interest rate of 20 percent per period.

3. The present value of an annuity of one dollar per period for n periods at interest rate i is denoted $a_{\overline{n}|i}$, and the corresponding future value of this annuity is denoted $s_{\overline{n}|i}$. Show that $s_{\overline{n}|i}$ equals $a_{\overline{n}|i}(1 + i)^n$.

4. Calculate the expected value, variance, standard deviation, semi-variance, and semi-deviation (square root of semi-variance) for each of the following probability distributions:

Net Profit	Probability	Sales	Probability
$ 75	.25	$400	.50
100	.50	500	.25
125	.25	600	.25

   In calculating semi-variances, the target net profit and target sales are assumed to be $110 and $550 respectively.

5. Suppose that investments A and B, each costing $15,000 and lasting one year, have the following profitability:

Profit (A)	Probability	Profit (B)	Probability
$4,000	.8	$2,000	.8
−1,000	.2	7,000	.2

   Which distribution of profit would an investor averse to risk prefer?

6. Determine how well common stock, as measured by the Dow-Jones industrial average, has served as a hedge against inflation during the last 25 years.

7. Redwood, Inc., with existing assets alone, is expected to generate perpetual annual net earnings of $300,000. The company, which is all-equity financed with 100,000 shares of common stock authorized and outstanding, follows a policy of paying out 40 percent of each year's earnings in dividends and reinvesting the balance. Reinvestments are expected to yield perpetual returns of 18 percent per annum. If investors require a 15 percent return, at what price will they appraise the shares of this company?

8. Repeat Problem 5 on the assumption that instead of reinvesting 40 percent of each year's earnings, the company reinvests a fixed amount of $80,000 each year.

REFERENCES

"Are the Institutions Wrecking Wall Street?" *Business Week* (June 2, 1973), pp. 58–66.

BAKER, H. KENT, and JOHN A. HASLEM, "Toward the Development of Client-Specified Valuation Models," *Journal of Finance* 29 (September, 1974), pp. 1255–1263.

BLUME, MARSHALL E., JEAN CROCKETT, and IRWIN FRIEND, "Stockownership in the United States: Characteristics and Trends," *Survey of Current Business* 54 (November, 1974), pp. 16–40.

BREALEY, RICHARD A., *An Introduction to Risk and Return from Common Stocks* (Cambridge: The M.I.T. Press, 1969).

HALEY, CHARLES W., and LAWRENCE D. SCHALL, *The Theory of Financial Decisions* (New York: McGraw-Hill Book Company, 1973).

HOGAN, WILLIAM W., and JAMES M. WARREN, "Toward the Development of an Equilibrium Capital-Market Model Based on Semivariance," *Journal of Financial and Quantitative Analysis* 9 (January, 1974), pp. 1–11.

LINTNER, JOHN, "Expectations, Mergers and Equilibrium in Purely Competitive Securities Markets," *American Economic Review* 61 (May, 1971), pp. 101–111.

LINTNER, JOHN, "Security Prices, Risk, and Maximal Gains from Diversification," *Journal of Finance* 20 (December, 1965), pp. 587–606.

LORIE, JAMES H., and MARY T. HAMILTON, *The Stock Market: Theories and Evidence* (Homewood: Richard D. Irwin, Inc., 1973).

MALKIEL, BURTON G., *A Random Walk Down Wall Street* (New York: W. W. Norton and Company, 1973).

MALKIEL, BURTON G., and J. G. CRAGG, "Expectations and the Structure of Share Prices," *American Economic Review* 60 (September, 1970), pp. 601–617.

MAO, JAMES C. T., "Survey of Capital Budgeting: Theory and Practice," *Journal of Finance* 25 (May, 1970), pp. 349–360.

MARKOWITZ, HARRY M., *Portfolio Selection* (New York: John Wiley and Sons, Inc., 1959).

MODIGLIANI, FRANCO, and MERTON H. MILLER, "Dividend Policy, Growth, and the Valuation of Shares," *Journal of Business* 34 (October, 1961), pp. 411–433.

REINHARDT, UWE E., *Mergers and Consolidations: A Corporate-Finance Approach* (Morristown, N.J.: General Learning Press, 1972).

SHARPE, WILLIAM F., "Capital Asset Prices: A Theory of Market Equilibrium Under Conditions of Risk," *Journal of Finance* 19 (September, 1964), pp. 425–442.

Part Two

Financial Planning and Control

3 Financial Analysis and Budgeting

Just as mathematics in a sense is the language of science, so accounting is the language of business. The financial executive is dependent on the accounting system for much of the data necessary to evaluate past performance and current position and for the financial framework used in planning and control. In this chapter, we shall begin with a discussion of the usefulness and limitations of ratio analysis—a simple technique for measuring a firm's liquidity, solvency, and profitability on the basis of the data in its income statement and balance sheet. We shall then consider the meaning, structure, and uses of the statement of funds, a versatile tool for explaining the change in a firm's net working capital or for describing a firm's overall financial strategy.

In the second part of the chapter, we shall deal with the budget process and the elements of a comprehensive budget. Here, the accounting system is used for planning and controlling future activities. The translation of a firm's operating, investment, and financing plans into dollars and cents, and the forecasting of the firm's liquidity, solvency, and profitability by means of a system of projected financial statements make up the budgeting process. The budget, once it is adopted, also serves as a useful yardstick for appraising actual performance. For the sake of simplicity in this chapter, we shall treat only fixed budgets—i.e., budgets whose components are calculated on the basis of a fixed level of sales. We shall postpone the consideration of budgets based on variable sales levels, as well as the application of management-science techniques, until Chapter 4.

FINANCIAL RATIO ANALYSIS

The ratios we will discuss are calculated from financial statements and can be grouped as measures of liquidity, of solvency, and of profitability. These ratios are useful to the financial executive not only for internal planning and control, but also for predicting how a firm's financial position and strength will be appraised by external securities investors. We must remember that the central aim of financial planning is to enhance the company's attractiveness to investors so that the common stock of the company will sell at the highest possible price.

Measures of Liquidity

Definition of Ratios. The ability to raise the cash necessary to meet a firm's debts is essential to its survival. In the long run, this ability, called "solvency," depends largely on the profitability and the degree of indebtedness of a firm; but, in the short run, even a potentially insolvent company may have sufficient cash resources to meet its currently maturing obligations. Table 3-1 defines three liquidity ratios for measuring a firm's ability to generate cash for meeting debt payments in the short run: the current ratio, the quick ratio, and the cash ratio.

The current ratio is an attempt to measure liquidity by expressing the company's current assets as a multiple of its current liabilities. Since only cash can be used directly to pay off debt, and since current assets also include accounts receivable and inventories, the measure is at best a crude index. It is possible to refine this ratio by supplementing it with data on the average time necessary to convert inventories and receivables into cash (i.e., the average selling period and the average collection period).[1] The quick ratio and cash ratio represent two conservative alternatives to the current ratio. When only cash and accounts receivable are included in the numerator, the resulting multiple is known as the quick ratio; when only cash is included, the result is the cash ratio. These ratios are calculated in Table 3-1 for a hypothetical company, Extron, Inc., which produces commercial and industrial lasers. Tables 3-2 and 3-3 give its financial statements for a recent year.

Interpretation. These three liquidity ratios suffer from a common defect: they present a static picture of what is essentially a dynamic process.[2] The liquid assets of a firm will rise or fall depending on whether the

---

[1] To calculate the average selling period, divide the finished-goods inventory by the cost of an average day's sales; to calculate the average collection period, divide the accounts receivable by the average day's sales.

[2] Cf. Kenneth W. Lemke, "The Evaluation of Liquidity: An Analytical Study," *Journal of Accounting Research* 8 (Spring, 1970), p. 61.

Table 3-1 Standard Financial Ratios (dollar amounts in thousands)

Ratio	Formula	Calculation for Extron, Inc.
Short-term Liquidity Ratios		
1. Current ratio	Current assets / Current liabilities	$14,700 / $ 8,300 = 1.77
2. Quick ratio	Current assets less inventory / Current liabilities	$ 9,300 / $ 8,300 = 1.12
3. Cash ratio	Cash and marketable securities / Current liabilities	$ 1,700 / $ 8,300 = 0.20
Long-term Solvency Ratios		
4. Debt-equity ratio	Total debt / Total equity	$16,000 / $13,200 = 1.21
5. Interest coverage ratio	*EBIT** / Interest expense	$ 5,200 / $ 650 = 8.00
6. Preferred-dividend coverage ratio	*EBIAT*** / Interest plus preferred dividend	No preferred stock
Profitability Ratios		
7. Asset turnover ratio	Sales / Total assets	$26,000 / $30,000 = 0.867
8. Operating profit margin	*EBIT* / Total sales	$ 5,200 / $26,000 = 0.200
9. Return on total assets	*EBIT* / Total assets	$ 5,200 / $30,000 = 0.173
10. Return on total equity	*EBIAT* less interest / Total equity	$ 2,730 / $14,000 = 0.195
11. Return on common equity	*EBIAT* less interest and pfd. div.† / Common equity	$ 2,730 / $14,000 = 0.195

* Earnings before interest and taxes, or simply operating income.
** Earnings before interest but after taxes, or equivalently operating income less taxes.
† *EBIAT* less interest and preferred dividend is the same as net income in Table 3-3.

combined effects of operations, new financing, and repayments produce a cash surplus or a cash deficit. If cash inflows and outflows are perfectly synchronized, a firm can meet its payments without holding any liquid assets. On the other hand, if the synchronization is imperfect, liquid assets are a useful buffer for absorbing temporary deficiencies. In the long run, however, a firm's cash balance, inventories, and accounts receivable are all necessary investments in that they cannot be permanently reduced without seriously disrupting the firm. Ultimately, therefore, the liquidity of a firm is based on the long-term balancing of cash inflows and outflows. In this dynamic context, the liquidity ratios fail to provide a sound basis for judging a firm's debt-paying ability.

Table 3-2 Extron, Inc., Balance Sheet, December 31, 19__ (in thousands)

Assets		
Current assets:		
Cash and marketable securities		$ 1,700
Accounts receivable (net)		7,600
Inventories		5,400
		$14,700
Plant and equipment	$13,900	
Less: accumulated depreciation	4,000	9,900
Deferred costs of research and development		1,800
Other assets		3,600
Total assets		$30,000
Liabilities and Equity		
Current liabilities:		
Notes payable to bank		$ 3,400
Accounts payable		3,900
Accrued liabilities		1,000
		$ 8,300
Long-term debt		7,700
Stockholders' equity:		
Common stock	$ 2,000	
Paid-in surplus	4,000	
Retained earnings	8,000	14,000
Total liabilities and equity		$30,000

The key instruments of liquidity planning and control by management are the cash budget and the statement of funds; but since the budgets prepared by corporate management are generally not available outside the firm, the current ratio and its variants have become the standard tools of external analysis. Two types of external analysis are common: trend analysis, which determines the change in a firm's liquidity over time; and intra-industry comparisons, which show a firm's liquidity relative to its competitors at a given time. To facilitate intra-industry comparisons, Dun and Bradstreet, Inc., annually publishes fourteen industry average ratios with interquartile ranges for 125 lines of business.[3] It calculates these ratios from the firms' most recent financial statements. In addition, the Robert Morris Associates, a national association of bank loan officers, publishes eleven ratios for 156

[3] See Dun and Bradstreet, Inc., *Key Business Ratios in 125 Lines;* Robert Morris Associates, *Statement Studies;* and Federal Trade Commission and Securities Exchange Commission, *Quarterly Financial Report for U.S. Manufacturing Corporations.*

Table 3-3 Extron, Inc., Income Statement, Year Ending December 31, 19__ (in thousands)

Net sales		$26,000
Cost of goods sold (including depreciation and amortization)		14,000
Gross margin		$12,000
Operating expenses		
Selling and administrative expenses	$ 4,600	
Research and development expenses	1,700	
Contribution to employee pension fund	500	6,800
Operating income		$ 5,200
Interest expense, net		650
Income before taxes		$ 4,550
Provision for income taxes		1,820
Net income		$ 2,730

lines of business. It calculates these ratios from the financial statements of companies to which banks have made loans. The Federal Trade Commission and the Securities Exchange Commission also jointly publish quarterly data, including financial ratios, on manufacturing companies. Corporate management does well to heed these ratios, since the investing public generally prefers better-than-average ratios.

Measures of Solvency

Definition of Ratios. A firm's long-term debt-paying ability depends partly on the size of its debt and partly on the burden of its interest expenses. To make adjustments for inter-firm differences in total assets, a company's indebtedness is usually measured by the ratio of its debt to equity capital. The higher this ratio, the greater the risk of insolvency is to the company. This ratio, however, considers only the amount of debt, not the interest rate on the debt. An alternative measure that considers both factors is the interest coverage ratio, defined as the ratio of the firm's earnings before interest and taxes (*EBIT*) to its total interest charges. For example, an interest coverage ratio of 3 means that the firm earns three times the amount of its interest payments. Obviously, the higher this coverage ratio, the greater is a firm's ability to pay its interest.

There is also a corresponding preferred-dividend coverage ratio, defined as the ratio of the firm's earnings before interest but after taxes (*EBIAT*) to its combined interest and preferred-dividend payments. Why is *EBIAT*, which is simply *EBIT* minus taxes, used here in place of *EBIT?*

We must remember that interest expenses, for income tax purposes, are deductible. Operating income (*EBIT*) must exceed interest expenses before any tax liability is incurred, and this means that, were it needed, the entire operating income could be used for meeting interest expenses. Thus, the interest coverage ratio which uses *EBIT* expresses the firm's ability to cover its interest payments. On the other hand, preferred dividends are not deductible, and income tax must be paid before preferred stockholders can expect dividends. Thus, the preferred-dividend coverage ratio which uses *EBIAT* expresses the firm's ability to cover both preferred dividend and interest payments.

We should also note that debt principal is excluded from the calculation of the interest coverage ratio. This is done because a firm operating at a profit and which is in sound financial condition can usually refund its debt on or before maturity; that is, it can pay off existing obligations by incurring new obligations. Similarly, since preferred stock does not have a maturity date, its principal amount is excluded from the calculation of the preferred-dividend coverage ratio.

Interpretation. We shall again use the data for Extron, Inc., to illustrate the meaning of our ratios (Table 3-1). At the end of 19__, Extron had a debt-to-equity ratio of 1.21, meaning that the value of the company's assets could shrink by as much as 45 percent (= \$1 ÷ \$2.21) before the stockholders' equity would be eliminated. The firm's operating income (*EBIT*) during the same year was 8 times as large as its interest expenses—i.e., operating income could fall to one-eighth of the 19__ level and still be adequate for payment of all interest expenses.

Is an interest-coverage ratio of eight sufficiently high to insure the long-run solvency of the Extron, Inc.? Instead of attempting a definite answer, let us observe that the margin of safety offered by a given coverage ratio varies inversely with the variability of the firm's operating income, which in turn depends on such factors as the nature of the products sold, the competitive position of the firm within the industry, and the monetary and fiscal policy of the government. A safe coverage for one company may be unsafe for another; simple rules of thumb are likely to be unreliable. Perhaps the most useful applications of these ratios are again trend analysis and intra-industry comparisons (the organizations that publish liquidity ratios also publish solvency ratios). Finally, what is an adequate coverage ratio also depends on how conservative the company's accounting practices are in reporting its income. If the company inflates its current reported income through such practices as taking an excessively long depreciation period or treating current expenses as capital expenditures, higher coverage ratios are obviously needed than if reported income were more conservatively calculated.

Measures of Profitability

For common stockholders, the key information in the financial statements is the ratio of net income after taxes to their total investment (line 11 in Table 3-1). Given a fixed amount invested by common stockholders, this profitability ratio varies directly with *EBIT* (the result of operating management) and inversely with the portion of *EBIT* paid out in interest, preferred dividends, and taxes (the result of financial management). We use various ratios to measure these two aspects of management.

Definition of Ratios. The efficiency with which operating management utilizes its resources is measured by the rate of return on total assets; i.e., the ratio between the before-tax operating income (*EBIT*) and total assets. One way operating management can become more efficient is to increase the asset-turnover rate—that is, to increase the sales volume generated per dollar of assets. However, this increase in efficiency may be offset if there is an accompanying decrease in the operating-profit margin, which is the ratio of operating income to sales. In other words, asset-turnover rate and operating-profit margin must be considered simultaneously in any evaluation of operating management. In fact, the return on total assets is the product of the asset-turnover rate and the operating-profit margin, which relationship may be written as follows:

$$\frac{EBIT}{\text{Total assets}} = \frac{\text{Sales}}{\text{Total assets}} \times \frac{EBIT}{\text{Sales}} \tag{3-1}$$

This is sometimes called the du Pont equation (E. I. du Pont de Nemours and Company was the first to utilize it), and it is useful in evaluating a company's operating efficiency.

Given the operating results, financial management can increase the rate of return on common equity by means of "leverage financing," which refers to the use of debt and/or preferred stock, instead of common stock, in a firm's capital structure. The degree by which the return on common equity is increased measures the efficiency of financial management. A simple example will clarify the relationship between financial leverage and return. Let us posit that Company X, with \$5,000 of common equity and \$5,000 of debt, makes an investment of \$10,000 on which it realizes a 20 percent (\$2,000) return at the end of the year. Tax rate on net income is 50 percent. The interest is only 8 percent (\$400), so the firm has an after-tax income of \$800, or 16 percent on its \$5,000 equity capital. This return is 6 points higher than the 10 percent after-tax return the common stockholders would have earned had they provided the entire \$10,000 investment themselves.

On the other hand, suppose business falls off and the company is able to realize a return on assets of, say, only 2 percent ($200). The interest must still be paid in full ($400), so the firm has an after-tax net income of −$200, or −4 percent on its $5,000 equity capital. This return is 5 points lower than the 1 percent after-tax return the common stockholders would have earned assuming all common equity financing. Since the results can be profitable or unprofitable, depending on business conditions, the desirability of debt financing cannot be inferred from the results of any one year. Debt financing is profitable only if it increases the return on common equity in the long run.

Although we have discussed only debt financing, it should be clear that the above example is also applicable to preferred-stock financing. If the return on total equity exceeds the preferred-dividend rate, then the return on common equity will exceed the return on total equity. The converse is also true.

Interpretation. Figure 3-1 presents a convenient way of visualizing the basic relationships which determine operating efficiency. The data in this figure are based on the Extron financial statements in Tables 3-2 and 3-3. Extron had sales of $26.0 million and total assets of $30.0 million. Dividing sales by total assets, we get an asset turnover ratio of .867, meaning that every dollar of assets generated 86.7 cents of sales. (To be more accurate, we should have used average assets during the year, rather than year-end figure.) Operating income (*EBIT*) was $5.2 million for the year. Dividing this amount by sales, we get an operating profit margin of 20 percent, meaning that every dollar of sales added 20 cents to operating income. This profit margin, multiplied by the asset-turnover ratio, gives us the 17.33 percent return in operating income which the company earned on its total assets.

Had Extron employed no debt financing, the before-tax return on common equity would have been the same as the return on total assets—17.33 percent. Since the company's average tax rate is 40 percent, the after-tax return would then be 10.4 percent. Since common equity totaled $14 million, after-tax earnings to common stockholders would have been $1.456 million. But in actuality, the company employed $16 million in debt; at a before-tax return of 17.33 percent, this capital contributed $2,773,333 to operating income (*EBIT*). The interest on this debt amounted to only $650,000, leaving a surplus of $2,123,333, which accrued to the common stockholders, who thus made a total after-tax profit of $2.73 million (= $1.456 million + $2.123 million × .6). In other words, the return on common equity was 19.5 percent, or nearly twice the 10.4 percent return without debt.

Should Extron eliminate financial leverage by replacing its $11.1 million of interest-bearing debt (bank loans + long-term debt) with common equity? Such a move would have three effects: first, the common stockholders would have to increase their investments in the company by $11.1

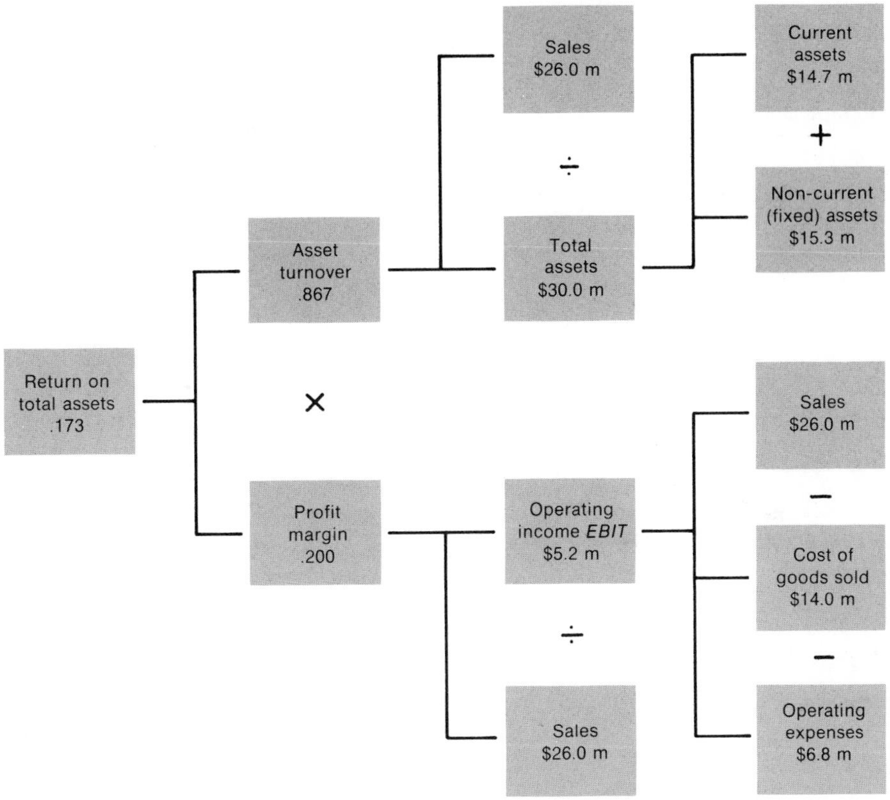

Figure 3-1 An Application of the du Pont Equation

million. Second, the stockholders' after-tax net profit would increase by 60 percent of the amount of interest savings (i.e., from \$2.73 million to \$3.12 million); and third, since debt repayment improves the quality of earnings, there would be a reduction in the rate at which security investors discount the new earnings. The first of these effects reduces the wealth of the stockholders; the second and third increase it. The Extron stockholders will be better off with 100 percent equity financing only if the increase in the value of their shares exceeds the \$11.1 million which would be used up in debt repayment. Given the \$390,000 increase in earnings, the increase in share value depends on the change in the discount rate, which, in turn, depends on the security investors' assessment of how much the risk in earnings is reduced by the elimination of debt. For example, if the security investors were discounting the earnings of Extron at, say, 14 percent with debt financing, then the new discount rate would have to drop to 10.19 percent in order for the value of the shares to increase by 11.1 million after debt repayment.[4] As we have mentioned, financial writers disagree on the possible effects of debt financing on the total value of a firm; we shall consider this subject in Chapter 13.

THE STATEMENT OF FUNDS

The funds statement is a useful accounting tool for managing liquidity and solvency and for formulating the broad strategy behind financial policy. This statement may be either historical or projected (*pro forma*); in either case it summarizes the changes in a firm's net working capital. However, since the preparation of the funds statement is well understood, we shall focus here on the statement's analytical structure and how it is useful to financial management.

Analytical Structure

The term "funds" is usually defined as net working capital—i.e., the excess of current assets over current liabilities. In terms of the balance sheet, this definition implies that

$$\text{Funds} = \text{Long-term debt} + \text{Equity} - \text{Fixed assets} \qquad (3\text{-}2)$$

This identity enables us to trace the effect of any transaction on a firm's current resources. Thus, given the fixed assets, any increase in long-term debt or in equity will increase funds; and given long-term debt and equity, any increase in fixed assets will decrease funds.

Eq. (3-2) provides the logic behind the classification of funds transactions into sources and uses. "Sources" are those transactions causing funds to increase and "uses" are those transactions causing funds to decrease. Since Table 3-4 presents these categories in a self-explanatory way, we shall limit ourselves to a few clarifying remarks. First, since depreciation is an expense that does not reduce working capital in the current period, it must be added back to current income in order to determine the contribution to working capital made by current operations. Second, the sale of fixed assets constitutes a source of working capital only if the proceeds increase current assets or decrease current liabilities. Thus, the exchange of a warehouse for an office building would have no effect on the funds statement; but if the exchange brings in, for example, a short-term promissory note, then funds are increased. Third, by the same reasoning, the issuance of a stock

[4] The new discount rate is obtained by solving the value for k in the following equation: (\$2.730 million/.14) + \$11.1 million = \$3.120 million/k.

Table 3-4 Classification of Funds Transactions

Sources		Uses	
1. Net income, adjusted for depreciation and other expenses not using working capital	xxx	1. Net loss, adjusted for depreciation and other expenses not using working capital	xxx
2. Sale of fixed assets	xxx	2. Purchase of fixed assets	xxx
3. Issuance of long-term debt or stock	xxx	3. Retirement of long-term debt or stock	xxx
	xxx		
4. Net increase in working capital	xxx	4. Payment of cash dividends	xxx
Total sources	xxx	Total uses	xxx

dividend (rather than one paid in cash) or the exchange of stock for long-term bonds has no implication for funds. On the other hand, cash repurchases of a company's own shares do reduce funds.

The definition of funds as net working capital is consistent with our emphasis on solvency and liquidity. But if the funds statement were to be used for formulating an overall investment and financing strategy, it would be more helpful to think of funds as the firm's total resources. In this case, we would focus on the flow of resources itself rather than on its effects on net working capital. This change in focus does not alter the classification of sources and uses, but it does necessitate a different form of presentation to indicate clearly the sort of information that W. M. Cole has called "where-got, where-gone" (see Table 3-5).[5]

Applications in Financial Management

The funds statement can be profitably employed to improve the management of working capital. Let us consider how a firm might run into liquidity crises while generating sizeable accounting profits. A company might have started business with the production of a good product but lacked sufficient capital. Let us assume that as sales expand, more and more cash is converted into accounts receivable and inventory, and the turnover periods lengthen due to increased competition. Accounts payable also increase as the consumption of raw materials increases. The firm is more profitable but less liquid than it was before. At this point, management might see an opportunity to expand its physical plant, if only financing were

[5] W. M. Cole's funds statement appeared in his *Accounts: Their Construction and Interpretation,* rev. ed. (Boston: Houghton Mifflin Company, 1915), pp. 127–132. For a survey of the different ways of presenting the funds statement, see Hector R. Anton and Robert M. Jaedicke, "Financial Statements—Statement of Funds and Cash Flows," in Sidney Davidson, ed.-in-chief, *Handbook of Modern Accounting* (New York: McGraw-Hill Book Company, 1970), Ch. 4.

available. If the firm decides to finance expansion by drawing on its working capital, the loss in liquidity could lead to a crisis.

Many actual companies have experienced such liquidity crises because management mistakenly thought that a profitable operation automatically produced a sound working-capital position. This is clearly an over-simplification since, as Table 3-4 shows, net income from operation is only one of many factors affecting working capital. If liquidity management is efficient, working capital will be available at the right moment in the right amount for the right duration. To achieve this result, management must anticipate all uses and sources of working capital by using a framework such as the funds statement. If such an analysis reveals a potential surplus, plans can be made to utilize the surplus profitably when it materializes. If analysis reveals a potential deficit, both uses and sources can be re-examined to see if sources can be increased or uses reduced.

The funds statement is also useful in the planning and control of a firm's overall investment and financing strategy. The information it provides can help the financial executive decide how much to invest in the firm and what method of financing to employ. A firm, for example, may be contemplating an expansion program which requires substantial capital expenditures over a period of years. In preparing the funds statement, the financial executive must ask if the proposed program is within the financial resources of the firm. He must also ask how profitable the new investments are relative to the cost of financing. The funds statement provides a useful framework for answering these questions. Once the size of the proposed investment program is fixed, the financial executive must then specify the sources of financing, whether it will be bank credit, financial leases, long-term bonds, preferred stock, common stock, retained earnings, or some combination of the above. The funds statement itself provides no answers, but it does force the financial executive to understand what sources are available and how much each costs before he actually launches a program.

An Example

Let us return to our example and see how the funds statement is useful. Extron, Inc., we remember, is a producer of commercial and industrial lasers. It was formed as a research-oriented firm, by a group of individuals who put up a total of $600,000. During the first two years, the business expanded, and the company needed more capital, so it sold 500,000 shares of common stock publicly for a total of $3.4 million. In the next five years, the company grew phenomenally: net sales rose from $5 million to $26 million; net profit rose from $0.45 million to $2.73 million; and total assets skyrocketed from $5.2 million to $30 million. Because of the great investment and financing during this period, Extron is an especially good subject for our purposes.

Table 3-5 Extron, Inc., Sources and Uses of Funds, a Five-Year Period (in thousands)

Sources		Uses	
Net income from operations	$ 5,640	Plant and equipment	$11,400
Provision for depreciation	2,900	Deferred R & D costs	2,100
Net increase in long-term debt	6,760	Increase in other assets	100
Proceeds from sale of common stock	5,000	Increase in net working capital	6,000
Total sources	$20,300	Total uses	$20,300

Table 3-5 presents Extron's funds statement for the five-year period, and it is arranged to bring out the firm's major financial decisions. During this period of rapid expansion, the company experienced a $20.3 million outflow of its funds. The largest components of this outflow were $11.4 million for fixed assets, $2.1 million for deferred-research-and-development expenditures, and $6 million for net working capital. Like other technology-oriented firms during that period, Extron did not charge its research-and-development costs immediately to the current accounting period; instead, they were recorded as a long-term investment and charged off systematically over the life of the related product (i.e., the cost is "deferred"—or, more accurately, capitalized). To finance the $20.3 million outflow, the company relied on three major sources: earnings retention ($5.64 million), the issuance of long-term debt (6.76 million), and the sale of common stock ($5 million). In addition, depreciation provision added $2.9 million to funds inflow.

The funds statement suggests several critical questions. Should the company have invested as much as it did and expanded its assets as rapidly as it did? Did the company allocate the $20.3 million among its different assets in the most profitable way? Was the method of financing the one most suitable for the company and its stockholders? Was it wise to rely on debt financing to such a great extent ($6.76 million), especially when the company is in such a competitive field? Did the firm utilize the best mix of long-term and short-term debt? Should it have relied so heavily on retained earnings in the equity portion of its financing? No dividends were paid during this period. Would it have been better to have paid out some earnings and raised part of the needed funds by issuing additional stock?

Any attempt to answer all these questions at once would require such complexity that we would be unable to see any single issue clearly. Hence, in this book we shall consider these questions one by one, using a partial equilibrium framework; that is, we shall study one issue at a time, treating the other factors as givens. This will enable us to reduce each question to manageable size. There is a hazard, though; we must be careful not to lose sight of the interrelationships involved. The funds statement itself should help us here, by providing a broad framework within which to view the various relationships.

BUDGET AND THE BUDGETING PROCESS

Earlier in the chapter, we described budgeting as the projection of financial statements in line with the management's specific goals. In this section, we shall first explain how one firm, the Noyes Corporation, uses its budgets for planning and control and then make some suggestions for improvement.

How One Company Budgets

The Noyes Corporation is a medium-sized sporting goods manufacturer producing a complete line of products. The company's activities are organized into divisions along product lines, with each divisional manager held responsible for the profitable operation of his product group. The company uses a detailed 1-year budget for controlling current operations and a condensed 5-year budget for long-range planning. No formal budgeting is projected beyond five years.

The company's basic budgetary documents include a Monthly Profit Plan, a Five-Year Operating Forecast, a Monthly Cash-Flow Projection, and a Five-Year Long Range Program. Of these four documents, the most basic is the Monthly Profit Plan, which is essentially a month-by-month projection of profit and loss for the coming year. On the basis of the sales forecast (or sales sub-budget) which he receives from the marketing manager, the company controller derives a production schedule for the coming year, making allowances for any planned changes in the inventory. From the production schedule, the controller derives the projected cost of goods sold month by month, which becomes the manufacturing sub-budget. Various other expense and income classifications are also each supported by a sub-budget, usually prepared by the executive in charge. By integrating the various sub-budgets, the controller produces the Monthly Profit Plan.

Besides this profit plan, produced annually, the company prepares a projection of the profit plan for the next five years. This is the Five-Year Operating Forecast. The procedure is the same as the above, with the difference, as mentioned, that the long-range plan is figured by years, not months. Also, some of the income and expense items are lumped together in order to condense the statement. This five-year plan is updated every year. Naturally, the upcoming year's profit plan is always the first year of the five-year plan.

The Five-Year Long-Range Program is based on the long-range sales forecast and its implications. This long-term budget focuses on capital expenditures, research and development programs, new-products programs, marketing programs, major sources of financing, and the company's long-run objectives. Finally, the Monthly Cash-Flow Projection is the standard statement of cash receipts and disbursements, derived from the current operating budget and the current portion of the long-range program.

Like most companies, the Noyes Corporation uses its annual profit plan to gauge the operating efficiency of the various divisions submitting sub-budgets. Once the profit plan has been submitted and approved by the management, it is not changed. At the end of each month, the controller collates each division's actual income and expense figures with the budget figures and tabulates comparisons for the month and for the year to date. Thus, at any given moment, a division has a record of its actual performance for year to date, as well as the targets for the remainder of the year.

We should ask how the financial executive allows for uncertainty in his forecasts, especially for the short-run (one-year) operating budget, and in particular whether the company makes any sensitivity tests to determine how the budget could change in response to variations in sales forecasts. No such sensitivity tests are actually made. Noyes uses only a single set of figures, not range estimates or probability distributions, in making its forecasts. Noyes thinks that the sales forecasts have been so reasonable that although there may be month-to-month error, the yearly forecasts have proved accurate enough that no probabilistic analysis is necessary. On closer examination, however, it is clear that Noyes' sales forecasts are deliberately cautious, so that any error is usually on the conservative side. In fact, error has been as high as 10 percent in certain years.

Also, how does the financial executive decide how much cash to keep on hand, and how does he insure that the company has enough cash for unexpected needs? Again, Noyes felt that this was not an important decision, because the company has always been able to meet cash payments. As it turns out, however, the company has always kept an excessively large amount of cash on hand. Its balance sheet shows that 10 percent of its assets are in the form of cash and short-term marketable securities. This primarily reflects the philosophy of the management: the company is publicly owned, but controlled by several financially conservative individuals who happen to be on the management team. The company has invested surplus cash in Treasury bills, but has no well-conceived plan for optimizing its short-term marketable securities portfolio.

Opportunities for Improvement

Quite simply, the company ought to increase the efficiency of its budgeting procedure through computerization. The budgets now take four full months to prepare manually. Computerization will allow the financial executive greater flexibility both in anticipating business uncertainties and in responding to unexpected variations from his original forecasts.

As it now stands, Noyes allows for uncertainty simply by building a slack into the budgetary forecasts. That is, sales are forecast on a conservative basis so that if there is an error, it is likely to be in actual sales exceeding the budget. This may be psychologically pleasing to the management, but such a budget could easily result in operating inefficiency, since understatement of sales leads to understatement of cash, accounts receivable, inventory, and plant and equipment needed to support the sales. A much more desirable way of dealing with uncertainty in sales is to forecast a probability distribution for sales, and with the computer derive a separate set of budgets for each possible value of sales in the distribution. Also, as we have seen, Noyes' budgets, once prepared, remain unchanged for the year. If the budgets were computerized, the controller could easily update them when there were major variations from the original budgetary assumptions.

A SIMPLIFIED EXAMPLE

To illustrate actual budget preparation, we shall use simplifying assumptions to project the income statement, the balance sheet, and the cash budget for a hypothetical company, the El Camelo Corporation.

Outline of Procedure

The steps outlined below are valid for the preparation of comprehensive budgets such as those adopted by Noyes Corporation as well as for the simple version we shall present.

(1) Since the ultimate justification of all business activities is sales, the sales forecast is the natural starting point in any budgeting process. Material purchases, accounts receivable, inventory, wage bills, operating expenses, capital expenditures, etc. must all be projected on the basis of anticipated sales. (A distinction should be made in the sales budget between cash sales and credit sales since there are implications for the timing of cash receipts.)

(2) After the sales budget comes the production budget: how much to produce and when. This budget derives from the simple principle that production in any period must equal current sales plus (less) the desired increase (decrease) in finished-goods inventory. This step therefore requires data on beginning inventory and the desired level of ending inventory.

(3) A given production schedule implies a given schedule of payments for material purchases and a given level of operating expenses. Operating expenses can be divided into variable expenses (those that vary with sales and production, such as direct labor, selling commission, etc.) and fixed

operating expenses (those which do not vary with sales and production, such as rent, depreciation, indirect labor, administrative expenses, etc.).

(4) The data in the third step, together with information on taxes, interest, and changes in inventory, enable us to project the income statement.

(5) If we have additional information on capital expenditures and financing plans, we shall be able to project the cash budget and the balance sheet.

(6) If a funds statement is needed, it can be derived from the income statement, the beginning and ending balance sheets, and certain supplementary information.

The Basic Data

(1) El Camelo Corporation is a manufacturer of a plastic household device which sells for $1 per unit. Ten percent of the firm's sales are retail sales for cash; the other 90 percent are wholesale on terms of "net 90"—i.e., the wholesalers are given 90 days to pay their bills in full. Bad debt is negligible. As of January 1, 19X1 (current year), the sales forecast for the coming year is $15 million for the first quarter, $14 million for the second quarter, $16 million for the third quarter, and $18 million for the fourth quarter. (2) The firm carries practically no raw materials inventory since quick delivery by the supplier makes it unnecessary. The company purchases only what it needs when it needs it on terms of 90 days net. Therefore, the $3.5 million of raw material purchased in the fourth quarter of last year (19X0) becomes due in the first quarter of this year (19X1). Company policy on finished-goods inventory is to have a sufficient number of physical units on hand at the end of each quarter to meet half the demand anticipated for the next quarter. The inventory on January 1, 19X1, totals 7.5 million units.

(3) To facilitate control, the management has established the following standard costs of production:[6]

Raw materials	$0.20 per unit of product
Direct labor	0.25 per unit of product
Other manufacturing expenses:	
Heat and light	$625,000 per quarter
Repairs and maintenance	375,000 per quarter
Depreciation	925,000 per quarter
Insurance	325,000 per quarter
Indirect labor	350,000 per quarter
Power	400,000 per quarter

[6] "Standard" costs are target costs—what products "should" cost, as opposed to actual, or "historical," costs. Standard costs are usually determined by material specifications and engineering studies.

Raw materials, as we have mentioned, are purchased on terms of "net 90." All other expenses (except, of course, depreciation) must be paid in cash in the period during which service is rendered. (4) Selling, administrative, and general expenses are expected to equal $3.413 million per quarter, payable in cash. (5) The firm has committed itself to a $4.5 million expansion program, which necessitates cash payments of $1.75 million in the third quarter and $2.75 million in the fourth quarter. To finance this expansion, the company has negotiated a five-year insurance-company loan of $4.5 million, of which $1.75 million will be available in the third quarter and $2.75 million in the fourth quarter. The company's bank has agreed to extend its $3.4 million loan for another year after it matures on May 1, 19X1.

(6) Total interest expenses for the year are estimated at $225,000 per quarter for the first two quarters, $260,000 for the third quarter, and $280,000 for the fourth quarter. (7) The current federal income tax payment always equals half of the prior quarter's taxable income. For the first quarter, $900,000 in taxes are due. (8) Company policy calls for 25 cents of

Table 3-6 El Camelo Corporation, Balance Sheet, December 31, 19X0

Assets		
Current assets:		
Cash and marketable securities		$ 935,000
Accounts receivable		13,808,000
Inventories—at cost or market, whichever is lower		4,810,000
Total current assets		$19,553,000
Plant and equipment	$36,798,000	
Less: accumulated depreciation	10,925,000	25,873,000
Total assets		$45,426,000
Liabilities and Equity		
Current liabilities:		
Short-term bank loan		$ 3,400,000
Accounts payable		3,500,000
Federal income taxes		900,000
Total current liabilities		$ 7,800,000
Long-term debt		10,306,000
Stockholders' equity		
Common stock	$10,000,000	
Capital surplus	5,000,000	
Retained earnings	12,320,000	27,320,000
Total liabilities and equity		$45,426,000

cash dividend per share during each quarter. (9) The firm values its inventory on the basis of cost (first-in, first-out) or market, whichever is lower. "First-in, first-out" means that the cost of goods sold is computed on the assumption that the goods held longest are sold or consumed first and that the goods remaining in inventory are those most recently purchased or produced. (10) The firm's balance sheet on December 31, 19X0 is presented above in Table 3-6.

Budget Preparation

We shall limit our solution here to the first quarter, but the calculation may easily be extended to subsequent quarters. Since first-quarter sales are estimated at 15,000,000 units, and a reduction in inventory of 500,000 units is desired, only 14,500,000 units need be produced during the first quarter. The production of these units requires the expenditure of $3,625,000 for direct labor, $2,900,000 for raw materials, and $3,000,000 for "other" manufacturing expenses. These cost figures, together with the change in inventory level, provide the basis for determining the cost of goods sold (see Table 3-7), which was the missing information needed to project the first-quarter income statement (Table 3-8).

Since 90 percent of the company's sales are on credit, only $1,500,000 worth of first-quarter sales will be for cash. But the year-end balance sheet shows $13,800,000 of accounts receivable which become collectible in the first quarter. Similarly, the $2,900,000 for raw materials will not be payable until the second quarter, but the year-end balance sheet shows $3,500,000 of accounts payable which become due this quarter. After these two ad-

Table 3-7 El Camelo Corporation, Cost-of-Goods-Sold Budget, First Quarter, 19X1

Raw material costs	$ 2,900,000
Direct labor	3,625,000
Other manufacturing expenses	3,000,000
Total cost of production	$ 9,525,000
(units produced)	(14,500,000)
(unit cost of production)	($0.657)
Add: beginning inventory	4,810,000
	$14,335,000
Less: ending inventory	4,598,000
Cost of goods sold	$ 9,737,000

Table 3-8 El Camelo Corporation, Income Statement, First Quarter, 19X1

Net sales	$15,000,000
Cost of goods sold	9,737,000
	$ 5,263,000
Selling, administrative, and general expenses	3,413,000
	$ 1,850,000
Interest expenses	225,000
	$ 1,625,000
Federal income tax	812,500
Net income	$ 812,500

justments have been made, the cash budget shows that the firm's balance sheet will have an ending cash balance of $2,005,000 (Table 3-9). And, finally, the beginning balance sheet, together with data on changes, enables us to project the values of other accounts in the ending balance sheet (Table 3-10).

Table 3-9 El Camelo Corporation, Cash Budget, First Quarter, 19X1

Beginning balance	$ 935,000
Budgeted receipts	
Collection of accounts receivable	13,808,000
Cash sales	1,500,000
Total cash available before financing	$16,243,000
Budgeted disbursements	
Accounts payable	3,500,000
Direct labor	3,625,000
Manufacturing expenses (except depreciation)	2,075,000
Selling, administration, and general expenses	3,413,000
Interest expenses	225,000
Federal income tax	900,000
Dividends	500,000
Plant expansion	0
Total cash disbursements	$14,238,000
Net financing	0
Ending cash balance	$ 2,005,000

Table 3-10 El Camelo Corporation, Balance Sheet, March 31, 19X1

Assets		
Current assets:		
Cash and marketable securities		$ 2,005,000
Accounts receivable		13,500,000
Inventories (7,000,000 units at $0.657 per unit)		4,598,000
Total current assets		$20,103,000
Plant and equipment	$36,798,000	
Less: accumulated depreciation	11,850,000	24,948,000
Total assets		$45,051,000
Liabilities and Equity		
Current liabilities:		
Short-term bank loan		$ 3,400,000
Accounts payable		2,900,000
Federal income tax		812,500
Total current liabilities		$ 7,112,500
Long-term debt		10,306,000
Stockholders' equity:		
Common stock	$10,000,000	
Capital surplus	5,000,000	
Retained earnings	12,632,500	27,632,500
Total liabilities and equity		$45,051,000

REVIEW QUESTIONS

1. What is financial ratio analysis? How is the information derived in this way of value to an executive in the financial management of his company? How would the emphasis of a financial manager differ from that of an external investor, such as a shareholder or creditor?
2. We classified financial ratios as measures of liquidity, solvency, and profitability. List and define the ratios in each category, indicating whether or not each ratio is an accurate measure. If the ratios are not accurate measures, how can they be improved?
3. True or false: If the after-tax return on total assets exceeds the return on equity, we have prima facie evidence that financial leverage is working to the advantage of the stockholders. (You may assume that there is only one class of equity: common stock.)
4. Identify the major inflows and outflows of cash in a typical firm. Within this dynamic framework, how reliable would you regard the standard liquidity ratios as predictors of the firm's bill-paying ability in the long run.

5. An alternative, but misleading, formula for calculating preferred-dividend coverage is the ratio of net earnings after interest and taxes to preferred dividends. Explain why the formula for preferred-dividend coverage given in Table 3-1 is preferable. (Hint: Apply both formulas to a company with preferred stock and compare the results with the company's interest coverage ratio.)
6. What is the du Pont equation? Explain its use as a tool for planning and controlling the efficiency of operating management. Can this equation be expanded to take account of the efficiency of financial management as well?
7. Explain the difference between a statement of funds and a statement of cash receipts and disbursements. Differentiate the ways in which these two statements are useful.
8. What is the difference between accounting and budgeting? How does each contribute to the financial management of a firm?
9. What is the meaning of the "Deferred Research and Development Costs" in the Extron funds statement? Why would a "deferred" cost be viewed as an application of funds?
10. Outline the key steps in the preparation of Noyes Corporation's budgets. In addition to those mentioned in the text, what other suggestions do you have for improving the budgeting process at Noyes?

PROBLEMS

1. Starting with the first-quarter budget, project the income statement, the balance sheet, and the cash budget for El Camelo for each of the remaining quarters of 19X1. Devise your own forms for presenting the various components of the budget and accompanying schedules.
2. In our discussion, we assumed that El Camelo appraised the value of its inventory on a first-in, first-out basis. How would the income statement and the balance sheet be affected if the company valued its inventory on a last-in, first-out basis?
3. Calculate the standard ratios for measuring liquidity, solvency, and profitability on the basis of the latest financial statements for the National Cash Register Company. Look up your own data.
4. Evaluate the operating efficiency of the Bethlehem Steel Company using the du Pont equation. Is this company more or less efficient than its competitors within the industry?
5. For the Detroit Edison Company (or another electric utility company), calculate the after-tax rate of return on total assets and compare it with the rate of return on total equity. Are the stockholders of Detroit Edison benefiting from the effect of debt leverage? If so, by how much? Use the most recent data available.
6. The annual reports of most companies contain, in addition to the usual income statement and balance sheet, a statement of the sources and uses of funds. Compile a ten-year funds statement for a growth company (e.g., IBM or Polaroid) and for a stable company (e.g., the Book-of-the-Month Club or Consumers

Power Company). Compare the statements, noting how the companies differ in their total demand for funds, distribution of funds among asset classes, sources of financing, and policy on cash dividends and external equity financing. Can the differences be explained in terms of differences in the nature of the product sold; rate of growth; management philosophy; past history; other factors?

REFERENCES

Accountants International Study Group, *The Funds Statement* (New York: American Institute of Certified Public Accountants, 1973).

ALTMAN, EDWARD I., *Corporate Bankruptcy in America* (Lexington: Heath Lexington Books, 1971).

ANTON, HECTOR R., and ROBERT K. JAEDICKE, "Financial Statements – Statement of Funds and Cash Flows," in Sidney Davidson, ed.-in-chief, *Handbook of Modern Accounting* (New York: McGraw-Hill Book Company, 1970), Ch. 4.

BEAVER, WILLIAM H., "Financial Ratios as Predictors of Failure," *Empirical Research in Accounting: Selected Studies, 1966* (Chicago: University of Chicago, 1967), pp. 71–102.

COLE, W. M., *Accounts: Their Construction and Interpretation,* rev. ed. (Boston: Houghton Mifflin Company, 1915).

DAVIDSON, SIDNEY, JAMES S. SCHINDLER, and ROMAN L. WEIL, *Accounting: The Language of Business* (Glen Ridge, N.J.: Thomas Horton and Daughters, Inc., 1974).

du Pont de Nemours, E. I., and Company, *Executive Committee Control Charts* (New York: American Management Association, 1960).

EDMISTER, ROBERT O., "An Empirical Test of Financial Ratio Analysis for Small Business Failure Prediction," *Journal of Financial and Quantitative Analysis* 7 (March, 1972), pp. 1477–1493.

HELFERT, ERICH A., *Techniques of Financial Analysis* (Homewood: Richard D. Irwin, Inc., 1972).

HORNGREN, CHARLES T., *Accounting for Management Control: An Introduction* (Englewood Cliffs: Prentice-Hall, Inc., 1974).

HORRIGAN, JAMES, "The Determination of Long-Term Credit Standing with Financial Ratios," *Emprical Research in Accounting: Selected Studies, 1966* (Chicago: University of Chicago, 1967), pp. 44–70.

KNIGHT, W. D., and E. H. WEINWURM, *Managerial Budgeting* (New York: The Macmillan Company, 1964).

LEMKE, KENNETH W., "The Evaluation of Liquidity: An Analytical Study," *Journal of Accounting Research* 8 (Spring, 1970), pp. 47–77.

LEV, BARUCH, *Financial Statement Analysis: A New Approach* (Englewood Cliffs: Prentice-Hall, Inc., 1974).

SHASHUA, L., and Y. GOLDSCHMIDT, "An Index for Evaluating Financial Performance," *Journal of Finance* 29 (June, 1974), pp. 797–814.

WELSCH, GLENN A., *Budgeting: Profit-Planning and Control* (Englewood Cliffs: Prentice-Hall, Inc., 1971).

4 Management Science in Planning and Control

The close relationship between budgeting and accounting should now be clear: since budgets are projected financial statements, an accounting framework must underlie every system of budgeting. It is not only accountants, however, from whom budgeting has received attention; in recent years, management scientists have enhanced both the flexibility and the usefulness of budgets by applying modern methods of quantitative analysis. In this chapter, we shall study four important advances: the automation of the budgeting process through computer modeling, the refinement of flexible budgeting through probability analysis, the optimization of product-mix decisions through linear programming, and the control of the risk of insolvency through simulation.

FINANCIAL BUDGETING AND THE COMPUTER

The Need for Computerization

The budget which we prepared in Chapter 3 for El Camelo Corporation was a fixed budget; that is, it was calculated on the basis of a given level of sales. In actual business, for purposes of both planning and control, the financial executive may wish to test the sensitivity of the budgeted figures to variations in the level of sales. The preparation of several sets of budgets under alternative assumptions about sales is generally known as "flexible budgeting." But sales volume is not the only possible variable. The financial executive may, for example, also wish to explore the budgetary implications of changing costs of production, different assumptions about future investment plans, competing methods of long-term and short-term financing, or alternative strategies for dividend payments. For our discussion, we shall broaden the concept of flexible budgeting accordingly.

Although the computer is useful in fixed budgeting, its greatest value stems from the extent to which it makes flexible budgeting feasible. The projection of even such a budget as the one we used for El Camelo for, say, the next ten years, would be extremely time-consuming; and yet it is only a skeleton budget, constructed on the basis of many simplifying assumptions. In reality, the contents of budgets are more detailed, the computations and adjustments more involved, and the administrative procedures more complex. In short, budgeting is a time-consuming and expensive operation. Fortunately, however, much of budgeting is a matter of simple arithmetical calculations according to various accounting rules—calculations which a computer can make with great speed and accuracy. With the aid of the computer, a financial executive can now make his budget system as comprehensive as he wishes, expand his planning horizon to include as many separate periods as he desires, and answer "what-if" questions for any number of sets of assumptions—all at reasonable cost and at a speed that insures that the budget will be up-to-date.

The Role of Models

A computer can carry out orders only if its instructions are clear and unambiguous. We can attain the required clarity and unambiguity by representing a firm's accounting framework as a system of equations. The resulting equations, called a model, will enable us to give the computer precise information about the firm's current financial position, projected level of operation, and plans for future investment and financing. It will also enable us to tell the computer the sequence of calculations to perform in preparing the budgets. Mathematical equations make it possible to spell out the exact relationships and steps in budget projections, from the initial data input to the final printout. The abstract model, in other words, provides a framework within which the financial executive can communicate with the inanimate computer.

The algebraic model also makes explicit the quantitative relationships among the budget variables, indicating the possible effects of a particular event or course of action on the firm's finances. For example, the financial executive may want to know how a new accounts receivable policy would affect his firm's immediate liquidity; or he may want to know the impact of a proposed investment on the company's cash flow and rate of return. The model gives corporate management a convenient way of experimenting with alternative courses of action before making a decision. The possibility of a comprehensive budget that could optimize all financial decisions at once is tantalizing; but, as we have already noted in another context, a general-equilibrium model would involve so many equations and variables that we would be unable to see any relationship clearly. In any case, no such comprehensive model has yet been constructed. Instead, we shall use budget models to generate financial data which we shall then use to optimize decisions one at a time. In this partial equilibrium approach, only the factors directly relevant to a decision are taken as variables. Treating the less immediate factors as given enables us to focus on the key variables affecting a decision.

An Application to El Camelo

The Model. Our budget model for El Camelo stresses the accounting relationships among the financial variables.[1] The symbols are defined in Table 4-1. Lower-case letters denote constants. Capital letters indicate variables. Thus, $SAL = s$ means that sales equals s units. Variables are dated by subscript according to the following principle: no subscript denotes the current period, "last" refers to the immediately preceding period, and "next" indicates the coming period. Selling price per unit, percentage of sales on credit, materials and labor costs, and the rate of income taxation are all assumed to be constant. Finally, we adopt the multiplication sign (*) and the division sign (/) to conform with standard practice in computer programming language.

Table 4-2 presents the equations needed to derive El Camelo's income statement in any given quarter. Eq. (4-1) states that the budget will be based on a projected sales of s units for the quarter. Eq. (4-2) translates sales into total revenue, divided between credit sales and cash sales in a ratio of a to $1 - a$. Eqs. (4-3) and (4-4) state that current production must equal current sales plus (minus) any increase (decrease) in inventory and that the firm's policy is to set its ending inventory at one-half the next quarterly sales. Given the production schedule, Eqs. (4-5) and (4-6) give the consumption of raw materials and direct labor, and Eq. (4-7) gives the manufacturing expenses (power, heat and light, depreciation, indirect labor, etc.). The sum of raw materials costs, direct labor costs, and manufacturing expenses is the total current cost of production.

Eqs. (4-8) through (4-11) give the cost of goods sold during the quarter, using the first-in, first-out method of inventory valuation. The cost of goods sold equals the total cost of production plus beginning inventory (valued at last quarter's unit-production cost) minus ending inventory (valued at the current quarter's unit-production cost). When the cost of goods sold is

---

[1] A similar model for financial projection can be found in James M. Warren and John P. Shelton, "A Simultaneous Equation Approach to Financial Planning," *Journal of Finance* 26 (December, 1971), pp. 1123–42.

Table 4-1 Definition of Symbols

Symbol	Definition
SAL	Sales in physical units
REV	Sales revenue in dollars
PPU	Production in physical units
IPU	Inventory of finished goods at end of period (in physical units)
INV	Inventory of finished goods at end of period (in dollars)
VRM	Value of raw materials used in production
VDL	Value of direct labor used in production (i.e., the wage bill)
FME	Total manufacturing expenses
POW	Power bill
HTL	Heat and light bill
REM	Repair and maintenance
DEP	Depreciation
INS	Insurance premium
IDL	Indirect labor cost
CGS	Cost of goods sold
TCP	Total cost of production
AVC	Average cost of production per unit of physical output
SAG	Selling, administrative, and general expenses
INT	Interest expense
NET	Net earnings after taxes
p	Selling price per unit of product
a	Percentage of sales on credit
b	Cost of raw materials per dollar of sales revenue
g	Cost of direct labor per dollar of sales revenue
τ	Rate of income taxation

subtracted from sales revenue, the difference is the gross margin, from which the firm must pay selling, administrative, and general expenses; interest on debt; and federal and state income taxes. Net profit, Eq. (4-12), is what is left over after all these expenses have been deducted. Thus, the equations in Table 4-2 outline step-by-step the procedure by which we projected El Camelo's income statement. When properly instructed, the computer will implement this model by going through exactly the same calculations.

Similar sets of equations can be set up for the cash budget and the balance sheet. The cash balance at the end of a period equals the beginning balance plus all receipts minus all disbursements. The cash budget is simply a systematic way of presenting this information of cash flows. The cash balance, of course, is only one of many accounts in a firm's balance sheet; the balance of any other account can be determined in the same way by noting the initial balance and adjusting for changes during the period. The reader will find it a useful exercise to attempt a model of El Camelo's cash budget and balance sheet.

Table 4-2 A Model of Income and Expenses

Sales forecast (in physical units and dollars)	
$SAL = s$	(4-1)
$REV = s * p = a * s * p + (1 - a) * s * p$	(4-2)
Production and inventory budget (in physical units)	
$PPU = IPU + SAL - IPU_{last}$	(4-3)
$IPU = 1/2 * SAL_{next}$	(4-4)
Requirements for raw materials and direct labor	
$VRM = b * Q * p$	(4-5)
$VDL = g * Q * p$	(4-6)
Manufacturing expense budget	
$FME = POW + HTL + DEP + IDL + REM + INS$	(4-7)
Cost-of-goods-sold budget	
$CGS = TCP + (INV_{last}) - INV$	(4-8)
where $TCP = VRM + VDL + FME$	(4-9)
$AVC = (TCP)/(PPU)$	(4-10)
$INV = IPU * AVC$	(4-11)
Net income projection	
$NET = (REV - CGS - SAG - INT) * (1 - \tau)$	(4-12)

The Computer Program. Once a budget model is formulated, it must be converted into a set of instructions for the computer to execute. Figure B-1 in Appendix B contains the computer program for projecting El Camelo's income statement on the basis of Eqs. (4-1) through (4-12). The same computer program also projects El Camelo's balance sheet and cash budget, based on another set of equations. Without going over these new equations one by one, we shall review the model's key assumptions. On the whole, these assumptions are similar to those we made in Chapter 3 when we projected El Camelo's balance sheet and cash budget by manual means:

1. The firm maintains enough finished goods inventory at the end of each quarter to meet half the demand anticipated for the next quarter, but there is no raw materials inventory.
2. All accounts receivable outstanding at the beginning of a quarter are collected during the quarter.
3. All accounts payable outstanding at the beginning of a quarter are paid during that quarter.
4. New investments are financed entirely by borrowings from banks and insurance companies. Money is borrowed at the beginnings of quarters and is repaid at the ends of quarters.
5. Taxes are figured on the basis of a fixed percentage of net income, and dividends are set at a fixed amount per share.

Although the above assumptions are oversimplified, certain realistic features can easily be added in any practical applications of the budget. For example, we assumed that any new investment will be financed entirely with borrowings. But we could assume instead that any new investment will be financed through a combination of debt, internal funds, and proceeds from sale of common stock. Moreover, we could impose constraints on the firm's cash position and its debt-to-equity ratio. The model itself will then be able to determine the amount of internal financing available and the division of external financing between stocks and bonds. This is only one example of practical improvements. An executive applying this model to a specific situation will no doubt find others.

FLEXIBLE BUDGETING WITH BREAK-EVEN ANALYSIS

The Nature of Break-Even Analysis

With a computer, one can easily calculate a company's profit for any assumed level of sales. The financial executive may, however, wish to know the quantitative relationship between sales and profit. Although the computer can solve specific problems, it cannot provide general abstract formulations, whereas the analytical method can. "Break-even analysis" is concerned with determining the algebraic relationship between sales and profit. The analysis is actually misnamed, since the goal of financial management is never merely to break even but to make a profit. Moreover, the profit should be high enough to compensate the firm for the opportunity costs of its capital investments, although break-even analyses generally ignore such costs. However, since the terminology is well established, we shall continue to use "break-even analysis" to indicate what might more accurately be termed volume-cost-profit analysis.

The Traditional Break-Even Analysis

Break-even analysis is based on the fundamental assumption that all costs can be classified as either fixed or variable. Variable costs are those which vary directly in proportion with the volume of production. In a manufacturing concern, raw materials, direct labor, selling commission, etc. are variable costs. Fixed costs, on the other hand, are those which remain fixed during the planning period regardless of variations in the volume of production. These would include such items as depreciation, property taxes, and executives' salaries. Since break-even analysis usually assumes equality between sales and production, we shall substitute sales for production in the following discussion.

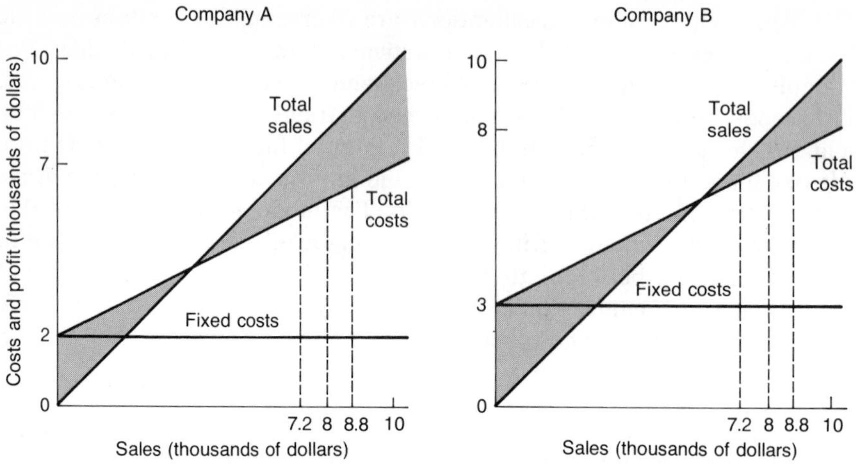

Figure 4-1 Break-Even Analysis

If there were no fixed costs, the net profit of a firm would be a constant percentage of sales, since break-even analysis also assumes selling price and average variable cost per unit of output to be constant. The presence of fixed costs means that the relationship between sales and profit is not actually a simple proportion. To determine the actual relationship, break-even analysis makes use of algebra. If we let p stand for the selling price of the product, v for unit-variable cost, F for total fixed cost, and Q for the number of units sold, then a firm's net profit Π can be written as:

$$\Pi = pQ - (vQ + F)$$

where pQ denotes total revenue and $(vQ + F)$ denotes total cost. We should note that if fixed costs equal zero, then $\Pi = (p - v)Q$. This latter relationship implies that (1) a unit increase in sales always results in a constant dollar increase in net profit, and (2) a given percentage increase in sales always results in an equi-proportionate increase in net profit.

The presence of fixed costs magnifies the percentage response of net profit to changes in sales. When F in the above equation is positive, an s percent increase in sale will cause net profit to increase from $(p - v)Q - F$ to $(p - v)(1 + s)Q - F$, for a gain of $s \dfrac{(p - v)Q}{(p - v)Q - F}$ percent. As an illustration, let us consider two firms producing the same product, which has a market price of \$1 per unit. The variable costs of production total 50¢ per unit for each company, but the fixed costs of production are \$3,000 for company B but only \$2,000 for company A. The resulting volume-cost-profit relationships are plotted in Figure 4-1, in which costs and revenue

Table 4-3 Profits At Different Levels of Sales (in dollars)

Company A				Company B			
Sales Revenue	Fixed Costs	Variable Costs	Net Profit	Sales Revenue	Fixed Costs	Variable Costs	Net Profit
$7,200	$2,000	$3,600	$1,600	$7,200	$3,000	$3,600	$ 600
8,000	2,000	4,000	2,000	8,000	3,000	4,000	1,000
8,800	2,000	4,400	2,400	8,800	3,000	4,400	1,400

are measured vertically and units of sales horizontally; net profit, then, is the vertical distance between the straight lines denoting total revenue and total cost. For convenience, this information is also presented in Table 4-3, in which costs and profit have been calculated for selected levels of sales.

Suppose that each company has sold 8,000 units in the year just ended, with a net profit of $2,000 for company A and $1,000 for company B (see Figure 4-1 or Table 4-3). If sales during the coming year were to fall by 10 percent (to 7,200 units), the net profit of firm A would decline by 20 percent (from $2,000 to $1,600) and that of firm B by 40 percent (from $1,000 to $600). What the example illustrates is this: the presence of fixed costs magnifies the percentage response of net profit to a given percentage change in sales; the higher the fixed costs, the greater the degree of magnification. This is why in periods of recession, profits often drop by a greater proportion than sales.

All of this has important implications for financial management. If a firm makes a product with an unstable demand, fixed costs should be kept at a low level in order to minimize fluctuations in net profit. Fixed costs may arise in connection with production or financing. It may be difficult to influence fixed costs of production, since they often reflect the technical engineering aspects of the manufacturing process; but the financial executive can exert direct control over the fixed costs of financing arising from leverage financing. When we discuss the optimal method of financing a business in Chapter 13, we shall distinguish between the magnification of profit fluctuation due to the presence of fixed operating expenses and that due to fixed financing charges. At that time, we shall see why the optimal use of leverage financing must take into account not only average profitability over a period of time but also the variability of profit within that period.

Probabilistic Break-Even Analysis

An important limitation of traditional break-even analysis is its assumption that the financial executive knows exactly how many units of his firm's product will be sold, whereas, in reality, demand forecast is at best an educated guess. But by using probability theory, we can take demand uncertainty into account.

Descriptive Statistics of **Π.** If demand Q is a random variable, then net profit Π is also, since net profit is uniquely determined by the number of units sold. In describing the probability distribution of a random variable, we have already introduced the mean as a measure of central tendency and the standard deviation as a measure of dispersion. Let us now explore the relationship between the mean and standard deviation of the net-profit variable and those of the demand variable.

Suppose that company A (whose cost, revenue, and profit data are given in Table 4-3) predicts that the demand for its product in the coming year will be 7,200 units, 8,000 units, or 8,800 units, with probabilities of .5, .25, and .25, respectively. Since demand uniquely determines net profit, these probabilities are also applicable to the corresponding net-profit figures. That is, net profit will be \$1,600, \$2,000, or \$2,400, with probabilities of .5, .25, and .25. (Selling price and costs are assumed to be unchanged.) To calculate the mean and the standard deviation of the demand (Q), we apply the appropriate formulas given in Chapter 2:

$$\mu_Q = \tfrac{1}{2}(7{,}200) + \tfrac{1}{4}(8{,}000) + \tfrac{1}{4}(8{,}800)$$
$$= 7{,}800$$
$$\sigma_Q = [\tfrac{1}{2}(7{,}200 - 7{,}800)^2 + \tfrac{1}{4}(8{,}000 - 7{,}800)^2 + \tfrac{1}{4}(8{,}800 - 7{,}800)^2]^{1/2}$$
$$= 663.35$$

Similar calculations show that the mean and the standard deviation of net profit (Π) are \$1,900 and \$331.67, respectively.

Interesting relationships exist between the two means and between the two standard deviations. These relationships can be derived mathematically, but we shall simply state them here without formal proof:[2]

$$\text{Mean of Net Profit} = (\text{Unit Contribution} \times \text{Mean of Demand}) - \text{Fixed Costs}$$

$$\text{Std. Dev. of Net Profit} = (\text{Unit Contribution} \times \text{Std. Dev. of Demand}),$$

where unit contribution is the profit contribution per unit of demand, as measured by the excess of selling price over unit variable cost. As an

[2] More generally, if $X = a + bY$, where X and Y are random variables, then $\mu_X = a + b\mu_Y$ and $\sigma_X = b\sigma_Y$.

exercise, the reader should verify these relationships for the data under consideration.

An Application. Knowing the mean and the standard deviation of net profit enables us to make certain probabilistic statements about a firm's net profit. For this example, let us assume that demand and hence net profit have normal probability distributions. We have already defined probability distribution as a table which assigns a probability to each of several values which a random variable may possibly take on. This information may also be presented graphically, usually with the values of the random variable measured along the horizontal axis and the corresponding probabilities along the vertical axis. The graphic representation of the normal distribution is the familiar bell-shaped curve (Figure 4-2), which has two relevant properties. First, the curve is symmetrical around the mean of the distribution, which means that if a random variable is distributed normally, there is a 50–50 chance that its value will be above the mean and a 50–50 chance that it will be below. And second, if μ and σ stand respectively for the mean and the standard deviation of a normally distributed random variable, then 68.27 percent of the area under the curve is included within the limits $\mu \pm 1\sigma$; 95.45 percent is within the limits $\mu \pm 2\sigma$; and 99.74 percent is within the limits $\mu \pm 3\sigma$.

To facilitate the use of the normal curve in probability analysis, statisticians have calculated the cumulative area under the curve in small incremental units from the lower limit of $\mu - 3\sigma$ to the upper limit of $\mu + 3\sigma$ (see any basic statistics text). Suppose that the demand for company A's product and hence the firm's net profit are distributed normally. We shall assume that net profit has a mean value of \$1,900 and a standard deviation of \$332. The financial executive may wish to know the probability that net profit will exceed \$2,500. We note that \$2,500 is 1.81 standard deviations to the right of the mean. Any table on normal distribution would show that

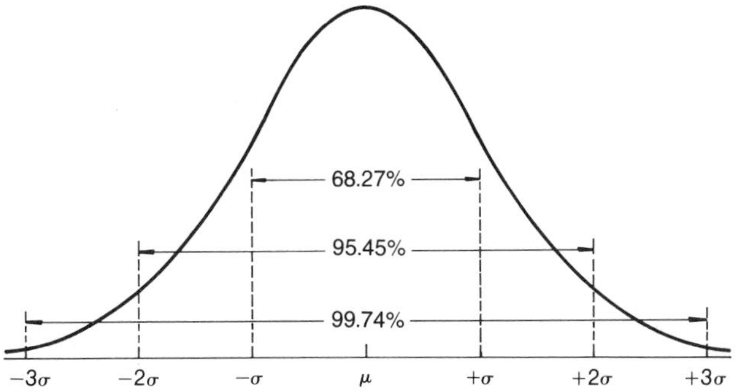

Figure 4-2 Area Under Normal Probability Distribution

96.48 percent of the area under the normal curve is to the left of the point $+1.81\sigma$. Since the total area under the curve is 1, this means that only 3.52 percent of the area under the curve is to the right of that point. In other words, there is a probability of 3.52 percent that the firm's net profit will exceed \$2,500. We can, of course, also find the probability that net profit will fall below a given level—say, \$1,500. Fifteen hundred dollars is 1.21 standard deviations to the left of the mean. Similar analysis would show that 11.31 percent of the area under the curve is to the left of the point -1.21σ; so the probability is 11.31 percent that net profit will be less than \$1,500. Finally, we can determine the probability that net profit will fall between two levels—say, between \$1,500 and \$2,500. We know that the combined probability of net profit being less than \$1,500 or more than \$2,500 equals 11.31% + 3.52%, or 14.83 percent. Therefore, the probability that net profit will be between \$1,500 and \$2,500 is 100% − 14.83%, or 85.17 percent.

LINEAR PROGRAMMING AND THE OPTIMAL PRODUCT-MIX

The Uses of Linear Programming

As an extension of budgeting, linear programming can be used to optimize the product-mix decision. In a multi-product firm, the projection of sales must be based on an assumption about the proportion in which the sales of the various products will be combined. (No product-mix decision came up in our earlier discussion since we assumed that El Camelo manufactured only one product.) Also, when a firm's cost structure changes, the impact on profit will depend on how the company adjusts the level and composition of its production. Linear programming is a valuable tool for determining what this adjustment should be.

Before we consider these applications, however, we should note that there are several other financial decisions to which this mathematical technique may be profitably applied. We have already noted the use of linear programming to determine the allocation of a fixed amount of funds among several competing investment projects (Chapter 1); and we shall consider it in more detail when we take up the study of capital budgeting in Part III. In addition, we shall use this technique to determine the best way to finance the short-term needs of a firm which experiences pronounced seasonal fluctuations and which has alternative sources of financing differing in cost and flexibility. Linear programming is also helpful in the management of bank-investment portfolios.[3]

[3] See Alfred Broaddus, "Linear Programming: A New Approach to Bank Portfolio Management," in Federal Reserve Bank of Richmond, *Monthly Review* 58 (November, 1972), pp. 1–11.

The Product-Mix Decision

The Problem. Let us imagine a firm, the Miracle Pharmaceutical Company (see Table 4-4), which produces two wonder drugs whose code names are SGP and PNZ. There are two bottlenecks in the production of these drugs: the company's fractional-distilling capacity and its blending capacity. The total distilling time available during the period for which we are planning is 160 hours; the total blending time available for the same period is 360 hours. The production of one ounce of SGP requires two hours of distilling time and two hours of blending time; each ounce of PNZ requires one hour of distilling time and four hours of blending time. SGP sells for $60 an ounce; PNZ, for $50 an ounce. Miracle Pharmaceutical can sell as much of each drug as it wishes at these prices. Half of the sales of each drug are on credit, collectible at the end of the following period. Materials, labor, and other variable costs total $35 an ounce for SGP and $30 an ounce for PNZ, payable in cash at the end of the current period. Subtracting the variable costs from selling price, we find that each unit of SGP contributes $25 to profit, while each unit of PNZ contributes $20.

Our decision must take into account, in addition to these data, the impact of product mix on the firm's cash position. The company's initial cash balance is $2,000, including the collection of past receivables. The amount of cash is increased by only 50 percent of the current sales, since the other 50 percent is on credit, collectible at the end of the next period. We must remember that expenses for labor, raw materials, and other variables must be

Table 4-4 Data for Product-Mix Decision

A. Plant capacity and requirements

Process	SGP (hr. per oz.)	PNZ (hr. per oz.)	Capacity (hrs.)
Distilling	2	1	160
Blending	2	4	360

B. Price, costs, and profits

Product	Price	Variable Costs	Profit Margin
SGP	$60	$35	$25
PNZ	50	30	20

C. Cash position

Initial balance	$2,000
Desired ending balance	1,500

paid in cash at the end of this period—after which the firm desires an ending cash balance of \$1,500.

Our problem is to determine how many ounces of each drug, in view of the given production and financial constraints, the company should produce in order to maximize profit and hence share value.

Linear Programming Formulation. Although the problem sounds simple, it would not be easy to solve without linear programming.[4] The difficulty stems from the fact that the optimal solution must take account simultaneously of all the constraints: plant capacity, technical coefficients of production (the proportions in which the factors of production are combined), and cash balance requirements. The reader might find it interesting to venture a numerical solution by some other means to compare with the optimal solution which we will reach with the aid of linear programming.

In this linear-programming formulation of the problem, x_1 and x_2 denote the number of ounces of SGP and PNZ, respectively, to be produced:

$$
\begin{array}{rl}
2x_1 + x_2 \leq 160 & \text{(capacity constraint)} \\
2x_1 + 4x_2 \leq 360 & \text{(capacity constraint)} \\
5x_1 + 5x_2 \leq 500 & \text{(liquidity constraint)} \\
x_1, x_2 \geq 0 & \text{(nonnegativity constraint)} \\
\text{Maximize } 25x_1 + 20x_2 & \text{(objective function)}
\end{array}
$$

The capacity constraints limit the use of the distiller to 160 hours and the blender to 360 hours. To understand the liquidity constraint, we must recall that half of the firm's sales are on credit, whereas all of its expenses must be paid in cash. The expression $5x_1 + 5x_2$ measures the net cash outflow associated with current operation;[5] if the firm is to have an ending cash balance of \$1,500, this outflow cannot exceed \$500. The nonnegativity constraint simply states that units of output cannot be negative. And the objective function defines the problem: to determine the values of x_1 and x_2 that will give the greatest possible profit ($= 25x_1 + 20x_2$) while satisfying all the constraints.

The Optimal Solution and Sensitivity Analysis

The Optimal Solution. The graphic solution of the problem involves two steps: first, we must find the set of "feasible" combinations—those

[4] For a more detailed explanation of linear programming, see my *Quantitative Analysis of Financial Decisions* (New York: The Macmillan Company, 1969), Chs. 3 and 4.

[5] Each ounce of SGP brings in \$60, but since half the sales are on credit, only \$30 are received in cash. Since SGP costs \$35 per ounce to produce, there is a net cash outflow of \$5 per ounce; similarly for PNZ.

which will satisfy all constraints; then, we must isolate the one combination which will produce the highest profit. In Figure 4-3, all sales combinations on or to the left of line I satisfy the distilling constraint; all combinations on or to the left of line I′ satisfy the blending constraint; all combinations on or to the left of line II satisfy the liquidity constraint; and all combinations in the first quadrant satisfy the nonnegativity constraint. Since all constraints must be satisfied simultaneously, the set of feasible combinations is the intersection of these four sets: the pentagonal area *abcde*.

To isolate the optimal solution, we introduce the concept of the equal-profit line, defined as the locus of all combinations of output that produce the same profit [see Figure 4-4(a)]. Any such line must be negatively inclined, with a slope determined by the relationship of the profit margin of SGP to that of PNZ. Thus, to earn $2,000 of profit, the firm can operate at output levels $x_1 = 0$ and $x_2 = 100$, or at $x_1 = 20$ and $x_2 = 75$, or at $x_1 = 40$ and $x_2 = 50$, etc. In fact, any combination of output satisfying the condition $x_2 = 100 - 1.25x_1$ will generate $2,000 of profit. There is, of course, a whole family of such lines, with each line representing a higher profit than the line to its left. Since the Miracle Pharmaceutical Company wishes to maximize profit, it would like to aim at the line farthest to the right. The point which represents the intersection of the set of feasible combinations with the line farthest to the right is the "corner" point *d*. The optimal policy, therefore, is to produce 60 ounces of SGP and 40 ounces of PNZ, with a resulting total profit contribution of $2,300.

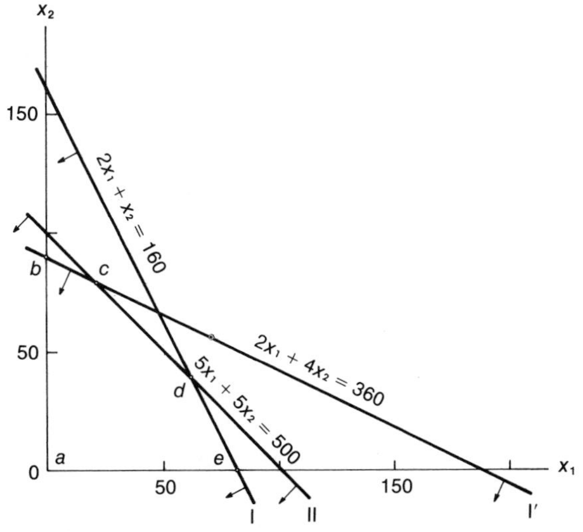

Figure 4-3 Constraints and Nonnegativity Conditions

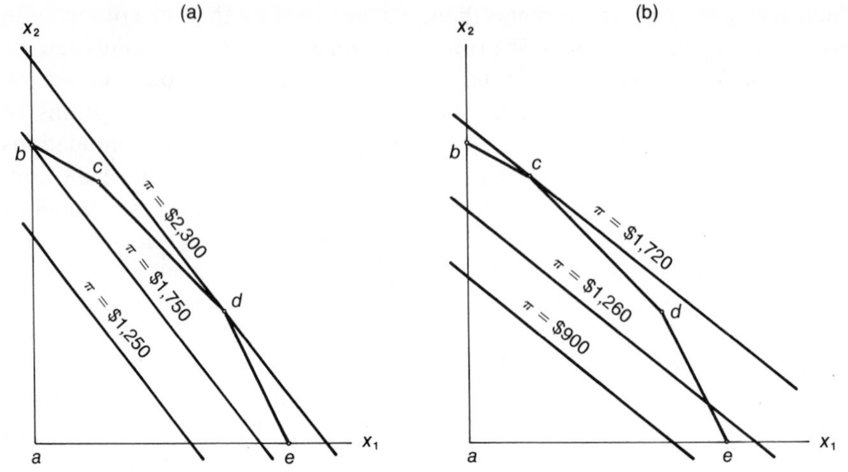

Figure 4-4 Determination of the Optimal Solution

The graphic approach to the problem has the serious drawback that it cannot easily be applied when there are three or more decision variables. A much more efficient method is the algebraic procedure known as the simplex algorithm, developed by George B. Dantzig. The technique is based on the fact (clear from the graphic solution) that the optimal solution must be represented by a point at a "corner" of the area of feasible combinations. (A corner point is one at the intersection of two constraints. The exception to the corner-point rule is the special case in which the equal-profit line has the same slope as one of the constraints; in that event, there will be infinitely many "optimal" solutions, but at least one of them will be a corner point.) The simplex method provides an efficient test for determining the more desirable of two combinations. Since there is only a finite number of corner points to be tested, repeated application of the simplex method leads us to the optimal solution.

The iterative nature of this technique suggests that the computations might be done by computer. And, indeed, efficient computer programs have been written which not only generate the optimal solution but also allow the decision-maker to test the effect on that solution of changes in production capacity, changes in the technical coefficients of production, and changes in price, cost, and profit margin. Various computer manufacturers have published manuals on the preparation of data input, the setting up of problems on the computer, and the interpretation of output. Familiarizing oneself with at least one of these manuals is a good investment of time.

Sensitivity Analysis. After obtaining the optimal solution, one may wish to know how sensitive the solution is to changes in any of the underlying data. Sensitivity analysis is in essence contingency planning, concerned with "what-if" questions. Suppose, for example, the prices of some raw materials were to rise, how should Miracle adjust its production so as to minimize the adverse impact on profit? The higher materials costs, let us say, cut the profit margin on SGP to $14 per ounce and that on PNZ to $18 per ounce. Hence, the company's objective function is:

$$\text{Maximize profit} = 14x_1 + 18x_2$$

In Figure 4-4(b), the feasible solution that maximizes this function is at corner point c. The company, therefore, should now produce 20 ounces of SGP and 80 ounces of PNZ, with a resulting profit of $1,720. This profit is smaller than before, but it is still the best attainable under the changed circumstances.

Cerro de Pasco is one well-known company that uses linear programming for its contingency planning.[6] The company, a subsidiary of Cerro Corporation, uses linear programming to determine how much of its zinc mining output should be sold as concentrate and how much should be refined to be sold as metals. This model, one of the most comprehensive in operation, is reported to contain 150 equations with some 370 variables. The same model is also used to formulate plans for meeting such contingencies as a fall in output prices, a jump in transportation costs, a wildcat strike, or a breakdown in key production facilities. Because metal prices are highly volatile, Cerro's management needed a tool to shorten their reaction time to sudden changes in internal and external conditions and the result was the linear programming model. Speaking from experience, the management notes that human judgment is still indispensable, since the model cannot take into account those political and social factors that may spell the difference between success and failure. The management, however, obviously found the zinc model valuable, since it is now planning similar models for the company's copper and lead operations.

SIMULATING THE RISK OF INSOLVENCY

The Simulation Model

"Simulation," used here to determine a firm's risk of insolvency, is a technique for evaluating the merits of alternative financial policies through experimentation on a mathematical model. A good model should specify correctly, with a minimum of details, the crucial relationships between the key variables in a situation requiring a decision. Using actual data, the model

---

[6] "A Computer Model to Upgrade Zinc Profits," *Business Week* (August 26, 1972), pp. 74–76.

can forecast the results that might be expected from a particular policy. By experimenting with several policies and comparing outcomes, the policy most likely to produce the desired results can be identified. If our mathematical models could always be solved quickly and cheaply, there would be no need for simulation, of course. But when mathematical models are too complex or costly to solve, simulation provides a useful alternative method.

The model for simulating the risk of insolvency consists of an equation which computes the net effect which a recession will have on a firm's cash inflows and outflows.[7] The equation is based on the following set of assumptions. A recession causes sales to decline and the average collection period on receivables to lengthen. Both these changes are of uncertain dimension, but the management is assumed to be able to specify the distribution of their probabilities during the recession. Moreover, not all cash outflows are of equal priority for maintaining a firm's solvency. For example, if a firm is short on cash, it can easily postpone dividend payments, major capital expenditures, and so on without risking or precipitating insolvency. In predicting a firm's solvency position, these cash expenditures are viewed as discretionary.

Other types of cash expenditures, however, must be made if the firm is to remain in business. Mandatory cash expenditures would include such items as interest payments, taxes, and manufacturing, selling and administrative expenses needed to maintain sales. Since our concern is with the risk of insolvency, only the mandatory cash outflows will be considered in the following equation for calculating the firm's cash balance at the end of a recession; all receipts are of course considered a part of the firm's cash inflow.

Consider a firm hit by a business recession lasting a given number of days. Assume that the sales of the firm are all on credit and that its debts are all refunded at maturity. Then, K_1, the firm's cash balance at the end of the recession, is given by the expression:

$$\underset{\text{Ending balance}}{\tilde{K}_1} = \underset{\text{Beginning balance}}{K_0} + \underset{\text{Inflow}}{\tilde{C}} - \underset{\text{Outflow}}{(\tilde{V} + F + I + \tilde{T})} \qquad (4\text{-}13)$$

where K_0 stands for the cash balance at the onset of the recession, C for collections on accounts receivable during the recession,[8] V for total variable

---

[7] This model was first presented by Gordon Donaldson in his *Corporate Debt Capacity* (Boston: Harvard Business School, 1961), Appendix B.

[8] $C = S_0 \times m + S_1 [n - m - \Delta m]$

where S_0 = pre-recession daily sales
S_1 = daily sales during the recession
n = length of recession in days
m = pre-recession average collection period, measured in days
Δm = increase in average collection period during the recession measured in days.

cash expenses (excluding taxes) during the recession, F for total fixed cash expenses (excluding interest), I for total interest payment, and T for total tax payment. Since sales volume is a random variable, so are C, V, T and K_1: the ~ indicates random variables as distinguished from constants.

If the probability distribution of the recession sales and collection period are known, we can calculate the probability that the firm's final cash balance K_1 will be negative. This probability will be designated as the firm's risk of cash insolvency.

Solution by Hand Calculation

A simple numerical example will demonstrate use of the model as a basis for simulation. Assume that the firm has an initial cash balance of $40, daily fixed cash expenses of $1.888, daily fixed non-cash expenses of $31.25¢, normal daily sales of $5.50, a normal collection period of 30 days, and a ratio of .4375 between variable cash expenses and sales. The probabilities of recession sales and collection slowdown are given in Table 4-5. These are "joint" probabilities because they refer to the simultaneous occurrence of two random variables. For example, during the recession there is a joint probability of .035 that daily sales will equal $5 *and* that the collection period will lengthen by 10 days. Assume further that the firm has a debt of $1,250 in its capital structure, with interest payable at 8 percent per year. Tax on corporate income is 50 percent. Given these data, what is the probability that the firm will become insolvent if hit by a recession lasting 360 days?

Before turning to computer simulation, we shall first solve this problem by hand calculation. Suppose during the recession, daily sales decline to $5 and the collection period lengthens by 10 days. For this combination of events, the company will have a cash balance at the end of the recession of $177.50, calculated in accordance with Eq. (4-13) as follows:

Beginning cash balance		$ 40.00
Cash inflows:		
Collection on pre-recession sales	$ 165.00	
Collection on post-recession sales	1,600.00	1,765.00
		$1,805.00
Cash outflows:		
Variable cash expenses	$ 787.50	
Fixed cash expenses	680.00	
Interest expense	100.00	
Income tax	60.00	1,627.50
Ending cash balance		$ 177.50

In Table 4-6 this ending cash balance appears along with sales of $5 and a lengthening in the collection period of 10 days, with a probability of

Table 4-5 Joint Probability Distribution of Recession Sales and Collection Period

	Increase in Collection Period				
Sales	10 Days	20 Days	30 Days	40 Days	Total
$5.00	.035	.040	.060	.015	.150
4.80	.015	.080	.080	.175	.350
4.30	.175	.080	.080	.015	.350
4.10	.015	.060	.040	.035	.150
Total	.240	.260	.260	.240	1.000

.035. The other sets of values in the table are calculated in the same way. Thus, there is a probability of .08 that recession sales will be $4.80 per day and the average collection period will lengthen by 20 days, with a resulting ending cash balance of $117.25, and so on. The table shows two possibilities in which the ending cash balance falls below zero: when recession sales drop to $4.30 or to $4.10, and the collection period lengthens by 40 days. These possibilities occur with a total probability of .05 (= .015 + .035), which is by definition the firm's risk of insolvency if it is hit by a recession lasting 360 days.

Table 4-6 Probability Distribution of Cash Balance at End of Recession

Cash balance K_I (dollars)	Sales and collection period: S_I (dollars)	Sales and collection period: Δm (days)	Probability of event
$177.50	$5.00	10	.035
127.50	5.00	20	.040
77.50	5.00	30	.060
27.50	5.00	40	.015
165.25	4.80	10	.015
117.25	4.80	20	.080
69.25	4.80	30	.080
21.25	4.80	40	.175
123.75	4.30	10	.175
80.75	4.30	20	.080
37.75	4.30	30	.080
−5.25	4.30	40	.015
91.25	4.10	10	.015
50.25	4.10	20	.060
9.25	4.10	30	.040
−31.75	4.10	40	.035

Computer Simulation

The first step in computer simulation is to generate random observations on recession sales and collection slowdown according to the joint probability distribution in Table 4-5. Three-digit decimals are generated randomly and the following meanings are attached to the numbers: any random number between 0 and .035 represents daily sales of \$5 *and* a collection slowdown of 10 days; any number between .036 and .075 represents daily sales of \$5 *and* a collection slowdown of 20 days; any number between .076 and .135 represents daily sales of \$5 *and* a collection slowdown of 30 days; and so on. Note that since 35 of the 1,000 3-digit decimals are assigned to daily sales of \$5 *and* a collection slowdown of 10 days, this joint event will be observed in the simulation with a probability of exactly .035. Similarly, we assigned 40 of the decimals to daily sales of \$5 *and* a collection slowdown of 20 days, so that this joint event will be observed with a probability of .04. The procedure, therefore, does generate these joint events with the desired frequencies.

Corresponding to any set of observed values for daily sales and collection period, the firm's final cash balance, K_1, can be computed using Eq. (4-13). We performed these calculations by hand earlier, but the computer can do the same calculations thousands of times faster. Running this experiment repeatedly will give us a probability distribution for K_1. The percentage of times that the value of K_1 falls below zero will show the firm's risk of insolvency. For this example, results based on 10,000 observations indicate that should the firm be hit by a recession of 360 days, the probability that the firm will become insolvent is approximately .0518. Sampling error explains the slight difference between this figure and the theoretical probability of .05 calculated earlier.

For some businesses, a probability of .05 represents a very high exposure to the risk of insolvency. If a recession lasting 360 days is not at all unlikely, then the company should take appropriate measures to reduce this risk exposure. The computer can also be used to test the sensitivity of the insolvency risk to other factors such as changes in the length of the recession, the extent of the collection slowdown, the size of the initial cash balance or initial debt, and the ratio of cash variable expenses to sales. The computer program for the simulation experiment is given in Figure B-2 of Appendix B.

REVIEW QUESTIONS

1. What are the benefits and costs associated with computerized budgeting? Are the benefits more likely to exceed the costs in a large firm or in a small firm?

2. What are the essential steps in computerizing the financial budgeting system? Explain the roles of financial accounting, mathematical modeling, and computer programming in the computerization process.
3. Identify the variables and constants in the model of income and expenses (Table 4-2) to which initial values must be assigned before the computer can make budgetary projections. From which division in the firm is each of these values most likely to come? Which figures are likely to be most precise, and which are determined more or less by subjective judgment?
4. Explain break-even analysis. Why is it misnamed? How can break-even analysis be used to improve a firm's operating, investment, and financing decisions?
5. A basic assumption of break-even analysis is that costs are either fixed or variable. Explain the distinction between fixed and variable costs. Which is each of the following: depreciation of plant and equipment, raw materials, sales commissions, interest charges on debt, salaries of top executives, heat and light, lubricant for machines, salaries of repairmen, and federal unemployment-compensation taxes?
6. What financial applications of linear programming can you think of besides the ones mentioned in the text?
7. Even though SGP's profit margin is \$25 per ounce, while PNZ's is only \$20 per ounce, we found that it was more profitable for Miracle Pharmaceutical to divide its productive capacity between the two drugs than to make only SGP. Explain the reason for this in terms that the firm's president, who may not be mathematically oriented, can understand.
8. You were asked to solve Miracle's product-mix decision by a method of your own choosing. Did you get the optimal solution? If not, what were the problems that you encountered?
9. How does simulation differ from optimization as a method of decision-making, and what factors would determine which method is the more appropriate to use in a given situation?
10. An important step in any simulation experiment is the generation of observations on those variables in the model whose values are random. Explain how these observations are obtained when the simulation is carried out on a computer.

PROBLEMS

1. Construct an algebraic model to represent El Camelo's cash budget and balance sheet. Use the figures given in Chapter 3 to test the financial projections derived from your model against the results presented in the text.
2. How will the model of income and expenses in Table 4-2 be changed if our assumptions are altered in the following ways:
   a. The number of units sold in the current period is $1{,}500 + 1.5 \times$ the level of last year's GNP.
   b. Inventory is now valued on a last-in, first-out basis. Goods produced in any period are sold either in that period or in the period following.

c. New policy calls for the finished-goods inventory at the end of each quarter to be equal to one third of the sales for the next quarter plus one fourth of the sales for the quarter after next.

d. The federal income-tax rate is τ on the first $50,000 of taxable income and τ' on taxable income beyond $50,000.

3. The General Cycle Corporation manufactures a standard line of children's bicycles. The total fixed cost of the product is $10,000 a year; the unit variable cost (labor, materials, sales commissions, etc.) is $20 per bicycle. Each bicycle sells for $50. We shall assume that current sales equals current production, so there is no inventory variation. Answer the following questions by means of both algebraic and graphic analysis:

   a. What is the firm's profit or loss if 400 bicycles are sold during the year?

   b. If sales increase by five percent, by what percentage will profit (loss) be increased (decreased)?

   c. At what level of sales will the firm break even? What would be the effect on the break-even point if fixed cost were only $7,500? If selling price were $45 per bicycle? If unit variable cost were $25 per bicycle?

4. Suppose that the vice-president of marketing at General Cycle estimates that next year's demand for his firm's product will be distributed normally with a mean of 400 bicycles and a standard deviation of 15 bicycles. Calculate the mean and the standard deviation of General Cycle's net profit. What is the probability that next year's net profit will exceed $3,000? Will drop below $1,100? Will fall between $1,100 and $3,000?

5. The Ajax Corporation manufactures two products: A and B. Product A sells for $100 per unit, with variable costs totaling $80 per unit. Product B sells for $60 per unit, with variable costs totaling $50 per unit. Production is constrained by a cutting capacity of 150 hours and an assembly capacity of 240 hours during the planning period. The production of A requires three hours of cutting time and two hours of assembly time per unit; the production of B requires one hour and five hours, respectively. What product mix will maximize the firm's profit? Formulate it as a linear-programming problem and solve it by the graphic method.

6. Given the production and liquidity constraints, and the costs and prices, the maximum profit that the Miracle Pharmaceutical Company could make was $2,300, by producing 60 ounces of SGP and 40 ounces of PNZ. By how much would the maximum profit be increased if the distilling capacity were increased by one hour? How is this information useful to the financial executive in deciding whether or not to expand distilling capacity? Given the present distilling and liquidity constraints, why would it not be profitable for the firm to expand its blending capacity?

7. In the simulation experiment, if recession sales drop to $4.30 per day and collection period lengthens by 20 days, the firm will have a cash balance at the end of the recession of $80.75. (See Table 4-6.) Use Eq. (4-13) to verify this ending cash balance.

8. (Special projects) The computer program for forecasting El Camelo's financial statements appears in Figure B-1 of Appendix B. Test the validity of this program by running it on a computer, using the data for El Camelo. Does the computer output agree with the results we have calculated by hand?

The computer program for the simulation experiment appears in Figure B-2 of Appendix B. Perform the simulation on a computer, using the data in the text. How sensitive is the firm's risk of insolvency to changes in the length of the recession, the extent of the collection slowdown, the size of the initial cash balance or initial debt, and the ratio of variable cash expenses to sales?

REFERENCES

"A Computer Model to Upgrade Zinc Profits," *Business Week* (August 26, 1972). pp. 74–76.

BROADDUS, ALFRED, "Linear Programming: A New Approach to Bank Portfolio Management," in Federal Reserve Bank of Richmond, *Monthly Review* 58 (November, 1972), pp. 1–11.

BROOKS, LEROY D., *Financial Management Decision Game* (Homewood: Richard D. Irwin, Inc., 1975).

CARLETON, WILLARD T., CHARLES L. DICK, and DAVID H. DOWNES, "Financial Policy Models: Theory and Practice," *Journal of Financial and Quantitative Analysis* 8 (December, 1973), pp. 691–709.

CHILDRESS, ROBERT L., *Sets, Matrices, and Linear Programming* (Englewood Cliffs: Prentice-Hall, Inc., 1974), Chs. 5, 6, and 7.

DONALDSON, GORDON, *Corporate Debt Capacity* (Boston: Harvard Business School, 1961), Appendix B.

GREENLAW, PAUL S., and M. WILLIAM FREY, *FINANSIM: A Financial Management Simulation* (Scranton: International Textbook Company, 1967).

HILLIER, FREDERICK S., and GERALD J. LIEBERMAN, *Operations Research* (San Francisco: Holden-Day, Inc., 1974), Chs. 2 and 15.

JARRETT, JEFFREY E., "An Approach to Cost-Volume-Profit Analysis Under Uncertainty," *Decision Sciences* 4 (July, 1973), pp. 405–420.

LIFSON, K. A., and BRIAN R. BLACKMARR, "Simulation and Optimization Models for Asset Deployment and Funds Sources Balancing Profit, Liquidity and Growth," *Journal of Bank Research* 3 (Autumn, 1973), pp. 239–255.

MAO, JAMES C. T., *Quantitative Analysis of Financial Decisions* (New York: The Macmillan Company, 1969), Chs. 3, 4, and 14.

MOORE, CARL L., *Profitable Applications of the Break-Even System* (Englewood Cliffs: Prentice-Hall, Inc., 1971).

WAGNER, JOHN, and LEROY J. PRYOR, "Simulation and the Budget: An Integrated Model," *Sloan Management Review* 12 (Winter, 1971), pp. 45–58.

WARREN, JAMES M., and JOHN P. SHELTON, "A Simultaneous Equation Approach to Financial Planning," *Journal of Finance* 26 (December, 1971), pp. 1123–42.

Part Three

Capital Budgeting

5 Investment Decisions Under Certainty (I)

Although budgeting is a useful tool, it does not provide a theory of decision-making, since budgeting in itself does not indicate which course of action is optimal. In Chapter 4, we saw how linear programming and probabilistic break-even analysis can be used to optimize the operating decisions of a firm. In this section (Chapters 5-9), we shall consider the theory of optimal investment decisions, first under the relatively simple conditions of certainty and then under the more realistic conditions of uncertainty.

THE NATURE OF INVESTMENT ANALYSIS

The term "investment" is used here to denote a firm's expenditures for long-lived assets, i.e., those assets whose costs and benefits are not immediate but spread over a period of time. For an industrial firm, these expenditures would include such investments as plant and equipment, working capital, marketing and advertising programs, research and development, mergers and acquisitions, and even repurchases of one's own common stock. Investment analysis is the same as what business executives refer to as capital budgeting: it involves that body of knowledge which deals with the optimal growth rate of a firm's total resources and the optimal allocation of these resources among specific assets.

The optimal investment program is the one that maximizes the value of a company's existing shares. Since this value depends on the firm's earning power, the first step in any investment analysis is to forecast the incremental earning power of the investment. We equate earning power here with cash flows, defined as the excess of receipts over all operating and financing costs, except depreciation (which is a noncash expense). Moreover, we assume that a firm knows its optimal financing plan (i.e., the division between debt, preferred stock and common equity), and that every investment is financed according to this plan. In deriving cash flows, all proceeds from the sale of debt and preferred stock are treated as cash inflows and all interest, preferred dividends, and principal repayments as cash outflows. Hence, the resulting cash flows are the flows accruing to the common stockholders. Once these cash flows are forecast, the financial executive must estimate how much they will enhance the firm's net worth. Obviously, an investment is profitable only if it increases the market value of a company's common shares.

Investment analysis, then, is a direct extension of valuation theory; Figure 5-1 describes the close relationship between securities valuation by investors and investment decision-making by financial executives. The amount, composition, and financing of a firm's assets determine the level, futurity, and uncertainty of its earning power. The basis on which this earning power is appraised by the securities investors provides the ultimate test for evaluating the merits of an investment decision. For this reason, investment theory derives from valuation theory criteria for comparing the relative attractiveness of earnings streams which differ in time pattern and in degree of uncertainty. Such criteria are necessary if the financial executive is to be able to distinguish those investments that will enhance a firm's share value from those that will not.

Investment analysis would be straightforward if the future returns on all investments were known with certainty; financial theory is well developed for appraising returns streams which differ only in level and futurity. Uncertainty, however, complicates the matter in at least two ways. First,

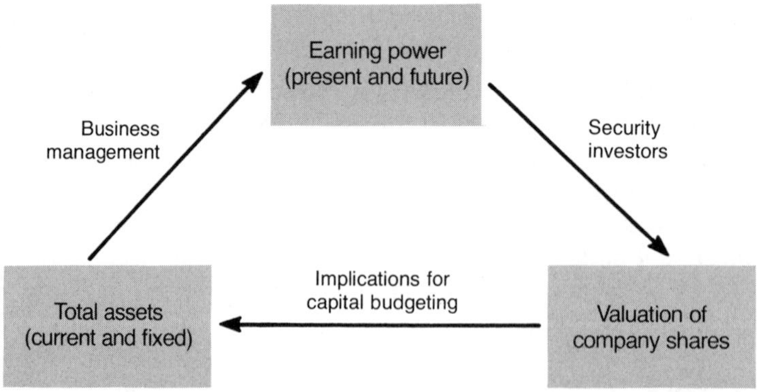

Figure 5-1 Security Valuation and Capital Budgeting Decisions

uncertainty makes it difficult for the analyst to forecast future investment returns. This is especially true in the case of long-lived assets, since forecasting inevitably becomes less accurate as the time horizon is extended. Second, under uncertainty the analyst cannot forecast the market's required rate of return with accuracy. The financial executive needs to know not only the risk-free interest rate, but also the risk premium required by securities investors to invest in the company's shares. The fact that the risk premium changes over time makes it difficult to forecast accurately the way an investment will affect share price.[1]

Because of the problems posed by uncertainty, our discussion will assume for the present the simple case of certainty. Here and in Chapter 6, we shall derive criteria of investment analysis for situations in which futurity is the only complicating factor. Then, in Chapters 7 and 8, we shall consider the concept and measurement of investment risk, as well as various ways of incorporating risk in investment analysis.

THE INVESTMENT PROCESS

The financial executive is not, of course, the only one involved in the investment process. Operating executives in marketing, production, engineering, and research and development also have important roles. We shall be better able to appreciate the theory of investment analysis if we first examine the financial executive's role in the origination, analysis, and final approval of investment proposals.

The Role of the Financial Executive

The source of an investment idea depends largely on whether the expenditure is routine or strategic. Routine investments are those expenditures which merely maintain or expand a firm's existing business, whereas strategic investments are those expenditures which give new direction to a firm's business. Routine investments may be made to reduce cost of production, to improve quality of output, or to increase physical capacity. Ideas for such investments will most likely come from a production manager. Strategic investments may involve the launching of a new product, a new product line, or an entirely new business. Ideas for such investments will most likely come from the top management, including the financial executive. But the initiative could also come from the other vice presidents, the president, or a member of the board of directors.

---

[1] The stationarity of risk premium is discussed in Burton G. Malkiel and John G. Cragg, "Expectation and the Structure of Share Prices," *American Economic Review* 60 (September, 1970), pp. 601–617.

New investment ideas are clearly essential for the survival and continued growth of any business. But once an idea is conceived, it must be analyzed. This is where the financial executive can make the greatest contribution. Many operating executives who specialize in marketing, engineering, or production are not very familiar with the concept and technique of investment analysis. The financial executive and his staff act as internal consultants and assist in the preparation of project proposals. They identify the relevant factors to be considered, anticipate changes which might affect investment return, work with others in gathering information, and assemble the material in logical form. The financial executive has another job as well. When top management receives capital budget proposals, it usually finds that various divisions have requested more than the amount available for investment. It is up to the financial executive to co-ordinate the proposals so that additional funds may be raised or projects trimmed to coincide with available funds.

Whether the financial executive plays a purely advisory role or an advisory-decision role depends in part on his position in the organizational structure of the firm and in part on the size of the investment project. In most companies, small-investment decisions are delegated to the operating executives. Large-investment decisions, usually handled at high levels (e.g., by the president, executive vice-president, or board of directors), generally involve the financial executive as a consultant. Participation in the final approval or rejection of a project depends on his position in the firm: for example, whether or not he is on the executive committee or sits in on the meetings of the board of directors. In any case, it is the financial executive who provides the objective analysis necessary for making investment decisions on a rational basis.

How One Firm Makes Investment Decisions

The Cameo Company is a soap and detergent manufacturer, organized by divisions along product lines. Each division has an assistant controller who is responsible for all of its financial functions, including the preparation of capital-expenditure proposals. Each assistant controller reports to both the corporate controller and the divisional operating executive. At the corporate level, the finance function is divided between the corporate controller and the treasurer. The former is responsible for planning and controlling operations; financial reporting and interpretations; protection of assets; and capital budgeting. The latter is responsible for acquisition of funds; management of cash and banking arrangements; and maintaining good investor relationships.

Let us suppose that the household-products division has an idea for a new product. The research-and-development division will probably be asked to analyze similar products made by competitors to see if the Cameo

Company can make equally good or better products for a competitive price. If this is feasible, the product manager, with the aid of the assistant controller, draws up a "profit plan" with estimates of the total necessary investment, the probable volume of sales, revenue and expenses, and cash flow. If the rate of return indicated by these estimates is acceptable, the proposal is submitted to the corporate management as part of the divisional 1-year and 5-year budget.

The corporate controller carefully re-analyzes the project proposal, checking the accuracy of the profitability forecasts. What rate of return will the firm get if it captures the predicted share of the market? What if it falls short of the target? or exceeds the target? The same sort of sensitivity analysis is applied to cost estimates. The controller must then consider another issue: if the new product is a complete failure, what else could the plant and equipment be used for? What "bail-out" protection is there? The controller must also consider whether the people making the proposal have tended to be overly optimistic or pessimistic in the past, and make allowances accordingly. Next, to assess its overall impact, the proposed project is set against the 5-year plan to see what effect the investment would have on the annual profit-and-loss statement, the balance sheet, the funds flow, and the financial ratios—that is, on the investing public's indicators of stock value.

The analysis must also take into account the overall investment picture. What is the *total* of funds available for investment? Since there are usually more projects than the company can fund, no investment can be considered only as an individual project but must be viewed as a part of the firm's overall plans. This portfolio approach also allows the management to take account of the possible correlations among the returns of different investment projects. Finally, the president of the company makes his decision on the basis of the analysis provided by the controller.

THE CASH-FLOW FRAMEWORK OF ANALYSIS

We are now ready to consider in detail the measurement of the attractiveness of an investment proposal. In this section, we shall justify the cash-flow framework of analysis; and in the following section, we shall analyze the merits of various criteria for appraising the worth of an investment considered as a series of cash flows.

Why Cash Flow?

Since the price of a share may be viewed as a function of its future adjusted earnings,[2] why is the value of an investment viewed instead as a

[2] The concept of adjusted earnings was defined in Chapter 2 above.

function of its future cash flows? Actually, the cash flow of an investment is equivalent to its adjusted earnings, so the difference is only one of terminology. Let us consider an investment costing $27,000 now, which the company plans to finance entirely with common equity. The investment is expected to generate accounting income (after depreciation) of $3,000 annually for the next 3 years, after which the investment will be scrapped with zero salvage value. Annual depreciation, let us say, is a constant $9,000. The cash flows, then, would consist of the initial outlay of $27,000 and the subsequent inflow of $12,000 (= $3,000 + $9,000) in each of the 3 years of project life.

Now, if investors in the stock market require a 10 percent return, by how much would such an investment increase or decrease the value of the company's existing common shares? In other words, what is the net present value of the investment? Using the earnings approach to valuation, we first examine the project's accounting income to see if proper adjustment has been made for the cost of the investment necessary to generate the income in the first place. The principle of accrual accounting requires that the initial cost of $27,000 be charged off as depreciation, not in a single year, but over the economic life of the project. This method of depreciation accounting facilitates the matching of revenue and expenses in income statements, but it creates a timing discrepancy between the actual outlay of $27,000 and the accounting recognition of this expense. The discrepancy can be removed, however, simply by reversing the accounting entries—that is, by treating the $27,000 as a cash outlay now and by adding the $9,000 of annual depreciation back to the annual accounting income of $3,000. The result is the following adjusted earnings series:

End of Year	0	1	2	3
Accounting income	—	$ 3,000	$ 3,000	$ 3,000
Deduct: Cost of investment	$27,000	—	—	—
Add: Depreciation	—	9,000	9,000	9,000
Adjusted earnings	−$27,000	$12,000	$12,000	$12,000

Since these figures are the same as the cash flows associated with the investment, the cash-flow analysis of investment is consistent with the earnings approach to share valuation.

To determine the net present value of the investment, we must discount the cash flow series at the cost of equity capital to the firm, which is the minimum rate of return an investment must earn if it is to be profitable. In Chapter 8, we shall express this minimum return as a function of the securities investors' required rate of return. For the moment, however, these two rates will be viewed as identical, and the terms used interchangeably. Discounting the cash flows at 10 percent, we get a net present value of

$2,842, the amount by which the investment will enhance the value of the company's existing shares.

Since the cash-flow analysis is equivalent to the earnings approach to share valuation and since the latter is equivalent to both the dividend approach and the investment-opportunities approach, the cash-flow framework is consistent with all three approaches to share valuation.

The Derivation of Cash Flow

Two Basic Rules. The cash flow of an investment must be determined on an incremental basis if the impact of the investment on the company's share value is to be assessed correctly. "Incremental basis" is the difference between the firm's expected cash flow with the investment and its expected cash flow without the investment. This calculation enables us to isolate the change in cash flow which is attributable to the investment.

This "with-and-without" framework is in sharp contrast to the "before-and-after" framework. The latter method compares the firm's expected cash flow after the proposed investment with its present cash flow, a comparison which may not indicate causal relationships clearly. For instance, a rise in cash flow may occur independent of the new investment, in which case this method would overstate the investment's benefits. On the other hand, it might understate the benefits of an investment by failing to indicate an investment's potential for retarding a decline in cash flow.

Our second basic rule is that the cash flow must be calculated on an after-tax basis. Since the corporate income-tax provision affects both the level and the timing of cash flows, we would be ignoring a critical factor if we made our calculations on a before-tax basis. There are several situations in which tax considerations may significantly alter the cash flow of an investment:[3]

1. Accelerated depreciation enables a firm to shift its tax payments from the early years of a project's life to its later years. Such postponements, equivalent to an interest-free loan from the government, may have a substantial effect on an investment's profitability.
2. The investment-tax-credit provision allows a firm to reduce its regular federal income-tax liability in any year by a certain percent of the cost of machinery and equipment purchased in that year; this may be viewed as a cash discount on the price of any new investment. Any unused tax credit may be carried forward to future years.

---

[3] For a comprehensive analysis of the impact of taxation on investment decisions, see James W. Edwards, *Effects of Federal Income Taxes on Capital Budgeting* (New York: National Association of Accountants, 1969).

Table 5-1 Shoe Machine Revenue and Cost Data

Annual sales (100,000 pairs @ $9.50 per pair)		$95,000
Variable costs		
Materials		$42,000
Manufacturing costs		
Direct labor	$18,000	
Repairs and maintenance	2,800	
Power	1,800	
Supplies and lubricants	1,400	
Taxes and insurance	1,500	
Depreciation	5,000	30,500
Selling costs		8,500
		$81,000
Prorated fixed costs		
Factory administration		$ 2,900
General administration		1,900
		$ 4,800

3. When an investment involves the sale of an existing asset at a gain, the tax on the gain is a cash outflow caused by the investment decision. Under the Revenue Act of 1962, as amended, the gain is divided into two parts: the amount representing the depreciation accumulated since 1961 and the amount (if any) in excess of that. The amount representing past depreciation is taxed at the normal income-tax rate; only the amount in excess is taxed at the preferential rate for capital gains.[4]
4. The problem of multiple tax rates may also arise when one decides to invest in subsidiaries in foreign countries, where tax laws may differ considerably from those in the United States. Before-tax cash flows are inadequate since they ignore these differences in international tax laws.

An Illustration. The following example, summarized in Table 5-1, will serve to illustrate the derivation of the cash flow associated with an investment.[5]

[4] To illustrate, suppose a machine with an expected economic life of 10 years was acquired on January 1, 1968 at a cost of $100,000. For tax purposes, it was depreciated using the double-declining-balance method with zero salvage value. On January 1, 1976, the machine was sold for $126,777, which was $110,000 above the book value on that date. Of the $110,000 gain, $83,223, the amount equalling the accumulated depreciation, would be taxed at the normal income tax rate, and only the excess of $26,777 at the preferential rate for capital gains. This example is adapted from James W. Edwards, *op. cit.*, pp. 62–63.

[5] Adapted from John H. Kempster, *Financial Analysis to Guide Capital Expenditure Decisions* (New York: National Association of Accountants, 1967), pp. 102–107.

The Red Shoe Manufacturing Company is planning to purchase a new machine in order to increase its production of men's shoes. The estimated cost of the machine is $25,000; its economic life is 5 years, at the end of which it will have no salvage value. The machine is expected to increase sales of men's shoes by 10,000 pairs per year; this increase will not affect the current selling price of $9.50 per pair. The firm expects the following variable costs of production (in dollars):

Materials	$ 4.20	per pair
Manufacturing costs		
Direct labor	1.80	per pair
Repairs and maintenance	2,800.00	per year
Power	1,800.00	per year
Supplies and lubricants	1,400.00	per year
Selling costs	0.85	per pair
Local taxes and insurance premium	6% of	machine cost

In addition to these variable costs, the investment will also assume its share of the fixed costs of administration: factory administration—9.51 percent of manufacturing costs; general administration—2.00 percent of sales. To operate the new machine, the firm also estimates that it must increase its investments in cash balance, accounts receivable, and inventories by $30,280. For the sake of simplicity, we shall assume that, in calculating its taxable income, the firm figures its depreciation on a straight-line basis. (The advantages of accelerated depreciation in postponing tax payments will be discussed in Chapter 9.) Income is assumed to be taxed at 50 percent.

Table 5-2 shows the derivation of the cash flow associated with the proposed investment. The $14,000 designated as profit contribution is the excess of sales over all variable costs (except income taxes), calculated on

Table 5-2 Annual Cash Flows from Shoe Machine

End of Year	0	1	2	3	4	5
Profit contribution	0	$14,000	$14,000	$14,000	$14,000	$14,000
Depreciation	0	5,000	5,000	5,000	5,000	5,000
Income tax payment	0	−7,000	−7,000	−7,000	−7,000	−7,000
Cash flow from operation	0	$12,000	$12,000	$12,000	$12,000	$12,000
Cost of shoe machine	−$25,000	0	0	0	0	0
Investment in working capital	− 30,280	0	0	0	0	30,280
Total cash flow	−$55,280	$12,000	$12,000	$12,000	$12,000	$42,280

a with-and-without basis. Since both factory- and general-administrative costs are fixed, they are ignored in the derivation of cash flow, even in the figuring of incremental tax payments. Working capital, unlike the new machine, is not used up; consequently, it is shown as a cash outlay at the beginning of the first year and as a recovery at the end of the fifth year. We shall use these data in the next section as we discuss criteria for investment.

INVESTMENT-ACCEPTANCE CRITERIA

Once the cash flow of an investment is known, how does one go about deciding whether or not the investment should be accepted? In this section, we shall discuss five criteria for acceptance: net present value, internal rate of return, benefit-cost ratio, payback period, and the accounting rate of return.

Assumptions

We will simplify our analysis with two assumptions: complete certainty about investment outcome, and a purely competitive capital market. Certainty means, first of all, that when a firm makes an investment, it knows exactly how much it will cost to produce its product, how many units it can sell, and at what price; it also means that when an investor buys a stock or bond, he knows exactly how much the company will earn, how much it will pay in dividends or interest, and for how much he can sell the stock or bond. Under certainty, the distinction between stocks and bonds disappears, and the return on each is identical. In fact, in a situation of certainty, all investments, whether real or financial, must yield the same return. If an investment were to yield a high return, making it an attractive outlet for funds, competition would force its market price up and drive down the rate of return. On the other hand, if an investment were to yield a low return, making it unattractive, lack of demand would force its market price down and drive up the rate of return. Thus, with the market in equilibrium, a single rate of return would obtain on all assets; we shall call this the "pure" or the "risk-free" rate of interest.

The chief characteristic of pure competition in any market is the atomistic nature of its participants. In a purely competitive capital market, buyers and sellers trade in such small quantities (relative to the overall size of the market) that the effect of any buyer or seller on the market price of a security is negligible. Buying and selling securities is equivalent to lending and borrowing money; pure competition, therefore, implies that both the supply of and the demand for funds are completely elastic at the prevailing rate of interest. Since the firm can always raise the funds it needs at the going interest rate, it can undertake all profitable investments, eliminating the need to choose among attractive proposals; the only decision at issue is whether to accept or reject any given investment. Of course, with opportunity for investment unrestricted, any investment that does not yield at least the risk-free rate of interest would be unprofitable. We turn now to criteria for distinguishing profitable investments from unprofitable ones.

The Net-Present-Value Criterion

According to the net-present-value (*NPV*) criterion, an investment should be accepted only if its *NPV* is positive—that is, only if it enhances the value of the company's outstanding shares; this criterion is the most direct approach in determining the profitability of an investment.

NPV can be defined mathematically by an algebraic formula. Let us consider an investment whose incremental benefits and costs are measured by the following pattern of cash flows:

End of year	0	1	2	. . .	$n-1$	n
Inflow	b_0	b_1	b_2	. . .	b_{n-1}	b_n
Outflow	c_0	c_1	c_2	. . .	c_{n-1}	c_n

If the cost of equity capital to the firm has a rate of k, the present values of the inflows and outflows are given, respectively, by these expressions:

$$B = b_0 + \frac{b_1}{(1+k)^1} + \frac{b_2}{(1+k)^2} + \cdots + \frac{b_n}{(1+k)^n}$$

$$C = c_0 + \frac{c_1}{(1+k)^1} + \frac{c_2}{(1+k)^2} + \cdots + \frac{c_n}{(1+k)^n}$$

The *net* present value of the investment, which is the excess of B over C, is represented by the formula:

$$NPV = a_0 + \frac{a_1}{(1+k)^1} + \frac{a_2}{(1+k)^2} + \cdots + \frac{a_n}{(1+k)^n} \qquad (5\text{-}1)$$

where $a_i = b_i - c_i$ is the net cash flow for year i.

The Red Shoe Company's shoe machine proposal provides a convenient set of cash-flow data with which to illustrate the *NPV* criterion. In Table 5-3, we see that if k, in this case the pure rate of interest, has a value of 8 percent, the investment has an *NPV* of \$13,240. This value was reached in two ways: (1) by calculating the present value of cash flows from operating the machine and subtracting from it the cost of the investment; and (2) by combining the cash flows from operation with the cost of the in-

Table 5-3 Net Present Value of the Shoe Machine*

End of Year	Cash Flow from Operation	Present Value	Cost of Investment	Present Value	Net Cash Flow	Present Value
0	$ 0	$ 0	−$55,280	−$55,280	−$55,280	−$55,280
1	12,000	11,111	0	0	12,000	11,111
2	12,000	10,288	0	0	12,000	10,288
3	12,000	9,526	0	0	12,000	9,526
4	12,000	8,820	0	0	12,000	8,820
5	42,280	28,775	0	0	42,000	28,775
Total		$68,520		−$55,280		$13,240

* $k = 8$ percent.

vestment and then discounting the combined flow. Predictably, both methods yield the same *NPV*. Since the *NPV* is positive, the company should accept this investment, according to the *NPV* criterion.

Eq. (5-1) shows that the *NPV* of an investment depends not only on the project's cash flows but also on the discount rate k. In a typical investment, an initial cash outlay is followed by net cash inflows. A high discount rate, by reducing the present value of these inflows, lowers the *NPV* of the investment. Figure 5-2 shows that the *NPV* of the shoe machine decreases as k increases, going from $35,000 when $k = 0$, to $0 when $k = 15$ percent and becoming negative when k is greater than 15 percent. The shoe machine, in other words, is a profitable investment not only when k is 8 percent, as we already know, but when k has any value lower than 15 percent.

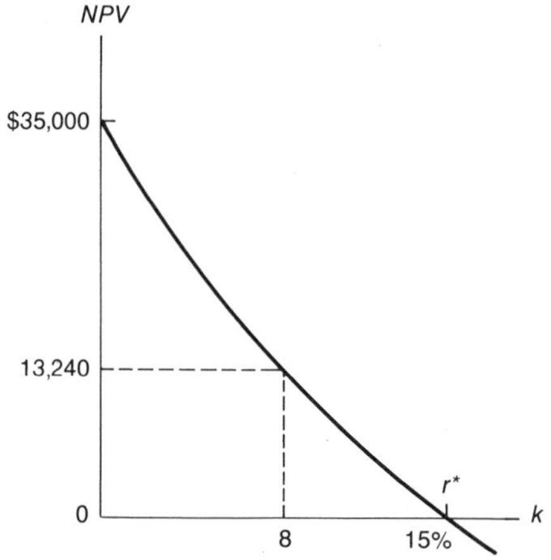

Figure 5-2 *NPV* of Shoe Machine as a Function of *k*

The Internal-Rate-of-Return Criterion

Although *NPV* is the most direct criterion for acceptance, it is not widely used in practice, since financial executives customarily think in terms of rates of return rather than absolute dollar gains. The internal-rate-of-return (*IRR*) criterion is similar to the *NPV* criterion in that both recognize the time value of money by discounting cash flows. However, whereas the *NPV* criterion appraises an investment directly by calculating its impact on the firm's share value, the *IRR* criterion appraises indirectly by comparing the rate of return on an investment with the cost of capital to the firm. An investment should be accepted if and only if return exceeds cost.

The *IRR* is an actuarial return, based not on the initial investment but on the actual investment, taking into account any capital recovered during the life of the project after the initial outlay. If we consider an investment which generates net cash flows of $a_0, a_1, \ldots, a_n$ at the end of years 0, 1, 2, . . . , n, respectively, then the *IRR* of the investment is the rate r^* which satisfies the condition:

$$0 = a_0 + \frac{a_1}{(1+r^*)^1} + \frac{a_2}{(1+r^*)^2} + \cdots + \frac{a_n}{(1+r^*)^n} \qquad (5\text{-}2)$$

Suppose an investment has an *IRR* of r^*. This means that if the investment is financed with funds borrowed at an interest rate of r^*, the cash inflows generated by the investment will be exactly enough to amortize the loan (i.e., to repay it with interest calculated on the actual balance) over the life of the project. Hence, when k denotes the cost of capital to a company, it will be worthwhile for the company to undertake any investment whose r^* is greater than k.

We should note that if k is substituted for r^*, the right-hand side of Eq. (5-2) becomes the formula for *NPV*. Hence, r^* may be defined alternatively as that value of k which makes the *NPV* of an investment zero. (See Figure 5-2.) Moreover, when k is smaller than r^*, *NPV* will be positive; when k is greater than r^*, *NPV* will be negative. *NPV* and *IRR* are, then, equivalent criteria, since both result in the same acceptance or rejection decision.

Table 5-4 illustrates the calculation of the *IRR* of the shoe machine by trial and error. A discount rate of 10 percent is too low, since it results in an *NPV* of \$9,010; a discount rate of 25 percent is too high, since the resulting *NPV* is −\$13,087. But at a discount rate of 15 percent, the *NPV* is \$0, indicating that we have found the exact *IRR*. An *IRR* of 15 percent means that if the firm finances the shoe machine with funds borrowed at an interest rate of 15 percent, the cash inflows from the investment will be exactly enough to amortize the loan over the life of the project (see Table

Table 5-4 Internal Rate of Return of the Shoe Machine

End of Year	Cash Flow	Present Values at 3 Trial Rates 10%	25%	15%
0	−$55,280	−$55,280	−$55,280	−$55,280
1	12,000	10,909	9,600	10,435
2	12,000	9,917	7,680	9,074
3	12,000	9,016	6,144	7,890
4	12,000	8,196	4,915	6,861
5	42,280	26,252	13,854	21,020
Total		$ 9,010	−$13,087	$0

5-5). In other words, the machine will be a profitable investment if funds are available at any rate lower than 15 percent. This is, of course, the same conclusion reached under the *NPV* criterion.

The Benefit-Cost-Ratio Criterion

The benefit-cost ratio, sometimes called the profitability index, is the ratio of the present value of the net cash flows from operation to the present value of the cost of the investment. Suppose an investment costs a_0 dollars now and generates net cash inflows of $a_1, a_2, \ldots, a_n$ at the end of years 1, 2, . . . , n, respectively. Its benefit-cost ratio, ϕ, is given by the formula:

$$\phi = \frac{1}{a_0}\left[\frac{a_1}{(1+k)^1} + \frac{a_2}{(1+k)^2} + \cdots + \frac{a_n}{(1+k)^n}\right] \qquad (5\text{-}3)$$

According to this criterion, an investment is acceptable only if its ratio ϕ is greater than one. To illustrate, consider the shoe-machine data in Table 5-3, which assumes a cost of capital k of 8 percent. Since the investment would cost $55,280 now and would generate net cash inflows with a present value of $68,520, the benefit-cost ratio is 1.24 and hence the project should be accepted if k is 8 percent.

Table 5-5 Schedule of Amortization

Year	Amount of Loan Outstanding	Annual Cash Inflow	Interest on Loan	Principal Repayment
1	$55,280	$12,000	$ 8,292	$ 3,708
2	51,572	12,000	7,736	4,264
3	47,308	12,000	7,096	4,904
4	42,404	12,000	6,361	5,639
5	36,765	42,280	5,515	36,765
Total		$90,280	$35,000	$55,280

The benefit-cost ratio deals with the ratio between the present value of costs and benefits, unlike the *NPV* criterion, which is concerned with the absolute difference between the two. When the benefit-cost ratio is greater than one, the *NPV* will be greater than zero, so the two criteria lead to the same acceptance or rejection decision. There is, however, one possible exception. When a firm is confronted with two mutually exclusive investments, the two criteria could lead to conflicting decisions. To illustrate, suppose there are two processes, A and B, for manufacturing a given product, A needing more investment than B. Process A costs $100,000 now and would generate future cash inflows with a present value of $125,000, so that it has an *NPV* of $25,000. Process B costs $70,000 now and would generate future benefits with a present value of $91,000, so that it has an *NPV* of $21,000. According to the *NPV* criterion, process A is clearly the better investment. However, process B has a ϕ of 1.30, compared with a ϕ of 1.25 for process A, so that according to the benefit-cost-ratio criterion, process B is the better investment.

The above inconsistency stems from the difference in the costs of the two investments. Process B is more profitable per dollar of investment than process A, but B costs $30,000 less than A, so that if the firm adopts B, it will have $30,000 available for supplemental investments. If these $30,000 can be invested to yield an *NPV* of more than $4,000, then process B should be chosen, since the company would then realize a combined *NPV* in excess of the $25,000 associated with process A. This decision is also consistent with the benefit-cost-ratio criterion. When two mutually exclusive investments of *equal* size are compared, the *NPV* and benefit-cost-ratio criteria always result in the same acceptance or rejection decision.

The Payback-Period Criterion

The payback-period criterion is primarily a crude method for evaluating risky investments. When risk is absent, the payback period may still be useful as a way of approximating the *IRR* of an investment. However, this approximation, as we shall see, is accurate only under special conditions.

According to this criterion, the attractiveness of an investment varies inversely with the length of its payback period, which is defined as the time required for an investment to pay back its initial cash outlay. If the annual cash returns from an investment are uniform, the payback period is indicated by the ratio between the initial cash outlay and the annual cash inflows. Thus, a printing press costing $10,000 and generating annual cash inflows of $4,000 for the next five years has a payback period of 2.5 years. If the annual cash returns vary in size, the payback period is the time required for the cumulative cash inflow to equal the initial cash outlay. In the case of the shoe machine, whose returns are unequal, it will take 4.2 years to recover the initial cash outlay of $55,280.

Under certain conditions, the payback period offers a quick and easy method of estimating investment return. Suppose, for example, an investment costs C dollars now and generates uniform annual cash inflows of a dollars for the next n years. The *IRR* of the investment, r^*, is the rate that satisfies the condition:

$$C = \frac{a}{(1+r^*)^1} + \frac{a}{(1+r^*)^2} + \cdots + \frac{a}{(1+r^*)^n}$$

Since the right-hand side of this equation is the present value of an annuity, we can rewrite the equation as follows:

$$C = a\left[\frac{1-(1+r^*)^{-n}}{r^*}\right] = \frac{a}{r^*} - \frac{a}{r^*}\left(\frac{1}{1+r^*}\right)^n$$

Transposing terms, we get:

$$r^* = \frac{a}{C} - \frac{a}{C}\left(\frac{1}{1+r^*}\right)^n \tag{5-4}$$

where a/C is the reciprocal of the payback period.

From Eq. (5-4), we see that if n is very large, then $\left(\frac{1}{1+r^*}\right)^n$ is small, so that a/C provides a reasonably good estimate of r^*. The error of estimation approaches zero as n approaches infinity. Thus, when an investment generates a perpetual series of uniform annual cash inflows, the reciprocal of the payback period is exactly the project's internal rate of return. But in other cases, the error of estimation may be substantial. In the case of the printing press, for example, whose annual cash inflows are uniform but not perpetual, the reciprocal of the payback period indicates a return of 40 percent, 12.5 percent higher than the actual *IRR* of 28.5 percent. Table 5-6 summarizes the relationship between the payback estimate a/C and the true value of *IRR* for other assumed values of the project's economic life.

Table 5-6 The Degree of Approximation of a/C to r^*

Project life n (years)	Payback Period C/a (years)	Reciprocal of Payback Period a/C (percent)	True Value of r^* (percent)
4	2.5	40.0%	22.0%
6	2.5	40.0	32.5
8	2.5	40.0	36.5
10	2.5	40.0	38.5
∞	2.5	40.0	40.0

In measuring the rate of return, then, the usefulness of the payback period is limited to special situations. Nonetheless, the payback period is widely used by business executives as a criterion (though not necessarily the only criterion) for investment decisions. The reason for this lies in the usefulness of the payback period as a measure of investment risk. In appraising projects whose cash flows are random, the management may wish to view distant cash flows as more risky than those of the near future. It may also wish to consider the distribution of this risk over the life of the project. The payback period provides a crude, but simple and direct means of incorporating these considerations into investment analysis.

The Accounting-Rate-of-Return Criterion

The main drawback of the accounting-rate-of-return criterion is that it ignores the time value of money. The return of an investment is calculated as:

$$\frac{\text{Average net profit after taxes}}{\text{Average invested capital}}$$

where both net profit and invested capital are values obtained from the company's books and both have been determined by conventional accounting methods. Incremental net profit from the shoe machine would average \$7,000 per year after taxes. With straight-line depreciation, the investment for the new machine proper would average \$12,500 yearly; when we add a \$30,280 investment in working capital, we get an average invested capital of \$42,780 yearly. The accounting rate of return, therefore, is 16.4 percent, which overstates the true return by 1.4 percent.

Clearly, the figure of 16.4 percent ignores the time value of money. As long as total net profit remains constant throughout the lifetime of the machine, the average net profit is unaffected by the timing of the receipt of the income. Furthermore, since the income is averaged, the effects of accelerated depreciation on advancing cash inflows are ignored. The accounting-rate-of-return is consequently not recommended as a criterion for investment analysis.

INVESTMENT DECISIONS AND INFLATION

Our analysis so far has been assuming a stable general price level, so that the cash flows are all expressed in dollars of constant purchasing power. The general price level, of course, does not always remain stable. If prices are expected to rise, the management may wish to evaluate the profitability of an investment in constant dollars. This adjustment can be achieved by simply including in the firm's required rate of return an allowance for inflation. The following analysis describes a procedure for calculating the *NPV* of an investment, taking into account this adjustment.

Uniform Price Changes

The extent to which inflation alters investment analysis depends on whether price changes are uniform or nonuniform. Price changes are said to be uniform if all prices (including costs) change by the same percentage; if the percentages differ, price changes are said to be nonuniform. To illustrate a case of uniform price changes, we shall return to the example of the cash flow generated by our shoe machine, assuming a constant price level (see Column 2 of Table 5-7). At an interest rate of 8 percent, we arrived earlier at an *NPV* of $13,240 (see Table 5-3).

Now suppose that starting with year 0, the price level increases at a rate of, say, 5 percent per year. The assumption of uniform price changes implies that all revenues and costs increase at the same rate, so that the cash flow increases proportionately (see Column 3, Table 5-7). Discounting the figures at 8 percent gives us the present values listed in Column 4. Because of inflation, however, these present values are not expressed in dollars of constant purchasing power. We can convert them into constant dollars by discounting each figure at the rate of inflation. Thus, assuming a constant annual inflation of 5 percent, the first-year cash flow would be multiplied by a factor of $\frac{1}{(1+.05)}$, the second year, $\frac{1}{(1+.05)^2}$, and so on. Adding up the resulting values, we get an *NPV* of $13,240, the same figure we calculated assuming a constant price level.

The above exercise demonstrates that in a period of inflation, if the cash flow of an investment increases at the same rate as the general price level, evaluating an investment using the method outlined in Table 5-7 gives

Table 5-7 Capital Budgeting Under Inflation

End of Year	Cash Flow Assuming Stable Prices	Cash Flow Assuming Inflation	Present Value in Current Dollars	Present Value in Constant Dollars
0	−$55,280	−$55,280	−$55,280	−$55,280
1	12,000	12,600	11,667	11,111
2	12,000	13,230	11,343	10,288
3	12,000	13,892	11,027	9,526
4	12,000	14,586	10,721	8,820
5	42,280	53,961	36,725	28,775
		Net Present Value of Investment		$13,240

results identical to an evaluation based on stable prices. This equivalence allows a simplified procedure for a firm whose investments meet the condition of uniform price changes. Simply evaluate investments as if prices will remain constant. Uniform price changes insure that results will be identical to those expressed in constant dollars.

Nonuniform Price Changes

In reality, of course, the net cash flow of an investment does not always vary at the same rate as the general price level. With regard to inflow, cash from an investment is a function of price (P) and quantity (Q) of output sold. When the general price level changes, the change in sales revenue ($P \times Q$) may vary more or less than the price level, depending on demand elasticity. If inflation is accompanied by a real increase in consumer income, a TV manufacturer, for example, may expect his sales revenue to rise, possibly more than the general price level does. But if inflation causes a drop in consumer real income, P may rise, but Q will drop, and sales revenue may increase less than the general price level.

On the side of cash outflow, a company may have long-term labor contracts, with wage rates fixed irrespective of price levels. Similarly, if a company has long-term debts, the interest and principal payments will be fixed, at least for the length of the contract. But the price of raw materials may be volatile. With so many divergent forces, it is pure coincidence if net cash flow varies at the same rate as the general price level. Each firm, therefore, must analyze its own situation to determine how the cash flow of its investments will change, and whether these changes will be sufficiently uniform to permit use of the simple procedure of assuming a stable price level.

The effect of the long-term borrowing on the variability of net cash flow deserves additional comment. Unlike labor contracts, usually short-term and specifying only wage rates, a debt contract may extend over 20 to 30 years, and it fixes not only the interest rate but also the amount of borrowing. In a period of rising prices, if a firm expects cash flow before debt-servicing to rise proportionately, then long-term borrowing with its fixed interest and principal payments will cause cash flow after debt-servicing to rise at a greater rate. In this situation, borrowing is clearly desirable. However, if the firm expects cash flow before debt-servicing not to rise proportionately, long-term debt may have the opposite effect, magnifying the shrinkage of net cash flow. Because it has this effect of magnification, debt financing is known as leverage financing, a topic we shall study in Chapters 13 and 14.

Finally, if a firm concludes that proportionality cannot be assumed, it must use the full procedure outlined in Table 5-7. That is, it must forecast the cash flow in current dollars, discount them at the pure rate of interest, and again at the expected rate of inflation. Taking our shoe machine, let us assume that the firm now wishes to evaluate the investment assuming an annual rate of inflation of 10 percent for the next 5 years. It forecasts the corresponding annual increases in cash flow under two assumptions:

Uniform increase	10%	10%	10%	10%	10%
Nonuniform increase	5	5	10	15	15

We already know that for the uniform case, the *NPV* of the shoe machine would be $13,240. But for the second case (nonuniform) the result will be different. The reader should determine intuitively whether this will be greater or less than in the first case, and do the actual computation to confirm his hypothesis.

REVIEW QUESTIONS

1. Explain the nature and scope of capital-expenditure analysis. What is the relationship between this type of analysis and the theory of share valuation?
2. What is the role of the financial executive in the investment-decision-making process? Is his role advisory or decision-making?
3. Since the value of a company may be viewed as the present value of its future earnings, why is it that, in evaluating investment projects, we view the value of an investment as the present value of its cash flows?
4. What is the difference between the net income associated with an investment and the cash flow of that investment? What is the difference between the before-and-after approach to deriving incremental cash flows and the with-and-without approach? Why should cash flow always be calculated on an after-tax basis in investment analysis?
5. How might the depreciation policy that a firm uses for tax purposes affect the profitability of an investment as measured by *IRR?* by *NPV?* by accounting rate of return? by payback period? by benefit-cost ratio?
6. Define the *NPV* of an investment. Why is the *NPV* criterion the most direct means of appraising the profitability of an investment?
7. Define the *IRR* of an investment. Why does the *IRR* criterion always lead to the same acceptance-rejection decision as the *NPV* criterion?
8. Explain the meaning and implications of assuming complete certainty and a purely competitive capital market. How do these assumptions simplify investment analysis?
9. Define the payback period of an investment. Does the reciprocal of the payback period provide an accurate measure of the internal rate of return of the investment? If not, how would you explain the fact that it is still widely used by business executives as a criterion for investment analysis?
10. Is the accounting rate of return a measure of true investment return? If not, why do many firms still use this criterion?

PROBLEMS

1. Hickel, Inc., which produces a consumer product, is thinking of replacing a semi-automated machine with a new, fully automated one. The present machine has a lifetime of 5 more years and a book value and a scrap value of zero; the new machine would cost $18,000 and have a lifetime of 5 years, with no scrap value at the end of that time.

   The firm sells 10,000 units of its product each year at a price of $7.57 per unit. The costs of production with the old machine have been as follows: the cost of materials has equalled 25 percent of sales, direct labor has taken another 25 percent of sales, and fixed costs have totalled $2,000 per year. But since the condition of the machine is deteriorating, the cost engineer estimates that the cost of direct labor will be 30 percent for the next 5 years. With the new machine, fixed costs would still be $2,000, and the cost of materials would still be 25 percent of sales; but the cost of direct labor would be only 15 percent of sales. The income-tax rate is 50 percent; and the firm uses straight-line depreciation.

   Assuming that the working-capital requirement is the same under both machines, calculate the cash flow from the new machine on a before-and-after basis and on a with-and-without basis.

2. (a) On the basis of the cash-flow data just derived, calculate the *IRR* of the new machine. According to the *IRR* criterion, is the investment acceptable if the cost of equity capital to the firm, *k*, is 10 percent? 15 percent? You may assume that the firm is financed completely with equity capital.

   (b) Calculate the *NPV* of the investment when the discount rate, *k*, is 10 percent; 15 percent. According to the *NPV* criterion, is the investment acceptable when *k* has either of these values?

3. (a) Calculate the *IRR* and the accounting rate of return for an investment which costs $37,910 now and which will generate the following incremental revenue, costs, depreciation, and taxes:

Year	1	2	3	4	5
Sales revenue	$19,537	$19,537	$19,537	$19,537	$19,537
Operating expenses	7,119	7,119	7,119	7,119	7,119
	$12,418	$12,418	$12,418	$12,418	$12,418
Depreciation	7,582	7,582	7,582	7,582	7,582
	$ 4,836	$ 4,836	$ 4,836	$ 4,836	$ 4,836
Taxes	2,418	2,418	2,418	2,418	2,418
Net income	$ 2,418	$ 2,418	$ 2,418	$ 2,418	$ 2,418

   (b) On the basis of the following sales revenues, calculate the *IRR* and the accounting rate of return:

Year	1	2	3	4	5
Sales Revenue	$39,074	$31,107	$9,769	$7,968	$9,767

   Note that the total revenue for the five years is the same as in part *a* ($97,685), but that the timing is altered. All other data are assumed to be unchanged.

(c) Calculate the *IRR* and the accounting rate of return, this time assuming that depreciation is figured on the basis of double-declining-balance.

4. A certain investment has the following cash flows:

End of Year	0	1	2	3	4	5
Cash Flow	−$410,000	$100,000	$100,000	$100,000	$100,000	$100,000

Graph the *NPV* of the project as a function of the discount rate, k. Determine the *IRR* of the project and compare it with the reciprocal of the payback period.

5. Suppose that the *IRR* of the above project is x percent. Draw up an amortization schedule to show that if the investment is financed with a loan of $410,000 at an interest rate of x percent, the cash inflow from the project will be exactly enough to amortize the loan over the life of the project.

6. Five years ago, J. Smith, Inc., purchased $100,000 worth of new machinery. Taking advantage of a 7 percent investment tax credit, the company deducted $7,000 from its income-tax liability for that year. Assume that, under the old law, it must reduce the depreciable cost of the new machine by $7,000, thus increasing its future taxable income by $7,000. If we assume a tax rate of 50 percent and a discount rate of 10 percent, what is the *NPV* of the investment tax credit if the machine is depreciated on a straight-line basis over a period of 10 years?

7. A machine with an expected economic life of 10 years was acquired on January 1, year 1, at a cost of $10,000. For tax purposes, it was depreciated by the double-declining-balance method with zero salvage value. The machine was sold on January 1, year 6, for $10,000. Was there any taxable gain from the sale? If so, what was the size of the gain and the related tax? You may assume that the tax on capital gain is 30 percent and that the tax on ordinary income is 50 percent.

8. The Jupiter Aircraft Company is considering the development and production of a new commercial airplane, model J-1070, with intercontinental range. The cash outlay required for the project will fall into three categories:

   R—the costs of research, development, testing, and evaluation.
   T—the costs of machine tools, plant, assembly jigs, needed to produce the airplanes.
   S—the costs of components and their assembly into the completed airplanes.

   For the J-1070 project, R and T are estimated at $882 million. These costs are usually incurred over a period of time, but we shall assume that the entire amount is paid at the beginning of year 1. The company expects to sell 100 J-1070's in year 1, 125 in year 2, 80 in year 3, 40 in year 4, 20 in year 5, and none thereafter. Because assembly workers become more efficient with experience on a new model, the company expects its S-costs to drop noticeably with time. Thus, although the plane's selling price is expected to remain constant over time, each J-1070 sold is expected to produce net cash inflows of $2 million during the first year of production, $4 million during the second year, and $5 million per year thereafter. You may assume that all cash flows are received at the end of each year.

   Calculate the net present value and the internal rate of return of this J-1070 project. Should the company accept this project if its cost of capital is 16 percent?

REFERENCES

BIERMAN, HAROLD, JR., and SEYMOUR SMIDT, *The Capital Budgeting Decision* (New York: The Macmillan Company, 1971).

BOWER, JOSEPH L., *Managing the Resource Allocation Process* (Homewood: Richard D. Irwin, Inc., 1972).

BROMWICH, MICHAEL, "Capital Budgeting—A Survey," *Journal of Business Finance* 2 (Autumn, 1970), pp. 3–26.

EDWARDS, JAMES W., *Effects of Federal Income Taxes on Capital Budgeting* (New York: National Association of Accountants, 1969).

HOSKINS, C. G., "Benefit-Cost Ratios Versus Net Present Value: Revisited," *Journal of Business Finance and Accounting* 1 (Summer, 1974), pp. 249–265.

KAHN, DOUGLAS A., *Basic Corporate Taxation* (Ann Arbor: The Institute of Continuing Legal Education, 1973).

KEMPSTER, JOHN H., *Financial Analysis to Guide Capital Expenditure Decisions* (New York: National Association of Accountants, 1967).

KLAMMER, THOMAS, "Empirical Evidence on the Adoption of Sophisticated Capital Budgeting Techniques," *Journal of Business* 45 (July, 1972), pp. 387–397.

LEWELLEN, WILBUR G., HOWARD P. LANSER, and JOHN J. MCCONNELL, "Payback Substitutes for Discounted Cash Flow," *Financial Management* 2 (Summer, 1973), pp. 17–23.

MALKIEL, BURTON G., and JOHN G. CRAGG, "Expectation and the Structure of Share Prices," *American Economic Review* 60 (September, 1970), pp. 601–617.

MAO, JAMES C. T., *Quantitative Analysis of Financial Decisions* (New York: The Macmillan Company, 1969), Ch. 6.

MAO, JAMES C. T., "Survey of Capital Budgeting: Theory and Practice," *Journal of Finance* 25 (May, 1970), pp. 349–360.

MURDICK, ROBERT G., and DONALD D. DEMING, *The Management of Capital Expenditures* (New York: McGraw-Hill Book Company, 1968).

PETTY, J. WILLIAM, DAVID F. SCOTT, JR., and MONROE M. BIRD, "The Capital Expenditure Decision-Making Process of Large Corporations," *Engineering Economist* 20 (Spring, 1975), pp. 159–172.

RABY, WILLIAM L., *The Income Tax and Business Decisions* (Englewood Cliffs: Prentice-Hall, Inc., 1972).

REINHARDT, U. E., "Break-Even Analysis for Lockheed's Tri Star: An Application of Financial Theory," *Journal of Finance* 28 (September, 1973), pp. 821–838.

SCHWAB, BERNHARD, and PETER LUSZTIG, "A Comparative Analysis of the Net Present Value and the Benefit-Cost Ratio as Measures of the Economic Desirability of Investments," *Journal of Finance* 24 (June, 1969), pp. 507–516.

WEAVER, JAMES B., "Organizing and Maintaining a Capital Expenditure Program," *Engineering Economist* 20 (Fall, 1974), pp. 1–36.

WEINGARTNER, M. H., "Some Views on the Payback Period and Capital Budgeting Decisions," *Management Science* 15 (August, 1969), pp. B-594 to B-607.

6 Investment Decisions Under Certainty (II)

In this chapter, we shall consider three aspects of investment decisions under conditions of certainty: the theory and application of multiple internal rates of return; the ranking of projects by *IRR* and by *NPV;* and the selection of investment portfolios by mathematical programming.

MULTIPLE INTERNAL RATES OF RETURN: THEORY

The Phenomenon

In the typical investment situation, the pattern of the net cash flow takes the form of an initial outlay followed by a series of cash inflows. In this type of "simple investments," a unique *IRR* is always associated with a given series of cash flows; and the *IRR* is a clear criterion for determining the profitability of an investment. But in actuality, the cash outflow associated with an investment may not be restricted to the initial period. In these "nonsimple investments," multiple *IRR*'s may be associated with a given series of cash flows, creating an ambiguous situation.

Sandy's Restaurants, Inc., is planning to set up a French restaurant at the Paris International Fair. It is a condition of the Fair that any participating commercial enterprise must pay for the removal of any structure which it puts up. Taking into account the cost of removal, Sandy's has estimated the cash flows associated with the restaurant as follows:

End of Year	0	1	2
Cash Flow	−$10,000	$30,000	−$22,100

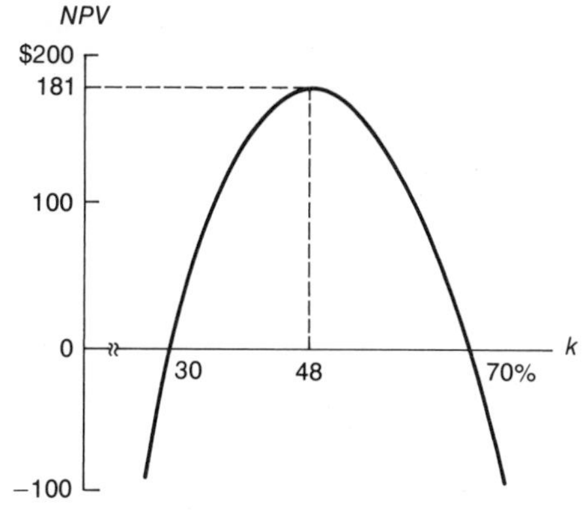

Figure 6-1 *NPV* of Sandy's Restaurant as a Function of *k*

The *IRR* of this investment is the value of r^* that satisfies the condition

$$\$10{,}000 = \frac{\$30{,}000}{(1 + r^*)^1} - \frac{\$22{,}000}{(1 + r^*)^2} \tag{6-1}$$

Solving this equation, we find that r^* has not one but two values: 30 percent and 70 percent.[1] Which is the correct measure of the return on this investment?

Before answering this question, let us calculate and plot the *NPV* for selected values of k, the cost of capital to the firm. Since conditions of certainty prevail, there is no distinction between the cost of equity capital and that of debt capital, and k is simply the risk-free rate of interest. In Table 6-1 and Figure 6-1, we find that the *NPV* is −$2,100 at $k = 0$ percent, $0 at $k = 30$ percent, reaches a maximum of $181 at $k = 48$ percent, falls to $0

Table 6-1 ***NPV* of Sandy's Restaurant as a Function of *k***

k	*NPV*	*k*	*NPV*
0	−$2,100	1.00	−$ 525
.10	− 992	1.10	− 725
.30	0	1.30	− 1,134
.48	181	1.50	− 1,536
.70	0	1.70	− 1,920

[1] The maximum number of *IRR*'s which an investment may have is determined by the number of sign reversals in the cash-flow series.

again at $k = 70$ percent, and finally becomes negative again when k is greater than 70 percent. The increase in *NPV* from −\$2,100 to \$181 as k increases from 0 to 48 percent is contrary to our normal expectation that *NPV* varies inversely with the discount rate k. We shall see that this phenomenon derives from the same source as the investment's multiple *IRR*'s.

Interpretation[2]

The internal rate of return is called internal because its value is supposedly internal to the investment, i.e., not affected by the cost of capital, k. This assumption is valid for simple investments but not necessarily for nonsimple investments. When an investment has multiple IRR's, we must specify the cost of capital before we can determine the rate of return.

Let us consider, as an example, Sandy's French Restaurant, which is a nonsimple investment by virtue of its negative salvage value. Part of the inflow of \$30,000 must be set aside as a reserve to cover the net cash outflow of \$22,100; consequently, only the remainder constitutes a return on the original investment of \$10,000. The amount of the necessary reserve clearly depends on the interest rate at which funds can be lent during the second year. The return on the original investment, therefore, cannot be independent of the cost of capital. If k is 10 percent, \$20,091 must be set aside to produce a value of \$22,100 at the end of the year. Thus, \$9,909 of the \$30,000 inflow constitutes a return on the investment, equivalent to a rate of −1 percent on the original investment of \$10,000. However, at a higher value of k, say 48 percent, less money (in this case, only \$14,932) need be set aside to produce a value of \$22,100 at the end of the year. The investment return in this situation would be \$15,068, equivalent to a rate of 51 percent on the original investment. Here, the rate of return is not independent of k but rises with k, as indicated in Table 6-2 and Figure 6-2. To distinguish this return from the *IRR*, we denote it simply as r, without the asterisk.

Table 6-2 Rate of Return of Sandy's Restaurant as a Function of k

k	r	k	r
0	−.21	1.00	.90
.10	−.01	1.10	.95
.30	.30	1.30	1.04
.48	.51	1.50	1.12
.70	.70	1.70	1.18

[2] The analysis here is based on my *Quantitative Analysis of Financial Decisions*, Ch. 6.

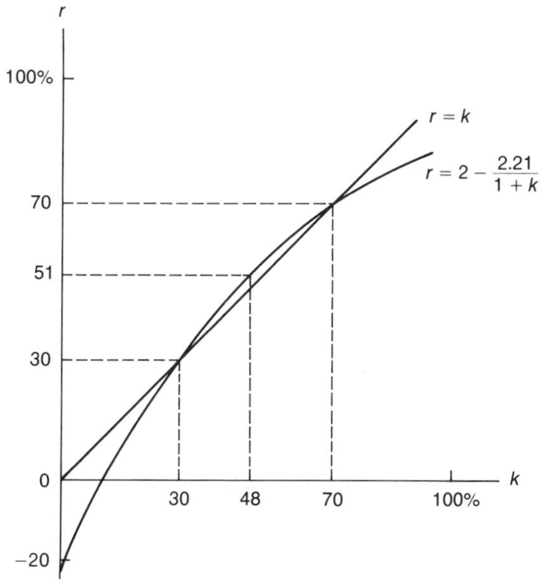

Figure 6-2 Rate of Return on Sandy's Restaurant as a Function of *k*

Sandy's French Restaurant is a "mixed" investment in that it is an investment as well as a financing transaction. Our example illustrates the dependence, for mixed investments, of both *NPV* and *IRR* on the cost of capital. But what light does this dependence shed on the phenomenon of multiple *IRR*'s? In Figure 6-2, a curve is drawn according to Eq. (6-2), which expresses r as a function of k:

$$\$10{,}000(1+r) = \left(\$30{,}000 - \frac{\$22{,}100}{1+k}\right) \tag{6-2}$$

The left-hand side of this equation is the value of Sandy's investment at the end of one year, assuming a rate of return r. The right-hand side is the net cash inflow at the end of year 1, after setting aside a reserve, varying with the cost of capital, k, for meeting future outflow. On this curve, r equals k at two points: .3 and .7, the *IRR*'s as calculated by Eq. (6-1). This result is expected since Eq. (6-1) and Eq. (6-2) become identical if k is equal to r. Thus, for an investment whose return r varies with k, the *IRR*'s are the values on the curve at which r happens to equal k. Since these values of k may or may not correspond to the actual cost of capital to the firm, no special significance should be attached to the concept of *IRR* when there are multiple values.

Once the rate of return is determined, analysis proceeds in the usual way. An investment is profitable only if its rate of return, *r*, exceeds the cost of capital, *k*. Since *r* exceeds *k* in the range between .3 and .7, Sandy's should invest in the French restaurant only if its cost of capital is between 30 percent and 70 percent. We should note that the same conclusion was reached by means of the *NPV* criterion, since the *NPV* was found to be positive only if *k* was between 30 percent and 70 percent. This finding shows that when multiple *IRR*'s are correctly understood, the *NPV* and *IRR* criteria still produce the same acceptance or rejection decision.

MULTIPLE INTERNAL RATES OF RETURN: APPLICATION

In this section, we shall describe a bank investment to show that the phenomenon of multiple *IRR*'s does arise in real business situations.

A Realistic Example

Leveraged leasing provides an interesting example of multiple *IRR*'s. This is a method commonly used by banks to provide equipment financing for airlines. A chief motive for lease financing is the possible tax benefit it brings. Suppose, for example, that the XYZ Airlines wants to buy a new airplane. If the company is losing money, it cannot benefit from the tax shield provided by depreciation and the investment tax credit resulting from ownership. The company may enter into a leasing arrangement with a profitable bank which, as owner of the equipment, makes full use of the tax shield and passes on part of the benefits to the lessee in the form of reduced rental payments.

The bank, as lessor, may try to increase the return on its investment even more, by introducing financial leverage directly into the lease. For example, instead of assuming full ownership, the bank may decide to put up only a fraction of the cost, borrowing the remainder from insurance companies. It not only benefits from the leverage, but also receives a larger tax shelter per dollar of its own investment. In terms of the bank's cash flows, such leases result in inflows during the early years, with outflows during the later years. The presence of cash outflows during the later part of the lease life means that the lease investment will have multiple *IRR*'s. Moreover, the true return to the bank is not independent of the bank's cost of capital, but, rather, related to it.

Table 6-3 illustrates how the bank may structure such a financial lease.[3] Notice that the cost of the aircraft is assumed to be $10 million, and

[3] This example is adapted from Robert C. Wiar, "Economic Implications of Multiple Rates of Return in the Leveraged Lease Context," *Journal of Finance* 28 (December, 1973), pp. 1278–79, Exhibit I.

Table 6-3 A Hypothetical Leveraged Lease

Asset:	Executive aircraft
Cost:	$10,000,000
Lease period:	15 years
Nominal rate of return:	8%
Annual rental income:	$1,168,296
Depreciation:	Sum-of-the-years-digits, 15 years, 5% salvage value
Total lender participation:	80%, non-recourse
Lender interest rate:	9%
Loan period:	15 years
Principal offset:	5 years
Lessor tax rate:	50%

the lease period 15 years. The nominal rate of return on the lease is 8 percent, which implies an annual rental income of $1,168,296. The bank will calculate its depreciation using the sum-of-the-years-digits method,[4] and will allow a salvage value of 5 percent. Of the $10 million, the bank will put up 20 percent, and borrow the remaining 80 percent from several life insurance companies. The borrowing is to be evidenced by a non-recourse promissory note, secured by an assignment of lease payments and a security interest in the equipment. The non-recourse feature means that the bank is not liable beyond its initial equity investment. The repayment on the loan is to be figured on a payment plan over 15 years, with 5 years principal deferment and then level payments over the next 10 years, with interest at 9 percent per annum. Notice also that the bank is subject to a marginal tax rate of 50 percent on its income.

Based on the above data, the lease is able to generate the cash flows shown in Table 6-4. Inflows in the early years result from significant tax

Table 6-4 Cash Flows from the Leveraged Lease (in dollars)

Year	Cash Flow	Year	Cash Flow
0	−$2,000,000	8	−$ 35,280
1	817,898	9	− 103,016
2	778,314	10	− 173,285
3	738,731	11	− 246,316
4	699,148	12	− 322,359
5	659,564	13	− 401,682
6	93,411	14	− 484,582
7	30,132	15	− 71,211

[4] The different methods of depreciation are explained below in Chapter 9.

savings due to accelerated depreciation and heavier interest payments; whereas, in later years, smaller depreciation and interest payments produce smaller tax savings and this results in cash outflows. The outflows in later years are also increased by principal repayments to life insurance companies. Given these cash flows, how does the rate of return on the lease vary with the cost of capital to the bank?

Analysis by Computer

Figure B-3 in Appendix B contains a computer program which calculates the rates of return of any investment as a function of the bank's cost of capital. The program employs the same theory that we used in analyzing the French restaurant. But the program is more general in that it is applicable to investments whose cash flows are spread over many time periods. Applying this program to the leveraged lease, we obtain the relationship between r and k shown in Figure 6-3.

In Figure 6-3, the horizontal axis measures k, while the vertical axis measures r. Curve BC traces the functional relationship between r and k. Line OA, drawn at 45° through the origin, has the property that every point on the line is equidistant from the two axes. Notice that OA and BC intersect at 0.2 percent and 22.8 percent, which are the rates we would have obtained using the standard formula for internal rate of return. But, as can be seen from the diagram, these are the values of r when r happens to be equal to k. Clearly, the cost of capital for a given firm may be other than

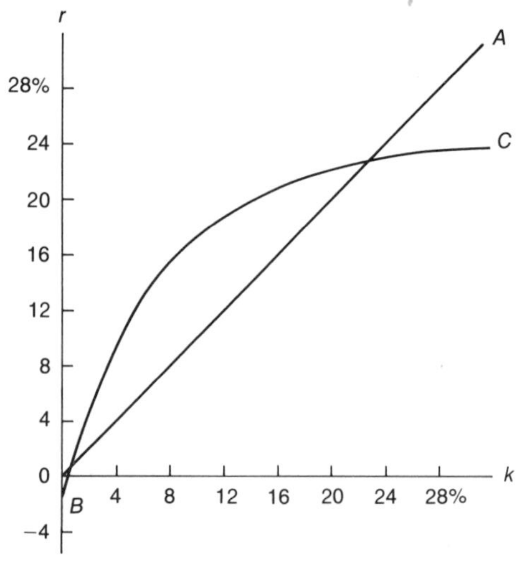

Figure 6-3 Rate of Return on the Leveraged Lease as a Function of k

either of these, meaning that the correct procedure is first to ascertain the value of k and then to read off the value of r from the curve BC.

Notice that where curve BC lies above OA, r is greater than the corresponding value of k. In this event, the lease is profitable to the bank. Conversely, when curve BC lies below OA, the opposite is the case and the lease is not profitable. In other words, the lease is profitable if and only if the cost of capital to the bank is between 0.2 percent and 22.8 percent. Hence, if the actual value of its k falls within this range, the bank should accept the lease investment.

IRR AND NPV AS RANKING CRITERIA

The Portfolio-Selection Decision

Until now, we have had to decide only whether a given investment was acceptable or unacceptable, since we have assumed unlimited funds. However, some firms operate under conditions of capital rationing—that is, the amount of funds available for investment is fixed. When the amount of capital to be invested is fixed, the firm must be able to decide not only which investments would be profitable and which unprofitable but also, since it cannot afford to undertake all profitable investments, what combination of projects will be most profitable. There are two approaches to this portfolio-selection problem: ranking, to be discussed here, and mathematical programming, to be discussed in the next section.

In ranking, the competing projects are listed in decreasing order on the basis of a given criterion, usually *IRR* or *NPV*. Projects may then be accepted in that order until the capital budget is exhausted. However, this approach poses a problem: rankings by the *IRR* criterion sometimes differ from rankings according to the *NPV* criterion. Financial writers have traced this problem to the different reinvestment rates assumed by the two criteria and have labeled the phenomenon the "reinvestment rate problem." When a common reinvestment rate is assumed, the seeming contradiction is avoided.

The Reinvestment Rate Problem[5]

An example will help to illustrate the possibility of inconsistency between *IRR* and *NPV* as criteria for ranking investments. The Space Exploration Corporation launches satellites to take and send back pictures of

---

[5] The discussion here is based in part on my paper "A New Graphic Analysis of Fisher's Rate of Return," *Cost and Management* 44 (November–December, 1970), pp. 24–27.

distant planets. It must choose between two projects, each of which costs \$100,000. Project J involves sending a satellite to planet J; no pictures could be sent back until the end of the 1-year traveling period, at which time the company would receive a \$120,000 cash payoff. In Project K, a satellite would be sent to a more distant planet, K; pictures could not be sent back until the end of a 5-year traveling period, at which time the firm would receive a cash payoff of \$201,140. Since we are still working under conditions of certainty, we shall assume that there is no risk, that the company knows that both ventures will be successful. The firm must bear in mind that the government will license a competitor to explore these planets, if Space Exploration Corporation decides not to.

Applying Eq. (5-2) to the cash-flow data, we find that the *IRR* of Project J is 20 percent, while that of Project K is 15 percent. If the projects are ranked by *IRR*, J is clearly preferable to K. However, the same decision would not in every case be reached on the basis of *NPV* ranking. In this case, since capital is rationed, the discount rate k in the *NPV* formula is the opportunity cost of capital, as measured by the rate of return of foregone investments. If this k equals 10 percent, Project J has an *NPV* of \$9,090:

$$NPV \text{ of J} = \frac{\$120{,}000}{(1 + .1)} - \$100{,}000 = \$9{,}090$$

On the other hand, Project K has an *NPV* of \$24,890:

$$NPV \text{ of K} = \frac{\$201{,}140}{(1 + .1)^5} - \$100{,}000 = \$24{,}890$$

The *IRR* and *NPV* rankings do not always conflict. We can see this by plotting the *NPV*'s of projects J and K as functions of the discount rate k. In Figure 6-4, *NPV* is measured along the vertical axis and the discount rate along the horizontal axis. The *IRR* of an investment, we recall, is that discount rate which produces an *NPV* of zero. The higher *IRR* ranking of J is reflected in the fact that the *NPV* function of J cuts the horizontal axis at 20 percent, whereas K cuts it at 15 percent. The *NPV* of J is greater than that of K when *NPV* is calculated using any discount rate greater than 13.8 percent, in which case *IRR* and *NPV* rankings agree. The rankings are contradictory, however, if a discount rate of 13.8 percent or less is used in calculating *NPV*.

Reconciliation

The conflicting rankings stem not from any actual contradiction but from contradictory assumptions about the rate at which funds may be

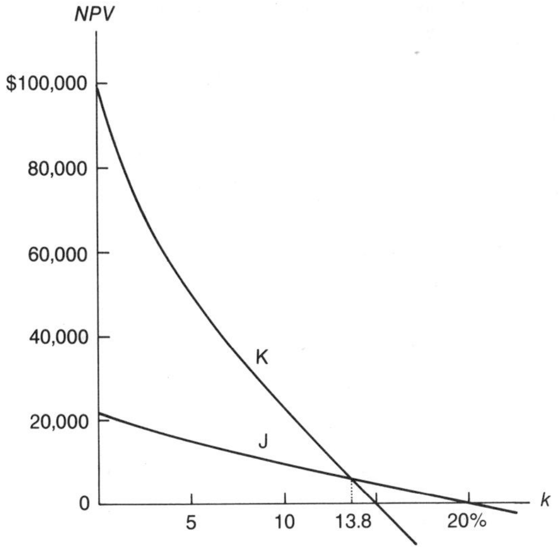

Figure 6-4 *NPV* Functions of Projects J and K

reinvested after they are released from a given project. The project to the farther planet, K, yields a 15-percent annual return over a 5-year period. Project J yields a higher annual rate (20 percent) but for only one year. Because of this difference in project life, the opportunity for reinvestment becomes a critical matter.

In ranking investments by *IRR,* the assumption is that funds released by the short-lived project can be reinvested to yield their own internal rate of return. On the other hand, in ranking investments by *NPV,* the reinvestment rate is assumed to equal the cost of capital. A firm's actual reinvestment rate, of course, may or may not coincide with either of these assumed rates. If it does not, projects with different economic lives can be correctly ranked only by comparing the sequences of investments implied by them. When a common reinvestment rate is used, both the *IRR* and the *NPV* criteria will produce the correct ranking of competing investment sequences.

In our example, by setting k at a rate of 10 percent, we assume that funds released from Project J (whose *IRR* is 20 percent) at the end of one year can be reinvested to yield a return of exactly 10 percent. Project J has the advantage of having a higher *IRR* (20 percent) than K (15 percent) for one year, but this is more than offset by its low (10 percent) reinvestment rate for the next four years. At a 10-percent reinvestment rate, Project K would be preferable even in terms of rate-of-return, since the $120,000 released by J at the end of the first year would increase to a total of only $175,700 by the end of the fifth year. Although J's *IRR* for a single year is

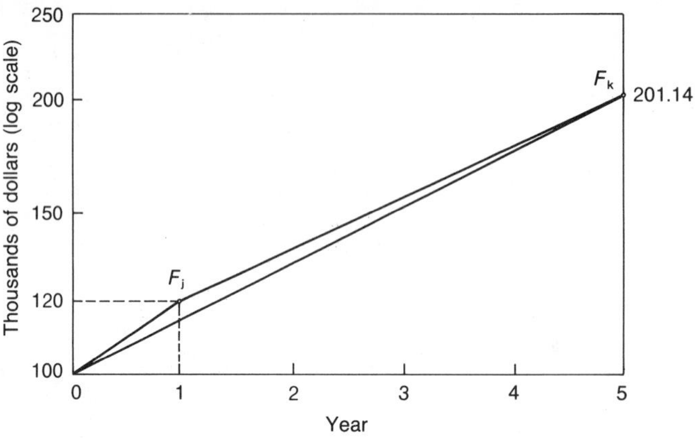

Figure 6-5 Fisher's Rate of Return as a Reinvestment Rate

20 percent, the sequence of investments implied by a choice of J would yield an overall return of only 12 percent for the 5-year period—3 percent lower than that of Project K. As this illustrates, the same rankings of competing projects result whether the *IRR* or *NPV* is used as a ranking criterion.

At a reinvestment rate of 10 percent, Project J is less attractive than Project K. How high would the reinvestment rate have to be for J to be at least as attractive as K? A simple graphic device can help us to find this break-even reinvestment rate, r_f. In Figure 6-5, the vertical axis is logarithmic (the rulings are not at distances of 1, 2, 3, etc. from the origin but at distances of log 1, log 2, log 3, etc.). Plotting dollar amounts on this scale is equivalent to plotting their logarithms on standard graph paper. Since Projects J and K each cost \$100,000, we are using \$100,000 as the value at the origin. At the end of the first year, Project J returns \$120,000 (including principal); at the end of the fifth year, Project K returns \$201,140. These amounts are designated as F_j, the future value of J and F_k, the future value of K, respectively. Now, at what rate (r_f) must F_j be reinvested in order for the future value of J at the end of the fifth year to be at least as great as the corresponding future value of K? To find r_f, we plot the line $F_j\ F_k$; the slope of this line is $\log(1 + r_f)$.[6] By subtracting one from the antilog of the slope, we find that r_f is 13.8 percent. Thus, at any reinvestment rate exceeding 13.8 percent, Project J and the subsequent reinvestments associated with it will rank higher than Project K whether the criterion is *NPV* or *IRR*.

---

[6] To prove this statement, observe that r_f satisfies the condition $F_j\,(1 + r_f)^4 = F_k$. Hence, $\log(1 + r_f) = (\log F_k - \log F_j)/4$ = slope of the line F_jF_k.

This break-even rate, r_f, is also called the Fisher's rate of return, because its value can be calculated using Irving Fisher's formula:

$$0 = \frac{(a_0 - b_0)}{(1 + r_f)^0} + \frac{(a_1 - b_1)}{(1 + r_f)^1} + \cdot \cdot \cdot + \frac{(a_n - b_n)}{(1 + r_f)^n} \qquad (6\text{-}3)$$

where the a's and b's are respectively the cash flows from any two investments being compared. The reader may wish to verify that for our example this equation indeed holds when r_f is set at 13.8 percent. Note that the rate r_f is that discount rate that equates the *NPV*'s of two investments. Thus, in Figure 6-4, r_f is the discount rate at which the *NPV* functions J and K intersect. For determining r_f, Figure 6-4 has the advantage of being easily applicable to investments with more than one cash inflow and one cash outflow. However, it does not demonstrate graphically that r_f is the reinvestment rate as clearly as does Figure 6-5.

Finally, the above standard analysis strongly suggests that the reinvestment rate matters only when projects are ranked inconsistently by *IRR* and *NPV*. This inference, however, is not valid. In Problem 5 at the end of this chapter, the reader will find that even when two projects are ranked consistently by *IRR* and *NPV*, reinvestment rate must be considered, and under certain conditions, the project with the higher *IRR* (or *NPV*) should not be selected.

Implications for Financing Decisions

The reinvestment rate problem, which arises when a firm must choose between two sequences of cash flows, has its counterpart in the refinancing rate problem. The reinvestment rate problem occurs under two situations: when capital is rationed or when projects are mutually exclusive. The refinancing rate problem, on the other hand, is more pervasive. It is present whether or not a firm's capital is rationed, since every financing method involves an exclusive decision. Financing an investment one way automatically excludes financing it in any other way. Every financing method, therefore, involves a choice between two or more cash flows, which means that the refinancing rate problem is potentially present whenever financing decisions are made.

This fact could greatly complicate a firm's financing decisions, but, fortunately, most financing decisions can be made without reference to the firm's refinancing rate. Suppose that a company is considering two alternative financing methods to raise a given sum of money. As a rule, one method will require a smaller payment in every time period throughout the transaction, and the choice of method is simple and clearcut. Sometimes, however, one method will require larger payments in the earlier periods and smaller payments in later periods. In that case, the choice of methods must take into account the firm's refinancing rate, i.e., the cost of meeting the larger payment during the earlier periods and the benefits of making the smaller payments in the later periods. The comparison of leasing and borrowing costs in Chapter 20 provides a realistic example of the refinancing rate problem. The decision to meet a long-term need by borrowing initially for a short time and later refinancing provides another everyday example.

SELECTION OF INVESTMENTS BY MATHEMATICAL PROGRAMMING

Why Mathematical Programming?

As a means of selecting investments, mathematical programming has several major advantages over the simpler method of ranking by *NPV* or by *IRR*. For instance, when a firm has a fixed amount of capital to allocate among various indivisible (all-or-nothing) projects, the ranking method does not always indicate the optimal portfolio.

A simple example will illustrate the point. Let us imagine a firm that has $55,000 to invest and only three projects to consider. Project X costs $50,000 and has an *NPV* of $10,000; Project Y costs $30,000 and has an *NPV* of $5,600; Project Z costs $25,000 and has an *NPV* of $4,800. Any sum left over is added to the firm's checking account which yields a negligible return. The acceptance of X, which has the largest single *NPV*, would exclude Y and Z, which together have an *NPV* of $10,400. When investments are indivisible, optimal portfolio selection requires that the *NPV* comparisons be applied to projects not only individually but also in combination. In this case, the same (nonoptimal) portfolio—Project X—would be selected when projects were ranked individually by *NPV*, whereas mathematical programming would select Projects Y and Z.

Project indivisibility is not the only circumstance favoring mathematical programming. Given the objective of share-value maximization, a firm may have a target pattern of growth for its reported earnings. There is statistical evidence that, given a firm's underlying earnings trend, the price-earnings ratio of its shares varies inversely with the degree of fluctuation around this trend. Hence, the impact of a new investment on the stability of future earnings is an important consideration in any investment decision. The method of ranking considers overall profitability, but not the distribution of profitability over time. On the other hand, a mathematical program can easily incorporate the requirement of a stable earnings' growth into its calculations.

A firm may have a target pattern not only for its earnings but also for its cash flows. If a company anticipates unusual expenditures in certain years, it may wish to have the net cash inflows from its new investments during those years. In other years, when expenditures are normal or below normal, the firm may not be so concerned. Cash-flow targets, like earnings targets, may be incorporated into mathematical programs as constraints.

Investment as an Integer Program

Integer programming may be thought of as linear programming in which the solution values must be integers; this requirement constitutes a recognition of the indivisibility of investments. Since the nature of integer programming does not concern us here, we shall omit the mathematical theory involved. We shall also simplify our example so that advanced solution techniques will not be necessary.

Formulation of the Problem.[7] The Northern Electronics Company has $250,000 to allocate among Projects A, B, C in a way that will maximize *NPV*. Table 6-5 presents the data for these projects, including the derivation of the accounting income and cash flows. Project A costs $125,000, B $103,000, and C $120,000; each has an economic life of five years. The firm is all equity financed, calculates depreciation on a straight-line basis, and is subject to a tax of 50 percent on its taxable income.

When capital is unlimited, the discount rate in the *NPV* formula is the cost of equity capital to the firm. However, as we mentioned before, when capital is rationed, the discount rate in the *NPV* formula is the opportunity cost of capital, as measured by the rate of return of foregone investments. Northern Electronics estimates that its opportunity cost is 15 percent. At a discount rate of 15 percent, Projects A, B, and C have net present values of $30,150, $7,010, and $8,420, respectively.

The firm is subject to three constraints in choosing its portfolio. First, the company anticipates a merger, in the near future, involving an exchange of stock; it therefore wishes its stock to sell at a favorable price. Accordingly, the company requires that the new investment contribute a total of at least $5,000 of net income in each of the first two years with a two-year total of at least $15,000. Second, to protect its liquidity, the firm imposes a constraint (in addition to its $250,000 investment limit) on the new investment's cash flow: it must contribute at least $120,000 to the firm's cash flow in the first two years (if part of the initial $250,000 is not spent, it may be counted toward the $120,000). Finally, since the investments are indivisible, each of the three projects must be accepted or rejected *in toto*. (Other constraints might arise from a shortage of skilled labor, the complementarity of projects, mutual exclusiveness between projects, etc.).

---

[7] For an account of how one company uses such a model in making investment decisions, see John K. Shank and A. Michael Burnell, "Smooth Your Earnings Growth Rate," *Harvard Business Review* 54 (January–February, 1974), pp. 136–141.

Table 6-5 Financial Data on Three Investments (in thousands of dollars)

Year	Cost of Project (1)	Taxable Income* (2)	Depre-ciation (3)	Income Tax (4)	Accounting Income (5) = (2) − (4)	Cash Inflow (6) = (5) + (3)
			Project A			
0	−125					
1		−3	25	0	−3	22
2		−5	25	0	−5	20
3		10	25	5	5	30
4		90	25	45	45	70
5		196	25	98	98	123
			Project B			
0	−103					
1		36	22	18	18	40
2		−1	21	0	−1	20
3		40	20	20	20	40
4		0	20	0	0	20
5		50	20	25	25	45
			Project C			
0	−120					
1		22	24	11	11	35
2		42	24	21	21	45
3		32	24	16	16	40
4		42	24	21	21	45
5		0	24	0	0	24

* Depreciation deducted.

The investment problem may be represented by the following integer program formulation:

$$\text{Maximize } NPV = 30{,}150x_1 + 7{,}010x_2 + 8{,}420x_3 \tag{6-4}$$

Subject to

$$
\begin{aligned}
&E_1 > 5{,}000,\ E_2 > 5{,}000 && \text{(earnings constraint)}\\
&E_1 + E_2 > 15{,}000 && \text{(earnings constraint)}\\
&C_1 + C_2 + U > 120{,}000 && \text{(cash constraint)}\\
&U = 250{,}000 - 125{,}000x_1 && \\
&\qquad -103{,}000x_2 - 120{,}000x_3 && \text{(definition of } U)\\
&x_i = 1 \text{ or } 0\ (i = 1, 2, 3) && \text{(indivisibility condition)}
\end{aligned}
\tag{6-5}
$$

where x_1, x_2, x_3, are the proportions of Projects A, B, C accepted; E_1 and E_2 are the combined net income contributions in years 1 and 2; C_1 and C_2 are the combined cash inflows generated in years 1 and 2; and U is the unspent portion of the $250,000. The problem is to find the values of x_1, x_2, and x_3 that satisfy the cash-flow, net-income, and indivisibility constraints, and at the same time maximize *NPV*. The requirement that the x_i's have values of only 0 or 1 insures that there will be no fractional projects in the optimal solution.

Solution by Enumeration. We shall solve the problem by means of complete enumeration. Since the three projects are indivisible, seven possible combinations are available to Northern Electronics: A, B, C, AB, AC, BC, and ABC. Each of these seven portfolios is tested against the net income and cash-flow constraints; those satisfying the constraints constitute the set of feasible portfolios. The *NPV* of each feasible portfolio is then calculated, and the portfolio that maximizes *NPV* is selected.

To facilitate the identification of feasible portfolios, we have summarized the yearly cash flow (Table 6-6) and the yearly accounting income (Table 6-7) of each project. The figures for portfolios A, B, and C are identical to those in Table 6-5; the figures for portfolios AB, AC, BC, and ABC are obtained by totaling their component figures.

All portfolios except ABC satisfy the cash-flow constraint. AB, for instance, although it generates only $102,000 in years 1 and 2, yields a $124,000 cash flow when we add the $22,000 left over from the initial $250,000. Next, we check the portfolios (except ABC, which has already been eliminated) against the net-income constraint; only C, AC, and BC satisfy this constraint. AB, for example, shows earnings of −$6,000 in the second year, which is clearly less than the annual target of $5,000; and the total for the 2 years is only $9,000. The three feasible portfolios, C, AC, and BC, have *NPV*'s of $8,420, and $38,570, and $15,430, respectively. The optimal portfolio is the one with the highest *NPV,* i.e., portfolio AC.

The same optimal solution would have been attained by ranking. Projects A, B, and C have *NPV*'s of $30,150, $7,010, and $8,420, respectively, and benefit-cost ratios of 1.241, 1.068, and 1.070, respectively. According to either criterion, A is more profitable than C, which is more

Table 6-6 Incremental Cash Flows from Different Portfolios (in thousands of dollars)

Project \ Year	0	1	2	3	4	5
A	−$125	$22	$20	$ 30	$ 70	$123
B	− 103	40	20	40	20	45
C	− 120	35	45	40	45	24
AB	− 228	62	40	70	90	168
AC	− 245	57	65	70	115	147
BC	− 223	75	65	80	65	69
ABC	− 348	97	85	110	135	192

Table 6-7 Incremental Earnings from Different Portfolios (in thousands of dollars)

Project \ Year	0	1	2	3	4	5
A	—	−$ 3	−$ 5	$ 5	$45	$ 98
B	—	18	− 1	20	0	25
C	—	11	21	16	21	0
AB	—	15	− 6	25	45	123
AC	—	8	16	21	66	98
BC	—	29	20	36	21	25
ABC	—	26	15	41	66	123

profitable than B. The optimal portfolio would therefore be a combination of A and C.

However, it is important to note that it is only a coincidence that ranking and mathematical programming led us to the same portfolio. To illustrate the point, let us change the cash flows of Projects A and C as follows:

End of Year	0	1	2	3	4	5
A	−$128,000	−$35,000	−$40,000	−$50,000	$100,000	$450,000
C	− 122,000	20,000	55,000	35,000	60,000	30,000

We find that A, B, and C have *NPV*'s of $59,350, $7,010, and $9,220, respectively, and benefit-cost ratios of 1.464, 1.068, and 1.075, respectively. Ranking would still lead us to portfolio AC, even though AC violates the cash constraint. By means of mathematical programming, which can take into account the indivisibility, the pattern of cash flow, and the pattern of net income of proposed investments, we find that the optimal portfolio is now BC.

REVIEW QUESTIONS

1. Explain the difference between simple and nonsimple investments. In what sense may we say that for some nonsimple investments, there are no rates of return internal to the project?
2. Describe the phenomenon of multiple *IRR*'s. When an investment has more than one *IRR*, which would you choose as the true measure of its rate of return? If none, how would you determine the profitability of the investment?
3. "When two projects are ranked consistently by *IRR* and *NPV*, the correct choice of project can be made without considering the reinvestment rate." Do you agree? Why or why not?

4. The discount rate r_f that equates the *NPV*'s of any two investments is known as Fisher's "rate of return over cost." How does this "break-even" rate of return contribute to our understanding of the possible discrepancy between *NPV* and *IRR* rankings?

5. Describe a situation in which project rankings according to *NPV* would not agree with rankings according to benefit-cost ratio. Which ranking criterion would you recommend to a firm that had to ration its capital among competing projects?

6. A firm which rations its capital can select its investment portfolio either by ranking or by mathematical programming. Discuss the advantages and disadvantages of each method.

7. Let $x_1, x_2, \ldots, x_5$ denote the fractions of investments 1, 2, . . . , 5, which a firm decides to undertake. Explain the meaning of the following set of constraints in a mathematical programming formulation:

   a. $x_1 + x_2 + x_3 \leq 1$
      $0 \leq x_i \leq 1 \quad (i = 1, 2, 3)$
      x_i is an integer.

   b. $-x_4 + x_5 \leq 0$
      $0 \leq x_i \leq 1 \quad (i = 4, 5)$
      x_i is an integer.

   (Hint: Experiment with different combinations of values of 0 and 1 for x_i. Which combinations are permitted and which are excluded by the constraints?)

8. In a mathematical programming model of investment decisions, Eugene M. Lerner and Alfred Rappaport stress the importance of consistency in reported earnings growth in determining share value. Consult their paper and compare their formulation with the one in this chapter. (See reference at end of chapter.)

9. The techniques of investment appraisal which we have been discussing are based on the assumption that the objective of an investment is to enhance the value of a company's shares. What modifications in technique would be necessary if the objective is to improve public welfare?

10. Imagine that you are the director of a local redevelopment agency trying to quantify the costs and benefits associated with a residential slum-clearance project. How would you measure the benefit of improved allocation of land resources? of improved fiscal position of local governments? of improved housing welfare?

PROBLEMS

1. In a widely-known example, J. H. Lorie and J. L. Savage posit the XYZ Oil Company, which has \$10,000 worth of oil underground. If the company uses the old machine (a slow pump), it will receive the \$10,000 at the end of two years; if it puts in a new, \$1,600 pump, it will receive the \$10,000 at the end of one year. Neither machine has a salvage value after the oil has been pumped.
   Determine the cash flow associated with the new pump. Calculate the *IRR*(s) and interpret the results. Is the investment profitable if the cost of capital to the firm is 10 percent? 40 percent? 300 percent? 500 percent?

2. Verify the cash flows from the leveraged lease, summarized in Table 6-4, by completing the calculations in the following table:

(in thousands of dollars)

End of Year	Equity Investment	Rental Income	Depreciation Expense	Interest Payment	Principal Repayment	Salvage Value	After-tax Cash Flow
0	−$2,000	$ 0	$ 0	$ 0	$ 0	$0	−$2,000
1	0	1,168	1,188	720	0	0	818
2	0	1,168	1,108	720	0	0	778
3	0	1,168	1,029	720	0	0	739
4	0	1,168	950	720	0	0	699
5	0	1,168	871	720	0	0	660
6	0	1,168	792	720	527	0	93
7	0	1,168	712	673	574	0	30
⋮	⋮	⋮	⋮	⋮	⋮	⋮	⋮
15							

3. Use the computer program in Figure B-3 of Appendix B to derive the functional relationship between r and k for a mixed investment of your own choosing.
4. Determine the discount rate which equates the NPV's of Projects X and Y, with the following cash flows:

End of Year	0	1	2	3	4	5
X	−$100,000	$125,000	0	0	0	0
Y	− 100,000	0	0	0	0	$228,000

   a. Show that the rankings of X and Y by IRR agree with rankings by NPV if the funds released by the short-lived Project X can be reinvested at a rate greater than the rate of discount just calculated.
   b. Which is the better investment, if funds released from Project X can be reinvested to yield a return of exactly 15 percent?
5. Calculate the IRR's, the NPV's, and Fisher's rate of return for Projects M and N, with the following cash flows:

End of Year	0	1	2	3	4	5
M	−$100,000	$115,000	0	0	0	0
N	− 100,000	0	0	0	0	$248,832

   Decide which is the better investment, if a firm must choose between the two. Be sure to state your assumptions regarding the firm's cost of capital and reinvestment rate.
6. How would you express E_1, E_2, C_1, and C_2, in the Northern Electronics problem, as functions of the decision variables x_1, x_2, and x_3?
7. Verify that, in the Northern Electronics problem, when the cash flow of Projects A and C are changed to:

End of Year	0	1	2	3	4	5
A	−$128,000	−$35,000	−$40,000	−$50,000	$100,000	$450,000
C	− 122,000	20,000	55,000	35,000	60,000	30,000

the optimal portfolio is BC, not AC.

8. The C-Tech Corporation is engaged in the manufacture of integrated circuits which form the electronic circuitry of computer memories, calculators, and other electronic devices. An important step in the manufacture of integrated circuits is the fabrication of photoplates. Although C-Tech possessed the internal capability to make the photoplates themselves, it had, due to problems in workload, chosen to buy its photoplate requirements from several suppliers. The company is now reconsidering whether or not it should fabricate the plates itself.

   The company estimates that if it keeps buying the photoplates, they will cost $90,000 annually for the next 3 years and $130,000 annually for the 2 years thereafter. If the company decides to make the photoplates itself, it will invest initially $100,000, but the same numbers of photoplates can be made at an incremental cash cost of only $60,000 annually for the next 3 years and $80,000 annually for the 2 years thereafter.

   Should C-Tech undertake to make the photoplates itself or continue to buy them from its suppliers? You may assume that the company has a planning horizon of 5 years for this make-or-buy decision and that its cost of capital is 13 percent.

REFERENCES

DE FARO, CLOVIS, "A Sufficient Condition for a Unique Nonnegative Internal Rate of Return: A Comment," *Journal of Financial and Quantitative Analysis* 8 (September, 1973), pp. 683–684.

DE FARO, CLOVIS, "On the Internal Rate of Return Criterion," *Engineering Economist* 19 (April–May, 1974), pp. 165–194.

DOENGES, R. CONRAD, "The 'Reinvestment Problem' in a Practical Perspective," *Financial Management* 1 (Spring, 1972), pp. 85–91.

DUDLEY, JR., CARLTON L., "A Note on Reinvestment Assumptions in Choosing Between Net Present Value and Internal Rate of Return," *Journal of Finance* 27 (September, 1972), pp. 907–915.

DYCKMAN, THOMAS R., and JAMES C. KINARD, "The Discounted Cash Flow Investment Decision Model with Accounting Income Constraints," *Decision Sciences* 4 (July, 1973), pp. 301–313.

LERNER, EUGENE M., and ALFRED RAPPAPORT, "Limit DCF in Capital Budgeting," *Harvard Business Review* 46 (September–October, 1968), pp. 133–139.

MAO, JAMES C. T., "A New Graphic Analysis of Fisher's Rate of Return," *Cost and Management* 44 (November–December, 1970), pp. 24–27.

MAO, JAMES C. T., *Quantitative Analysis of Financial Decisions* (New York: The Macmillan Company, 1969), Chs. 6 and 7.

NORSTRØM, CARL J., "A Sufficient Condition for a Unique Nonnegative Internal Rate of Return," *Journal of Financial and Quantitative Analysis* 7 (June, 1972), pp. 1835–1839.

Osteryoung, Jerome, *Capital Budgeting: Long-Term Assets Selection* (Columbus: Grid Inc., 1974).

PETERS, G. H., *Cost-Benefit Analysis and Public Expenditures* (London: The Institute of Economic Affairs, 1973).

PETTWAY, RICHARD H., "Integer Programming in Capital Budgeting: A Note on Computational Experience," *Journal of Financial and Quantitative Analysis* 8 (September, 1973), pp. 665–672.

SHANK, JOHN K., and A. MICHAEL BURNELL, "Smooth Your Earnings Growth Rate," *Harvard Business Review* 54 (January–February, 1974), pp. 136–141.

SOLOMON, EZRA, "The Arithmetic of Capital Budgeting Decisions," *Journal of Business* 29 (April, 1956), pp. 124–129.

TEICHROEW, DANIEL, ALEXANDER A. ROBICHEK, and MICHAEL MONTALBANO, "An Analysis of Criteria for Investment and Financing Decisions Under Certainty," *Management Science* 12 (November, 1965), pp. 151–179.

WIAR, ROBERT C., "Economic Implications of Multiple Rates of Return in the Leveraged Lease Context," *Journal of Finance* 28 (December, 1973), pp. 1275–1286.

7 Investment Decisions Under Uncertainty (I)

A critical assumption underlying Chapters 5 and 6 has been the condition of certainty. When uncertainty prevails, as it does in actuality, the cash flows of an investment become random variables. Consequently, we need a method of investment appraisal which will take into account the randomness of cash flows as well as their futurity. In this chapter, we shall present the risk-adjusted discount-rate approach and the certainty-equivalent approach. We shall then discuss various means of quantifying risk. Finally, we shall propose a practical procedure for incorporating risk into investment decisions.

THE RISK-ADJUSTED DISCOUNT-RATE APPROACH

The Approach

We have already introduced the risk-adjusted discount-rate approach to valuation in Chapter 2, although at that time we did not designate it by that name. We assumed that securities investors, in appraising the value of a stock, know the expected value of the stock's earning power for each future time period. They calculate present values by discounting the expected earning power at a constant rate that compensates for both futurity and uncertainty. The value of the stock is the sum of these present values.

A similar procedure is used in analyzing capital expenditures. The management of a firm is assumed to know the expected cash flows of an investment for each future time period. These figures are forecast on the assumption that the firm employs the optimal mix of debt financing and equity financing, taking into account the risk characteristics of the investment. (The forecasts are made on the basis of the optimal proportions even though the actual mix may or may not correspond initially to the long-run ideal.) Present values can then be calculated by discounting these expected cash flows at a constant rate which compensates for both futurity and uncertainty. The *NPV* of the investment will be the sum of these present values. An investment is profitable, of course, if and only if its *NPV* is positive.

Although this approach is relatively straightforward, two aspects require clarification. First, in deriving the cash flows of an investment, we treat all proceeds from the sale of debt and preferred stock as cash inflows and all interest, preferred dividends, and principal repayments as cash outflows. Hence, the resulting cash flows are those accruing to the common stockholders. A corollary of this method of calculating cash flows is that the appropriate risk-adjusted discount rate is the cost of common equity to the company. In actual practice, however, most financial analysts calculate their cash flows without separating out the effects of debt and preferred stock financing, so that their cash flows are those accruing to the company as a whole. They then equate the risk-adjusted discount rate with the weighted average of the costs of debt, preferred stock, and common equity, following the proportions in the firm's capital structure. As we shall see later, this average-cost-of-capital method produces correct results only in the presence of special assumptions.

The second aspect to be clarified is the use of a constant discount rate for calculating the present values of the cash flows of an investment in all future time periods. When cash flows differ in both futurity and uncertainty, is it reasonable to assume that investors will use the same discount rate to determine the present values of all future cash flows? Of course not; in fact, only rarely would the futurity and the uncertainty of cash flows call for a constant discount rate for all periods. Since most firms can forecast investment outcome accurately only for the very near future, the risk-adjusted discount rate tends to rise rapidly as a function of time. Given the expected cash flow and the corresponding discount rate for each time period, the *NPV* of an investment is uniquely determined. Now, for these same cash flows, we can find a constant discount rate which would produce the same *NPV* as that produced by the set of variable discount rates. When financial writers speak of discounting future cash flows at a constant rate, they are actually referring to a weighted average of the set of variable rates for the time periods in question.

An Example

The Peters Tool Company is thinking of installing a new, special-purpose lathe, costing $30,000, to replace an old lathe that is becoming inefficient due to wear and tear. To pay for the lathe, the company would provide \$20,000 from internally generated funds and would borrow the other \$10,000 from an insurance company at an interest rate of 8 percent, with the interest payable annually and the principal due in a lump sum at the end of the third year. The old lathe has no book value and no salvage value, but its working life could be stretched another 3 years if necessary. However, since it is rapidly declining in efficiency, its replacement is expected to enhance the firm's earnings before interest but after taxes (*EBIAT*) by \$800, \$800, and \$10,800, respectively, for the next 3 years. (The numbers, by chance, equal in absolute value the interest and principal repayments in the table below.) These *EBIAT*'s are sums after deducting depreciation, which the firm figures on a straight-line basis. Since the lathe is used for a product with a transitory demand, the economic life of a new lathe is estimated at only 3 years, with no salvage value.

These data mean that the new lathe would have the following incremental effects on the cash flows accruing to the common stockholders:

End of Year	0	1	2	3
Cost of investment	−\$30,000			
Loan proceeds	10,000			
EBIAT plus depreciation		\$10,800	\$10,800	\$20,800
Interest and principal repayments		−800	−800	−10,800
Cash flow	−\$20,000	\$10,000	\$10,000	\$10,000

In deriving these cash flows, the total investment of \$30,000 is treated as an outflow at the end of year 0 (i.e., now), and the loan of \$10,000 as an inflow. The annual interest charge of \$800 is treated as an outflow in each year, and the principal repayment of \$10,000 is treated as an outflow at the end of year 3. Annual depreciation, a noncash expense, is added back to the corresponding *EBIAT*. The resulting cash flows are the relevant figures for appraising the worth of the investment.

Let us suppose that the risk of the investment is such that, although the risk-free interest rate is only 4 percent, the firm requires an annual return of 9.474 percent on the first-period inflow, 15.555 percent on the second-period inflow, and 73.333 percent on the third-period inflow. Using these required returns as discount rates, we get an NPV of −\$1,456.20:

$$NPV = -\$20{,}000 + \frac{\$10{,}000}{(1+.09474)^1} + \frac{\$10{,}000}{(1+.15555)^2} + \frac{\$10{,}000}{(1+.73333)^3}$$

$$= -\$20{,}000 + \$9{,}134.60 + \$7{,}488.90 + \$1{,}920.30 = -\$1{,}456.20$$

Hence, the new lathe is not a profitable investment.

We could have obtained the same *NPV* of −$1,456.20 by discounting the cash flows of all three periods at a constant rate *k:*

$$NPV = -\$20{,}000 + \frac{\$10{,}000}{(1+k)^1} + \frac{\$10{,}000}{(1+k)^2} + \frac{\$10{,}000}{(1+k)^3} = -\$1{,}456.20$$

The value of *k* in this equation is found by trial and error to be approximately 28.5 percent. It is this constant rate that financial writers have in mind when they speak of the risk-adjusted discount rate as a single rate.

THE AVERAGE-COST-OF-CAPITAL APPROACH

A Common Error

Even financial writers often equate the average-cost-of-capital approach with the risk-adjusted discount-rate approach to investment appraisal. In the former case, the cash flows of an investment are calculated as one flow which accrues to the capital suppliers as a whole, including common stockholders, preferred stockholders, and creditors. The rate at which the expected cash flows are discounted is the weighted average of the costs of debt, preferred stock, and common equity, according to the proportions in the firm's capital structure. The *NPV* of an investment, calculated in this way, is then thought to be an accurate measure of the investment's effect on the value of the company's common shares. This reasoning, however, as our analysis will show, is incorrect; the average-cost-of-capital approach and the risk-adjusted discount-rate approach nearly always yield different results.

Let us consider an investment of $10,000 now which is expected to generate gross after-tax cash flows (i.e., *EBIAT* plus depreciation) of $12,000 annually at the end of the first, second, and third years and $16,000 at the end of the fourth year. These flows are "gross" in that loan proceeds have not been added to inflows nor the interest and principal repayments on the loan to outflows. These flows also recognize that the interest on any new debt is an added deduction for tax purposes. For simplicity, our calculations assume that the ABC Company has no preferred stock outstanding and that it plans to finance the investment with $4,000 of debt capital and $6,000 of retained earnings. The debt capital is to carry an interest rate of 7 percent, with interest payable annually and the principal due in a lump sum at the end of the fourth year. The firm requires an annual return of 12 percent on the equity portion of the investment.

To calculate the *NPV* by means of the risk-adjusted discount rate, we first note that the investment would have the following incremental effects on the residual cash flows accruing to the common stockholders:

End of Year	0	1	2	3	4
Cost of investment	−$10,000				
Loan proceeds	4,000				
EBIAT plus depreciation		$12,000	$12,000	$12,000	$16,000
Interest and principal repayments		−280	−280	−280	−4,280
Cash flow	−$ 6,000	$11,720	$11,720	$11,720	$11,720

Discounting this series at the 12-percent rate of return required on equity, we get an *NPV* of $29,600.

Using the average-cost-of-capital approach, we ignore the effect of debt financing when we calculate the expected cash flows:

End of Year	0	1	2	3	4
Cost of investment	−$10,000				
EBIAT plus depreciation		$12,000	$12,000	$12,000	$16,000
Cash flow	−$10,000	$12,000	$12,000	$12,000	$16,000

Although the firm requires a 12-percent return on its equity capital, the cost of its debt capital is only 7 percent per annum. Since debt and equity are combined in a ratio of 2 to 3, the average cost of capital to the firm is 10 percent ($= \frac{2}{5} \times 7\% + \frac{3}{5} \times 12\%$).[1] Discounting the above cash flows at 10 percent, we find that the investment has an *NPV* of $30,770—an overstatement of $1,170, or approximately 4 percent.

This discrepancy is clear evidence that the two methods of investment appraisal which we have been discussing are not equivalent. Given the fact that the cash-flow figures of an investment are at best only educated guesses, an error in calculating *NPV* of only 4 or 5 percent probably does not have any significant effect on a firm's investment decisions except in the case of marginal projects. Nevertheless, since the average-cost-of-capital method has no advantages over the risk-adjusted discount-rate method even at the practical level (both methods require the same amount of information and computation), we prefer the latter, which yields the theoretically correct value of *NPV*.

[1] The interest rate used for calculating this average is the before-tax rate, because our cash flow (*EBIAT* + depreciation) includes the actual amount of interest paid, without adjusting for its tax benefits. Most other writers calculate the average cost of capital using the after-tax interest rate, because their cash flows include interest payments after adjusting for the tax benefits. The two approaches give similar results, and the choice does not affect the validity of the discussion in this section.

Special Conditions and Limitations

Theory. There is one situation in which the average-cost-of-capital approach and the risk-adjusted discount-rate approach are mathematically equivalent. In this situation, three conditions must obtain: (1) the economic life of an investment must be perpetual; (2) the expected cash flows from the investment must be constant in size and in their division between creditors and stockholders; and (3) the equity portion of the investment must be appraised at market value, not at cost, in calculating the weights used in averaging the costs of debt and equity. These conditions insure that the *NPV* of the investment, calculated by the average-cost-of-capital method, is theoretically correct.

To explain how these conditions are derived, let us consider an investment costing a_0 dollars now and which is expected to generate after-tax cash inflows (*EBIAT* + depreciation) of $a_1, a_2, \ldots, a_n$ at the end of years 1, 2, . . . , *n*, respectively. To finance the investment, the firm would use S dollars of common equity, with a required return of k_e, and L dollars of debt, at an interest rate of k_i. The debt is to be fully amortized over n years, with payments of $a'_1, a'_2, \ldots, a'_n$ at the end of years 1, 2, . . . , *n*, respectively. We shall denote $a_t - a'_t$, the cash flow accuring to the common stockholders, simply as a''_t. Observe that at the time of the investment $\sum_{t=1}^{n} \frac{a'_t}{(1+k_i)^t}$ equals the amount of debt financing and $\sum_{t=1}^{n} \frac{a''_t}{(1+k_e)^t}$ equals the market value of the equity portion of the investment.

Using these notations, we now express the *NPV* of the investment according to the risk-adjusted discount-rate approach:

$$NPV_1 = \underbrace{\sum_{t=1}^{n} \frac{a''_t}{(1+k_e)^t}}_{\substack{\text{Market value}\\ \text{of equity}\\ \text{investment}}} - \underbrace{S}_{\substack{\text{Cost of}\\ \text{equity}\\ \text{investment}}} \tag{7-1}$$

The expression that corresponds to the average-cost-of-capital approach is the following:

$$NPV_2 = \underbrace{\sum_{t=1}^{n} \frac{a_t}{(1+\rho)^t}}_{\substack{\text{Market value}\\ \text{of total}\\ \text{investment}}} - \underbrace{S}_{\substack{\text{Cost of}\\ \text{equity}\\ \text{investment}}} - \underbrace{L}_{\substack{\text{Amount}\\ \text{of debt}\\ \text{financing}}} \tag{7-2}$$

where ρ is the weighted average of the costs of debt and equity. This latter approach is theoretically correct only if NPV_2 equals NPV_1. Accordingly, we equate the formula for NPV_2 to that for NPV_1 and inquire under what conditions this equality will always hold. The conditions are found to be: (1) n must be infinite, (2) a_t, a'_t, and a''_t must all be constant, and (3) the market value of equity capital must be used in calculating the weights in the formula for ρ.

An Example. To illustrate these conditions, let us consider an investment which costs $12,000 and is expected to generate perpetual cash inflows (*EBIAT* + depreciation) of $1,000 per year. To finance the investment, the ABC Company would use $2,000 of its own capital, with a required return of 10 percent, and $10,000 of permanent debt, at a fixed interest rate of 6 percent. According to the risk-adjusted discount-rate approach, the investment's effects on common stockholders would be as follows:

End of Year	0	1	2	3	. . .	∞
Cash Flow	−$2,000	$400	$400	$400	. . .	$400

Discounting the perpetual annual cash inflow of $400 at the 10-percent required return, we get a market value of $4,000 for the equity portion of the investment. Since the cost of this equity is $2,000, the *NPV* of the investment is therefore $2,000:

$$NPV_1 = \underbrace{\sum_{t=1}^{\infty} \frac{\$400}{(1+.1)^t}}_{\text{Market value of equity investment}} - \underbrace{\$2{,}000}_{\text{Cost of equity investment}} = \$2{,}000$$

By the average-cost-of-capital method, *NPV* is calculated on the basis of these cash flows:

End of Year	0	1	2	3	. . .
Cash Flow	−$12,000	$1,000	$1,000	$1,000	. . .

If the equity portion of the investment is appraised at its market value of $4,000, the weighted average cost of capital turns out to be 7.14 percent ($= \frac{2}{7} \times 10\% + \frac{5}{7} \times 6\%$). Discounting the perpetual annual cash inflow of $1,000 at 7.14 percent, we find that the investment has a total market value of $14,000. Since the total cost is $12,000, the investment has an *NPV* of $2,000, the theoretically correct figure:

$$NPV_2 = \underbrace{\sum_{t=1}^{\infty} \frac{\$1{,}000}{(1+.0714)^t}}_{\text{Market value of total investment}} - \underbrace{\$2{,}000}_{\text{Cost of equity investment}} - \underbrace{\$10{,}000}_{\text{Amount of debt financing}} = \$2{,}000$$

But in order to arrive at this correct result, the company must know the market value of the investment—which is precisely what the company is trying to find out. This example reinforces our already-stated preference for the risk-adjusted discount-rate method.

THE CERTAINTY-EQUIVALENT APPROACH (I)

The Approach

Let us imagine that an investor is faced with the alternatives of receiving at a future time t either a sure sum Y or an uncertain sum with an expected value X. Given the value of X and the associated risk, there is some value of Y at which the investor will view the two alternatives as equally attractive. This critical value of Y is known as the certainty equivalent of the uncertain sum whose expected value in this case is X.

Suppose now that X_1, X_2, and X_3 denote the expected cash flows from an investment. We can calculate the NPV of the investment according to either of two variants of the certainty-equivalent method of investment appraisal. Under variant I, we convert the expected cash flows into their certainty equivalents and then discount them at an appropriate rate to determine their NPV. Since the certainty equivalents are viewed as riskless sums, the appropriate discount rate will be the risk-free interest rate. Under variant II, we reverse the procedure. First, we discount the expected cash flows at the risk-free interest rate to determine their expected NPV, which we then convert into its certainty equivalent. Thus, whereas in the risk-adjusted discount-rate approach, risk affects NPV through the rate of discount, in the certainty-equivalent approach, risk affects NPV through a factor which converts risky sums into their certainty equivalents.

Variant I of the certainty-equivalent approach can be depicted graphically. In Figure 7-1, the points (a_0, b_0), (a_1, b_1), and (a_2, b_2) represent the expected cash flows a_0, a_1, a_2, received at time t with b_0, b_1, b_2 units of risk, respectively. We shall assume that the three combinations of risk and return are valued equally by investors in the market place. Since investors are generally risk-averse, this equality will obtain only if $a_2 > a_1 > a_0$ *and* $b_2 > b_1 > b_0$. That is, investors will value equally two different expected sums to be received at the same time if and only if the larger sum has a correspondingly higher degree of risk. The curve which passes through the various possible combinations which have equal values is known as the equal-market-valuation curve.

At point (a_0, b_0), the degree of risk, b_0, is zero; that is, this point denotes a sum a_0 which is certain to be realized at time t. By definition, then, a_0 is the certainty equivalent of every risky sum on the equal-market-valuation curve J. To determine the present market value of a risky future sum—say,

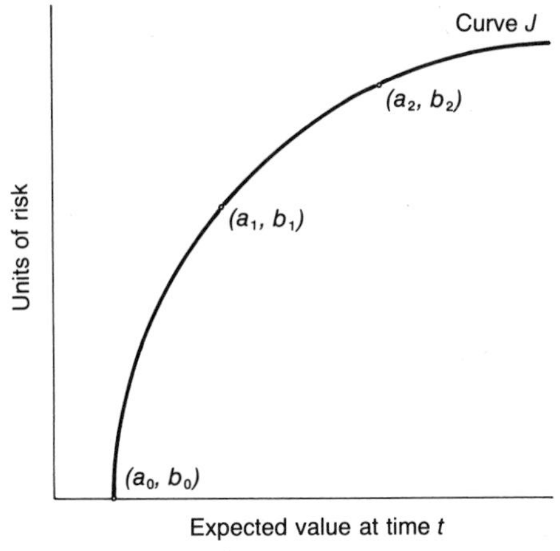

Figure 7-1 The Equal-Market-Valuation Curve

(a_2, b_2)—on this curve, we first multiply the expected value a_2 by a fraction α to reduce a_2 to its certainty equivalent. The fraction α is a ratio whose value will be smaller the greater the degree of risk and the stronger the market's aversion to risk. Since α is not an observable market statistic, the management must estimate its value on a subjective basis. Once the certainty equivalent, a_0 in this case, is known, its present value is obtained by discounting at the risk-free interest rate. An investment typically has cash flows in several time periods. The *NPV* of the investment is the sum of the present values of all its cash flows, each calculated in this way.

An Example

The $30,000 lathe that the Peters Tool Company is thinking of buying will cost the firm $20,000 in equity capital. It is expected to generate cash flows of $10,000 at the end of each of the three years of its economic life, with each inflow more risky than the last. If the risks are such that the company converts these inflows into their certainty equivalents at ratios of 95/100, 81/100, and 27/125, respectively, the *NPV* of the lathe is −$1,456.20:

$$NPV = -\$20{,}000 + \frac{(95/100)(\$10{,}000)}{(1+.04)^1} + \frac{(81/100)(\$10{,}000)}{(1+.04)^2} + \frac{(27/125)(\$10{,}000)}{(1+.04)^3}$$

$$= -\$20{,}000 + \$9{,}134.60 + \$7{,}488.90 + \$1{,}920.30 = -\$1{,}456.20$$

where the risk-free rate of interest is 4 percent.

This result agrees with that obtained by the risk-adjusted discount-rate method not only in *NPV* but also in the components of *NPV*. Is this term-by-term correspondence predictable or merely a coincidence? Let us approach this question by writing out the alternative expressions for the present value of the risky sum with an expected value of $\bar{X}$ dollars at time t:

Certainty-equivalent method: $$\frac{\alpha \bar{X}}{(1+i)^t}$$

Risk-adjusted discount-rate method: $$\frac{\bar{X}}{(1+k)^t}$$

where α is the certainty-equivalent conversion ratio, i is the risk-free interest rate, and k is the risk-adjusted discount rate. The present values of the risky sum as derived by the two methods will be identical only if

$$\frac{\alpha \bar{X}}{(1+i)^t} = \frac{\bar{X}}{(1+k)^t}$$

This equality implies that k, i, t and α are related according to the expression:

$$k = \frac{1+i}{\alpha^{1/t}} - 1 \tag{7-3}$$

The lathe example, which was constructed to satisfy condition (7-3), demonstrates that if one is consistent, the two methods will yield the same *NPV* for a given investment.

THE CERTAINTY-EQUIVALENT APPROACH (II)

The Approach

Under variant II, we first discount the expected cash flows at the risk-free interest rate to determine the investment's expected net present value. We then convert this $E(NPV)$ into its certainty equivalent by subtracting from it an allowance for risk, which is generally measured as $V(NPV)$, the variance of *NPV*. To implement this method, therefore, we need formulas for calculating the $E(NPV)$ and $V(NPV)$ of an investment.

Formula for E(NPV). Suppose an investment is expected to generate random cash flows of A_0, A_1, and A_2 at the end of years 0, 1, and 2, respectively. The *NPV* of the investment, viewed as a random variable, is represented by the equation:

$$NPV = A_0 + \frac{A_1}{(1+i)^1} + \frac{A_2}{(1+i)^2} \tag{7-4}$$

where i, for previously discussed reasons, is the risk-free rate of interest. We use the same basic equation to calculate the expected value:

$$E(NPV) = a_0 + \frac{a_1}{(1+i)^1} + \frac{a_2}{(1+i)^2} \tag{7-5}$$

where a_0, a_1, and a_2 denote the expected values of A_0, A_1, and A_2, respectively. That is, to compute $E(NPV)$, we simply replace the random cash flows by their respective expected values. This procedure is valid irrespective of whether or not the cash flows are correlated.

Formulas for V(NPV). To calculate $V(NPV)$, we need to know the variances of A_0, A_1, and A_2, which we label as σ_0^2, σ_1^2, and σ_2^2, respectively. We also need to know all of the possible covariances between pairs of A_0, A_1, and A_2, which we label σ_{01}, σ_{02}, and σ_{12}, respectively. Using these notations and applying a standard formula,[2] we get:

$$V(NPV) = \sigma_0^2 + \frac{\sigma_1^2}{(1+i)^2} + \frac{\sigma_2^2}{(1+i)^4} + \frac{2\sigma_{01}}{(1+i)^1} + \frac{2\sigma_{02}}{(1+i)^2} + \frac{2\sigma_{12}}{(1+i)^3} \tag{7-6}$$

where i, as before, is the risk-free interest rate.

Frederick S. Hillier considered two special cases which greatly simplified the expression we reached in Eq. (7-6): the case of zero correlation and the case of perfect correlation.[3] If the cash flow in any period is uncorrelated with that in any other period, all covariances between cash flows will be zero, and (7-6) reduces to:

$$V(NPV) = \sigma_0^2 + \frac{\sigma_1^2}{(1+i)^2} + \frac{\sigma_2^2}{(1+i)^4} \tag{7-7}$$

That is, $V(NPV)$ equals the sum of the variances of the individual terms on the right-hand side of Eq. (7-4).

Perfect correlation means that the values of the cash flows in any two periods are systematically related. Specifically, when correlation is perfect, if the cash flow in any period deviates from its mean value by s standard deviations, then the cash flow in any other period will also deviate from *its*

---

[2] In general, if X, Y, Z are random variables, and a, b, c are constants, then $V(aX + bY + cZ) = a^2V(X) + b^2V(Y) + c^2V(Z) + 2abCov(X,Y) + 2acCov(X,Z) + 2bcCov(Y,Z)$.

[3] Frederick S. Hillier, "The Derivation of Probabilistic Information for the Evaluation of Risky Investments," *Management Science* 9 (April, 1963), pp. 443–457.

mean by s standard deviations. Mathematically, perfect correlation between two random variables X and Y means that their coefficient of correlation, ρ, has a value of one. By definition,

$$\rho = \frac{\sigma_{XY}}{\sigma_X \sigma_Y}$$

where σ_{XY} is the covariance between X and Y, and σ_X and σ_Y are respectively the standard deviations of X and Y. Hence, $\rho = 1$ means that σ_{XY} equals $\sigma_X \sigma_Y$. Using this equality in Eq. (7-6) and simplifying, we get:

$$V(NPV) = \left[\sigma_0 + \frac{\sigma_1}{(1+i)^1} + \frac{\sigma_2}{(1+i)^2}\right]^2 \tag{7-8}$$

That is, by replacing the cash flows in Eq. (7-4) with their respective standard deviations and then squaring the result, we get the $V(NPV)$.

Although Eqs. (7-7) and (7-8) are based on investments with economic life of two years, they can be generalized to economic life of n years:

$$V(NPV) = \sigma_0^2 + \frac{\sigma_1^2}{(1+i)^2} + \cdots + \frac{\sigma_n^2}{(1+i)^{2n}} \tag{7-9}$$

$$V(NPV) = \left[\sigma_0 + \frac{\sigma_1}{(1+i)^1} + \cdots + \frac{\sigma_n}{(1+i)^n}\right]^2 \tag{7-10}$$

An Example

Let us return once again to the lathe, which will cost the firm \$20,000 in equity capital. The future cash flows of this cost-saving investment are random variables with expected values of \$10,000 annually for the next 3 years. Applying Eq. (7-5), we find that the lathe has an expected NPV of \$7,750, calculated as follows:

$$E(NPV) = -\$20{,}000 + \frac{\$10{,}000}{(1+.04)^1} + \frac{\$10{,}000}{(1+.04)^2} + \frac{\$10{,}000}{(1+.04)^3} = \$7{,}750$$

where i, the risk-free interest rate, is assumed to be 4 percent in this case.

With regard to $V(NPV)$, we observe that although Eqs. (7-7) and (7-8) are directly applicable to the two extreme cases of complete independence and perfect correlation, an appropriate combination of the two can be used for any intermediate situation. For illustration, suppose that the cash flows from the lathe are partly independent and partly correlated. The cash flows, let us say, are composed of three independent annual inflows, each with an expected value of \$4,000 and a standard deviation of \$150, *and* three perfectly correlated annual inflows, each with an expected value of $6,000 and a standard deviation of $250—totaling our expected cash flow of $10,000 in each year. To calculate the $V(NPV)$ of the whole project, we simply apply Eq. (7-7) to the independent flows and Eq. (7-8) to the perfectly correlated flows:

$$V(NPV) = 0 + \frac{(150)^2}{(1+.04)^2} + \frac{(150)^2}{(1+.04)^4} + \frac{(150)^2}{(1+.04)^6} + \left[\frac{250}{(1+.04)^1} + \frac{250}{(1+.04)^2} + \frac{250}{(1+.04)^3}\right]^2 = 539{,}138$$

This figure for variance is equivalent to a standard deviation (σ)—or the square root of the variance—of $735.

Thus, the lathe has an $E(NPV)$ of $7,750, which measures return, and a $\sigma(NPV)$ of $735, which measures risk. The next step in the investment appraisal is to convert the $E(NPV)$ into its certainty equivalent by deducting from it an allowance for risk:

$$\begin{aligned} NPV &= E(NPV) - \lambda[\sigma(NPV)] \\ &= \$7{,}750 - \lambda(\$735) \end{aligned}$$

where λ denotes the market price of risk. The investing public generally regards return as desirable and risk as undesirable. They will accept more risk only when offered a higher return, and will accept a lower return only when offered less risk. The market price of risk, λ, is the ratio at which the investing public trades off risk for return or vice versa. Since this trade-off ratio is not directly observable, the management is forced to estimate its value subjectively. This explains why intuition and judgment will always play a key role in investment decisions under conditions of uncertainty.

In the above equation, a λ of, say, 10 means that a $1-increase in $\sigma(NPV)$ would leave the market valuation of the lathe unchanged if there is a corresponding $10-increase in $E(NPV)$. Earlier, using variant I, we found that the lathe has a certainty equivalent NPV of −$1,456.20. This NPV was calculated assuming a particular set of values for the α's, the certainty-equivalent conversion ratios. If we accept these assumed values, then λ must be equal to 12.52, since this is the value which would produce the same NPV and thus preserve consistency between the two variants of the certainty-equivalent approach. In practice, of course, a firm's estimates of λ and α may sometimes be inconsistent, in which case the two NPV's will be different. Calculating NPV in two different ways, therefore, provides the firm with a useful check on the internal consistency of its basic assumptions.

So far, we have been dealing with the calculation of $V(NPV)$ for a single project viewed in isolation. When a firm undertakes more than one investment, the portfolio approach is necessary whenever the *NPV*'s of the various projects under consideration are statistically correlated. If the *NPV*'s are independent, and hence uncorrelated, the *V*(*NPV*) of a portfolio is simply the sum of the individual *V*(*NPV*)'s. If the *NPV*'s are correlated, the *V*(*NPV*) of a portfolio is the sum of the individual *V*(*NPV*)'s *plus* the sum of all possible covariances between pairs of projects. In that case, equating a project's risk with its own *V*(*NPV*) may result in an under- or overestimation (depending on whether the sum of the covariances is positive or negative) of the project's contribution to portfolio risk. The projects of one firm may also be correlated with those of other firms. However, we shall not extend the portfolio concept beyond the limits of a single firm. This limitation is consistent with the specific-security approach to share valuation which we accepted in Chapter 2.

TOWARD A REALISTIC VIEW OF INVESTMENT RISK

V(*NPV*) has become the most widely used measure of investment risk. In this section, we shall explain the origin of *V*(*NPV*), point out its theoretical drawbacks, and then describe some alternative risk measures which theorists have recently proposed.

Origin of V(NPV)

Frederick S. Hillier was the first to propose *V*(*NPV*) as a measure of investment risk. At the time of Hillier's proposal in 1963, H. M. Markowitz had already developed his model of portfolio selection (see Chapter 2). This model assumed that securities investors chose their optimal securities portfolios on the basis of the expected value (*E*) and variance (*V*) of portfolio returns. We may conjecture that Markowitz's *E–V* criterion played a role in Hillier's choice of variance as a statistical measure of risk. In any case, we may ask why it was the variance of *NPV* that was chosen. This is apparently a carry-over from investment analysis under conditions of certainty: when cash flows are certain, the *NPV* of an investment is the theoretically correct measure of its contribution to the market value of the company's shares. When the cash flows are random variables, the *NPV* of an investment also becomes a random variable. It may have appeared reasonable to Hillier, as it did to others of us at that time, to measure the risk of an investment by the variance of its *NPV*. However, as we shall see, financial writers are beginning to realize that this approach has certain shortcomings.

Drawbacks of V(NPV)

A first drawback of *V*(*NPV*) as a measure of investment risk is its insensitivity to the time patterns of cash flow and net income that underlie an investment. This will be clearer if we consider a firm which must choose between two competing investment portfolios. Each portfolio has an economic life of 5 years; each costs \$3,000 now. Their annual net incomes and cash flows, as summarized in Table 7-1, have different expected values but identical variances. For the sake of simplicity, the net incomes and cash flows for each portfolio are assumed to be uncorrelated between time periods.

Assuming a risk-free interest rate of 6 percent and applying Eq. (7-7), we find that portfolios A and B have identical $V(NPV)$'s of 53,593. The portfolios therefore appear to be equal in risk. The typical financial executive, however, would probably view B as less risky than A, since B's net incomes show steady growth, while those for A are unstable. As we mentioned before, the price-earnings ratio of a company's shares tends to vary directly with the firm's earnings stability. In the present comparison between A and B, $V(NPV)$ fails to reveal the important difference in earnings stability.

A second drawback of $V(NPV)$ as a measure of investment risk relates to the concept of variance itself. Whether one is dealing with a single random variable (e.g., net income or cash flow in a single period) or with the sum of a number of random variables (e.g., the NPV of a project or of a portfolio), variance is defined in terms of the squared deviations from the mean of the

Table 7-1 Data on Two Investment Portfolios

Year	0	1	2	3	4	5
Project A						
Initial outlay	−\$3,000					
Expected net income		\$1,400	\$3,400	\$1,400	−\$ 120	\$1,400
Depreciation		600	600	600	600	600
Expected cash flow	−\$3,000	\$2,000	\$4,000	\$2,000	\$ 480	\$2,000
Variance of net income		15,000	15,000	15,000	15,000	15,000
Variance of cash flow		15,000	15,000	15,000	15,000	15,000
Project B						
Initial outlay	−\$3,000					
Expected net income		\$ 800	\$1,200	\$1,700	\$2,000	\$2,000
Depreciation		600	600	600	600	600
Expected cash flow	−\$3,000	\$1,400	\$1,800	\$2,300	\$2,600	\$2,600
Variance of net income		15,000	15,000	15,000	15,000	15,000
Variance of cash flow		15,000	15,000	15,000	15,000	15,000

random variable(s) involved. In comparing two investments, variance measures their risks from the means of the respective probability distributions. It does not allow for the possibility of measuring risks from a common point of reference—for example, the management's target rate of return. Nor does variance distinguish between positive and negative deviations from the mean; both contribute equally to risk. However, many decision-makers in fact think of risk only as "downside" deviations.

Recent Developments

Financial theorists, aware of the importance of earnings and cash-flow patterns over time, have dealt with them in a variety of ways. E. M. Lerner and A. Rappaport have constructed a linear-programming model of capital budgeting which incorporates earnings growth as an explicit constraint;[4] the objective becomes the choice of the portfolio with the highest *NPV*, given that earnings per share must grow at a specified rate. John K. Shank and A. Michael Burnell's model is similar.[5] In both models, however, earnings and cash flows are viewed as constants, rather than as random variables; consequently, neither model is directly applicable to investment decisions under uncertainty.

To take cash-flow pattern into account, James C. Van Horne suggested that we supplement $V(NPV)$ with an index of uncertainty resolution.[6] This index assumes that the speed with which uncertainty is resolved is an important aspect of investment risk. Let us suppose, for example, that a firm must choose between two investments with identical $V(NPV)$'s and identical economic lives. The uncertainty of one investment, however, is concentrated in the early years of the investment's life, whereas the uncertainty of the other is concentrated in the late years. Despite their identical economic lives and $V(NPV)$'s, the investments are not equally risky, since they present different opportunities for balancing risk over time. Van Horne's measure, by expressing risk as a function of time, enables a firm to regulate not only the total risk of an investment program but also the distribution of this risk over time.

A third suggestion was aimed at replacing variance with a better measure of investment risk. This suggestion introduces two features—the use of a target return and the distinction between positive and negative deviations. In two articles, the latter written in collaboration with John F. Brewster, I have advocated using $S(NPV)$, the semi-variance of *NPV*, as a

---

[4] E. M. Lerner and A. Rappaport, "Limit DCF in Capital Budgeting," *Harvard Business Review* 46 (September-October, 1968), pp. 133–139.

[5] John K. Shank and A. Michael Burnell, "Smooth Your Earnings Growth Rate," *Harvard Business Review* 52 (January-February, 1974), pp. 136–141.

[6] James C. Van Horne, "The Analysis of Uncertainty Resolution in Capital Budgeting for New Products," *Management Science* 15 (April, 1969), pp. B376–B386.

measure of risk.[7] Starting with the joint probability distribution of project *NPV*'s, we developed a step-by-step procedure for calculating the $S(NPV)$ of any given portfolio. Unfortunately, $S(NPV)$ is sufficiently more difficult to calculate than $V(NPV)$ that I now favor the use of $V(NPV)$ for practical reasons, especially since its drawbacks can be remedied in other ways.

Finally, some writers have reinterpreted the payback criterion as a tool for decision-making under uncertainty. The payback period of an investment was originally viewed as a proxy for return, since the value of the period's reciprocal was found to approximate the investment's *IRR*. This view, however, has given way to the realization that payback period is used by financial executives primarily as a crude but convenient measure of investment risk. In most cases, the distant cash flows of an investment are more uncertain than those of the near future. The payback criterion takes this difference into account by viewing the cash flows during the payback period as assured and by viewing the subsequent cash flows as virtually nonexistent. In addition, the payback period can also serve as an index of uncertainty resolution. As H. Martin Weingartner has observed, the shorter the payback period, the sooner is the profitability of an investment likely to be known.[8] By balancing payback periods, a firm is able to control the distribution of its investment risk over time.

AN OPERATING PROCEDURE

We shall now outline an operating procedure for making investment decisions based on the risk-adjusted discount-rate approach.

Practical Considerations

Although the certainty-equivalent approach and the risk-adjusted discount-rate approach will yield the same *NPV* for a given investment, there is a practical reason for preferring the latter method. Suppose, for example, that a firm knows the expected cash flows from an investment, the degree of risk present in these flows, and the risk-free interest rate. Depending on which method is used, the company must forecast either the ratios which the market will use in converting risky sums into their certainty

[7] James C. T. Mao and John F. Brewster, "An E–S_h Model of Capital Budgeting," *Engineering Economist* 15 (January-February, 1970), pp. 103–121; see also my "Models of Capital Budgeting, E–V vs. E–S," *Journal of Financial and Quantitative Analysis* 4 (January, 1970), pp. 657–675.

[8] H. Martin Weingartner, "Some New Views on the Payback Period and Capital Budgeting Decisions," *Management Science* 15 (August, 1969), pp. B594-B607. David Durand expresses a similar view in his "Payout Period, Time Spread and Duration: Aids to Judgment in Capital Budgeting," *Journal of Bank Research* 5 (Spring, 1974), pp. 20–34.

equivalents or the risk premium which the market will demand beyond the risk-free interest rate. Since there are many studies on the risk-return relationship for different classes of securities, it is usually easier to forecast the risk premium. The relationships established by these studies are averages and may not be directly applicable either to the firm or to the project; nevertheless, they provide a useful benchmark, lacking in the certainty-equivalent approach.

The Procedure

Let us suppose that an unspecified amount of capital for investment is to be raised in some fixed proportion of debt financing and equity financing. The firm must decide whether or not such a financing-investment venture would be profitable.

The following five-step procedure is a suggested means of finding the optimal investment program:

1. Forecast the expected earnings and the expected after-tax cash flows for each project in the list of potential investments.
2. Set earnings and cash-flow targets for each year of the firm's planning horizon. Only those portfolios reaching or exceeding the targets are "feasible."
3. Each feasible portfolio has a particular degree of risk, as measured by the variance of net present value. On the basis of this risk, forecast the rate of return on the company's shares which would be required by the market if that portfolio were the one chosen.
4. Given the market's required rate of return, calculate the cost of equity capital to the firm (see Chapter 8). Use this cost to determine the *NPV* of the corresponding portfolio.
5. From the set of feasible portfolios, select the one with the highest expected *NPV* (use the integer-programming method explained in Chapter 6).

We should note that these five steps do not represent a capital-rationing situation. Since the amount of capital is unlimited, a firm can experiment with different amounts of investible funds. The firm will push its investments until the return on its marginal project is equal to its cost of capital. The implied equality between the cost of capital and reinvestment rate justifies the use of the *NPV* selection criterion in the usual way. However, when capital is rationed, the reinvestment rate will exceed the cost of capital, and the calculation of *NPV* must take account of this divergence. In particular, step 4 in the above procedure must be modified as follows:

4. Calculate the net future value (NFV) of a given portfolio by compounding the cash flows at the firm's reinvestment rate to the end of the firm's planning horizon. Discount this NFV at the appropriate cost of capital (from step 3) to determine the NPV of this portfolio.

Although we go through the intermediate steps of calculating NFV, the final selection is still based on NPV. The NFV criterion will pick out the same optimal portfolio as the NPV criterion if the market views all portfolios as equally risky. When this necessary condition is not met, the market discount rate will be different for different portfolios. In that case, the NPV criterion must be used, since it is NPV, not NFV, that measures the increase in the market value of the company's shares.

REVIEW QUESTIONS

1. Outline the risk-adjusted discount-rate approach to investment appraisal; explain how it differs from the average-cost-of-capital approach.
2. Define the certainty equivalent of a risky sum. Outline the certainty-equivalent approach to investment appraisal. How does it differ from the risk-adjusted discount-rate approach?
3. Suppose that a firm calculates the expected NPV of an investment in two ways: by discounting the expected cash flows at the investment's risk-adjusted discount rate, and at the risk-free rate of interest. Explain the relationship between the two resulting expected NPV's.
4. A certain investment is partly debt financed and partly equity financed. How should the loan proceeds and the debt charges be handled in deriving the cash flows of the investment for the purpose of calculating NPV? Does your answer depend on which approach to investment appraisal you are using?
5. If a firm uses a constant risk-adjusted discount rate to discount the cash flows at different points in time, this means that the firm regards the risks in the cash flows (as measured by the certainty-equivalent conversion ratio α) to be constant over time. Do you agree? Why or why not?
6. What are the major shortcomings of $V(NPV)$ as a measure of investment risk and how might these shortcomings be remedied?
7. Why is the portfolio approach to investment decisions necessary under uncertainty even if the firm is not faced with the problems of capital rationing and project indivisibility?
8. Discuss the theoretical shortcomings of the payback period as a criterion of investment appraisal. How do you account for the fact that this criterion is still widely used in business even though many financial writers have dismissed it as misleading and worthless?
9. In Eqs. (7-9) and (7-10), why would it be wrong to equate i with the risk-adjusted discount rate? What is the correct value of i?

10. Give examples of investments whose cash flows at different times have high correlation, moderate correlation, and low correlation. Also, list pairs of investments whose *NPV*'s might have high, moderate, and low correlations.

PROBLEMS

1. Peninsula Publishers is thinking of investing in a new printing press costing \$50,000 which is expected to generate net after-tax cash flows of \$46,000 at the end of each of the next three years. Although the risk-free interest rate is only 8 percent, the risk of the investment is such that the firm considers it appropriate to assign a risk-adjusted discount rate of 12.5 percent to the first inflow, 20 percent to the second, and 80 percent to the third.

   Calculate the *NPV* of this investment. Find the uniform discount rate which would produce the same *NPV* as that produced by the set of variable discount rates.
2. Evaluate Peninsula Publishers' investment using the certainty-equivalent method, assuming that the risk-free interest rate is 8 percent and that the firm assigns a certainty-equivalent conversion ratio of 96/100 to the first inflow, 81/100 to the second, and 27/125 to the third. Did you get the same *NPV* that you got in Problem 1? Is there term-by-term equality? How would your answer be affected if the uniform discount rate of Problem 1 were used to calculate not only the overall *NPV* but also the present value of each cash flow?
3. A \$20,000 investment is expected to generate the following cash flows:

End of Year	0	1	2	3
Cost of investment	−\$20,000			
EBIAT + depreciation		\$9,000	\$9,000	\$15,000
Cash flow	−\$20,000	\$9,000	\$9,000	\$15,000

   To finance the investment, the company plans to use \$10,000 of debt capital and \$10,000 of equity capital. The debt capital is to carry an interest rate of 8 percent, with interest payable annually and the principal due in a lump sum at the end of the third year. The firm requires an annual return of 12 percent on the equity capital.

   Calculate the *NPV* of this investment using the average-cost-of-capital method. Show that the result differs from the correct value resulting from the risk-adjusted discount-rate method.
4. Suppose that in Figure 7-1, $a_0 = \$10$, $a_1 = \$12$, $a_2 = \$15$, and $t = 5$ years. Using the certainty-equivalent approach, an investor places a present value of \$6.07 on the sum (a_0, b_0), implying a risk-free interest rate of 10.5 percent. Determine the ratio at which this investor would convert a_1 and a_2 into certainty equivalents. (Hint: $[a_0, b_0]$, $[a_1, b_1]$, and $[a_2, b_2]$ are all on the same equal-market-valuation curve for this investor.)
5. Calculate the $V(NPV)$ of the Peters lathe on the new assumption that (a) the cash flows are independent of one another, and (b) the cash flows are perfectly correlated. Assuming the $E(NPV)$ of the lathe has a certainty equivalent of −\$1,456.20, what is the implied market price of risk (λ) in each case?

6. Saturn Aircraft Company forecasts that its S-111 project, which costs $425 million now, would generate cash inflows during the next 3 years as follows: 3 independent annual inflows, each with an expected value of $150 million and a standard deviation of $12 million, *and* 3 perfectly correlated annual inflows, each with an expected value of $250 million and a standard deviation of $15 million. Calculate the $E(NPV)$ and $V(NPV)$ of the project, assuming a risk-free interest rate of 7 percent. What do your results indicate about the profitability of the S-111 project?

7. Calculate the $E(NPV)$ and $V(NPV)$ of a portfolio of 3 investments (a, b, c), assuming that the NPV's of these investments have the following means (E), variances (V), and covariances (C):

$E_a = 500$	$V_a = 2{,}500$	$C_{ab} = 400$
$E_b = 400$	$V_b = 900$	$C_{ac} = 225$
$E_c = 600$	$V_c = 1{,}600$	$C_{bc} = 100$

8. John Hoffman invested $100,000 two years ago to form Floating Dream, Inc., to manufacture high-quality waterbeds. He estimated that the cash flow from the operation would average $44,000 annually for the 6-year life of the production facilities. Actual cash inflow was only $25,000 in each of the first two years; and by the end of the second year it was clear that Hoffman's original forecasts were overly optimistic. The cash flows for the four remaining years were reestimated at $15,000, $15,000, $5,000, and $5,000.

The firm is now thinking of converting its operation to the manufacture of plastic rowboats. It would cost $8,500 to make the conversion, but the cash flows for the four remaining years would be raised to $17,500 annually. On the other hand, sales of a night table specially designed to go with the waterbed brought in an additional annual net cash flow of $2,000, which will be forfeited if the company discontinues the manufacture of waterbeds.

Calculate the *NPV* of this $8,500-conversion project, assuming a risk-adjusted discount rate of 14 percent.

REFERENCES

ARDITTI, FRED D., "The Weighted Average Cost of Capital: Some Questions on Its Definition, Interpretation, and Use," *Journal of Finance* 28 (September, 1973), pp. 1001–1007.

BOWER, RICHARD S., and DONALD R. LESSARD, "An Operational Approach to Risk-Screening," *Journal of Finance* 28 (May, 1973), pp. 321–337.

CHEN, HOUNG-YHI., "Valuation Under Uncertainty," *Journal of Financial and Quantitative Analysis* 2 (September, 1967), pp. 313–326.

DURAND, DAVID, "Payout Period, Time Spread and Duration: Aids to Judgment in Capital Budgeting," *Journal of Bank Research* 5 (Spring, 1974), pp. 20–34.

DYCKMAN, THOMAS R., and JAMES C. KINARD, "The Discounted Cash Flow Investment Decision Model with Accounting Income Constraints," *Decision Sciences* 4 (July, 1973), pp. 301–313.

HERTZ, DAVID B., "Investment Policies that Pay Off," *Harvard Business Review* 46 (January–February, 1968), pp. 96–108.

HILLIER, FREDERICK S., "A Basic Model for Capital Budgeting of Risky Interrelated Projects," *Engineering Economist* 17 (October–November, 1971), pp. 1–30.

HILLIER, FREDERICK S., "The Derivation of Probabilistic Information for the Evaluation of Risky Investments," *Management Science* 9 (April, 1963), pp. 443–457.

JOY, O. MAURICE, and JERRY O. BRADLEY, "A Note on Sensitivity Analysis of Rates of Return," *Journal of Finance* 28 (December, 1973), pp. 1255–1261.

KRYZANOWSKI, LAWRENCE, PETER LUSZTIG, and BERNHARD SCHWAB, "Monte Carlo Simulation and Capital Expenditure Decisions: A Case Study," *Engineering Economist* 18 (October–November, 1972), pp. 31–48.

LERNER, E. M., and A. RAPPAPORT, "Limit DCF in Capital Budgeting," *Harvard Business Review* 46 (September–October, 1968), pp. 133–139.

MAO, JAMES C. T., *Quantitative Analysis of Financial Decisions* (New York: The Macmillan Company, 1969), Ch. 8.

MAO, JAMES C. T., and JOHN F. BREWSTER, "An E–S_h Model of Capital Budgeting," *Engineering Economist* 15 (January–February, 1970), pp. 103–121.

ROBICHEK, ALEXANDER A., and STEWART C. MYERS, "Conceptual Problems in the Use of Risk-Adjusted Discount Rates," *Journal of Finance* 21 (December, 1966), pp. 727–730.

SHANK, JOHN K., and A. MICHAEL BURNELL, "Smooth Your Earnings Growth Rate," *Harvard Business Review* 52 (January–February, 1974), pp. 136–141.

VAN HORNE, JAMES C., "The Analysis of Uncertainty Resolution in Capital Budgeting for New Products," *Management Science* 15 (April, 1969), pp. B376–B386.

WEINGARTNER, H. MARTIN, "Some New Views on the Payback Period and Capital Budgeting Decisions," *Management Science* 15 (August, 1969), pp. B594–B607.

8 Investment Decisions Under Uncertainty (II)

At the end of the last chapter, we outlined a five-step procedure for applying the risk-adjusted discount-rate approach to a firm's investment decisions. Since this procedure uses the *NPV* formula, it requires that we use the cost of common equity to the firm as the discount rate. Here, we shall see how this cost of equity capital is related to the market-capitalization rate—i.e., the rate of return on the firm's common stock required by the security investors. We shall first consider those cases in which the new investment does not alter the firm's risk and therefore does not alter the market-capitalization rate; we shall assume that we are dealing with "static" (non-growth) firms. Later we shall drop the assumption of no growth. We shall also discuss the case in which the new investment does alter risk and hence the market-capitalization rate; the relationship between the cost of equity capital and the market-capitalization rate is more complicated here and will lead us into modifications of our formulas. In the third section of this chapter, we shall present two practical procedures for estimating the market-capitalization rate, one using the interview method and the other the regression method. Finally, we shall report on a survey of relevant investment practices.

THE COST OF COMMON EQUITY

There are essentially two ways in which a firm can finance the common-equity portion of its investment expenditures: externally, by the sale of new shares; or internally, by the retention of earnings. The mechanics of selling securities and the relative advantages of debt versus equity financing will be discussed in later chapters; here we shall present formulas for calculating the cost of common equity obtained through each of these two methods.[1]

Symbols and Assumptions

Let us first define the list of symbols to be used in the following analysis:

n_0 = number of shares outstanding before new financing

n_1 = number of new shares sold to existing stockholders

n_2 = number of new shares sold to new stockholders

n = number of shares outstanding after new financing

C = total amount of equity capital raised

P = current market price of the company's shares

P' = price at which new shares are sold

k_e = cost of common equity capital to the firm

y = market-capitalization rate (i.e., security investors' required rate of return)

E = expected per-share earnings if new transaction is not undertaken

r = the uniform perpetual after-tax rate of return which the new equity capital is expected to earn

τ = rate of taxation on personal income.

We shall assume for the moment that we are considering a static (non-growth) company, whose market-capitalization rate is given by the reciprocal of the price-earnings ratio of the firm's shares. We shall also assume that the new investment and financing will not alter the firm's risk characteristics. The latter assumption implies that the market-capitalization rate y is unaffected by the transaction; the impact of the new investment on the market value of the existing shares may therefore be measured simply by comparing the size of the earnings with and without the new investment.

The Sale of New Shares

Break-even Analysis. The method used for determining the cost of common equity is essentially that of break-even analysis. Let us look at

[1] The discussion here is based on my *Quantitative Analysis of Financial Decisions,* Ch. 10.

Educational Toys, Inc., which, with existing assets alone, is expected to generate adjusted annual earnings of $180,000 perpetually. The firm has 125,000 shares of common stock outstanding. These shares have a total market value of $1,500,000, which implies that the security investors capitalize the earnings at 12 percent. In order to raise $250,000 of equity capital, the company issued 25,000 new shares at a price of $10 per share, $2 below the market price of $12 per share. Current stockholders purchased 40 percent of the new issue (10,000 shares); "outsiders" purchased the remaining 60 percent (15,000 shares). The existing stockholders were not given the pre-emptive right to subscribe to the new shares at a favored price; they purchased their new shares on the same terms as the outsiders. Given these facts, what is the cost of this common equity to the firm? That is, what is the *minimum* rate of return on the new investment at which the original stockholders will be at least as well off as they were before the new issue?

A key concept in this break-even analysis is "earnings dilution." When outsiders purchase 15,000 shares of the new issue, they become entitled to 10 percent (they own 15,000 of 150,000 shares) of every dollar of the firm's earnings. The extent to which the new stockholders are entitled to share in the earnings associated with the previously existing assets is the measure of the earnings dilution suffered by the original stockholders. This earnings dilution is the price that the original stockholders pay for the advantage of receiving 90 percent of the earnings of the new investment while contributing only 40 percent to its cost. Let us assume that the after-tax profit on the new investment is such that the firm receives a uniform perpetual annual return of r on the equity portion ($250,000) of the investment. For the original stockholders to be as well off as they were formerly, their share of the incremental earnings must compensate them not only for the 10 percent earnings dilution but also for the normal 12 percent return (the market-capitalization rate), which their new $100,000 investment would have earned had the funds been invested in other companies of comparable risk.

This break-even condition may be stated algebraically by the following equation:

$$\underbrace{(90\%)(\$250{,}000)(r)}_{\substack{\text{Incremental}\\ \text{earnings}}} = \underbrace{(10\%)(\$180{,}000)}_{\substack{\text{Earnings}\\ \text{dilution}}} + \underbrace{(12\%)(\$100{,}000)}_{\substack{\text{Normal}\\ \text{return}}}$$

The value of r in this equation is the cost of common equity capital, since it is the minimum rate that the new investment must earn to enhance the wealth of the original stockholders. In this case, r—and hence k_e—is 13.33 percent.

General Formulas. The cost of common equity can also be calculated by using general formulas. If we replace the numbers in the preceding break-even condition by the symbols which represent them, we get

$$\underbrace{\left(\frac{n_0+n_1}{n}\right)(Cr)}_{\text{Incremental earnings}} = \underbrace{\left(\frac{n_2}{n}\right)(En_0)}_{\text{Earnings dilution}} + \underbrace{y(n_1P')}_{\text{Normal return}} \tag{8-1}$$

To find the cost of common equity capital, we substitute k_e for r in (8-1) and solve for it:

$$k_e = \frac{n_0n_2}{(nn_1+n_0n_2)}\frac{P}{P'}y + \frac{nn_1}{(nn_1+n_0n_2)}y \tag{8-2}$$

Fortunately, this equation has rather simple economic interpretations.

Three possible cases may be distinguished. First, the entire issue may be sold to the original stockholders. In that case, $n_2 = 0$ and $n = n_0 + n_1$, so that Eq. (8-2) reduces to:

$$k_e = y \tag{8-3}$$

That is, the cost of equity capital is the same as the market-capitalization rate. For Educational Toys, this is 12 percent. Second, the entire issue may be sold to outsiders. In that case, $n_1 = 0$, $n = n_0 + n_2$, so that Eq. (8-2) reduces to:

$$k_e = \frac{P}{P'}y \tag{8-4}$$

In this situation, k_e varies directly with the market-capitalization rate and inversely with the size of the discount at which the new shares are sold. In our example, since P is 20 percent higher than P', the cost of equity capital would have been 1.2 × 12 percent, or 14.4 percent. Third, the new issue may be divided between the existing stockholders and outsiders. In that case, Eq. (8-2) cannot be simplified, but it can be written more succinctly as:

$$k_e = w\left(\frac{P}{P'}y\right) + (1-w)y \tag{8-5}$$

where w equals $\frac{n_0n_2}{(nn_1+n_0n_2)}$. The cost of equity capital is now revealed as a weighted average of the costs in the other two cases. This relationship was not demonstrated by the break-even analysis. Working out Eq. (8-5) with the data for Educational Toys' mixed financing, we get a cost of equity capital of 13.33 percent, the same value obtained by break-even analysis.

Privileged Subscription

The common stockholders of many companies have the pre-emptive right to subscribe to any new issue of common stock (or of securities convertible into common stock) on a pro-rata basis. In some states, firms are legally obligated to provide this right; in states where the pre-emptive right is not mandatory, it is often written into corporation charters. When new common stock is offered through privileged subscription, the holder of each previously existing share is entitled to one right. The number of rights needed to subscribe to one new share is determined by the ratio of existing shares to new shares. This ratio R (known as the subscription ratio), together with the degree of underpricing (the extent to which P' is below P), determines the market value of a right. Stockholders may either exercise or sell their rights.

If the corporation charter of Educational Toys provided stockholders with this pre-emptive right, how would this affect the computation of the cost of equity capital to the firm? In order for the outsiders to purchase their 15,000 shares of the new issue under conditions of privileged subscription, they must first purchase 15,000 $\times$ R rights from the existing stockholders. (In this case, R = 125,000/25,000 = 5.) The cost of equity capital to the firm will depend in part on the amount received by the existing stockholders for the sale of their rights. The current market price of a share is \$12; the subscription price is only \$10. We shall assume that \$12 is the on-right market price, i.e., the price includes the value of the share proper plus the value of one right.[2] It takes \$12 $\times$ 5 to purchase enough shares to detach the 5 (=R) rights necessary to buy one share for \$10. After the rights have been exercised, the investor will have 6 ex-right shares costing \$70, or \$11⅔ each. Since the on-right market price is \$12 a share, each right is worth 33⅓¢.

For the privilege of subscribing to 15,000 shares at \$10 per share, the new stockholders must pay a total of \$25,000 (= 5 $\times$ 15,000 $\times$ 33⅓¢) to the existing stockholders for relinquishing the necessary number of pre-emptive rights. Since the existing stockholders receive this \$25,000 compensation, their net investment in this transaction is not \$100,000 but only

[2] For the distinction between "on-right" and "ex-right" prices, see the discussion of rights offerings in Chapter 17.

\$75,000. When we make this change, the original break-even condition becomes:

$$(90\%)(\$250{,}000)(r) = (10\%)(\$180{,}000) + (12\%)(\$75{,}000)$$

Substituting k_e for r and solving, we find that the cost of equity capital is 12 percent, the same figure we got for the case in which all securities are sold to existing stockholders.

What this example illustrates is that the sale of new shares to outsiders at a discount does not increase the cost of equity capital to the firm above the market-capitalization rate y, provided that the existing stockholders have pre-emptive rights and are thus assured of adequate compensation through the sale of some or all of their rights to the outsiders. So far, we have ignored the inevitable costs involved in selling new securities. In practice, these costs should be expressed as a percentage of the capital raised and added to the figure computed by one of the formulas above.

Retained Earnings

The market capitalizes the earnings of Educational Toys at y. This means that any investor may earn a return of y either by investing his funds in the shares of this company or by investing in the shares of any other firm of comparable risk. The cost of retained earnings to the company would be identical to this opportunity cost y, except for the impact of the personal income tax. When a company makes a profit, the stockholders can get that profit only if the net income is declared in dividends. If the stockholder is subject to a marginal tax rate τ, only $\$(1-\tau)$ is left for reinvestment out of every dividend dollar. But if the dividend dollar is retained by the company, the firm will have the whole dollar to reinvest on behalf of the stockholder. Consequently, the cost of retained earnings is indicated not by y but by $(1-\tau)y$.

A possible objection to this formulation is that if a firm reinvests its earnings, the only way a stockholder can realize his earnings in cash is to sell part of his holdings, in which case he is subject to capital gains tax. However, if we assume that the stockholder would have reinvested his dividend proceeds, the cost of retained earnings is not increased above $(1-\tau)y$, since the capital gains tax would apply whenever he sells his investment. If the stockholders of Educational Toys are subject on the average to a marginal tax rate of 40 percent, the cost of retained earnings is only 7.2 percent ($= .6 \times .12$). The tax advantage, together with the fact that no selling costs are involved in retained earnings, makes retained earnings the least expensive of all forms of equity capital.

For easy reference, Table 8-1 summarizes the formulas for computing the cost of common equity and their application to Educational Toys.

Table 8-1 Formulas for the Cost of Common Equity

Method of Financing	Algebraic Expression*	Application to Educational Toys
New shares sold to:		
Existing stockholders	y	12.0%
New stockholders	$\frac{P}{P'}y$	14.4
Both groups	$w\frac{P}{P'}y + (1 - w)y$	13.3
Privileged subscription	y	12.0
Retained earnings	$(1 - \tau)y$	7.2

* Assuming a constant market-capitalization rate.

TWO IMPORTANT QUALIFICATIONS

The Effect of Earnings Growth

We have seen that the cost of equity capital depends largely on the market-capitalization rate, modified by such factors as flotation expenses and the method of financing actually used. The market-capitalization rate is sometimes equated with the reciprocal of the price-earnings ratio of the company's shares. However, this procedure is correct only if the firm is static. If growth is expected, the reciprocal of the price-earnings ratio would underestimate the market-capitalization rate by an amount varying directly with the growth potential of the firm.

The Case of Exponential Growth. Exponential growth occurs when a company grows by a constant percentage each year. In this case, we can explain the underestimate by going back to stock valuation Eq. (2-8) presented in Chapter 2:

$$P_0 = \frac{E}{y} + \left(\frac{bE}{y - br}\right)\left(\frac{r - y}{y}\right) \tag{8-6}$$

where P_0 represents current share price, E the uniform perpetual earnings generated by existing assets alone, b the percentage of each year's earnings that is reinvested, r the perpetual annual rate of return on reinvestments, and y the market-capitalization rate. In Chapter 2, the unknown was P_0; here, since we are using the equation to estimate the market-capitalization rate, the unknown is y.

The example used in Chapter 2 to illustrate Eq. (2-8) as a valuation formula can be used here to illustrate the above equation as a formula for determining market-capitalization rate. We are dealing with an all-equity firm with 25,000 shares outstanding. Its existing assets alone are expected to generate perpetual annual earnings of \$50,000 – i.e., \$2 per share. The firm has a policy of paying out 60 percent of each year's earnings in dividends and reinvesting the balance; reinvestments are expected to yield perpetual returns of 15 percent per annum. Our question is, if the company's stock sells at \$20 per share, at what discount rate are the security investors capitalizing the company's earnings? In this case, E = \$2 per share, $b = .40$, $r = .15$, and $P_0 = \$20$. Solving Eq. (8-6) with these values, we find that the market-capitalization rate y is exactly 12 percent. Had we equated y with the reciprocal of the price-earnings ratio in this example, we would have a rate of 10 percent (=\$2/\$20), as much as two full percentage points below the actual capitalization rate.

It is interesting to note in this connection that shares of IBM sold at a price-earnings ratio of about 50 in the bull market of 1961. If one ignored IBM's obvious growth potential, one might conclude that security investors were willing to supply equity capital to IBM at a required rate of return of only 2 percent per annum (1/50) while they were demanding an interest rate of 4 percent on funds loaned to the United States government. The paradox can easily be accounted for by considering IBM's growth potential. Investors are willing to pay a high price for IBM's shares relative to the company's current earnings because they expect earnings to increase rapidly. The cost of equity capital to IBM was actually considerably higher than two percent even in years with a high price-earnings ratio.

The Case of Constant Growth. Eq. (8-6) assumes an exponential growth for a firm's investments and its earnings and dividends. If the growth rate is slower (e.g., if the company reinvests a constant dollar amount I each year at a rate of return of r), the market-capitalization rate is implied by Eq. (2-7) of Chapter 2:

$$P_0 = \frac{E}{y} + \frac{I}{y}\left(\frac{r-y}{y}\right) \tag{8-7}$$

For our example, $E = \$2$, $I = \$0.80$ ($= \$2 \times .4$), and $r = .15$; so a share price of \$20 implies a market capitalization rate of 11.3 percent, which is still more than one percentage point above the 10 percent figure for E/P_0.

We should note that for any given share price, the market-capitalization rate implied by (8-7) is lower than that implied by (8-6). In Figure 8-1, this difference is reflected in the fact that y' always lies below y. The graph also includes a curve relating E/P_0 to P_0. In both kinds of growth, the extent to which E/P_0 underestimates y increases as the actual value of y decreases. This is because growth potential, which E/P_0 ignores, takes on greater significance as y decreases.

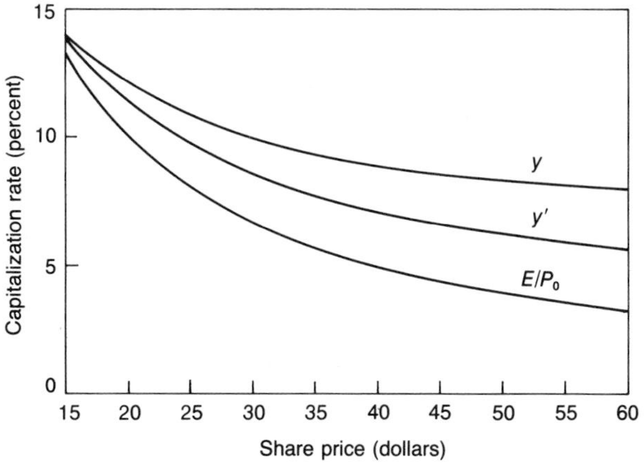

Figure 8-1 Capitalization Rate-Share Price Relationship for a Growth Company

The Effect of Changing Risk

The formulas presented in the first part of this chapter require a second qualification as well. These formulas were derived on the assumption that the risk characteristics of the firm are unaffected by the new investment-and-financing transaction. This assumption may be valid for many investments, particularly those which expand or replace existing or related product lines. But new investments may alter a company's risk profile by taking the firm into new product areas—when, for example, an office-equipment manufacturer such as SCM enters into the production of food items, or a sewing-machine manufacturer such as Singer begins to make television sets, or a consumer-finance company such as GAC enters the field of land development. When a firm's risk is altered, its market-capitalization rate changes. This change necessarily affects the market valuation of the earnings generated both by the already existing assets and by the new investment. In determining its cost of capital, the firm clearly must take into account the effects of such a revaluation.

To illustrate, let us again consider Educational Toys. This time, let us assume that the new issue of common stock is to be sold entirely to the existing stockholders; the other data remain unchanged. The new investment alters the risk characteristics of the firm so that the market-capitalization rate rises from the original 12 percent to 12.5 percent. Before the new transaction, the company had 125,000 shares outstanding, on which it earned \$180,000 yearly; at a market-capitalization rate of 12 percent, these shares had a total market value of \$1,500,000. The new financing costs the stockholders \$250,000 in cash, after which they hold 150,000 (= 125,000 + 25,000) shares, with a total annual earnings of \$180,000 + \$250,000r

(where r, as before, is the perpetual annual return on the new investment). Since the market now capitalizes the earnings at 12.5 percent, the 150,000 shares have a market value of (\$180,000 + \$250,000r)/.125. For the existing stockholders to be as well off as they were before, this value must exceed the value of their original holdings by \$250,000, the amount paid for the 25,000 new shares. This break-even condition may be written as:

$$\frac{\$180{,}000 + \$250{,}000r}{.125} - \$250{,}000 = \$1{,}500{,}000 \tag{8-8}$$

Solving this equation, we find that r, and hence the cost of equity capital k_e, is 15.5 percent. The increase of the market-capitalization rate from 12 percent to 12.5 percent raises the cost of equity capital from 12 percent to 15.5 percent. This is to be expected, since the return on the new investment must now compensate the stockholders for the lower asset value brought about by the higher market-capitalization rate.

To generalize the break-even condition, we replace the numbers in Eq. (8-8) with the symbols which represent them:

$$\frac{n_0E + n_1P'r}{y_2} - n_1P' = \frac{n_0E}{y_1} \tag{8-9}$$

where the left-hand side represents the total value of the shares held by stockholders, less the amount paid for the new shares; and the right-hand side represents the value of the holdings before the new transaction. Substituting k_e for r and solving for k_e, we get the following expression for the cost of equity capital:

$$k_e = \frac{n_0E}{n_1P'}\left(\frac{y_2}{y_1} - 1\right) + y_2 \tag{8-10}$$

If $y_2 = y_1$ (that is, if there is no change in the market-capitalization rate), (8-10) reduces to (8-3), and the cost of equity capital is equal to the constant market-capitalization rate. Otherwise, k_e will be higher or lower than y_2, according to whether y_2 is greater or less than y_1. This is predictable since, if y_2 is greater than y_1, the return on the new investment must compensate the stockholders for the accompanying depreciation in share value. If y_2 is less than y_1, the stockholders receive partial compensation from the appreciation in share value brought about by the lower market-capitalization rate and, consequently, can afford to accept a return on the new investment which is lower than the market-capitalization rate.

The other formulas in Table 8-1 can be modified in similar ways to take into account possible changes in the market-capitalization rate.

ESTIMATING THE MARKET-CAPITALIZATION RATE

Despite the exactness of our formulas, the cost of equity capital can never be determined precisely since its key determinant, the market-capitalization rate, must necessarily be based on forecasts of the company's earning power and growth potential. The manager will therefore find it very useful to have a method to check the accuracy of his forecast about the market-capitalization rate. In this section, we shall look at studies illustrating two different methods of making such a check: investor-opinion survey and regression analysis.

Investor-Opinion Survey

Obviously, the most direct way of finding out what rate of return investors require on a particular stock is to ask the investors themselves. Harold Bierman, Jr. and Clayton P. Alderfer used this method to determine the cost of equity capital to four companies: American Telephone and Telegraph, Standard Oil of New Jersey, General Motors, and Xerox.[3]

The Study. The study was conducted in 1968 by means of a questionnaire mailed to 250 members of The Financial Analysts Federation and selected at random from the membership directory. In designing the questionnaire, Bierman and Alderfer viewed the investors as setting the price of a share according to the present value of its future dividends:

$$P_0 = \frac{D_1}{(1+y)} + \frac{D_2}{(1+y)^2} + \frac{D_3}{(1+y)^3} + \cdots \tag{8-11}$$

where y is the market-capitalization rate sought by the investors. Since the price of a share, P_0, is known, the market-capitalization rate will be uniquely determined once the dividend expectations from now to perpetuity are known. But whereas investors may have only a vague idea of all future dividends, they may have a clearer idea of dividends and share price expected at the end of one year. Since the share price at the end of one year may be viewed as the present value of all future dividends from that time, Eq. (8-11) may be written as:

$$P_0 = \frac{D_1 + P_1}{(1+y)^1} \tag{8-12}$$

[3] Harold Bierman, Jr. and Clayton P. Alderfer, "Estimating the Cost of Capital, A Different Approach," *Decision Sciences* 1 (January–April, 1970), pp. 40–53.

Table 8-2 Estimates of Percentage Price Appreciation

Number of Responses	Company Name	Mean Percentage Appreciation	Standard Deviation
74	AT&T	.047	.047
79	Standard Oil (N.J.)	.088	.044
74	GM	.099	.060
75	Xerox	.151	.110

Source: Bierman and Alderfer, "Estimating the Cost of Capital, A Different Approach," *Decision Sciences*, 1 (January–April, 1970), p. 43.

Solving for y, we get

$$y = \frac{D_1}{P_0} + \left(\frac{P_1}{P_0} - 1\right) \tag{8-13}$$

The market-capitalization rate, in other words, equals the expected current dividend yield plus the expected 1-year appreciation in share price. Accordingly, the analysts surveyed were asked to give their best estimates of the appreciation in share price and, given this expected price appreciation, the *minimum* dividend rate they would want before purchasing shares in the four companies indicated.

The Results. Of the 250 analysts surveyed, 87 returned questionnaires "that were answered in a manner that enabled them to be processed." Table 8-2 summarizes the estimates of percentage price appreciation, and Table 8-3 summarizes the data on required dividends. Fewer responses are listed in Table 8-3 than in Table 8-2 because the analysts were asked not to answer that question "unless they thought the dividend rate was consistent with the projected price appreciation, and they would be willing to purchase the stock with this dividend and price appreciation."

Combining the results of Tables 8-2 and 8-3, we get the following market-capitalization rates for the four companies:

AT&T	9.7%	GM	14.9%
Standard Oil (N.J.)	13.7%	Xerox	16.9%

Regression Analysis

Bierman and Alderfer's study found the investors' required rate of return, given the risk of the firm at the time of the survey; it did not indicate how the rate would change if new investments were to alter the firms' risk. This point may be clarified by drawing an analogy with the parallel differ-

Table 8-3 Required Dividends to Accompany Price Appreciation

Number of Responses	Company Name	Mean Dividend Rate	Standard Deviation
67	AT&T	.050	.0124
69	Standard Oil (N.J.)	.049	.0122
65	GM	.050	.0121
75	Xerox	.018	.0234

Source: Bierman and Alderfer, *op. cit.*, p. 43.

ence between the quantity of a product demanded at a given price and the demand schedule of that product, the latter being a functional relationship between price and quantity.

The purpose of investor-opinion survey differs from that of regression analysis in that the latter seeks to find the functional relationship between risk and return. Of the several studies in this area, we shall briefly summarize two: that of Robert M. Soldofsky and Roger L. Miller[4] because of its broad scope and that of Alexander A. Robichek, Richard A. Cohn, and John J. Pringle[5] because of its more recent data.

The Soldofsky-Miller (SM) Study. SM derived "risk-premium curves," representing the functional relationships between risk and return, from a broad sample of long-term securities, including corporate and government bonds and preferred stock, as well as common stock. The study covered the 17-year period 1950–1966 and several sub-periods. Because of the homogeneity of government bonds, only three different long-term bonds were included (long-term defined as having at least a 15-year term). The corporate bonds were divided into five risk classes according to ratings by Moody's, a commercial rating agency; within each risk class, a minimum of 10 bonds were selected from industrials, a minimum of 10 from utilities, and a minimum of 10 from railroads. Preferred stocks were divided into three risk classes according to ratings by Standard and Poor; a minimum of 15 stocks were selected from each class. Common stock was divided into six risk classes, and a minimum of 10 stocks were selected from each. The annual rate of return for the securities selected was calculated by expressing the interest (or dividend) income plus capital appreciation as a percentage of the

[4] Robert M. Soldofsky and Roger L. Miller, "Risk-Premium Curves for Different Classes of Long-Term Securities, 1950–1966," *Journal of Finance* 24 (June, 1969), pp. 429–446.

[5] Alexander A. Robichek, Richard A. Cohn, and John J. Pringle, "Returns on Alternative Investment Media and Implications for Portfolio Construction," *Journal of Business* 45 (July, 1972), pp. 427–443.

market price of the security at the beginning of the year. The average value and standard deviation of return are then calculated for government bonds and for each risk class of corporate bonds, of preferred stock, and of common stock.

For clarity, let us look in greater detail at the procedure applied to government bonds. In this case, there are 17 annual returns. The return on the government bonds for the 17-year period is defined as the geometric mean (μ) of these returns; the risk (σ) is defined as the standard deviation of the 17 returns. Thus, government bonds have a mean of .0167 and a standard deviation of .0512. (Similarly, Aaa corporate bonds have a mean of .0131 and a standard deviation of .0402; etc.) The risk-return function is obtained by regressing the standard deviation of return on the mean rate of return, using data on different classes of securities.

The Results. The results of the regression analysis for the 17-year period are summarized in the equation:

$$\sigma = \underset{(.00797)}{.0349} + \underset{(.0798)}{.878}\mu \qquad R^2 = .9099 \tag{8-14}$$

where the numbers in parentheses are the standard errors of the corresponding regression coefficients. The fact that the standard errors are small relative to the regression coefficients gives us confidence in the accuracy of the estimated regression coefficients. "$R^2 = .9099$" means that 91 percent of the variation in σ (the risk) is explained by the variation in μ (the return).

The economic meaning of the risk-return function becomes clearer if we rewrite (8-14) as:

$$\mu = -.0397 + 1.139\sigma \tag{8-15}$$

Eq. (8-15) can be used to predict the mean return realized on a given class of securities if we know the risk. For example, the return on high-grade common stock during 1950–1966 had a standard deviation of 16.5 percent; substituting this value for σ in Eq. (8-15), we get a predicted return of slightly less than 15 percent. The actual return realized by this class of stock during 1950–1966 was 16.6 percent; the prediction is not perfectly accurate since the equation describes an average relationship between risk and return for many different classes of securities.

The risk-return function is intended to aid financial executives in forecasting the effects of new investments on the rate of return on the company's shares required by security investors. For the equation to be useful in this way, we must be able to rely on the constancy of the relationship between risk and return over time. Hence, SM also derived regression equations for two 8-year and three 5-year sub-periods. They found that both the level and the slope of the risk-return function change considerably over time. This finding means that the financial executive must not only estimate the risk-return relationship at a given time; he must also forecast its change over time. For this reason, choosing an appropriate cost of capital is probably the most difficult step in capital budgeting under conditions of uncertainty.

The Robichek, Cohn, and Pringle (RCP) Study. Strictly speaking, the RCP study is not a regression study in that it did not compute a regression equation between risk and return. But the study did present in tabular form the functional relationship between risk and return, which is the essence of any regression analysis. RCP calculated the risk and return associated with a broad spectrum of assets for the 20-year period 1949–1969. The list of assets included common stocks in the United States and two other countries, U.S. government and corporate bonds, real estate, and commodity futures. As before, the annual rate of return for any asset was calculated by expressing the current income, plus capital appreciation, as a percentage of the price of the asset at the beginning of the year. From the one-year returns, the geometric mean and standard deviation of return was then calculated for each type of asset.

The Results. Table 8-4 summarizes the mean and standard deviation of return for each of the 12 types of assets. We have arranged the assets in the order of their standard deviations, in order to bring out more clearly the relationship between risk and return. The data seem to indicate that the two variables are positively correlated: an increase in the standard deviation tends to be accompanied by a corresponding increase in mean return.

Table 8-4 Risk-Return Relationship for 12 Different Assets, 1949–1969

Asset	Geometric Mean of Annual Returns	Standard Deviation of Annual Returns
Treasury bills	3.00	1.60
Bethlehem Steel 2¾s of 7/15/70	2.00	3.40
Farm real estate	9.47	4.50
U.S. government 2½s of 3/15/70–65	2.37	4.68
Canadian Pacific perpetuals 4s	1.40	5.71
S&P utilities	8.60	12.43
Australian stocks	6.82	14.22
S&P industrials	11.63	17.55
Japanese stocks	18.94	41.30
Wheat futures	−22.88	64.07
Cotton futures	3.80	66.77
Copper futures	26.60	244.02

Source: Alexander A. Robichek, Richard A. Cohn, and John J. Pringle, "Returns on Alternative Investment Media and Implications for Portfolio Construction," *Journal of Business* 45 (July, 1972), pp. 431–432, Table 1. (Copyright © 1972 by the University of Chicago. All rights reserved.)

We could quantify this risk-return relationship more exactly by using regression analysis. Our objective here is to derive an equation for predicting the cost of common equity. Looking at Table 8-4, we see that the mean return and standard deviation for commodity futures and Japanese common stocks are noticeably outside the normal range for U.S. common stocks. We therefore exclude them from our regression analysis. There remain eight pairs of data in our sample. Regressing standard deviation on mean return, we get:

$$\sigma = \underset{(2.79290)}{1.89} + \underset{(0.41292)}{1.09\mu} \qquad R^2 = .5332 \tag{8-16}$$

Because of the small R^2 and the large standard errors, the present results are not as reliable as those of Soldofsky and Miller. But the exercise does illustrate again how one can use market data to estimate the relationship between risk and return.

A SURVEY OF BUSINESS PRACTICE

A few years ago, I conducted all-day interviews with the financial executives of each of eight medium-sized and large firms representing five different industries: electronics, aerospace, petroleum, household equipment, and office equipment. My purpose was to ascertain the financial executives' concept of risk, their method of incorporating risk in investment decisions, and their criteria for investment selection.[6]

The Concept of Risk

Standard finance theory measures risk by the variance of return. Is this the same measure that financial executives use to quantify risk in actual investment decisions? Below are the responses of the executives interviewed when asked what they understood by the term "investment risk":

1. Risk is the prospect of not meeting the target rate of return. That is the risk, isn't it? If you are 100 percent sure of making the target return, then it is a zero-risk proposition.
2. Risk is financial in nature. It is primarily concerned with downside deviations from the target rate of return. However, if there is a good chance of coming out better than you forecast, that is negative risk (a sweetener), which is taken into account in determining the security of an investment.
3. There are three things that concern me in evaluating the risk of an investment: the chances of losses exceeding a certain percent of my total

[6] The material in this section is based on my "Survey of Capital Budgeting: Theory and Practice," *Journal of Finance* 25 (May, 1970), pp. 349–360.

equity, the chances of earning the required rate of return, and the chances of breaking even on a cash-flow basis. Cash break-even is kind of a survival point. (The investment decisions in this company are few but large in size.)

4. There are some projects in the company which I don't think are going to pay off, and I disagree with the fellows who are running the show. These projects are risky investments. Also, I never worry about the project return going above the target return. Risk is what might happen when the return is going to be less.

These comments suggest that when an investment decision involves a relatively small portion of the firm's resources, risk is considered primarily in terms of not meeting the target rate of return; but when an investment calls for a large portion of the company's resources, risk also involves the danger of insolvency. In addition, the executives' emphasis on downside risk suggests that their concept of risk is better described by semi-variance than by ordinary variance.

The Method of Incorporating Risk

Whatever concept of risk is accepted, risk must be incorporated into investment analysis in such a way that, given two investments with different returns and different risks, the relative attractiveness of investments can be compared. Two approaches to this problem—the risk-adjusted discount-rate method and the certainty-equivalent method—have already been discussed in Chapter 7. The executives interviewed tend to use the former approach.

Quantification of Risk. Although all of the executives talked about the concept of probability, none of them used an explicit probabilistic framework for investment analysis. The operating division proposing a project is responsible for forecasting the incremental cash flows associated with the investment; three sets of figures are generally forecast: optimistic, pessimistic, and most likely. The optimistic and pessimistic figures indicate the range of possibilities; the "most likely" figure is not the mode: it is a conservative estimate which the executives view as having a .75 probability of being met or exceeded.

Usually, the chief financial executive receives an investment analysis which uses the most likely figures and states all of the underlying assumptions. The executives were asked which aspects of these analyses were most instrumental in their decisions. Here are three of their responses:

1. The project justification may run into volumes, but I am still going to ask my project manager one question: why do you believe we can get a 5, 10, or 15 percent share of the market against our competition? If he sells me

on this and on the accuracy of his cost estimate, then it is a worthwhile risk venture.

2. Before committing myself, I ask what else can we use the investments for, if things should go wrong. A project may have a fast payout, but it is not a good investment if we can't hedge our risk of failure.

3. Sometimes I make a decision truly on the basis that I have enthusiastic support from the people that are going to implement it. I also look at their track record.

Essentially, the financial executive tries to make a check on the accuracy of the most likely figure; he modifies the projected outcome by considering the human factor and by introducing a contingency plan. His dilemma grows out of the uncertain nature of the forecasts; his real problem is to find a reliable probability distribution of investment return on which to base his decision.

Setting the Discount Rate. Once the probabilistic assessment is made, how does the financial executive determine the risk-adjusted discount rate (in business parlance, the "minimum cutoff rate")[7] for deciding whether a given investment is acceptable or unacceptable? Cutoff rates are set with the objective of maximizing share value, but the connection is indirect; the current market price of the firm's shares did not directly enter into the determination of these rates in any of the companies studied. Since the stock market is subject to cyclical influences, current share prices are generally regarded as an unreliable index of the share's long-run economic value. Instead, all of the companies started from a set of operating targets, expressed either as required rates of return on invested capital or as a required rate of growth in earnings per share. These targets take into account the relative performance of other firms (e.g., as reported in *Fortune*'s annual survey) and the results which the investing community might expect the company to show, adjusted for differences in risk. As this suggests, the immediate targets imply the ultimate objective of maximizing share value, although indirectly. Finally, a minimum cutoff rate is set at a level consistent with the attainment of the corporate objectives.

In every company surveyed, the minimum cutoff rate was quite a bit higher than what might reasonably be considered the market-capitalization rate. In a comprehensive study, researchers at the University of Chicago found that common stockholders realized a long-run return of about 9.3 percent;[8] but in my survey, the minimum cutoff was at least 18 percent after taxes. There are four possible ways of accounting for this difference. First,

[7] This is not actually a single rate, but a structure of rates, with the applicable rate varying with the particular risk class (e.g., expansion, replacement, etc.) to which an investment belongs.

[8] James H. Lorie and Mary T. Hamilton, *The Stock Market, Theories and Evidence* (Homewood: Richard D. Irwin, Inc., 1973), p. 31.

people proposing new projects tend to be optimistic, so management sets the cutoff rates quite high to allow for "slippage." Second, there might be mandatory investments (e.g., washrooms, cafeterias, and safety devices) which produce little or no financial returns. The rate of return on other investments must be large enough to account for these. Third, being conservative, most executives require a high expected rate of return on every investment in order to reduce the likelihood of loss on any of them. A fourth explanation is the concern over future reinvestment when new shares will be issued to finance an immediate investment. Since a new issue causes a permanent increase in the number of the firm's shares, the company must consider not only the profitability of the new investment but also the opportunities for future reinvestment. Requiring a high return on a current project may be viewed as protection in case returns on future reinvestments fail to meet expectations.

Diversification Strategy. Although all of the firms use the portfolio approach to investment, they do not use it for the reasons or in the ways that current theory assumes. Standard finance theory sees the financial executive as presented with the mean, variance, and covariances of the cash flows associated with various investments; the executive chooses the portfolio of investments with the best combination of risk and return. But in actuality, since the project analyses are submitted independently by the divisions concerned, the risk assessment makes no allowance for the covariances between projects. The proposals received by top management simply do not contain the figures necessary for evaluating project risks on a portfolio basis in the manner indicated by current theory.

The executives were asked how they did in fact introduce the portfolio approach into their investment decisions, or, more specifically, what was the objective and method of diversification. In general, they consider diversification of major activities only and use long-range plans (usually covering five years) to provide broad guidelines for the operating divisions. The plans may emphasize existing activities, change the emphasis within existing activities, or incorporate brand-new ideas or products. In formulating the plans, the executives view the company's many activities in terms of large, global areas rather than particular, isolated investments. Details of variance and covariance are generally left in the background. In theory, diversification is concerned with stabilizing the earnings stream; but in practice, the executive more often seeks long-term growth.

Criteria of Investment Selection

In the present discussion, we have been using the term "return" in a general sense, not defining it specifically as internal rate of return, net present value, payback period, or accounting rate of return; this generality has enabled us to concentrate our attention on the concept of risk. Current theory generally regards *IRR* or its equivalent *NPV* as a better measure of return than either the payback period or the accounting rate of return since, under conditions of certainty, the investment with the highest *IRR* results in the highest value for the firm, other factors being equal. Unfortunately, this preference has been carried over to conditions of uncertainty without sufficient critical analysis. Both the payback period and the accounting rate of return are regarded as inferior measures since they are, at best, only approximations of *IRR*. However, since the payback period is usually justified as a means of measuring risk, a more relevant criticism is its limited applicability as a method of risk analysis. And the effect of a new investment on accounting profit must be taken into account, since reported earnings do affect share prices, and share-value maximization is the goal.

Of the eight companies questioned about investment criteria, two use *IRR* primarily; four use a combination of payback period and accounting rate of return; and two use accounting profit, payback period, and an "exposure index" which measures the probability that the maximum investment loss will exceed a specified percentage of the firm's total equity. The two companies relying primarily on *IRR* are growth companies with closely held stock which finances growth through internal generation of funds, and the typical investment of these firms is small relative to total resources. The four companies using payback period and accounting rate of return are publicly held companies which rely heavily on external sources to finance growth; these firms are in businesses which are fairly risky and competitive. The two remaining companies are similar to these four in terms of stock ownership and in their reliance on outside capital; but their investments are more risky because of strong intra-industry competition and because the investments are few but large.

These findings suggest that the payback period is primarily a measure of risk. The accounting rate of return, since it is what the financial community focuses on, is an especially important measure if the company is widely held and relies on external sources of financing. The *IRR* is most likely to be the major criterion in firms which are closely held, which are not particularly worried by erratic patterns in their per-share earnings, which finance themselves, and which make investments small enough that the risk of any single investment is not critical.

REVIEW QUESTIONS

1. Define the concept of the cost of common equity capital; explain its significance in a firm's investment-decision process.
2. How is a firm's cost of common equity capital related to the rate of return on the company's shares required by securities investors? How is this relation-

ship affected by the method of equity financing employed? by the cost of floating new securities? by the tax on income and on capital gains?

3. During the bull market of 1961, IBM stock sold at a price-earnings ratio of about 50. Does this mean that investors were willing to supply equity capital to IBM at a cost of 2 percent (= 1/50), even though at the same time they were demanding an interest rate of 4 percent on funds lent to the U.S. government? Explain.

4. Some theorists have argued that a firm should reach its investment decisions independently of its financing decisions. That is, an investment project should be accepted or rejected strictly on its own merit, without regard to the method of financing which would be used; the latter factor is considered relevant only after a decision to accept a project has been made. Do you agree or disagree? Why?

5. Many firms consider the issuance of new shares a very costly way to raise new capital; some, in fact, will not employ this method of financing under any circumstances. Do the cost-of-equity-capital formulas derived in this chapter provide economic justification for such a position?

6. If you were the president of a company, would you use Bierman and Alderfer's investor-survey method to determine the cost of equity capital? You may make any assumptions regarding the size of the company, the number of stockholders, product lines, etc.; but be sure to indicate how your assumptions affect your answer. If your answer is yes, design an appropriate questionnaire and indicate how much confidence you would have in the figure obtained this way. If your answer is no, describe the method that you would use instead.

7. What is a "risk-premium curve," and how is it derived statistically? How would you use such a curve to estimate the cost of equity capital to a company? Do you regard an estimate obtained in this way as more or less reliable than one obtained by the investor-survey method?

8. Based on the records of 900 corporations, William J. Baumol and his associates found through regression analysis that investments financed by new common stock produced significantly greater increases in earnings than investments financed by retained earnings or new debt. What economic and/or behavioral hypotheses would you offer to explain this finding?

9. According to the last section of this chapter, the management of the firms surveyed tended to set their cutoff rates considerably above the capitalization rate on the company's shares required by the market. Would you recommend a lower cutoff? Why or why not?

10. Compare the survey of business practices discussed in the last section of this chapter with the theory of investment decision put forth in Chapter 7 and this chapter. Point out salient differences and similarities. Can you make any suggestions for improving theory and/or practice?

PROBLEMS

1. Phoenix Instruments, Inc., has 1 million shares of common stock outstanding, with annual earnings of \$3.5 million (or \$3.50 per share). The market-capitalization rate on the firm's shares is 14 percent, so each share sells at \$25. The com-

pany wishes to raise $4 million by selling 200,000 new shares at $20 per share—20 percent below the current market price. The existing stockholders have no pre-emptive right; if they wish to buy some of the new shares, they may do so on the same terms as outsiders. The firm is static. You may assume that the new investment will not alter the market-capitalization rate of 14 percent.

What is the cost of this new equity capital to the firm if the new issue is purchased entirely by the existing stockholders? entirely by outsiders? 40 percent by outsiders and 60 percent by the existing stockholders?

2. (a) If the risk characteristics of Phoenix Instruments' new investment are such that the market-capitalization rate is increased from 14 to 15 percent, what would be the cost of the new equity capital if the new issue were purchased entirely by the existing stockholders?

   (b) If Phoenix Instruments were a growth company, what would the new equity capital cost the firm if the new issue were bought entirely by outsiders? (You may assume either a constant or an exponential growth rate.)

   (c) If the existing stockholders had a pre-emptive right, what would the cost of equity capital be if the new issue were purchased 40 percent by outsiders and 60 percent by the existing stockholders?

3. On April 11, 19X9, the Magic-Foto Corporation, a manufacturer of photo equipment and supplies, offered 1 million shares of common stock at $32 per share. Although the stock had sold for $40 per share earlier in the year, the most recent (April 10) price was $38 per share. The company set the new subscription price at $32 per share to insure the success of the offering. Since the already existing stockholders had a pre-emptive right, they had the opportunity to subscribe to additional shares at a ratio of one additional share for each 20 shares already held. The table below summarizes Magic-Foto's annual sales, earnings, dividends, and share prices for the last 5 years.

Year	19X4	19X5	19X6	19X7	19X8
Sales (in millions)	$55	$81	$127	$150	$180
Total earnings (in millions)	7	10	19	23	27
Earnings per share	0.35	0.50	0.95	1.15	1.35
Dividends per share	0.07	0.10	0.20	0.24	0.27
Share price					
High	9¼	20	26½	40¼	43
Low	6½	10⅜	20⅞	28¾	32¼

   Assume that the cost of selling the new securities is 2½ percent of the capital raised, and that the new investment does not alter the market's capitalization rate on the firm's shares. On the basis of these data, calculate the cost of the new equity capital.

4. The common shares of the Eastern Sierra Corporation, a manufacturer of business paper, include no pre-emptive right. On February 9, 19X8, Eastern Sierra made a public offering of 400,000 shares of common stock at a price of $25 per share (net price after all selling commissions). The firm's annual sales, earnings, dividends, and share prices for the last 5 fiscal years are summarized below.

Year	19X3	19X4	19X5	19X6	19X7
Sales (in millions)	$158.8	$166.0	$178.5	$185.0	$180.7
Total earnings (in millions)	11.0	10.0	11.2	11.6	11.4
Earnings per share	2.75	2.50	2.80	2.90	2.85
Dividends per share	0.80	0.80	0.82	0.82	0.82
Share price					
High	30¼	28¾	28	30¼	28½
Low	20½	20	19½	23	19⅞

Assuming that the company's shares have an equilibrium market price of $27, calculate the cost of the new equity capital.

5. Suppose that following Soldofsky and Miller's method you find the following values for the geometric means and standard deviations of return realized on different classes of assets during one 8-year period:

G.M.	.03	.06	.06	.08	.09	.10	.20	.25	.32	.35
S.D.	.02	.06	.08	.07	.07	.10	.26	.20	.22	.25

Estimate the risk-return function for these assets and interpret your results.

REFERENCES

ALBERTS, W. W., and S. H. ARCHER, "Some Evidence on the Effect of Company Size on the Cost of Equity Capital," *Journal of Financial and Quantitative Analysis* 8 (March, 1973), pp. 229–242.

BAUMOL, WILLIAM J., PEGGY HEIM, BURTON G. MALKIEL, and RICHARD E. QUANDT, "Earnings Retention, New Capital and the Growth of the Firm," *Review of Economics and Statistics* 52 (November, 1970), pp. 345–355.

BERNSTEIN, PETER L., "What Rate of Return Can You 'Reasonably' Expect?" *Journal of Finance* 28 (May, 1973), pp. 273–282.

BIERMAN, HAROLD, JR., and CLAYTON P. ALDERFER, "Estimating the Cost of Capital, A Different Approach," *Decision Sciences* 1 (January-April, 1970), pp. 40–53.

BIERMAN, HAROLD, JR., DAVID H. DOWNES, and JEROME E. HASS, "Closed-Form Stock Price Models," *Journal of Financial and Quantitative Analysis* 7 (June, 1972), pp. 1797–1808.

BOWER, JOSEPH, *Managing the Resource Allocation Process* (Homewood: Richard D. Irwin, Inc., 1972).

BREALEY, RICHARD A., *Security Prices in a Competitive Market* (Cambridge: The M.I.T. Press, 1971), Chs. 8 and 9.

BREALEY, RICHARD A., *An Introduction to Risk and Return from Common Stocks* (Cambridge: The M.I.T. Press, 1969).

KLAMMER, THOMAS, "Empirical Evidence of the Adoption of Sophisticated Capital Budgeting Techniques," *Journal of Business* 45 (July, 1972), pp. 387–397.

LORIE, JAMES H., and MARY T. HAMILTON, *The Stock Market, Theory and Evidence* (Homewood: Richard D. Irwin, Inc., 1973), Ch. 2.

MALKIEL, BURTON G., and JOHN G. CRAGG, "Expectations and the Structure of Share Prices," *American Economic Review* 60 (September, 1970), pp. 601–617.

MAO, JAMES C. T., *Quantitative Analysis of Financial Decisions* (New York: The Macmillan Company, 1969), Ch. 10.

MAO, JAMES C. T., "Survey of Capital Budgeting: Theory and Practice," *Journal of Finance* 25 (May, 1970), pp. 349–360.

ROBICHEK, ALEXANDER A., RICHARD A. COHN, and JOHN J. PRINGLE, "Returns on Alternative Investment Media and Implications for Portfolio Construction," *Journal of Business* 45 (July, 1972), pp. 427–443.

SOLDOFSKY, ROBERT M., and ROGER L. MILLER, "Risk-Premium Curves for Different Classes of Long-Term Securities, 1950–1966," *Journal of Finance* 24 (June, 1969), pp. 429–446.

TAYLOR, WALTON, "A Note on Mao's Growth Stock–Investment Opportunities Approach," *Journal of Finance* 29 (December, 1974), pp. 1573–1576.

9 Management of Fixed Assets

The assets of a firm are usually classified as fixed capital (plant and equipment) and working capital (cash, accounts receivable, and inventories). Our study of investment decisions was concerned with the acquisition of fixed assets; but the goals of investment analysis cannot be fully realized unless the assets, once acquired, are managed as profitably as possible. In Chapter 4, we learned how mathematical programming, by leading us to the optimal product mix, can ensure the efficient utilization of plant and equipment. Here, we shall take up five other aspects of the management of fixed capital: methods of tax depreciation, retirement decisions, replacement decisions, divestment decisions, and post-audit procedures. The management of working capital will be discussed in the next three chapters.

THE "BEST" TAX-DEPRECIATION METHOD

The Problem

For a corporation subject to a 50 percent tax rate on its incremental income, saving \$1 in tax is equivalent to increasing its before-tax income by \$2. A firm's tax burden can be minimized through the proper choice of a method of tax depreciation. The purpose of depreciation in accounting is to distribute the cost of long-lived assets over the useful lives of those assets so that revenues and expenses may be closely matched. Federal income-tax law recognizes depreciation as a business expense and allows it to be deducted from current revenues when computing income subject to taxation. Moreover, the law permits several methods of tax depreciation, which may be different from the method which the firm uses in its report to the financial community. While these tax methods do not affect the total amount of depreciation, nor, consequently, total tax savings, they do affect the timing of the savings. The problem is to choose the method that allows the firm to deduct the greatest amounts of depreciation in the early years, so that funds otherwise representing tax payments can be reinvested (at least temporarily) by the firm.

Methods of Tax Depreciation

Under current tax laws, a firm may choose any of three methods of calculating depreciation for tax purposes: the straight-line method (SL), the double-declining-balance method (DDB), and the sum-of-the-years-digits method (SYD).[1] The last two are "accelerated-depreciation" methods: compared with the straight-line method, they involve an acceleration of the rate of depreciation.

The Straight-Line Method. The assumption underlying SL depreciation is that the asset will wear out at a constant rate as a function of time. Annual depreciation, accordingly, is a constant equal to the basis of depreciation (the cost of the asset less its salvage value) divided by the estimated economic life of the asset. Equivalently, if we designate the reciprocal of the estimated life as the rate of depreciation, the annual depreciation will equal the basis of depreciation times this rate. This constancy in annual depreciation means that when depreciation is plotted as a function of time, the result is a straight line; hence, the name.

The 1954 Internal Revenue Code, as amended, gives a break to the taxpayer in determining salvage value. The Code permits the taxpayer to recognize no salvage value for an asset if the salvage value is less than 10 percent of the original cost; if the salvage value is greater than 10 percent, only the portion in excess of 10 percent is treated as salvage.[2] If, for example, a $1,000 asset with an estimated economic life of four years has an estimated salvage value of $150, only $50 (= $150 – 10% of $1,000) need be recognized as salvage for tax purposes. In this case, the maximum allowable depreciation is $950 (= $1,000 – $50). An estimated life of four years implies an annual rate of depreciation of one fourth, or 25 percent. Multiplying the $950 basis of depreciation by 25 percent, we get an annual depreciation of $237.50 (see Table 9-1 A).

---

[1] Other permissible methods, rarely used, will not be considered here.

[2] See Section 167(f) of the Internal Revenue Code of 1954.

Table 9-1 Three Methods of Depreciating a Sample Asset

A. Straight-Line Method

Year	Rate (1)	Basis of Depreciation (2)	Depreciation (3) = (1) × (2)
1	25%	$950.00	$237.50
2	25	950.00	237.50
3	25	950.00	237.50
4	25	950.00	237.50
Total	100%	–	$950.00

B. Double-Declining-Balance Method

Year	Rate (1)	Basis of Depreciation (2)	Depreciation (3) = (1) × (2)
1	50%	$1,000.00	$500.00
2	50	500.00	250.00
3	50	250.00	125.00
4	SL	125.00	75.00
Total	–	–	$950.00

C. Sum-of-the-Years-Digits Method

Year	Rate (1)	Basis of Depreciation (2)	Depreciation (3) = (1) × (2)
1	4/10	$950.00	$380.00
2	3/10	950.00	285.00
3	2/10	950.00	190.00
4	1/10	950.00	95.00
Total	100%	–	$950.00

The straight-line method of depreciation is still used by many companies for simplicity and clarity in their reports to stockholders, even though they may use other methods for tax purposes. This is permissible since the federal income-tax law does not require conformity between the depreciation method used for taxes and that used for financial reporting.

The Double-Declining-Balance Method. During World War II and again during the Korean Conflict, firms engaged in defense production were permitted to depreciate their assets at an accelerated pace; the Internal Revenue Code of 1954 installed accelerated depreciation on a permanent basis and extended the privilege to other types of business. DDB is one of the two systems of acceleration permitted by law. Under this plan, the rate of depreciation permitted is twice ("double") that of the SL method. Moreover, whereas the basis of depreciation in the SL method is cost less salvage value (a constant), the basis in the DDB method is cost, ignoring salvage, less cumulative depreciation for each year ("declining balance"). Given the life and salvage value of an asset, there is a unique rate which, applied to the declining balance, will depreciate the asset to its exact salvage value at the end of its life.[3] This rate, however, is often different from that allowed under the DDB method, and hence the DDB method may result in over- or under-depreciation. To counteract this shortcoming, the law permits a taxpayer to shift from DDB to SL at any time during the life of the asset.

Since the annual depreciation rate for our sample $1,000 asset was 25 percent under SL, the corresponding rate under DDB will be 50 percent. For the first year, the basis of depreciation is the full $1,000; multiplying by 50 percent, we get $500 of depreciation for the first year (see Table 9-1 B). Subtracting this $500 from the $1,000 gives us a basis of depreciation of $500 for the second year; multiplying by 50 percent, we get $250 of depreciation for the second year. Repeating the procedure, we get $125 of depreciation for the third year. By the fourth year, the basis of depreciation would be $125; but a maximum of only $75 of depreciation is allowed for the remaining years because the law requires that the total depreciation not exceed cost less salvage value—in this case, after adjusting for the 10 percent "free" salvage, $950. If the firm shifts now to SL, the full $75 can be written off immediately, since the asset has a service life of only four years. DDB would have produced a corresponding depreciation of only $62.50 (= $125 × 50%). Therefore, the company is assumed to shift to SL for the fourth year.

The Sum-of-the-Years-Digits Method. According to the second method of accelerated depreciation permitted by the Internal Revenue Code of 1954, a separate fraction (rate of depreciation) is calculated for each period. The numerator of this fraction is the number of years remaining, calculated from the beginning of the period in question. The denominator is the sum of the digits, 1, 2, . . . , n, where n is the economic life of the asset in years: e.g., if the asset has an economic life of four years, the denominator is the sum of $1 + 2 + 3 + 4 = 10$. For any given economic life, the denominator, obviously, is constant; only the numerator changes. In any given year, depreciation is equal to the rate for that year times the basis of depreciation, which, as in the SL method, is constant and equal to cost less salvage value (subject to the 10% clause).

---

[3] Earl A. Spiller, Jr., *Financial Accounting* (Homewood: Richard D. Irwin, Inc., 1971), p. 278.

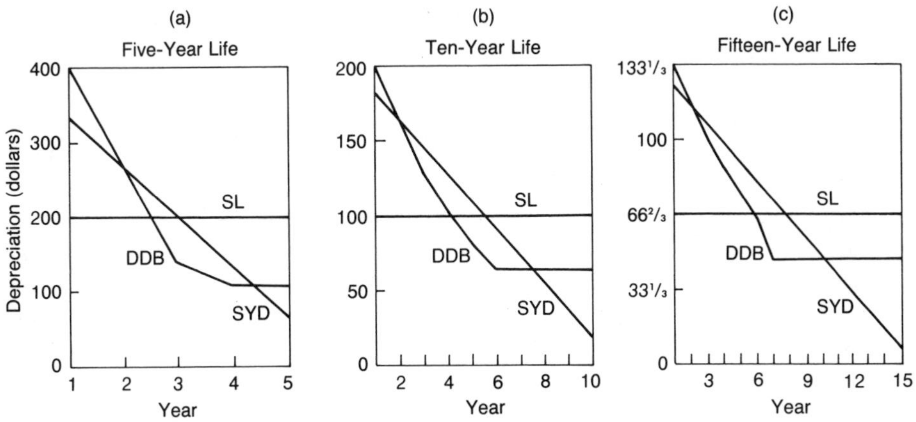

Figure 9-1 Annual Depreciation (SL, SYD, and DDB) on a $1,000 Asset

Since our sample asset has an estimated economic life of four years, the relevant fractions are 4/10, 3/10, 2/10, and 1/10. Multiplying the appropriate fraction by the constant basis of depreciation ($950) gives us the amount of depreciation for the year in question (see Table 9-1 C). Unlike DDB, SYD does lead to full depreciation over the life of the asset.

A Comparison of the Alternative Methods

Theoretical Analysis. The total tax savings permitted to a firm is a constant, regardless of the method of depreciation; and we shall assume that the method of depreciation does not substantially alter the quality of a firm's cash-flow stream. Thus, the market-capitalization rate remains unchanged. The best depreciation method, then, is the one which most advances the timing of the depreciation, since early realization of tax savings enhances the cash-flow available for early reinvestment.

Figure 9-1 compares the annual depreciation under SL, DDB, and SYD of a $1,000 asset (with no salvage value beyond the 10 percent "free" salvage) for economic lives of 5, 10, and 15 years. The SL "curve" is a horizontal line (since straight-line depreciation is a constant); the DDB curve first declines and then straightens out (reflecting the changeover at that point to SL); and the SYD curve declines continuously. We should note that the SL line intersects the DDB and SYD curves once each: up until the point of intersection, both DDB and SYD have greater values than SL; after that point of intersection, SL has the largest value. In other words, both DDB and SYD advance the timing of depreciation and hence both are superior to SL as methods of depreciation.

This still does not tell us which of the two acceleration methods is preferable. The comparison of DDB and SYD is complicated by the fact that their curves intersect not once but twice. As we can see in the graphs in Figure 9-1, DDB has the advantage over SYD of advancing part of the tax savings of the middle years to the first year—and the disadvantage of delaying part of the savings of the middle years to the later years. Any evaluation must therefore consider the amount moved forward relative to the amount postponed, as well as the rate of return at which the tax savings can be reinvested. An exact formula can no doubt be derived to express the comparative advantage as a function of economic life, salvage value, and reinvestment rate; but even without such a formula, several basic relationships are obvious.

First, since the advantage of DDB stems from its large tax savings in the first year, a high reinvestment rate makes DDB more advantageous. Second, a high salvage value also shifts the advantage toward DDB, since the salvage value reduces the first-year tax savings under SYD (whose basis of depreciation is cost less salvage) but does not affect DDB. Third, a long estimated economic life has the opposite effect of weakening DDB's advantage, since the first year's depreciation is reduced proportionately more than under SYD. Sidney Davidson and David F. Drake reached the same conclusions by experimenting with various combinations of estimated economic lives, salvage values, and reinvestment rates.[4] They concluded that SYD is preferable to DDB when the following conditions are simultaneously true: the salvage value of the asset is less than 10 percent of its cost; the estimated life of the asset is 8 years or longer; and the reinvestment rate is less than 50 percent. Note that these conditions apply to most assets.

An Example. Let us look more closely at the example depicted by graph (b) in Figure 9-1. The asset has a cost of $1,000, an estimated life of 10 years, and no salvage value in excess of 10 percent of the cost. We shall assume the firm's reinvestment rate to be 10 percent and the switch from DDB to SL to be made at the optimal time, year 6 in this case. We shall also assume the rate of taxation to be a constant, independent of the method of depreciation.

Since the choice of depreciation methods involves mutually exclusive alternatives, the decision must take into account the rate at which the resulting tax savings can be reinvested. Consequently, we make our comparison in terms of the future values of the series of depreciation charges, computed with the firm's reinvestment rate of 10 percent. Since share-value maximization is its objective, a firm may be more concerned with present value than with future value. However, in this situation, evaluation in terms of future

[4] See Sidney Davidson and David F. Drake, "The 'Best' Tax Depreciation Method—1964," *Journal of Business* 37 (July, 1964), pp. 258–260.

Table 9-2 Future Values of Depreciation on a $1,000 Asset: DDB vs. SYD

	SYD		DDB*	
Year	Depreciation	Future Value†	Depreciation	Future Value†
1	$181.82	$428.73	$200.00	$471.59
2	163.64	350.78	160.00	342.97
3	145.45	283.44	128.00	249.44
4	127.27	225.47	102.40	181.41
5	109.09	175.69	81.92	131.93
6	90.91	133.10	65.54	95.96
7	72.73	96.80	65.54	87.23
8	54.55	66.00	65.54	79.30
9	36.36	40.00	65.54	72.09
10	18.18	18.18	65.54	65.54
Total		$1,818.19		$1,777.46

* Switch to SL in year 6.
† Reinvestment rate = 10%.

value is permissible since we assume that the market-capitalization rate is unaffected by the method of depreciation; hence, a large future value indicates a large present value. By using future value as a guide, we avoid using the net-present-value formula, which assumes that the firm's reinvestment rate is equal to its market-capitalization rate. This latter equality may not always hold.

As Table 9-2 shows, at a compounding rate of 10 percent, the depreciation series associated with SYD has a future value of $1,818.19, whereas that associated with DDB has a future value of only $1,777.46; SYD is therefore preferable. In order to check the sensitivity of this finding to changes in the reinvestment rate, we have carried out the comparison for rates from 0 to 100 percent, at increments of 10 percent. The summary in Figure 9-2 (b) shows that the SYD method of depreciation leads to a higher future value at all reinvestment rates between 0 and 66 percent. Since the circumstances of this example (10-year life, no salvage value over 10 percent, and a reinvestment rate between 0 and 66 percent) are representative of the vast majority of depreciable assets, our results help to explain why SYD is the primary method of depreciation used in industry.

For the sake of comprehensiveness, graphs A and C in Figure 9-2 extend our comparisons to cases involving estimated economic lives of 5 years and 15 years. For a 5-year life, DDB is consistently preferable to SYD, with its preferability increasing with the reinvestment rate; but for a 15-year life, DDB is preferable to SYD only if the reinvestment rate is greater than 83 percent. A shorter economic life shifts the advantage to DDB since a short life creates a significant increase in first-year depreciation under DDB, which, we recall, is the source of DDB's merit.

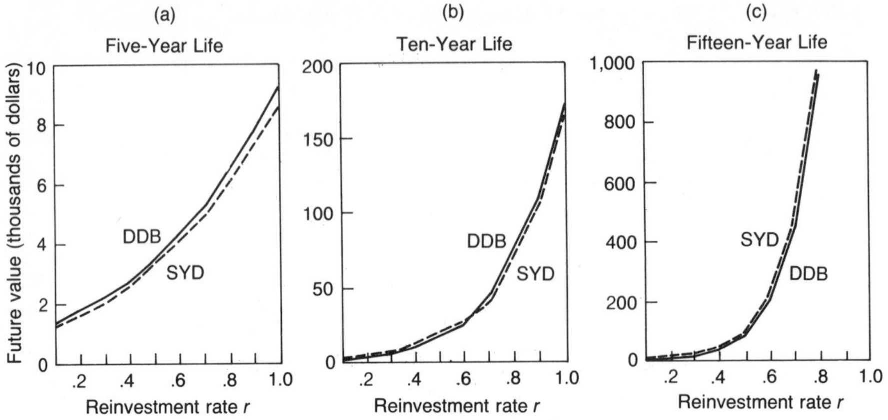

Figure 9-2 Future Value of Depreciation (DDB vs. SYD) for a $1,000 Asset

RETIREMENT DECISIONS

The Problem

We turn now to another aspect of fixed capital management: equipment retirement decisions. The luxury liner *Queen Mary* was retired from service when Cunard sold it for $2.5 million to the City of Long Beach, California, which planned to turn it into a floating hotel and convention center. Although the ship was still seaworthy, its economic life as a passenger liner was at an end, since its operation no longer generated sufficient profit to warrant foregoing the opportunity for recovery of capital by resale. The point of a retirement decision is to determine the best time to salvage an asset through resale or scrappage, whether the asset be an ocean liner, a lathe, a printing press, a bulldozer, or a helicopter.

Retirement decisions are "terminal" decisions in that they assume that an asset withdrawn from its original activity will not be replaced by a comparable asset. A firm may not replace an asset after its retirement for any of several reasons: the future demand for the product may be too low; the costs of production may be too high; or, aside from profitability, the owner-operator may himself have decided to retire. Our analysis of retirement, whatever its reasons, assumes nonreplacement. We shall discuss the replacement decision in the next section.

The Method of Analysis

The analysis of a retirement decision, like the analysis of depreciation, involves the comparison of two cash-flow streams. The retirement question asks when it is best to switch from the cash flows derived from an asset's current activity (including any future salvage value) to the cash flows that would be received if the asset were sold or scrapped immediately.

Estimating Cash Flows. The relevant cash flows for retirement decisions are the incremental figures calculated on a with-and-without basis. Gordon Shillinglaw has offered several pointers for improving the accuracy of these forecasts:[5]

First, Shillinglaw reminds us that the total loss in sales revenue may be larger or smaller than the revenue directly associated with the plant and equipment retired. If the firm makes other products that are close substitutes for one another (e.g., slide rules and electronic mini-calculators), dropping one product may cause some customers to shift their demand to other products made by the same company. On the other hand, if there is a complementary relationship among a firm's products (e.g., golf clubs and golf balls), dropping one product may lead to a decline in the sales of the related products.

Second, if the discontinuation of a product does lead to an increase (decrease) in the sales and output of a substitute (complementary) product, the resulting change in the cost of production must be taken into consideration in determining cash flows.

Third, if some units of the product to be discontinued are normally sold at cost to other divisions of the same company, discontinuation will force the other divisions to purchase these items from external sources at a higher price. This increased outlay should be viewed as a cash outflow associated with the retirement decision.

Fourth, the determination of cash flows must take into account the tax effects of any capital gain or loss resulting from retirement of the asset in question.

And finally, when a fixed asset is retired, the financial executive must remember to count as a cash inflow the working capital (cash, accounts receivable, and inventories) released as a result of the reduced activity.

Comparing Cash-Flow Series. Let us suppose that the cash flows generated by the continued use of an asset are expected to be $a_1, a_2, \ldots, a_n$ during years $1, 2, \ldots, n$, where n is the last year of the maximum remaining physical life of the asset. Let us further suppose that the salvage values of the asset at the end of years $1, 2, \ldots, n$, respectively, would be $S_1, S_2, \ldots, S_n$. The question, then, is, what is the best time to retire the asset? We may approach the problem either directly or indirectly.

[5] Shillinglaw was concerned primarily with the divestment of entire operating divisions, but his comments are basically applicable to equipment retirement as well. See his "Profit Analysis for Abandonment Decisions," in Solomon, ed., *The Management of Corporate Capital,* pp. 269–281.

Since the asset has a maximum physical life of n remaining years, there are n opportunities for retirement (namely, one at the end of each year). We may calculate directly the cash-flow series associated with the asset supposing it to be retired at the end of each year; we then have n series to compare. Since these n series are mutually exclusive, a sound decision must take into account the specific opportunities for reinvestment at each possible retirement time. The future value of each cash-flow series may then be calculated using the firm's reinvestment rate as the compounding rate. This focus on future value, as we have noted elsewhere, assumes that the market-capitalization rate is unaffected by the retirement period selected; if the rate is affected, each future value should be discounted at the appropriate discount rate, and the selection should be made on the basis of present value.

We may approach the same problem indirectly by asking whether it is better to retire the asset at the end of year j or at the end of year $j+1$. If the firm has a reinvestment rate of r, then retirement at the end of year j is to be preferred if

$$\underbrace{S_j(1+r) - S_{j+1}}_{\text{Decline in salvage value}} > \underbrace{a_{j+1}}_{\text{Cash flow from operation}} \qquad (9\text{-}1)$$

This inequality states that postponing retirement from j to $j+1$ is undesirable if a_{j+1} (the cash flow from operation in the year $j+1$) is less than $S_j(1+r) - S_{j+1}$ (the corresponding decline in the salvage value of the asset). S_j is multiplied by $1+r$ since S_j—the salvage value realizable at the end of year j—can be reinvested at a return of r one year before S_{j+1} is received. In a similar way, we can derive formulas for comparing the advisability of retirement at the ends of years j vs. $j+2$, j vs. $j+3$, etc. These formulas permit us to determine whether it is best to retire at the end of year 1 vs. 2, 3, . . . , n; at the end of year 2 vs. 3, 4, . . . , n; etc. Since this approach involves a great deal of computation, we shall use only the direct approach to illustrate our example.

An Example

The Wildcat Transport Company provides scenic bus tours, cruises in San Francisco Bay, and helicopter shuttle service between the San Francisco International Airport and local airports in Palo Alto and San Jose. The helicopter division operates one helicopter with a maximum remaining physical life of six years. The company has a contract with a group of Bay Area companies to shuttle executives between the airports for the next six years, but Wildcat Transport may terminate the service at any time on a one-year notice. The contract assures a stable revenue; but the costs of maintenance and operation are expected to increase rapidly, so that the cash flows from operation are expected to fall as follows:

End of Year	1	2	3	4	5	6
Cash Flow	$190,000	$150,000	$110,000	$50,000	$10,000	−$30,000

The helicopter has the following salvage values at the end of each year (remember that Wildcat cannot retire the helicopter before the end of the first year because of the notice clause):

End of Year	1	2	3	4	5	6
Salvage Value	$220,000	$120,000	$70,000	$30,000	$20,000	$0

The company's plan is to discontinue its shuttle service after this helicopter reaches the end of its economic life.

If Wildcat Transport has a reinvestment rate of 14 percent, when should it retire the helicopter? We begin by calculating directly the cash-flow series associated with retirement at the end of each year (see Table 9-3). If the firm retires the helicopter at the end of the first year, the company would receive $190,000 from operation and $220,000 from salvage—a total of $410,000; at the end of the second year, the firm would receive $150,000 from operation during the second year, and $120,000 from salvage—a total of $270,000, in addition to the $190,000 from operation during the first year; etc. We then compute the future value of each cash-flow series, by compounding the individual cash flows at the firm's reinvestment rate. For example, the series associated with retirement at the end of the third year has a value of $885,849 at the end of the 6-year horizon, computed in the following way:

Cash Flow	Compound Value Factor	Future Value
$190,000	$(1+.14)^5$	$365,828
150,000	$(1+.14)^4$	253,344
180,000	$(1+.14)^3$	266,677
Total		$885,849

As Table 9-3 shows, the highest future value is that associated with retirement at the end of the fourth year.

Table 9-3 Cash Flows and Future Values of Six Retirement Policies

Retire at End of Year	Cash Flow at Year-End 1	2	3	4	5	6	Future Value of Series
1	$410,000						$789,418
2	190,000	$270,000					821,847
3	190,000	150,000	$180,000				885,849
4	190,000	150,000	110,000	$80,000			886,109
5	190,000	150,000	110,000	50,000	$30,000		881,321
6	190,000	150,000	110,000	50,000	10,000	−$30,000	828,521

REPLACEMENT DECISIONS

The Problem

Whereas retirement decisions are terminal decisions, replacement decisions view the end of the economic life of one asset as the occasion for acquiring a comparable asset. Replacement decisions therefore involve a longer planning horizon. We could, of course, study successive replacements of a given asset as isolated decisions unrelated to one another. But for any ongoing business it is more realistic to treat successive replacements as a chain of interrelated decisions. Taking this longer view, we have then to determine the optimal replacement cycle—that is, the best time-interval between successive replacements.

Replacement decisions are affected by the two economic variables affecting retirement decisions—the cash flows from operation and the salvage value of the asset—plus, for obvious reasons, a third variable: the cost of the asset. A short replacement cycle has two advantages: since operating and maintenance costs are generally low in the early years of an asset's life, early replacement increases annual cash inflows; and the salvage value of an asset is clearly higher early in its life than in later years. The disadvantage, however, of a short replacement cycle is the large capital expenditures.

An Example

Let us imagine that Wildcat Transport is currently contemplating the purchase of a new helicopter for $350,000. The helicopter will generate the same operating cash flow and salvage value as the one in the retirement example. For the sake of simplicity, assume that the planning horizon is 12 years (in actuality, an ongoing business would probably have an infinite planning horizon) and that helicopter technology will remain constant during this period, so that the characteristics—and hence cash flows—associated with any future replacement helicopter will be identical. In order to decide whether or not to go ahead with the proposed purchase, the management must know the optimal replacement cycle.

Since we assume that the helicopter has a maximum physical life of 6 years, the replacement cycle has 6 possible values. The most direct approach, as in the case of retirement decisions, is to determine the cash flows associated with each policy, calculate the future values, and select the replacement date with the highest future value. All six cash-flow series are summarized in Table 9-4; the derivation of the series for replacement at the end of the third year is shown schematically here:

Year	0	1	2	3	4	5	6	7	8	9	10	11	12
						(in thousands of dollars)							
Cash flow	−350	190	150	180									
				−350	190	150	180						
							−350	190	150	180			
										−350	190	150	180
Total	−350	190	150	−170	190	150	−170	190	150	−170	190	150	180

At a reinvestment rate of 14 percent, this series of cash flows has a future value of $629,000 at the end of the 12-year horizon. The future values of the other cash-flow series are calculated in the same manner and presented in Table 9-4. The figures indicate that the highest future value can be obtained by operating the helicopter for three years before replacing it.

We said earlier that in determining the optimal retirement period, it is necessary to balance cash flow from operation against decline in salvage value. In making replacement decisions, we must consider not only these factors but also the benefits of increased operating efficiency vs. the cost of frequent replacement. Consequently, the optimal replacement period is shorter than the optimal retirement period, since assets generally become obsolete before they become worthless.

DIVESTMENT DECISIONS

The Problem

Some investments, though carefully planned, simply do not work out as well as expected. The financial executive in such cases needs to know whether and when to bail out. In financial literature, bail-out decisions are sometimes called "abandonment" decisions, but we prefer the term "divestment." In popular usage, "abandonment" implies getting rid of assets judged to be worthless, whereas divestment decisions arise precisely because the assets still do have value and we must determine the best way to

Table 9-4 Cash Flows and Future Values of Six Replacement Policies (in thousands of dollars)

Replace at End of Year	Cash Flow at Year-End													Future Value of Series*
	0	1	2	3	4	5	6	7	8	9	10	11	12	
1	–$350	$ 60	$ 60	$ 60	$ 60	$ 60	$ 60	$ 60	$ 60	$ 60	$ 60	$ 60	$410	$300
2	– 350	190	– 80	190	– 80	190	– 80	190	– 80	190	– 80	190	270	404
3	– 350	190	150	–170	190	150	–170	190	150	–170	190	150	180	629
4	– 350	190	150	110	–270	190	150	110	–270	190	150	110	80	503
5	– 350	190	150	110	50	–320	190	150	110	50	–320	190	270	409
6	– 350	190	150	110	50	10	–380	190	150	110	50	10	– 30	193

* The reinvestment rate is assumed to be 14 percent.

manage them. Furthermore, when a new investment is being evaluated, the financial executive must also consider future divestment opportunities in order to assess its attractiveness correctly. The same analytical framework applies whether divestment is an actual event or a mere contingency.

Divestment decisions may have to be made about a product line, a division, or even an entire operating subsidiary, in contrast with retirement and replacement decisions, which generally concern a specific asset. Otherwise, divestment decisions basically resemble retirement and replacement decisions, in that the problem is to determine the optimal service life of an asset or a group of assets. Hence, the same analysis applies to all of these decisions, but a divestment decision has two aspects which complicate the analysis.

First, cash flows are generally more difficult to forecast for an operating division or an entire subsidiary than for a specific asset. For example, Proctor and Gamble probably could not forecast cash flows from its soap and detergent division as accurately as it could from a new saponification unit for converting fats and oils into soap. Similarly, General Motors probably could not forecast cash flows from its Frigidaire Division as accurately as it could from a new high-speed drill used in making refrigerators. For that reason, we shall assume in the divestment example below that the cash flows are known only probabilistically.

The second aspect of divestment which complicates the analysis is choosing the appropriate reinvestment rate for evaluating alternative cash flows. Retirement and replacement typically involve amounts which are small relative to the size of the firm and, therefore, are easily reinvested. The reinvestment rate, then, is the return on the new investment. Divestment, on the other hand, often involves amounts which are large relative to the size of the firm, and when large divestments occur, many firms in recent years have used the proceeds to repurchase their own outstanding stocks and bonds. If we view such repurchases like any other investments, their returns would consist simply of the interest and/or dividend savings to the company. The reinvestment rate, then, is these savings expressed as a percentage of the amount invested.

An Example

Recognizing the possibility of future divestment can have a significant effect on the acceptability of a proposed investment. To simplify our example, we shall assume the reinvestment rate equals the firm's cost of capital, so that the *NPV* criterion applies. According to this criterion, a firm should divest itself of an asset if the *NPV* resulting from continued operation is less than the price at which the asset can be sold.

Dillon Brewing Company is a producer and distributor of beer and other light alcoholic beverages. As a side venture, Dillon's management plans to acquire Deerfield Minerals Company, which produces a certain metal oxide from its mines. The acquisition will cost $1,600,000, and the mines have only a 3-year supply of the oxide left. The chemists have recently discovered a new use for the oxide, and this new use is the major source of uncertainty in the future price of the oxide.

Dillon forecasts that the acquisition is expected to generate cash flows during the next 3 years as depicted in Figure 9-3. In year 1, there is an equal

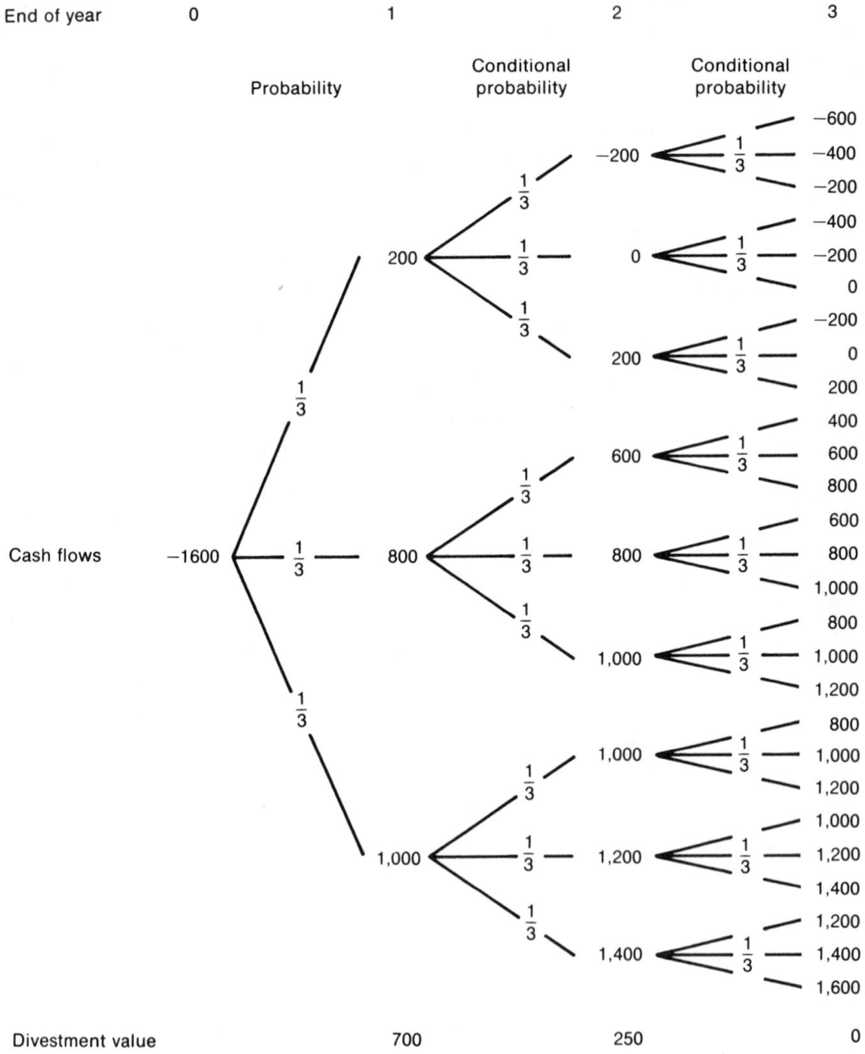

Figure 9-3 Deerfield's Cash Flows and Divestment Value (in thousands of dollars)

probability (1/3) that cash flows will be \$200,000, \$800,000, or \$1,000,000. If cash flow in year 1 is \$200,000, then there is an equal "conditional" probability (1/3) that cash flow in year 2 will be −\$200,000, \$0, or \$200,000.[6] If cash flow in year 2 is −\$200,000, then there is an equal conditional probability (1/3) that cash flow in year 3 will be −\$600,000, −\$400,000, or −\$200,000. The other branches of the cash-flow diagram have similar interpretations. Dillon also forecasts that if it chooses to divest itself of the mining operation at the end of year 1, it will be able to get a price of \$700,000; at the end of year 2, \$250,000; and at the end of year 3, \$0. Suppose the appropriate risk-adjusted discount rate is 14 percent. How is the *NPV* of this acquisition affected by the divestment opportunities?

First, without considering divestment opportunities, let us calculate the *NPV* of the acquisition.[7] For each of the 27 possible cash-flow sequences (branches) we can calculate an *NPV* using 14 percent as the discount rate. (See Table 9-5.) Each of these 27 *NPV*'s is equally likely to occur, with a probability of $(1/3)^3$, or 1/27. Taking a simple average of these 27 values, we get an expected *NPV* for the Deerfield Minerals Company equal to −\$97,300. If we assume that once the company undertakes the investment it is committed to its operation over its entire estimated life, the acquisition is clearly unprofitable.

Realistically, however, we must allow for the possibility of future divestment. Dillon Brewing Company, of course, will consider divestment of Deerfield only if first-year results of the mining business are discouraging. Suppose the cash flow from Deerfield in year 1 totaled only \$200,000. Dillon has to decide whether to bail out or to continue the operation. Given the first year's figure of \$200,000, the only cash-flow sequences that could follow for years 2 and 3 are those 9 branches at the top of Figure 9-3. At a discount rate of 14 percent, these cash flows have an expected *NPV* of −\$153,900 at the end of year 1. Since the divestment value is \$700,000 at the end of year 1, it is more profitable for the firm to bail out. But would it be more profitable to divest at the end of year 2 than at the end of year 1? Since divestment value decreases with time, and since the *NPV* of cash flows in year 2 is clearly not positive, deferring divestment does not pay in this case. Given a cash flow of \$200,000 in year 1, the best strategy is to divest immediately.

If Dillon divests itself of Deerfield at the end of year 1, its cash flow in year 1 will total \$900,000. Moreover, this sum will replace all 9 branches of the cash-flow sequences at the top of the cash-flow diagram in Figure 9-3. Calculated with the revised cash-flow figures, the expected *NPV* of the Deerfield acquisition is \$152,400. Allowing for the possibility of divestment

---

[6] "Conditional" describes the fact that the probability distribution in year 2 is dependent on the actual cash flow in year 1.

[7] All calculations for this problem were done on the computer, using the program in Figure B-4 of Appendix B.

Table 9-5 Calculating Deerfield's Expected Net Present Value* (in thousands of dollars)

Cash-Flow Sequence	Probability of Sequence	Cash Flow at End of Year 0	1	2	3	NPV
1	1/27	−$1,600	$200	−$200	−$600	−$1,983.4
2	1/27	− 1,600	200	− 200	− 400	− 1,848.4
3	1/27	− 1,600	200	− 200	− 200	− 1,713.5
4	1/27	− 1,600	200	0	− 400	− 1,694.6
5	1/27	− 1,600	200	0	− 200	− 1,559.6
⋮	⋮	⋮	⋮	⋮	⋮	⋮
27	1/27	− 1,600	1,000	1,400	1,600	1,434.4
		Expected Value of *NPV*				−$ 97.3

* Assuming no bail-out opportunities.

has revealed an apparently unprofitable acquisition to be a worthwhile and profitable business venture.

POST-AUDIT

Benefits of Post-Audit

The familiar warning "GIGO"—garbage in, garbage out—applies to computers as well as to other analytical tools. Post-audits provide a means of verifying the accuracy of data used in capital-budgeting analysis. Such feedback on the performance of past investments can be of great value not only in pinpointing areas for improvement in current operations but also in the control and planning of new capital expenditures.

When planning, some analysts tend to be consistently optimistic in their forecasts of the future costs and benefits of projects, while others tend to be pessimistic. Both groups of analysts are more likely to exercise objectivity if they realize that their forecasts will be post-audited. In addition, post-audits, by revealing errors in previous decisions, help the firm identify corrective measures for avoiding the same mistakes in the future.

In the area of control, post-audits deal with the effective implementation of already-made investment decisions. Three major questions are pertinent here. Have the intended cost reductions or profit additions been realized—and if not, why not? What problems, both in the quality and in the implementation of the original decision, can be corrected? Are the problems severe enough to warrant consideration of a bailout from the project?

The Process

Which Projects? Since auditing all projects would be extravagantly expensive in terms of both time and money, many companies audit all projects over a certain size, but only a portion of the others. These other projects may be selected for audit according to various criteria. The projects chosen may, for example, belong to certain categories: e.g., intended cost reductions; pilot projects related to proposals for future large investments; projects with the largest relative prospective incremental profits; or projects difficult to assess in terms of financial results, such as those involving significant intangibles. A combination of these approaches would be most likely to give a relatively complete picture of the state of current operations.

Responsibility and Timing. An important factor in any post-audit is the delegation of responsibility. In one sense, it seems most logical for the review of a project to be carried out by the person who originally developed it, since he presumably is especially familiar with it and is in the best position to judge how effectively the plans are being implemented. On the other hand, since he has a vested interest in the project's success, it may be difficult for him to be totally objective. An outsider may be less efficient, but more objective. Many firms try to combine the advantages of both approaches by having post-audits done jointly by the project originator and by representatives from the controller and engineering staffs. Other firms have post-audits done by the originators with random spot-checks by outsiders. In any case, it is important that the originators not be made to feel that their work is being reviewed punitively, since this may lead to excessive conservatism in the future.

If the greatest benefits are to be obtained, a post-audit should not be postponed too long, since the time lost in implementing improvements may be costly; however, if the study is made too soon, the auditors may view as weaknesses problems that are due simply to the newness of the project. The post-audit schedule should therefore be fairly flexible, allowing time for the "debugging" stage to pass. Most firms make their audits within a year. In simple cases, this is all that is needed; but frequently a later audit is indicated if the project's performance is likely to change over time, if the estimate of the project's lifetime is critical, or if there are significant "in-flight" adjustments made on the original project.

Interpretation of Data. Even with the benefits of hindsight, post-audits cannot lead to unambiguous conclusions regarding project performance, since the cash flows used to justify an investment are derived on a with-and-without basis rather than a before-and-after basis. In other words, the forecasts include both the cash flows generated directly by the investment and those indirectly attributable to it. But whereas actual performance records can be used to evaluate the forecasts of the direct component, there is no apt standard for evaluating the indirect component. Because of this, many firms confine their post-audits to the direct component; but such an audit of only one side of investment performance is obviously inadequate.

The real difficulty of a post-audit, then, stems from the need to determine what a firm's performance would have been had the project not been undertaken. Since this will obviously not show up in the accounting records, the auditor must use any available information to create his own "without" data. Fortunately, not every variable in the investment decision is subject to this conceptual exercise; only the critical variables need be examined in this way. For example, if the justification for acquiring a machine was direct labor-saving, the audit should focus on direct labor costs; while if the rationale for introducing a new product line was protection of the market share, the audit should focus on industry and company sales. In the latter case, it is also necessary to ask what the firm's share of the market would have been without the new product line—a much more difficult question than what labor costs would have been without a new machine. But, easy or difficult, these assessments must be made if post-audits are to cover both direct and indirect cash flows. Only in this way can a post-audit lead to a meaningful comparison of a project's actual performance with the original forecast.

REVIEW QUESTIONS

1. Explain the nature of asset-management decisions. How do they differ from capital-budgeting decisions? Give illustrative examples of each.
2. Review the du Pont equation (Chapter 3) for controlling the rate of return on a firm's total investment. Which variables or ratios of variables are influenced by asset-management decisions? How? Give examples.
3. In 1962, two changes were made in tax laws which eased depreciation rules. Section 167(f) of the Tax Code provides for the 10 percent free salvage already discussed; and the Treasury's Depreciation Guidelines shortened the service lives of many asset categories (service lives have been further shortened since then). What general effect do these changes have on the relative advantages of SL, DDB, and SYD depreciation for tax purposes, as measured by the present value of the tax savings associated with each method?
4. When we determine the best tax-depreciation method by maximizing the future value of depreciation charges, we assume that the market-capitalization rate is unaffected by the methods selected. What modifications in analytical procedure would be necessary if the market-capitalization rate was affected? Outline the computational steps for implementing the modified procedure.
5. How do replacement decisions differ from retirement and divestment decisions? How do these differences affect the analytical framework used to optimize each sort of decision?

6. Discuss the practical problems involved in estimating the incremental cash flows associated with retirement and divestment decisions. Illustrate with examples.

7. Explain how the optimal replacement period for a piece of equipment is affected by the firm's planning horizon, the cost of equipment, the salvage value, and the firm's reinvestment rate. (You may answer this question within the framework of either the direct or the indirect approach to the problem.)

8. Explain in terms of economic logic why the optimal replacement period for a given piece of equipment is always equal to or shorter than the optimal retirement period. What role, if any, does a firm's cost of capital have in your explanation?

9. The Alpha Petroleum Company, a large independent producer of gas and oil, also purchases, feeds, and sells cattle. Alpha is considering selling its cattle operation and using the entire proceeds to repurchase 500,000 (about 1/20) of its outstanding common shares. Outline a procedure for analyzing this decision and explain how your analysis might differ if the proceeds from the sales of the cattle operation were intended not for share repurchase, but for expanding Alpha's refining facilities.

10. Suppose you have been asked to post-audit a new-product decision. You may decide for what company you are working, what product you are reviewing, what information you will ask for, and whom you will ask for data. What kind of analysis would you make? How would you intend the results of your study to be used? Relate these particulars to your concept of the purpose of post-audit.

PROBLEMS

1. Determine the tax-depreciation charges under each method of depreciation (SL, DDB, and SYD) on an asset which cost \$1,000, has an estimated economic life of 10 years, and has a salvage value of \$130.
2. Suppose an asset costs C dollars, has an economic life of n years, and has no salvage value. The annual depreciation under the three methods of depreciation are given by the formulas:

$$SL_t = \frac{C}{n};\ SYD_t = \frac{2C(n-t+1)}{n(n+1)};\ DDB_t = \frac{2C}{n}\left(1-\frac{2}{n}\right)^{t-1}$$

where $1 \le t \le n$. Graph SL_t, SY_t, and DDB_t as a function of t, assuming $C =$ \$1,000,000 and $n = 8$.
3. Figure 9-2 compares the future values of depreciation charges under DDB with those under SYD. Construct for graph (b) a new series of data by subtracting DDB depreciation from the corresponding SYD depreciation. Calculate and graph the *NPV* of this new series as a function of the discount rate for the range 0 to 1 at increments of .1. What value would you expect this *NPV* to have at a discount rate of 0 percent? 66 percent? Be sure to explain your reasoning.

4. Suppose that the salvage values and the cash flows from operation associated with Wildcat Transport's helicopter are as follows:

End of Year	1	2	3	4	5	6
Operation	$240,000	$200,000	$120,000	$43,000	$25,000	$4,000
Salvage value	250,000	170,000	100,000	70,000	50,000	0

Determine the optimal retirement period at a reinvestment rate of 15 percent. Given a 12-year planning horizon and the same reinvestment rate, determine the optimal replacement period.

5. CNB Inc. invested $10,000 in a project with a 3-year economic life. During year 1, the company received a cash flow of only $1,500 from the project. Given this fact, the company now forecasts the cash flows for years 2 and 3 as follows:

End of Year 2		End of Year 3	
Cash Flow (dollars)	Probability	Cash Flow (dollars)	Conditional Probability
		−3,000	1/3
−1,000	1/3	−2,000	1/3
		−1,000	1/3
		−2,000	1/3
500	1/3	−1,000	1/3
		0	1/3
		−1,000	1/3
1,000	1/3	0	1/3
		1,000	1/3

Suppose that the appropriate risk-adjusted discount rate is 12 percent and that the project has divestment values of $500, $450, and $0 at the end of years 1, 2, and 3, respectively. In view of the first year's record, should CNB divest itself of the project before the end of year 3? If so, when?

6. (a) Complete the Deerfield cash-flow data in Table 9-5, and then calculate $E(NPV)$ and $V(NPV)$ using a risk-free interest rate of 7 percent. To save time, you may wish to use the computer program in Figure B-4 of Appendix B.

(b) Repeat the above exercise, now allowing for the possibility of future divestment.

7. BBA, Inc., wishes to buy a 2-year license from the government to operate a hunting resort. The company is given two alternatives: purchase the license outright for $10,000; or purchase the license for $12,000, with the option of selling it back at the end of one year for $4,000. Suppose that BBA expects the cash flow from operation to be as follows:

Year 1		Year 2	
Cash Flow	Probability	Cash Flow	Conditional Probability
$8,000	.7	$10,000	.5
		6,000	.5
2,000	.3	3,000	.5
		1,000	.5

Which alternative will be more profitable, assuming that BBA uses a discount rate of 0 percent and is neutral toward risk?

REFERENCES

BIERMAN, HAROLD, JR., "Accelerated Depreciation and Rate Regulation," *Accounting Review* 44 (January, 1969), pp. 65–78.

BRIGHAM, EUGENE F., and TIMOTHY J. NANTELL, "Normalization Versus Flow Through for Utility Companies Using Liberalized Tax Depreciation," *Accounting Review* 49 (July, 1974), pp. 436–447.

DAVIDSON, SIDNEY, and DAVID F. DRAKE, "Capital Budgeting and the 'Best' Tax Depreciation Method," *Journal of Business* 34 (October, 1961), pp. 442–52.

DAVIDSON, SIDNEY, and DAVID F. DRAKE, "The 'Best' Tax Depreciation Method—1964," *Journal of Business* 37 (July, 1964), pp. 258–260.

EDWARDS, JAMES W., *Effects of Federal Income Taxes on Capital Budgeting* (New York: National Association of Accountants, 1969).

GRANT, EUGENE L., AND W. GRANT IRESON, *Principles of Engineering Economy* (New York: The Ronald Press, 1970), Ch. 17.

HACKAMACK, LAWRENCE C., *Making Equipment-Replacement Decisions* (New York: American Management Association, 1969).

JARRETT, JEFFREY E., "An Abandonment Decision Model," *Engineering Economist* 19 (Fall, 1973), pp. 35–46.

MURRAY, ALAN P., *Depreciation* (Cambridge: International Tax Program, Harward Law School, 1971).

RABY, WILLIAM L., *The Income Tax and Business Decisions* (Englewood Cliffs: Prentice-Hall, Inc., 1972).

ROBICHEK, ALEXANDER A., and JAMES C. VAN HORNE, "Abandonment Value and Capital Budgeting," *Journal of Finance* 22 (December, 1967), pp. 577–589.

SCHNELL, JAMES S., and ROY S. NICOLOSI, "Capital Expenditure Feedback: Project Reappraisal," *Engineering Economist* 19 (July–August, 1974), pp. 253–261.

SHILLINGLAW, GORDON, "Profit Analysis for Abandonment Decisions," in Ezra Solomon, ed., *The Management of Corporate Capital* (New York: The Free Press of Glencoe, Inc., 1959), pp. 269–281.

SHORE, BARRY, *Operations Management* (New York: McGraw-Hill Book Company, 1973), Ch. 3.

SIEMENS, NICOLAI, C. H. MARTING, and FRANK GREENWOOD, *Operations Research* (New York: The Free Press, 1973), Ch. 3.

SPILLER, EARL A., JR., *Financial Accounting* (Homewood: Richard D. Irwin, Inc., 1971), Ch. 9.

TERBORGH, GEORGE, *Business Investment Management* (Washington, D.C.: Machinery and Allied Products Institute and Council for Technological Advancement, 1967), Ch. 21.

Part Four

Working Capital Management

10 Management of Cash and Cash Resources

Since cash receipts and expenditures are seldom perfectly synchronized or completely predictable, all firms must hold a cash balance to insure financial solvency; and since production, sales, and collections take place neither simultaneously nor instantaneously, all firms must have a sizeable amount of accounts receivable and inventories. In a typical manufacturing firm, these working-capital assets, as they are called, represent about 50 percent of the total assets; in wholesale and retailing firms, about 70 percent; in electric and gas utilities, about 8 percent. On the average, they account for slightly more than 48 percent of the total assets of all firms.[1] Such sizeable investments make working-capital management crucial for the financial executive. In Chapters 5–9, we treated the decision to invest in working capital as an integral part of capital-budgeting analysis and assumed in that analysis that working capital was optimally managed. But until now we have not discussed either the function of working capital or specific techniques for its optimal management. We shall now do so.

From the point of view of financial management, the significant difference between working capital and fixed capital lies not in their physical forms but in their divisibility and liquidity. Cash, inventory, and receivables may be increased or decreased in small units, whereas plant and equipment must be purchased on an all-or-nothing basis. The divisibility of working capital means that in setting levels of cash balance and inventories, a firm may choose to limit working capital to immediate needs. Such a hand-to-mouth policy minimizes investments but increases the risk of shortages or "stockouts." In this chapter we will discuss cash management, and in

[1] Based on data in corporate income tax returns, released annually by the IRS.

Chapter 11, inventory management; both help the financial executive to balance the cost of larger investments against the penalties of shortages. We should note, however, that since receivables necessarily coincide with actual use, prestocking is not an issue. Here, divisibility permits the firm to adjust its policy precisely and frequently.

Besides being more divisible, working capital is more liquid (i.e., nearer to cash) than fixed capital. Both the liquidity and the divisibility of working capital have implications for a firm's financing decisions. The greater the percentage of assets a firm invests in working capital, the greater its liquidity, and the greater reliance it can place on debt financing without incurring excessive risk of insolvency. Moreover, because working capital is divisible, a firm can vary its investments in working capital according to its immediate needs. To benefit from this innate flexibility of working capital, the firm must maintain flexibility in its financing arrangements. It must consider not only the relative costs of different sources of financing but also whether funds can be returned to their sources when the immediate needs for working capital subside. Later, in Chapter 21, we shall present a linear program for solving this financing problem.

THE SCOPE OF CASH MANAGEMENT

The Cash-Flow Diagram

In Chapter 3, we stressed the importance of viewing the management of cash as a dynamic process. This viewpoint underlies the cash-flow diagram in Figure 10-1, which depicts the generation and disposition of cash

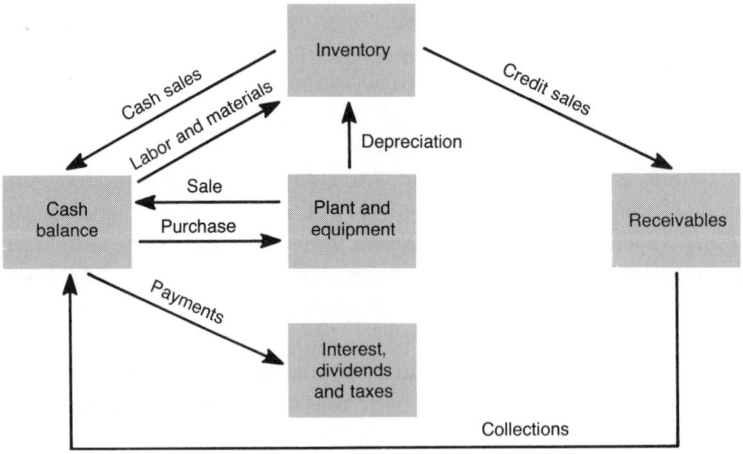

Figure 10-1 Circular Flow of Cash

in a typical manufacturing firm. The arrows indicate the direction of flow. Depending on the relative amounts of cash flowing in and out, the firm experiences a surplus or deficit.

With cash subject to so many forces, we might expect inflows and outflows to be frequently, if not constantly, in a state of imbalance. But a firm's survival depends on always having sufficient cash to discharge its obligations on time. Cash management, therefore, is ultimately concerned with minimizing the risk of insolvency through the balancing of cash inflows and outflows. Careful planning is necessary if the firm is to avoid taking drastic emergency measures or carrying an excessively large amount of cash, which may be costly in terms of income foregone.

Cash-Management Decisions

If cash receipts and disbursements were perfectly synchronized and could be forecast with complete certainty, a firm would need no cash balance. But since this ideal situation never exists, several cash-management decisions must be made. First, the firm must project the cash surplus or deficit for each period of the firm's planning horizon. Typically, a firm uses the cash budget for this. Second, given that projection, the firm must decide what amount of cash resources to hold, taking into account the probabilistic nature of the projection, the opportunity cost of excess liquidity, and the penalty for cash deficiency. Third, a firm should know what techniques are available for economizing by accelerating cash inflows and decelerating cash outflows. And finally, given the size of cash resources, a firm must decide how the total should be divided between bank balances and marketable securities.

FORECASTING CASH REQUIREMENTS

The Cash Budget

The first step in cash management is the preparation of the cash budget. As an illustration, we could return to the quarterly cash budgets of El Camelo, the hypothetical company in Chapter 2. However, in order to exercise a tighter control over cash, most firms use a shorter budgeting period. Hence, we shall construct a new 1-year cash budget with the month as the basic budgeting period.

We shall study the cash budget of Fancycraft, Inc., a hypothetical firm which manufactures greeting cards and gift-wrapping paper.[2] Because of the nature of the business, Fancycraft's sales vary seasonally, although

[2] This example is adapted from my article, "Application of Linear Programming to Short-Term Financing Decisions," *Engineering Economist* 13 (July–August, 1968), pp. 221–241.

Table 10-1 Fancycraft's Sales Forecast for the Next Twelve Months

Month	Sales	Month	Sales
January	$183,000	July	$150,000
February	183,000	August	150,000
March	183,000	September	150,000
April	83,000	October	250,000
May	83,000	November	250,000
June	83,000	December	250,000

the product line does include such stable items as birthday cards, thank-you notes, and some wrapping paper. Since the bulk of the company's revenue comes from sales for Valentine's Day, Easter, Halloween, Thanksgiving, and Christmas, sales are generally lowest in the second quarter of the year and highest in the fourth quarter. Table 10-1 forecasts the monthly breakdown of sales revenues for the coming year.

For every dollar in sales, Fancycraft incurs 50¢ in production costs: 25¢ for labor, 12.5¢ for materials, 6.25¢ in cash overhead, and 6.25¢ in depreciation. The firm also has fixed selling and administrative expenses of $70,000 per month, and pays taxes and dividends at a rate of $25,000 per quarter. Products are sold on a "net 90" basis (i.e., full payment is due in 90 days). Current production is equal to the sales level forecast for three months later. Labor and cash-overhead expenses are paid in cash in the month they are incurred; materials are paid for on a "net 90" basis. Selling and administrative costs are paid in cash every 90 days (January, April, July, and October). Dividends and taxes are also paid quarterly (March, June, September, and December). A $20,000 sinking-fund payment is made in January and again in July. During the last quarter of last year, monthly sales totaled $200,000. During the first quarter of next year, monthly sales are expected to total $183,000. The production department has two $100,000 plates on order, one to be delivered in January, the other in June.

The cash budget in Table 10-2 was prepared from this information with the aid of a computer program (see Figure B-5 in Appendix B). Looking at the figures for January, we see that collection is made for sales from last October, that payments for materials total 12.5 percent of current sales (the forecast of which, we recall, determined the production for October), and that payments for labor and cash overhead total 31.25 percent of the sales forecast for next April (which determines current production). The other disbursements are givens. Subtracting disbursements from receipts, we get a net deficit for January of $179,000. The monthly figures indicate that the firm will have a cumulative deficit in eight of the twelve months, with the largest cumulative deficit—$304,000—in October.

Table 10-2 Fancycraft's Cash Budget for the Next Twelve Months*
(in thousands of dollars)

Item	Jan.	Feb.	Mar.	Apr.	May	June	July	Aug.	Sept.	Oct.	Nov.	Dec.
Cash receipts due to operations												
Accounts receivable	200	200	200	183	183	183	83	83	83	150	150	150
Cash disbursements due to operations												
Purchase of materials	23	23	23	10	10	10	19	19	19	31	31	31
Labor and cash overhead	26	26	26	47	47	47	78	78	78	57	57	57
Selling and administrative expenses	210	0	0	210	0	0	210	0	0	210	0	0
Net flow due to operations	−59	151	151	−84	126	126	−224	−14	−14	−148	62	62
Other cash disbursements												
Dividends and taxes	0	0	25	0	0	25	0	0	25	0	0	25
Sinking fund	20	0	0	0	0	0	20	0	0	0	0	0
Purchase of plates	100	0	0	0	0	100	0	0	0	0	0	0
Monthly surplus (+) or deficit (−)	−179	+151	+126	−84	+126	+ 1	−244	− 14	− 39	−148	+ 62	+ 37
Cumulative surplus (+) or deficit (−)	−179	− 28	+ 99	+14	+140	+141	−103	−117	−156	−304	−242	−205

* Figures have been rounded off.

Sensitivity Analysis

Management tends to view the firm's overall plan (of which the cash budget is a part) with more confidence than the facts may justify, since the plan has already been agreed upon and serves as a fixed target. In cash budgeting, we must especially avoid this pitfall by undertaking sensitivity analysis (contingency planning) to cope with unexpected events that might affect the firm's cash flows. For most firms, the key source of uncertainty is the volume of sales. Table 10-3 shows the monthly surplus (or deficits) in Fancycraft's cash budget, revised on the assumption that sales forecasts are uniformly 10 percent above, 10 percent below, 20 percent above, and 20 percent below the basic forecast.

The results show that a given percentage change in sales forecasts does not bring about the same percentage change in projected cash requirements. For example, in the April budget, a 10-percent increase in sales and collections causes the net cash flow to change from −$84,300 to −$71,700, decreasing the deficit by 14.9 percent. This disproportionate change can be explained algebraically. Sales and cash requirements would vary equiproportionately if all cash receipts and disbursements were constant proportions of sales. The cash budget, however, includes several payments whose values are independent of sales. The presence of these fixed payments magnifies the response of cash requirements to variations in sales. The degree of this magnification is given by the formula:

$$c = s\left(\frac{V}{V + F}\right) \tag{10-1}$$

where c is the percentage change in total cash requirement; s, the percentage change in sales; V, the variable net cash flows (receipts minus disbursements); and F, the fixed net cash flows (receipts minus disbursements). Thus, in the April budget (see Table 10-2), $V = \$183{,}000 - \$10{,}400 -$

Table 10-3 Sensitivity of Fancycraft's Cash Budget to the Level of Sales (in thousands of dollars)

Sales Forecast	Jan.	Feb.	Mar.	Apr.	May	June	July	Aug.	Sept.	Oct.	Nov.	Dec.
+20%	−189	+141	+116	−59	+151	+26	−247	−17	−42	−136	+74	+49
+10%	−184	+146	+121	−72	+138	+13	−245	−15	−40	−142	+68	+43
Basic*	−179	+151	+126	−84	+126	+ 1	−244	−14	−39	−148	+62	+37
−10%	−174	+156	+131	−97	+113	−12	−243	−13	−38	−155	+55	+30
−20%	−169	+161	+136	−109	+101	−24	−241	−11	−36	−161	+49	+24

* Identical with line 8 of Table 10–2.
"+" indicates surplus and "−" indicates deficit.

$46,900 = $125,700; $F = -\$210{,}000$; and $V/(V+F) = -1.49$. A 10-percent increase in sales consequently results in a 14.9 percent decrease in the original deficit of $84,300.

In managing cash under uncertainty, it is not enough merely to ask hypothetically how the cash budget would be affected if the assumptions underlying it were not met. It is vital also to know the probabilities of various possible events, since the anticipatory measures that should be taken will depend on these probabilities. In Chapter 4, we showed how a firm can use computer simulation to determine the risk of insolvency should it be hit by a business recession. The simulation model is general enough that it can also be used to explore the liquidity implications of changes in the ratio of debt to equity, level of capital expenditures, and dividend payout. Since the model was presented in detail earlier, we shall not take it up again here.

MAINTAINING SOLVENCY UNDER UNCERTAINTY

Resources of Financial Mobility

If an unexpected deficit develops in a firm's cash budget, it can be met with what Gordon Donaldson calls the firm's resources of financial mobility.[3] These take two forms: instant and negotiated resources.

Instant Resources. Cash is obviously the ultimate in liquidity and the most instant resource. Firms maintain a cash balance for transactions purposes and for meeting planned cash-flow deficits. Only the amount in excess of these needs is available for unexpected cash drains.

A second instant resource is the unused portion of a firm's line of credit. A line of credit is an informal agreement between a firm and a bank, whereby the firm is given the privilege of borrowing any sum up to a set amount at the going interest rate. A line of credit generally has to be renewed annually; but during its term, the firm may borrow as often as it wishes, usually simply by making a telephone call, so long as its borrowings do not exceed the stipulated amount.

Negotiated Resources. All mobile financial resources except cash and credit lines require either internal or external negotiation and consequently entail various degrees of delay and uncertainty. New bank loans may involve extensive negotiations and even then may not be available in the amount or on the terms desired. Issuing long-term debt and common stock

---

[3] Gordon Donaldson, *Strategy for Financial Mobility* (Boston: Graduate School of Business Administration, Harvard University, 1969), Ch. 11.

requires planning with an investment banker, registration with the Securities and Exchange Commission, and public distribution. All this may take many months, and even then success will depend on conditions in the capital market.

Another way to meet an unexpected cash deficit is to reduce planned outflows. If the deficit is due to low sales, the obvious counter-move is to scale down production; the savings in operating expenses will help to alleviate the deficit. But the speed with which operating expenses can be reduced will depend on how quickly production workers can be laid off and how willing operating executives are to work with a reduced inventory. Realizing the full effect of these economy measures will take months. Capital expenditures are generally easier to curtail than operating expenses, since they are not directly related to current cash generation. Various classes of investments may be reconsidered, depending on the intensity and duration of the deficit. But any re-ordering of priorities requires the consent of the operating management, so that, again, reductions of cash outflow take time.

If current common-stock dividends are liberal, cutting the dividend rate could yield substantial immediate cash "savings." Such a change in the dividend policy must be evaluated in terms of the firm's long-run financial strategy. Security investors are generally willing to accept a low dividend rate if they are convinced that the firm can reinvest its earnings at a higher-than-normal rate of return; but if investors see the low dividend rate as a sign of financial weakness, a cut can severely depress the market value of the firm's common shares.

If the deficit is developing slowly, the firm may consider the time-consuming process of negotiating the sale of some of its earning assets. But this should be done only as a last resort, since the liquidation of part of the company's earning power is too important a step to be made with a weak bargaining position, incomplete data, and under pressures of time.

Of the above sources of financial mobility, only three—surplus cash, line of credit, and negotiated bank loans—are relatively quick, certain, and without adverse effects on operations. Cash management should concentrate on these three.

The Optimal Amount of Liquid Resources

A hypothetical example[4] will illustrate how the optimal amount of unused bank loans and contingency cash balance is determined by balancing the cost of such holdings against the cost of illiquidity and possible insolvency. The Southfield Tool Company, a manufacturer of automobile

[4] This analysis is adapted from an example in Harold Bierman, Jr., and Alan K. McAdams, *Management Decisions for Cash and Marketable Securities* (Ithaca: Graduate School of Business and Public Administration, Cornell University, 1962), pp. 51–54.

Table 10-4 The Excess Demand for Cash (in millions)

Cumulative Cash Deficit	Size of Liquid Holdings			
	$1	$2	$3	$4
$1	0	0	0	0
2	+1	0	0	0
3	+2	+1	0	0
4	+3	+2	+1	0

"+" indicates an excess of cumulative cash deficit over initial liquid holdings; "0" indicates equality or surplus.

parts, is having difficulty with its union over wage negotiations, and a strike seems imminent. The financial management forecasts that, depending on the duration of the strike and the number of plants struck, the firm could have cumulative cash-flow deficits ranging from $1 million to $4 million over the next 12 months. The firm could, of course, insure against financial embarrassment by holding $4 million in liquid reserves. But money is tight at this time, and the cost of holding excess cash and unused bank loans is 9 percent for the 12-month period. On the other hand, if inadequate liquid reserves lead to a disruption in research and capital-expenditure programs, the firm's long-run earning power will suffer. The management places a value of $150,000 on such a disruption if the cumulative cash deficit exceeds liquid reserves by $1 million; $350,000 if the difference is $2 million; and $550,000 if the difference is $3 million. Southfield Tool keeps a minimum of $1 million in liquid reserves and must decide whether to up it to 2, 3, or 4 million dollars. We shall designate the alternatives as policies 1, 2, 3, and 4, respectively.

Table 10-4 shows the excess demand for cash associated with each policy under various assumptions regarding initial liquidity and the size of anticipated deficits. Thus, under policy 1, the excess demand for cash varies from $0 to $3 million as the cumulative cash-flow deficit varies from $1 million to $4 million. The excess demands are assigned costs on the basis of their disruptive impact on the firm's operation; $150,000 for $1 million; $350,000 for $2 million; and $550,000 for $3 million. When we add a flat fee of 9 percent of the initial liquid asset holdings, we get the cost matrix on the right side of Table 10-5.

The matrix shows the cost involved for each cash-management policy at each level of excess cash demand. But this information is not useful in decision-making until a probability distribution is assigned to the random variable: excess cash demand. Management can then calculate the expected costs associated with each policy simply by averaging the costs, using the probabilities as weights. Given the distribution shown in the table, policy

Table 10-5 Determining the Expected Cost of Holding Different Amounts of Liquid Resources

Cumulative Cash Deficit	Probability	Size of Initial Liquid Holdings			
		$1M	$2M	$3M	$4M
$1M	.05	$ 90,000	$180,000	$270,000	$360,000
2M	.50	240,000	180,000	270,000	360,000
3M	.40	340,000	330,000	270,000	360,000
4M	.05	440,000	430,000	420,000	360,000
Expected cost		$332,500	$257,500	$277,500	$360,000

2 is optimal, since it has the smallest expected cost: $257,500. Policy 4 would give absolute security but at a disproportionate cost: $360,000. It is possible, of course, that the management may wish to consider, in addition to expected costs, the risk associated with each policy. It may do this by calculating the variance or semi-variance (or some other measure of risk) of the cost of providing liquidity. In theoretical terms, the important thing here is the effect of the cash-management policy on the probability distribution of the firm's earnings as a whole. But as a practical matter, it may be inconvenient and even unnecessary to determine this in every case. Except for major decisions, it is generally more feasible to consider a set of policies, eliminate those with obviously unacceptable risks, and from the remaining alternatives choose the one with the lowest expected cost.

MOBILIZING THE IN-TRANSIT CASH BALANCE

The Size of Possible Gain

A firm still needs a cash balance on a daily basis for bridging the time gap between payment of expenses and collection of revenue even if the monthly cash budgets show no deficits. This in-transit cash balance can be minimized by accelerated collection of receipts and tightened control over disbursements. In many cases the savings can be substantial. General Electric, let us suppose, makes sales averaging $35 million per day. If collection were advanced by only one day, General Electric could reduce its bank borrowing by $35 million, and at an interest rate of, say, 10 percent, the savings in interest would be $3.5 million per year. We might also remember the situation a few years ago when the State of Alaska leased the oil rights on the north slope of Prudhoe Bay. The various bidders were required to submit certified checks as deposits on their bids, and since these checks were drawn on Chicago and New York banks, it was profitable for the State to charter a plane in order to collect the funds sooner than they could have through normal business channels. On $900 million, at 8 percent interest, the income was $197,300 per day.

Accelerating Receipts

The key to accelerating receipts lies in reducing float, as in the case of the Alaska auction. Float is the money tied up in the collection process between the time the customer mails his check and the time the money becomes available to the firm for disbursement. The time required for postal delivery varies with the weather, the season, and the distance; and even after a check has been received and deposited, the bank must collect the money before the firm can draw against the deposit. When checks are collected through the Federal Reserve System, the collecting bank receives a credit in its Federal Reserve account according to a fixed time schedule based on distance. Although this time deferral is less than the actual collection time, it may be two full days.

Many firms reduce float by means of decentralized collection and regional banking.[5] Customers are instructed to mail their checks to local sales offices located strategically to minimize mail delays. Once the checks are received, they are funneled into regional banks, which keep company headquarters informed of daily deposits. To avoid unnecessary cross-country transfer of funds, regional collections are used for that region's disbursements; this way, only the surplus in each account need be transferred to the central office for reinvestment. General Electric, for example, has 170 plant locations, hundreds of sales offices which are also used as collection points, and 450 commercial banks whose services it employs. The company collects from its customers at no less than 500 locations, including 175 lock-boxes (see below). When large sums are forthcoming in single payments, the firm bypasses the mailing system completely by sending a messenger. Once the money is collected, GE follows the procedure already described, channeling funds into a network of regional banks.

The lock-box system is another way to reduce float. A lock box is a post office box held by a bank to receive the client's remittance mail. The bank picks up remittances, processes them, and credits the firm's account. When the lock boxes are strategically located, remittances should take no more than 1 day in transit. Banks normally charge a fee in addition to requiring a minimum compensating balance. The amount in excess of the compensating balance may be automatically transferred to company headquarters, drawn by the company's treasurer at his discretion, or drawn by local operating units to meet local disbursements.

---

[5] James F. Lordan, "A Profile of Corporate Cash Management," *The Magazine of Bank Administration* 48 (April, 1972), pp. 15–19. For the General Electric example, see Reginald H. Jones, "Face to Face with Cash Management: How One Company Does It," *Financial Executive* 37 (September, 1969), pp. 37–39.

Controlling Disbursements

The control of disbursements centers on scheduling and centralizing payables. Since the objective is to conserve cash, payments should be scheduled so that bills are not paid before they are actually due. An extreme case is that of one large firm which never mails checks until after 3:00 P.M. the day bills are due. Moreover, the checks are always drawn on remote banks to increase the time that the firm has use of its money before the checks are collected. Centralizing payables minimizes the working balances needed by subsidiaries and divisions. Pooling at company headquarters permits the efficient utilization of funds that might otherwise be stalled at the divisional level.

Do these elaborate schemes for reduction of float and control of disbursements actually pay off? During the mid-1960's, when General Electric's annual sales were only $.5 billion, it operated with cash and marketable securities totaling slightly over $600 million. Today, when its annual sales exceeded $1.2 billion, G.E. is able to get by with cash and marketable securities of approximately $330 million. Reginald H. Jones, former Vice-President of Finance and now Chairman of the Board, attributed the reduction in cash balances to the effective application of the techniques we have been discussing.[6]

INVESTING THE CASH BALANCE: THEORY AND PRACTICE

Investment Media[7]

The financial executive is also responsible for the investment of cash assets, which, in some companies, total millions or even hundreds of millions of dollars. Since the cash assets are held primarily to insure liquidity and solvency, such investments should be both easily marketable and safe. In the short-term money market, these criteria are met by U.S. Treasury obligations, federal agency obligations, negotiable certificates of deposits, and commercial paper.

Treasury Bills. Treasury bills are a debt instrument which the U.S. Treasury issues in order to borrow money for short-term periods. They are available in seven denominations, from $1,000 to $1 million, and in four maturities, from 3 to 6 months. When first issued, Treasury bills may be purchased at auction from the Federal Reserve Banks. After the initial

---

[6] Jones, *op. cit.*, pp. 37–39.

[7] For more details on investment media, see Bank of America's *Money Market Investments and Investment Vocabulary* (San Francisco, 1974).

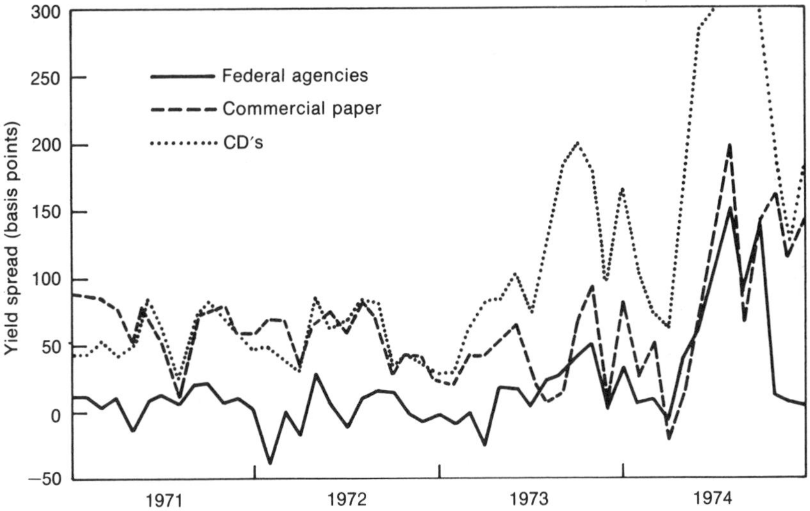

Source: Securities Investment Division, Bank of America.

Figure 10-2 Yield Spreads from 3-Month Treasury Bills of Selected Short-Term Instruments

offering they may be purchased in the secondary market from dealers in government securities, who maintain a regular inventory. Treasury bills are sold on a discount basis: that is, the investor receives his interest as the difference between the purchase price and the maturity value (or resale price). Since they are the safest as well as the most marketable, Treasury bills have the lowest yield of the various money-market instruments (see comparisons in Figure 10-2).

Treasury Certificates, Notes, and Bonds. The U.S. Treasury also issues certificates of indebtedness, notes, and bonds, with maturities respectively of 9 to 12 months, 1 to 7 years, and 7 years and over. The same dealers who handle Treasury bills also handle these three. Unlike bills, however, certificates, notes, and bonds carry fixed-interest coupons, so that the investor receives his interest in the form of periodic payments. Because certificates, notes, and bonds have longer maturities, their market prices are more sensitive to any easing or tightening of general credit conditions. However, as the securities approach their maturity dates, their prices become as stable as those of Treasury bills.

Federal Agency Issues. Five government-sponsored agencies issue their own securities: Federal Home Loan Banks (FHLB), Federal Land Banks (FLB), the Federal National Mortgage Association (FNMA), Banks for Cooperatives (BC), and Federal Intermediate Credit Banks

(FICB). In addition, the Federal Financing Bank (FFB) issues securities on behalf of the smaller federal agencies. The yield on these issues is slightly higher than that on Treasury issues, but lower than that of the other competing money-market instruments.

Negotiable Certificates of Deposit. A certificate of deposit (CD) is a receipt issued by a commercial bank for funds deposited. It entitles the bearer to the amount deposited plus accrued interest, on the date specified in the contract. Negotiable CD's were first introduced by a New York bank in 1961. This negotiability—which distinguishes the new CD's from CD's issued prior to 1961—means that an investor who purchased a CD in good faith is protected by law from anyone who might have a prior claim to it. Because these certificates are negotiable and because government-securities dealers are willing to keep them in inventory, they are a highly liquid investment.

Both the denomination and the maturity of a CD can be tailored to suit the needs of the original investor. Typically, CD's have denominations of \$100,000, \$500,000, or \$1,000,000 and maturities of 30 to 360 days, so that they may be more easily traded in the secondary market. The contractual interest rate at the time of issue is subject to Federal Reserve regulation. Once a CD has been issued, however, its price in the secondary market is determined by the forces of supply and demand, and the effective yield may go above or below the contractual rate. The yield on CD's lies between that from federal-agency issues and that from commercial paper.

Commercial Paper. Commercial paper means the unsecured short-term promissory notes, of two types, issued by large, well-known corporations. Direct paper, or finance-company paper, is issued continually by finance companies (such as General Motors Acceptance Corporation and C.I.T. Financial Corporation). These companies sell commercial paper in such large quantities that it is worth their while to have their own department and staff to place their paper with the investor directly. Dealer paper is issued by non-finance companies, such as industrials, public utilities, and transportation. Their issues are smaller and less frequent and are therefore sold through commercial-paper dealers.

Commercial paper generally matures in three to nine months, since notes with a longer maturity must be registered with the SEC, a requirement which entails time and cost. They are typically issued in denominations of \$100,000, or larger. Like Treasury bills, commercial paper is sold on a discount basis, rather than at an explicit rate of interest. Since the secondary market for commercial paper is not active, the investor should choose a note with a maturity that corresponds to his future needs. Due to the weak marketability and greater credit risk, the return obtainable on commercial paper is higher than that on any of the other money-market instruments.

State and Municipal Obligations. Obligations issued by both state and municipal governments are called "municipals." Some, such as one-year revenue-anticipation notes, are short-term; others are long-term investments which become short-term with time. Since the interest on these investments is exempt from federal income tax, the yield is attractive for corporations paying taxes. As for commercial paper, the secondary market for municipals is weak; therefore the investor must take care to plan his needs precisely so that he will not be forced to sell his holdings prematurely. Most state and municipal obligations are of high investment quality.

A Theoretical Model

The following probabilistic model describes a useful procedure for determining the proper distribution of the firm's cash resources between interest-bearing securities and cash.

The Problem. Let us suppose that Northland, Inc., describes its demand for cash by the probabilistic matrix:

Amount Demanded	Period 1	Period 2
\$10,000	3/5	1/3
20,000	1/5	1/3
30,000	1/5	1/3

where the fractions in the columns describe the probability distribution of the cash demand for each period. It is assumed that the demand can take on only three possible values and that the probability distributions for the two periods are independent of each other. It is further assumed that the management has already decided to hold \$40,000 worth of cash resources at the beginning of its two-period planning horizon. We shall assume, in addition, that all purchases of marketable securities are made at the beginning of a period, that cash demands materialize in the middle of a period, and that, if it is necessary to sell securities to meet these demands, this is done in the middle of a period. Each buying or selling transaction involves a transaction cost of $\$50 + .002Q$, where Q is the value of the securities bought or sold. The interest rate on marketable securities is 2 percent per period; but because of the inconvenience of selling at midperiod, securities sold then not only forfeit the interest for that period but are assigned a penalty of one-half percent for the period. The problem is how much of the cash balance to invest in marketable securities and how much to hold in cash, bearing in mind that the objective is to maximize expected net income.

The Analysis. The problem is difficult to solve analytically, since it involves sequential decision-making. Therefore, instead of deriving a general formula for the optimal strategy, we shall present a convenient method for calculating the expected net income associated with any strategy that management may wish to evaluate.

Let us suppose, for example, that the management is considering the strategy of investing, in each of two successive periods, the excess of its liquid resources over the expected cash demand for the period. The "tree" diagram (Figure 10-3) shows the relevant data for such a strategy. At the beginning of Period 1, the firm holds \$16,000 in cash (C), or the amount of its expected cash demand for that period; the remaining \$24,000 is invested in marketable securities (M), at a transactions cost (T) of \$98. Recall that there are three possible cash demands for the period. First, if the demand turns out to be \$10,000 (probability = 3/5), the cash balance will be reduced to \$6,000 at the end of Period 1; and the firm will receive interest income (I) of \$480 (= \$24,000 × 2%) for the period. Second, if the demand turns out to be \$20,000 (probability = 1/5), the cash balance will be \$0 at the end of Period 1; and the firm will be forced to sell \$4,000 worth of marketable securities (M) at midperiod, reducing its interest income to \$380 (= \$20,000 × 2% − \$4,000 × 1/2%) for the period—and there will be a transactions cost of \$58. Third, if the demand is \$30,000 (probability = 1/5), at the end of Period 1 the firm will have \$0 of cash balance, \$10,000 of marketable securities, and \$130 in interest income, but the firm must spend \$78 to cover transactions costs.

Next we need to relate this strategy's results at the end of Period 1 to the various possible cash demands during Period 2. These demands are \$10,000, \$20,000, and \$30,000, each with a probability of 1/3. We calculate the values of C, M, I, and T for Period 2 just as we did for Period 1. We can now calculate the expected net income for this strategy over the two periods, and we do this by taking the weighted average of the net incomes for each of the 9 possible sequences of cash demands. The net income for each such sequence is the sum of the interest incomes in the two periods minus the transaction costs, and the associated probability is the product of the probabilities for each period. For example, for the first possible sequence in Figure 10-3, the net income is \$480 + \$200 − \$98 − \$78 = \$504, and the probability is $\frac{3}{5} \times \frac{1}{3} = \frac{1}{5}$. The weighted average is the sum of the various net incomes times their probabilities and, in this case, is \$242.

The same procedure can be used to evaluate other investment strategies. A firm may wish to consider the possibility of always investing the excess of current resources over some amount functionally related to both the expected cash demand and the semi-variance of that demand; or, it may consider always investing a percentage of the company's current resources, with the percentage varying with the expected cash demand. Whatever the strategy, the method outlined gives a basis for selection.

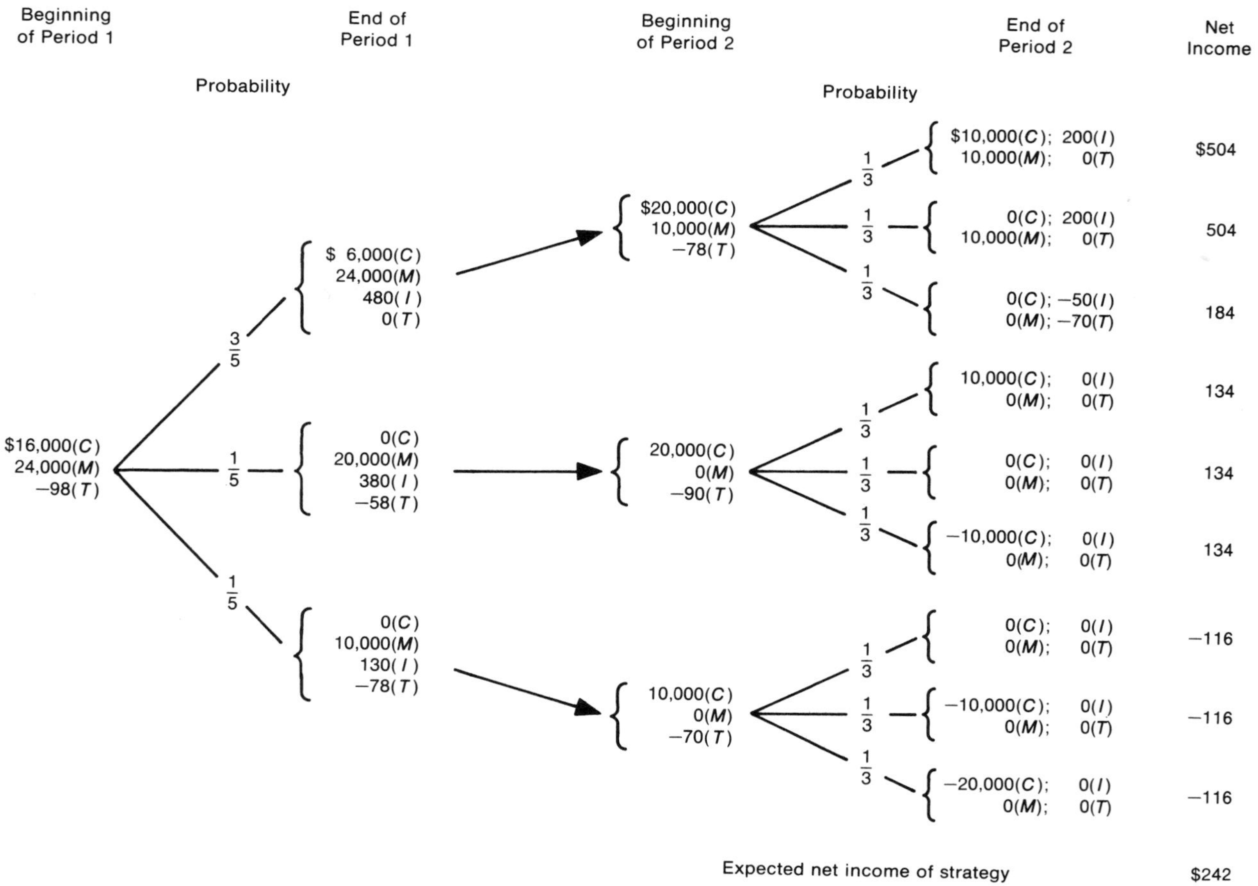

Figure 10-3 Tree Diagram for Analyzing an Investment Strategy

A Practical Modification

In order to limit the amount of computation in the example, we assumed that Northland, Inc., had a planning horizon of only two periods. Actually, however, it is not uncommon for firms to look 12 or 13 weeks ahead when making cash-management decisions. If we had assumed that Northland had a 13-period planning horizon, the decision tree would have had 3^{13} branches instead of the 3^2 branches shown in Figure 10-3, and the computation would have been burdensome even for a computer. To be practical, we must modify the model so that the computation will be manageable. The modification described here is based on the procedure used in an actual electronics firm, which has total assets of about $200 million, of which $5 million is in the form of cash and marketable securities. Due to its sizeable cash resources, the firm can afford a cash manager, who devotes a third of his time to managing the marketable-securities portfolio.

The Basic Procedure. This firm uses a 13-week cash budget in which cash receipts and disbursements are forecast week by week. The 13-week forecast, which is updated every week, contains the information on which the cash manager bases his investment decisions.

Let us imagine that at a given moment the company has J million dollars in cash resources, all in the form of cash. The cash manager must decide how much to hold in cash and how much to invest in marketable securities and at what maturities. He may view the J million dollars as consisting of J layers of $1 million each (an even more refined analysis could be made by considering $2J$ half-million-dollar layers or $4J$ quarter-million-dollar layers). For each layer, the cash manager estimates the probability that the funds will be needed to meet payments at the end of one week, at the end of two weeks, and so on through the thirteenth week; the probabilities are based on the assumption that the money in an "upper" layer will be spent before the money in a "lower" layer.

The first $1 million may be invested in securities maturing in 1 week, 2 weeks, . . . , or 13 weeks. Given the probabilities that funds will be needed at various points in time, the cash manager can calculate the expected net income associated with the strategy of investing funds at a certain maturity, taking into account the interest rate, transactions costs, and any penalties for selling before maturity. If the expected net income is negative for every strategy, the cash manager infers that the funds in that layer should be held in cash rather than invested. If some or all of the expected net incomes are positive, the optimal strategy is to invest in securities of the maturity that is expected to yield the highest net income.

The analysis for each layer indicates whether or not the funds in that layer should be invested in marketable securities, and, if so, at what maturities. In other words, a completed analysis specifies the maturity structure as well as the quantity of securities to be purchased.

Table 10-6 Probability of the Timing of Future Cash Needs

	Need Materializes at the End of			
	Period 1	Period 2	Period 3	Period 4
First layer of $10,000	.80	.20	0	0
Second layer of $10,000	0	.55	.45	0
Third layer of $10,000	0	0	.10	.90

A Numerical Example. Let us take a simple example. The XYZ Company has $30,000 in cash resources at the beginning of Period 1; the cash manager employs a 4-period planning horizon. All securities are assumed to yield an interest return of .3 percent per period if held to maturity but only .2 percent per period if sold before maturity. Each buying or selling transaction involves a transactions cost of $\$12 + .002Q$, where Q is the value of the securities. How much of the $30,000 should be invested in securities and at what maturities?

The cash manager first divides the $30,000 into three layers and then, on the basis of the projected cash budget, estimates the respective probabilities that each layer will be needed to meet payments at the end of Period 1, Period 2, Period 3, and Period 4, as summarized in Table 10-6.

Next, the cash manager calculates the expected net income for each maturity strategy possible for the first layer. If securities maturing in one period are purchased and a need for cash materializes at the end of the first period, the firm receives an interest income of $30 ($= \$10{,}000 \times .003$) but incurs transactions costs of $32 ($= \$12 + \$10{,}000 \times .002$), resulting in a net loss of $2.00. If a need for cash materializes at the end of Period 2, the firm receives an interest income of $60 ($= 2 \times \$10{,}000 \times .003$) but incurs transactions costs of $64 ($= 2[\$12 + \$10{,}000 \times .002]$), giving a net loss of $4.00. The assumption here is that funds invested in securities maturing before the need for cash arises are reinvested in securities with the same original maturity. Since the probability of cash needs at the end of the third and fourth periods is zero, the incomes associated with such an eventuality need not be calculated. Taking a weighted average of $-\$2.00$ and $-\$4.00$, using the respective probabilities as weights, we get $-\$2.40$ ($= -\$2 \times .8 - \$4 \times .2$). The result is the total net income expected from investing the first layer of funds in securities with a maturity of one period.

Table 10-7 summarizes the expected net incomes associated with various maturity strategies for each of the three layers of XYZ's cash balance. Since all strategies yield a negative net income for the first layer, that $10,000 should be withheld as cash. For the second and third layers, the largest expected net incomes are $12.90 and $78.80. To maximize returns, then, the second layer should be invested in marketable securities with a 3-period maturity, and the third layer in marketable securities with a 4-period maturity.

Table 10-7 Expected Net Income from Security Investments

	Maturity of 1 Period	Maturity of 2 Periods	Maturity of 3 Periods	Maturity of 4 Periods
First layer of $10,000	−$2.40	−$29.60	−$40.00	−$40.00
Second layer of $10,000	− 4.90	+ 8.20	+ 12.90	− 15.00
Third layer of $10,000	− 7.80	+ 48.80	+ 18.40	+ 78.80

Relation to the Theoretical Model. This practical model is an adaptation of the theoretical model because the same probabilistic information underlies both models; the significant difference is the way the information is processed. In the theoretical model, the probabilities of cash demands are diagrammed as a decision tree. For any given investment strategy, a net income figure is calculated for each branch of the tree; the average of these net incomes, weighted according to the probabilities, indicates the profitability of the strategy. The computation time involved makes this process economically infeasible except in the simplest situations.

The practical model requires that the cash manager pre-process the probabilistic information, in an attempt to avoid the computational bottleneck. We assume he understands the decision tree, from which he infers the sort of probabilistic summary presented in Table 10-6. The total cash balance is divided into layers, and the likelihood that each layer will be needed for payments at the end of any given period is measured probabilistically. This pre-processing reduces the subsequent computation to manageable proportions.

REVIEW QUESTIONS

1. How do working-capital decisions differ from fixed-capital decisions? How and how much are these differences related to the greater divisibility of working capital?
2. Below are the amounts of cash assets, accounts receivable, and inventory, expressed as a percentage of total assets, shown on the balance sheets of the companies listed:

	An Electric Utility	A Finance Company	An Electronics Manufacturer
Cash assets	1.01%	3.79%	1.53%
Accounts receivable	2.14	70.72	32.34
Inventory	2.74	0	32.54
	5.89%	74.51%	66.41%

How would you explain the differences between these companies in terms of the businesses in which they are engaged?

3. Suppose that in order to control inflation, the government shifts from an easy to a restrictive monetary and fiscal policy. If your firm produces a consumer durable (say, washers and dryers), how would you expect the policy shift to affect your net cash flow from operations? Would you expect the inflow to be affected more or less than the outflow? Which components of each would be involved? Why?
4. Fixed cash payments tend to magnify the effect that a given percentage change in sales will have on a firm's net cash flow. Do you see any similarity between this phenomenon and the leverage effect of fixed costs in standard break-even analysis?
5. List the resources of financial mobility of a typical manufacturing firm. In what order is the firm likely to mobilize these resources in meeting a cash-flow deficit? Explain your reasoning.
6. For each item in your list (question 5), explain how the speed, size, and certainty of mobility would be affected by:
   a. an increase in the firm's planning horizon from three months to six months;
   b. a shift from a tight to an easy Federal Reserve policy;
   c. a change in Regulation Q permitting commercial banks to pay a higher interest rate on savings deposits;
   d. a lowered Moody's credit rating on the firm's long-term bonds.
7. Business economists have observed that strained liquidity positions tend to be a feature of an economy in transition between business expansion and contraction. Do you think this statement is equally true of the general economy and of individual firms? Explain.
8. What factors determine the amount of float involved in the collection of accounts receivable? How do the regional-banking system and the lock-box system reduce float?
9. List the major types of money-market securities suitable for investing a firm's temporary surplus funds. Compare their relative advantages and disadvantages in terms of safety, marketability, and yield.
10. Look up the most recent money market yields on each of the following types of securities: Treasury bills, federal agency issues, prime commercial paper, and CD's. Calculate the yield spreads among the various issues and explain the factors primarily responsible.

PROBLEMS

1. Derive Fancycraft's cash budget assuming that quarterly selling and administrative expenses are \$20,000 + ⅓ of the quarter's sales (instead of the original uniform \$210,000 per quarter). For this and the next 3 problems, you are encouraged to use the computer program in Figure B-5 of Appendix B, but be sure to modify the program to incorporate any necessary changes.
2. Maintaining the figures from Problem 1 for selling and administrative expenses, derive Fancycraft's cash budget if sales forecasts are uniformly 10 percent higher. What is the corresponding percentage increase in cash-flow surplus for the month of March? Using Eq. (10-1), explain the relationship between the two percentage increases.

3. The cash budget in Table 10-2 assumes that Fancycraft sells its products on terms of net 90. Derive next year's budget assuming that the company changes its credit terms to net 30 effective January 1. Use the same monthly sales forecasts as for this year, and reset selling and administrative expenses at the original uniform level of $210,000 per quarter.
4. The cash budget in Table 10-2 assumes that the company produces each month what it expects to sell three months later. Derive next year's budget assuming that starting January 1 the company will produce only every other month and in that month will produce what it expects to sell during two months, two and three months later. That is, the firm will produce in January for March and April, in March for May and June, and so forth. Assume that everything else will remain the same as in the original model.
5. Suppose that a firm has uniform daily sales of $50,000. By instituting regional banking and collection and a lock-box system, the firm could reduce collection time. How much would float be reduced if collection time were reduced by half a day? one day? two days?
6. Rework the tree-diagram example (see Figure 10-3) on the assumption that the company always invests 50 percent of its liquid resources in marketable securities at the beginning of each period. Use the planning horizon, transaction costs, interest rates, probability distribution, and independence assumption given in the text example.
7. Check the numerical example of the practical model by verifying the entire set of expected net income figures in Table 10-7.

REFERENCES

Bank of America, *Money Market Instruments and Investment Vocabulary* (San Francisco, 1974).

BIERMAN, HAROLD, JR., and ALAN K. MCADAMS, *Management Decisions for Cash and Marketable Securities* (Ithaca: Graduate School of Business and Public Administration, Cornell University, 1962).

BUDIN, MORRIS, and A. T. EAPEN, "Cash Generation in Business Operations: Some Simulation Models," *Journal of Finance* 25 (December, 1970), pp. 1091–1107.

CALMAN, ROBERT F., *Linear Programming and Cash Management/CASH ALPHA* (Cambridge: The M.I.T. Press, 1968).

DONALDSON, GORDON, *Strategy for Financial Mobility* (Boston: Graduate School of Business Administration, Harvard University, 1969).

First National Bank of Chicago, *Cash Management* (Chicago: 1975).

FISHER, DAVID I., *Cash Management in the Moderate-Sized Company* (New York: The Conference Board, 1972).

JONES, REGINALD H., "Face to Face with Cash Management: How One Company Does It," *Financial Executive* 37 (September, 1969), pp. 37–39.

KRAUS, ALAN, CHRISTIAN JANSSEN, and ALAN MCADAMS, "The Lock-Box Location Problem," *Journal of Bank Research* 1 (Autumn, 1970), pp. 51–58.

LORDAN, JAMES F., "A Profile of Corporate Cash Management," *The Magazine of Bank Administration* 48 (April, 1972), pp. 15–19.

LORDAN, JAMES F., *The Banking Side of Corporate Cash Management* (Boston: Financial Publishing Company, 1973).

MAO, JAMES C. T., "Application of Linear Programming to Short-Term Financing Decisions," *Engineering Economist* 13 (July–August, 1968), pp. 221–241.

MURRAY, ROGER F., "The Penn Central Debacle: Lessons for Financial Analysis," *Journal of Finance* 26 (May, 1971), pp. 327–332.

ORGLER, YAIR E., *Cash Management: Methods and Models* (Belmont: Wadsworth Publishing Company, Inc., 1970).

ORR, DANIEL, *Cash Management and the Demand for Money* (New York: Praeger Publishers, 1970).

"Penn Central Files Bankruptcy Petition for Rail Unit After U.S. Reneges on Aid," *Wall Street Journal* (June 22, 1970), p. 3.

SALOMON BROTHERS, *An Analytical Record of Yields and Yield Spreads* (New York: 1972), and subsequent annual supplements.

SMITH, KEITH V., *Management of Working Capital* (St. Paul: West Publishing Company, 1974).

SMITH, KEITH V., "State of the Art of Working Capital Management," *Financial Management* 2 (Autumn, 1973), pp. 50–55.

U.S. Department of Treasury, Internal Revenue Service, *Statistics of Income—Corporation Income Tax Returns* (Washington, D.C.: U.S. Government Printing Office, annual).

11 Management of Inventory

Perhaps the only businessman who is entirely free of the management of inventory and receivables is a street-corner vocalist who performs only for cash. Even the owner of a barber shop or a coin-operated car wash, providing services on a cash basis, must carry a minimal amount of raw-materials inventory, such as shaving cream or detergent. Most businesses, of course, carry greater amounts of inventory and receivables. Safeway Stores, for example, carries 44.1 percent of its total assets in inventory and 2.0 percent in receivables, and Ford Motor Company carries 26.0 percent in inventory and 9.5 percent in receivables.[1] The combined figures for all corporations are 7.5 percent and 23.7 percent, respectively.[2] In Chapter 10, we identified the functions of cash and presented techniques for managing the cash position in the most efficient way. In this and the following chapter, we shall consider inventory management and accounts-receivable management, in that order. We shall assume that a firm will consider only alternatives that avoid an unacceptable liquidity position.

THE PROBLEM OF INVENTORY MANAGEMENT

Inventory management is concerned, first, with determining what order quantity maximizes the excess of benefits over costs and, second, with

[1] Based on recent published reports of the respective companies.

[2] Based on data in the corporate income tax returns, released annually by the Internal Revenue Service.

choosing the method of inventory valuation that minimizes the firm's income-tax liability. We shall begin by discussing how optimal order quantity is determined.

The Benefits of Inventory

The most direct approach to inventory management is to identify the benefits and costs associated with inventories. It is obvious that management would like to reduce inventory, since that would free capital to earn additional profit; but this is not always desirable. Often the benefits of a large inventory exceed the costs of carrying it. We need to define the functions of inventory and their benefits.

Transit Inventories. Let us consider a simple production-distribution system with raw materials flowing from the supplier to a manufacturer who processes the materials and sells the finished product to distributors who, in turn, sell to the ultimate consumers:

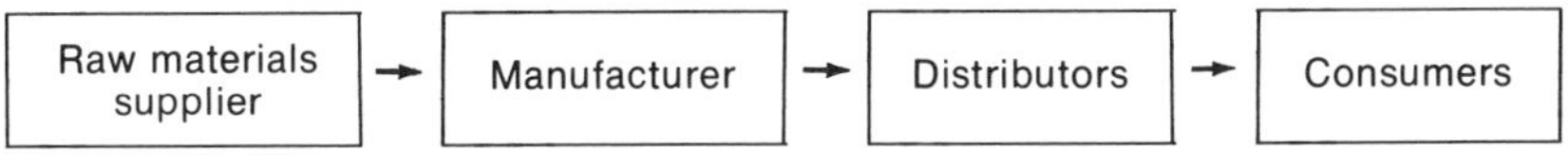

Since it takes time to move goods from one location to the next, inventory in transit needs to be considered. On the average, this transit inventory is equal to $D \times t$, where D is the average rate of demand and t is the shipping time between two points. Thus, if a distributor sells 200 units of a product each week, and the shipping time from the manufacturer to him is a week and a half, the average inventory in transit will be 300 units (= 200 × 1.5).

Although transit inventory is generally thought of as the movement of inventory among firms, it also includes the work in process between the production centers within a firm. Work in process differs from other transit inventories in that it undergoes physical transformation while in transit, and also in that its transit time is determined primarily by the state of manufacturing technology, rather than transportation technology. Within the framework of inventory analysis, however, both the rate of demand and the state of technology (transportation as well as manufacturing) are usually viewed as data beyond the control of the decision-maker. Standard inventory analysis, therefore, is not concerned with optimizing the size of transit inventories: it is assumed that these inventories are already the smallest possible under existing technological conditions.

Decoupling Inventories. Another kind of inventory decouples the successive operations in a firm's production and distribution systems. Such decoupling allows the rates of any two successive operations to diverge from each other without disrupting the functioning of the system, and so permits the firm to take full advantage of possible economies in purchasing, manufacturing, or marketing. Three kinds of decoupling inventories may be distinguished: economic-order quantity (*EOQ*) inventories, safety stocks, and seasonal stocks.

EOQ inventories are maintained whenever a firm finds it economical to buy or make a product in larger quantities than it can use or sell immediately. For example, in a production run, the manufacturer incurs certain costs which are relatively fixed regardless of the number of units produced. These include the costs of preparing the machines, writing production orders, and supervising workers. Similarly, in ordering raw materials from vendors, the manufacturer incurs certain costs (e.g., the costs of making requisitions, checking receipts, and handling payments) which are constant regardless of the size of the order. The same principle holds, of course, when orders for the final product are placed by the distributor. Consequently, by ordering and producing in large (i.e., lot-size) quantities, the fixed costs can be spread over a large number of units, reducing the cost per unit.

Safety stocks would be unnecessary if a firm could predict with certainty the rate of sales of its products. In that case, the firm could wait until existing inventory was reduced to zero before restoring it to the *EOQ* level, although it would still, of course, be necessary to place purchase and production orders in advance to allow for lead time. Since demand is, however, in fact uncertain, the possibility always exists that the actual rate of sales may exceed the predicted rate. In that event, if there were no safety stocks to meet the unexpected demand, customers—whether distributors or ultimate consumers—would have to wait for their orders to be filled, which would lead to ill will and/or lost sales. Moreover, if the inventory is not finished goods but raw materials or work in process, shortages can cause shut-downs, resulting in intermittent production, extra cost of unemployment-insurance compensation, idle time out for core workers, and extra costs for rescheduling when production is resumed. Safety stocks provide security against such a contingency by reducing the portion of the lead-time interval during which the firm is liable to shortages.

Seasonal stocks are maintained primarily to reduce the costs of production. The management of a firm whose rate of demand is seasonal rather than constant may adjust the production rate either to conform strictly to sales or else to follow a reasonably uniform schedule, meeting peak-season sales with inventories accumulated during the off-season months. The latter plan is generally more economical since it stabilizes employment, improves employee morale, and also permits full utilization of the physical plant and equipment.

The Costs of Inventory

Determining the amount of inventory to hold requires a knowledge of the costs as well as the benefits of inventory. The benefits increase at a less-than-proportionate rate as the size of the inventory increases, while the costs tend to increase at a more-than-proportionate rate. The optimal inventory size, then, is that at which the costs of an additional inventory unit are balanced by the corresponding benefits.

Inventory costs arise from the handling, storing, risk-bearing, and financing of inventories. They include the costs of receiving or dispatching materials and products to and from the warehouse; storage expenses such as rent, utilities, insurance, and taxes; the risk of value shrinkage through obsolescence, forced sales, and spoilage; and the cost of capital invested in inventories. In computing financing costs, some firms use the rate of interest as a measure of the cost of capital invested in inventory. This procedure tends to understate the true financing cost, since a firm's borrowing must always be supported by a proportionate amount of equity financing. In fact, inventory investment is not a separate undertaking, but an integral part of a firm's capital expenditure decisions. If a firm uses a certain discount rate in calculating the *NPV* of a capital project, it should use the same discount rate in determining the cost of financing whatever inventory is needed to support the project.

The risk of value shrinkage also deserves special comment. Obsolescence is most probable for stylized merchandise. When fashion changes, any manufacturer or distributor caught with an oversupply of old styles receives a costly lesson in obsolescence. In the toy market, products generally remain in style for only nine to twelve months, and last year's stock can usually be sold only at a substantial discount. Technological innovations may also cause obsolescence. Many electronics firms use the concept of exponential decay to estimate the effect of obsolescence on the value of stored items. But even when obsolescence is not an issue, a firm is always exposed to the risk of forced liquidation if it overestimates the market demand and fails to make prompt adjustments in its purchasing or production schedule. National income statistics reveal that the turning points in aggregate business inventories have generally lagged behind the turning points in gross national product. Furthermore, the inventory adjustments seem to have been sizeable, since liquidations, once initiated, have generally lasted several quarters. Finally, inventory shrinkage may also result from deterioration, breakage, or other physical causes. Of the various costs, value shrinkage is most likely to increase more than proportionately with the size of the inventory.

The Role of Mathematical Models

Inventory management makes heavy use of mathematical modeling, and we should be cognizant of both the usefulness and the limitations of such models. To begin with, since the number of relevant variables is large and their interactions are complex, inventory theorists have been forced to adopt simplifying assumptions, some of which are quite unrealistic. Standard inventory analysis typically assumes, for example, that a firm's annual sales are uniform, without seasonal variations. Such an assumption makes it possible to solve the *EOQ* inventory problem as a relatively simple pure-inventory problem, rather than as a more complex production-scheduling problem; but it detracts from the general applicability of the model.

Moreover, the standard models for optimizing *EOQ* inventories and safety stocks assume that the following factors, or at least their probability distributions, are known: rate of demand, set-up cost, handling and storage costs, cost of capital, procurement lead time, and obsolescence and spoilage costs. The danger is that mathematical modeling may be so appealing that the analyst forgets that the results are derived from assumptions which are themselves an integral part of the inventory-management problem. For caution's sake, several questions should precede any mathematical analysis. Is the forecast of the rate of demand as accurate as possible, and is the forecast being conveyed to the purchasing, production, and sales departments promptly enough for them to minimize unplanned inventory accumulations? Have all possible measures been taken to minimize fluctuations in production and inventory levels by stabilizing the rate of sales, both seasonally and cyclically? Is the product design sufficiently advanced to minimize the risk of obsolescence for stored merchandise, and is there a vigorous policy for disposing of obsolete items so that unavoidable losses may be kept to a minimum? Can the production lead time be reduced, so that the present degree of safety may be attained with a smaller investment in safety stocks? Are the most efficient data-processing methods being used to minimize the costs of handling inventories?

Mathematical models are undeniably important in inventory management. But one must be sure to consider the underlying assumptions of the models so that factors assumed as given are in their most favorable state. With this in mind, we turn to the models for determining the optimal *EOQ* inventory and the optimal safety stocks.

THE OPTIMAL EOQ INVENTORY

The inventory model we shall first discuss is based on the assumptions of infinite shortage costs and infinite production rates. The first assumption means that demand must be met at all times and that no shortages are permitted. The second assumption means that when a production order is placed, the entire quantity is produced instantaneously. These assumptions will be modified later in order to incorporate more realistic conditions.

The concept of *EOQ* inventory is applicable to both the purchase of raw materials and the production of intermediate and finished items. For ease of discussion, however, we shall focus on the finished goods inventory as determined by the optimal size of a production run. Since safety stocks will be considered in the next section, we shall assume conditions of certainty for the present.

The Graphical Approach

Modern Scientific Laboratories (MSL) produces a full line of educational toys, including an electronic device called a "flip-flop," more technically known as a bistable multivibrator, which serves as the basic unit for building a digital computer. Let us suppose that the firm expects a demand for 14,400 flip-flops per year (i.e., 40 units per day) with no seasonal variations, that the set-up cost for each production run is \$125, and that carrying costs (handling, storage, spoilage, and financing) are 40 cents per unit per year. For the present, let us also assume that production lead time is zero, that the production capacity is infinite (i.e., the entire run is delivered into inventory at once), and that no shortages are permitted. If the objective is to minimize cost, how many flip-flops should be produced in each run, how frequent should runs be, and what is the optimal level of inventory?

The optimal size of a production run is determined by balancing two opposing forces: the fixed set-up cost, which favors large runs, and the proportionate inventory-carrying cost, which favors small runs. If the size of each run is R units, then $14{,}400/R$ runs will be needed to satisfy the annual demand for flip-flops. The production cycle t_c (i.e., time between runs) will be $R/40$ days, since the rate of demand is 40 units per day. The inventory level will follow the pattern in Figure 11-1, starting with R units at the beginning of each cycle and declining to zero at the end, implying an average inventory of $R/2$. Table 11-1 shows the total set-up cost ($\$125 \times 14{,}400/R$) and the total carrying cost ($\$0.40 \times R/2$) for producing the annual demand of 14,400 units, using runs of various sizes. Figure 11-2 presents the same

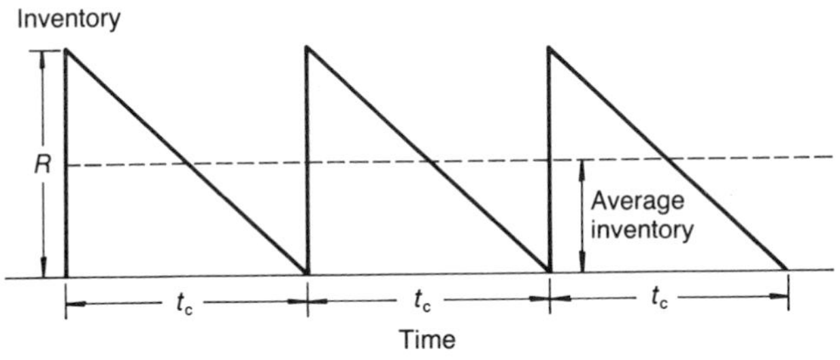

Figure 11-1 Inventory Pattern (Infinite Production Capacity)

Table 11-1 Determining the Optimal Production Run

Size of Run (R)	Annual Set-Up Cost*	Annual Carrying Cost**	Total Cost
1,000	$1,800	$ 200	$2,000
2,000	900	400	1,300
3,000	600	600	1,200
4,000	450	800	1,250
5,000	360	1,000	1,360

* $125 × 14,400/$R$.
** $0.40 × R/2.

data as a graph. As the graph and table show, a run of 3,000 units reduces total inventory cost for the year to a minimum of $1,200, half set-up cost and half carrying cost. Optimally, then, there would be 4.8 (= 14,400/3,000) runs, spaced 75 (= 3,000/40) days apart, and resulting in an average inventory of 1,500 (= 3,000/2) units.

We should be careful to note that the above solution minimizes the total of set-up and carrying costs, rather than the present value of these costs. We have already included the cost of inventory financing among the carrying costs; discounting them would therefore count the cost of financing twice. Hence, our optimal solution is simply to minimize the undiscounted total of the set-up and carrying costs.

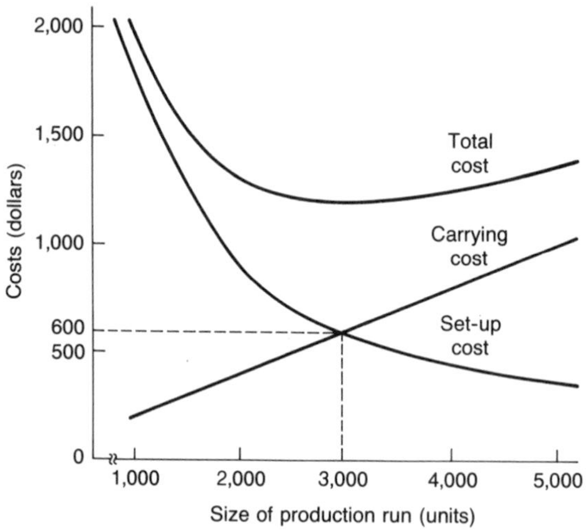

Figure 11-2 Determining the Optimal Production Run

Algebraic Formulation

In order to derive mathematical formulas for quick calculation of the optimal production run and *EOQ* inventory, let us begin with the total-cost (*TC*) function which the firm is trying to minimize:

$$\underset{\text{Total cost}}{TC} = \underset{\text{Set-up cost}}{C_s(D/R)} + \underset{\text{Carrying cost}}{C_1(R/2)} \tag{11-1}$$

where D is the annual demand, R the size of production run, C_s the set-up cost per run, and C_1 the annual carrying cost per unit of inventory. Note that D/R is the number of times set-up costs are incurred and that $R/2$ is the size of the average inventory during the year. The value of R that will minimize TC is obtained by setting the derivative of TC with respect to R equal to zero. This gives us the following formula for optimal production run:

$$R = \sqrt{\frac{2C_sD}{C_1}} \tag{11-2}$$

From formula (11-2), it follows that:

$$\text{Length of one cycle } (t_c) = R \div \frac{D}{360} = 360\sqrt{\frac{2C_s}{C_1D}} \tag{11-3}$$

$$\text{Average } EOQ \text{ inventory } (I_a) = R \div 2 = \sqrt{\frac{C_sD}{2C_1}} \tag{11-4}$$

In our example, $D = 14{,}400$ units per year, $C_s = \$125$, and $C_1 = \$0.40$ per unit per year. Substituting these values gives the following results:

$$\text{Optimal production run } (R) = \sqrt{\frac{2 \times 125 \times 14{,}400}{.4}} = 3{,}000 \text{ units}$$

$$\text{Length of one cycle } (t_c) = 360\sqrt{\frac{2 \times 125}{.4 \times 14{,}400}} = 75 \text{ days}$$

$$\text{Average } EOQ \text{ inventory } (I_a) = \sqrt{\frac{125 \times 14{,}400}{2 \times .4}} = 1{,}500 \text{ units}$$

$$\text{Total cost } (TC) = 125\ (14{,}400/3{,}000) + 0.40\ (3{,}000/2) = \$1{,}200$$

These are the same results obtained graphically.

Eq. (11-4) reveals an important property of optimal inventory: its size varies directly with the square root of demand and inversely with the square root of carrying costs. The presence of the square root in the formula indicates that optimal inventory increases less than proportionately with sales and decreases less than proportionately with carrying costs. Some firms set inventory levels in accordance with a certain number of weeks of expected sales or use. The point just noted suggests that such a procedure would probably be nonoptimal for a firm carrying various items with significantly different sales and cost characteristics.

Minimizing inventory cost is fully consistent with the capital budgeting criterion of maximizing net present value. Let us suppose that a firm must choose between two inventory policies. One policy entails fewer production runs and lower set-up costs but requires a larger investment in inventory. Viewed as a capital budgeting decision, the larger investment can be justified if and only if the savings in set-up costs exceed the extra costs of carrying the larger inventory. Minimizing Eq. (11-1), the cost function, ensures that this requirement is met.

Two Modifications

Finite Shortage Costs. Our analysis assumed that customer demand was to be met at all times, an assumption tantamount to setting the cost of shortages at infinity. Realistically, shortage costs are finite; and a firm may find it sound to be periodically out of stock, since such a policy reduces both the number of production runs and the size of the average inventory. However, the savings in set-up and carrying costs must be weighed against the corresponding shortage costs. Figure 11-3 shows the inventory pattern when production capacity is infinite but shortage costs are finite. During each production cycle t_c, the firm has a positive inventory during the subperiod t_1 and a negative inventory (i.e., a shortage) during the subperiod t_2.

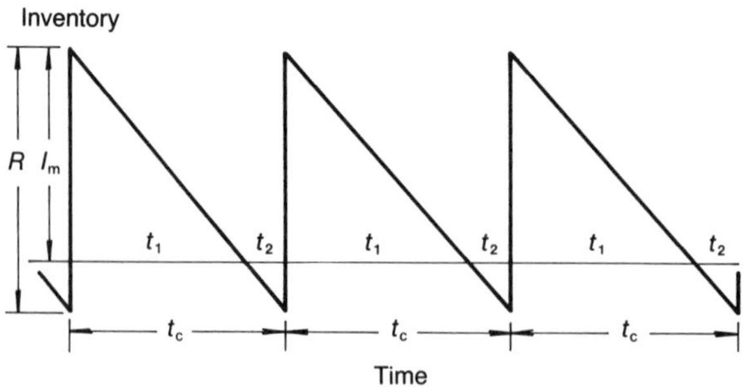

Figure 11-3 Inventory Pattern (Finite Shortage Costs)

The maximum inventory, I_m, reached at the beginning of each cycle, is always smaller than the production run R, since part of each run must be used immediately to meet accumulated back orders.

Our knowledge of the inventory pattern permits us to derive separate formulas for the optimal values of the production run and the maximum inventory. Using standard methods of optimization, we obtain:[3]

$$R = \sqrt{\frac{2C_sD}{C_1}}\sqrt{\frac{C_1 + C_2}{C_2}} \qquad (11\text{-}5)$$

$$I_m = \sqrt{\frac{2C_sD}{C_1}}\sqrt{\frac{C_2}{C_1 + C_2}} \qquad (11\text{-}6)$$

where the new variable C_2 stands for shortage cost. Thus, for MSL, if C_2 is \$0.81 per unit per year, the optimal production run, R, is 3,666.67 units:

$$R = \sqrt{\frac{2 \times 125 \times 14{,}400}{.4}}\sqrt{\frac{.4 + .81}{.81}} = 3{,}666.67 \text{ units}$$

Since the demand is 40 units per day, the implied production cycle, t_c, is 91.66 days:

$$t_c = R \div \frac{D}{360} = 3{,}666.67 \div \frac{14{,}400}{360} = 91.66 \text{ days}$$

Although each run produces 3,666.67 units, the maximum inventory I_m is only 2,454.54 units:

$$I_m = \sqrt{\frac{2 \times 125 \times 14{,}400}{.4}}\sqrt{\frac{.81}{.4 + .81}} = 2{,}454.54 \text{ units}$$

Maximum inventory is smaller than the run size because 1,212.13 units of each production run are used to meet previous demands. This optimal solution implies that the firm sells from inventory during the first 61.36 (= 2,454.54 ÷ 40) days of each cycle and that during the remaining 30.30 (= 1,212.13 ÷ 40) days of the cycle, it is out of stock.

To calculate total cost, we observe that (1) the average inventory during the first subperiod (61.36 days) is equal to half of the value of I_m; i.e., 1,227.27 units per day, and (2) the average shortage during the second subperiod (30.30 days) is equal to half the difference between R and I_m; i.e., 606.06 units per day. Hence, the total cost of this strategy is \$982, calculated as follows:

---

[3] For the derivation of these formulas, see Elwood S. Buffa and William H. Taubert, *Production-Inventory Systems: Planning and Control* (Homewood: Richard D. Irwin, Inc., 1972), pp. 76–78.

$$TC = 125\left(\frac{14{,}400}{3{,}666.67}\right) + 0.4(1{,}227.27)\left(\frac{61.36}{91.66}\right) + 0.8(606.06)\left(\frac{30.30}{91.66}\right) = \$982$$

Total cost Set-up cost Carrying cost Shortage cost

This figure is \$218 or 18 percent less than the \$1,200 figure when no shortages are permitted. This sizeable reduction in total cost can be traced to the drop in both set-up cost and carrying cost.

Finite Production Rate. Our previous analysis still assumed that when a production order is placed, the entire order quantity is delivered into inventory at once. This is the infinite capacity assumption. Actually, however, it takes time to fill production orders, and as a result, the inventory pattern does not follow that depicted in Figure 11-3. We would like to modify the finite shortage cost model to deal with this problem, but such an integration would be overly complex. We can, however, present general observations about the effect of finite production rates on inventory costs and policy.

We assume that the production rate is set by management in order to maximize the efficiency of its facilities. The production rate is thus as high as possible, and this is what led us to assume infinite capacity in the first place. But the production rate is not infinite, and we should ask ourselves what effect this has on the size of the production run. Let us call p the daily production rate, d the daily demand, and R the size of the run. Maximum inventory size, reached at the end of each production run, is then given by the expression $(p - d)R/p$, where $(p - d)$ is the daily addition to inventory, and R/p is the number of days in a production run. The expression can be simplified to $(1 - d/p)R$, and this has several implications. The maximum inventory is smaller if p is finite rather than infinite, as in our previous assumption, and thus both average inventory and carrying costs are also smaller. The smaller carrying costs in turn justify larger (and fewer) runs, which in turn reduce set-up costs to meet a given demand. We can also see the conditions under which the finite production rates affect inventory policy. If p is much greater than d, there is only a small effect, and we can return to the infinite capacity model. As p approaches d, however, the effects on inventory can be sizeable and total costs can be significantly reduced if finite capacity is taken into account.[4]

THE OPTIMAL SAFETY STOCK

The assumption of infinite capacity means that a company can fill any production order with a zero lead time. As we mentioned, this assumption

[4] For a more precise formulation of the effects, see Buffa and Taubert, *op. cit.*, pp. 83–91.

is unrealistic. However, as long as we assume a constant rate of demand, the existence of a positive production lead time does not alter the optimal values of production run, interval between runs, and inventory size; the only difference is that each production run must begin earlier to account for the lead time. But if demand is random, a safety stock is needed to control the risk of stockouts (shortages) during the lead time. Below we shall describe a probabilistic method for determining the optimal level of safety stock.

The ideal safety-stock level is that which minimizes the expected total-inventory cost, including the cost of inventory stockouts. In practice, however, it is difficult to quantify the cost of stockouts; most firms set their safety stocks at a level high enough to ensure that the risk of stockouts during lead time will not exceed a given probability. Assuming that lead time is constant and that demand is the only source of uncertainty, one may proceed as follows:

(1) Specify the probability distribution of demand during the production lead time. Derive the cumulative probability distribution of demand, which will be a curve showing the chances that the demand will exceed any given level.

(2) On this graph of the cumulative distribution, find the total number of units demanded which corresponds to the maximum acceptable risk of stockout. This is called the "reasonable" maximum demand.

(3) The excess of the reasonable maximum over the normally expected demand indicates the desired safety-stock level.

To illustrate this procedure, we shall assume that it takes MSL 7 days to fill a production order, so that it must initiate a new production run whenever the inventory reaches the 7-day level of 280 units. If the demand is a constant 40 units per day, no shortages will occur. However, if the demand is random with an expected value of 40, demand may exceed expectations, resulting in shortages. To control this risk, the firm may wish to maintain a safety stock beyond its normal inventory.

Let us suppose that the frequency distribution in Figure 11-4(a) shows the probability distribution of demand for flip-flops. On this basis, we can construct the cumulative distribution in Figure 11-4(b), which gives the probability that the demand will exceed any indicated level. The probability is 1 that the demand will exceed 10 units per day, .95 that it will exceed 20 units per day, .85 that it will exceed 30 units per day, etc. This cumulative distribution shows that if MSL sets the maximum acceptable risk of stockouts at .05, it must be prepared to meet a demand as high as 50 units per day. In other words, if MSL maintains a "reasonable" maximum stock of 350 units (50×7), the probability of stockouts during its production lead time will be exactly .05. Note that under conditions of certainty, 280 units will normally still be on hand when a new run is initiated. Hence, only 70 units—the difference between the "reasonable" maximum inventory and the normal reorder-point inventory—are being held as safety stock.

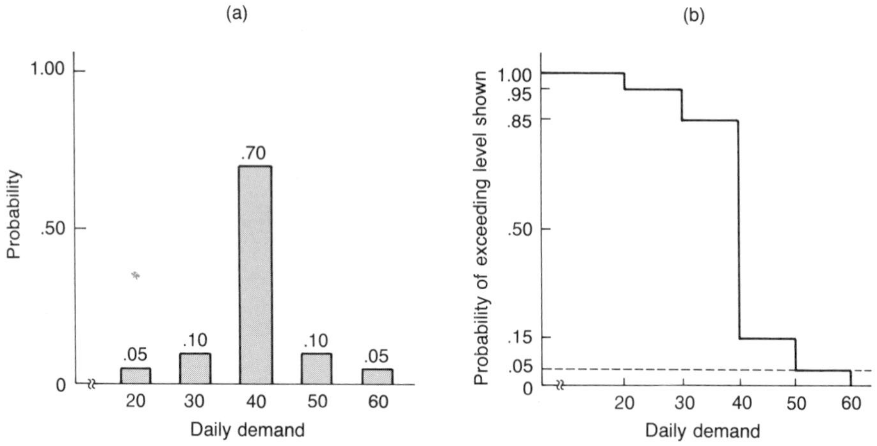

Figure 11-4 Probability Distribution of Daily Demand for Flip-Flops

VALUATION OF INVENTORY

We now turn to the second aspect of inventory management: the method of inventory valuation that minimizes a firm's income-tax liability. While both cash and accounts receivables are by nature monetary claims expressed in unequivocal figures, inventories consist of raw materials, work in process, and finished goods. These are tangible assets which may be weighed, measured, or counted, but their values must be assigned according to some accounting convention. In this section, we shall study the various bases for assigning values to inventory, and their effects on reported income and on the associated income-tax liability.

The Effect on Income Determination

A basic principle in accounting is the matching of expenses and revenues by period. One key expense in any period is the cost of the goods sold in that period. The cost of goods sold equals, by definition, the value of initial inventory and current purchases less the value of final inventory. The method of inventory valuation, therefore, plays a critical role in determining both the cost of goods sold and the firm's taxable income.

In a world of stable prices, inventory valuation and income accounting would be relatively simple. If all units of an item were acquired at a constant unit cost, both the units sold and the units remaining in inventory would be valued at this constant cost and there would be no need to distinguish one unit from another. But with changing prices, units acquired at different times have different costs. In determining the net income of a given period, the accountant can view the units sold as either low-cost units or high-cost units.

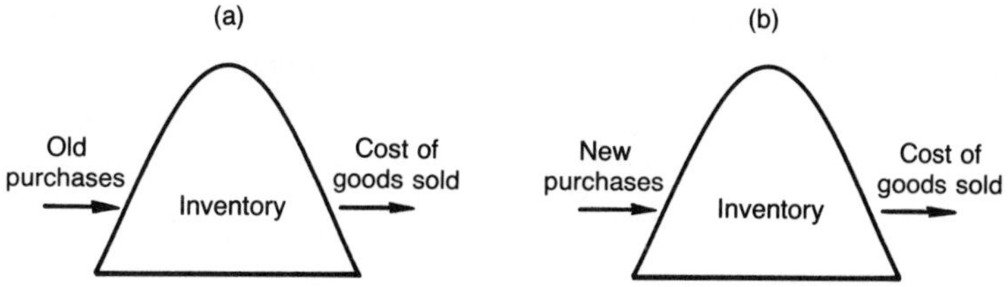

Figure 11-5 Flow of Costs: FIFO vs. LIFO

In a period of rising prices, the former option is associated with the FIFO (first-in, first-out) convention and the latter with the LIFO (last-in, first-out) convention; in a period of falling prices, the converse is true. If a low cost is assigned to the units sold, the effect is an increase in current income-tax liability and in ending-inventory valuation, since the remaining units will be identified as high-cost units. If a high cost is assigned to the units sold, the effect is the reverse. Clearly, the financial executive cannot be neutral toward the two procedures. The relative advantages of each will be clearer if we first compare the mechanics of the two approaches.

FIFO and LIFO Procedures

Under the first-in, first-out method of inventory valuation, the cost of goods sold is computed on the assumption that the goods held longest are sold or consumed first and that the goods remaining in inventory are those most recently purchased or produced. Under the last-in, first-out method, the opposite assumption holds. (See Figure 11-5.)

We can illustrate the difference between these procedures by considering the XYZ Company, which at the beginning of a year held 10,000 units of a certain item, valued at $1.00 per unit. We assume that prices up to that time were stable, so that the $1.00 cost per unit is consistent with either method. During the year, however, prices changed, and the firm purchased 10,000 additional units, half at $1.20 per unit and half at $1.40 per unit—an average cost of $1.30 per unit. Ten thousand units were sold during the year, so that the ending physical inventory was 10,000 units, the same as the initial inventory. We now wish to calculate the cost of the goods sold during the year and the value of the ending inventory.

According to the FIFO procedure, we find that the cost of goods sold was $10,000 and the ending inventory $13,000:

Cost of goods sold:	
10,000 units @ $1.00/unit	$10,000
Ending inventory:	
5,000 units @ $1.20/unit	$ 6,000
5,000 units @ $1.40/unit	7,000
	$13,000

The LIFO method, on the other hand, shows a higher total for the cost of goods sold and a smaller value for the ending inventory:

Cost of goods sold:	
5,000 units @ $1.20/unit	$ 6,000
5,000 units @ $1.40/unit	7,000
	$13,000
Ending inventory:	
10,000 units @ $1.00/unit	$10,000

In this example, the price of the item was assumed to have risen during the year. If the price had fallen, the LIFO approach would have resulted in a lower cost of goods sold and a greater ending inventory than FIFO.

FIFO or LIFO?

Until 1938, LIFO was not a legally accepted method of inventory valuation in determining a firm's net profit for income-tax purposes. Some firms nevertheless adopted this convention for financial reporting in order to produce a more meaningful income statement. In a period of rising prices, FIFO overstates current profitability, since the costs charged against current revenues are the oldest costs, and thus likely to have been incurred when prices were lower. Reported profits therefore represent a combination of profit from current operation and any inventory profit due to inflation. Since the firm must replace inventory at higher prices, the firm's ability to maintain its operation will be impaired to the extent that taxes or dividends are paid from this inventory profit. Similarly, in a period of falling prices, FIFO will understate current profits, but this problem is less serious.

LIFO, on the other hand, since it uses the current cost of goods sold, excludes inventory profit (or loss) from currently reported profit. It avoids both the problem of taxation on profit necessary to rebuild inventory, and the clamor of stockholders for larger dividends out of this same profit. If the accountant wishes to recognize this type of profit or loss, even though it is still unrealized, he may debit (or credit) the inventory account and credit (or debit) an appropriate equity adjustment account. The advantage of this two-step process is that both current profit and ending inventory are calculated on the basis of the most recent cost figures.[5]

In 1938, responding to pressure from business, Congress authorized for the first time the use of LIFO by those industries (e.g., nonferrous and tanning) which normally have large inventory profits or losses. The Revenue Act of 1939 extended this authorization to all taxpayers, provided they

[5] This two-step procedure was recommended by Harold Bierman and Allan Drebin in their *Managerial Accounting* (New York: The Macmillan Company, 1972), pp. 341–347.

comply with certain Treasury regulations. The original 1938 authorization had carried the conformity condition that firms using LIFO for tax purposes must use it also for reports to stockholders. This condition was substantially relaxed in 1939, enabling many firms to adopt LIFO for tax purposes in anticipation of wartime inflation and the resulting appreciation in inventory value. Under FIFO, firms would have had to report this appreciation as current profit and would have been under pressure to use the cash needed to restore physical inventory at the higher prices, for taxes based on the higher reported profit. The LIFO method permitted many companies to avoid this potential cash squeeze. The conformity condition was reimposed in 1975.

The XYZ example cited above shows clearly that in a year of rising prices, LIFO shows a smaller taxable income than FIFO. But are these savings permanent, or will the same method cancel them out in later years? Under certain conditions, LIFO may yield immediate tax savings but over a longer period may result in increased total tax payments. Once LIFO has been adopted for tax purposes, it may be abandoned only with the consent and subject to the stipulations of the Commissioner of the Internal Revenue Service. The choice between LIFO and FIFO must therefore be made with the long-run effect in mind.

A major factor in the permanence of these tax savings is the future course of price movement.[6] If we extend the XYZ example to a second year, we may distinguish three possibilities: the price level in year 2 may (continue to) rise; it may stabilize; or it may fall. Let us suppose first that unit cost increases from $1.30 in year 1 to $1.50 in year 2 and that 10,000 units are purchased at this higher price. During year 2, the firm sells 10,000 units, so the ending and beginning physical inventories are the same. LIFO will indicate that the cost of goods sold in year 2 was $15,000, based on the most recent acquisition cost; this figure is $2,000 higher than the corresponding $13,000 for FIFO (see Table 11-2). In this situation, LIFO will report a smaller taxable income for year 2 than FIFO. But if unit cost falls in year 2, say to $1.10, the relation between the LIFO- and FIFO-figures will be reversed; and LIFO will show the larger taxable income. Finally, let us suppose that unit cost is the same in year 2 as in year 1. In that case, both procedures will show a $13,000 cost of goods sold in year 2, and the method chosen will have no effect on the amount of taxable income.

The analysis in Table 11-2 provides the basis for the following conclusions regarding the permanency of LIFO tax savings. First, in a year of rising prices, LIFO will show a smaller taxable income than FIFO. Second, once the transition to LIFO has been made, future price levels will deter-

[6] The following discussion is based on J. Keith Butters, *The Effects of Taxation on Inventory Accounting and Policies* (Boston: Graduate School of Business Administration, Harvard University, 1949), pp. 70–83; see also William L. Raby, *The Income Tax and Business Decisions* (Englewood Cliffs: Prentice-Hall, Inc., 1972), Ch. 12.

Table 11-2 The Effect of Price Level on Inventory Value and Cost of Goods Sold

A. FIFO

	Year 1		*Year 2*	
	Rising Prices	Rising Prices	Stable Prices	Falling Prices
Ending inventory	$13,000	$15,000	$13,000	$11,000
Cost of goods sold	10,000	13,000	13,000	13,000

B. LIFO

	Year 1		*Year 2*	
	Rising Prices	Rising Prices	Stable Prices	Falling Prices
Ending inventory	$10,000	$10,000	$10,000	$10,000
Cost of goods sold	13,000	15,000	13,000	11,000

mine whether or not LIFO will continue to report a smaller taxable income. LIFO will be more advantageous than FIFO only if prices continue to rise. Third, even if future prices are such that both procedures show the same total taxable income over a period of years, a firm still cannot afford to be neutral toward LIFO and FIFO. To the extent that tax rates are progressive and are higher in years of rising prices, FIFO will result in larger total tax liabilities than LIFO. Finally, if a firm expects substantial inventory liquidation (as opposed to the constant level of inventory that we have been assuming) in a period of rising prices, the LIFO cost of goods sold will be computed on the basis of more distant, lower prices, resulting in considerable taxable income in the years of liquidation. If these years coincide with high tax rates on corporate profits, LIFO would put a firm at a severe disadvantage.[7] The choice of LIFO should therefore include an awareness of the possible cost of liquidating inventories.

REVIEW QUESTIONS

1. The optimal inventory size is that at which the benefits of an additional inventory unit equal the corresponding costs. What are these costs and benefits, and what is the relative significance of each in determining the optimal inventory size?
2. How might the viewpoints of production, sales, and purchasing executives differ from the viewpoint of the financial executive in formulating a firm's

[7] This explains why some companies chose not to adopt LIFO at the beginning of World War II, even though they foresaw a period of rapidly rising prices.

inventory policy? How should the financial executive resolve these differences if and when they arise?

3. One textbook publisher keeps a two-year supply of every text on its active list of publications. For certain lines of business, it is not optimal to follow a uniform policy of setting inventory levels in accordance with a fixed number of weeks of expected sales or use. Is such a policy optimal for the textbook publisher? If so, why?

4. Relative to the basic inventory model summarized in Eq. (11-1) and Eq. (11-2), the assumption of finite shortage costs results in larger optimal runs and smaller total costs. What is the economic explanation for this?

5. In Problem 4 of Chapter 10, you were asked to use a computer program to analyze the effect on Fancycraft's 12-month budget of a change in inventory policy. In general terms, what does the computer output reveal about the effects of that change on the company's cash flows? Make sure you distinguish between the short-run and the long-run effects.

6. One variable in the formula for optimal inventory size is the cost of financing. In applying the formula, would you equate the cost of financing with the firm's borrowing cost, the cost of equity, a weighted average, or something else? Justify your answer.

7. How would the following developments affect the optimal size of a firm's inventory:

   a. Orders are placed with a more distant shipper because of the price discount he offers.

   b. Generally higher prices are expected.

   c. Automatic handling lowers the cost of receiving and inspecting inventory.

   d. Demand for the final product becomes less stable.

   e. The Federal Reserve discount rate is increased sharply.

   Relate your discussion to the formulas developed in this chapter, indicating the variables through which the inventory decision is affected.

8. How might a firm reduce inventory cost by having suppliers carry some of the raw-materials inventory and customers some of the finished-goods inventory? Give examples. What considerations would prevent the company from carrying this approach to the ultimate end of having suppliers and customers carry all of these inventories?

9. How is the permanency of tax savings in the shift from FIFO to LIFO affected by future price movements? future tax rates on corporate profits? future levels of physical inventory?

10. Many firms chose not to adopt LIFO at the beginning of World War II even though they foresaw a period of sharply rising prices. Explain the financial logic behind this decision.

PROBLEMS

1. (a) Moonbeam, Inc., is trying to determine the optimal inventory and optimal production run for its electronic toaster, model K-57. The carrying cost is $1

per unit per year; the firm expects to sell 7,200 units a year (i.e., 20 a day). What figures must the company be using as its set-up cost if it decides on a 1,200-unit optimal production run and a 600-unit optimal average inventory? You may assume that shortage costs and production capacity are both infinite.

(b) Using this set-up cost, employ graphical analysis (cf. Figure 11-2) to show that 1,200 units does minimize the total cost of inventory.

2. (a) What is the total annual inventory cost associated with the optimal production run of 1,200 units in Problem 1? How is this cost divided between set-up costs and carrying costs?

(b) How much would this total cost rise if the firm decided on production runs of 1,000 units? 1,400 units?

3. Rework Problem 1(a) assuming that shortage costs are not infinite, but \$2.25 per unit per year.

4. The New Outlook Press, a publisher of travel books, is ready to print a new travel book about Paris. The company must decide how big the first and subsequent printings should be. They forecast annual sales of 10,800 copies for the first 3 years. Each printing has a set-up cost of \$1,500. The cost of carrying the inventory is estimated at 40 cents per copy per year. Given these data, what is the optimal size of a printing run for this book, assuming conditions of certainty prevail? What must be the ratio between set-up costs and carrying costs to justify a run of 21,600 copies (that is, 2 years' anticipated demand)?

5. Suppose that Educational Instruments, Inc., faces a demand for pocket calculators which is described by the following probability distribution:

Units Demanded	Probability	Units Demanded	Probability
200	.1	700	.025
300	.1	800	.025
400	.6	900	.0125
500	.1	1,000	.00625
600	.025	1,100	.00625

What size inventory should the firm hold if the maximum acceptable risk of stockouts is .05? .025? .0125? What aspect of the probability distribution explains the disproportionate increase in the required size of inventory as the maximum acceptable risk of stockouts decreases?

6. (a) At the beginning of year 1, Eaton's Stores had 10,000 boxes of stationery, valued at \$1.00 per box. During the year, the store purchased 5,000 boxes of stationery at \$1.05 per box, 3,000 boxes at \$0.95, and 2,000 boxes at \$1.05, in that order. The store also sold 8,500 boxes during the year. Use both FIFO and LIFO to determine the cost of goods sold and the value of the ending inventory.

(b) Extend your computation to year 2, during which the firm purchased 7,000 units and sold 10,000. Assume that the acquisition cost in year 2 was \$0.75 per box. Repeat your calculations assuming that the acquisition cost was \$1.50 per box.

REFERENCES

BERANEK, WILLIAM, "Financial Implications of Lot-Size Inventory Models," *Management Science* 13 (April, 1967), pp. 401–408.

BIERMAN, HAROLD, JR., and ALLAN DREBIN, *Managerial Accounting* (New York: The Macmillan Company, 1972), Ch. 15.

BUFFA, ELWOOD S., *Basic Production Management* (New York: John Wiley & Sons, Inc., 1975), Chs. 13 and 14.

BUFFA, ELWOOD S., and W. H. TAUBERT, *Production-Inventory Systems: Planning and Control* (Homewood: Richard D. Irwin, Inc., 1972).

BUTTERS, J. KEITH, *Effects of Taxation on Inventory Accounting and Policies* (Boston: Graduate School of Business Administration, Harvard University, 1949).

FRANCIS, JACK CLARK, "Has the Inventory Cycle Lost Its Oomph?" in Federal Reserve Bank of Philadelphia, *Business Review* (February, 1973), pp. 19–27.

HILLIER, FREDERICK S., and GERALD J. LIEBERMAN, *Operations Research* (San Francisco: Holden-Day, Inc., 1974), Ch. 11.

HOFFMAN, RAYMOND A., and HENRY GUNDERS, *Inventories: Control, Costing, and Effect Upon Income and Taxes* (New York: The Ronald Press Company, 1970).

KNUDSEN, JOHN W., "Inventory Investment—A Volatile Component of GNP," Federal Reserve Bank of Kansas City, *Monthly Review* (February, 1972), pp. 3–10.

MAGEE, JOHN F., and DAVID M. BOODMAN, *Production Planning and Inventory Control* (New York: McGraw-Hill Book Company, 1967).

NILAND, POWELL, *Production Planning, Scheduling, and Inventory Control* (London: The Macmillan Company, 1970).

RABY, WILLIAM L., *The Income Tax and Business Decisions* (Englewood Cliffs: Prentice-Hall, Inc., 1972), Ch. 12.

SCHIFF, MICHAEL, and ZVI LIEBER, "A Model for the Integration of Credit and Inventory Management," *Journal of Finance* 29 (March, 1974), pp. 133–140.

SHORE, BARRY, *Operations Management* (New York: McGraw-Hill Book Company, 1973), Ch. 14.

TRIPPI, ROBERT R., and DONALD E. LEWIN, "A Present Value Formulation of the Classical EOQ Problem," *Decision Sciences* 5 (January, 1974), pp. 30–35.

U.S. Department of Treasury, Internal Revenue Service, *Statistics of Income—Corporation Income Tax Returns* (Washington, D.C.: U.S. Government Printing Office, annual).

12 Management of Accounts Receivable

The accounts receivable of a firm indicate the amount of credit extended to other firms when goods and services are sold. In general, accounts receivable take the form of open accounts, in which the selling firm simply records the amount of credit sales in an accounting entry, without requiring written evidence of obligation from the purchasing firm. On the books of the firms receiving credit, the amounts owed appear as accounts payable. The use of accounts payable as a source of financing will be considered in Chapter 21; for the present, we are concerned only with the management of accounts receivable, from the viewpoint of the credit-granting firm.

The investment in accounts receivable for all nonfinancial corporations is now 1.5 times the investment in inventories.[1] Until 1953, inventories had consistently exceeded accounts receivable; but the higher growth rates since then have caused accounts receivable to soar 50 percent over inventories. This growth, which shows no sign of abating, combined with the relative lack of intensive study by financial theorists, makes accounts-receivable management a rich area for improvement.

THE PROBLEM OF ACCOUNTS-RECEIVABLE MANAGEMENT

If a firm could achieve a given sales volume without extending credit, it would naturally prefer to do so. With all sales in cash, the company could

[1] The 1.5 ratio is based on the pre-1972 SEC working capital series, which has since been replaced. The new data, however, indicate that accounts receivable and inventories have been increasing at about the same rate since 1972; thus, if the old series were extended, the 1.5 ratio would still be valid.

eliminate not only its investment in accounts receivable, but also any related costs of credit administration (e.g., costs of credit analysis, record keeping, collection, and bad-debt losses). As a rule, however, sales volume tends to vary inversely with the ease with which the firm's credit is extended. A stringent credit policy will reduce investments in accounts receivable and related costs, but it may also reduce sales and net profit. On the other hand, too liberal a credit policy may lead to an excessive increase in receivables investment and administrative costs and may thus depress profits even though stimulating sales. In formulating a credit policy, the financial executive must consider financial as well as marketing implications. The optimal policy maximizes the firm's expected profit, subject to the condition that the risk of bad debt does not exceed some maximum acceptable level.

Although the financial executive is concerned with the firm's investments in both inventories and accounts receivable, his control over accounts receivable is less direct. After *EOQ* inventory and safety stock are calculated, a firm can use its production policy to adjust inventory directly to conform to an optimal level. In accounts-receivable management, the firm can establish a general framework for its credit operation, but it cannot force its customers to pay cash if they prefer credit—or on credit if they prefer cash. Control, therefore, is only indirect: a firm regulates the amount and quality of its accounts receivables by altering the terms of sales, the standards for approving credit, and the collection policy for delinquent accounts. Decisions affecting these three variables constitute the central aspects of accounts-receivable management.

Two additional comments are needed to place our analysis in the proper perspective. First, this chapter deals primarily with the profit implications of alternative policies. These policies, like inventory policies, have important effects on the size and timing of a firm's cash flows. We have already studied liquidity implications in Chapter 10, and we shall assume here that a firm will consider only those alternatives which avoid an unacceptable liquidity position.

Second, a firm may avoid accounts-receivable management altogether by turning over credit analysis and collection to a factoring company, which in effect becomes the firm's hired credit-management department. Factors actually have a broader function since, like finance companies and banks, they also engage in the financing of receivables. Factoring of receivables will be discussed in Chapter 21 when we take up methods of short-term financing.

THE OPTIMAL TERMS OF SALES

In finance literature, the expression "terms of sales" refers only to the terms of payment. In this section, we shall see how financial analysis can optimize the terms by which a firm sells its product on credit.

Standard Terms of Sales

The terms of sales include three decision variables: the cash discount d, the discount period t, and the (total) credit period T. The cash discount specifies the amount (usually expressed as a percentage of sales) that the customer may deduct from his invoice if he pays on or before the end of the discount period. The credit period is the time up to the date on which an outstanding account becomes delinquent. The total credit period is usually longer than the discount period; in other words, a customer who is willing to forfeit the discount may take longer to pay his bill. If a firm sells its goods on terms of "2/10, net 30," the buyer is given a 2 percent discount if he pays within 10 days of the invoice date; or he may pay the net amount within 30 days. Since this discount is equivalent to an annual interest rate of $2\% \times {}^{365}/_{20}$, or 36.5 percent, foregoing the discount is in effect very costly.

The discount period, if there is one, is usually 10 days; but, depending on the industry, the discount may vary from 1/2 to 10 percent, and the credit period may vary from 30 to 90 days. Theodore N. Beckman and Ronald S. Foster, in a comprehensive study, list the customary terms of sales for a selected sampling of industries:[2]

Boxes	1/10, net 30	Lard	2/10, net 60
Candy (bulk)	2/10, net 60	Preserves	2/10, net 30
Gray goods	3/10, net 60	Tin plates	2/10, net 30
Hats (Panama)	2/10, net 30	Varnishes	1/10, net 30

Although there is great diversity in the terms of sales from industry to industry, the authors found considerable uniformity within a given industry and from year to year.

What we have been discussing is often called "ordinary terms of sales," since they do not incorporate special features such as extra terms or seasonal dating. The term "7/10, 60 extra," for example, granted by the manufacturer of worsted fabrics, means that 7 percent may be deducted from the bill if payment is made within 70 days (the 10-day discount period plus 60 extra days) of the invoice date. In effect, then, "7/10, 60 extra" is equivalent to "7/70, net 70."

Industries whose sales show pronounced seasonal patterns often use seasonal dating. A manufacturer who wishes to stabilize production without carrying a finished-goods inventory during the off season may stimulate off-season sales to wholesalers by extending the credit period so that it coincides with the season of peak retail demand. The advantage of this system to the wholesaler is that his supply is assured at a known price. The advantages to the manufacturer are that he can reduce both storage and production costs, and also gauge demand more accurately. The effect of

[2] Theodore N. Beckman and Ronald S. Foster, *Credits and Collections* (New York: McGraw-Hill Book Company, 1969), pp. 697–704.

seasonal dating, like that of extra terms, is to lengthen the credit period, which has the disadvantage of increasing financing costs.

Optimizing the Terms of Sales

Many firms set terms of sales merely on industry practice or historical evolution, ignoring the opportunity of using these terms to influence their investment in accounts receivable and the volume of sales and profits. In this section, we shall present a simple model for choosing between two alternative sets of terms, viewing the terms as an integral part of the firm's pricing policy.

Effective Price. A firm may sell its product either for cash or on credit; if on credit, either with or without a cash discount. Selling on credit, especially with a cash discount, is equivalent to reducing the cash price. The effect of this reduction on the physical quantity of the product demanded depends partly on the size of the reduction and partly on the elasticity of the demand.

What is the effective price to a purchaser when goods are offered on terms of "2/10, net 30"? If each unit of the product is priced at $1.00, then the customer must pay 98 cents in cash per unit within 10 days from the invoice date, assuming he takes advantage of the discount. If money carries an annual return of 12 percent for the customer, the 10 days of free credit have an implicit value of about 1/3¢ (= 98¢ × .12 × 10/365) per unit. Subtracting this implicit value from 98 cents gives an effective price of 97.68 cents, which is equivalent to a 3.3 percent reduction in cash price. In general, the effective price is given by the formula:

$$P - Pd - P(1-d)\frac{kt}{365} \qquad (12\text{-}1)$$

where P represents the invoice price, d the cash discount, t the discount period, and k the value of money to the customers. That is, the effective price to the customers equals the invoice price minus cash discount minus the value of free credit during the discount period.

Our definition assumes that all customers take the cash discount. This is generally true, since the cost of trade credit is so high that few firms will find its use financially justifiable. There are, of course, some companies that have weak financial positions and such limited access to the capital market that they are unable to take advantage of cash discounts. But these few firms present such a high default risk that many companies prefer not to sell to them at all. Consequently, the optimal solution based on an analysis of discounting customers is not likely to differ much from that based on an analysis of all customers. Considering only discounting customers, then, simplifies the analysis without substantially affecting the results.

Financial Analysis. The return on investment (*ROI*) provides a convenient guide in choosing between competing terms of sales. Let us say that a firm is selling its products on the terms of Policy X but is considering changing to Policy Y. The *ROI* analysis requires two items as data input: the change in accounts-receivable investment attributable to the policy shift, and the resulting change in net income under the new policy. The *ROI* itself is the ratio of the increment (decrement) in net income to the corresponding increment (decrement) in accounts-receivable investment. Whether or not a policy shift is profitable depends, therefore, on whether the *ROI* is greater or less than the opportunity cost of capital to the firm.

The change in accounts-receivable investment is determined jointly by the receivables turnover rate and the change in sales. The change in company's net income is determined jointly by the firm's cost structure and the change in sales. To illustrate the calculation, let us suppose that current Policy X has terms of "2/10, net 30" and contemplated Policy Y has terms of "3/10, net 30." The company currently sells 50,000 units annually at $10 per unit. The elasticity of demand is estimated at 3.0, meaning that a 1 percent change in (effective) price would cause a 3 percent corresponding change in the number of units sold. Bad debt losses equal 2 percent of sales; selling and administrative expenses come to 25 percent of sales; and production costs[3] total 35 percent of sales. Sales here mean sales before the cash discount. Net income is taxed at a rate of 50 percent. If the cost of capital to both the firm and its customers is 15 percent, which sales terms are more profitable?

Table 12-1 presents the data for choosing between policies. Applying formula (12-1), we find that shifting from Policy X to Policy Y lowers the effective price to the customers from $9.76 to $9.66 per unit, a reduction of about 1 percent (line 2). Since demand elasticity is 3.0, this price reduction may be expected to increase annual demand from 500,000 units to 515,000 units. The policy shift also reduces the sales proceeds to the company from $9.80 to $9.70 per unit, but gross sales may be expected to increase from $4,900,000 to $4,995,500. Subtracting 2 percent for bad debt losses, we arrive at a corresponding increase in net sales from $4,800,000 to $4,982,500 (line 7). From the net sales receipts, the firm must pay selling and administrative expenses, production costs, and income taxes. Subtracting these expenses gives net incomes of $900,000 and $901,250 for Policies X and Y, respectively (line 12). Thus, the new sales terms are expected to increase net income by $1,250.

Both policies offer cash discounts attractive enough to induce all customers to pay by the end of the 10-day discount period. This means that the firm's accounts receivable will equal, on the average, 1/36 of annual

[3] Production cost will be interpreted broadly here to include the cost of carrying any additional inventory caused by the increase in sales.

Table 12-1 Choosing Between Two Sets of Terms of Sales

Line		Policy X	Policy Y
1	Full price	$ 10.00	$ 10.00
2	Effective price to customers	9.76	9.66
3	Proceeds to company	9.80	9.70
4	Annual demand (units)	500,000	515,000
5	Gross sales receipts	4,900,000	4,995,500
6	Bad debt losses	100,000	103,000
7	Net sales receipts	4,800,000	4,892,500
8	Selling and administrative expenses	1,250,000	1,287,500
9	Production costs	1,750,000	1,802,500
10	Income before taxes	1,800,000	1,802,500
11	Income taxes	900,000	901,250
12	Net income	900,000	901,250

sales. Thus, to finance the credit sales under Policy Y, the firm would have to increase its investment in receivables by about $2,650 (= [$4,995,500 − $4,900,000] ÷ 36). The annual required return on this additional investment is 15 percent, or $398:

$$\text{Required Return} = \$2{,}650 \times .15 = \$398$$

Since this required return is only one third the anticipated profit increment of $1,250, Policy Y is clearly the more profitable.

To clarify the connection between *ROI* analysis and discounted cash flow, let us note that the shift from Policy X to Policy Y entails an initial investment of $2,650 in accounts receivable and a subsequent permanent increase in annual net income (and hence cash inflows) of $1,250. Since the cost of capital is 15 percent, or $398, we see that the policy shift, viewed as an investment, has a positive net present value. We note also that the analysis assumes that there is no increase in the firm's physical plant and equipment since an increase would involve a major decision in its own right and should not be considered merely as a by-product of accounts-receivable policy.

The conditions under which Policy Y has been shown to be superior should be kept in mind. Any change in the elasticity of demand or in the bad-debt ratio could alter the relative attractiveness of the policies. Moreover, the analysis establishes only the superiority of Policy Y over Policy X. To seek out the optimal credit policy, we could, as in the inventory model, set up an objective function expressing company profit as a function of credit terms, taking into account their effects on effective price, units demanded, and costs, and use calculus to determine which credit policy maximizes net profit. But in practice, because of tradition or competitive pressure, a company is not likely to consider more than a limited number of alternatives. Thus, the simpler procedure we have outlined is adequate for almost all cases.

EVALUATION OF CREDIT RISK

Any firm would refuse credit to a customer if it knew at the time of the sale that the customer would later default. But in reality, the firm cannot always be certain that it will be able to collect. The credit manager must decide whether or not to grant credit by balancing the potential loss if the customer defaults against the potential profit if he pays, according to the probability that each situation will materialize. The purpose of all credit analyses is to determine the values of these probabilities.

Information for Credit Decisions

In any information processing, the quality of the output depends on the quality of the information used as input. To assess credit risk accurately, the credit manager must know what information to look for and where. For most customers, much of the needed information will already have been compiled by one of the several mercantile credit agencies. But even when this information can be purchased, the credit manager will be able to make better use of it if he understands why the data are significant and how they were collected.[4]

Who Is the Borrower? When a firm sells on credit, the credit manager wants to know any historical information that might shed light on the customer's credit rating. When Mr. Endicott, a wholesale distributor of prescription drugs, sends in an order, the drug manufacturer's credit manager wants to know several things. How long has Endicott been operating his present business? If his previous experience was primarily in sales, does he also know how to buy and finance? What does the record show about his past payment habits? And have there been any suits or litigations which might give a clue to his moral character?

How Does His Business Operate? Whether the customer is a wholesaler, retailer, or manufacturer, the credit manager will want to know what product(s) he sells and the distribution of sales if there is more than one product. He also wants to know what territory and class of trade the customer caters to; what terms of sales he offers; and his inventory policy. Does

[4] The following discussion is based on Dun and Bradstreet, Inc., *Ten Keys to Basic Credits and Collections* (1973).

he maintain a wider selection of products and a larger safety stock than his competitors? Since the nature of a business and its method of operation have a direct impact on financial figures, an understanding of these factors will enable the credit manager to interpret the customer's financial statements in a meaningful way.

How Are His Finances? If a customer has adequate liquidity, he will be able to pay his bills promptly. Chapter 10 showed how cash budgeting could be used to forecast a firm's ability to meet maturing obligations. Ideally, the same type of cash-flow information should be the basis for assessing the customer's ability to pay, but the credit manager usually has access only to the customer's balance sheet and income statement. The credit manager may proceed simply by starting with the customer's monthly sales and deducting the operating expenses (rent, utilities, salaries, taxes, etc.), which shows him the amount available for paying creditors. The relationship between this residual amount and the customer's debt determines his ability to pay his bills promptly. The meaning of financial statistics may also be brought out through ratio analysis, which has already been discussed in Chapter 3.

Credit Ratings by Mercantile Agencies

A number of mercantile agencies specialize in collecting credit information on business units. Dun and Bradstreet, Inc., is perhaps the best known and most comprehensive of these agencies. Dun and Bradstreet subscribers receive a Reference Book, revised six times a year, containing listings for nearly three million businesses in the United States and Canada. Each listing gives the firm's name, standard industrial classification, line of business, starting date, and—most important—the Dun-and-Bradstreet rating based on the credit information collected by the agency.

Dun-and-Bradstreet ratings consist of a combination of numerals and letters (e.g., 3A1, EE2, FF#). As explained in the Reference Book, each rating indicates the subject firm's net worth as well as a composite appraisal based on factors such as integrity, experience, financial condition, and payment record. In addition to the Reference Book, Dun and Bradstreet sells more detailed credit reports on individual companies. Credit ratings, though generally reliable, are not infallible. The Baptist Foundation of America, for example, was rated early in the 1970's as having $20 million in assets, when actually it had assets of only $15,000 and liabilities in the millions.[5] With its rating, the Foundation was able to continue borrowing from investors who later regretted their investments.

---

[5] Based on hearings before the Select Committee on Crime, House of Representatives, 92nd Congress.

An L. D. Model of Credit Evaluation

Credit rating is essentially a subjective method of estimating the probability that a customer will default. But we can make the process more objective by using a linear-discriminant model for our forecasts.[6]

The Model. Linear-discriminant analysis is a statistical technique for classifying the members of a population according to their characteristics. In accounts-receivable management, a firm must classify credit applicants according to the likelihood of default. Assuming that there are significant differences between the characteristics of good and bad risks, we use linear-discriminant analysis to identify these characteristics and to determine the relative weight of each characteristic as it contributes to the probability of default. Once a numerical weighting system is devised, the score of a prospective customer enables the credit manager to assign a probability to the risk of default.

Central to the model is the idea that a firm's credit score may be expressed mathematically as a function of a set of distinguishing characteristics:

$$S = a + b_1X_1 + b_2X_2 + \cdots + b_nX_n \qquad (12\text{-}2)$$

The value of S, the credit score, varies between 0 (bad risk) and 1 (good risk). $X_1, X_2, \ldots, X_n$ are the characteristics (e.g., total capital, debt-equity ratio, past payment record) that determine a firm's credit score; and $b_1, b_2, \ldots, b_n$ are constant coefficients that indicate the relative weight of each characteristic in the scoring process. The presence of constant a implies that the linear relationship is a general one—i.e., not a special one that forces a to equal zero.

The credit manager begins by classifying a representative sample of his customers as good or bad risks, depending on their actual payment records during a given time period. The good risks are assigned S values of 1 and the bad risks S values of 0. If the credit manager has kept a record of the relevant characteristics for each customer in his sample, he can assign each a set of n values describing the credit profile in terms of the n variables $X_1, X_2, \ldots, X_n$. By regressing the X's on S, he can determine the values of the constants $a, b_1, b_2, \ldots, b_n$ that will make Eq. (12-2) agree as closely as possible with the statistical data. Once the values of the constants are

[6] A number of writers have suggested the use of a linear-discriminant model for credit analysis. See, for example: David C. Ewert, "Trade Credit Management: Selection of Accounts Receivable Using a Statistical Model," Paper No. 236 issued by the Institute for Research in the Behavioral, Economic, and Management Sciences at Purdue University, March, 1969; and C. D. Batt and Terrence R. Fowkes, "The Development and Use of Credit Scoring Schemes," in Samuel Eilon and Terrence R. Fowkes, eds., *Applications of Management Science in Banking and Finance* (Epping, Essex: Gower Press, 1972), Ch. 13.

known, Eq. (12-2) can be used to forecast credit risk. When a prospective customer applies for credit, his X values are combined with the values of the constants in accordance with Eq. (12-2) to give a point score, which will enable the credit manager to determine the probability of default.

A Case Study. In a research paper, David C. Ewert reports an interesting application of this model.[7] Ewert studied a sample of 507 customers from the credit files of a manufacturer; 298 were good risks, 209 bad. The total was divided into two subgroups: a working sample of 307 (198 good risks and 109 bad) to estimate the forecasting equation, and a holdout sample of 200 to test the validity of the equation.

After experimenting with numerous characteristics, Ewert decided on two models, one with nine variables, one with seventeen. The nine variables of the simpler model are all available from the Dun and Bradstreet report, and Ewert found that this simpler model is almost as predictive as the more complex one. Table 12-2 gives a summary of the nine variables, together with the regression coefficients and t-values associated with the model. With two exceptions, these variables all come from the firm's suppliers and indicate how long and on what terms the supplier has sold the account, how the

Table 12-2 A Linear Discriminant Analysis of Accounts Receivable

Variable	Coefficient	t-Value
Intercept term	.4498	–
Percentage of suppliers reporting slow payments	–.4023	–7.0
Percentage of suppliers reporting COD terms	–.5047	–4.5
Percentage of suppliers reporting accounts in for collection	–.5229	–6.8
Percentage of suppliers reporting credit refused	–.8617	–5.0
Percentage of suppliers reporting selling account three years or more	.2086	5.3
Highest amount of credit granted ($9,000 ceiling)	.002	5.3
Past due amount owed suppliers ($2,000 ceiling)	–.0102	–4.7
Composite credit rating given by Dun & Bradstreet*	.2956	7.6
Appearance of physical premise*	.1321	4.1

* Yes = 1; No = 0.
Source: Ewert, *op. cit.*, p. 14.

[7] The following discussion is based on the paper by Ewert cited above.

debts have been paid, how much credit has been extended, and how much is overdue. In other words, a customer's past payment record is the best index to future credit worthiness. Ewert also showed that financial ratios contribute little to an enlarged model's predictive power, and so omitted them. The advantage of his simple model to the credit manager should be obvious. He has a quick and external source by which he can make credit decisions.

When Ewert applied his model to the control sample, the comparison of score distributions in the two groups provided a measure of the model's predictive accuracy. Table 12–3 shows the cumulative frequency distributions for good-risk and bad-risk firms receiving a given score or lower. Only 5 percent of the good risks scored .298 or lower, compared with 49 percent of the bad risks; only 1 percent of the bad risks scored .763 or higher, compared with 51 percent of the good risks. These results indicate that the model can discriminate effectively between good and bad risks.

What does any given credit score reveal about the probability that a firm will default? We can illustrate this by Figure 12-1. The circle represents the entire body of prospective customers. Prior to any analysis, the credit manager estimates that a certain percentage of the customers will be good risks, a certain percentage bad. The horizontal line represents this division between good and bad risks. The shaded areas represent those customers who score a given value or less. Let us assume that we have a customer who scores this value. He can either be a good risk, or a bad risk: if a good risk, he falls into area A_1; if a bad risk, in area A_2. We can easily see that the probability he will be a good risk, given that score, is the ratio of area A_1 to the total shaded areas, $A_1 + A_2$. Conversely, the risk of default is the ratio of area A_2 to this combined shaded area, or $A_2/(A_1 + A_2)$.

Table 12-3 Cumulative Frequency of Firms Receiving a Given Score or Lower

Credit Score	Good-Risk Firms	Bad-Risk Firms
.208	0%	35%
.226	2	36
.298	5	49
.356	6	58
.543	16	76
.577	17	82
.596	20	85
.699	34	97
.763	49	99
.898	75	100

Source: Ewert, *op. cit.*, p. 17.

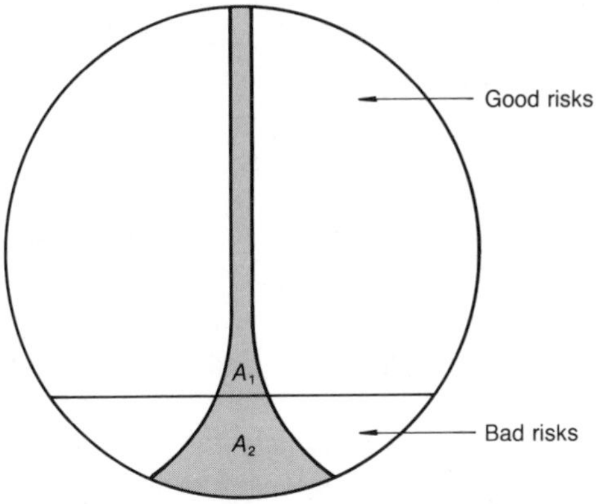

Figure 12-1 Deriving Probability of Default from Credit Scores

We should note that areas A_1 and A_2 are also probabilities. Expressed as percentages of the total circle, A_1 and A_2 are the respective probabilities that a good risk and a bad risk will receive a given score or less, when each customer is viewed as a member of the total clientele. Suppose that a given firm knows from past experience alone that 90 percent of its customers will be good risks and 10 percent will be bad. Suppose also a prospective customer receives a credit score of .226. What inference does this score have for our given firm? If we look at Table 12-3, we see that the probability a good risk will score .226 or less is .02. Therefore, $A_1 = .9 \times .02 = .018$; and similarly, $A_2 = .1 \times .36 = .036$. Substituting these values into the formula $A_2/(A_1 + A_2)$, we conclude that there is a .67 (= .036/.054) probability that a prospective customer scoring .226 or less will default. This figure enables the credit manager to distinguish more easily and more sharply between good and bad risks.

A CRITERION FOR GRANTING OR REFUSING CREDIT

Once the credit manager has arrived at a probability of default for each prospective customer, he must decide which customers are to be accepted and which rejected. This section considers a criterion of acceptance designed to maximize the firm's expected profit, subject to a risk constraint.

A Risk-Return Criterion

Let us begin by considering a company whose clientele consists of a large number of relatively small firms. We shall modify our previous method of calculating net profit in one way: unlike Table 12-1, where bad-debt losses were taken as a constant, we now shall assume only a probabilistic knowledge. We now express π_j, the profit associated with customer *j*, as:

$$(\pi_j) = s_j - cs_j - B_j \tag{12-3}$$

where s_j is the sales to customer *j*, B_j is bad-debt losses, and c is the ratio of incremental costs to incremental sales. (Incremental costs include production costs, selling and administration costs, income tax, *and* required return on invested capital.) Whereas s_j and c are constants, B_j is a random variable.

The probability that *j* will default is p_j. B_j equals s_j (total sales, which we can also call a total loss) with probability p_j and 0 (no loss) with probability $1 - p_j$, giving B_j an expected value of $p_j s_j$. The expected profit from selling to customer *j* is therefore:

$$E(\pi_j) = (1 - c)s_j - p_j s_j \tag{12-4}$$

Since all the customers are roughly the same size, it is most convenient to consider expected profit per dollar of sales. Dividing (12-4) by s_j, the sales to *j*, we get:

$$\frac{E(\pi_j)}{s_j} = (1 - c) - p_j \tag{12-5}$$

That is, the expected profit per dollar of sales to *j* is equal to the gross margin $(1 - c)$ less *j*'s probability of default. Thus, for the company in Table 12-4, with a gross margin of 40 percent, selling to a customer with a 15 percent chance of default yields an expected profit of 25 cents for every dollar of sales.

Moreover, we define the risk of selling to customer *j* as the expected bad debt. Expected bad-debt loss is $p_j s_j$, so risk per dollar of sales is simply p_j. In other words, the risk per dollar of sales equals the probability of default and is independent of the gross profit margin. Selling to a customer with a 15 percent chance of default therefore exposes a firm to an expected bad-debt loss of 15 cents on every dollar of sales.

Once the firm has calculated the expected profit and risk for each customer, the customers are ranked according to risk of default, starting with the lowest risk. The larger the risk, the smaller the expected profit; consequently, ranking risk in ascending order is equivalent to ranking expected profit in descending order. The customers highest on the list promise both more profit and less risk. The problem of criterion, then, is simply to determine how far down this list the firm may profitably sell on credit. The credit manager needs a cutoff point for dividing the list into customers to whom the firm will sell on credit and those to whom it will sell only for cash.

The criterion we recommend is the maximization of the firm's total expected profit, subject to the constraint that total expected bad-debt losses do not exceed some specified percentage of sales. In setting the cutoff point, the firm will naturally be influenced by the size of its gross margin of profit, since the expected profit from selling to a given customer varies directly with the profit margin. A customer who is not an acceptable risk to a firm with a low profit margin may be an acceptable risk to a firm with a higher profit margin.

Our risk-return criterion is not identical with the simple maximization of a firm's total expected profit. Under the latter criterion, every customer is an acceptable risk as long as there is some expected profit from selling to him. Under our criterion, however, even a customer with a positive expected profit may be rejected if his probability of default is such that selling to him causes the firm to violate its risk constraint. Because the constraint on expected bad debt takes precedence over the simple maximization of expected profit, adherence to the risk-return criterion may force expected profit below its unconstrained maximum.

We must also consider how well expected bad debt losses, our risk measure, predict actual bad-debt losses. The prediction will be reasonably accurate if the number of customers is large, individual purchases are small, and sales are broadly distributed among a wide range of customers so that their bad-debt losses are not highly correlated. One could, of course, make an even more accurate prediction by taking into account both the expected value and the variance of bad-debt losses; but this would involve more computation and would also necessitate data on the variances and covariances of the customers' default risks. A single measure of risk makes the procedure simpler and is sufficiently accurate for the fairly common situation described.

A Numerical Example

Table 12-4 shows the items to be calculated before the risk-return criterion can be applied. The firm is assumed to have 100 prospective customers, each wanting to buy $100 worth of goods on credit. These customers have been grouped into 10 risk classes (Column 1) according to their probabilities of default; Class I is the least risky. Column 2 shows the dollar sales volume for each class, found by multiplying the number of customers in each class by $100. The probabilities of default appear in Column 3; the same figures indicate the expected bad-debt losses for each dollar of sales to the customers in that class. Column 4 gives the expected profits per dollar of sales, which is the gross profit margin (40 percent) less the expected

Table 12-4 The Effect of Credit Sales on Expected Profit and Bad-Debt Losses

Risk Class (1)	Sales (2)	Default Probability (3)	Expected Profit per Dollar of Sales (4)	Cumulative Expected Profit (5)	Cumulative Expected Bad-Debt Losses: Amount (6)	Cumulative Expected Bad-Debt Losses: % of Sales (7)
I	$1,000	.001	.399	$ 399	$ 1	.10%
II	4,000	.005	.395	1,979	21	.42
III	3,000	.010	.390	3,149	51	.64
IV	1,000	.015	.385	3,534	66	.73
V	300	.050	.350	3,639	81	.87
VI	200	.100	.300	3,699	101	1.06
VII	200	.200	.200	3,739	141	1.45
VIII	100	.350	.050	3,744	176	1.80
IX	100	.450	−.050	3,739	221	2.23
X	100	.500	−.100	3,729	271	2.71

bad-debt loss. For each class, we now multiply sales (Col. 2) by expected profit per dollar (Col. 4), which gives us the total expected profit for the class: e.g., $399 for Class I, $1,580 for Class II, $1,170 for Class III, etc. Column 5 gives the successive cumulative sum of these profits. Similarly, multiplying sales by the expected bad debt per dollar of sales gives the total expected bad debt for each class. The successive cumulative sums of these losses are given in Column 6 and are presented as a percentage of the corresponding sales in Column 7.

To implement the risk-return criterion, we first graph the data given in Columns 5 and 7. Figure 12-2 shows that as a firm sells to increasingly risky

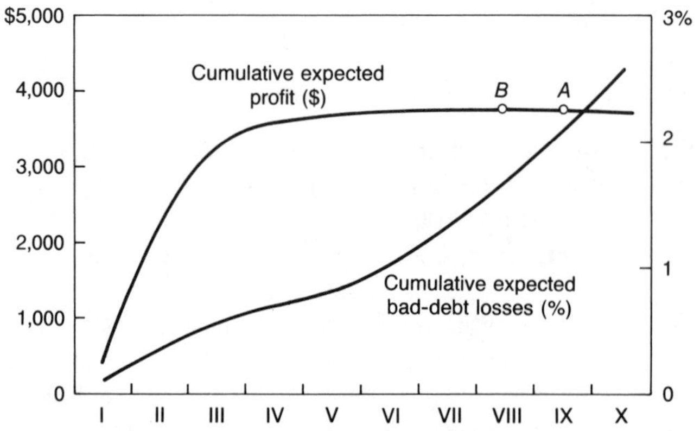

Figure 12-2 Determining the Optimal Credit Policy

customers, the cumulative expected profit first increases, then decreases; but the cumulative expected credit loss increases continuously as a percentage of sales. Let us suppose that a firm's policy is to maximize expected profit subject to the constraint that expected bad debts do not exceed 2.5 percent of sales. The risk constraint would permit the firm to sell to all customers in Classes I through IX, but the profit-maximization objective excludes Class IX, since the marginal contribution of that class to expected profit is negative. By limiting sales to Classes I through VIII, the firm not only reduces its expected bad-debt ratio, but also increases its expected profit to $3,744, the maximum attainable, represented on the graph by Point *A*. In this case, the optimal solution is the same as it would have been without a risk constraint; but that is not always true. If, for example, the firm tightened the risk constraint, limiting the expected bad-debt ratio to 1.5 percent, the new optimal solution would be at Point *B* (selling only to Classes I through VII), whereas the unconstrained optimum is still Point *A*. Since a firm's market value depends on both the size *and* the quality of the company's earnings stream, a risk-return criterion is superior to a criterion that aims only at maximizing expected profit.

Decisions on Large Customers

If a firm sells to a few large customers, as well as to small ones, the expected bad-debt ratio is not a suitable measure of risk because it may not accurately predict bad-debt losses. A large customer may be viewed as a conglomeration of small customers whose bad-debt losses are perfectly correlated. This correlation increases the likelihood that the actual bad-debt ratio may take on extreme values, particularly if the large customers account for a significant percentage of total sales and if their probabilities of default are high. When selling on credit to large customers, the firm is concerned less with the expected bad debt than with the maximum possible loss and the implications of the loss for the firm's survival. If a given loss would result in insolvency, the firm might well decide not to make the sale, even if the probability of loss is only slight.

To be safe, the firm should determine what maximum loss is acceptable for any single account and how this maximum varies with the probability of its occurring. Each large account should then be analyzed to determine its probability of default. The firm may also wish to refine its figures by forecasting the time of customer payments and converting the payments to their present values. The firm will grant the customer credit only if he falls within the firm's risk and return constraints.

Even a customer, large or small, that seems to fall outside the constraints should be viewed only as a conditional "no." The customer or the firm's own salesmen may be able to provide information which may tip the balance in favor of credit. Or the customer may be a reasonable risk if 50 percent of his purchases are on credit and 50 percent are for cash. The credit manager should explore these possibilities before refusing credit altogether; and even a refusal should be diplomatic, since the customer may be a desirable prospect in the future. Moreover, special considerations may convert a "no" to a "yes" even without a change in the customer's credit rating. When a firm is introducing a new product, for example, management may want to loosen credit standards so that more customers can be introduced to the new line. Or, idle production and marketing resources during a recession may make sales to marginal accounts more profitable than they would be if the firm were already operating at full capacity. The credit manager, in short, must consider both the direct and the indirect implications of his decisions.

COLLECTION OF ACCOUNTS RECEIVABLE

If a customer pays when his bill is due, the cash manager will want to effect the transfer of funds as quickly as possible. This aspect of collection has already been discussed in Chapter 10. Here, we shall consider only the second aspect of collection policy: collecting overdue accounts.

Formulating a Collection Policy

The credit manager must decide how much money should be spent on collection efforts and whether the firm's policy should be lenient or tough.[8] A lenient policy stresses letters and telephone calls; a tough policy emphasizes personal visits, legal action, and the use of collection agencies. A tough policy is generally more expensive to implement. Which policy is desirable depends on how closely sales and bad-debt losses are related to collection efforts. Once this relationship has been ascertained, the technique used to optimize credit policy can be applied to optimize collection policy. Instead of repeating this exercise, we shall elaborate on the interrelationship of credit and collection policies.

Let us suppose that a credit manager is considering 5 collection policies and 5 credit standards: $C_1 \ldots C_5$ and $S_1 \ldots S_5$, respectively, in increasing degrees of toughness. For a given collection policy, an overly lenient credit standard will increase bad-debt losses excessively, while an overly tough standard will decrease sales excessively. Therefore, each of the profit functions in Figure 12-3 is shown to reach a maximum at some intermediate credit standard. The same pattern of increasing, then decreasing, return holds for collection policies. This is why the lower profit functions are associated with very lenient and very tough collection policies, while the higher functions are associated with intermediate—more reasonable—

[8] For more on collection procedure, see Thomas Guybon Hutson and John Butterworth, *Management of Trade Credit* (London: Gower Press, 1968), Ch. 7.

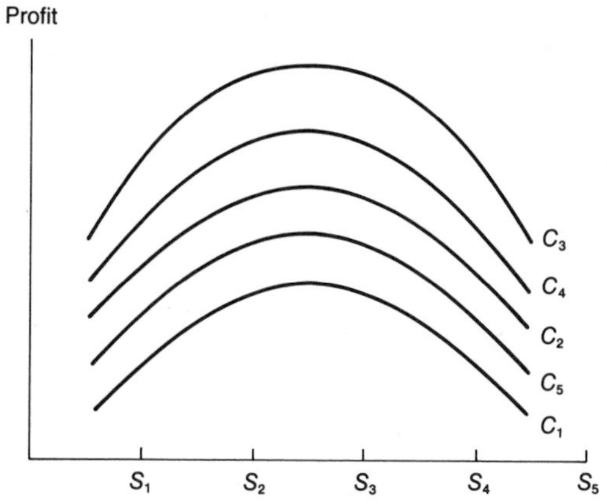

Figure 12-3 Determining the Optimal Credit-Collection Policy

policies. In the example, the highest profit is obtained by using collection policy C_3 along with credit standard S_3, a combination that maximizes profit with respect to both collection and credit. Financial executives are apt to characterize collection policy C_3 as "maximum recovery of delinquent accounts without undue loss of customer goodwill."

Monitoring Collection Experience

The credit manager has the additional responsibility of monitoring the firm's collection experience, both to control operations and to ascertain the quality of outstanding receivables. Two commonly used monitoring devices are the average collection period and the aging schedule of receivables. The average collection period is calculated by dividing accounts receivable outstanding by the average daily credit sales. The resulting period indicates the number of average daily credit sales outstanding in receivables (*DSO*). Management may also want to know how long the receivables have been on the books. This information is given by the aging schedule, which classifies receivables according to the duration they have been outstanding.

These monitoring devices have the virtue of simplicity, but they also have limitations. First, when a credit sale is made, a slow payment will not be recognized perhaps until an unacceptable amount of time has elapsed. Second, both devices are subject to aberrations when the rate of sales is changing. In a month of rising sales, accounts receivable will rise by the amount of the credit sales, but not to the level that the new sales and collection pattern will eventually bring about. Consequently, even though the collection experience remains unchanged, the monitoring indices will show an improvement whenever sales are rising—and conversely, a deterioration whenever sales are falling. Finally, actual payment record is a function of both credit and collection policies, but these indices do not distinguish between the two.

REVIEW QUESTIONS

1. What are the central aspects of accounts-receivable management? To what extent does the efficient management of accounts receivable depend on the accurate forecasting of future sales?
2. In Problem 3 of Chapter 10, you were asked to use a computer program to analyze the effect on Fancycraft's 12-month cash budget of a change in the firm's accounts-receivable policy. Discuss what the computer output revealed about the effects of the change on the company's cash flows. Make sure you distinguish between the short-run and the long-run effects.
3. Define "terms of sales." How do the various elements of ordinary terms affect the effective selling price of a product?
4. An airplane manufacturer sells to a few large customers, whereas a department store has many small customers. In imposing a risk constraint on credit sales, which company would be more concerned with minimizing the risk of insolvency? What would be the primary importance of the risk constraint for the other firm?
5. Discuss the equivalence or non-equivalence of the *DCF* (discounted-cash-flow) analysis used in standard capital-budgeting analysis and the *ROI* (return-on-investment) analysis used in Table 12-1.
6. The Dun and Bradstreet Reference Book includes these items:

52 51 Smith, Adam Co.	* Hwr 9 DD1
15 11 Reinke Construction Co.	Constr 7 FF3

   What information do these entries give about each company's industry's classification, incorporation status, line of business, starting date, and credit worthiness? Consult the Key in the Dun and Bradstreet Reference Book.
7. David Ewert's linear-discriminant model expresses the credit worthiness of a firm as a function of 9 variables. List these variables, indicating which are most important in determining a firm's credit score. Explain the relative importance of the characteristics.
8. Universal Airlines, Inc., operates a fleet of 24 jumbo jetliners connecting major North American cities with major resort cities in Australia, Europe, and Asia. Because of the recession, the planes are flying at only 50 percent of capacity. To stimulate sales, the company has initiated a "fly-now, pay-much-later" plan, whereby the customer puts nothing down and makes the payment over the next 24 months. Moreover, flight agents have been instructed to accept all customers, with no credit check. Discuss the economics of this credit decision in terms of the risk-return criterion. How would your answer be affected if this were a period of prosperity, with the planes already operating at 90 percent of capacity?
9. Mr. Kline owns a jewelry store. Hit by the recession, he is trying to devise ways to stimulate sales. Mr. Kline reasons: "If a customer defaults on a credit

sale, the bad debt is tax deductible. Since I am in the 60 percent tax bracket, each dollar of bad debt saves me 60 cents in taxes. My goods cost me only 30 percent of sales, so I make 30 cents (= 60¢ − 30¢) per dollar even if the customer defaults. I should therefore sell to anyone, regardless of credit position, and should require no money down." Is Mr. Kline's reasoning sound? Why or why not? If not, would a liberal credit policy be justified if a down payment were required?

10. Charles Edwards is the new credit manager of Malloy Toys, Inc. In his first six months at Malloy, Edwards reduced the firm's bad debt from 2 percent of sales to 1/4 percent, and increased the rate of receivables turnover from 4 to 8. What inference can you draw regarding the probable effect of Edwards' efforts on the company's profitability?

PROBLEMS

1. A certain firm sells its product at $8 per unit on terms of 1/10, net 30. Customers currently buy 10,000 units annually; their demand is estimated to have a price elasticity of 1.8. What would be the effect on effective price and quantity demanded if the firm changed its selling terms to 2/10, net 30? 1/20, net 30? 1/10, net 60? You may assume that money yields an annual return of 12 percent to the customers.
2. In an earlier example, changing terms of sales from Policy X to Policy Y was shown to increase profit by $1,250 (Table 12-1). Assuming that the demand elasticity could be 2, 3, or 4, with probabilities of .2, .5, and .3, respectively, determine the expected increase in profit that would now be associated with a shift from Policy X to Policy Y.
3. M-Ray, Inc., a new company, manufactures a product which is sold directly to consumers at a price paid in 12 equal monthly installments. Suppose that its monthly sales are a constant $50,000, what will the amount of its receivables at the end of 6 months? 12 months? 18 months? And what is the general formula for determining this amount?
4. Suppose that a prospective customer scores .500 according to Ewert's model of credit evaluation. What does this indicate about the probability that he will default? Illustrate your calculations with a diagram similar to Figure 12-1. Assume that past experience shows that 85 percent of all customers are good risks and 15 percent are bad risks.
5. Re-compute the data in Table 12-4 assuming that the 100 customers are distributed among the ten risk classes as follows: 10 in Class I, 20 in II, 40 in III, 10 in IV, 5 in V, 5 in VI, 4 in VII, 3 in VIII, 2 in IX, and 1 in X. To which risk classes should the firm sell if the objective is to maximize expected profit subject to the constraint that the ratio of expected bad-debt losses to sales not exceed 2.5 percent? 3.5 percent? 4.5 percent?
6. A company selling on terms of net 30 finds that only 50 percent of its accounts are paid by the end of 30 days, an additional 30 percent being paid by the end of 60 days, and the last 20 percent being paid by the end of 90 days. The rate of sales has been a steady $100 per day. The equilibrium relationships among sales, collection, accounts receivable (amounts and age distribution), and *DSO* may be visualized in this manner:

Month	0	1	2	3	4
Sales	$3,000	$3,000	$3,000	$3,000	$3,000
Collections		1,500	1,500	1,500	1,500
			900	900	900
				600	600
Receivables	$3,000	$4,500	$5,100	$5,100	$5,100
% Current	100%	66.7%	58.8%	58.8%	58.8%
% 1 mo. overdue	0	33.3	29.4	29.4	29.4
% 2 mos. overdue	0	0	11.8	11.8	11.8
DSO	30 days	45 days	51 days	51 days	51 days

Suppose that in the fifth month sales increase permanently to $200 a day ($6,000/month). Show that in the fifth and sixth months, even with no change in the firm's collection experience, the *DSO* statistic and the aging schedule will show improvement. How long will it take before equilibrium relationships are restored?

REFERENCES

BATT, C. D., and TERRENCE R. FOWKES, "The Development and Use of Credit Scoring Schemes," in Samuel Eilon and Terrence R. Fowkes, eds., *Applications of Management Science in Banking and Finance* (Epping, Essex: Gower Press, 1972), Ch. 13.

BECKMAN, THEODORE N., and RONALD S. FOSTER, *Credits and Collections* (New York: McGraw-Hill Book Company, 1969).

BENISHAY, HASKEL, "Managerial Controls of Accounts Receivable: A Deterministic Approach," *Journal of Accounting Research* 3 (Spring, 1965), pp. 114–132.

BENISHAY, HASKEL, "A Stochastic Model of Credit Sales Debt," *Journal of the American Statistical Association* 61 (December, 1966), pp. 1010–1028.

BROSKY, JOHN J., *The Implicit Cost of Trade Credit and Theory of Optimal Terms of Sales* (New York: Credit Research Foundation, Inc., 1969).

DAVEY, PATRICK J., *Managing Trade Receivables* (New York: The Conference Board, 1972).

DUN & BRADSTREET, INC., *Ten Keys to Basic Credits and Collections* (New York: 1973).

EWERT, DAVID C., "Trade Credit Management: Selection of Accounts Receivable Using a Statistical Model," Paper No. 236 issued by the Institute for Research in the Behavioral, Economic, and Management Sciences at Purdue University, March, 1969.

HUTSON, THOMAS GUYBON, and JOHN BUTTERWORTH, *Management of Trade Credit* (London: Gower Press, 1968).

LEWELLEN, WILBUR G., and ROBERT O. EDMISTER, "A General Model for Accounts-Receivable Analysis and Control," *Journal of Financial and Quantitative Analysis* 8 (March, 1973), pp. 195–206.

MAO, JAMES C. T., and CARL E. SÄRNDAL, "Controlling Risk in Accounts Receivable Management," *Journal of Business Finance and Accounting* 1 (Autumn, 1974), pp. 395–403.

MEHTA, DILEEP R., *Working Capital Management* (Englewood Cliffs: Prentice-Hall, Inc., 1974), Chs. 1-3.

ORGLER, YAIR E., "Evaluation of Bank Consumer Loans with Credit Scoring Models," *Journal of Bank Research* 2 (Spring, 1971), pp. 31–37.

SCHIFF, MICHAEL, and ZVI LIEBER, "A Model for the Integration of Credit and Inventory Management," *Journal of Finance* 29 (March, 1974), pp. 133–140.

STANCILL, McN. JAMES, *The Management of Working Capital* (Scranton: Intext Educational Publishers, 1971), Ch. 4.

U.S. Congress, *Organized Crime*. Hearings before the Select Committee on Crime, House of Representatives, 92nd Congress, 1st Session (Washington, D.C., 1972).

Part Five

Capital Structure and Dividend Policy

13 The Debt-Capacity Decision

FINANCING-POLICY DECISIONS

Nature

This chapter marks an important shift in the focus of our discussion. Whereas Chapters 5 through 12 dealt with the acquisition and management of assets, Chapters 13 through 21 will deal with the best pattern for financing those assets. In terms of the balance sheet, the shift is from asset accounts to liability and equity accounts. Of course, our earlier analysis did not totally ignore financing considerations. The profitability of an investment was evaluated in terms of the cash flows accruing to the common stockholders, and we assumed that the investment was optimally financed. That assumption simplified the analysis by letting us optimize the investment decision while taking the financing decision as given. Now, however, investment is the constant and financing will be viewed as the variable.

In general, a firm obtains its funds from two sources: debt and equity. Debt capital is externally generated, whereas equity is either internally or externally generated; but what truly distinguishes the two is that debt involves a credit relationship, whereas equity involves an ownership relationship. Equity may take the form of either preferred stock or common stock (see Chapters 17 and 19). Because preferred dividends are semi-fixed, we shall view preferred stock as a variant of debt in our analysis of capital structure.

A financial executive must make several basic policy decisions in regard to the two basic forms of financing: (1) Should his firm utilize debt financing; and if so, what is the optimal mix of debt and equity? (2) If debt is used, what is the optimal mix of short- and long-term financing; and how is this mix influenced by interest-rate expectations and liquidity considerations? (3) When equity capital is used, to what extent should it be generated internally through retention of earnings and to what extent should it be obtained externally through the sale of new shares? This chapter will deal with the first of these questions; the others will be covered in the next two chapters.

These questions are called policy decisions because they deal with general principles rather than with the specifics of financing. In debt and equity financing, for example, we deal primarily with the optimal debt-to-equity ratio, not with the various methods of financing. Similarly, in considering the maturity structure of debt, we use a simple short-/long-term dichotomy, considering neither the distinctions between bank loans, insurance-company loans, commercial paper, debentures, financial leases, etc., nor the relative advantages of each in a particular situation. In choosing between internal and external equity financing, we focus on the optimal dividend payout, not on the practical problems of selling new shares or administering dividends.

The practical aspects must, of course, be understood if the policy decisions are to be implemented successfully. Chapter 16 describes the forces of supply and demand in the capital market as well as the ways of raising funds in this market. Chapters 17 through 19 deal with the nature of common stock, preferred stock, and long-term debt, and those features of debt and equity contracts that have a bearing on the liquidity and profitability of the issuing firm. Chapters 20 and 21 present a similar treatment of intermediate- and short-term financing.

Diversity

To understand the scope of financing-policy decisions, let us examine the financing patterns actually employed by several well-known corporations. We shall confine the debt-financing decision to interest-bearing debt. Non-interest-bearing debt, such as accounts payable and accruals, are so clearly beneficial to the company that no analysis is needed. Accruals and accounts payable are also called spontaneous debt, since they vary spontaneously with a firm's business volume. According to this framework, then, total assets less spontaneous credit give the net amount which a firm must finance. The use of spontaneous credit does, however, reduce other forms of debt that a firm can safely incur. For this reason, the capital structure percentages calculated for our sample companies in Table 13-1 include both their spontaneous credit and interest-bearing debt.

As Table 13-1 shows, there is great diversity in the ways various companies finance themselves. For example, both Detroit Edison and GMAC have a much higher debt-to-equity ratio than Maytag or U.S. Gypsum.

Table 13-1 The Capital Structures of a Sample of Companies (in percent)

	Detroit Edison	Safeway Stores	U.S. Gypsum	Maytag	Alcoa	GMAC
Short-term debt	11.4	38.4	24.2	20.3	10.9	58.1
Long-term debt	47.0	12.7	3.1	0	39.1	33.8
Capital stock	31.4	7.2	15.5	27.8	5.9	4.4
Retained earnings	10.2	41.7	57.2	51.9	44.1	3.7
	100.0	100.0	100.0	100.0	100.0	100.0

Source: Company annual reports.

Safeway Stores has a ratio close to Alcoa's; but the liabilities of the former are primarily short-term while those of the latter are chiefly long-term. The firms in the sample differ also in relative reliance on internal financing, as suggested by their retained earnings to total asset ratios. Presumably, the capital structure of a firm at any given moment reflects the cumulative result of all past attempts to optimize the pattern of financing. Accordingly, certain principles must lie behind the relatively heavy borrowing by electric utilities and finance companies, the relatively light borrowing by manufacturers of building materials and electrical appliances, the relatively heavy reliance on short-term debt by retail food stores, the relatively heavy reliance on long-term debt by producers of metals, and the diversity of dividend policies among our sample companies. We shall attempt to discover the underlying principles in such diverse financing-policy decisions.

DEFINING THE DEBT-CAPACITY PROBLEM

In order to separate the debt-vs.-equity decision from the debt-maturity decision, we shall assume that all debts have the same maturity. The two decisions are actually interrelated and will be viewed as such in our later discussion of the maturity-structure decision. But here we will deal only with the debt-vs.-equity decision and ask this simple question: given the physical assets of a firm, what total amount of debt financing will maximize the firm's market value?

How Debt Affects Value

We shall consider a firm whose assets are expected to generate the net-operating-income (*EBIT*) stream depicted in Figure 13-1. Under Plan A (Figure 13-1[a]), a constant amount I is allocated annually to interest payments, leaving a variable amount E as the annual income of the common stockholders. Associated with this division of *EBIT* is a corresponding market value assigned to the firm by security investors. The I dollars of

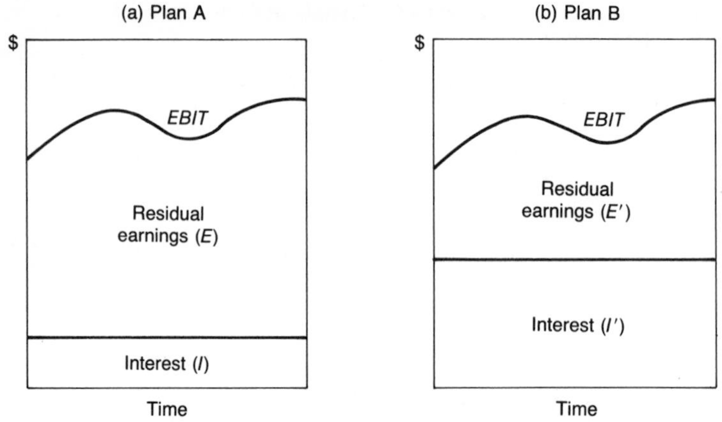

Figure 13-1 Dividing the Income Stream

annual interest payments will support a certain amount of debt, and the E dollars of annual earnings will support a certain amount of equity. The combined value of debt and equity is the total market value of the firm.

Under Plan B (Figure 13-1[b]), a constant amount, I', greater than I, is allocated annually to interest payments, leaving a variable amount E', smaller than E, as annual residual earnings. Plan B would enhance the market value of the firm *if* the interest rate and earnings-capitalization rate remained unchanged. There are two reasons for this observation. First, since interest is tax-deductible, Plan B would yield a greater tax savings than Plan A. And second, since interest payments are less risky than residual earnings, each dollar of interest would have a higher market valuation than a dollar of residual earnings. Therefore, even without tax savings, shifting income from residual earnings to interest payments would increase the firm's total market valuation.

In fact, however, the earnings-capitalization and interest rates do not remain constant when the division of $EBIT$ is altered. In any firm, both $EBIT$ and residual earnings are random variables; and given the variability of $EBIT$, the variability of residual earnings tends to increase directly with the size of the firm's fixed interest payments. Large interest commitments also increase the risk of cash insolvency. Consequently, as a firm goes more heavily into debt, security investors will demand higher rates of return to compensate for the increased risk. To the firm, this means that investors will capitalize both interest payments and residual earnings at a higher discount rate.

Moreover, debt financing may affect even the firm's long-run ability to generate net operating income. Excessive debt, for example, may reduce liquidity so much that the firm will be unable to undertake profitable investments. In extreme situations, low liquidity may force bankruptcy. It is not true, therefore, that replacing equity with debt will always increase a firm's market value. Whether the value of the firm in Figure 13-1 will be greater under Plan A or under Plan B depends on the effect of various levels of debt financing on the firm's *EBIT* and on the rates at which earnings are capitalized. The market value will be greater under Plan B only if either the market values of both debt and equity increase or if the increase in the market value of debt more than offsets any decline in the market value of equity. Given a firm's assets, the central problem in the debt-vs.-equity decision is to determine the level of debt financing that will maximize the firm's market value.

A Clarifying Comment

Why, one may ask, if the objective is to maximize share value, should the firm care about maximizing the combined market value of its debt and equity? The maximization of share value is a valid objective for any transaction not involving the transfer of assets between the corporation and its stockholders. When transfer is involved, the objective becomes to maximize the stockholders' total net assets. Let us say that a firm, which has no debt at present, is considering two financing policies. Under Plan A the firm has a market value of $100,000, made up of $25,000 of debt and $75,000 of equity. Under Plan B, the firm borrows $40,000, using $15,000 of the proceeds to retire a portion of the common shares, so that the company still has the same amount of cash at its disposal as under Plan A. Increasing debt will reduce the stockholders' earnings and increase the rate at which they are capitalized, causing the market value of the company shares to decline. The stockholders, however, will still be better off, provided that the share-repurchase payments they receive exceed the decline in the market value of their shares. This will happen if the market value of the firm under Plan B (before share repurchase) exceeds the original $100,000 of Plan A. Maximizing total market value maximizes the wealth of the stockholders.

Note that we have viewed a firm's capital structure as a long-run decision—no debt has yet been incurred. In this situation, the change in the firm's total value will exactly equal the new borrowing and its effect on the value of the common stock. As we have seen, maximizing total value is the objective. However, when a firm already has some debt outstanding, the value of that debt may be adversely affected by the new borrowing. In this short-run situation, the change in total value of the firm will equal the new borrowing, its effect on common stock, *and* its effect on the already outstanding debt. Even a decrease in total value, then, when accompanied by a sizeable decrease in the market value of old debt, could produce an increase in the value of common stock. Conversely, an increase in total value does not preclude a decrease in the value of common stock. In the short run, therefore, the focus should be on maximizing the wealth of common stockholders directly, in terms of both common stock value and cash benefits. But, even when a firm is able to exploit the short-run immobility of existing debt, it should not lose sight of the long-run need to refund the existing debt when it eventually matures. Chapter 23 considers measures to change a firm's existing capital structure, called recapitalization, taking into account both the short- and long-run implications. Here we are taking the long view.

THE EFFECTS OF DEBT FINANCING

Debt financing, then, affects the firm's value through two main channels: the division of the firm's net operating income between interest payments and residual earnings; and the rates at which security investors capitalize interest payments and residual earnings received from the firm. Given net operating income, an increase in interest expenses inevitably reduces residual earnings; but since interest expenses lead to tax savings, the reduction in residual earnings will be smaller than the corresponding increase in interest payments. Since these accounting relationships need no more elaboration, let us turn our attention to the effects of debt financing on the

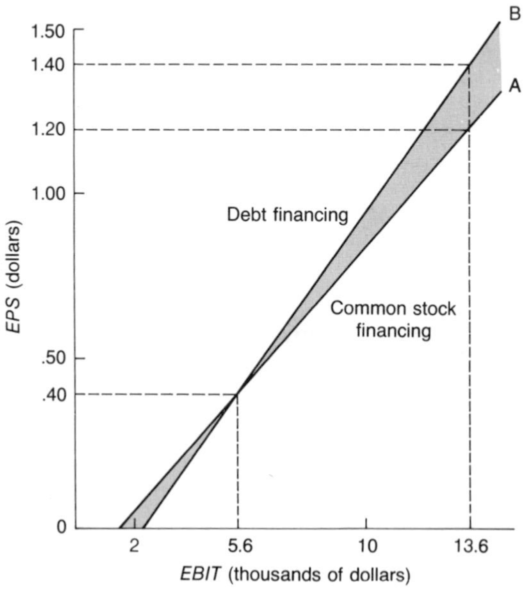

Figure 13-2 The Effect of Debt Financing on *EPS*

variability of earnings and on the risk of insolvency. These are the factors that prompt investors to demand higher rates of return.

The Variability of EPS

Fluctuations in the net operating income of a firm give rise to fluctuations in earnings per share. The *EPS* of the firm in Figure 13-2 will fluctuate more under Plan B than under Plan A because of the larger fixed interest payments under Plan B. The two plans differ also in the number of shares outstanding since Plan B uses more debt financing. A simple graphic technique may be used to determine the *EPS* corresponding to any given *EBIT* under each financing alternative.

Let us suppose that the Lamda Company currently generates an annual operating income of $13,600. Under Plan A, the firm has $20,000 of 8 percent debt, requiring $1,600 in annual interest payments. Assuming a 50 percent tax rate, the 5,000 shares of common equity will be entitled to an annual income of $6,000 (= .5[$13,600 − $1,600]). At a capitalization rate of, say, 12 percent, these 5,000 shares will have a total value of $50,000. Under Plan B, the firm increases its debt from $20,000 to $30,000 and uses the $10,000 in proceeds to retire 1,000 shares of stock. Assuming the interest rate on debt remains at 8 percent, we can calculate the *EPS* corresponding to any given level of net operating income (*EBIT*):

$$\text{Plan A} \qquad EPS = \frac{(EBIT - \$20{,}000 \times .08)(1 - .5)}{5{,}000}$$

$$\text{Plan B} \qquad EPS = \frac{(EBIT - \$30{,}000 \times .08)(1 - .5)}{4{,}000}$$

Thus, if *EBIT* is $2,000, *EPS* will be 4 cents under Plan A and −5 cents under Plan B; but if *EBIT* is $13,600, *EPS* will be $1.20 under Plan A and $1.40 under Plan B.

Figure 13-2 shows graphically the relationship between *EBIT* and *EPS*. The relationship of *EPS* under Plan B to *EPS* under Plan A depends on whether *EBIT* is greater than, equal to, or less than $5,600. We must note that the relative attractiveness of the two plans cannot be ascertained simply by comparing the resulting *EPS*'s, partly because there are fewer remaining shares under Plan B and partly because the added debt in Plan B will cause the earnings-capitalization rate to rise. In our example, the stockholders had an original holding of 5,000 shares valued at $50,000. Under Plan B, since they received $10,000 for selling 1,000 shares to the company, their wealth will be increased if the value of the remaining 4,000 shares does not fall below $40,000, or, equivalently, if the price per share does not fall below the original $10. We know that if *EBIT* is $13,600, *EPS* under Plan B will be \$1.40. The stockholders, therefore, will be better off under Plan B as long as the added debt financing does not cause the earnings-capitalization rate to rise above 14 percent.

Figure 13-2 also provides a useful visual means of studying the effect of debt financing on the variability of *EPS*. The two slopes associated with Plans A and B reveal that as *EBIT* changes over time, the fluctuation in *EPS* varies directly with the firm's reliance on debt financing. Moreover, the greater its reliance on debt, as in Plan B, the greater the fluctuation in *EPS;* the less its reliance, as in Plan A, the less the fluctuation in *EPS*.

A Variability Index

We can devise an index to quantify the extent to which debt financing magnifies the degree of earnings variability. This index is applicable to both total earnings and per-share earnings, but now we shall focus on the former. The variability of total earnings (E) is derived from the variability of net operating income (X). By accounting definition, E and X are related according to the equation:

$$\underset{\text{Residual earnings}}{E} = \underset{\text{Taxable income}}{(X - \mathrm{I})} - \underset{\text{Income tax}}{(X - I)\tau} \tag{13-1}$$

where τ is the tax rate on corporate income and I is the fixed interest payment. From Eq. (13-1), it can be shown that when net operating income changes by x percent, residual earnings will change by e percent, where[1]

$$e = x\frac{X}{X - I} \tag{13-2}$$

Since $X/(X - I)$ is greater than 1, a given change in X results in a greater than proportionate change in residual earnings. Additionally, given X, the value of $X/(X - I)$ varies directly with I, so that the greater the fixed interest expenses, the greater the degree of magnification. Consequently, the ratio of $X/(X - I)$ measures the degree of financial leverage in a firm's capital structure.

Financial leverage must be distinguished from the related concept of operating leverage. Operating leverage describes the magnifying process by which sales affect net operating income, while financial leverage describes the magnifying process by which net operating income affects residual earnings. Net operating income is defined as sales minus operating expenses,

---

[1] $E = (X - I)(1 - \tau)$, $E' = [(1 + x)\ X - I](1 - \tau)$, and hence $e = (E' - E)/E = xX/(X - I)$.

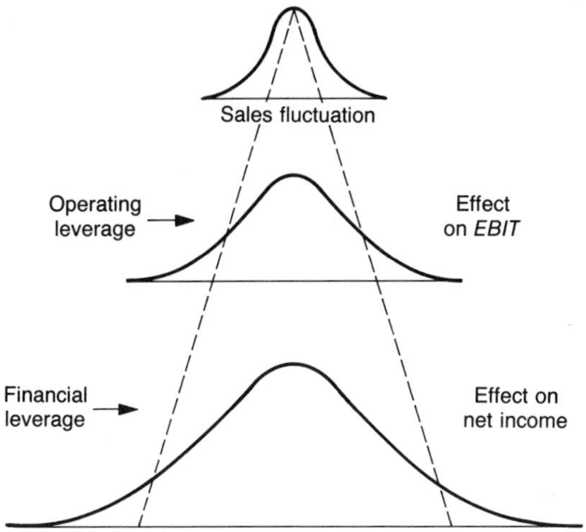

Figure 13-3 Operating Leverage vs. Financial Leverage

some of which are variable, others fixed. Fixed operating expenses serve as the fulcrum in operating leverage, just as fixed interest payments provide the fulcrum in financial leverage. Figure 13-3 shows that a given change in sales is magnified successively by the two levers to produce a greater than proportionate change in residual earnings. In determining debt capacity, the financial executive must usually take sales fluctuations and the degree of operating leverage as givens; but he may directly control financial leverage through borrowing activities. Debt financing, therefore, provides a means for the financial executive to exercise some control over the variability of residual earnings.

Let us return to Eq. (13-2), using the data for the Lamda Company. In Table 13-2, we assume that the company's net operating income rises from \$10,000 to \$13,600, an increase of 36 percent. As the calculations show, residual earnings under Plan A rise from \$4,200 to \$6,000, an increase of 42.9 percent; under Plan B, they rise from \$3,800 to \$5,600, an increase of 47.4 percent. These results are the same as those implied by Eq. (13-2). The table also indicates that *EPS* shows the same percentage change as total earnings. This was predictable since *EPS* is simply total earnings divided by the number of outstanding shares. Thus, for any two points on a given line in Figure 13-2, the relationship between the percentage change in net operating income and the corresponding percentage change in *EPS* is defined precisely by Eq. (13-2). This formula, therefore, is valid for both *EPS* and total earnings.

Table 13-2 The Effect of Debt Financing on the Variability of Earnings

	Plan A		Plan B	
Net operating income	$10,000	$13,600	$10,000	$13,600
Interest expense	1,600	1,600	2,400	2,400
Taxable income	$ 8,400	$12,000	$ 7,600	$11,200
Income tax	4,200	6,000	3,800	5,600
Residual earnings	$ 4,200	$ 6,000	$ 3,800	$ 5,600
Number of shares	5,000	5,000	4,000	4,000
EPS	$ 0.84	$ 1.20	$ 0.95	$ 1.40

The Risk of Insolvency

Viewing the debt-capacity decision solely as a matter of dividing income between interest and net earnings can be misleading, for it does not take into account the relative priority of claims: interest must be paid before any earnings can accrue to the stockholders. Debt financing also involves repayment of principal, whether in lump sum or in installments. Both principal repayments and interest are contractual, so that default on either will force the firm into insolvency. In our simulation of cash management in Chapter 4, we determined the risk of insolvency in a situation with a fixed amount of interest-bearing debt in addition to accruals and accounts payable. Here we shall suggest ways of extending simulation to determine how the risk of insolvency varies with changes in the amount of debt, the interest rate, and other contractual terms.

To review, the model dealt with a firm's contingency planning for a business recession. The following data were given: the duration of the recession; the severity of sales decline; the costs of manufacture, selling, and administration; the expected slowdown in collection of receivables; and the amount of interest and taxes. The firm had a given initial cash balance, and insolvency was said to occur if and when the firm experienced a cumulative cash deficit larger than this initial balance. The experiment was made more realistic by treating recession sales and collection slowdown both as random variables.

This model can easily be used to highlight the cash-flow implications of a company's debt policy. In the original formulation, the amount of debt was a constant, requiring no amortization of principal. The interest rate, too, was fixed and assumed constant. But if the company wishes to consider different amounts and/or types of debt, we can easily vary the amount, interest rate, and repayment schedule in the model. If the new money is for plant expansion, we may also specify the construction period and when the new investment will begin to pay off. This time schedule will enable us to distinguish between the short-run and long-run effects on the firm's liquidity and profitability.

The management is also interested in how a particular debt policy will be judged by the security investors and credit rating agencies which use the company's published financial statements. The same data used in simulation can be used to project the company's *pro forma* statements under alternative debt policies. A *pro forma* financial statement is a construct designed to project a hypothetical future or past, to illustrate what would be or would have been the financial statements if some conditions were to exist or had existed. In this case, we are comparing the financial statements which would result from following alternative debt policies. The computer program B-1, Appendix B, written to project the financial statements of El Camelo Corporation, can easily be adapted to make these comparisons.

Again, one might wonder why the financial executive should worry about the risk of insolvency. Why shouldn't he concentrate exclusively on maximizing the value of the firm and leave the assessment of insolvency risk to the security investors? Two answers may be suggested. First, the financial executive cannot maximize the value of his firm unless he can predict how debt financing will affect the firm's borrowing rate and earnings-capitalization rate. Such a prediction requires a knowledge of the way security investors assess a firm's risk of insolvency.

Second, even when the firm's market value is maximized, the financial executive still needs to be able to assess the risk of insolvency independently of the security investors. This is partly because security investors are looking in from the outside and therefore must base their assessments on the limited data in published statements. The financial executive, with greater access to detailed information, should be able to make a more accurate forecast. Moreover, even when the financial executive and the security investors agree on the risk of insolvency, their attitudes toward the risk may differ. Investment by security investors—particularly institutional investors—in a given company may represent only a small percentage of their portfolios. Diversification enables these investors to accept a degree of risk on a single security that might be quite unacceptable to the financial executive, who worries about the very survival of the company. He must be sure that the level of debt financing that maximizes the firm's value does not violate his risk constraint. If it does violate this constraint, his optimal strategy is simply to substitute equity for debt until the risk of insolvency is reduced to an acceptable level.

DETERMINING THE OPTIMAL DEBT-TO-EQUITY RATIO

A firm that is presently financed solely by equity may wish to decide how much of its equity capital should be replaced by debt capital. Simulation will determine the risk of insolvency associated with each level of proposed debt financing. Those levels of debt with unacceptably high risks are rejected outright; the others are designated "feasible." Of those feasible levels, the one that maximizes the value of the firm should be chosen.

An Analytical Model

Suppose a firm expects that its annual net operating income will be $\bar{X}$ dollars perpetually. This figure assumes continual replacement of existing assets, but no net investments, and therefore the firm's residual earnings equal its adjusted earnings as defined in Chapter 2. Given this earnings potential, the firm wishes to maximize its total market value through appropriate financing. The question is how to divide $\bar{X}$ dollars between interest, taxes, and residual earnings so that the total market value of the firm's debt and equity will be the highest possible. If interest payments are I dollars, residual earnings will be $(\bar{X} - I)(1 - \tau)$, where τ is the tax rate on income. The sum of interest and residual earnings thus exceeds residual earnings without debt by τI. That is,

$$\underbrace{I}_{\substack{\text{Interest}\\ \text{expense}}} + \underbrace{(\bar{X} - I)(1 - \tau)}_{\substack{\text{Residual}\\ \text{earnings}\\ \text{(with debt)}}} = \underbrace{\bar{X}(1 - \tau)}_{\substack{\text{Residual}\\ \text{earnings}\\ \text{(no debt)}}} + \underbrace{I\tau}_{\substack{\text{Tax}\\ \text{benefit}}} \qquad (13\text{-}3)$$

where $I\tau$ measures the tax savings associated with I dollars of interest.

When net operating income is divided between interest and residual earnings according to Eq. (13-3), the market value, V, of a firm is given by the equation:

$$V = \underbrace{\frac{I}{k_i}}_{\substack{\text{Value of}\\ \text{debt}}} + \underbrace{\frac{(\bar{X} - I)(1 - \tau)}{k_e}}_{\substack{\text{Value of}\\ \text{equity}}} \qquad (13\text{-}4)$$

where k_i and k_e are, respectively, the rates at which the creditors and the stockholders of the company capitalize their income streams. Since interest payments bring tax benefits, and since $k_e > k_i$, the market value of a firm will increase with every increase in debt *provided* that both k_e and k_i remain constant as debt is substituted for equity (see Figures 13-4[a] and 13-4[b]). But this provision cannot be satisfied, since the greater risk of insolvency and the greater variability of residual earnings will cause both rates to rise (see Figures 13-4[c] and 13-4[d]). Initially, the rise will be so slow that firm market value will in fact increase with debt financing. But as the debt-to-equity ratio approaches some critical level, the rise in k_e and k_i will accelerate, so that any increase in debt financing beyond a certain point will only

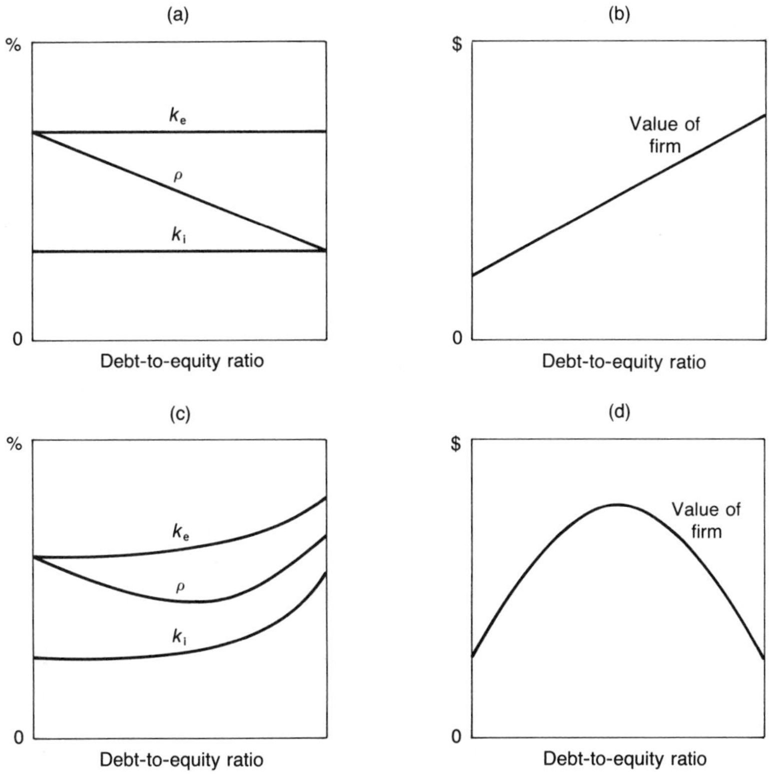

Figure 13-4 Capital Structure and Valuation

reduce the value of the firm. The symbol ρ in the figure is the average cost of capital, defined as the weighted average of k_e and k_i. The connection between ρ and firm valuation will be explained shortly.

Let us suppose that Champion, Inc., is expected to generate an annual net operating income of \$10,000 perpetually. In predicting k_e and k_i, the financial executive must take into account the nature of the firm's business, the liquidity of its assets, its long-run economic outlook, the standards of its lenders, the capital structure of comparable firms, and the investors' concept of risk and their attitudes toward it. He concludes that if Champion employs no debt, its borrowing and earnings-capitalization rates will be 7 percent and 9.5 percent, respectively; if it employs \$20,000 of debt, the respective rates will be 7.5 percent and 10 percent; if it employs \$30,000 of debt, the rates will be 8 percent and 11 percent; and at \$40,000 of debt, the rates will be 9.5 percent and 13.5 percent, respectively. With a tax rate of 50 percent, debt financing does increase the firm's value if it is kept within "reasonable" limits (see Table 13-3). For Champion, Inc., the limit is

Table 13-3 Valuation of Champion, Inc.

Debt (L)	$L = \$0$	$L = \$20{,}000$	$L = \$30{,}000$	$L = \$40{,}000$
Net operating income	$10,000	$10,000	$10,000	$10,000
Interest ($k_i \times L$)	0	1,500	2,400	3,800
Taxable income	$10,000	$ 8,500	$ 7,600	$ 6,200
Income tax	5,000	4,250	3,800	3,100
Residual earnings	$ 5,000	$ 4,250	$ 3,800	$ 3,100
Value of equity (S)	$52,632	$42,500	$34,545	$22,963
Total value ($S + L$)	$52,632	$62,500	$64,545*	$62,963

* Optimal.

$30,000; at this level of debt, the firm attains its maximum market value, $64,545.

Our example was simplified, since we assumed that the effects of debt financing on the values of k_i and k_e were known. In practice, the values of k_i and k_e must be forecast. The subjectivity of forecast makes accuracy difficult. Forecasting is complicated further because the relation between k_i and k_e tends to change with the business conditions, so that a capital structure that is optimal at one time may be nonoptimal at another time. In optimizing its capital structure, the management naturally should be alert to current opportunities in the capital market. Sometimes interest rate on debt may be especially low; at other times the price of the company stock may be especially high. But the company also needs a long-run debt policy as a safeguard against any tendency to excessive debt financing which might result from the optimism of a particular period. The best strategy is to optimize the firm's capital structure on the basis of the long-run relationship between k_i and k_e. Such a strategy minimizes both fluctuations in market value and deviations from optimal value.

The example was also simplified in its assumption of equal maturity for all debts, which eliminated many of the questions of dynamics arising when a firm has the option of borrowing funds of different maturities. Champion, for example, would have to determine what percentage of its debt should be long-term and what percentage should be short-term. It must then decide whether the long-term portion should be borrowed at once or whether the firm should begin with temporary short-term borrowing and then shift to long-term later. These issues will be treated in the next chapter on debt-maturity and timing decisions.

Comparison with Modigliani and Miller's Model

The preceding model is different from that which Franco Modigliani and Merton H. Miller used in reaching their independence hypothesis. In a well-known article, Modigliani and Miller (MM) contended that a firm's value is independent of its debt-to-equity ratio, assuming no income tax.[2] MM agree that the tax benefit, if present, does cause the firm's value to vary with debt financing. They argue, however, that tax benefit is the only factor which causes a dependency relation. Otherwise, they argue, two firms which are identical except for their capital structures are completely substitutable in the eyes of investors, and therefore have the same value. Our position is that there are factors other than tax benefit which cause a firm's value to vary with its debt-to-equity ratio.

An example will help explain the logic of Modigliani and Miller's independence hypothesis. Suppose that Champion, Inc., must decide whether to include $20,000 of 7.5 percent debt in its capital structure, or to use only equity financing. The difference is the presence of leverage in the former case and its absence in the latter. Since income tax is assumed to be nonexistent, the entire $10,000 of Champion's *EBIT* would constitute residual earnings for a nonlevered company. Capitalizing this pure equity stream at the appropriate rate of 9.5 percent would give a total market value for the firm of $105,260. As a levered company, Champion would be $20,000 debt financed, meaning that—according to the independence hypothesis—the value of its equity would have to be $85,260: the value of Champion as a nonlevered firm less the amount of debt financing.

MM attempt to prove their independence hypothesis by considering the case when "two" firms, identical in every respect except that one is levered and one nonlevered, have different market values. Suppose, in the Champion example, that debt financing results in a total market value of $120,000 (= $20,000 of debt + $100,000 of equity). MM claim that arbitrage operations would force this higher value back down to the equilibrium level of $105,260. If an investor owned 10 percent of the shares in the levered firm, his portion of the residual earnings would be .1($10,000 − $1,500), or $850. If he decides to substitute personal leverage for corporate leverage by selling his 10 percent for $10,000 and matching this sum with a $2,000 personal loan at 7.5 percent interest (the same rate that the levered firm pays on its debt), he would have a total of $12,000 with which he could buy an 11.40 percent ownership in the nonlevered company. His share in the residual earnings would now be .114 × $10,000, or $1,140. He must, of course, pay $150 in interest on his bank loan, but his net income would still be $140 greater than the $850 he received from his shares in the levered firm.

MM believe that investors consider personal leverage no riskier than corporate leverage as long as the debt-to-equity ratio remains the same. The investor would thus have a strong income motive to engage in arbitrage.

[2] Franco Modigliani and Merton H. Miller, "The Cost of Capital, Corporation Finance, and the Theory of Investment," *American Economic Review* 48 (June, 1958), pp. 261–97.

But the sale of his levered shares would force down the price of these shares. Conversely, if levered shares had sold for less than nonlevered shares, the opposite arbitrage would have driven up the price of the nonlevered shares. Thus, levered and nonlevered shares would have the same market value. We, on the other hand, believe that personal leverage and corporate leverage are not perfect substitutes. The reason is that a stockholder in a corporation is protected by limited liability, whereas a person who borrows on his own is subject to unlimited liability. In our model, therefore, it is possible for debt financing to increase the value of a firm, even assuming no income tax.

The difference between our position and that of MM can also be expressed in terms of a firm's average cost of capital. Since taxes are assumed to be nonexistent, no tax benefits can arise from debt financing. Hence,

$$\underset{\text{Net operating income}}{\bar{X}} = \underset{\text{Interest expense}}{I} + \underset{\text{Residual earnings}}{(\bar{X} - I)} \tag{13-5}$$

By definition, $k_i = I/L$ and $k_e = (\bar{X} - I)/S$, where L and S stand respectively for the market values of Champion's debt and equity. Substituting these definitions into Eq. (13-5) and dividing each side of the resulting equation by the total value V of the firm, we get

$$\frac{\bar{X}}{V} = k_i \frac{L}{V} + k_e \frac{S}{L} \tag{13-6}$$

The right-hand side of Eq. (13-6) is the firm's average cost of capital, ρ, defined as the weighted average of k_i and k_e, with the proportions of debt and equity in the capital structure acting as weights. Given $\bar{X}$, a constant V implies a constant ρ. The independence hypothesis, therefore, implies that the firm's average cost of capital is also unaffected by the firm's debt-to-equity ratio.

In Figure 13-5, the horizontal line AA' depicts the average cost of capital according to MM. The height of line AA' is determined by the average cost of capital when the firm is financed totally by equity; it is not affected by the degree of debt financing. By contrast, the model that we have presented assumes that, even ignoring the tax-deductibility of interest, moderate amounts of debt financing will enhance a firm's value. Personal leverage is in fact more risky than corporate leverage, so the two are not perfectly substitutable. Moreover, many financial institutions are required by law to confine their investments to high-grade bonds, a shortage of which would make them willing to pay prices higher than those implied by Modigliani and Miller's model. Our position implies that there is some debt ratio that will maximize the value of the firm and that the average cost of capital will be U-shaped, as shown by curve AA' in Figure 13-5.

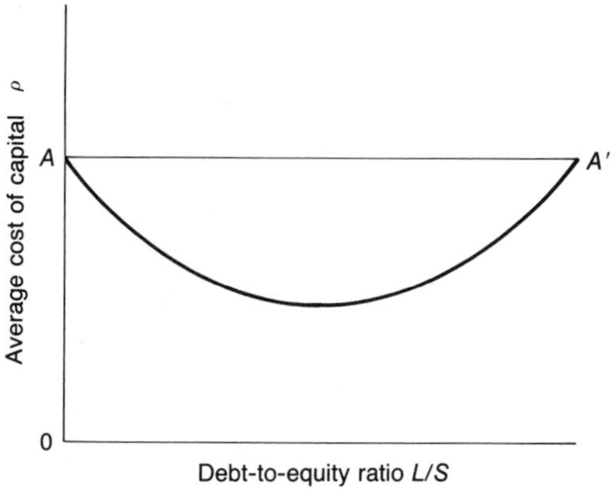

Figure 13-5 Capital Structure and Average Cost of Capital

The Explanatory Power of the Model

Our model is normative in that it prescribes the way a firm should formulate its debt policy. We can use our model to explain the different capital structures of Detroit Edison and General Motors Acceptance Corporation, two of the firms in Table 13-1. If the model provides a good explanation, we may have more confidence in its relevance. If not, the sample capital structures may be nonoptimal, or our theory may lack empirical validity, or both.

Nearly 60 percent of Detroit Edison's assets are financed with debt. How can we explain this relatively high debt-to-equity ratio? The chief characteristic of Detroit Edison, for debt-capacity decisions, is the stability of its net operating income, due to the stability of the firm's sales revenue. Detroit Edison, sells electricity to residential, commercial, and industrial consumers. Since electricity is a low-priced necessity, consumer demand for it tends to be independent of changes in business conditions. Commercial and industrial demands are somewhat more sensitive to these changes; but the company's revenue is partly protected by the "step-down" rate structure, which prices electric power on a sliding scale, so that any drop in physical consumption will reduce revenue less than proportionately. The long-run growth trend will also modify any cyclical setbacks which might otherwise strain the firm's resources. The resulting stability in net operating income explains why investors are willing to accept a high debt-to-equity ratio without demanding very high rates of return. In the future, however, considering the energy crisis and Detroit Edison's location in the heart of the automobile industry, the company may decide on a more conservative capital structure.

An even higher percentage—90 percent—of GMAC's total assets are financed with debt; furthermore, over half of this debt has maturities of one year or less. The net operating income of GMAC, since it varies with the sale of automobiles, is noticeably less stable than that of Detroit Edison. Some factor other than income stability is therefore needed to account for GMAC's high debt-to-equity ratio. This principle is to be found in the nature of GMAC's assets. An examination of the balance sheet will show that about two percent of the firm's total assets are cash and marketable securities, one percent is fixed assets, and 97 percent are accounts receivable. The liquidity of these receivables guards against their apparent vulnerability in terms of cash requirements. If net operating income dropped, it would probably be because the firm was making fewer loans and therefore collecting less interest. A decrease in business volume would be automatically accompanied by contraction and liquidation of accounts receivable, the chief assets. GMAC's assets thus contain within themselves the ability to pay off debt when earnings and sales volume fall. Asset liquidity, not income stability, makes it optimal for GMAC to use as much debt financing as it actually does.

Public utilities and finance companies provide extreme cases of stability and liquidity, respectively. Most businesses have less stable incomes than those of public utilities; few firms have assets as liquid as those of finance companies. Each firm has a peculiar combination of asset liquidity and earning stability; on the basis of this combination, security investors will assess the risk of investment and will decide how their required rates of return will vary with the extent of the firm's debt financing. We can forecast the k_i and k_e functions of a firm, calculate the optimal capital structure, and compare this with the pattern of financing actually employed. But this will not test our model because there is no objective way to verify forecasts of the k_i and k_e functions. Moreover, our model is more useful in explaining differences in the capital structures of firms with widely differing industrial characteristics than those of firms with basically similar characteristics.

Also, if we use our model to study the capital structures of individual firms, we should be alert to special factors beyond our general formulation. For example, debt financing in some companies may be artificially suppressed because the majority of stockholders favor earnings retention in order to convert dividends into capital gains. Debt financing may also be suppressed if management incorrectly views retained earnings as cost-free and therefore preferable to the issuance of either interest-bearing debt or new common stock. In some companies, distortion occurs when management refuses to borrow for fear that creditors may interfere with internal decisions. These factors do not apply to all firms at all times; but when they are present, they modify, sometimes significantly, the results that might be expected from a straightforward application of our model.

CORPORATE DEBT POLICY: INTERVIEW FINDINGS

We shall now present aspects of corporate debt policy, based on two interview studies, one conducted by Gordon Donaldson[3] and the other by myself.[4] The findings by Donaldson will be so identified; the others will be my own. Since my presentation here includes my interpretations of Donaldson's results, the interested reader should consult his original study. This discussion will include three sections: the objectives of debt financing, corporate control over the risk of insolvency, and procedures for maximization of share value.

Objectives

Do financial executives actually design their capital structures in order to maximize the values of their firms? Two extreme positions may be distinguished; in general, however, my interviews indicate that most firms follow an intermediate course.

According to one extreme position, a firm should take maximum advantage of its borrowing capacity consistent with the need for safety. The financial executive of a chemical company explained the logic of this position as follows:

> The overriding objective is a high-rate return on total equity or earnings per share. To help achieve this objective, you need as much leverage as you could qualify for in the industry. You can usually do best interest-wise if you rely on both long-term and short-term debt. But you must never forget to keep your company liquid, because if a credit crunch comes, your credit can evaporate awfully fast. It is important therefore to have in reserve some unused borrowing power.

Share-value maximization, although not explicitly mentioned, is clearly consistent with this objective.

At the other extreme is the policy of not relying on debt financing at all. This "no-debt" policy generally refers only to long-term debt, not to spontaneous credit or other short-term debt. At first glance, such a policy seems inconsistent with the objective of share-value maximization; but in fact there are at least two situations in which even our optimizing model would require a no-debt policy. First, some firms (e.g., steel companies and aircraft manufacturers) have largely fixed assets and highly unstable net

---

[3] Gordon Donaldson, *Corporate Debt Policy* (Boston: Graduate School of Business Administration, Harvard University, 1961).

[4] My findings, unpublished elsewhere, are based partly on personal interviews of company executives and partly on written replies to questions which I posed by mail.

operating incomes. Long-term debt financing might well violate the risk constraints of these firms. Second, when the main stockholders are in high income-tax brackets, their wealth is maximized through internal financing rather than through external borrowing. As the executive of an electronics firm said, "If we pay dividends, we would have to borrow money and pay interest on that. Moreover, the dividends would mostly go to Uncle Sam."

As we have mentioned, some executives erroneously view retained earnings as cost-free. It is true that retained earnings do not obligate a company to make payments comparable to the interest on debt; but if the earnings were distributed, they could earn income for the stockholders. The cost of retained earnings thus should be measured by the return that stockholders would have earned on their funds had they received them. To the extent that the cost-free view of retained earnings leads to a no-debt policy, it is nonoptimal and inconsistent with our model.

The Risk of Insolvency

From his interviews, Donaldson identified seven decision rules which guide debt policy in the firms he studied.[5] Although all seven affect both risk and return, two are particularly aimed at controlling the risk of insolvency.

The first rule limits the principal amount of long-term debt to a fixed percentage of the combined value of debt and equity. In some companies, debt financing is undertaken up to this limit; the companies could have utilized more debt were it not for this risk constraint. The constraint keeps the actual debt-to-equity ratio to a level below that of the unconstrained optimum. In other companies, the limit is a theoretical percentage considerably above the actual debt ratio. These companies could safely have incurred more debt but refrained because of the possible adverse effect on market valuation. In this case, the actual debt-to-equity ratio is identical with the unconstrained optimum.

The second rule Donaldson identifies indirectly regulates the amount of borrowing by limiting the ratio of "times fixed charges earned." The earnings available to pay debt charges must exceed the actual debt charges by a set margin, and this earnings-coverage requirement is generally some multiple of the annual interest charges or of interest plus principal repayments. The margin is designed to protect against the risk of insolvency due to an inability to meet fixed charges. The coverage requirement also affects valuation, although it is directed mainly at insolvency.

Financial executives in my interviews revealed the same awareness of the risk of insolvency associated with borrowing. Before actually borrowing, a firm will nearly always prepare a set of *pro forma* financial statements

---

[5] Donaldson, *op. cit.*, pp. 93–107. The interpretations are my own.

to see how the possible debt will affect the company's *EPS* and its debt-to-equity and interest-coverage ratios. In addition, several executives I interviewed stressed the possible threat to solvency of short-term borrowing. Even a company in a sound position may run into a short-term crisis and be unable to refinance its maturing obligations in a tight capital market. This prompted one executive to say, "The dominant consideration is never to get caught short. That is why we may for the sake of liquidity lengthen the maturity of our debt even though short-term funds may be cheaper and more flexible."

Maximizing the Value of the Firm

The risk of insolvency limits debt financing to a maximum level consistent with safety. The financial executive must determine what level within this limit will maximize the total market value of the firm. To do this, he must know how various debt ratios will affect the cost of his debt and equity financing. This, in turn, requires that he know how investors measure risk, how debt financing affects these measures, and what compensation investors demand for accepting risk. Most theorists use the variance of return as a measure of risk, although, as we have indicated, semi-variance may be more appropriate. Theorists have also had limited success in measuring the remuneration that investors require for assuming risk. How, then, do firms optimize their debt levels in practice?

Donaldson cites two frequently followed guidelines: "Borrow the maximum available at the prime [interest] rate," and "Borrow the maximum consistent with an 'A' rating."[6] Since bond rating determines the rate of interest, the two rules are similar, for both are aimed at locating the point on the capital supply schedules (i.e., the k_i and k_e functions) at which the curves begin to turn sharply upward. It is at this point that the marginal cost of debt financing becomes prohibitively high, so that any additional debt would lower the firm's market value. Earlier we mentioned that firms use the debt-to-equity and interest-coverage ratios to control the risk of insolvency. These controls may also be viewed as a means of maximizing share value by keeping both k_i and k_e within reasonable bounds. In my findings, nearly all firms seem to have fairly clear targets for debt-to-equity and interest-coverage ratios, which they constantly aim for.

Some theorists may disagree with this practical approach since it views the capital supply schedules as step functions rather than as smooth, continuously rising functions. But as a guide to action, it is sufficiently accurate, especially if, as many writers and practitioners believe, there is no single optimal debt ratio but rather a range of ratios that will maximize the value of a firm. If we plot total firm value as a function of debt ratio, we get not a

[6] Donaldson, *op. cit.*, pp. 97–100. The interpretations are my own.

single peak representing a unique optimum but a plateau representing multiple optima. It is the existence of this range, rather than a single point, that makes the practical approach acceptable despite its crudity.

REVIEW QUESTIONS

1. Taking the long-run view of capital structure, why should a firm be guided by the objective of maximizing the total value of the firm rather than the value of its common shares? In the short run, why would a firm find some other objective advantageous and what might it be?
2. Two nonfinancial executives of an electronics firm were overheard exchanging divergent views on financing policy: "You know the after-tax interest rate is lower than the yield on our stock. It's a mystery why we don't have as much debt in our capitalization as the finance companies do. If we did, the rate of return on our equity would double." "I disagree. Financing has no effect on the levels of our sales or production. We earn x dollars a year, which won't be affected by the way we finance our operations. Why ask for trouble by going into debt." Which line of reasoning would lead to the optimal capital structure for this firm?
3. Why is debt financing called financial leverage? How does this differ from operating leverage? If one were to measure the degree of financial and operating leverage in a sample of firms, would the relationship between the two be positive or negative? Why?
4. List the major factors to be considered in determining the optimal debt ratio for a firm's capital structure. Explain how and why each item affects the ratio.
5. Summarize Modigliani and Miller's independence hypothesis. What key assumptions must hold for it to be valid?
6. The capital structures of a commercial bank, an electric utility, a large department store, and a small textbook publisher are summarized below in random order. Match the firms with the data and explain the process by which you reached your conclusion.

	A	B	C	D
Short-term debt	11%	94%	33%	39%
Long-term debt	46	1	23	0
Preferred stock	10	0	3	0
Common stock and surplus	33	5	41	61
	100%	100%	100%	100%

7. What kinds of capital structures would you recommend to firms in these industries: commercial airlines, uranium mining, automobile manufacturing, general merchandising, and accounts-receivable factoring? Find the actual composite capital structures for these industries and account for any divergences from your recommendations.
8. Interview studies have the advantage of revealing ways in which both theory and practice may be improved. In the light of the findings presented in this chapter, how might debt-to-equity-ratio decisions be improved? Could theory be recast in a more readily applicable form?

9. A firm's capital structure is dynamic, changing with each transaction. Some transactions are undertaken explicitly to alter capital structure, e.g., the conversion of bonds or preferred stock into common stock. How would such conversions affect a firm's risk of insolvency and the expected value and variance of its net income? For extra credit, illustrate your discussion with the financial data of companies that have recently made such conversions.

10. If a firm incorrectly assumes that retained earnings are cost-free, how will its capital structure be distorted? How will this in turn distort the company's investment decisions?

PROBLEMS

1. Using the data in the latest annual reports, calculate the degrees of financial and operating leverage used by Carolina Power and Light, Cunningham Drug Stores, and Anheuser-Busch, Inc. Since annual reports do not usually distinguish between fixed and variable operating expenses, you will have to estimate that division on the basis of your knowledge of these companies. If you wish, you may make the calculations for firms with which you are familiar.

2. A group of investors is promoting a company that will manufacture and market a complete line of space-age garden products. The cost of the enterprise is estimated at $1 million. The promoters have narrowed their financing alternatives to two. Either they will put up the entire amount themselves in return for 100,000 shares of common stock, or else they will put up $600,000 in return for 60,000 shares and raise the remaining $400,000 by selling bonds at 8 percent. The company is expected to generate an annual net operating income of $380,000. The tax rate is 50 percent. Determine the functional relationship under each plan between net operating income and *EPS*. Graph your results.

   If the earnings-capitalization rate is 12 percent under Plan A and 13 percent under Plan B, which plan will enhance the wealth of the promoters more? Which plan would be preferable if the rate were 12 percent under Plan A and 16 percent under Plan B?

3. Determine the optimal level of debt financing for Champion, Inc., our text example, on the basis of the following relationships among the level of debt (L), the rate of interest (k_i), and the earnings-capitalization rate (k_e):

L	k_i	k_e
$ 0	7.0%	9.5%
20,000	7.5	10.0
30,000	9.0	12.5
40,000	11.0	15.5

4. (a) Using the data in Table 13-3, calculate the average cost of capital (ρ) associated with each level of debt. How does ρ respond to changes in the amount of debt? to changes in the debt-to-equity ratio?

   (b) Repeat your calculations assuming a tax rate of zero. How do your results contradict MM's independence hypothesis?

5. According to MM's theory, if there were no income tax, Champion, Inc., would have a value of $105,260, independent of its capital structure. Construct a table similar to 13-3 based on the independence hypothesis, and use Eq. (13-6) to

show that the average cost of capital is also independent of the firm's capital structure.

6. Listed below are the balance sheet and income statement of the Mid-State Power and Light Company. To meet expanding demand for electricity, the company has decided to invest $40 million in a new generating plant. The company is considering two alternatives—all debt financing at 9 percent interest, or $25 million of debt at 8.5 percent and the issuance of 600,000 shares of common stock at $25 per share. Prepare the *pro forma* balance sheet and income statement corresponding to each method of financing and compare the effects of these two methods on debt-to-equity and interest-coverage ratios and on *EPS*. You may assume that each additional dollar of company assets adds 15 cents to net operating income.

Mid-State Power and Light Company, Balance Sheet, December 31, Year 1 (in thousands of dollars)

Utility plant		Capitalization	
Original cost	$525,943	Preferred stock	$ 59,300
Accumulated depreciation	124,326	Common stock (8,000,000 shs.)	85,000
	$401,617	Retained earnings	33,371
		Long-term debt	184,422
Other assets			$362,093
Cash	$ 2,880		
Accounts receivable	6,996	Current liabilities	
Fuel (at cost)	9,555	Notes payable	25,731
Materials and supplies	5,473	Accounts payable	20,123
Miscellaneous	140	Accruals	18,714
	$ 25,044		$ 64,568
Total assets	$426,661	Total liabilities and equity	$426,661

Mid-State Power and Light Company Income Statement, Year 1 (in thousands of dollars)

Operating revenues	$130,000
Operating expenses	70,000
Operating income	$ 60,000
Other income	2,400
Income before interest charges	$ 62,400
Interest charges	14,000
Taxable income	$ 48,400
Income taxes (40%)	19,360
After-tax income	$ 29,040
Preferred dividends	2,000
Net income	$ 27,040
Common dividends	17,600
Transfer to retained earnings	$ 9,440

REFERENCES

ANG, JAMES S., and KIRITKUMAR A. PATEL, "Bond Rating Methods: Comparison and Validation," *Journal of Finance* 30 (May, 1975), pp. 631–640.

BREALEY, RICHARD A., *Security Prices in a Competitive Market* (Cambridge: The M.I.T. Press, 1971), Ch. 3.

COHAN, AVERY B., *The Risk Structure of Interest Rates* (Morristown: General Learning Press, 1973).

DONALDSON, GORDON, *Corporate Debt Capacity* (Boston: Graduate School of Business Administration, Harvard University, 1961).

DONALDSON, GORDON, *Strategy for Financial Mobility* (Boston: Graduate School of Business Administration, Harvard University, 1969).

DURAND, DAVID, "Costs of Debt and Equity Funds for Business: Trends and Problems of Measurement," *Conference on Research in Business Finance* (New York: National Bureau of Economic Research, 1952), pp. 215–247.

FAMA, EUGENE F., and MERTON H. MILLER, *The Theory of Finance* (New York: Holt, Rinehart and Winston, 1972), Ch. 4.

GORDON, M. J., "Towards a Theory of Financial Distress," *Journal of Finance* 26 (May, 1971), pp. 347–356.

HALEY, CHARLES W., and LAWRENCE D. SCHALL, *The Theory of Financial Decisions* (New York: McGraw-Hill Book Company, 1973), Chs. 10 and 11.

HARKINS, EDWIN P., and FRANCIS J. WALSH, JR., *Corporate Debt Management* (New York: The Conference Board, 1968).

MALKIEL, BURTON G., *The Debt-Equity Combination of the Firm and the Cost of Capital: An Introductory Analysis* (New York: General Learning Press, 1971).

MODIGLIANI, FRANCO, and MERTON H. MILLER, "Corporation Income Taxes and the Cost of Capital: A Correction," *American Economic Review* 53 (June, 1963), pp. 433–443.

MODIGLIANI, FRANCO, and MERTON H. MILLER, "The Cost of Capital, Corporation Finance, and the Theory of Investment," *American Economic Review* 48 (June, 1958), pp. 261–297.

PINCHES, GEORGE E., and KENT A. MINGO, "A Multivariate Analysis of Industrial Bond Rating," *Journal of Finance* 28 (March, 1973), pp. 1–18.

"Recent Developments in Corporate Finance," *Federal Reserve Bulletin* 61 (August, 1975), pp. 463–471.

"Recent Patterns of Corporate External Financing," *Federal Reserve Bulletin* 59 (December, 1973), pp. 837–846.

STIGLITZ, JOSEPH E., "A Re-Examination of the Modigliani-Miller Theorem," *American Economic Review* 59 (December, 1969), pp. 784–793.

STIGLITZ, JOSEPH E., "Some Aspects of the Pure Theory of Corporate Finance: Bankruptcies and Take-Overs," *The Bell Journal of Economics and Management Science* 3 (Autumn, 1972), pp. 458–482.

WALSH, FRANCIS J., JR., *Planning Corporate Capital Structures* (New York: The Conference Board, 1972).

WHITE, WILLIAM L., "Debt Management and the Form of Business Financing," *Journal of Finance* 29 (May, 1974), pp. 565–577.

14 Debt-Maturity and Timing Decisions

In the last chapter, we dealt strictly with the optimal debt-to-equity ratio. By assuming all debt to have the same maturity, we were able to avoid the debt-maturity decision. When this assumption is dropped, more alternatives become available, making the financing decision more complex. In addition to determining the amount of debt, the financial executive must also decide on the ratio of long-term to short-term debt and the appropriate time to issue each type of debt.

We shall start by assuming that the financial executive does not expect interest rates to change. This assumption sets aside the timing decision and allows us to focus first on the maturity decision. In reality, capital markets are never static and interest rates do fluctuate over time. Hence, if static analysis calls for some long-term debt, the financial executive must decide whether the possibility of falling interest rates might make it wiser to begin long-term financing with short-term debt and to refinance later. Similarly, if static analysis calls for some permanent short-term debt, the financial executive must decide whether higher interest rates in the future might make long-term debt now less expensive. We shall consider these timing decisions after our initial analysis of the debt-maturity decision under conditions of static interest rates.

When interest rates are static, the chief determinants of the optimal maturity structure are the relative costs of long- and short-term debt and the risk of insolvency associated with these kinds of debt. We shall begin by considering the difference in long- and short-term interest rates and the effects of this difference on the relative costs of long- and short-term borrowing.

LONG-TERM VS. SHORT-TERM BORROWING COSTS

Difference in Interest Rates

Debt maturity varies from a few days to more than 30 years. The relationship between the maturities and yields of comparable securities is known as the term structure of interest rates; its graphic presentation is called the yield curve.[1] "Comparable securities" are those which are the same in all characteristics except term to maturity. To compare long- and short-term interest rates, we should examine the whole array of rates, but for the sake of simplicity we shall restrict the comparison to two rates: the yields on Aaa corporate bonds as an example of long-term rates; and those on prime commercial paper as an example of short-term rates. Figure 14-1 shows the annual levels of these rates from 1925 through 1974, while Figure 14-2 shows the annual excess of the long-term rate over the short-term rate for the same

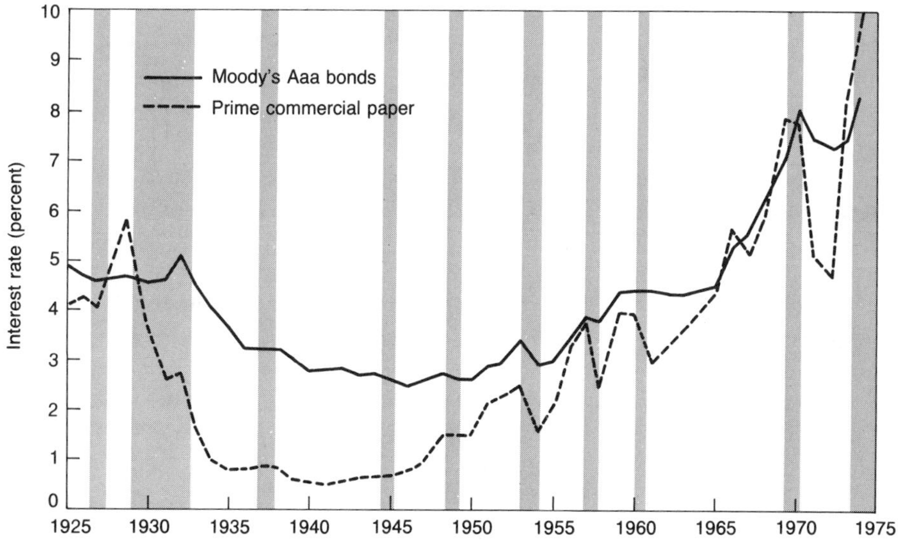

Shaded areas indicate recession.

Sources: Moody's Investors Service and *Federal Reserve Bulletin*.

Figure 14-1 Long-Term vs. Short-Term Interest Rates

[1] Here, bond yield refers to the rate of return that an investor will realize on his funds if he pays the market price for a bond and holds it to maturity. This yield to maturity is calculated by finding that discount rate that equates the present value of all future interest and principal payments to the price of the bond.

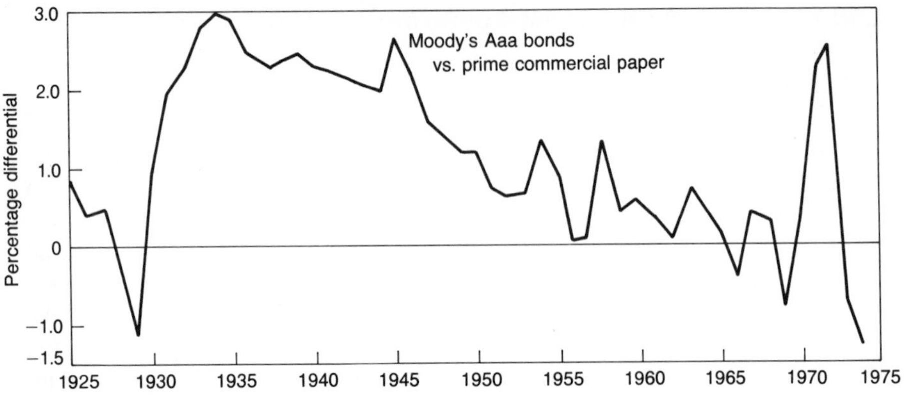

Sources: Same as Figure 14-1.

Figure 14-2 Interest Rate Differential: Long- and Short-Term

period. During this period, there were only 6 years (1928, 1929, 1966, 1969, 1973, 1974) in which the long-term rate was lower than the short-term: the greatest difference was in 1974, when Aaa corporate bonds yielded 8.56 percent and prime commercial paper yielded 9.83 percent, a difference of 1.27 percent. In the other 44 years, the long-term rate exceeded the short-term rate by 0.5 percent about half of the time, by 1.5 percent a quarter of the time, and by 2.5 percent the other quarter of the time. For the period as a whole, the short-term average was 2.96 percent, while the long-term average was 4.14 percent, giving the short-term rate an advantage of 1.18 percent—an advantage, at least, from the point of view of the borrowing corporations.

Since the interest rates in Figure 14-1 represent the yields to security investors, they are not an exact measure of the historical costs of long- and short-term borrowing (see Table 14-1). These rates are the yield on "seasoned" issues—that is, issues which have been outstanding for at least a few months. A firm floating a new bond issue must offer a premium return of about .17 percent;[2] no comparable premium is offered on commercial paper. On new issues, therefore, the short-term rate averages 1.35 (= 1.18 + .17) percent less than the long-term rate. Whether this difference will continue is not easy to predict.

---

[2] Joseph W. Conard and Mark W. Frankena, "The Yield Spread Between New and Seasoned Corporate Bonds, 1952–63," in Jack M. Guttentag and Phillip Cagen, eds., *Essays on Interest Rates* (New York: National Bureau of Economic Research, 1969), p. 144. For more recent data, see John D. Rea, "The Yield Spread Between Newly Issued and Seasoned Corporate Bonds," in Federal Reserve Bank of Kansas City, *Monthly Review* (June, 1974), pp. 3–9.

Table 14-1 Historical Costs of Long- and Short-Term Debt

	Aaa Corporate Bonds	Prime Commercial Paper	Difference
Interest rate on seasoned issues*	4.14%	2.96%	1.18%
New vs. seasoned yield†	.17	0	.17
Interest rate on new issues	4.31%	2.96%	1.35%
Issue costs	.06	.55	−.49
Total costs	4.37%	3.51%	0.86%

* 1925–1974 average.
† 1952–1963 average.
Source: See Figure 14-1 and the accompanying text.

Difference in Issue Cost

There is another reason why the interest rates in Figure 14-1 are not an exact measure of the historical costs of long- and short-term borrowing. Corporate bonds and commercial paper have had different issue costs, which typically ran as follows.[3] The cost of issuing bonds varied from 1.2 percent of the gross proceeds for large issues to 3.2 percent for small issues; the average was about 1.5 percent, which is equivalent to .06 percent per annum for a 25-year bond (see Table 14-1). The cost of issuing 9-month commercial paper was 1/8 of one percent per transaction, which is about .17 percent per annum. However, commercial paper also had to be secured by an open line of bank credit, and we may assume that each dollar of commercial paper had to be backed by 75 cents of bank credit, which in turn had to be supported by 7.5 cents of compensating balance. We may also assume that each dollar of compensating balance had to be borrowed, and historically, the interest rate was 5 percent per annum. This, in effect, increased the cost of commercial paper by .38 percent per annum, making the total issue cost .55 percent per annum. Since the issue cost for corporate bonds was .06 percent per annum, the historical difference in costs between long- and short-term debt must be adjusted by .49 percent; and since the interest difference, as shown before, has been 1.35 percent, short-term debt has had a net annual cost advantage to the borrower of .86 percent.

The fact that short-term rates, even when adjusted for issue costs, are generally lower than long-term rates does not in itself mean that short-term borrowing is less costly; it is less costly only if the interest-rate level does not change over time. When interest rates change, short-term rates which are lower than contemporary long-term rates may yet be higher than long-term rates at a later time. In that case, a company needs a timing strategy,

[3] Burton G. Malkiel, *The Term Structure of Interest Rates* (Princeton: Princeton University Press, 1966), pp. 129–132.

which we shall take up later when we drop the assumption that the level of future interest rates will be static.

Difference in Flexibility

Not only the interest-rate differential but also the greater flexibility of short-term debt makes this form of borrowing less costly. When a firm's need for funds subsides, short-term debt can be returned to the lender(s) more easily than long-term. The borrowers of long-term funds may, of course, initiate a call for redemption. But if bonds are redeemed before maturity, the indenture generally requires that the borrower pay the bondholders a premium as compensation for the inconvenience and cost of having to advance the time of their reinvestments. If the indenture prohibits redemption during, say, the first five years, the borrower will probably invest any accumulated surplus in money-market instruments such as Treasury bills and commercial paper. But unless the period is one of tight money, the interest income from such temporary investments will be less than the interest expense which the firm pays to obtain these funds.

To quantify the value of flexibility, let us consider a company which utilizes $1 million in capital over an extended period. The funds may be raised either by selling long-term bonds or by borrowing from banks, both at 8 percent. If the funds are fully utilized all the time, the interest expense will be $80,000 per annum under either alternative, and flexibility is not an issue. But let us assume that the needs for funds are not continuous and that they are needed for only three months each year. A 3-month bank loan would cost the firm $20,000 (= $80,000 ÷ 4) in interest expenses. A long-term bond would still cost $80,000 annually, but the expense would be partly offset by the income from the investment of temporary surplus funds. If the reinvestment rate is 6 percent, investing $1 million for nine months would bring $45,000. The net long-term cost would be $35,000, which is still more than the short-term cost. The value of flexibility, in other words, depends on the variability in the demand for funds and on the opportunity for temporary reinvestment.

The difference in flexibility tends to reinforce the cost advantage of short-term debt over long-term debt. Thus, under static assumptions, cost considerations strongly favor short-term financing. But, as we shall see, a realistic maturity policy must consider two other factors: the risk of insolvency and the future level of interest rates.

UNDERSTANDING THE INTEREST-RATE STRUCTURE

Before considering the risk of insolvency, let us study the yield curve, to gain a better understanding of the structure of interest rates. A yield

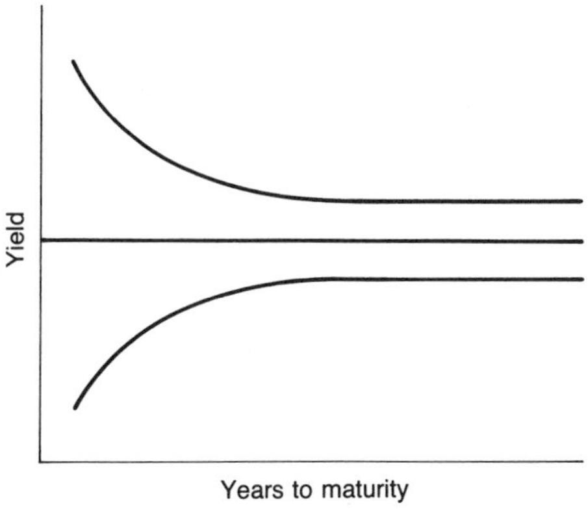

Figure 14-3 Types of Yield Curves

curve, as mentioned before, shows how interest rate varies with maturity for debt securities of comparable quality. The curve is upward sloping, level, or downward sloping depending on whether short-term rates are lower than, equal to, or higher than long-term rates (see Figure 14-3). The financial executives will need to know why the yield curves have historically sloped upward and whether or not this pattern is likely to continue. Various theories attempt to explain the term-structure of interest rates, and we shall now outline the expectations theory, the market-segmentation theory, and the eclectic theory.[4]

The Expectations Theory

According to this theory, the structure of interest rates at a given moment is determined by the market's (i.e., the investors') expectations regarding the future course of interest rates. Four assumptions are involved: all securities under consideration are comparable in all respects except term to maturity; all investors have identical expectations regarding future interest rates; all investors are motivated solely by the objective of profit maximization; and transactions costs are zero. The theory then maintains that the interest rate on two-year bonds must be mathematically related to the current one-year rate and to the one-year rate expected one year hence; the rate on three-year bonds must be similarly related to the current one-year rate and to the one-year rates expected one and two years hence; etc. The mathematical relationship must be one that will insure that the investor with a given investment horizon will realize a constant return on his funds

[4] Friedrich A. Lutz and John M. Culbertson are the most articulate exponents of the expectations theory and the market-segmentation theory, respectively. The discussion here is based on the succinct restatement by Malkiel, *op. cit.*, Ch. 2.

regardless of the maturity of the securities purchased. Thus, given the current short-term rate and a series of expected future short-term rates, the interest-rate structure is uniquely determined.

The mechanism behind this unique structure is the process of arbitrage. Let us say that an investor with funds to invest for two years may choose either a two-year bond or two successive investments in one-year bonds. The returns from the two investments must be equal; otherwise, the investor will divert his funds from the less profitable source to the more profitable. This condition of equilibrium will hold if $R(2)$, the two-year (i.e., long-term) rate, and r_1 and r_2, the one-year (i.e., short-term) rates, bear the following relationship to each other:

$$[1 + R(2)] = [(1 + r_1)(1 + r_2')]^{1/2} \tag{14-1}$$

where the symbol (′) indicates that the rate is a forecast. Thus, if the current one-year rate (r_1) is 8 percent and the expected one-year rate for year 2 (r_2') is 9 percent, then the current two-year rate ($R[2]$) must be approximately 8.5 percent. If $R(2)$ is greater than 8.5 percent, the investor will shift his funds from short-term to long-term bonds, causing the short-term rate to rise and the long-term to fall; if $R(2)$ is less than 8.5 percent, the reverse phenomenon will occur. The condition prescribed in Eq. (14-1) must be met exactly for a state of equilibrium to hold.

Although our example covers only two time periods, the formula may be generalized for an n-period investment horizon:

$$1 + R(n) = [(1 + r_1)(1 + r_2')(1 + r_3') \cdots (1 + r_n')]^{1/n} \tag{14-2}$$

Just as the two-year rate was the geometric average of the current one-year rate and the expected one-year rate for the second year, so the n-year rate will be the geometric average of the current one-year rate and the expected one-year rates for each of the next $(n - 1)$ years. The formula implies that an investor purchasing a 30-year bond knows not only the current one-year rate but also the one-year rates expected for each of the next 29 years. Some writers object to this assumption, since few bond investors can forecast such distant interest rates.

Eq. (14-2) may also be used to explain any of the three rate structures depicted in Figure 14-3. If the short-term rates form a declining (level, or rising) series, then the corresponding long-term average must be less than (equal to, or greater than) the current short-term rate. According to the expectations theory, it follows that a falling yield curve is due to an expected fall in short-term rates; a level yield curve is due to an expected constancy in short-term rates; and a rising curve is due to an expected increase.

The Market-Segmentation Theory

The expectations theory states that the investor is indifferent to the maturity structure of his securities holdings and will shift freely among securities of varying maturities if a shift will enhance his return during the investment period. It follows that changes in the maturity structure of the existing supply of bonds will have no effect on the structure of interest rates unless expectations are also affected. This supposed independence of interest rate structure and maturity structure has been criticized by institutionalists, who argue that the market for capital is less unified and fluid than the expectationists maintain.

The institutionalists regard the capital market as segmented. Borrowers and lenders are assumed to have rigid preferences regarding the particular maturity segment of the market in which they will operate. Lenders such as commercial banks are assumed, because of their liquidity needs, to purchase short-term bonds only; life-insurance companies, because of their earnings requirements, are assumed to purchase only long-term bonds. Borrowers such as public utilities are assumed, because of their large investments in fixed assets, to issue only long-term debt; while finance companies, because of their asset liquidity, are assumed to issue only short-term debt. Carried to its extreme, then, the market-segmentation theory views the long- and short-term capital markets as totally separate, distinct, and independent. Since the interest rate of each market is determined by forces of supply and demand that are unique to that market, the long-term and short-term rates are also independent.

The Eclectic Theory

The eclectic theory combines elements of both other theories and offers a more balanced explanation of the structure of interest rates.[5] This approach acknowledges the importance of investor expectations but rejects the behavioral assumption that investors are able to forecast short-term rates far into the future. Instead, bond investors are assumed to form expectations only of the "normal range" of interest rates. If current rates are near the upper bound for this range, future rates are more likely to fall than to rise. Investors will then prefer long-term over short-term bonds, and this preference will create a downward-sloping yield curve. Conversely, if current rates are near the lower bound, the yield curve will be upward-sloping.

While the expectations theory attaches no significance to the maturity structure of debt, the eclectic theory recognizes that different investor and

[5] The eclectic theory is essentially Malkiel's attempt to synthesize the expectations and market-segmentation theories of interest-rate structure. "The eclectic theory" is my term.

issuer groups have quite different maturity preferences; but it does not view this segmentation as complete. As the eclectics point out, if market segmentation were complete, the maturity structure of outstanding debt for each class of borrowers or lenders would not change over time—a conclusion which is not supported by the evidence. When interest rates are high, financial institutions lengthen the average maturity of their holdings and corporations shift their borrowing from long- to short-term debt; when interest rates are low, the opposite behavior is generally observed.

The eclectic theory also explains how transactions costs affect the structure of interest rates. According to the expectations theory, when interest rates are in equilibrium, a bond purchaser has no maturity preferences because, given his investment period, he can realize the same return on either a long- or short-term security. But even if the capital market were completely unified and fluid, this reasoning would be valid only if transactions costs were zero. Actually, investors can minimize these costs by buying bonds whose maturities coincide with the desired investment period. Debt maturity does make a difference. If most investors have investment periods shorter than the maturities of available securities, the yield curve will slope upward, since a higher long-term rate will be needed to induce additional investors to buy long-term bonds. Conversely, if most investors have investment periods longer than the available maturities, the yield curve will slope downward. The former case is, however, far more likely, since most firms require relatively permanent financing.

THE RISK OF INSOLVENCY

We have seen that the interest-rate structure, issue costs, and flexibility all favor short-term borrowing. On the other hand, rising interest rates may shift the relative advantage in favor of long-term borrowing. However, even if future interest rates were to remain constant, we would still expect firms to employ some long-term financing. The reason is the effect of short-term financing on a firm's risk of insolvency, and this risk varies directly with the frequency of refunding and inversely with asset liquidity.

Debt Maturity and the Probability of Default

The maturity structure of debt affects the risk of insolvency primarily through the frequency of refunding. As one executive observes, short-term debt may be cheaper, but it increases the chances of being "caught short." By way of illustration, let us consider a firm that needs $5 million in capital over a 20-year planning horizon. If the money is raised through 10-year notes, one refunding operation will take place during that time; but if 1-year notes are used, there will be nineteen such operations. At each refunding, there is at least a slight chance that the operation will be unsuccessful, forcing the firm to default on its obligations. Therefore, other things being equal, the risk of insolvency varies directly with the frequency of refunding.

Independence Over Time. Our hypothetical firm needs M dollars in capital over a period of n years. On the basis of past experience, the financial executive forecasts that there are k chances out of n that any given year will be a "good" year for successful refunding of maturing debt. If the need to refund occurs in a "bad" year, bankruptcy will be inevitable. We shall temporarily assume that the financial conditions are independent over time; that is, the fact that year t was good has no effect on the probability that any succeeding year will be good. Given the length of the planning horizon, the number of refundings, r, varies inversely with the maturity of the debt. Since k/n is the probability that any given year will be good, k/n is also the probability that the first refunding will be successful. By virtue of the independence assumption, k/n is also the probability that any future refunding will be successful, given that all previous refundings have succeeded. If the firm is to remain solvent, all r refundings must succeed. The probability of this event is

$$P(S) = (k/n)^r \tag{14-3}$$

Accordingly, the probability of default may be expressed:

$$1 - P(S) = 1 - (k/n)^r \tag{14-4}$$

Eq. (14-4) enables us to calculate the risk of insolvency as a function of the frequency of refunding. Table 14-2 shows the values of $1 - P(S)$ for various values of k/n and r. We can see that for a firm which is financially strong (let us say, $k/n \geq .990$), the cumulative risk of default associated with r refundings is approximately r times the basic risk for one refunding. For a weak firm ($k/n < .990$), the cumulative risk of default does not increase

Table 14-2 The Probability of Default as a Function of the Frequency of Refunding: Independent Model

k/n \ r	1	2	3	4	5	6	7	8
.996	.004	.008	.012	.016	.020	.024	.028	.032
.993	.007	.014	.021	.028	.035	.041	.048	.055
.990	.010	.020	.030	.039	.049	.059	.068	.077
.980	.020	.040	.059	.078	.096	.114	.132	.149
.975	.025	.049	.073	.096	.119	.141	.162	.183
.900	.100	.190	.271	.344	.410	.469	.522	.570
.800	.200	.360	.488	.590	.672	.738	.790	.832

proportionately with the number of debt refundings, but since the basic risk is large, the cumulative risk soon becomes overwhelming. Short-term financing of long-term investments, therefore, is riskier for a financially weak firm than for a financially strong one; but we should note it can be risky for a strong firm as well.

Dependence Over Time. The preceding model unrealistically assumed that the risk in a given year is independent of that in the others, which means all might be good years or all bad. An alternative is to assume that there will be k good years and $(n-k)$ bad ones. We will also assume all possible sequences of good and bad years are equally likely. In this revised model the probability that any given year will be good is not independent of the past record, since the planning horizon is divided in a fixed proportion between good and bad years. To determine the risk of default, we again let r stand for the number of refunding operations. Solvency demands that none of the r refundings fall in a bad year. The probability of a successful first refunding is k/n, the overall percentage of good years during the planning horizon. A successful first refunding will reduce the probability that the next year will be good from k/n to $(k-1)/(n-1)$. We again use S to denote the success of all r refundings and $P(S)$ to denote the probability of this outcome:

$$P(S) = \left(\frac{k}{n}\right)\left(\frac{k-1}{n-1}\right)\cdots\left(\frac{k-r+1}{n-r+1}\right) \tag{14-5}$$

The probability of default is

$$1 - P(S) = 1 - \left(\frac{k}{n}\right)\left(\frac{k-1}{n-1}\right)\cdots\left(\frac{k-r+1}{n-r+1}\right) \tag{14-6}$$

Table 14-3 gives the values of $1 - P(S)$ for various values of k/n and r under the dependence assumption. A comparison with Table 14-2 shows that the

Table 14-3 The Probability of Default as a Function of the Frequency of Refunding: Dependent Model*

k/n \ r	1	2	3	4	5	6	7	8
.996	.004	.008	.013	.018	.023	.029	.035	.043
.993	.007	.014	.022	.031	.040	.050	.061	.074
.990	.010	.021	.032	.044	.057	.071	.087	.104
.980	.020	.041	.063	.087	.111	.138	.167	.198
.975	.025	.051	.078	.107	.138	.170	.205	.242
.900	.100	.196	.289	.378	.463	.543	.619	.691
.800	.200	.371	.516	.637	.736	.815	.877	.923

* This table is calculated assuming a 15-year planning horizon.

dependent model yields higher cumulative risks when a firm engages in frequent refundings. The difference between the two tables becomes more significant for both strong and weak firms if the number of refundings, r, exceeds three. These results reinforce our earlier conclusion that short-term financing of long-term investments is risky.

Asset Liquidity and the Probability of Default

The above tables reveal that firms with low basic risks have a small probability of default even as refundings increase in frequency. Firms in some industries, therefore, can engage heavily in short-term financing without endangering their solvency. Almost invariably, these are companies whose assets are highly liquid. Asset liquidity enhances a firm's ability to generate internally funds which may be used, if necessary, to meet maturing obligations. Healthy internal cash flows make it easier for the firm to obtain external funds as well.

Since different firms have different assets, we need a way to measure asset liquidity. By the liquidity of an asset, we mean the ratio between the immediate value that can be realized upon quick sale and the full value that can be realized if all useful preparations may be made before sale.[6] Thus, if V' is immediate cash value and V is full cash value, asset liquidity is measured by the ratio V'/V. Since quick sales generally result in a selling price below full value, the liquidity index V'/V for any given asset will have a value less than one. Figure 14-4 shows the curves that result when V'/V is

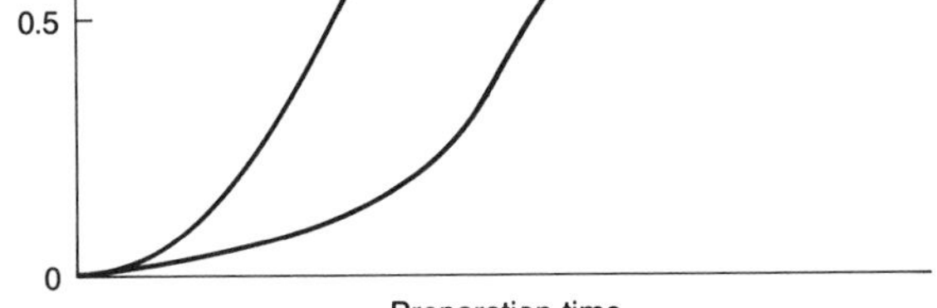

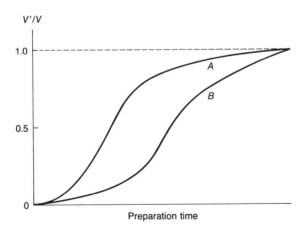

Figure 14-4 Index of Asset Liquidity

[6] This is the definition of liquidity used by James L. Pierce in his paper, "Commercial Bank Liquidity," *Federal Reserve Bulletin* 52 (August, 1966), pp. 1093–1101.

plotted against preparation time. The S-shape implies that preparation time before sale is subject to phases of increasing and decreasing returns. The actual curves shown are only examples; any curve would slope upwards since realizable value increases with preparation time before sale.

The asset represented by Curve *A* in Figure 14-4 is more liquid than that represented by Curve *B:* the firm can realize the full economic value of asset A more readily than that of asset B. If *A* represents accounts receivable, the corresponding curve for cash and marketable securities will be to the left of *A*. If *B* represents equipment, the corresponding curve for land and buildings will lie to the right of *B*. Each firm has a spectrum of assets whose varying degrees of liquidity may be depicted by a family of such curves. Although *A* and *B* refer here to individual assets, we may easily derive a composite curve for each firm by averaging the individual curves, using the relative sizes of the assets as weights. We will find that commercial banks, savings-and-loan associations, and finance companies are considerably more liquid than electric utilities, railroads, and steel manufacturers. This difference explains why the former groups can easily incur heavy short-term indebtedness, while the latter should not.

It is asset liquidity, not earnings stability, that permits a firm to borrow a large proportion of its funds on a short-term basis. For example, an electric utility has highly stable earnings and cash flows but largely illiquid assets, and should therefore avoid short-term debts. Liquid assets can provide a ready source of cash if the firm is having difficulty refinancing its short-term debt, but earnings stability offers no such protection against large demands on cash.

The debt-maturity decision is closely related to the debt-capacity decision, and in practice the two must be made simultaneously. The financial executive must specify not only the level of debt financing but also the maturity composition of any given level of debt. However, the procedure for optimizing debt policy remains as presented: each composite strategy must be tested for the risk of insolvency and those strategies with excessive risks eliminated. For each remaining strategy, the financial executive must forecast the interest rate and earnings yield (k_i and k_e) that are likely to prevail. The optimal debt policy is the one that will maximize the value of the firm. Since risk must be balanced against cost, the optimal policy for most firms calls for some combination of long- and short-term debt.

THE TIMING DECISION

Effect of Interest-Rate Fluctuations

We shall now recognize that interest rates do fluctuate and that this necessitates timing decisions. Under static conditions, management would decide on a given level of debt and the division of this debt between long- and short-term. Timing would not be a factor in implementing this decision. In reality, interest rates do fluctuate cyclically, and a firm can benefit from these fluctuations if it times its security offerings skillfully.

Suppose, for example, a firm's analysis calls for a certain amount of long-term debt financing. If interest rates are expected to fall, the firm may do better to postpone its borrowing until the interest rates have fallen. This may require postponing the firm's investments as well. Industrial companies, in general, can do this more easily than, for example, public utilities. If the investments cannot be postponed, much the same interest savings can be realized by short-term borrowing first and long-term refinancing later. Thus, short-term borrowing may be a way to defer a long-term commitment. Similarly, if repeated short-term borrowing is being considered and interest rates are expected to rise, the firm may be able to save interest by long-term borrowing. Thus, long-term borrowing may be a way to advance the timing of a series of short-term borrowings. We see, then, that a maturity decision is also a timing decision.

A Cyclical Debt Strategy

An upward-sloping yield curve does not mean that continual short-term borrowing will necessarily minimize a firm's interest costs. Long-term borrowing may be cheaper if the company can time its bond issues to coincide with the low in the cycle of interest rates. Returning to Figure 14-1, let us examine the behavior of interest rates during the entire period since 1925. Three general observations seem warranted:

1. Short-term interest rates tend to be more volatile than long-term rates.
2. Short-term rates tend to exceed long-term rates in years of tight money and to fall below long-term rates in years of easy money.
3. Fluctuations of both rates conform to fluctuations in general business conditions. The rates tend to be high in years of prosperity and low in years of recession.

The observations suggest a typical pattern of interest-rate cycles such as the one depicted in Figure 14-5. J. Fred Weston and Eugene F. Brigham have observed that businesses have frequently relied heavily on short-term debt during the early phases of business recovery because of the need to build up working capital assets and the desire to take advantage of the lower short-term rates.[7] The tendency is to delay long-term borrowing until

[7] See their *Managerial Finance* (New York: Holt, Rinehart and Winston, 1969), pp. 782–783.

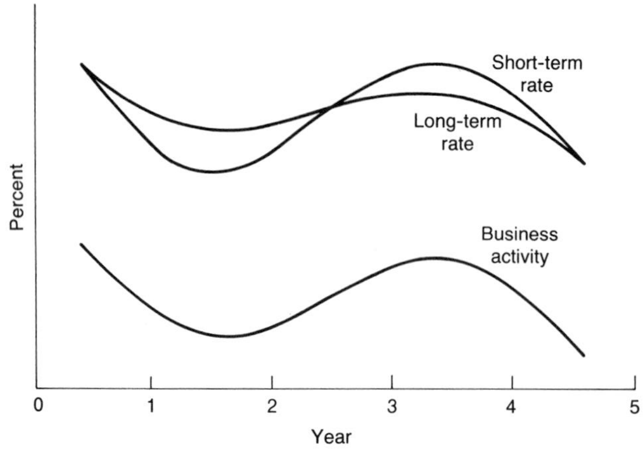

Figure 14-5 Cyclical Fluctuations of Interest Rates

the short-term rate overtakes the long-term. In the long view, this timing is the reverse of the optimal strategy. Using short-term debt when the general level of interest is low may result in savings during the initial months, but only at the cost of losing the opportunity to sell long-term bonds at the low point of the interest-rate cycle. Similarly, long-term borrowing when interest rates in general are up may produce an initial savings but at the cost of the firm's being committed to high rates for years to come. Instead, short-term debt should be used temporarily until long-term rates fall. The problem is, of course, more difficult in practice, since forecasting changes in interest rates is not so easy as discussing them.

An Actual Timing Decision

We shall now show how one company implemented this cyclical strategy by using debt maturity to effectively postpone its long-term borrowing in a tight money market. A firm we shall call the Waverly Company needed to raise $50 million in a lump sum for use over the next 25 years. The firm had been confronted with a 9 percent rate of interest, hence they had postponed their borrowing. Then the interest rate fell below 8 percent, but management still believed the current level to be too high and expected it to fall further. The borrowing, however, could not be deferred any longer, and after considering several strategies, the firm arrived at two alternatives: it could issue noncallable 5-year notes at 8 percent, refunding the issue after the 5 years with a 20-year issue at a new rate; or it could issue at 7.75 percent 25-year bonds with a 5-year non-call provision (at the end of 5 years, the bonds would be callable at 107.5 percent of face value). The first al-

Table 14-4 Forecast of Interest Rate Five Years Hence

Interest Rate	6%	6.5%	7%	7.5%	8%
Probability	.2	.2	.2	.2	.2

ternative would permit the company to return the funds to the lenders without any prepayment penalty at the end of 5 years, which would be desirable if interest rates were to fall. The second alternative would enable the firm to pay a slightly lower interest rate for the first 5 years; but if interest remained high after 5 years, the bonds could be left outstanding, saving issue costs.

Issue costs (including compensation for the investment banker as well as printing costs, legal fees, registration fees, etc.) totaled 1 percent of the gross proceeds. The tax on net income was 50 percent. The firm's interest-rate forecast is given by the probability distribution in Table 14-4. Under these circumstances, Waverly had to determine which plan minimized the expected financing costs to the company over the 25-year horizon.

Table 14-5 shows Waverly's computations. Under the first strategy, the firm would incur \$500,000 in issue costs on two occasions. Interest expenses for the first 5 years would be \$4 million annually; for the next 20 years, interest expense would be a random variable between \$3 million and \$4 million annually, with an expectation of \$3.5 million annually for the 20 years. To insure that funds would be available to pay off the maturing debt at the end of 5 years, the firm would float the new 20-year issue a month ahead of time; therefore, there would also be one month of overlapping interest, costing an extra \$291,667 (= \$3,500,000 ÷ 12). The company required a minimum return of 10 percent on its relatively safe investments. Using 10 percent as the discount rate, Waverly found that the enumerated costs had a total expected present value of \$34,656,596. Since each dollar of expense yields 50 cents in tax savings, the present value of the net costs was \$17,328,298.

Under the second strategy, the firm would incur \$500,000 in issue costs now and another \$500,000 if it decided to refund the original issue at the end of five years. Whether or not refunding would be profitable was determined by comparing interest savings and the cost of refunding. The economics of refunding will be treated in Chapter 18; here, we assume that the break-even interest rate was 7.2 percent—that is, refunding would be profitable only if the new interest rate was less than 7.2 percent. According to Table 14-4, the probability that the rate would be less than 7.2 percent was .6. In other words, the second issue cost had an expected value of \$500,000 × .6 = \$300,000. Interest expenses for the first 5 years would be \$3.875 million annually. For the next 20 years, the firm would pay the same annual interest if it decided not to refund; this bears a probability of .4. If

Table 14-5 Choosing Between Two Financing Strategies

	Amount	Present Value
Strategy I (5-Year Notes)		
Issue Costs		
Start of year 1	$ 500,000	$ 500,000
End of year 5	500,000	310,460
Regular interest payments		
Years 1 to 5	4,000,000/yr.	15,163,160
Years 6 to 25	3,500,000*/yr.	18,501,875*
Overlapping interest	291,667*	181,101
		$34,656,596
Tax savings		17,328,298
Net expected financing costs		$17,328,298*
Strategy II (25-Year Bonds)		
Issue Costs		
Start of year 1	$ 500,000	$ 500,000
End of year 5	300,000*	186,275*
Regular interest payments		
Years 1 to 5	3,875,000/yr.	14,689,310
Years 6 to 25	3,500,000*/yr.	18,501,875*
Overlapping interest	175,000*	108,662*
Call premium	2,250,000*	1,397,070*
		$35,383,192
Tax savings		17,691,596
Net expected financing costs		$17,691,596*

Note: Numbers with asterisks (*) are expected values.

the interest rate dropped enough to trigger refunding, the rate might be 7.0 percent, 6.5 percent, or 6.0 percent, each with a probability of .2 and with respective annual interest expenses of $3.5 million, $3.25 million, and $3 million. The annual interest expense for years 6 through 20 therefore had an expected value of $3.5 million. Overlapping interest and call premiums had expected values of $175,000 and $2.25 million, respectively. At a discount rate of 10 percent, these costs had a total expected present value of $35,383,192; when tax savings were deducted, the net expected cost was $17,691,596. Since this was more costly than the first alternative, Waverly issued the 5-year notes at 8 percent.

The size of the call premium was critical in determining which alternative was less costly. As Table 14-5 shows, both issue costs and interest expenses would have been lower under the second strategy; but these advantages were more than offset by the call premium that the firm would have had to pay if the debt had been refunded. If the call premium had been smaller, the second plan might have been the more advantageous.

Because of their shorter maturity, however, the 5-year notes created a greater risk of insolvency for the firm. Since Waverly was financially strong, this was not significant; but if the short maturity had caused the company's risk constraint to be violated, the 5-year issue should have been rejected despite its lower cost.

POLICY GUIDELINES: A SYNTHESIS

The Need for a Synthesis

To summarize, the chief factors in maturity and timing decisions are the relative costs of short- and long-term borrowing, the risk of insolvency in different maturity structures, and the expected level of future interest rates. Because the problem is complex, we have discussed these determinants separately, considering one variable at a time, taking other factors as constants. This approach simplifies the analysis, but the financial executive must reach his decision considering all factors simultaneously. Therefore, we shall attempt to distill from our findings three basic principles as a guide for action.

Ideally, we would like to construct a model to quantify the effects of these determinants on optimal maturity and timing decisions. Such a model should take into account the level and structure of interest rates, present and future, the liquidity of the company's assets, the level and stability of its earnings, its expected cash receipts and disbursements, and the effect of debt maturity on borrowing capacity and cost. Such a model would be too complex to construct here. Fortunately, however, the principles underlying maturity and timing decisions are quite simple, and even without a quantitative model, the financial executive can implement them.

Policy Guidelines

First and foremost, debt-maturity and timing decisions must not increase a firm's risk of insolvency beyond acceptable limits. In this chapter, we did not show how to test whether a particular maturity structure will meet a firm's solvency requirement, but earlier we did introduce a model which can be adapted to do so. The model simulated the risk of insolvency when a firm was hit by a business recession. By simulating with different maturity structures, we can determine which are compatible with the maximum risk of insolvency the firm is willing to tolerate. We shall assume for the following discussion that solvency permits a mixture of short- and long-term debt.

Second, debt-maturity and timing decisions must consider management's expectation of future interest rates. We can distinguish two forms of expectations. In the first case, the financial executive expects the level of interest rates to remain unchanged, so that there are no timing decisions, only maturity decisions. The strategy then should be to rely as much on short-term debt as solvency permits, because interest-rate structure and flexibility both favor short-term debt. We have seen that historically short-term rates average lower than long-term rates. Flexibility means that the company can return funds to the lenders when the need subsides without having to pay the penalty often required by long-term lenders. There are, however, two qualifications. The company may want to retain a reserve of short-term borrowing power to be able to take advantage of good buys when opportunities arise. Also, the company may have a target credit rating for its securities, with which its maturity policy must not interfere.

In the second case, the financial executive expects the level of interest rates to fluctuate cyclically. We shall assume that he has an idea of the "normal range" of interest rates. If current rates are near the upper band for this range, future rates are more likely to fall than to rise. The firm should postpone its borrowing if possible. If borrowing cannot be postponed, the firm should rely on short-term funds (even though they may carry a higher rate than long-term funds) so that it will not be committed to long-term funds at high rates. Conversely, if current rates are near the lower band for the normal range, future rates are more likely to rise than to fall. The firm should rely on long-term funds (even if they carry a higher rate than short-term funds) so that it may secure the low long-term rates.

Third, debt-maturity and timing decisions must consider the value of a reserve of unused short-term borrowing power. Such a reserve, as mentioned before, enables a firm to take advantage of good buys; equally important, it also adds to a firm's financial maneuverability. Suppose a company needs additional working capital to support an increase in sales. Short-term financing enables the firm to meet these needs without making an immediate long-term commitment. Such maneuverability is especially important if company sales are volatile. In such a situation, long-term borrowing can be costly if the demand for additional working capital turns out to be only temporary. Short-term loans meet the immediate needs, giving the firm more time to determine how permanent its funds requirements are.

A CASE STUDY IN DEBT FINANCING

To integrate theory and practice, let us examine the way the General Motors Acceptance Corporation (GMAC) utilizes debt to finance its operations. GMAC, which is owned wholly by the General Motors Corporation, is a sales finance company whose primary business is to finance the distribution of new automobiles manufactured by the parent company. Like other sales finance companies, GMAC extends credit to dealers, so they can carry GM inventory, and to buyers, so they can pay in installments. Consequently, notes receivable constitute over 95 percent of GMAC's assets. These receivables are generally secured and are well diversified, among both customers and geographical regions. The standard term of repayment is about 36 months for new cars, less for used cars. The notes are therefore not only safe but extremely liquid. In fact, on any balance-sheet date, the amount of receivables collectable within a year is nearly 90 percent of the firm's total debt payable within a year. Since automobile financing hinges on automobile sales, which are variable, the volume of receivables is subject to sharp seasonal and cyclical fluctuations. Both the liquidity and the variability of the receivables influence the way debt is utilized at GMAC.

The liquidity and safety of receivables permit GMAC to operate with a high debt-to-equity ratio and a debt structure with a short maturity.[8] In fact, GMAC finances 90 percent of its assets with debt, and in recent years 40 to 60 percent of its debt has been short-term. While the liquidity and safety of the receivables permit this pattern, they do not necessitate it. There must be an economic justification. Debt financing will presumably increase the firm's expected earnings, but it will also magnify earnings variability. However, GMAC has an automatic stabilizer, which will moderate this magnification: if net operating income drops, it will happen because the firm is doing a smaller volume of business; but with fewer new extensions, cash outflow will fall below cash inflows from repayments. The net cash inflow will thus enable GMAC to repay its short-term debt, undoing at least some of the financial leverage.

This automatic stabilizer can only reduce fluctuations, not eliminate them. As long as new credit extensions fluctuate seasonally and cyclically, net income will do the same. The ability to undo a part of leverage with surplus funds reduces the fluctuation in net income, moderating the leverage effect of debt financing. But the question remains: to what extent does debt financing increase the rate at which securities investors capitalize the net income generated by GMAC? In all likelihood, the net effect is such that debt financing enhances the total market value of the firm. This, at any rate, must have been the conclusion reached by GMAC.

GMAC must have a timing strategy to cope with the cyclical fluctuations of interest rates. Perhaps because of the difficulty of forecasting future interest rates, GMAC's long-term debt strategy seems to be primarily "dollar averaging," which obviates the need for interest-rate forecasts. Under this system, debt maturity is structured so that a relatively constant amount of debt is refinanced at regular intervals. The purpose is to stabilize the annual cost of money by paying a moving average of the interest rates over time. This policy has been in effect at GMAC for many years, so that today about one twentieth of its intermediate- and long-term debt matures and is refinanced each year. Staggered maturity also reduces the risk of in-

---

[8] All information on GMAC's debt policy is based on data published in the annual reports of the company.

solvency, but this seems to be less of a consideration for GMAC than for others. There is also some evidence that interest-rate expectations may have led to an increased reliance on short-term borrowing in recent years: during the period 1961–1965, short-term debt averaged about 35 percent of the total indebtedness; but since 1965, the average increased dramatically to over 50 percent, coinciding with rising interest rates during those years. GMAC may have viewed the interest rates of those years as abnormally high and expected a drop; reliance on short-term debt, as we have noted, is consistent with an expectation of falling interest rates.

REVIEW QUESTIONS

1. Historically, short-term interest rates have generally been lower than the contemporary long-term rates. Does this mean that concentrating on short-term borrowing will automatically be less costly than concentrating on long-term borrowing? Why or why not?
2. Figure 14-1 shows the relationship between the yield on Aaa corporate bonds and the yield on prime commercial paper for the period since 1925. How must these rates be adjusted before they may be used to measure the actual cost of long- and short-term borrowing?
3. Explain the expectations theory of the term structure of interest rates. How does it differ from the market-segmentation theory? With which do you agree?
4. Finance companies are said to have an automatic stabilizer moderating the degree of leverage associated with a given level of debt financing. What is this stabilizer and how does it work? In what other types of business would you expect to find such a stabilizer?
5. Why, other factors being equal, does short-term debt financing create so much greater a risk of insolvency for a financially weak company than for a financially strong company? Using the economic concepts behind Eqs. (14-4) and (14-6), present your explanations in words rather than symbols.
6. Describe the cyclical fluctuations of short- and long-term interest rates over time. Discuss the implications of this pattern for the optimal timing of a firm's debt financing.
7. What is dollar averaging as applied to the timing of a firm's long-term debt issues? What is its purpose and how is it implemented?
8. Commenting on debt-maturity and timing decisions, the treasurer of a packaged food producer states, "As a general rule, our policy is to fund working capital increases and fixed asset expenditures on a short-term basis (commercial paper) until it reaches a level where it is economical to fund long." Explain why it would not be economical for the company to finance every increase in its capital needs with long-term funds.
9. Chemical New York Corporation is a one-bank holding company whose principal asset is the capital stock of the Chemical Bank. In 1974, the Corporation sold \$150 million of debt, splitting the offering in two parts: \$100 million of 25-year debentures and \$50 million of 8-year notes. What considerations might have prompted Chemical to divide its new debt into two parts?

10. What major factors would determine your debt maturity and timing policy if you were the treasurer of Southern Bell, a wholly-owned subsidiary of American Telephone and Telegraph Company? In what ways might your policy be different from that of an industrial company?

PROBLEMS

1. Let us posit that the current year is year 1 with a one-year interest rate of 9 percent and that the expected rates for years 2, 3, and 4 are 8 percent, 7 percent, and 6 percent, respectively. According to the expectations theory, what will be the current yield on a two-year bond when equilibrium is reached? What return will an investor realize if he buys a three-year bond and sells it after holding for one year?
2. Using Eq. (14-2), show that if investors expect future one-year interest rates to rise, the yield curve will be monotonically increasing. You may either prove this proposition analytically or illustrate it with a numerical example.
3. Suppose that the basic risk of the XYZ Company is such that its ratio k/n has a value of only .7. Using Eq. (14-4), calculate the firm's risk of insolvency as a function of frequency of refunding. Compare your results with those obtained using Eq. (14-6) and assuming a planning horizon of 20 years.
4. The financial executive of Waverly predicts the following probability distribution (instead of the one in Table 14-4) for market interest rates at the end of year 5:

Interest Rate	6%	6.5%	7.0%	7.5%	8.0%
Probability	.1	.1	.6	.1	.1

   a. How does this change in forecast affect the relative attractiveness of Strategies I and II? Explain why and verify your position.
   b. Suppose that the 25-year bond were callable in five years at a premium of only 5.0 percent, instead of the 7.5 percent assumed in Table 14-5. How would this affect the relative advantages of the two strategies? Verify your conclusions.
5. In Table 14-5, the following expected values were given for Strategy II:

Issue costs (end of year 5)	\$ 300,000
Annual interest (years 6 through 25)	3,500,000
Overlapping interest	175,000
Call premium	2,250,000

   Verify the accuracy of these figures.
6. Look up the maturity structure of GMAC's short-, intermediate-, and long-term debt. What is the weighted average interest rate on its total interest-bearing debt? How much will this average rate be affected if and when the \$100 million worth of 5 percent debentures due March 15, 1981, is refunded with a new \$100 million issue at an interest rate of 10 percent?

REFERENCES

AIGNER, D. J., and C. M. SPRENKLE, "On Optimal Financing of Cyclical Cash Needs," *Journal of Finance* 28 (December, 1973), pp. 1249–1254.

Board of Governors of The Federal Reserve System, *Historical Chart Book, 1975* (Washington, D.C., 1975).

BOOT, JOHN C. G., and GEORGE M. FRANKFURTER, "The Dynamics of Corporate Debt Management, Decision Rules, and Some Empirical Evidence," *Journal of Financial and Quantitative Analysis* 7 (September, 1972), pp. 1957–1965.

CACY, J. A., and MARY HAMBLIN, "Trends and Cycles in Credit Market Borrowing," in Federal Reserve Bank of Kansas City, *Monthly Review* (March, 1974), pp. 3–12.

CONARD, JOSEPH W., and MARK W. FRANKENA. "The Yield Spread Between New and Seasoned Corporate Bonds, 1952–63," in Jack M. Guttentag and Phillip Cagan, eds., *Essays on Interest Rates,* Vol. 1 (New York: National Bureau of Economic Research, 1969), Ch. 5.

CRAGG, JOHN G., and NEVINS D. BAXTER, "The Issuing of Corporate Securities," *Journal of Political Economy* 78 (November–December, 1970), pp. 1310–1324.

DODDS, J. C., and J. L. FORD, *Expectations, Uncertainty and the Term Structure of Interest Rates* (London: Martin Robertson and Company Ltd., 1974).

LITZENBERGER, ROBERT H., and DAVID P. RUTENBERG, "Size and Timing of Corporate Bond Flotations," *Journal of Financial and Quantitative Analysis* 7 (January, 1972), pp. 1343–1359.

MALKIEL, BURTON G., *The Term Structure of Interest Rates* (Princeton: Princeton University Press, 1966).

MICHAELSEN, JACOB B., *The Term Structure of Interest Rates* (New York: Intext Educational Publishers, 1973).

PIERCE, JAMES L., "Commercial Bank Liquidity," *Federal Reserve Bulletin* 52 (August, 1966), pp. 1093–1101.

REA, JOHN D., "The Yield Spread Between Newly Issued and Seasoned Corporate Bonds," in Federal Reserve Bank of Kansas City, *Monthly Review* (June, 1974), pp. 3–9.

Salomon Brothers, *An Analytical Record of Yields and Yield Spreads* (New York: 1972), and subsequent annual supplements.

WESTON, J. FRED, and EUGENE F. BRIGHAM, *Managerial Finance* (New York: Holt, Rinehart and Winston, 1969), Ch. 23.

15 Dividend Policy, Internal Financing, and Growth

Once a firm has decided upon its optimal debt-to-equity ratio, it must next determine what percentage of equity financing it will obtain externally through the issuance of new stock and what percentage internally through the retention of earnings. Since cash dividend payments are the obverse of earnings retention, dividend policy is inextricably related to internal-financing policy. Some writers argue that dividend policy is a mere detail. From the corporate viewpoint, they argue that while it is true that dividends decrease retained earnings, the decrease can be offset by funds obtained by the sale of new shares. From the shareholders' viewpoint, they argue, dividends increase the shareholders' immediate cash balance, but the increase is at the cost of higher share values which would have prevailed had the dividends been retained. However, these arguments are valid only if there are no taxes and no transaction costs, if corporations can raise equity capital in unlimited amounts, and if investors discount all future dividends at a constant rate. Only under these circumstances will dividend policy be a trivial matter.

Actual complications or "imperfections" cause different dividend policies to affect the wealth of shareholders differently. For example, not all companies have access to the equity-capital market, and in this case, dividends will reduce the funds available for investment, slowing the rate of growth. Even firms that can raise equity capital externally may find that personal income tax and the cost of issuing stock may cause their shareholders to prefer retained earnings over dividends. On the other hand, the same stockholders may have an opposite preference because the current dividend is a certainty, whereas retained earnings are less safe. This chapter will deal with the principles of optimizing dividend policy in the light of these complications. Related transactions, such as stock dividends, stock splits, and repurchase of shares will also be considered.

THE DIVIDEND SETTING

Quantitative Significance

Let us summarize the annual record of corporate (after-tax) profits and dividends from 1950 through 1974. Over the entire 25 years, all private corporations earned a total profit of $928 billion after taxes, of which $424 billion was paid out in dividends, implying an average payout ratio of 46 percent.[1] The annual payout ratio has been reasonably stable, varying between 40 and 50 percent in the majority of cases.

To understand fully the significance of dividends, however, we must also compare retained earnings (the obverse of dividends) to the total sources and uses of funds by corporations. The figures here refer only to a subset of all corporations, namely, the nonfarm, nonfinancial corporations. Over the same 25 years, these corporations increased their net assets by $1,150 billion, of which $790 billion was financed externally (debt and stock issues) and $360 billion was financed internally by retention of earnings.[2] Thus, for every dollar increase in assets, about 31 cents was financed internally. External capital included $720 billion of debt and $71 billion of stock. If we exclude debt from our comparison, so that the comparison is strictly between internal and external equity, the ratio is 5.05; that is, for every dollar of stock issued, $5.05 is supplied by retained earnings. Excluding several years during which the total stock outstanding actually decreased, the ratio of retained earnings to new stock issue varied from 1.5 to 21, with 6 being the most common ratio.

The asset figures given above are net of depreciation charges; that is, the increase in assets represents gross additions minus the current depreciation allowances. Over the same 25 years, depreciation totaled $822 billion. If we were to figure assets on a gross basis, this depreciation would have to be added back as an adjustment to net profits. Depreciation is, in effect, an internal source of funds. When depreciation is thus viewed, internal financing accounted for 60 percent of total corporate financing during this period, with the annual ratio varying between 55 and 65 percent.

The Analytical Framework

The optimal dividend policy is the one that maximizes stockholders' wealth. Dividend policy is complex because, depending on the circumstances,

[1] *Economic Report of the President,* various issues.
[2] *Survey of Current Business,* various issues.

Table 15-1 Effects of Dividend Policy on Share Price

	Low Dividend		High Dividend
No access to equity market	$(EPS)_a$	$>$	$(EPS)_b$
	k_a	$>$	k_b
	P_a	?	P_b
Easy access to equity market	$(EPS)_c$	$>$	$(EPS)_d$
	k_c	$=$	k_d
	P_c	$>$	P_d

it may involve either an investment decision or a financing decision. It is an investment decision if a company does not have access to the equity market and increased dividend payments reduce the size of its investments. It is a financing decision if the company does have access to the equity market and increased dividend payments cause the company to issue new stock. (In this case, we assume debt financing is not under consideration.) Thus, a firm may finance its cash dividends either by reducing investments or by issuing stock. To optimize dividend policy, we must distinguish between the investment and financing viewpoints and determine which is relevant to the particular situation.

Although dividend payments may be varied incrementally, we shall consider only the choice between a high and a low dividend policy. Table 15-1 outlines the effects of dividend policy on share valuation under two assumptions regarding the company's access to the equity market. When not accompanied by external equity financing, a liberal dividend policy reduces investments and, therefore, $(EPS)_a > (EPS)_b$. The resulting slower growth in EPS also lowers the investor's required rate of return, and, therefore, $k_a > k_b$. Whether share price will be higher or lower depends on the relationship between the depressing effect of a smaller EPS and the stimulating effect of a lower capitalization rate, and, therefore, P_a ? P_b. On the other hand, if a liberal dividend policy is accompanied by external equity financing, both investments and total earnings will be maintained. However, the external financing increases the number of shares outstanding, so $(EPS)_c > (EPS)_d$. But since the earnings growth rate remains the same, the capitalization rate remains unchanged, i.e., $k_c = k_d$. The smaller $(EPS)_d$, therefore, must indicate a lower share price.

Since dividend payment is not an internal transaction but rather an external transfer of funds from the corporation to its stockholders, the goal of optimal dividend policy is the maximization of the shareholders' wealth. The wealth of a shareholder, of course, is determined not only by share price but also by the cash dividends he receives and the taxes he must pay. A high dividend payout gives the stockholders more cash now and less cash in the future; a low payout will have the opposite effect. Which policy is better depends on the value of current dividends forgone relative to future dividends gained. In general, the appeal of a high payout stems from the certainty of near dividends compared with distant dividends. The appeal of a low payout stems from the prospect of large increases in future dividends if the company can invest its retained earnings at above normal rates of return. To the extent attractive future dividends lead to higher future share prices, a low payout also offers the shareholder the opportunity to convert his current dividend income (taxable as regular income) into capital gains. The tax on capital gains is half of the marginal rate on ordinary income, subject to a maximum of 25 percent on the first $50,000 of capital gains, and 35 percent on anything over $50,000. This possible tax benefit and the trade-off between current and future cash dividends are the critical considerations in determining dividend policy.

THE OPTIMAL PAYOUT RATIO

A New Company

Because of their different circumstances, new firms view dividend policy primarily as an investment decision while established firms view it primarily as a financing decision. BAX, Inc., has $500,000 of invested capital, all equity financed, divided into 10,000 shares of common stock. The existing assets are expected to generate yearly after-tax earnings of $50,000 ($5 per share). Because the firm is new, it has no access to the external capital market, even though it operates profitably. Any increase in dividend payments must therefore reduce investment expenditures dollar for dollar. The company's investment opportunities are such that every dollar of retained earnings produces an annual after-tax return of 15 percent. The company is choosing between two dividend policies: pay 70 percent of each year's earnings in dividends and retain 30 percent, or pay 50 percent and retain 50 percent. Increasing the retention ratio shifts dividends from the present to the future. Since future dividends are less certain than near-term dividends, investors generally raise their required rate of return as a firm lowers its payout ratio. The management of BAX estimates that at a high payout ratio of 70 percent, investors will require an 11.5 percent return; at a low payout ratio of 50 percent, they will require a 12 percent return. The typical stockholder of BAX is subject to a marginal tax of 40 percent on ordinary income and a flat tax of 20 percent on capital gain. Given these circumstances, the firm must decide which payout ratio will maximize the wealth of its stockholders.

Table 15-2 Effects of Dividend Policy L vs. Policy H*

	Policy L			Policy H		
Year	*EPS*	*DPS* ($k = .120$)	*P*	*EPS*	*DPS* ($k = .115$)	*P*
1	$5.00	$2.50	$55.56	$5.00	$3.50	$50.00
2	5.38	2.69	59.72	5.23	3.66	52.25
3	5.78	2.89	64.20	5.46	3.82	54.60
4	6.21	3.11	69.02	5.71	3.99	57.06
5	6.68	3.34	74.19	5.96	4.17	59.63
6	7.18	3.59	79.76	6.23	4.36	62.31
7	7.72	3.86	85.74	6.51	4.56	65.11
8	8.29	4.15	92.17	6.80	4.76	68.04
9	8.92	4.46	99.08	7.11	4.98	71.10
10	9.59	4.79	106.51	7.43	5.20	74.30

* *EPS and DPS* are end-of-year figures, but *P* is a beginning-of-year figure.

Effect on Share Price. Table 15-2 shows the effect of dividend policy on share price. For convenience we shall designate the low (50 percent) payout as Policy L and the high (70 percent) payout as Policy H. During the first year, the firm is expected to generate $5 of earnings per share. At the end of the year, $2.50 of this $5 would be paid in dividends under Policy L; under Policy H, $3.50. Under Policy L, 50 percent of each year's earnings is reinvested at a return of 15 percent, so that both *EPS* and *DPS* (dividends per share) will grow at an annual rate of 7.5 percent. Columns 2 and 3 list the values of *EPS* and *DPS*, after rounding, for the first 10 years.[3]

The price of a share may be viewed as the present value of *all* future dividends. Therefore, under Policy L, the price at the beginning of year 1 (P_1) of a BAX share can be calculated by discounting the future dividends at 12 percent (the investors' required rate of return):

$$P_1 = \frac{\$2.50}{(1 + .12)} + \frac{\$2.69}{(1 + .12)^2} + \frac{\$2.89}{(1 + .12)^3} + \cdots$$

The right-hand side of this equation is an infinite geometric series, so that

$$P_1 = \frac{\$2.50}{.12 - .075} = \$55.56 \qquad (15\text{-}1)$$

In other words, P_1 is equal to the dividend in year 1 divided by the excess of its dividend-capitalization rate over the dividend growth rate. Similarly, at the beginning of year 2:

[3] These values were calculated using four decimal places, but, due to rounding, some of the results may appear not to agree.

$$P_2 = \frac{\$2.69}{.12 - .075} = \$59.72 \qquad (15\text{-}2)$$

Policy L differs from Policy H not only in the dividend payments of the base period but also in the rate of dividend growth. These differences account for the higher share price under Policy L (see Columns 4 and 7).

Effect on Shareholders' Wealth. In view of these results, what can we say about the relative effects of Policies L and H on the wealth of shareholders? If an investor sold one share of BAX stock at the beginning of year 1, he would receive a price of \$55.56 under Policy L, or \$50.00 under Policy H. He would be better off by \$5.56 under Policy L. If he sold the share at the beginning of year 2, Policy L would yield him a share price of \$59.72 plus a dividend of \$2.50; Policy H would yield \$52.25 plus \$3.50. Assuming that investors require a return of 12 percent under Policy L and and 11.5 percent under H, we find that at these discount rates Policy L produces a present value of \$55.56 (= \$62.22/1.12); Policy H, \$50.00 (= \$55.75/1.115). Policy L thus increases the wealth of shareholders again by \$5.56 more per share than Policy H. Further computation would demonstrate that no matter when the stockholder sells, he will be ahead \$5.56 (in present value) with Policy L (see Table 15-3, Part A).

The above results depend critically on our assumptions about the investors' dividend-capitalization rate and the company's return on its

Table 15-3 Dividend Policy and Shareholders' Wealth

A. Before Personal Tax

Holding Period	Dividend Policy	Cash Flow at End of Year 1	2	3	4	5	Present Value
3 Years	L	\$2.50	\$2.69	\$71.91	\$ 0	\$ 0	\$55.56
	H	3.50	3.66	60.88	0	0	50.00
5 Years	L	2.50	2.69	2.89	3.11	83.10	55.56
	H	3.50	3.66	3.82	3.99	66.48	50.00

B. After Personal Tax

Holding Period	Dividend Policy	Cash Flow at End of Year 1	2	3	4	5	Present Value
3 Years	L	\$1.50	\$1.61	\$62.10	\$ 0	\$ 0	\$46.82
	H	2.10	2.20	56.94	0	0	44.73
5 Years	L	1.50	1.61	1.73	1.87	74.81	47.50
	H	2.10	2.20	2.29	2.39	61.35	43.10

investments. We assumed a dividend-capitalization rate of 11.5 percent under Policy H, only .5 percent below the 12 percent rate under Policy L. If the company's stockholders prefer near dividends to distant dividends, they may choose a capitalization rate under Policy H lower than we assumed, in which case they could prefer a high payout policy. Also, we assumed that the company has unlimited opportunities to invest retained earnings at 15 percent, which tends to favor a low payout. More limited or less profitable investment opportunities could make a high payout policy preferable.

We must not forget to consider the implications of personal tax. The tax impact invariably favors a low-payout policy for two reasons. First, a low payout shifts taxable income from the present to the future, thus postponing taxes; second, a low payout converts ordinary income into capital gains, generally taxable at a maximum of only 25 percent. To measure the tax benefit, we must know the investor's holding period, his tax bracket, and the price he paid for his share. Let us say that a typical BAX stockholder holds his shares for three years, is taxed 40 percent on his regular income and 20 percent on capital gains, and initially paid $45 per share. This stockholder receives a present value per share of $46.82 under Policy L or $44.73 under H, a difference of $2.09 (see Table 15-3, Part B). The present values for a 5-year holding period would be $47.50 and $43.10, respectively, a difference of $4.40. For BAX, a low payout was preferable even before considering personal income tax; the introduction of taxes reinforces this preference. Here, of course, we have shown only that L is preferable to H. To find the optimal of all policies, the analysis must cover a wider range of payout ratios considering all possible ratios between L and H. The principle, however, remains unchanged.

Since personal tax favors a low payout ratio, why is the excess of the present value of L over H smaller on an after- than on a before-tax basis? There is really no contradiction here, since the present values in Table 15-3 reflect the combined effects of payout, reinvestment rate (r), dividend-capitalization rate (k), and taxation. If we wish to isolate the pure tax effect, we must make k equal to r, so that in the absence of tax the present values of L and H would be equal. The actual difference when taxes are introduced may then be attributed directly to the tax effect. Given the preferential treatment of capital gains, this effect will always favor Policy L.

An Established Company

With all other circumstances remaining the same, let us suppose that BAX is an established firm with easy access to the external capital market. Might it not then benefit the stockholders if the company were to issue enough new shares each year to be able to raise the payout level to 100 percent and yet still maintain investments at Policy L's level of 50 percent

Table 15-4 Effects of Dividend Policy S

Year	*EPS*	*DPS*	*P*
1	$5.00	$5.00	$55.24
2	5.12	2.56	56.87
3	5.50	2.75	61.13
4	5.92	2.96	65.71
5	6.36	3.18	70.64
6	6.84	3.42	75.96
7	7.35	3.67	81.64
8	7.90	3.95	87.78
9	8.49	4.25	94.36
10	9.13	4.56	101.42

of the earnings? For simplicity, we shall assume the 100 percent payout only for one year, that is, whatever our decision, we assume that after year 1 the firm will adopt a 50 percent payout level and finance its investments solely with retained earnings.

Effect on Share Price. In year 1, BAX generates $50,000 in after-tax earnings. The choice is now between Policy L (paying out $25,000 and reinvesting $25,000) and Policy S (paying out $50,000, investing $25,000, and issuing $25,000 worth of new stock). Issuing stock is an expensive process, involving legal, accounting, underwriting, and marketing expenses. Moreover, in order to insure the success of the issue, new shares must often be priced slightly lower than the current market price. If each new share brings the company a net $50, a total of 500 new shares must be sold in order to raise $25,000. Since investments are maintained at a level of $25,000, total earnings will grow at the same rate under Policy S as under L. But since there are 500 more shares, *EPS* and *DPS* will be proportionately lower in all future years. The investors' required rate of return may be affected. Because the 100 percent payout is only for one period, we shall assume its effect on the required rate to be negligible, and shall continue using a 12 percent rate. Table 15-4 shows *EPS, DPS,* and corresponding stock prices under Policy S for each of the first 10 years. After the first year, all figures are lower under Policy S than under Policy L (see Table 15-2); Policy S's only advantage is in first-year dividends.

Effect on Shareholders' Wealth. Our approach is again to consider an investor holding one share of BAX for varying periods. If he sells immediately, he receives $55.24 under Policy S or $55.56 under Policy L. If he sells at the beginning of year 2, he will receive a price of $56.87 plus a dividend of $5 under Policy S; under L, $59.72 plus $2.50. At a discount rate of 12 percent, the present values of Policies S and L are $55.24 and $55.56, respectively. Computation will show that, whatever the holding period, the investor is 32 cents ahead (in present value) under Policy L. This result should have been expected, since the decision was really whether to finance investments by retained earnings or by stock issue. External equity capital is generally more costly than retained earnings.

We have again assumed no personal tax. But since personal taxation favors high retention, Policy L is still preferable. We must note, however, that since the company maintains its investments under either policy, the above result does not depend on our assumption about the company's return on investments. But the result still does depend critically on our assumption that because the high payout is only temporary, the dividend-capitalization rate remains at 12 percent. Some companies, however, continue their high payout policy, while repeatedly raising new capital by issuing new stock. In particular, public utilities frequently do this. Such a policy shifts dividends from the future to the present. If the company's stockholders are conservative, like those of public utilities, and consider a near dividend safer than a distant one, they may lower their required rate of return, putting a higher valuation on the company's shares because of its high payout. In that case, Policy S is preferable.

If we consider both the new firm and the established firm, we may make four generalizations. First, firms with profitable investments are justified in retaining a greater percentage of their earnings. Second, the preferential tax treatment of capital gains favors high retention of earnings and low payout. Third, the cost of issuing new common stock also favors high retention and low payout. And finally, these factors favoring low payout can be partially or totally offset by the increase in the investors' required rate of return which generally accompanies a high retention rate.

IMPLEMENTATION OF DIVIDEND POLICY

The implementation of a long-run payout ratio involves three short-run problems: the timing, legal, and procedural aspects of dividend policy.

Timing Pattern of Dividends

If analysis indicates an optimal payout ratio, if a firm adheres to this fixed ratio, and if *EPS* fluctuates over time, then *DPS* will also fluctuate. It is still possible, however, to construct a *DPS* series that will minimize fluctuation while still conforming to the long-run payout ratio. Uniroyal, the nation's third largest rubber fabricator, provides a good example. Figure 15-1 shows Uniroyal's *EPS* and *DPS* for 1965–1974; during this time, the company paid out 51.5 percent of its total earnings. Although its earnings showed a considerable degree of instability, its *DPS* was relatively stable: 55 cents in 1965, 60 cents annually from 1966 to 1968, and

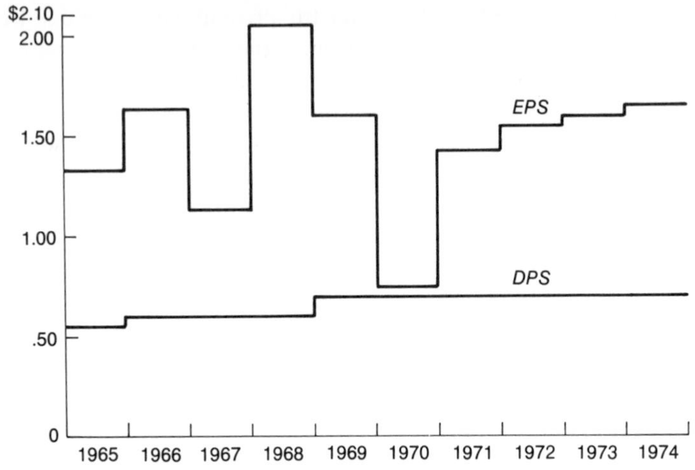

Figure 15-1 Uniroyal's Dividend Payout

70 cents after that. The annual payout ratio ranged from 35.3 percent (1968) to 96.9 percent (1970). Thus, by varying yearly payout ratio, Uniroyal was able to achieve a reasonably stable *DPS* in spite of a fluctuating *EPS*.

Dividend stability over time is desirable because, other things being equal, investors value a firm's shares more highly if its dividends are regular. There are three reasons for this. First, when a firm retains a portion of its earnings, investors will value its shares more highly if they anticipate that current reinvestments will yield predictably larger dividends in the future; a stable dividend policy encourages this anticipation. Second, investors being generally risk averse, they prefer stable over fluctuating dividends. Third, dividend stability may also widen the market for the company's shares by qualifying them for institutional investment. A firm with an uninterrupted pattern of dividends may be placed on legal lists of securities, prepared by government agencies, for investment by pension funds, insurance companies, savings banks, etc. A company's name may be removed from these lists if dividends are cut.

Legality of Dividends

Dividend payments must conform to the statutes of the states in which a firm is incorporated. Although laws vary, they generally require dividend payments to meet one or more of three tests: the balance-sheet surplus test, the insolvency test, and the current-profits test.[4]

[4] For a more thorough discussion of these tests, see Paul M. Van Arsdell, *Corporation Finance* (New York: The Ronald Press Company, 1968), pp. 1204–1220.

The balance-sheet surplus test allows a firm to declare a dividend only if the company shows a positive balance in the surplus account of its balance sheet. This criterion views the stockholders' equity as composed of two parts: legal capital, that portion which is impounded for the protection of creditors; and surplus, the remainder, available for dividends. The legal concept of distributable surplus does not always coincide with the accounting concept of surplus. Accountants distinguish between earned surplus, which arises from profitable operations, and capital surplus, which may have a variety of sources (excess paid over par or stated value of stock, writedown of par value, transfer from earned surplus, etc.). Earned surplus is a legal source of dividends, but state laws differ greatly on capital surplus. In Delaware and Nevada, for example, paid-in surplus is available for cash dividends on both preferred and common shares; but in Michigan and Illinois on preferred shares only; and in South Carolina and Hawaii, on neither. In Delaware, surplus created by a writedown of par value may be used for dividends; but not in some other states.

The solvency test prohibits a company from declaring a dividend if the firm is insolvent or would be rendered insolvent by payment of the dividend. This test is one of the criteria in New York and Virginia, and the only criterion in New Hampshire.

The current-profits test permits dividends from current profits, if any, even if there is a deficit on the balance sheet. California and Delaware are among the states permitting such dividends.

Dividend payments may be further restricted by covenants in bond indentures and loan agreements. During the period 1972–1974, the dividend increase of the country's 10,000 largest corporations was regulated by a federal Committee on Interest Rates and Dividends.

Procedural Aspects

If a stockholder sells his shares after the declaration but before the payment of a dividend, does the dividend go to the original shareholder or the new buyer? And when will the recipient get his check? These questions are answered by reference to four dates in dividend-payment procedure:

1. Date of declaration—the date on which the dividend is formally declared by the board of directors.
2. Date of record—usually two weeks after the date of declaration. The dividend is paid to those stockholders whose names are on the list of shareholders on that date.
3. Date of payment—the date on which actual payment is made; this is usually two weeks after the date of record and is also specified in the formal declaration.

4. Ex-dividend date—set by the stock exchange on which the firm's shares are traded. The New York Stock Exchange, for example, uses a four-day delivery system: stocks must be delivered on or before the fourth full business day after the sale. Consequently, if a share is purchased before the close of the fourth full business day before the date of record, the dividend goes to the new buyer; the stock is said to be traded dividend-on. If the sale occurs after that time, the seller retains the dividend; the stock is said to be traded ex-dividend.

DIVIDEND POLICY IN PRACTICE

Theoretically, the long-run payout ratio should vary with the profitability of reinvestment, the investors' required rate of return, the tax differential on ordinary income and capital gains, and the expenses associated with the issue of common stock. Also important is the accuracy of reported earnings in measuring a firm's true profitability. In this section, we shall study the actual payout ratios of typical companies, examining the factors guiding their policies.

The Long-Term Payout Ratio

Company Data. United States corporations have been paying out close to 50 percent of their after-tax profits in dividends. The table below shows the target payout ratios and the actual ratios of four companies:

Company	Target Payout	1970–71 Average	1972–74 Average
Bristol-Myers	50%	50%	42%
Detroit Edison	70–75	78	80
Purex	50	128	58
Whirlpool	50	45	35

Our sample is too small to permit generalization, but James Walter studied 80 firms and drew three conclusions.[5] First, most firms with payout ratios over 50 percent are public utilities. Second, 50 percent is a widespread target ratio. And third, the average ratio is a good clue to the target payout ratio, if one exists.

Determinants of Payout Ratio. Two studies indicate that actual firms stress the same considerations that we regarded as theoretically important.

[5] James E. Walter, *Dividend Policy and Enterprise Valuation* (Belmont: Wadsworth Publishing Company, Inc., 1967), p. 33.

In an interview study, Lowell Laporte questioned the chief executives of 130 moderate-sized companies.[6] He found that a major consideration in determining the payout ratio was the need for funds to finance further growth; a countervailing factor is the desire of stockholders for some current income. The actual ratio constitutes a compromise. A number of subordinate factors also play a role. For example, since it is undesirable to cut dividends, some firms set their ratios at a level that can be maintained in bad as well as good years. On the other hand, some firms pay out more than they deem financially prudent lest the IRS apply a penalty tax on excessive retentions.

Laporte's conclusions were based on firms with fewer than 2,000 employees. My own study of ten larger companies confirmed his basic findings and added two new factors.[7] First, since large companies have access to the capital market, they give greater consideration to the effect of dividend policy on the firm's ability to sell stock. The chief executive of an electric utility told me, "As we look forward to external financing in the $300 million to $400 million range, this means that substantial common equity financing will be required. Naturally, the dividend policy of the company has a direct bearing on the attitude of the investors in this type of security." Second, since the shares of large companies tend to be widely dispersed, none of the firms was very concerned with keeping dividends low in order to minimize personal tax liability. In Laporte's sample of smaller firms, on the other hand, the desire to convert current income into capital gains was occasionally so strong that no dividends at all were paid.

Retained Earnings vs. Stock Financing. Laporte's survey covered 122 firms, 22 of which had paid no cash dividends during the five years preceding his study; most of these 22 had in fact never paid a dividend. The main reason that a profitable firm pays no dividends is that it needs to retain all internally generated funds for expansion. Theoretically, these companies could have paid dividends and simultaneously issued new stock; but because they are relatively small, they probably could not have sold stock externally. Moreover, as our analysis has shown, retained earnings are less costly than external equity financing. A no-dividend policy is therefore sound under these circumstances.

Sometimes, however, stock financing is unavoidable. If a private firm wants to go public, for example, the sale of stock is obviously necessary, costly though it may be. Or, when one company acquires another, the stockholders of the acquired firm may wish, for tax reasons, to be paid in stock rather than in cash. But the most important reason is that retained earnings, being less certain in timing and amount, are unsuitable for meeting

---

[6] Lowell Laporte, *Dividend Policy in the Smaller Company* (New York: The Conference Board, 1969).

[7] My findings are based partly on personal interviews of company executives and partly on written replies to questions I posed by mail.

sudden needs. A firm must therefore resort to a stock or bond issue when growth requirements exceed the amount of funds generated internally.

Stability of Dividends

Factual Evidence. Most firms do not view a target ratio as a fixed ratio to be adhered to year in and year out. Rather, the target ratio is a long-run objective. When earnings fluctuate, the payout ratio is varied so that the size of annual dividends is reasonably stable. Since the financial community favors regular dividends, share value is higher when dividends are stable. Moreover, many stockholders rely on regular dividends to supplement their income.

When a firm's dividends show a long-term upward trend, stability generally means smoothing out the dividend series to minimize reversals. This concept is embodied in Keith V. Smith's "increasing-stream hypothesis of dividend policy."[8] According to this hypothesis, "the board of directors deliberately avoids dividend cuts if at all possible and attempts to construct over time an increasing, or at least a nondecreasing, record of cash dividend payments." A corollary of the hypothesis is that "when it is no longer possible to avoid a dividend cut, directors will make a single cut large enough so that subsequent cuts are avoided."

To test this hypothesis, Smith examined the annual dividend records of 900 firms from 1948 through 1966, as given on the Standard and Poor's Compustat industrial tape. Smith calculated annual percentage changes in *EPS* and *DPS* for each firm for each of the 19 years. The total 14,367 usable observations included 5,099 instances of *EPS* decrease but only 1,807 instances of *DPS* decrease. Smith also examined the sequence of dividend changes over time for each firm to determine the longest consecutive decreases and the longest consecutive increases in dividends. He found that 254 of the 900 firms had never cut dividends, and 313 others had never made cuts in two or more consecutive periods. The series of dividend increases were noticeably longer than the series of decreases. All of Smith's findings thus support his hypothesis.

Adaptive Mechanism. Given the aim of increasing dividend streams, how is dividend policy implemented in the face of fluctuating and uncertain earnings? My survey revealed a fairly common response:

> We gradually raise dividends as our earnings increase. We would not cut dividends unless there were a prolonged and deep drop in earnings.
>
> We would raise dividends above the current level when a trend of increased earnings had been clearly established. We would cut dividends only if earnings

[8] Keith V. Smith, "Increasing Stream Hypothesis of Corporate Dividend Policy," *California Management Review* 15 (Fall, 1971), pp. 56–64.

fell sharply from the average of the last few years and continued at depressed levels for at least two years.

This procedure was noted first by John Lintner in his statistical study of dividend policy.[9] He called the device "partial adaptation" and formulated it analytically:

$$D_t - D_{t-1} = a + c(gE_t - D_{t-1}) \tag{15-3}$$

where D_t is dividends this year, D_{t-1} is dividends last year, E_t is earnings this year, g is the target payout ratio, and a and c are positive constants. The change in current dividend $(D_t - D_{t-1})$ is thus expressed as a function of the divergence between actual and target dividends $(gE_t - D_{t-1})$. Moreover, a positive value for a means that companies are reluctant to cut dividends, and a fractional value for c means that dividend adjustments are not instantaneous. Lintner found that, for his sample of companies, this model gives a good explanation of corporate dividend policy.

Dividends and Inflation

The preceding studies were made in periods when the price level was relatively stable, so that reported earnings were a good measure of the firm's true profitability. However, a period of rapid inflation will distort reported earnings, with major implications for corporate dividend policy. As we mentioned in Chapter 11, an important source of distortion is the presence of inventory profits in reported earnings. Since the company must replace inventory at higher prices, inventory profit is not available for distribution. A similar overstatement of profit occurs when depreciation is figured on the basis of original cost. This latter problem is not so serious, however, because most firms compute depreciation on an accelerated basis, partially offsetting the profit overstatement.

A dramatic example of earnings distortion caused by inventory profits comes from the reported earnings of U.S. nonfinancial corporations for the third quarter of 1974. With double-digit inflation, after-tax earnings rose to an annual rate of \$76.9 billion, of which \$33.2 billion in dividends were paid out. This seems to be a fairly modest 43.2 percent; but Department of Commerce figures show that \$51.7 billion of those earnings were inventory profits, leaving only \$25.2 billion in real profits. The payout ratio, therefore, was really 131.7 percent. While the 43.2 percent figure is close to the commonly stated target of 50 percent, 131.7 percent is clearly unsustainable. If inflation continues at a high rate, we may expect corporations to cut the dividend payout ratio considerably.

---

[9] John Lintner, "Distribution of Incomes of Corporations Among Dividends, Retained Earnings, and Taxes," *American Economic Review* 46 (May, 1956), pp. 97–113.

STOCK DIVIDENDS AND STOCK SPLITS

Stock Dividends vs. Stock Splits

A stock dividend is the pro-rata issue of stock to existing shareholders, accompanied by a simultaneous capitalization of surplus on the firm's balance sheet. The capitalization of the XYZ Company, for example, might look like this before a stock dividend:

Common stock (par value $25 a share)	
Authorized—200,000 shares	
Issued —100,000 shares	$2,500,000
Earned surplus	1,000,000

The shares have a fair market value of $30 per share. After a 25 percent stock dividend is declared and issued, each stockholder will have 25 percent more shares than previously, and the company's new capitalization will be:

Common stock (par value $25 a share)	
Authorized—200,000 shares	
Issued —125,000 shares	$3,125,000
Capital surplus	125,000
Earned surplus	250,000

For each share issued in the stock dividend, XYZ transfers $30 (the fair market value of the share) from the earned-surplus account; $25 (the par value of the share) goes to the common-stock account, and $5 goes into a capital-surplus account. This "capitalization" of earned surplus notifies the stockholders that the firm regards the capitalized $750,000 as permanently reinvested.

A stock split is the pro-rata issue of stock to existing stockholders with a corresponding reduction in the par value of the stock. If XYZ had effected a 5-for-4 split instead of a 25 percent dividend, the new balance sheet would read:

Common stock (par value $20 a share)	
Authorized—200,000 shares	
Issued —125,000 shares	$2,500,000
Earned surplus	1,000,000

A stock split has no effect on the surplus accounts. The increased number of shares causes the par value to be reduced from $25 to $20. In either case, a stockholder's proportionate interest remains the same. Since stock dividends and splits are so similar, we shall treat them together.

Reasons for Stock Dividends and Stock Splits

Before the stock dividend, XYZ was earning and retaining $3 per share. After the dividend, a person who previously owned one share will own 1.25 shares, but his *EPS* will drop from $3 to $2.40. If the share price drops proportionately from $30 to $24, the total market value of his shares will, however, remain the same.

XYZ had previously paid out 50 percent of its earnings, i.e., $1.50 per share, in dividends. Suppose it continues to pay out $1.50 per share. Since there are now 25 percent more shares, the total of cash dividends increases by 25 percent. If this were the only purpose of the stock dividend, it could have been accomplished more easily and less expensively without a stock dividend by increasing *DPS*.

It is when personal tax is taken into account that the benefit to shareholders of a stock dividend becomes clear. Cash dividends are always taxable; stock dividends are generally not immediately taxable. There are, however, two cases in which stock dividends are immediately taxable: when the shareholder had the option of receiving his dividend in either cash, property, or stock; and when some shareholders received property but others received stock, so that their relative interests in the corporation are changed. But these are rare cases, and most stock dividends are tax-free. When shares are later sold, any gain will of course be taxable—but only at the preferential rate for capital gains.

Two qualifications must be noted. First, the sale of stock involves a brokerage fee, which must be subtracted from the net benefit. Second, when a firm pays cash dividends, each shareholder's proportionate interest remains unchanged; but if a shareholder receives a stock dividend and sells it for cash, his proportionate interest is reduced.

We have been assuming that a stock dividend will cause a drop in *EPS, DPS, and* share price. But it is also possible that share price might fall less than proportionately because the lower price puts the stock within a more popular trading range. The general purpose of a stock split, in fact, is to stimulate the demand for a company's shares by making them more available to investors with limited resources. In some cases, however, when a company feels its stock is in too low a trading range, it will effect a reverse split in order to shed the negative image of a "cheap" stock.

Effects on Market Price of Shares

Early Findings. Do stock dividends and splits actually benefit stockholders by producing a greater total market value for their shares? C. Austin Barker was one of the first to study the effects of stock dividends and splits on share prices.[10] Since his conclusions are similar for dividends and splits, and since later research has concentrated on splits, we shall present only the findings on stock splits.

It is difficult to isolate the effects of the split itself from those of extraneous factors, such as dividend policy and stock-market trends. Barker examined the splits of the New York Stock Exchange during the periods 1951–53 and 1954–55. For each split, he computed a "price relative" by dividing the price six months after the split by the price (adjusted for the split ratio) twelve months before the split. The "relatives" were deflated by the industry stock price index to remove the effect of market trend. Barker then classified the stocks into those that raised dividends at the time of the split and those that did not. He found that the "price relatives" increased for those companies that increased dividends but fell or remained constant for those that did not. Barker's conclusion was that any favorable price effect was the result of the increased cash dividend, not the split itself.

Recent Findings. Keith B. Johnson criticized two aspects of Barker's study.[11] First, Barker actually studied the effect of dividend policy in general, not the effect of stock splits, since his sample included only split stocks, with no control group. Second, Barker's list of extraneous factors included only changes in dividends and in the stock-price index, whereas changes in earnings are also a factor and should therefore have been held constant.

Johnson used regression analysis to test the hypothesis that stock splits have no significant price effect when the effects of earnings, dividends, and market index are removed. His sample included 73 firms listed on the New York Stock Exchange that had been split two-to-one during the year 1959; 73 unsplit stocks were included for comparison. For each stock, price observations were made 12 months apart: 7.5 months before the split and 4.5 months after. In the regression equation, relative price change was the dependent variable; earnings, dividends, market index, and split status were the independent variables. Contrary to Barker's findings, Johnson concluded that "there is a significant relative price change associated with a stock split, after taking into consideration the other factors included in the models."

Johnson's study was in turn followed by W. H. Hausman, R. R. West, and J. A. Largay's hypothesis that most of the price effect that Johnson attributed to the split had in fact occurred before the split.[12] For each firm in Johnson's sample, they obtained three additional price observations within

---

[10] C. Austin Barker, "Effective Stock Splits," *Harvard Business Review* 34 (January–February, 1956), pp. 101–106; "Stock Splits in a Bull Market," *Harvard Business Review* 35 (May–June, 1957), pp. 72–79.

[11] Keith B. Johnson, "Stock Splits and Price Change," *Journal of Finance* 21 (December, 1966), pp. 675–686.

[12] W. H. Hausman, R. R. West, and J. A. Largay, "Stock Splits, Price Changes, and Trading Profits: A Synthesis," *Journal of Business* 44 (January, 1971), pp. 69–77.

the original twelve-month period. When they ran regressions for all possible time periods, they found that split status has the greatest association with share-price appreciation during the four weeks preceding the announcement of the split. This finding raises the possibility that price appreciation may be due at least partly to the favorable developments underlying the decision to split stock. No scientific determination has yet been made.

REPURCHASE OF SHARES

A firm may repurchase its own shares either on the open market or by a standing offer to repurchase a given number of shares at a fixed price. (Again, we are speaking of common shares.) Essentially, such repurchases are a device to enable the common stockholders to withdraw profits from a corporation and have those withdrawals treated by the tax authorities as sales transactions, taxable only at the capital-gains rate. Before elaborating on this, let us first specify our analytical framework.

The Decision Framework

Every share repurchase decision is simultaneously an investment decision, a capital structure decision, and a dividend decision. Share repurchase is an investment decision because a firm may use its funds either for this or for plant and equipment. We made this point in Chapter 9 when a company considered using the proceeds from a divestment to reacquire its own shares. Share repurchase is a capital structure decision because a firm may use its funds either for this or for debt retirement. We shall comment on this decision in Chapter 23 when we analyze recapitalizations involving common stock. Finally, share repurchase is also a dividend decision because both cash dividends and share repurchase are methods whereby a company can distribute cash to its stockholders. Here, we shall view share repurchase solely as a dividend decision.

In announcing plans to repurchase shares, a firm often states that its purpose is to provide treasury shares for use in possible future acquisitions and for fulfilling obligations to employee stock plans. "Purpose" here refers to the uses to which the shares are put *after* they are acquired. This does not alter the fact that the act of repurchase is essentially a means of distributing cash to the shareholders and, as such, can be meaningfully evaluated only by comparing it with the cash dividend alternative. There is of course one important difference between the alternatives: all stockholders participate uniformly in dividend payments but not in repurchase transactions. According to tax laws, such disproportionate redemption qualifies stockholders for the capital-gains rate; otherwise, repurchase places stockholders under income-tax law governing dividend payments.

Tax Status of Share Repurchases

It does not take a tax attorney to see the advantage of using repurchases to siphon off cash to shareholders. If one investor owned 100 percent of the shares of a corporation, and the corporation repurchased 5 percent of his shares for cash, would the repurchase be a dividend payment, yielding ordinary income, or a true sale, yielding capital gains? After repurchase, the single stockholder still owns all of the firm's outstanding shares: his proportionate interest in the company is unchanged. For this reason, tax laws consider repurchases of this nature essentially equivalent to dividends and tax them as such.

Nevertheless, share repurchase can reduce taxes. When repurchase is made by a company with widely held shares, the proportionate interests of the various stockholders will in all probability be altered. In these cases of disproportionate redemption, federal law treats share repurchases not as cash dividends but as true sales resulting in capital gains (or losses). The condition of disproportionate redemption is critical: if redemption is done proportionately, the cash received by the stockholders is taxed as dividends, according to the ordinarily higher rates.

How important is it to the stockholder to have his proportionate interest in a corporation remain unchanged? To most stockholders, absolute wealth is more important; in fact, some even prefer disproportionate redemption as a means of distribution because it gives stockholders the option either of accepting the distribution or of postponing their acceptance, whereas they have no chance to postpone a cash dividend. Share repurchase offers corporations a perfect device for distributing profits in cash to stockholders in a way permitting these monies to be taxed as capital gains.

Shares may be repurchased not only by the issuing company but by related firms as well. For example, if a group of investors controls both Corporations A and B, Corporation A may acquire the common stock of Corporation B; this is called acquisition by a brother-or-sister company. Or, if Corporation A controls Corporation B, Corporation B may acquire the common stock of A; this is acquisition by a subsidiary company. In either case, even if the issuing company is not directly involved, tax authorities will view the acquisition as redemption by the issuing company. The redemption may be taxed either as dividend or capital gain, depending on how the transaction would have been treated if the repurchase had been made directly by the issuing company.

Effect on Shareholders' Wealth

There are stockholders who sell their shares back to the company and those who keep their shares. The tax advantage for the selling stockholders is now clear. But what about the continuing stockholders?

Let us say that XYZ earns $3 per share and pays $1.50 per share in cash dividends, and that its shares sell for $30. A stockholder owning one share therefore has one share worth $30 plus $1.50 in cash from his dividend. But if the company uses its dividend funds for share repurchase instead of dividends, each $1.50 (otherwise paid out in dividends) will reduce outstanding stock by 1/20 of a share; *EPS* for the continuing stockholder will thus rise by approximately 1/20, from $3 to $3.158. Even if we assume conservatively that the price-earnings ratio remains at ten, each share will now have a price of $31.58. The continuing stockholder owning one share will now have a share worth $31.58 instead of a share worth $30 plus $1.50 in cash. His cash dividend is converted into capital gains, and in addition he profits by 8 cents. Moreover, he may decide on his own when best to realize his capital gain.[13] Since fewer shares are now outstanding, *EPS* may be expected to grow more rapidly in the future. If this growth causes the price-earnings ratio to rise, share price will climb above $31.58, giving the shareholder a still greater profit. The tax benefit and price appreciation are the major reasons for the growing importance of share repurchase in recent years.

REVIEW QUESTIONS

1. For each of the following firms, prepare an appropriate statement of dividend policy:
   a. a small, rapidly growing electronics firm with closely held ownership
   b. one of the nation's largest chemical manufacturers
   c. an electric utility firm in the Southeast
   d. a wholesale firm selling Maine lobsters in St. Louis
   e. a medium sized department store.

   Compare your statements, noting similarities and differences regarding payout ratio, stability and regularity of dividends, stock dividends, and share repurchase. What factors did you consider in formulating your statements?
2. Is dividend policy a financing decision or an investment decision? What is the correct approach for determining dividend policy? How does dividend policy affect share value? Which variables determine share price; how does dividend policy affect these variables?
3. Examine the statement of funds in the latest annual reports of any five of these companies: American Telephone and Telegraph, Southwestern Public Service, Bell and Howell, Charles Pfizer, Westinghouse, Coleman Company, Foxboro, Sinclair Oil, Lucky Stores, Polaroid. What were the major sources of funds for

[13] We assume that the repurchase of stock is made at a market price prevailing before the repurchase is announced. In actuality, the repurchase price may be somewhat higher, since the selling stockholders may demand a division of the potential benefits. In this case, our calculations should be slightly modified; the benefits for continuing stockholders may be slightly lower.

each company? What major uses competed with dividends for the firm's cash resources?

4. Since the cost of retained earnings is lower than the cost of stock financing, why do dividend-paying companies ever issue common stock? Would the shareholders of these firms be better off if the companies eliminated cash dividends as a means of reducing the size of common-stock offerings?
5. What is Keith V. Smith's increasing-stream hypothesis of dividend policy? Cite the empirical evidence supporting this hypothesis. What is John Lintner's partial adaptation hypothesis of dividend policy? What is the connection between Lintner's hypothesis and Smith's?
6. How do the balance-sheet surplus test, the solvency test, and the current-profits test affect the legality of dividend payments?
7. What is the difference between a stock dividend and a stock split? What are the reasons for undertaking each?
8. Summarize the findings of Barker; Johnson; and Hausman, West, and Largay on the effect of stock splits on share prices. What is the implication for financial management if the greatest part of the effect occurs before the date of the split?
9. Do you agree with the current tax treatment of disproportionately redeemed share repurchases or do you feel that all repurchases should be treated as dividends? If the latter, what administrative problems would be involved in implementing the new tax regulation?
10. A corporation has two important means of assisting its stockholders to convert potential dividend income into capital gains. It may reinvest earnings, or it may repurchase shares. What is the essential difference between these two methods? Under what conditions is each appropriate?

PROBLEMS

1. Calculate *EPS*, *DPS*, and share price for BAX, assuming a long-run retention ratio b of 65 percent, a reinvestment-return rate r of 10 percent, and an investors' required rate of return k of 14 percent. Compare your results with those in Table 15-2, which were derived from different values of b, r, and k. Interpret your comparison.
2. Calculate *EPS*, *DPS*, and share price for BAX under each of the following sets of assumptions:

$$b = .4 \qquad r = .12 \qquad k = .12$$
$$b = .2 \qquad r = .12 \qquad k = .12$$

   Ignoring taxes, which policy yields the greater wealth to a stockholder with a 3-year holding period? How would your conclusion be affected if he is subject to a 50 percent tax rate on ordinary income and 25 percent on capital gains?

3. (a) On June 1, 19XX, the Boyle Company (Del.) asked its stockholders to approve two measures:

   (i) to increase its capital surplus by $515,200 by reducing the par value of its common shares from $1.00 to $.50 per share.

(ii) to use the existing and the newly created capital surplus to offset a deficit in the retained-earnings account.

What might be the purpose of this accounting adjustment?

(b) Before the adjustment, the capital-stock and surplus accounts of Boyle appear as follows:

Preferred stock ($4 par value)	
121,200 shares issued	$ 484,800
Common stock ($1 par value)	
1,030,400 shares issued	$1,030,400
Paid-in capital	3,670,150
Retained earnings (deficit)	−3,530,700

How will the accounts read after the adjustment?

4. Suppose that Denton, Inc., had the following capitalization:

Common stock ($1 par value)	
1,000,000 shares issued	$1,000,000
Capital surplus	500,000
Earned surplus	500,000

What would be the amounts in each account after a 100 percent stock dividend? after a 2-for-1 stock split?

5. The Starr Corporation produces vehicles and vehicle components, and industrial power transmission systems and components. Its dividends and earnings records are given below. Do these records conform to Lintner's model of partial adaptation? If so, estimate c, the speed-of-adjustment coefficient.

Year	19X0	19X1	19X2	19X3	19X4	19X5	19X6	19X7	19X8	19X9
EPS	1.16	1.39	1.80	2.36	2.76	1.68	2.30	2.76	2.01	2.44
DPS	0.72	0.72	0.76	0.86	1.00	1.00	1.10	1.15	1.15	1.15

6. Find a company that has recently made an offer to repurchase its own common stock for cash. On the basis of published information, analyze the effect of the repurchase on the wealth of selling and of continuing stockholders.

REFERENCES

BARKER, C. AUSTIN, "Effective Stock Splits," *Harvard Business Review* 34 (January–February, 1956), pp. 101–106.

BARKER, C. AUSTIN, "Stock Splits in a Bull Market," *Harvard Business Review* 35 (May–June, 1957), pp. 72–79.

BREALEY, RICHARD A., *Security Prices in a Competitive Market* (Cambridge: The M.I.T. Press, 1971), Ch. 2.

BRIGHAM, EUGENE F., and MYRON J. GORDON, "Leverage, Dividend Policy, and the Cost of Capital," *Journal of Finance* 23 (March, 1968), pp. 85–103.

BRITTAIN, JOHN A., *Corporate Dividend Policy* (Washington, D.C.: The Brookings Institution, 1966).

ELLIS, CHARLES D., and ALLAN E. YOUNG, *The Repurchase of Common Stock* (New York: The Ronald Press Company, 1971).

ELTON, EDWIN J., and MARTIN J. GRUBER, "The Effect of Share Repurchases on the Value of the Firm," *Journal of Finance* 23 (March, 1968), pp. 135–149.

FAMA, EUGENE F., and MERTON H. MILLER, *The Theory of Finance* (New York: Holt, Rinehart and Winston, 1972), Ch. 2.

FINN, FRANK J., "Stock Splits: Prior and Subsequent Price Relationships," *Journal of Business Finance and Accounting* 1 (Spring, 1974), pp. 93–108.

HAUSMAN, W. H., R. R. WEST, and J. A. LARGAY, "Stock Splits, Price Changes, and Trading Profits: A Synthesis," *Journal of Business* 44 (January, 1971), pp. 69–77.

JOHNSON, KEITH B., "Stock Splits and Price Change," *Journal of Finance* 21 (December, 1966), pp. 675–686.

KAHN, DOUGLAS A., *Basic Corporate Taxation* (Ann Arbor: The Institute of Continuing Legal Education, 1973).

LAPORTE, LOWELL, *Dividend Policy in the Smaller Company* (New York: The Conference Board, 1969).

LINTNER, JOHN. "Distribution of Incomes of Corporations Among Dividends, Retained Earnings and Taxes," *American Economic Review* 46 (May, 1956), pp. 97–113.

Moody's Handbook of Common Stocks (1975).

SMITH, KEITH V., "Increasing Stream Hypothesis of Corporate Dividend Policy," *California Management Review* 15 (Fall, 1971), pp. 56–64.

VAN ARSDELL, PAUL M., *Corporation Finance* (New York: The Ronald Press Company, 1968).

VAN HORNE, JAMES C., and JOHN G. MCDONALD, "Dividend Policy and New Equity Financing," *Journal of Finance* 26 (May, 1971), pp. 507–519.

WALTER, JAMES E., *Dividend Policy and Enterprise Valuation* (Belmont: Wadsworth Publishing Company, Inc., 1967).

WATTS, ROSS, "The Information Content of Dividends," *Journal of Business* 46 (April, 1973), pp. 191–211.

Part Six

Long-Term Financing

16 The Marketing of Stocks and Bonds

A firm whose fund requirements exceed the amount generated internally must resort to external financing. External funds may be obtained for short periods (one year or less) through short-term loans, trade credit, or commercial paper; for intermediate durations (one to ten years) through term loans or leasing; and for long durations (more than ten years) through the sale of stocks and bonds. The issue and sale of stocks and bonds are our present concerns.

Once a firm decides upon a stock or a bond issue, a series of questions arises. Should the issue be offered publicly to the investing community at large or privately to a limited number of investors? What are the advantages and disadvantages of each method of sale? (Both cost and non-cost factors must be taken into account.) Which Wall-Street firms specialize in the marketing of new securities, and how do they operate? What fees do these companies charge? Can the issuing firm save money by performing some of the selling functions itself? What internal costs are involved? Which are out-of-pocket and which are overhead items? What government rules and regulations apply to the sale? Since the issuing firm wants to sell its securities at the best possible price, it will want to know who the potential purchasers are, where they are located, how much they have to invest, and what types of securities they prefer. It will also be necessary to know who the competing fund-raisers are, their demands for funds, and the terms on which they offer their securities to potential investors.

THE MARKET FOR LONG-TERM CAPITAL

The Nature of the Capital Market

The capital market, like any commodity market, is the place where the forces of supply and demand interact. The commodity here is money capital, or loanable funds. In any time period, the supply of loanable funds is made up of three components: savings, new money, and dishoarding. Savings is the result of consuming less than one's income; new money is created when banks make loans or purchase securities; dishoarding is the activation of idle cash balances. Arrayed against this supply are the demands of individuals, businesses, and governments. Individuals borrow to pay for homes, durables, education, etc.; businesses, to augment working capital, expand physical facilities, etc.; and governments, to meet budgetary deficits. We shall deal primarily with the supply and demand for long-term funds, but we should remember that the division of the capital market into long- and short-term sectors is artificial since the two sectors are closely interrelated.

The capital market includes not only the organized stock exchanges, where traders actually congregate, but also the over-the-counter (OTC) market, consisting of a large number of securities firms that carry on their transactions only by telephone. The organized exchanges confine trading to outstanding (old) securities. Moreover, each exchange has a list of the securities that it has approved for trading; securities are listed only if they are issued by companies that have applied for listing and have met certain requirements. On the other hand, the OTC market encompasses three kinds of transactions: initial distribution of new securities; block (large) transactions, involving outstanding securities; and trading in unlisted outstanding securities. Whereas the organized exchanges operate on an auction basis, OTC prices are reached by negotiation. The OTC market has a much larger trading volume than the organized exchanges.

The capital market is split as well into primary and secondary markets. The initial distribution of new securities is said to take place in the primary market, while trading in outstanding securities occurs in the secondary market. In public offerings, investment bankers generally serve as middlemen between the corporate issuer and the ultimate investors; in private placements, the corporation deals directly with the investors. This chapter will deal with the primary market, as it pertains to corporate finance, and with the role of the investment banker in this market.

An Overall View

Flow-of-funds accounts provide a useful means by which to understand the capital market, its components, and their interrelationships. In Chapter 3, we saw that the funds statement could show us how a firm obtains and

Table 16-1 Sources and Uses of Long-Term Funds, 1974*

Sources	Billions	Percent	Uses	Billions	Percent
Savings institutions	$57.5	51.6%	Mortgages	$56.5	50.7%
Commercial banks	28.8	25.8	Corporate bonds	21.2	19.0
Government agencies	13.9	12.5	Corporate stocks	3.8	3.4
Corporations	.7	0.6	State and local debt	16.3	14.6
Individuals and others	10.6	9.5	Others	13.7	12.3
Total	$111.5	100.0%	Total	$111.5	100.0%

* Estimated.
Source: Bankers Trust Company, *Credit and Capital Markets 1975* (New York: 1975), p. T2.

utilizes its funds; the same type of analysis can be applied to larger economic groups. The flow-of-funds data are a set of accounts that trace the financial flows among the various sectors of the economy. Whereas national-income statistics divide total spendings into consumption, investment, and government expenditures, flow-of-funds data indicate the channels and methods through which these spendings are financed. These data are thus particularly useful in analyzing the forces of supply and demand in the market for loanable funds.

Table 16-1 summarizes, for non-federal sectors of the economy, the sources and uses of long-term capital during 1974. A total of $111.5 billion in long-term capital was raised by users, of which 50.7 percent was raised by real-estate mortgagors; 19.0 percent and 3.4 percent by issuers of corporate bonds and stock, respectively; 14.6 percent by state and local governments; and 12.3 percent by others. Since these are historical figures, the amount of funds used must have equaled the amount supplied. Savings institutions (life insurance firms, private pension funds, state and local retirement funds, fire- and casualty-insurance companies, savings-and-loan associations, mutual savings banks, and investment companies) supplied 51.6 percent of the total. Commercial banks supplied 25.8 percent, government agencies 12.5 percent, corporations 0.6 percent, and individuals and "others" 9.5 percent.

The Corporate Sector

Gross New Issues. In 1974, as Table 16-1 shows, corporations increased their outstanding bonds and stocks by $21.2 billion and $3.8 billion, respectively. The gross new issues were even larger: $31.6 billion and $8.3 billion, respectively. The differences between these two sets of figures are due to the year's securities retirements: bond refunding, share repurchase, liquidation, etc. The financial executive is, of course, concerned also with total new issues, not just the increase beyond issues outstanding. The

Table 16-2 Gross New Issues of Corporate Bonds and Stocks

	1964	1967	1970	1974*
Bonds	74.3%	81.9%	76.2%	79.2%
Stocks	25.7	18.1	23.8	20.8
Total (in percent)	100.0%	100.0%	100.0%	100.0%
Total (in billions)	$14.4	$26.0	$38.7	$39.9

* Estimated.
Source: Bankers Trust Company, *Credit and Capital Markets 1975*, pp. T10-T11.

distribution of gross new issues between bonds and stocks for selected years between 1964 and 1974 is shown in Table 16-2.

The amount and distribution of corporate-securities issues can be accounted for by corporate liquidity and the respective costs of debt and equity. In 1974, for example, corporations borrowed heavily in the bond market to meet both fixed and working capital requirements. Many companies anticipated increased capital expenditures, but few had foreseen the impact of double-digit inflation which resulted in vastly increased investments in inventory and accounts receivable. Large expenditures reduced corporate liquidity, forcing them to raise capital externally; and the Federal Reserve's restrictive credit policy depressed stock prices, so that corporations turned to the bond market to raise much of their needed capital requirements.

Major Investors. Table 16-3 summarizes all the investors in corporate securities for selected years from 1964 through 1974. As a result of the institutionalization of personal savings over the past several decades, financial institutions are now by far the largest investors in corporate securities.

Table 16-3 Investors in Corporate Bonds and Stocks (in percent)

	1964	1967	1970	1974*
Life insurance companies	29.5	25.7	10.9	24.7
Private pension funds	48.7	33.9	25.5	19.8
State and local retirement funds	29.5	24.0	21.4	32.9
Fire and casualty insurance companies	3.8	8.2	8.9	3.3
Mutual savings banks	−1.3	11.5	4.8	2.6
Investment companies	14.1	8.2	6.1	.3
Savings institutions	124.3	111.5	77.6	83.6
Commercial banks	1.3	.5	1.0	1.3
Individuals and others	−25.6	−12.0	21.4	15.1
Total	100.0	100.0	100.0	100.0

* Estimated.
Source: Bankers Trust Company, *Credit and Capital Markets 1975*, pp. T10–T11.

There are, however, significant differences in the investment patterns of various types of financial institutions. These differences stem largely from varying legal constraints and varying requirements regarding safety of principal, liquidity, and yield. Life insurance companies tend to buy bonds, whereas mutual funds generally buy stocks. Pension funds and fire-and-casualty insurance companies usually buy stocks and bonds equally. Commercial banks are prohibited by law from investing in corporate securities; and savings-and-loan associations, being specialists in home-mortgage financing, do not contribute to corporate financing. Individuals, attracted by high bond yields, have been significant buyers of bonds since 1967, but their sales of stock have frequently been larger than their purchases of bonds, so that the net effect is negative. Individuals' purchases of shares in investment companies are not included in this calculation since they are considered as part of the institutional supply of funds.

Methods of Sale. In general, a corporation can market its securities in either of two ways: by offering them publicly to the investing community at large or by placing them privately with a small number of investors. When the offering is public, a group of investment bankers usually serve as middlemen. The price at which the corporation sells its securities to the bankers may be determined by direct negotiation with the bankers or by competitive bidding. Table 16-4 summarizes corporate financing by method of sale for selected years between 1964 and 1974.

The data in the table result from a combination of complex economic factors, both long- and short-term. In 1964, 60 percent of all corporate securities were sold privately, which was a continuation of an upward trend in private placements that had begun in the 1930's. The 60 percent, however, represented an aberration—in that year, AT&T raised over $1.2 billion in new money, which greatly reduced the need for many of its subsidiaries to engage in public financing on their own. Because this sum was not fully underwritten, the *Investment Dealers' Digest* did not include it in its public offering figure. Otherwise, public offering and private placements would be roughly equal, as in the two previous years. In 1967, tight money reduced credit availability overall, but especially in the private placement market. Many firms which had the option of borrowing in either market, shifted from

Table 16-4 Methods of Security Distribution

	1964	1967	1970	1974
Public Offering				
Direct negotiation	26.3%	51.7%	66.3%	58.2%
Competitive bidding	13.6	16.2	16.7	16.6
Private Placement	60.1	32.1	17.0	25.2
Total	100.0%	100.0%	100.0%	100.0%

Source: *Investment Dealers' Digest*, various issues.

private to public. The shift also received a stimulus when many individuals, as mentioned before, withdrew funds from their savings accounts to buy bonds directly in the open market.

The year 1970 was one of easy money in which we would expect private placements to gain. But because the economy was depressed, individuals borrowed heavily against their insurance policies, reducing the amount which insurance companies had available for private placements. Again, in 1974, large policy loans had depleted the funds of insurance companies; however, the year was one of tight money and many companies found it more attractive to raise their capital publicly. We would expect, therefore, an increase in the percentage of securities publicly offered. Our 1974 figure of 74.8 percent, though lower than 1970, is in fact 10 percent higher than that of the previous year.

NEGOTIATED PUBLIC OFFERINGS

What Is a Public Offering?

A precise definition of a public offering is important because it determines whether or not an issue is subject to the registration requirements of the Securities Act of 1933, which requires that a firm selling new securities disclose financial and other information, on the basis of which investors may appraise the merits of the securities. The information must be set forth in a registration statement filed with the Securities and Exchange Commission (SEC). Unless the issue is privately placed or otherwise exempt, the firm cannot sell it until the registration statement becomes effective on the twentieth day after filing. For reasons which we shall consider later, many firms prefer to offer their securities in such a way that the registration statement will not be necessary.

The main exemption is security sales "not involving any public offering."[1] The Securities Act itself, however, defines neither public nor private offering. Instead, the terms are interpreted by the SEC in its administration of the Act. Five criteria have been established for private placements:[2]

1. Manner of offering: there can be no general advertising or general solicitation in the offering of the securities.
2. Nature of offerees: the offerees must possess such knowledge and experience in financial matters so that they are capable of evaluating the merits and risks of the prospective investment. Moreover, all offerees must be able to bear the economic risk of the securities.

[1] Section 4(2) of the Securities Act of 1933, as amended.

[2] See SEC Rule 146, which became effective in June, 1974.

3. Availability of information: the offeree should have access to the sort of information that would normally be contained in a registration statement.
4. Number of offerees: there can be no more than 35 purchasers of the issuer's securities in any 12-month period.
5. Investment intent: the securities are being purchased for long-term investment, not for immediate resale. Intent is generally documented on the basis of confidential letters from the investors. In addition, a sale is more likely to be considered private if the corporation stamps on the security instrument a legend warning other investors that the original transaction was private.

The Role of Investment Bankers

The term "investment banker" is actually a misnomer since the banker does not invest in the securities of the issuing corporation.[3] He is strictly a middleman, originating, underwriting, and distributing the security. "Origination" refers to the investment banker's negotiations with the corporation, which result in his managing the distribution of the firm's securities. The term covers not only the initial contact and negotiation of rate of compensation, but also advice on broad financial policy, such as capital structure, timing, and pricing of an offering. "Underwriting" guarantees the corporation that it will receive full payment on a set date whether or not the underwriter is successful in marketing the issue; in effect, the corporation sells its issue to the underwriter at the negotiated price. "Distribution" is the actual selling of the security to the individual and institutional investors.

Although origination must precede any offering made through an investment banker, the other two functions do not accompany all offerings. If the investment banker both underwrites and distributes, the resulting agreement is an outright purchase, also called a firm commitment. If the investment banker underwrites the entire issue but distributes only a fraction of it, the result is a standby agreement. This type of agreement is used when a corporation sells stock to present stockholders: the investment banker guarantees the success of the entire offering, but distributes only those shares to which present stockholders do not subscribe. Finally, if an investment banker distributes but does not underwrite, the result is a best-effort agreement. This type of contract is used when the issue is particularly risky either because the issuing firm is financially weak or because the issue is over-priced. It is also used when an issue is so attractive that its success is assured.

---

[3] Comprehensive studies of investment banking functions include those by Merwin H. Waterman, *Investment Banking Functions* (Ann Arbor: Bureau of Business Research, The University of Michigan, 1958); Irwin Friend and others, *Investment Banking and the New Issues Market* (Cleveland: The World Publishing Company, 1967); and Vincent P. Carosso, *Investment Banking in America* (Cambridge: Harvard University Press, 1970).

Offering Procedure

Selection of an Investment Banker. An investment banker should be chosen systematically. Major investment bankers (e.g., Morgan Stanley & Co., Lehman Brothers, The First Boston Corporation) operate nationally and internationally and have a minimum-size criterion for underwriting. Minor investment bankers operate regionally and locally, and some lack the experience and the capital to handle large issue. The geographic market and the size of an issue thus automatically limit the number of investment bankers suitable for originating and managing the issue.

To judge its list of candidates, a firm should apply the criterion of functional suitability. For example, if the firm wants its securities to be distributed widely, it should select a banker with a strong organization for retail distribution; if the firm is making its first public offering, it will need a banker with experience in "going public." Most firms use a variety of financing methods: stocks, bonds, term loans, sale-and-lease-back, commercial paper, warrants, options, convertibles, financial subsidiaries, and private placements. The investment banker should be versatile enough to assist with the firm's overall financing plan. Finally, since the public offering price is subject to negotiation between the firm and the banker, the financial executive should be alert to the danger of underpricing.

Underwriting Agreements. The contract between the issuing corporation and its investment banker consists of a letter of intent and a formal underwriting agreement. The letter of intent records the tentative terms reached during early negotiations; it usually concerns underwriting compensation, allocation of expenses (legal fees, printing, advertising, etc.), steps to be taken by the corporation prior to the offering, and the schedule of the offering. There will also be a *tentative* agreement, written or oral, on the price of the public offering.

After the letter of intent is signed, the formal documents for the SEC registration are prepared and filed. In time, the registration will go into effect. A few days before the effective date, a formal underwriting agreement will be signed. This document covers the same items as the letter of intent, with two additions: the investment banker's commitment to purchase the issue from the corporation at the public price, along with a statement of the commission he will charge for his services; and the details of the closing operation, i.e., the time and place of securities delivery and cash payment. These agreements are binding unless the banker invokes the "market-out" clause, which permits an investment banker to withdraw from his commitment if a drastic market break occurs between the signing of the underwriting agreement and the closing date.

Although the corporation has direct dealings only with the originating banker, many bankers are involved. To spread the risk, the originating banker invites other bankers to participate in the underwriting. All of the underwriting bankers may sell the securities; other bankers may be asked to help with the selling without participating in the underwriting. Purchase-group and selling-group agreements may thus arise among the bankers, but the corporation will not be directly involved with these.

Processing of Formal Documents. The most important formal document is the registration statement that the issuer must file with the SEC; the investment banker usually assists in the preparation of this statement. The corporation must disclose the major provisions of the security, the intended use of the proceeds, the corporation's business and profitability, its capital structure, and its general financial condition. The law provides that a registration shall become effective on the 20th day after filing. However, if the SEC finds the statement incomplete or inaccurate, it will instruct the company to file a clarifying or correcting amendment. If one or more such amendments are required, the securities may not legally be offered for sale until 20 days after the filing of the final amendment.

Any actual sale must be preceded or accompanied by a final prospectus, containing the same type of information as that in the registration statement. The prospectus is a selling device, and should be designed with that in mind. If a prospectus is sent to a potential customer before the effective date, its cover must state that the registration is not yet effective and that the prospectus is only information, not an offer to sell. Since the statement is printed in red, a preliminary prospectus is called a "red herring prospectus." Brief newspaper advertisements are also permitted; because of their brevity, they are known as "tombstone advertisements."

An offering must comply not only with federal laws but also with state statutes (blue-sky laws) governing security sales. These regulations cover anti-fraud provisions, registration requirements, and the licensing of security salesmen. The investment banker usually sees to it that these statutes are complied with.

Post-Effective Date Activities. Speed in selling an issue is important in minimizing the underwriting group's exposure to adverse market developments. During the offering period, the managing banker may fix the market price of the new security at the public-offering level in order to insulate the new issue from temporary oversupplies. The corporation is a bystander whose primary interest is in the forthcoming closing date (usually seven days after the effective date), when it will deliver the securities to the banker in return for full payment of the sum agreed upon.

Costs of Flotation

The cost of flotation includes spread, extras, and "other" expenses. Spread is the excess of the public-offering price over the price received by the corporation from the investment banker. When the FMC Corporation sold $100 million worth of 9.5%, 25-year debentures through a group of investment bankers headed by Kidder, Peabody & Co. and Lehman Brothers, the following information appeared on the cover of the prospectus (see Figure 16-1). The bankers purchased the entire issue for $98,125,000, planning to resell it to the public for $99 million—an anticipated commission or "spread" of .875 percent of the face value. The public price per bond was $990; the proceeds to the corporation were $981.25, leaving the banker a gross profit of $8.75 per bond.

Whereas spread is an investment banker's cash compensation, "extras" are his noncash compensation. Extras may be "cheap stocks" (corporation stocks at bargain prices), warrants or options on the company's shares, or rights of first refusal in handling future issues. Extras, however, are used only in the sale of weak issues, when the normal range of spread does not adequately compensate the investment banker for the risk he assumes. "Other" expenses include printing costs, accounting and legal fees, and registration fees. The spread, extras (if any), plus the other expenses make up the total cost to the corporation of selling its securities.

Much more data are published on spread and "other" expenses than on extras. The *Investment Dealers' Digest* classifies all securities as straight debt, convertible debt, preferred stock, and common stock. Table 16-5 summarizes the average cost of floating each of these classes. The table shows that total cost (excluding extras) varies from 1.26 percent for straight debt to 7.41 percent for common stock, with an overall average of 3.75 percent. Since equity securities involve greater risk and selling effort, common stock and convertibles have higher spreads than preferred stock and straight debt. "Other" expenses vary directly with spread, generally equalling about one fourth of the spread. No information on extras was reported. In another study, Craig A. Simmons reported the use of cheap stocks in slightly over half of all 1971 offerings of unseasoned common stocks. He estimated that these cheap stocks have generally equalled about 8.4 percent of the total number of shares offered for public sale, but made no estimate of the dollar value of such extras.[4]

Morris Mendelson used multiple-regression analysis to determine which characteristics of an issue may best be used to predict the percentage of spread, and found that spread on common stock is inversely correlated with share price, size of the company, and size of the issue.[5] Mendelson also presented a summary of a similar study by Avery Cohan, who reached substantially the same conclusions concerning the spread on straight-debt

---

[4] Craig A. Simmons, *An Economic Analysis of the 1971 New Issues Market* (Washington, D.C.: Office of Economic Research, Securities and Exchange Commission, 1973), pp. 48–52.

[5] Morris Mendelson, "Underwriting Compensations," in Irwin Friend and others, *op. cit.*, pp. 428–449. Mendelson also summarizes the results of a similar study by Avery Cohan on pp. 407–411 and 413–415.

PROSPECTUS

$100,000,000

FMC FMC Corporation

9½% Sinking Fund Debentures due January 15, 2000

Prior to January 15, 1985, the Debentures may not be refunded at an interest cost of less than 9.61% per annum. Otherwise, the Debentures may be redeemed at any time as set forth herein. Interest on the Debentures is payable on January 15 and July 15 in each year.

Mandatory sinking fund payments commencing in 1986 will retire 92.4% of the Debentures prior to maturity. FMC has the option to increase the sinking fund payment in any year by an amount not exceeding the mandatory sinking fund payment for that year.

Application has been made to list the Debentures on the New York Stock Exchange.

THESE SECURITIES HAVE NOT BEEN APPROVED OR DISAPPROVED BY THE SECURITIES AND EXCHANGE COMMISSION NOR HAS THE COMMISSION PASSED UPON THE ACCURACY OR ADEQUACY OF THIS PROSPECTUS. ANY REPRESENTATION TO THE CONTRARY IS A CRIMINAL OFFENSE.

	Price to Public(1)	Underwriting Discounts and Commissions(2)	Proceeds to Company(1)(3)
Per Debenture	99%	0.875%	98.125%
Total	$99,000,000	$875,000	$98,125,000

(1) Plus accrued interest from January 15, 1975, to date of delivery.

(2) FMC has agreed to indemnify the Underwriters against certain civil liabilities, including liabilities under the Securities Act of 1933.

(3) Before deducting expenses payable by FMC, estimated at $290,000.

The Debentures are offered by the several Underwriters subject to receipt and acceptance by them and the right to reject any order in whole or in part. It is expected that delivery of Debentures offered by the Underwriters will be made on or about January 30, 1975, at the office of Kidder, Peabody & Co. Incorporated, 10 Hanover Square, New York, New York. Debentures are being offered to certain institutions through the Underwriters for later delivery pursuant to Delayed Delivery Contracts with FMC as described herein under "Delayed Delivery Arrangements."

Kidder, Peabody & Co.
Incorporated

Lehman Brothers
Incorporated

The date of this Prospectus is January 23, 1975

Figure 16-1 Cover Page of a Prospectus

Table 16-5 Cost of Flotation of All Underwritten Issues, 1969 (percent of gross proceeds)

Type of Security	Spread	"Other" Expenses	Total
Straight debt	1.01	0.25	1.26
Preferred stock	1.36	0.28	1.65
Convertible debt	2.10	0.63	2.73
Common stock	6.01	1.40	7.41
All issues	3.02	0.73	3.75

Source: Roger Hillstrom and Robert King, *1960–1969 A Decade of Corporate and International Finance* (New York: Investment Dealers' Digest, Inc., 1971), p. 16.

issues. Share price and company size are proxies for the quality of the issue and therefore inversely correlated with spread. The inverse relationship between spread and issue size is explained by the universal presence of fixed costs, in investment banking as in any other business. The percentage of "other" expenses also decreases with increasing issue size, and so, therefore, does total flotation cost, when expressed as a percentage of the size of the offering.

COMPETITIVE PUBLIC OFFERINGS

Background and Scope

Competitive bidding is the direct result of the 1939 investigation of monopolies by the Temporary National Economic Committee (TNEC). The contention was that investment bankers, with their monopoly power, had been paying their corporate customers less than the best prices for their negotiated offerings. More competition, it was believed, would force investment bankers to agree to lower underwriting spreads and higher public-offering prices. The results of the TNEC investigation led to the promulgation in 1941 of SEC Rule U-50, which requires public utilities under SEC jurisdiction to offer their securities by competitive bidding; that is, the investment bankers must compete for the issues through sealed bids. The SEC decision prompted the Interstate Commerce Commission and the Federal Power Commission to make similar requirements for railroads and utilities, respectively, under their jurisdictions. Some securities, however, such as stocks, rights offerings, and small issues, are regularly exempt.

Approximately 25 percent of all issues underwritten during the period 1964–1973 were competitive offerings, while 75 percent were negotiated.[6]

[6] Based on data in *Investment Dealers' Digest,* various issues.

Most competitive bidding involves debt issues, with competitively offered debt accounting for nearly half of all debt offerings. Competitive offerings of stocks are relatively insignificant, accounting for less than 10 percent of stocks in recent years. Of the competitive offerings, most are utility and railroad issues, since industrial companies very seldom use the method of competitive bidding.

Offering Procedures

The procedures for competitive bidding naturally differ from those for negotiations. When, in response to news of a forthcoming competitive offering, an investment banker initiates the formation of a bidding account, he will be in competition with other groups of bidders for account members with strong capital and good selling organizations. If the issue is large, the need to share the underwriting risk among many bankers may limit the bidders to two or three groups; if the offering is small, ten or more groups may be in competition.

The corporation must satisfy the same registration requirements as one which makes a negotiated offering. The issuing company must prepare a registration statement, containing detailed information about the company and the securities offered. The company will send to any potential bidder a copy of the registration statement, along with an invitation to bid. The invitation describes the form, content, submission, and acceptance of bids. Current practice calls for the bid to be for the entire issue and to specify both the coupon rate and the proceeds to the company. The bid must be accompanied by a cash deposit, usually about 2 percent of the principal amount of the issue. The invitation will also state the date and time by which the bid must be submitted, as well as the terms of the purchase. The winning bid is determined by the lowest cost of capital to the issuing company, which reserves the right to return all bids unopened or to reject all bids after opening them.

A week or two before the registration becomes effective, the issuing firm usually holds a meeting at which the officers of the company are available to review with prospective bidders the information in the registration statement and prospectus. After the meeting, each member of a bidding group decides on the appropriate bid; he will be influenced especially by the current prices of outstanding bonds with similar features and ratings. On the day before the bidding, the members of each group meet to exchange their views so that the managing firm will have time to mediate if there are important differences within the group. It is important to note that an account member may withdraw from the underwriting agreement if the bid price at the final meeting, the next day, is not to his liking. During mediation, the managing banker must try to reconcile two conflicting forces: he wants the bid to be high enough to win the issue but low enough to keep most of the account members in the group. On the day of the bidding, each group assembles; its managing banker announces its bid price and sends it to the representative of the issuing company. Within a short time, the group knows whether or not it has won; and the issuing company knows to which group its bonds are sold and at what price.

Costs of Flotation

The *Investment Dealers' Digest,* in publishing data on flotation costs, does not distinguish between negotiated and competitive offerings. We can, however, ascertain the costs of floating an issue, competitive or otherwise, by examining the issuer's registration statement and prospectus. Thus, consider the case of Oklahoma Gas and Electric Company, which sold \$75 million worth of $8^3/_8$ percent, 30-year bonds in a competitive offering in 1974. The major saving in competitive bidding is theoretically in the reduction of underwriting spread. In the case of OG&E, the winning bid of 100.463 (percent of face value) was submitted by Morgan Stanley and Company who re-offered the securities to the public at 101.38, for a spread of .917 percent. In its registration statement, the company also reported "other" expenses of \$105,000, or .14 percent of gross amount of issue. Total flotation costs to OG&E, therefore, were 1.057 percent of gross amount of issue. In the same year, Delmarva Power and Light Company sold slightly over \$19 million of its common stock in a competitive offering. The total cost of flotation was 5 percent, made of 4.6 percent of spread and .4 percent of "other" expenses.

Competitive bidding may affect the public-offering price of the new securities. To satisfy the issuing corporation, the investment banker should price an issue at or near its true market value; but to minimize his own underwriting risk, he should price the issue below its true market value. By comparing the fixed public-offering price with the first free-market quotation, one can tell whether the investment banker has under- or over-priced the issue. Table 16-6 shows the frequency of under- and over-pricing for 125 bond issues, based on data collected by Merwin H. Waterman. Since security appraisal is an art, errors in judgment are unavoidable. If the prices are intended to be unbiased, positive and negative errors should be equally likely. It cannot be pure chance, then, that among competitive offerings, underpriced issues were only 9/10 as frequent as over-priced issues, but in negotiated offerings underpriced issues were more than twice as frequent as overpriced. The financial executive should take into account this price difference in measuring the true cost of selling securities competitively.

It may at first seem surprising that competitive bidding is not used in industrial issues, since there would be the prospect of a lower cost of money. But, first, the managements of many firms value strongly the full range of

Table 16-6 Public Offering Prices of 125 Bond Issues

Relative to First Market Quotation	Negotiated Offering	Competitive Bidding	Total
Over pricing	6	57	63
Exact pricing	1	4	5
Under pricing	14	43	57
Total	21	104	125

Source: Based on data in Waterman, *op. cit.*, pp. 164–169.

services which investment bankers make available only to their continuing customers. Second, competitive bidding is more suited to securities with uniform and standard features, such as those of utilities and railroads, rather than those of industrials. Some industrials, however, do use this method.

PRIVATE PLACEMENT OF SECURITIES

The Method of Private Placement

Securities sold by private placement need not be registered since the Securities Act of 1933 exempts transactions not involving public offerings. As Figure 16-2 indicates, the percentage of corporate bonds privately placed showed a steady upward trend from 1935 through 1965; the greatest growth was during the years immediately after World War II, when corporations placed large amounts of debt with life-insurance companies and pension funds. From 1966 through 1970, the trend reversed itself, because institutional investors concerned with liquidity favored the greater marketability of publicly-traded securities. Since then, the percentage has fluctuated between 22 and 40 percent, reflecting primarily the cash position of insurance companies and pension funds and their aggressiveness in seeking private investments in a given year.

In its exemption of private placement, Congress originally had in mind the direct sale of bonds or notes to financial institutions that generally purchase for long-term investment and are knowledgeable enough not to need the protection of registration. This type of transaction still dominates private placements quantitatively. But private placement has been used increasingly by small firms selling stocks and bonds which are convertible into stock. When straight debt is placed privately by a small company, the debt is frequently sold jointly with common stock (or warrants to purchase stock) at a single price. These packages are called unit offerings.

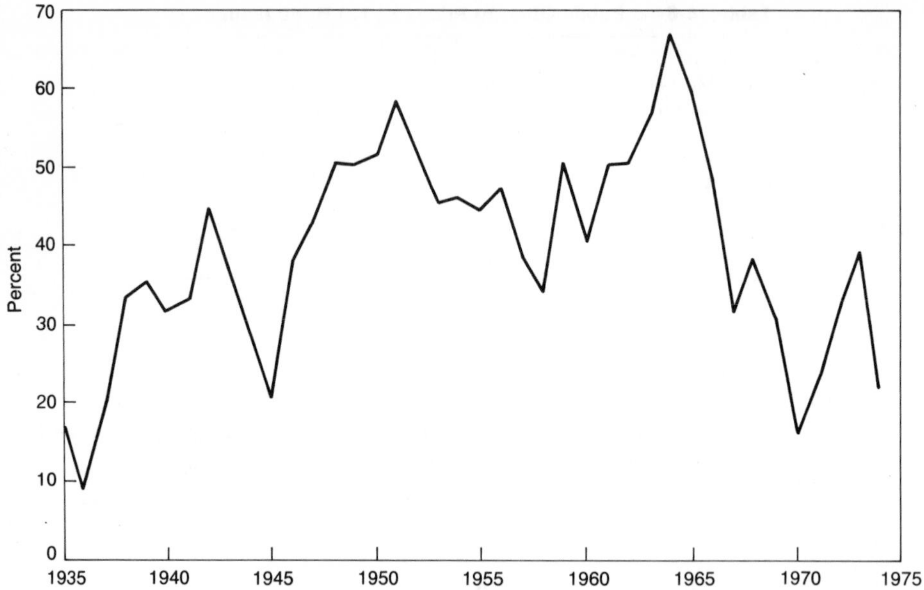

Source: Securities and Exchange Commission.

Figure 16-2 Percentage of Corporate Bonds Privately Placed

Reasons for Private Placement

Large Companies. Large companies often use private placement for reasons different from those of small companies. Private placement has five major advantages for large firms:[7]

1. Speed: a private placement may take a few days or a few weeks to complete. On the other hand, a public offering may take six months, during which the company's financial plan may be upset by adverse market developments. Speed is even more crucial if the money is needed for takeover bids and mergers.
2. Initial savings: underwriting spread is eliminated. The issuing company may still have to pay a fee, if the placement is arranged by an investment banker, but the fee is much smaller than the usual spread. At least as important is the greater simplicity of private placement, calling for less of the executive's time.

[7] Eli Shapiro and Charles R. Wolf, *The Role of Private Placements in Corporate Finance* (Boston: Graduate School of Business Administration, Harvard University, 1972), Ch. 2.

3. Tailor-made terms: the issuing company can negotiate terms, such as "delayed take-down," to fit its own needs. In delayed take-down, the firm may draw on the funds borrowed over a period of time rather than all at once; the company may have to pay a fee on the amount not immediately drawn, but even this is less costly than paying full interest.
4. Flexible credit standards: if a firm has a low credit rating because of, say, a temporary earnings setback, an insurance company that has dealt with the firm and understands its problems may be willing to pay a better price for the firm's securities than investors at large would pay. The issuing firm could thus avoid the heavy penalties imposed on weak issues by the impersonal public capital market.
5. Off-balance-sheet financing: in financing plant and equipment, a firm may borrow money through a subsidiary in such a way that the debt does not appear on its own balance sheet. Private placement of the subsidiary debt minimizes undesirable publicity of increased borrowing.

On the other hand, private placement does have three disadvantages from the borrower's viewpoint:

1. No open-market repurchases: if a company's bonds are traded publicly, the company can repurchase its bonds at a discount, if and when the market rate of interest rises above the coupon rate. If the bonds are privately placed, there is, of course, no opportunity for such open-market repurchases.
2. High interest rates: while the private lenders have flexible credit standards, they do charge slightly higher interest rates than lenders in the public market. For companies that have the alternative of public offering, the higher interest rate could be a deterrent to private borrowing.
3. Restrictive covenants: private loan agreements generally contain more restrictive covenants than a public offering. The restrictions increase the protection for the lender but decrease the operating flexibility of the borrower.

Small Companies. Because of either small size or weak financial position, some firms lack ready access to the public market and therefore have weak bargaining powers.[8] For these firms, the comments already made

[8] See Benjamin R. Makela, ed., *How to Use and Invest in Letter Stock* (New York: Presidents Publishing House, Inc., 1970), for many useful insights on fund raising by small firms in the private capital market.

need two qualifications. First, the savings in registration expenses is less permanent for small firms than for large ones. Large companies usually place their debt with insurance companies that buy for long-term investment and therefore contemplate no resale. But small companies generally place equity issues with venture capitalists who may wish to resell in two or three years. Such resales must usually be registered. In a typical case, the issuer must bear the cost of this delayed registration; but even if the investor pays, he takes the registration cost into account in determining the price he is willing to pay for the stock. In such a situation, therefore, private placement only postpones registration expenses. In other words, the savings on registration expenses will be permanent only if a firm places its debt with a lender that will hold it till maturity.

Second, market reception is a critical factor prompting many small firms to use private placement. We have already mentioned the advantage for lesser-known or financially weak firms in dealing with private lenders with flexible credit standards. For small firms issuing stock, another aspect of market reception stems from the possible impact of the new issue on the market price of its already outstanding shares. If the shares are selling at a high price but the market is thin because few shares are outstanding, then the new issue, if offered publicly, might lower the market price significantly. Private placement can keep the new shares off the market at least temporarily. If the company is contemplating a merger or the issue of stock options, a high share price is beneficial even in a thin market.

GOVERNMENT REGULATIONS

The Securities Act of 1933 governs the sale of new securities and should not be confused with the Securities Exchange Act of 1934, which governs trading in outstanding securities.

Sale of New Securities

The sale of new securities must conform to the following governmental regulations:

1. An issuer may not offer his securities to the investing public until his registration statement with the SEC has become effective.
2. Between the filing date and the effective date of registration, a red-herring prospectus and tombstone advertisements are permitted as ways of informing potential investors of the offering.
3. The actual sale of securities is permitted only after the effective date; each sale must be preceded or accompanied by a copy of the final prospectus.

4. The registration requirements apply to any middleman purchasing a security from an issuer for the purpose of reselling it to the public.
5. Exemptions from registration requirements are granted to some types of securities and transactions: e.g., private placements; government obligations; intrastate offerings; securities issued by banks, savings-and-loan associations, and certain railroads; securities with an original maturity of nine months or less; and small issues under certain conditions.

Resale of Private Offerings

Although private placements are exempt from registration at initial sale, registration may be required if the securities are later offered for resale. If the securities are resold in another private transaction, the exemption naturally applies again. But even if the securities are distributed publicly, the offering may still be exempt if the initial purchaser can prove to the SEC that his original intent was investment, not resale. The SEC's judgment of the investor's intention is presumably influenced by factors such as the purchaser's business, his relationship with the issuer, and the length of time he has held the securities.

Uncertainty is unavoidable in dealing with subjective intent, but it has at least been reduced by Rule 144, which permits the resale of privately placed securities without registration if five conditions are met:[9]

1. The person making the resale must have owned the securities for at least two years.
2. For unlisted securities, the amount sold during any 6-month period must not exceed one percent of the class of securities outstanding; for listed securities, the amount must not exceed one percent of the class outstanding *or* the weekly trading volume for the preceding four weeks, whichever is smaller.
3. The sale must be made through a broker who neither solicits customers nor receives more than the normal brokerage commission.
4. The public must have access to certain information (balance sheet, income statement, etc.) about the issuer.
5. The SEC must be informed of the sale.

Even though the resale of privately placed securities does not directly involve the issuing firm, the transaction affects the company's ability to place securities privately in the first place.

[9] See SEC Rule 144, which became effective in April, 1972.

Private placements should be distinguished from securities issued in exchange for assets in merger transactions. The latter securities were formerly exempt from registration, not because they represented private transactions, but because the SEC viewed them as no sale. Since 1973, the SEC has discarded the no-sale theory of mergers and has required a special form of registration for such securities. The securities received by the controlling stockholders of the selling company in a merger are restricted; they cannot, for example, be offered publicly without a new registration. Otherwise, their sale is also governed by Rule 144, as we shall see in the chapter on mergers and acquisitions.

REVIEW QUESTIONS

1. What is the magnitude of total demand for long-term capital? What percentage of this demand is attributable to the corporate sector? Who are the major purchasers of corporate securities? Against whom must corporations compete for funds?
2. What is the accounting relationship between new issues of securities, retirements, and net change in securities outstanding? Do the numbers on the use side of the flow-of-funds in Table 16-1 refer to "new issues" or "net changes in outstanding issues"? Retained earnings and depreciation, two major sources of long-term corporate financing, do not appear in the flow-of-funds table; why not?
3. Explain the direct effects of each of the following transactions on the data on new issues, retirements, and net changes in outstanding issues: GMAC refunds a bond issue; Studebaker-Worthington repurchases 50,000 shares of its common stock to be held in treasury; AW Liquidating Company pays a cash liquidating dividend on its common stock; AT&T sells debentures with warrants to purchase common shares; McDonald Corporation forces conversion of its 4.5 percent debentures; a small unknown company privately places a debt issue and keeps the transaction confidential.
4. Describe the essential characteristics of a securities offering which would qualify it as a private placement. Under the Securities Act of 1933, what are the prospectus and registration requirements for publicly offered securities?
5. What are the functions of an investment banker? Which of these functions are performed in an outright-purchase agreement? in a standby agreement? in a best-effort agreement? If you were the major owner of a uranium-prospecting corporation and were making a public offering of your shares for the first time, which type of underwriting agreement would be the most appropriate? Why?
6. Compare the procedures for negotiated public offerings with those for competitive public offerings from the viewpoints of the corporate issuer and the investment banker.
7. Locate the following information in the prospectus of any recent security issue: the name of the company; the amount, description, and purpose of the issue; the price to the public, the proceeds to the company, and the underwriting spread (how much of the spread is allowed to dealers and brokers for

finding the ultimate purchasers?); the number of investment bankers who signed the underwriting agreement; and the type of agreement: firm commitment, standby, or best-effort.

8. The Mobil Oil Corporation registered with the SEC a two-part offering of \$200 million of 30-year debentures and \$100 million of $7\frac{1}{2}$-year notes. A few months later, the firm announced that it had privately placed a long-term debt issue with an insurance company and that it was cancelling its scheduled public offerings. What are the advantages of private placement compared with public offerings? Which of these advantages are most relevant to a large corporation like Mobil Oil?

9. The costs of selling an issue publicly are composed of the underwriting spread and "other" expenses. Explain the nature of each component, its magnitude relative to gross proceeds, and the characteristics of an issue that would determine this magnitude. Should a firm take into account any other selling expenses?

10. How does the Securities Act of 1933 restrict the marketability of privately placed securities? May privately placed securities be offered to the public at a later date without registration? If so, under what conditions? If registration is required, who usually pays the costs: the issuer or the private investor?

PROBLEMS

1. The prospectuses of two common-stock issues contain the following information on pricing and on underwriting commissions:

530,000 Shares
Measurex Corporation

	Price to Public	Underwriting Commissions	Proceeds to Company
Per Share	\$20.25	\$1.15	\$19.10
Total	\$10,732,500	\$609,500	\$10,123,000

3,000,000 Shares
The Detroit Edison Company

	Price to Public	Underwriting Commissions	Proceeds to Company
Per Share	\$17.00	\$.67	\$16.33
Total	\$51,000,000	\$2,010,000	\$48,990,000

Express the underwriting commissions as percentages of the price to the public. Why is the commission rate for Detroit Edison's offering significantly lower than that for Measurex's? (You may assume that the issues were offered in 1974 at approximately the same time; in other words, market conditions are the same for both offerings.) Compare your answer with the variables that Morris Mendelson found significant in explaining the spread on common-stock issues.

2. The prospectuses of two debt issues contain the following information on pricing and underwriting commissions:

United States Gypsum Company
$75 million 7.875%, 30-year Debentures

	Price to Public	Underwriting Commissions	Proceeds to Company
Per Unit	99.500%	0.875%	98.625%
Total	$74,625,000	$656,250	$73,968,750

Macy Credit Corporation
$50 million 8%, 8-year Debentures

	Price to Public	Underwriting Commissions	Proceeds to Company
Per Unit	100%	.7%	99.3%
Total	$50,000,000	$350,000	$49,650,000

For each issue, compute the yield to an investor who purchases the bonds at the offering price and holds them to maturity. By how much does this yield exceed the effective interest cost to the company?

3. The Upstate Power and Light Company received the following bids on its $30 million of 30-year first mortgage bonds:

Bidding Group	Coupon Rate	Price to Company	Price to Public
A	$9\frac{1}{8}$%	99.057	99.75
B	$9\frac{1}{4}$%	100.317	101.00
C	$9\frac{1}{4}$%	100.300	101.00

Which is the winning bid, as determined by the lowest "annual cost of money"? The company defines the annual cost as the yield to maturity, carried out to the nearest 1/1,000 of one percent, calculated on the basis of proceeds to the company and by reference to a table of bond yields.

4. The XYZ Corporation must choose between a public offering and private placement as a way to raise $10 million of debt capital. It could sell $10 million of 7-year notes at 7.8 percent interest. The cost of flotation would be 3 percent of gross proceeds: 2 percent underwriting compensation and 1 percent "other" expenses. If the debt were privately placed, the terms of the loan agreement would be the same except that the interest rate would be 8.3 percent. In private placement, there would be no underwriting compensation but the firm would have to pay a finder's fee of .5 percent of gross proceeds. Because of the savings in registration fees, printing and engraving costs, accountants' fees, and legal fees, "other" expenses would be only one third as great as the corresponding costs for a public offering. In terms of present value, which method of financing would cost the company less? How much less? You should assume that the firm's opportunity cost of capital is 13.5 percent and that the private investor would hold the debt to maturity.

5. Suppose that XYZ has placed its issue privately and that the lender has given XYZ the option of "delayed take-down" so that XYZ may draw the funds as it needs them. XYZ has agreed to pay a commitment fee of .75 percent per annum on the unused balance from the date of the loan agreement; but interest is paid only from the time that funds are actually drawn. Suppose that XYZ expects with equal probabilities that its borrowing pattern will be either Pattern A or Pattern B:

Year	1	2	3	4 to 7
		(in millions)		
Pattern A	$7	$7	$7	$10 (annually)
Pattern B	5	6	9	10 (annually)

Suppose also that the firm's policy calls for investing temporary surplus funds in safe marketable securities whose yield is not expected to exceed 7 percent per annum. Calculate the expected present value to XYZ of the delayed take-down provision.

6. After losing money for two consecutive years, the Beta Marketing Company needed $35 million in Year 3 to strengthen its working-capital position. The firm obtained the money privately by issuing a 20-year note carrying 7.5 percent interest and convertible into common stock at $12 a share (i.e., one share for each $12 of debt). At the time of the agreement, Beta's stock was selling at a market price of $10 per share. Suppose that by Year 6 (now), the price of company stock has risen to $15 per share. What has the money borrowed cost Beta so far?

REFERENCES

Bankers Trust Company, *Credit and Capital Markets* (New York: annual).

CAROSSO, VINCENT P., *Investment Banking in America* (Cambridge: Harvard University Press, 1970).

CONNELLY, JULIE, "Shaking Up the Underwriting Syndicates," *Institutional Investor* 8 (March, 1974), pp. 52–58, 106–108.

DE MOTT, JOHN S., "A New Era for Private Placements," *Institutional Investor* 8 (January, 1974), pp. 105–106.

DOUGALL, HERBERT E., and JACK E. GAUMNITZ, *Capital Markets and Institutions* (Englewood Cliffs: Prentice-Hall, Inc., 1975).

FRIEND, IRWIN, and others, *Investment Banking and the New Issues Market* (Cleveland: The World Publishing Company, 1967).

GOLDSMITH, RAYMOND W., *Capital Market Analysis and the Financial Accounts of the Nation* (Morristown: General Learning Corporation, 1972).

HAYES, SAMUEL L., III, "Investment Banking: Power Structure in Flux," *Harvard Business Review* 49 (March–April, 1971), pp. 136–152.

HILLSTROM, ROGER, and ROBERT KING, *1960–1969 A Decade of Corporate and International Finance* (New York: Investment Dealers' Digest, Inc., 1971).

LOGUE, DENNIS E., and JOHN R. LINDVALL, "The Behavior of Investment Bankers: An Econometric Investigation," *Journal of Finance* 29 (March, 1974), pp. 203–215.

LOSS, LOUIS, *Securities Regulation,* 6 vols. (Boston: Little, Brown and Company, 1961–1969).

MAKELA, BENJAMIN R., ed., *How to Use and Invest in Letter Stock* (New York: Presidents Publishing House, Inc., 1970).

PRELL, MICHAEL J., "How Well Do the Experts Forecast Interest Rates?" in Federal Reserve Bank of Kansas City, *Monthly Review* (September–October, 1973), pp. 3–13.

REA, JOHN D., and PEGGY BROCKSCHMIDT, "The Relationship Between Publicly Offered and Privately Placed Corporate Bonds," in Federal Reserve Bank of Kansas City, *Monthly Review* (November, 1973), pp. 11–20.

ROBINSON, ROLAND I., and DWAYNE WRIGHTSMAN, *Financial Markets: The Accumulation and Allocation of Wealth* (New York: McGraw-Hill Book Company, 1974).

Securities and Exchange Commission, *Cost of Flotation of Registered Equity Issues 1963–1965* (Washington, D.C.: U.S. Government Printing Office, 1970).

SHAPIRO, ELI, and CHARLES R. WOLF, *The Role of Private Placements in Corporate Finance* (Boston: Graduate School of Business Administration, Harvard University, 1972).

SIMMONS, CRAIG A., *An Economic Analysis of the 1971 New Issues Market* (Washington, D.C.: Office of Economic Research, Securities and Exchange Commission, 1973).

TALLMAN, GARY D., DAVID F. RUSH, and RONALD W. MELICHER, "Competitive Versus Negotiated Underwriting Costs for Regulated Industries," *Financial Management* 3 (Summer, 1974), pp. 49–55.

THACKERAY, JOHN, "Regional Investment Banking Digs In," *Corporate Financing* 4 (May–June, 1972), pp. 27–36.

WATERMAN, MERWIN H., *Investment Banking Functions* (Ann Arbor: Bureau of Business Research, The University of Michigan, 1958).

17 Common Stock Financing

The optimal debt-to-equity ratio and the procedures for negotiated and competitive offerings are only a part of what the financial executive should know about common stock financing. In this chapter, we shall consider the nature of common stock, the sale of common stock through rights, the choice between rights offering and direct sales, and the problems of raising venture capital. But first we need to know why corporations issue common stock.

WHY ISSUE COMMON STOCK?

In light of our discussion in Chapter 15, it may seem strange that companies issue common stock. Tax incentives, after all, may make internal financing more attractive than external financing to management and existing stockholders. Also, the sale of common stock entails flotation costs, which are avoided by earnings retention. Nonetheless, there are at least four situations in which a firm will issue common stock rather than rely on internal financing.

1. *Going public*. The shares of many firms are closely held because the owners want independence and privacy. But it may at some point become advantageous to go public—i.e., to make the company's shares available to the investing public. Many firms follow this course not only to raise capital, but also to create a public market for their shares. A public market is in itself desirable because it gives the shares greater marketability and gives the firm access to the public capital market. An initial public offering

usually includes existing as well as newly issued shares, so that current owners may convert part of their holdings into cash and so that the total offering is large enough to make the subsequent market more viable.

2. *Supplementing retained earnings.* The retained earnings of public utilities and private hospitals, for example, cannot sustain the rate at which assets must be expanded. Corporations in this situation must periodically augment their equity bases by issuing common stock (or securities convertible into common stock) in order to maintain the proper ratio between debt and equity. Many small but rapidly growing firms find themselves in the same situation.

3. *Special tax benefits.* In mergers, the stockholders of the selling company can postpone the payment of capital-gains tax if they receive their payments in stock. In remunerating executives, stock options have advantages over cash compensations, as well. Even though a firm might be able to make cash payments, stock may be issued because of the tax benefits to the recipient.

4. *Good will.* Some firms own important businesses in countries whose governments follow strongly nationalistic economic policies. The sale of common stock to indigenous investors makes the firm more welcome in the host country.

THE RIGHTS OF COMMON STOCKHOLDERS

When a group of investors participates in a corporation, it must agree on the apportionment of risk, return, and control. Creditors and preferred stockholders have first claim on earnings and assets, but they have no control (except under special conditions). Common stockholders are residual owners, with various rights relating to their position in the apportionment. We shall now outline these rights.

Earnings

Common stock is attractive to stockholders because of the residual earnings it is expected to generate. Residual earnings are the net earnings of a firm after all charges (operating expenses, interest charges, preferred dividends, and taxes) have been deducted. When sales are insufficient to meet these charges, residual earnings will be negative; but since most prior charges are fixed in amount, any increase in sales will yield a disproportionately large increase in residual earnings. Common stockholders thus have the opportunity for maximum profit as well as maximum loss. It is the prospect of maximum profit that induces many investors to run the risks of common-stock investment.

A stockholder's claim to his pro rata share of the earnings does not automatically entitle him to immediate dividends. To optimize dividend policy, a firm must consider its investment opportunities, its cash-flow forecast, restrictive covenants in credit agreements, current profit, balance-sheet surplus, the stockholders' tax positions, etc. Management must use the firm's resources in the long-run interest of the stockholders. Therefore, even if the firm is showing a profit, management may decide that no immediate dividends are justified. Such a decision is usually final. In rare cases (e.g., Dodge vs. Ford Motor Company), stockholders can take court action to force a firm to alter its dividend policy;[1] for the most part, however, the courts view dividend policy as a business decision to be left to the discretion of management.

Assets

In the event of liquidation, common stockholders have the right to participate in the pro rata distribution of assets after all prior claims have been met. Common stockholders should be aware of the distinction between the book value and the market value of assets. Book value is the value on the firm's balance sheet; market value is the amount for which the assets can actually be sold. Since book value is based on cost and market value on economic worth, the two need not be identical. When the two values differ, the resulting loss (or profit) is borne entirely by the common stockholders. Since most liquidations occur because assets no longer generate sufficient earnings, liquidation is more likely to result in book losses than in book profits. A stockholder may realize a profit if he bought his shares at an average price below the actual liquidation value, and some security analysts even specialize in locating stocks whose liquidation values exceed their current market prices. Such situations are, however, quite rare. Usually, common stocks derive their value not from the possibility of liquidation but from the prospect of profitable operation.

Control over Management

As residual owners, common stockholders have primary control over the management of a corporation. They exercise this control through the right to vote for directors who oversee the operating management. It is the responsibility of the directors to set broad policies for operating management so that corporate affairs will be executed in the way that will maximize the

[1] In 1916, the Ford Motor Company showed on its balance sheet $112 million in surplus and $54 million in cash and municipal bonds; but only $1.2 million was paid in dividends. The Dodge brothers, who owned 10 percent of the stock, sued Ford and won a court order compelling an extra dividend of more than $19 million. For details see William L. Cary, *Corporations: Cases and Materials* (Mineola: The Foundation Press, Inc., 1969), pp. 1580–1583.

firm's market value. Directors are usually elected at an annual stockholders' meeting, at which one may vote either in person or by proxy (a written statement authorizing someone else to vote in a specified way). Since most stockholders either return signed proxies or ignore the meeting altogether, the management is usually able to perpetuate its position even if controlling substantially less than 50 percent of the total voting stock.

Occasionally, an outside group uses a proxy contest to try to wrest control from the current management. (In a famous contest, for example, Robert R. Young and William White fought over the control of New York Central Railroad; Young, the outsider, eventually won.) Outsiders tend to be at a disadvantage in proxy fights since the present management can mobilize corporate resources. Outsiders often respond simply by attempting to buy a controlling interest through public tender offers; proxies are then solicited only if additional anti-management votes are needed. Existing managements are most vulnerable if they control only a small percentage of the shares and if the stockholders are dissatisfied with the company's earnings and dividend records. Under these conditions, the chances of a successful takeover bid are greatly increased.

Voting Procedures

Voting procedures determine the minimum percentage of ownership needed to insure the election of a given number of the board of directors. Each share normally has one vote per director; if nine directors are to be elected, the owner of 100 shares thus has 900 votes. There are two kinds of voting: straight and cumulative. Under straight voting, a stockholder cannot allocate to any candidate more than one vote per share held; our sample shareholder, for example, could cast a maximum of 100 votes for one candidate. Clearly, straight voting permits no minority representation: a group controlling a simple majority can elect the entire board of directors. Cumulative voting, however, creates the possibility of minority representation. Under cumulative voting, a stockholder may cast all his (say, 900) votes for a single candidate, or may distribute his votes among any or all of the candidates. The maximum number of votes that a stockholder may cast for any candidate is thus limited only by the number of votes at his disposal. Minority groups may therefore have representation proportionate to their investment. In some states (e.g., Delaware and New Jersey), cumulative voting is permitted; in others (e.g., Kentucky and Nebraska), cumulative voting is mandatory.

Let us determine the minimum number of shares that a group must control under cumulative voting conditions in order to elect a given number d of its candidates. We shall use D to designate the total number of directors to be elected; S, the total number of voting shares; and s, the number of shares controlled by this group. There is then a total of DS votes to be cast, of which one group controls Ds votes and the opposing group controls $D(S - s)$ votes. The first group would fail to elect its slate of d directors only if the opposing group succeeded in electing $D - d + 1$ of their candidates. The first group can provide a maximum of Ds/d votes for each candidate; the opposing group, $D(S - s)/(D - d + 1)$ votes. Clearly, the first group can elect d directors if and only if

$$\frac{Ds}{d} > \frac{D(S - s)}{D - d + 1}$$

This inequality, when simplified, gives the following formula for s, the minimum number of shares needed to elect d directors:

$$s = \frac{dS}{1 + D} + 1 \tag{17-1}$$

It is also possible to solve for d, so that if a group knows how many shares it controls, it can determine how many directors it may elect. Thus,

$$d = \frac{(s - 1)(1 + D)}{S} \tag{17-2}$$

To illustrate Eq. (17-2), let us suppose that the XYZ Company has 10,000 outstanding shares, of which the management controls 7,400 shares and a dissident group controls 2,600. All nine directors are up for election. There are 14 candidates, nine of whom are sponsored by management and five by the dissidents. Eq. (17-2) tells us that, by cumulating their votes, the dissidents can be sure of electing two of their five candidates:

$$d = \frac{(2{,}600 - 1)(1 + 9)}{10{,}000} = 2.599$$

This result assumes that management concentrates its votes on seven candidates, the number it can be sure of electing. If management attempts to elect more than seven directors, perhaps by casting 7,400 votes for each of its nine candidates, and if the dissidents know about this intention, the dissidents can elect three directors by casting 7,800 votes for each. It is, of course, logical to assume that each group will concentrate its votes optimally. Eq. (17-2) is based on this assumption.

In Table 17-1, we use Eq. (17-1) to calculate the values of s corresponding to various combinations of values for D and d. The total number of voting shares is assumed throughout the table to be 10,000. The table reveals two points about cumulative voting. First, whatever the size of the board, a simple majority in ownership guarantees only a majority on the

Table 17-1 Number of Shares Needed to Elect a Specified Number of Directors*

d \ D	5	7	9	11	13
1	1,668	1,251	1,001	834	715
2	3,335	2,501	2,001	1,667	1,429
3	5,001	3,751	3,001	2,501	2,143
4	6,668	5,001	4,001	3,334	2,858
5	8,335	6,251	5,001	4,167	3,572
6	10,001	7,501	6,001	5,001	4,286
7	11,668	8,751	7,001	5,834	5,001

* Total number of voting shares (S) = 10,000.

board of directors (under straight voting, a majority in ownership guaranteed the election of the entire board). Second, the minimum number of shares needed to elect a given number of directors varies inversely with the number of directors up for election.

Some firms use this second principle to thwart minority representation. In XYZ's case, for example, if the board consisted of five directors instead of nine, the dissident group could be assured of electing only one candidate. The dissidents could also be excluded by staggering the terms of directorships, so that only a portion of the board is elected each year. The legality of staggered terms is, however, dependent on the state in which the firm is incorporated.

Pre-emptive Right

The pre-emptive right gives current stockholders the first opportunity to subscribe on a pro rata basis to any new shares issued by the firm. If exercised, this right enables a stockholder to maintain his proportionate interest in the earnings, assets, and control of the company. If sold, the pre-emptive right protects the stockholder against any loss arising from the sale of new shares to outsiders at a discount from the market price. The theory and the legal status of stockholders' pre-emptive rights will be taken up later in this chapter.

FEATURES OF COMMON STOCK

There are three features of common stock that management can influence by design—par value, classification, and listing.

Par Value[2]

The par value of a stock is its nominal or face value. The setting of par value is based on the premise that a corporation should designate a minimum amount of its common equity as protection for creditors. The par value is printed on the face of a stock certificate, and in some states the stock may not be issued below par. Where par-value shares may be sold below par, such shares are considered not "fully paid." If the firm becomes insolvent, creditors may hold the original purchasers of non-fully paid shares personally liable for the amount of the discount.

If the market price of a stock drops below its par value, the firm's ability to sell new stock will of course be hampered where state law prohibits below-par shares. Even where the law permits such sales, the threat of future assessment would severely restrict the marketability of new shares. "No-par" shares, permitted in most states, provide the obvious solution. But no-par shares, too, have disadvantages. When shares have no par, some states levy incorporation tax and annual franchise tax as if each share had a par value of $100. Many companies therefore find it economical to set par values at $1 or $2, or even 10 cents or 20 cents, per share. These low par values not only reduce tax payments but also permit greater pricing flexibility when new shares are sold.

Classified Stock

All common stocks are residual with respect to the claims of both creditors and preferred stockholders. But occasionally a corporation wishes to differentiate the claims of common stockholders even further. This may be done by distinguishing between Class A and Class B common stocks.

Such classifications may be control related, dividend related, or asset related.[3] A good example of control-related classification is the common stock of Pennzoil Offshore Gas Operators (POGO). Class A and Class B have identical claims on dividends and assets but different voting rights. For the first six years after issue (in 1970), each share of A stock has six votes; each share of B, one vote. From November, 1976 on, all shares have one vote. When POGO was formed in 1970, the company raised $130 million by selling to the general public 130,000 units, each consisting of a $1,000 principal amount of debentures and 33 shares of B stock. Each debenture was convertible into 166.67 shares of common stock (Class B prior to November, 1976) at the option of the company. Immediately before the sale,

---

[2] For the legal aspects of shares with and without par value, see Harry G. Henn, *Law of Corporations* (St. Paul, Minn.: West Publishing Company, 1970), pp. 291–293 and 305–310.

[3] Cf. Robert M. Soldofsky, "Classified Common Stock," *The Business Lawyer* 23 (April, 1968), pp. 899–902.

Pennzoil United (founder of POGO) bought 17,333,333 shares of A stock at $2 per share. Even assuming the conversion of all debentures, this transaction enabled Pennzoil United to control more than 80 percent of the total voting power for six years by putting up only 21 percent of the investment. The same device was used again in the financing of Pennzoil Louisiana and Texas Offshore (PLATO).

The stock of Calandra Industries provides an example of dividend-related classification. In this case, cash dividends may be declared on A stock with none on B stock; and if cash dividends are declared on B, at least three-and-a-half times as great a dividend must be declared on A. At his option, a holder of B shares can convert his stock into A shares at a fixed rate. This kind of classification is useful when a privately held company wishes to create a public market for its shares. A liberal dividend policy may help to establish a reasonable market for the firm's shares. But the owners may prefer, for tax reasons, to keep their dividend income small. By selling A stock to the public and holding convertible B stock for themselves, the owners can prepare the way for the eventual sale of their shares without meanwhile exposing themselves to the full impact of the ordinary tax rate.

Classification may also be used to give one class of stock a prior claim in liquidation. Suppose that a promoter pays $10,000 for 100,000 shares in a brand new company he has founded and that after a year of operation the firm decides to float 100,000 new shares at $5 per share. The earnings prospects of the firm may justify the $5 price; but the new shares will be more marketable if potential investors can be assured that the founder, who paid only 10 cents a share, will not insist on equal participation in the assets in case of dissolution. The founder can give this assurance by classifying the stock so that the new shareholders receive prior liquidation rights.

Listing

Once a company is able to meet the listing requirements of the exchanges, it must decide if it wants to list its shares. Many companies list their shares simply to gain prestige; but listing also has the tangible advantage of giving a firm's shares broader distribution, which, in turn, enhances the company's ability to raise capital. Also, listed shares have a greater acceptability (over unlisted shares) as a means of payment in mergers and acquisitions. On the other hand, listing may be harmful if the disclosure requirement forces the revelation of information on sales, profit margin, and net profit that the management would otherwise keep confidential for reasons of competition. Moreover, when a company is listed, even a temporary setback may cause enough adverse publicity to damage the firm's credit rating. If bad publicity coincides with planned financing, the cost of capital to the firm could be substantially increased. After weighing the advantages and drawbacks, several well-known companies—e.g., American Express, Anheuser-Busch, and Pabst—have chosen not to list. For these companies, whose shares are traded actively in the OTC market, listing would, at best, broaden the distribution of shares only marginally. For less well-known companies, however, listing could contribute significantly to the marketability of their shares.

SELLING STOCK THROUGH RIGHTS

All shares sold must first be authorized by articles of incorporation. Authorized shares are said to be issued once they are sold, and these shares are said to be either outstanding stock, if they are purchased by the general public, or treasury stock, if repurchased by the company. There are two ways of selling common stock: through rights offerings to existing stockholders and through direct sales to investors at large. The dollar volume of common shares sold through rights is about twice that sold directly.[4]

The Procedure of Rights Offerings

In a rights offering, current stockholders are given the first opportunity to subscribe to new shares, at a set price on a pro rata basis. Each share is entitled to one right, evidenced by a transferable warrant, and must be exercised within a certain period of time, usually two or three weeks. The ratio of old shares to new shares is the subscription ratio. Since the subscription price is usually below the current market price, rights have monetary value and can be traded during the subscription period. A stockholder may thus sell any rights that he does not plan to use himself. In general, a stockholder may also purchase unsubscribed shares from the company at the subscription price, subject to pre-announced allotment procedures.

If one sells his shares after a rights offering is announced, but before the rights are issued, who is entitled to the rights? Whoever receives the rights, how much time does he have before they expire? These questions may best be answered by referring to four dates of an actual rights offering:

1. *Date of announcement* (July 17). This is the date on which the company publicly announces the offering.
2. *Record date* (July 27). Subscription warrants are mailed to stockholders whose names appear on the list of official stockholders as of the date of record.

---

[4] Securities and Exchange Commission, *Cost of Flotation of Registered Equity Issues, 1963–1965* (Washington, D.C.: Government Printing Office, 1970), pp. 4–5.

3. *Ex-rights date* (July 28). As a rule, stocks are traded on the New York Stock Exchange on an "ex-rights" basis on the day following the first day's trading in the rights. Anyone buying his shares on an ex-rights basis is not entitled to the rights even though he may receive them in the mail.
4. *Expiration date* (August 15). This is the date, usually two to three weeks after the date of record, on which rights expire.

Although the subscription discount increases the chances for success of a rights offering, risks still exist. If uncontrollable factors cause the price of shares to fall below the subscription price, stockholders will not exercise their rights. In a standby agreement, the risk is shifted to an investment banker, who agrees to buy any unsubscribed shares. Underwriting compensation for standby agreements may be computed in two ways. In a two-fee deal, the investment banker gets a basic fee for risk-bearing on all shares, plus an extra fee for selling unsubscribed shares. In a one-fee deal, the banker gets one basic fee for all shares; this fee may be viewed as a weighted average of the components of a two-fee deal.

Rights Offering Is Not a Privilege

A rights offering is also known as a "privileged subscription," presumably because the subscription price is lower than the market price. However, if shares are correctly priced in the market, stockholders derive no benefit from the below-market subscription price; and if shares are undervalued, stockholders actually incur a loss to the extent that they decide to sell rather than to exercise their rights. We prefer the term "rights offering," since it avoids the implication of special financial privilege.

Let us illustrate the principle that, given a fixed amount of capital to be raised, the shareholders' wealth is independent of the subscription price of the new stock. Suppose that Solvang Industries decides to raise $2.5 million of new capital through a rights offering. At a subscription price of $25 per share, 100,000 new shares must be issued. One million shares are currently outstanding, giving a subscription ratio of 10 to 1. We may assume that the entire issue will be subscribed by current stockholders and that the market correctly (in the opinion of management) values the ex-right price of the shares at $32.76. This price implies that the company shares will have a total value of $36,036,000 after the rights offering. If the subscription price is changed to $20, the company can raise the same amount of capital by issuing 125,000 shares. Although the number of shares is now different, the investing public could be expected to place the same *aggregate* value of $36,036,000 on the firm's common stock. In each situation, the current stockholders have to pay a total of \$2,500,000 for the new shares. Their wealth is therefore independent of the price at which they subscribe to the new shares.

Effects of Undersubscription

We shall define a subscription discount as the amount by which the subscription price falls below the market price of a share. It should be distinguished from a market discount, which is the amount by which the market price falls below the true value of a share. We have shown that, in the absence of a market discount, the stockholders' wealth is independent of the subscription discount. This independence relation holds only if the current shareholders subscribe to the entire new issue. If the current stockholders undersubscribe, they incur a loss which varies directly with the size of the subscription discount and the degree of undersubscription. The sale of rights, however, provides nonsubscribing stockholders with the exact amount needed to offset this loss.

The Solvang situation can show us how rights protect stockholders. Let us return to the original assumptions of 100,000 shares at \$25 per share and a correct ex-right market valuation of \$32.76 per share. But instead of a 100 percent subscription, let us now assume that the current stockholders sell 30 percent of their rights. Since the subscription price is \$7.76 below the ex-right market price and since the subscription ratio is 10 to 1, each right is worth 77.6 cents, according to the equation:

$$V = \frac{M - B}{R} \tag{17-3}$$

where M stands for the ex-right market price, B represents the subscription price, R is the subscription ratio, and V is the theoretical value of one right. The sale of 300,000 rights thus produces a cash inflow of \$232,800 for the nonsubscribing shareholders.

This cash inflow is the exact sum needed to offset the loss associated with a 30 percent undersubscription. Table 17-2 compares the wealth of the current stockholders under two subscription percentages: 70 percent and 100 percent. With a 100 percent subscription, the stockholders' shareholdings have an aggregate value of \$36,036,000; but the \$2,500,000 contribution in subscription prices produces a net value of \$33,536,000. The corresponding net position for a 70 percent subscription is \$33,303,200, or \$232,800 less. This loss, due to undersubscription, is offset exactly by the proceeds from the sale of the rights that the current stockholders choose not to exercise themselves.

Table 17-2 The Effect of Undersubscription on the Wealth of Current Shareholders

	100% Subscription	70% Subscription
Number of shares owned	1,100,000	1,070,000
True value per share	$32.76	$32.76
Total value of shares owned	$36,036,000	$35,053,200
Less: Payment for new shares	2,500,000	1,750,000
	$33,536,000	$33,303,200
Add: Proceeds from sale of rights	0	232,800
Shareholders' wealth	$33,536,000	$33,536,000

Effects of Market Discount

So far, we have been assuming that the only discount is the subscription discount. When market price and true value are equal, there is no market discount. But there are two reasons why a rights offering might result in a temporary market undervaluation. First, the investing public does not have immediate knowledge of the productivity of the firm's planned new investments. Second, although all new issues of common stock dilute earnings per share, the dilution is greater in a rights offering because the new shares are usually offered to the existing stockholders at a substantial discount from the market price. If the investing public is preoccupied with per-share earnings, neglecting total earnings, the market price will probably suffer at least temporarily. If a firm's shares sell at a market discount and the current stockholders do not subscribe to the entire new issue, then the rights themselves will be undervalued and the sale of rights will therefore not fully compensate the stockholders for the loss associated with the undersubscription.

To see the effect of market undervaluation of shares, let us introduce a $2 market discount into the Solvang example. The management still estimates the true value of common equity to be $36,036,000, or $32.76 per share, but the market now values the equity at only $33,836,000, or $30.76 per share. Each right consequently has two values:

$$\text{True value of one right} = \frac{\$32.76 - \$25.00}{10} = 77.6¢$$

$$\text{Market value of one right} = \frac{\$30.76 - \$25.00}{10} = 57.6¢$$

The sale of each right thus results in a 20 cents loss to the selling stockholder. If current stockholders sell 30 percent of their rights, the total loss due to undersubscription will be $60,000 (= 20¢ × 300,000).

Table 17-3 The Effect of Market Discount on the Wealth of Current Shareholders

	100% Subscription	70% Subscription
Number of shares owned	1,100,000	1,070,000
True value per share	$32.76	$32.76
Total value of shares owned	$36,036,000	$35,053,200
Less: Payment for new shares	2,500,000	1,750,000
	$33,536,000	$33,303,200
Add: Proceeds from sale of rights	0	172,800
Shareholders' wealth	$33,536,000	$33,476,000

Table 17-3 enables us to see the $60,000 in the context of the stockholders' total wealth. If current stockholders subscribe the entire issue, their final net position will be $33,536,000; this figure takes into account the true value of shares owned, subscription payments, and the sale of rights. If stockholders subscribe only 70 percent of the issue, and sell the remaining rights, their final position is $33,476,000, or $60,000 less. We know that if market price and true value coincide, rights protect stockholders against any loss due to undersubscription; the $60,000 loss is therefore directly attributable to market undervaluation. The sale of rights, then, protects only against subscription discounts, not against possible market discounts.

Effects of Subscription Discount

We have just seen that, when a share is undervalued, stockholders suffer a loss when they undersubscribe. We shall now show that the magnitude of the loss, if the share is undervalued, increases as the subscription price decreases.[5]

Let us suppose that the Solvang subscription price is $12.50; 200,000 shares must now be issued in order to raise the $2,500,000. Management still values the total equity at $36,036,000, but this now implies a price of $30.03 per share. The market still values the equity at $33,836,000, which now implies a price of $28.20 per share. Each right now has two new values:

$$\text{True value of one right} = \frac{\$30.03 - \$12.50}{5} = \$3.51$$

$$\text{Market value of one right} = \frac{\$28.20 - \$12.50}{5} = \$3.14$$

[5] For the theory underlying this statement, see Michael Jones-Lee, "Underwriting of Rights Issues – A Theoretical Justification," *Journal of Business Finance* 3 (Spring, 1971), pp. 20–25.

The sale of each right results in a 37 cents loss to the selling stockholder. If current stockholders sell 30 percent of all rights, the total loss will be $110,000, or $50,000 more than the loss at a subscription price of $25.

What is the explanation for this inverse relationship between the subscription discount and the current stockholders' wealth when the shares are undervalued? We should note that the current stockholders will break even only if they subscribe to the entire issue. The size of their loss depends both on the degree of undersubscription and on the percentage of the firm's total equity offered for subscription. This percentage of the total equity is the hidden factor here; it in fact increases with the subscription discount, since a larger discount requires the issue of more shares to raise a given amount of capital. In Solvang's case, we assume that the stockholders will sell a constant 30 percent of their rights, and as a result, the actual loss due to undersubscription varies only with the percentage of total equity put up for subscription.

The Optimal Subscription Price

The financial executive must try to set the subscription price high enough to minimize possible cost to stockholders who sell their rights, but low enough to minimize the cost of underwriting the offering. The optimal subscription price minimizes the total of these two costs.

The Solvang management assumes that current stockholders will sell 30 percent of their rights and narrows its choice of subscription price to five possibilities: $30, $25, $20, $15, and $12.50 (see Table 17-4). Predictably, as the subscription price decreases, the loss due to undersubscription increases—but the risk, and hence the cost, of underwriting decreases. On an after-tax basis, Solvang's underwriting cost decreases from 2.5 percent of gross proceeds to .25 percent. As the last column of Table 17-4 shows, a subscription price of $25 is optimal since it minimizes the total of the two components of cost.

This optimization criterion assumes that every stockholder sells the same percentage of his rights. Minimizing costs would thus minimize the cost for every stockholder. The decision becomes more difficult, however,

Table 17-4 Setting the Optimal Subscription Price

Subscription Price	Loss Due to 30% Undersubscription	Cost of Underwriting	Total
$30.00	$ 50,700	$62,500	$113,200
25.00	60,000	33,750	93,750
20.00	73,200	31,250	104,450
15.00	94,200	12,500	106,700
12.50	110,000	6,250	116,250

if we assume that the sale of rights is limited to a portion of the stockholders. The loss due to undersubscription would then be concentrated in this group, while any savings in underwriting costs would be shared by all the stockholders. Minimizing total costs thus does not optimize the wealth of every stockholder. When this conflict of interest exists, the financial management must decide whether or not to place the welfare of stockholders who exercise their rights above that of stockholders who do not. In terms of fairness, the two groups should be treated equally. On the other hand, one may argue pragmatically that stockholders who subscribe to the new issue should be rewarded for their loyalty. Our analysis conforms to this latter approach.

For two reasons, a firm should protect its stockholders against selling rights at undervalued prices even though it clearly need not offer similar protection against selling actual shares at low prices. First, most stockholders do not understand rights offerings well enough to realize that the sale of rights might be unprotected against market undervaluation. Second, stockholders sell shares of their own volition, but they may be forced to sell rights if they lack the funds to subscribe to the new shares. Therefore, the company has a responsibility to minimize the potential loss to those current stockholders who must sell their rights.

RIGHTS OFFERING VS. PUBLIC OFFERING

A firm may decide to offer its common stock to the investing public without the prior use of subscription rights. Investment bankers usually serve as middlemen in these public offerings. But how does a company choose between a rights offering and a public offering?

Constraining Factors

Pre-emptive Right. If shareholders have pre-emptive rights, the company must give them the first opportunity to subscribe on a pro rata basis to any new issue of shares. Two general types of laws govern pre-emptive rights. In some states (e.g., New York and Ohio), pre-emptive rights are assumed unless the articles of incorporation explicitly deny them; in others (e.g., Delaware and California), pre-emptive rights are assumed not to exist unless the articles explicitly provide for them. A company may bypass its shareholders' pre-emptive rights only by a charter amendment or a stockholder waiver.

Even when the pre-emptive right is in effect, four types of security transactions are usually unaffected: continuing sales of original shares (initial financing); sales of treasury stock (acquired through share repurchase); issue of stock in exchange for non-cash assets (as in mergers and acquisitions); and the issue of stock in exchange for debt.

Ownership Composition. A firm considering a rights offering should consider how many stockholders it has and how the ownership is distributed among them. A broad ownership improves the chances of a successful offering. This explains why public utilities more frequently sell common stock through rights than do manufacturing companies. Data published by the SEC support this conclusion.

If a firm's target ownership composition differs from its actual composition, a public offering may be used to achieve its goal. For example, if the shares of a company are concentrated in a few founding stockholders, public offering is the only way to broaden its ownership. For the same reason, a firm wishing to sell common stock abroad, to gain the goodwill of foreign governments, should avoid rights offerings, which would only augment ownership among current stockholders. A public offering would also be wise for a closely held company which desires listing on an exchange but is unable to meet the required volume of shares outstanding and the required number of stockholders; a rights offering would not be effective for achieving these objectives.

Financial Factors

Market Discount. After constraints have been considered, financial factors must be taken into account. If a firm's shares are undervalued by a market discount, a rights offering would seem to be indicated because current stockholders need subscription rights as protection against losses arising from the sale to outsiders of undervalued shares. The sale of rights, as we have said, offers no protection against market discounts; only the exercise of rights can protect against loss. But in a rights offering, current stockholders at least have the right of first refusal, whereas in a public offering they would be in competition with the entire investing public.

Dilution of EPS. Shares are normally sold at a lower price in a rights offering than in a direct offering. In the 1974 American Electric Power Company's rights offering, for example, the subscription price was $23.25, or $1.875 lower than the market price. In Delmarva Power and Light's contemporary public offering, shares were sold at $13.75, only 12.5 cents below the market price. A rights offering necessitates the issue of more shares than a public offering and thus leads to a greater dilution of *EPS* than a public offering does. This dilution is in fact as innocuous as the *EPS* reduction caused by a stock split. But although it is obvious to everyone that a two-for-one split cuts *EPS* in half, many investors do not understand a rights offering well enough to make proper allowances in interpreting a firm's earnings trend. Share prices therefore may perform better in a public offering than in a rights offering.

Table 17-5 Underwriting Compensation on Common Stock Issues, 1963–1965 (percent of proceeds)

Size of Issue ($ million)	Public Offering	Rights Offering
Under 0.3	9.4	1.7
0.3–0.5	9.9	8.3
0.5–1.0	9.4	3.6
1.0–2.0	8.7	5.4
2.0–5.0	7.3	2.9
5.0–10.0	6.0	3.6
10.0–20.0	5.0	1.2
20.0–50.0	4.9	2.0
50.0–100.0	2.9	1.4
100.0–500.0	2.0	1.9

Source: Securities and Exchange Commission, *Cost of Flotation of Registered Equity Issues, 1963–1965* (Washington, D.C., 1970), p. 26.

Costs of Flotation. Rights offerings involve relatively low risks and selling efforts on the part of investment bankers. When the rights are used, the subscription discount lessens the risk of undersubscription and the standby agreement limits the banker's selling efforts to the unsubscribed portion of an issue. In a public offering, the smaller price discount gives the investment banker less protection against possible adverse market or corporate developments; moreover, selling costs are higher since the current shareholders no longer form a captive market. These differences in risk and selling expenses are reflected in the relative size of underwriting compensations for the two types of offering, as shown in Table 17-5.

The underwriting cost of a rights offering, unlike that of a public offering, does not show a consistently inverse relationship to the size of the issue. ("Other" expenses do not vary significantly according to the type of offering and therefore do not affect our comparison.) In a rights offering, the rate of compensation depends not only on the size of the issue but also on the investment banker's risk and selling efforts, two factors less closely correlated with size in a rights offering than in a public offering. If we could isolate pure effects, we would no doubt find a more consistent inverse relationship between the size of issue and underwriting compensation than that shown in Table 17-5; after all, investment bankers incur fixed as well as variable costs and so their fees do not rise proportionately with issue size. Unfortunately, SEC data are insufficient for such precision.

Taxation of Rights. The receipt of subscription rights does not constitute taxable income for stockholders, and the exercise of their rights does not give rise to an immediately taxable gain or loss. But the sale of rights, if it results in capital gain or loss, does have immediate tax implications. The value of a sold right is the amount received; the cost of the right, however, must be interpolated since the right was acquired, not separately, but as a part of the original share. Under the law, the original cost of a share is allocated between the ex-right share and the right, on the basis of their respective market values when rights are issued.

Let us say that an investor who paid \$100 for a share receives one right at a time that an ex-right share is selling for \$120 and a right for \$5. Of the original cost, \$96 (= \$100 × 120/125) is assigned to the ex-right share and \$4 to the right. If the value of a right is more than 15 percent of the value of a share, this sort of allocation is mandatory. Otherwise, the taxpayer may either use this allocation or assign a cost of zero to the right, letting the taxable base of his share remain at the original cost. The immediate capital-gains tax (or capital-loss deduction) will vary with the kind of allocation.

Whether there is a gain or a loss, the immediate tax impact will be offset by an opposite change in future tax payments. Other things being equal, share value decreases by the exact value of a right when a stock goes ex-right. The sale of rights simply advances the timing of the tax payment or deduction. The impact on shareholders' wealth is thus relatively small, and tax considerations should be only a marginal factor in the choice of offering method.

RAISING VENTURE CAPITAL

So far, we have concentrated on well-established firms with ready public markets for their common shares. But many smaller, less well-known companies, especially those in start-up or take-off situations, also need external equity financing. In a start-up situation, capital is needed to develop and test the validity of a yet untried idea. In a take-off situation, a firm beginning to operate profitably needs additional fixed and working capital at a rate that exceeds earnings retention. Although a start-up is clearly riskier, both situations are risky. Since the conservative investing public generally avoids start-up and take-off investments, the firms must seek out venture capitalists, whose strategy is to accept high risk along with the prospect of a correspondingly high payoff.

Sources of Venture Capital

Venture capital is available from several sources: individual investors, investment bankers, industrial corporations, insurance companies, mutual funds, venture-capital companies, and small-business investment companies

(SBIC's). Individuals, including friends and relatives as well as professional investors, constitute the largest single source of venture capital. Investment bankers, industrial corporations, and insurance companies have separate main businesses, but many have special divisions or subsidiaries to make venture investments on the side. Mutual funds, primarily for the management of the pooled resources of small investors, have traditionally been invested in well-known companies; but funds are sometimes put into venture capital when an above-average return is sought. Venture-capital companies are organized solely to invest venture capital; a few are public but most are private.

Although they are a kind of venture-capital company, SBIC's form a separate group because they are organized under the Small Business Investment Act of 1958, the purpose of which is to stimulate and supplement small-business financing. The Act provides the SBIC's, which are licensed and regulated by the Small Business Administration, with assistance through federal-agency loans and income-tax concessions. SBIC's have always been authorized to make term loans to firms qualifying as small businesses and to buy convertible debentures from these companies. Now they may also invest in stocks and warrants. When making loans, SBIC's must conform to regulations governing maximum interest rate, minimum and maximum maturity, and prepayment privileges; moreover, an SBIC may invest no more than 20 percent of its capital and surplus in any one firm. Another regulation preserves the independence of firms financed by SBIC's: unlike other venture capitalists, SBIC's may not gain control of the firms they finance. If circumstances force control upon them, divestment must take place within a reasonable time.

The financial executive seeking risk capital should realize that although the goal of capital gain is common to all venture capitalists, modes of operation vary. Preferences differ especially regarding the amount of financing, the degree of control over management, the type of industry (e.g., natural resources, electronics, ecology), and the type and maturity of the company (e.g., public or private; start-up or take-off). Venture-capitalist directories provide a convenient catalogue of these differences.

The Financing Agreement

Once a venture capitalist is satisfied with the integrity and competence of a firm's management, with the validity of its profit-making idea, and with its competitive position, he must decide which financing vehicle to employ in committing his funds. The wish for an above-normal return precludes straight-debt financing at a fixed rate of interest. Invariably, the capitalist will seek equity participation by investing in common stock or in debentures convertible into common stock or in a straight loan with warrants entitling him to buy common stock at a fixed price.[6] A conversion feature stays in effect as long as the debt is outstanding, but a warrant has an expiration date often distinct from the time of the debt's maturity. Venture capitalists generally prefer debt financing with equity features to straight equity investments. The reason is that if the firm fails and has to be sold, the capitalists, as creditors, will have prior claims on assets. The firm's owners may also wish to use convertibles and warrants, though for a different reason: the fixed price assigned to common stock for conversion purposes or for purchase with warrants is usually higher than the market price. The sale of common stock at a figure above the current price reduces the dilution of ownership, a result especially important to small, growing companies.

Since purchases by venture capitalists are private transactions, the securities may later be sold to the public only in limited amounts and under restricted conditions, unless they are registered with the SEC. Since securities can be registered only by the issuer, venture capitalists commonly demand a registration agreement with the firm. The agreement usually states that holders of a certain fraction (say, 1/3) of the security can require that the firm file a registration agreement on their behalf; the expenses of registration may be borne either by the firm or by the investors, depending on the agreement. Or a "piggyback" provision may allow the holders of privately placed securities to be included in the firm's own registration. Since registration is costly and time-consuming, it is important for a firm to limit the frequency of registration requests and see to it that those requesting registration bear a proportionate part of the expense.

To bargain effectively, the venture capitalist must formulate his objectives clearly. Terms will be reached only if the two sides can agree on the value of the business with and without the new financing and on the division of the incremental value. Valuation is difficult since there is little or no operating record on which to base the projection of future earnings. Moreover, the management of the firm naturally wishes to retain operating control, which could create a problem for the venture capitalist if the management turns out to be incompetent. A financing agreement may be structured in several ways; but, in any case, each side must keep its control and valuation objectives clearly in mind.

REVIEW QUESTIONS

1. Since retained earnings is a cheaper source of equity capital than a new stock offering, why do U.S. corporations issue millions of dollars worth of common stock each year? What are the major reasons for issuing common stock? Illustrate each reason with one or two recent examples.

[6] Stock-purchase warrants should be distinguished from the subscription warrants used in rights offerings. The context in which the terms are used should make the distinction clear.

2. What is cumulative voting? How does it differ from straight voting? Explain the purpose of cumulative voting and the ways management can defeat that purpose. What is the legal status of cumulative voting?

3. What are the main reasons for classifying common stock? Give a recent example for each reason.

4. What are the advantages and disadvantages of listing a stock on an exchange? Do you think that all companies over a certain size should be required by law to list their stocks?

5. A rights offering is also known as a privileged subscription. Which term is preferable? Why?

6. In a rights offering, what is the difference between a subscription discount and a market discount? When both types of discounts exist, how much do the proceeds from the sale of rights protect current stockholders against possible loss due to undersubscription?

7. By setting the subscription price sufficiently low, a firm could virtually guarantee the success of a rights offering and thus lower expenses by eliminating the need for underwriting. Why, then, in spite of this possibility, are most rights offerings underwritten by investment bankers?

8. American Electric Power Company sold 7 million shares of common stock in a 1974 rights offering. The subscription price was $23.25 per share; the underwriting commission was 10 cents per share on shares subscribed by the current stockholders and 48.8 cents per share on shares purchased by the investment bankers. At the time of the offering, 64,078,000 shares were outstanding, trading at about $25 per share. Two weeks later, Delmarva Power and Light Company sold 1,400,000 shares of common stock in a public offering. At the time, 13,548,000 shares were outstanding, trading at about $13.50 per share. What might have prompted one company to use a rights offering and the other to use a public offering?

9. A venture capitalist often invests funds in a venture firm by means of a financial instrument known as convertible debentures. Why is this instrument attractive both to the venture capitalist and to the venture firm?

10. An alternative to convertible debentures is straight debt financing combined with warrants to purchase common stock. In comparing these alternatives, the executive of a firm reasons that the latter is preferable: when the warrants are exercised, he would receive cash, which could be invested; there would be no corresponding cash inflow from the conversion of debentures. Do you agree with this reasoning.

PROBLEMS

1. A group of dissident stockholders and the management of Square Toe, Inc., are engaged in a proxy contest over the control of the company. One million shares are outstanding, 37 percent of which are controlled by management, 23 percent by the dissidents, and 40 percent by independents. Of the 9-member board of directors, only three are now up for re-election. The dissidents believe that by spending $100,000, $200,000, $300,000, or $400,000 on proxy solicitation, they could garner 10 percent, 30 percent, 50 percent, or 70 percent, respectively, of

the independent votes. In order to elect two of their candidates, how much should the dissidents spend on proxy solicitation? Assume that cumulative voting is employed.

2. Pennzoil Louisiana and Texas Offshore (PLATO) was formed by Pennzoil Company to participate in competitive bidding for federal oil and gas leases in the Gulf of Mexico. At the time of formation (1972) PLATO's capitalization consisted of:

   $130,000,000 Convertible Subordinated Debentures due 1979
   (Interest at 1% through October 1, 1975 and at 6% thereafter)
   28,166,666 shares of Class A common stock, $1 par value
   5,200,000 shares of Class B common stock, $1 par value.

   Pennzoil Company and its subsidiary bought all the A stock for $56,333,332 and sold to the investing public all B stock and the convertible debt for a total of $130,000,000. Until November 1, 1976, Class A common stock has nine votes per share at stockholders' meetings; Class B has one vote per share. After November 1, 1976, all shares of common stock have one vote each. Moreover, the holder of any debenture has the option of converting each $1,000 principal amount into 160 shares of Class B common stock at any time prior to May 1, 1979. What percentage of the total investment in PLATO did Pennzoil put up? What percentage of control did it get?

3. A northeast electric company sold 1 million shares of common stock in a rights offering, the prospectus of which gave the following information about the underwriting commission:

	Subscription Price	Underwriting Commission		Proceeds to Company	
		Minimum	Maximum	Maximum	Minimum
Per Share	$36.75	$.25	$.85	$36.50	$35.90

   The minimum commission applies to shares subscribed by stockholders; the maximum applies to shares purchased by the investment banker.

   If current stockholders subscribe to only two thirds of the issue, what will be the underwriting commissions to the investment banker? What will be the net proceeds to the company?

4. XYZ is offering its holders of common stock the right to subscribe to new shares at the rate of one share for each five shares of common stock currently held. The subscription price is $32 per share, and the market price is $36; 800,000 shares are outstanding. How much capital is being raised? What is the theoretical value of one right? Assuming that the market valuation is correct, by how much will the wealth of the stockholders be changed if they exercise 75 percent of their rights and sell the remaining 25 percent?

5. The Solvang example showed us that if a firm's shares are undervalued, the sale of rights does not fully protect shareholders against loss due to undersubscription; moreover, the loss increases with the degree of the subscription discount:

Subscription Price	$12.50	$15.00	$20.00	$25.00	$30.00
Loss Due to Under-subscription (30%)	$110,000	$94,200	$73,200	$60,000	$50,700

Verify the given loss figures that correspond to the subscription prices of $15, $20, and $25.

6. Michael Jones-Lee (see his article in the References) has derived the relationship between subscription price and the shareholders' loss due to undersubscription:

$$Z = \left(\frac{n_1}{n_1 + n_2}\right)(\alpha\beta)$$

where n_1 is the number of shares outstanding, n_2 is the number of new shares in the rights offering, α is the percentage of rights sold, β is the market undervaluation, and Z is the change in the wealth of current stockholders associated with unit change in n_2. Explain in words the economic logic underlying this relationship.

REFERENCES

ARANOW, EDWARD ROSS, and HERBERT A. EINHORN, *Tender Offers for Corporate Control* (New York: Columbia University Press, 1973).

AUSTIN, DOUGLAS V., and JAY A. FISHMAN, *Corporations in Conflict—The Tender Offer* (Ann Arbor: Masterco Press, Inc., 1970).

BEAR, ROBERT M., and ANTHONY J. CURLEY, "Unseasoned Equity Financing," *Journal of Financial and Quantitative Analysis* 10 (June, 1975), pp. 311–325.

BREALEY, RICHARD A., *Security Prices in a Competitive Market* (Cambridge: The M.I.T. Press, 1971), Chs. 6, 8, and 9.

BROWN, J. MICHAEL, "Post-Offering Experience of Companies Going Public," *Journal of Business* 43 (January, 1970), pp. 10–18.

CARY, WILLIAM L., *Corporations: Cases and Materials* (Mineola: The Foundation Press, Inc., 1969), Chs. 8 and 9.

FURST, RICHARD W., "Does Listing Increase the Market Price of Common Stocks?" *Journal of Business* 43 (April, 1970), pp. 174–180.

HENN, HARRY G., *Law of Corporations* (St. Paul: West Publishing Company, 1970), Ch. 8.

JONES-LEE, MICHAEL, "Underwriting of Rights Issues—A Theoretical Justification," *Journal of Business Finance* 3 (Spring, 1971), pp. 20–25.

MCDONALD, JOHN G., and BERTRAND C. JACQUILLAT, "Pricing of Initial Equity Issues: The French Sealed-Bid Auction," *Journal of Business* 47 (January, 1974), pp. 37–47.

NEUBERGER, BRIAN M., and CARL T. HAMMOND, "A Study of Underwriters' Experience with Unseasoned New Issues," *Journal of Financial and Quantitative Analysis* 9 (March, 1974), pp. 165–177.

REILLY, FRANK K., "Further Evidence on Short-Run Results for New Issue Investors," *Journal of Financial and Quantitative Analysis* 8 (January, 1973), pp. 83–90.

RUBEL, STANLEY M., *Guide to Venture Capital Sources: Third Edition* (Chicago: Capital Publishing Corporation, 1974).

Securities and Exchange Commission, *Cost of Flotation of Registered Equity Issues, 1963–1965* (Washington, D.C.: Government Printing Office, 1970).

SIMMONS, CRAIG A., *An Economic Analysis of the 1971 New Issues Market* (Washington, D.C.: Office of Economic Research, Securities and Exchange Commission, 1973).

SOLDOFSKY, ROBERT M., "Classified Common Stock," *The Business Lawyer* 23 (April, 1968), pp. 899–902.

STOLL, HANS R., and ANTHONY J. CURLEY, "Small Business and the New Issues Market for Equities," *Journal of Financial and Quantitative Analysis* 5 (September, 1970), pp. 309–322.

WALSH, CORNELIUS F., "Does Listing Increase the Market Price of Common Stocks?—Comment," *Journal of Business* 46 (October, 1973), pp. 616–620.

WINTER, ELMER L., *Complete Guide to Making a Public Stock Offering* (Englewood Cliffs: Prentice-Hall, Inc., 1972).

18 Long-Term Debt Financing

In discussing the theory of debt financing, we assumed that, except for differences in maturity, all debt instruments had identical contractual features. In practice, debt financing has many variations. The firm's objective is to choose the combination of alternatives that minimizes the overall financing cost.

THE FINANCING INSTRUMENT

The Nature of Bonds

The sale of bonds enables corporations to borrow money on a long-term basis. The debtor-creditor relationship is defined in the bond contract, which consists of two parts: the bond certificate and the bond indenture. The bond certificate contains the basic contractual terms: the principal, also known as face value or par value, is the amount owed; maturity is the date on which the company promises to repay the principal; and the coupon rate of interest determines the amount of the periodic interest payments.

The bond indenture is an agreement between the corporation and a trustee covering the obligation of the corporation, the rights of the bondholders, and the responsibilities of the trustee. The indenture enables the corporation to deal with its bondholders collectively through the trustee who legally represents them. Since a trustee must command the confidence of the investors, his qualifications, duties, and responsibilities are strictly regulated by the Trust Indenture Act of 1939. Under the terms of the Act, the trustee must be an independent institution with no possible conflict of interest; the debtor corporation must supply the trustee with all data necessary to determine whether or not the terms of indenture have been fully met; and, in case of default, the trustee must act as a prudent man would in conducting his own affairs.

Since a bond is evidence of debt, failure to meet interest payments constitutes an act of default. Bondholders may take legal action to enforce their claim; and, in the event of default, they generally have the right (provided by the "acceleration clause") to declare the entire bond issue due immediately. If the company could not pay interest, it would obviously have even greater difficulty paying both interest and principal. Debt financing thus usually increases the risk of insolvency. There is another type of bond, however, called an income bond, on which the interest is contingent, not fixed. Although the principal must be paid when due, interest is payable only if it is actually earned. Most income bonds stem from the financial restructuring of companies that have failed; these firms offer income bonds to replace fixed-interest bonds so that their fixed payments will be reduced. The holders of the fixed-interest bonds are often willing to accept the exchange in the hope that permitting the failed company to remain in operation will yield a greater value than liquidation.

Since bondholders are creditors, they have no voting rights and hence no voice in management. But their approval is needed if the firm wishes to modify the bond indenture even slightly.

Contractual Features

Bonds may be classified according to the factor emphasized: the pledge of assets, the repayment scheme, the inclusion of "equity sweeteners," or the tax status.

Pledge of Assets. To appeal to investors, a corporation may pledge specific assets against its bonds. "Unsecured" bonds, known as debentures, of course, are legal obligations of the corporation; but they are backed only by the firm's general credit. "Secured" bonds, however, pledge specific assets to which, in case of default, the bondholders have prior claim. Any secured debt remaining after the pledged assets have been exhausted ranks with the firm's other general obligations.

Secured bonds may be further classified according to the nature of the assets pledged: fixed assets, equipment, or security. In a mortgage bond, the pledge is a mortgage or lien on the firm's fixed assets. A mortgage is called open-ended if there is no ceiling on the debt issuable under the lien, limited open-ended if there is a ceiling on the debt but the ceiling has not been reached, and closed-ended if the ceiling has already been reached. In some mortgages, the company pledges only its existing assets. The bondholders of an open-ended mortgage may demand an "after-acquired" clause: the firm must pledge not only its existing assets but also any assets acquired after the date of the mortgage. In a closed-ended mortgage, an after-acquired clause means that any additional borrowing may at best involve a second mortgage, which generally carries a higher rate of interest. It is therefore desirable to avoid the combination of a closed-end mortgage and an after-acquired clause. In fact, because of the growth orientation of American business, most mortgage bonds are open-ended.

Equipment trust certificates are backed by the pledge of equipment (e.g., railroad rolling stock, oil tankers, commercial aircraft). These certificates are typically issued under a lease agreement known as the Philadelphia Plan. Under this plan, the user corporation places an order with an equipment manufacturer, who works according to the specifications. The user corporation generally agrees to pay 20 percent down when it places the order. When the equipment is ready, the company sells equipment trust certificates to the public for the balance. The title to the equipment passes from the manufacturer to a designated trustee; each certificate represents a proportionate interest in the trust. The trustee then leases the equipment to the user at a rental sufficient to amortize both the principal and the interest, usually for 15 years.[1] At the end of the lease, after all payments have been made, the user company takes over the title to all equipment subject to the trust. The standard nature of railroad rolling stock and of aircraft makes them good collateral because of their resale value. The quality of equipment trust certificates is further enhanced because they typically have serial maturity, reducing the principal systematically. Equipment trust certificates generally have high credit ratings and relatively low interest rates.

Collateral trust bonds are issued by corporations pledging the securities of another company, usually a subsidiary of the issuer; the proceeds are reloaned by the parent company to the subsidiary. The subsidiary is thus able to save on financing costs, since the money is borrowed on the credit of the parent firm, which usually has a higher credit rating than any of its subsidiaries. Ryder System, Inc., and Metro-Goldwyn-Mayer, Inc., for example, have both issued collateral trust bonds.

Debentures are backed by a company's general credit. Since debentures are unsecured, holders would want to foreclose further corporate borrowings that might relegate their own position to a junior status. The debenture holders may therefore insist on either a negative pledge clause, in which the corporation agrees not to pledge any of its assets, or an affirmative pledge clause, in which the corporation agrees to secure the debenture holders equally and ratably if any asset is pledged.

---

[1] The IRS does not view this transaction as a true lease, but as debt financing. Thus, railroads are permitted to deduct interest and depreciation as expenses, but not the "lease" payments.

Table 18-1 Effect of Subordination on Payment of Creditor Claims

Types of Claim	Amount of Claim	Payments Without Subordination	Payments with Subordination
Senior debentures	$ 6,000	$3,000	$4,500
Subordinated debentures	3,000	1,500	0
General creditors	1,000	500	500
Total	$10,000	$5,000	$5,000

Frequently, by offering an increased interest rate as a reward, a corporation is able to borrow from debenture holders with the understanding that the holders' claims on assets in case of insolvency will be subordinate to those of "senior" creditors. In other words, until the senior creditors receive the full amount of their claims, the subordinated creditors receive nothing because their proportionate share of claims goes to the senior creditors. Let us suppose, for example, that XYZ has liabilities totaling $10,000: $6,000 to senior debenture holders, $3,000 to subordinated debenture holders, and $1,000 to general creditors (see Table 18-1). Liquidation of assets yields only $5,000. Without subordination, each group of creditors would receive half its claims: $3,000, $1,500, and $500, respectively. With subordination, senior creditors get $4,500, subordinated debenture holders receive nothing, and general creditors get $500. In fact, if liquidation yielded $6,667, the senior creditors, because of their priority over subordinated debt, would recover their entire $6,000. Issuing subordinated debentures to protect senior creditors may assist a corporation in obtaining its senior credit.

Repayment Schemes. Although all corporate bonds have a maturity date, the single-payment scheme may be modified by a call option, a sinking-fund provision, or serial maturity.

A callable bond is one which the issuing company can redeem in whole or in part at its option before maturity. Unless a bond is called for sinking-fund purposes, it will be redeemed at face value plus a small call premium. A typical schedule of premiums is that of General Electric's $300 million issue of 8.5%, 30-year sinking-fund debentures, due in 2004. In the first year, the call premium is equivalent to one year's interest. After that, it decreases by a constant amount each year until it is reduced to zero 5 years before maturity.

A call option is valuable because it enables a firm to refinance its outstanding debt at a lower effective cost if and when the market interest rate falls. If bonds are noncallable, refunding will not result in interest savings because the old bonds must be repurchased in the open market at prices reflecting their higher coupon rate. Interest savings is not the only incentive for recalling bonds. A firm may wish to remove restrictive covenants, to return surplus funds, to alter debt maturity, or to improve its debt-to-equity ratio. Each of these objectives could be achieved through open-market purchases, but the call option is a safety valve in case the firm's bids for its bonds forces the bond price artificially high. Finally, a call option may be used to force the conversion of convertible bonds, as we shall see later in this chapter.

To the bondholder, a call option is clearly a drawback, since he will have to take the time and trouble to reinvest the proceeds from the recalled bonds—often in a period of low interest rates. The bondholder therefore wishes to avoid a call option altogether or at least to defer it for a period of years. In the General Electric issue, indenture prohibits the company, during the first ten years, from redeeming its debentures with borrowed money costing less than 8.50 percent annually. Other factors being equal, a callable bond will sell at a lower market price than a noncallable bond.

Many bond indentures have sinking-fund provisions, requiring the issuer to make annual deposits of cash with a trustee for the systematic retirement of the sinking-fund bonds. The provisions of the $300 million issue of General Electric debentures are typical. Each year from 1985 through 2003, General Electric must pay the trustee an amount sufficient to redeem $11,850,000 of the principal. If, however, the bonds are trading below par value, the company is allowed to meet its sinking-fund payments with bonds purchased in the open market. The company's failure to meet any sinking-fund payment constitutes default.

Once begun, the General Electric payments are fixed in amounts large enough to eliminate 75 percent of the debt by maturity. Other companies, however, may make other arrangements. Annual payments may be contingent (e.g., equal to a set percentage of the year's earnings) or variable (e.g., equal to a set percentage of the debt outstanding). Or the debt may be fully amortized, leaving a zero balance at maturity. General Electric's option of either calling the bonds or purchasing them in the open market is standard: it insures that a firm need pay no more than par value to redeem sinking-fund bonds. Of course, if the bonds are selling above par value, they will be redeemed at the sinking-fund redemption price and the bondholders will suffer a loss. But even so, investors generally favor sinking funds; and issuers can get relatively high prices for bonds with a sinking-fund provision.

In a serial bond issue, some of the bonds mature automatically each year until final maturity. A bondholder thus knows exactly when his bond will be repaid. In a sinking-fund issue, on the other hand, all bonds mature together, so the holder knows only that his bonds may be selected (usually by lottery) for early redemption. The specified maturity of serial bonds enables investors to choose the maturities best suited to their portfolios. The issuer, in turn, is able to reach a greater portion of the investing public by offering a range of maturities.

Equity Features. Investors in bonds are generally more averse to risk than investors in stocks. Some investors like an intermediate position, combining the safety of bonds with participation in growth potential of common stock. To attract these investors, corporations issue bonds with equity features: convertible bonds, bonds with warrants, and exchangeable bonds. A convertible bond may be exchanged, at the option of the bondholder, for common stock of the same company. A bond-warrant issue combines a straight bond with stock-purchase warrants which entitle the holder to buy common stock, usually of the same firm, at a specified price. An exchangeable bond may be traded, at the option of the bondholder, for the common stock of another company, which the issuer holds as an investment.

Tax Status. Although most corporate bonds are taxable, there are two kinds that are tax-exempt (i.e., the investors pay no federal income tax on interest from the bonds): the industrial development bond and the pollution control bond. In both cases, the procedure is that the bonds are offered by a municipal agency, and proceeds used to buy the needed equipment which is then leased or sold on installment to the company. The company is obligated to make payments sufficient to pay all amounts due on the bonds. The tax-exempt status of the bonds enables these bonds to be sold at an interest rate much below ordinary corporate bonds. Since 1968 each company's industrial development bonds have been limited to $5 million per county. Pollution control bonds can be issued in amounts sufficient to pay the full cost of the project.

THE EFFECTIVE RATE OF INTEREST

Basic Equations

To calculate k_i, the effective rate of interest, we find the discount rate that equates the present value of all future interest and principal payments with the net price of the bond. The following equation calculates the after-tax value of k_i, assuming that none of the debt is repaid before final maturity:

$$P - C = \frac{rF - T}{(1 + k_i)} + \frac{rF - T}{(1 + k_i)^2} + \cdots + \frac{rF - T}{(1 + k_i)^n} + \frac{F}{(1 + k_i)^n} \qquad (18\text{-}1)$$

where P is the public offering price of the bond; C is the issue cost; r is the coupon rate of interest; F is the face value of the bond; n is the maturity expressed in years; and T is the annual tax impact of the interest payment, issue cost, and bond discount (or premium). That is,

$$T = \left(rF + \frac{C}{n} + \frac{F-P}{n}\right)\tau$$

where rF is the annual interest payment; C/n is the annualized issue cost; $(F - P)/n$ is the annualized bond discount (or premium); and τ is the marginal rate of taxation.

Calculating k_i by using Eq. (18-1) can be time-consuming without a computer.[2] Fortunately, however, the regularity of the annual payments enables us to use a simpler formula to estimate k_i:

$$k_i = \frac{\left(rF + \frac{C}{n} + \frac{F-P}{n}\right)(1-\tau)}{[F + (P - C)]/2} \tag{18-2}$$

In this formula, the numerator is the annual financing cost, composed of the interest payment rF, the issue cost C/n, and the bond discount or premium $(F - P)/n$. The factor $(1 - \tau)$ adjusts for the tax savings. The denominator is the average amount of financing obtained—an average of the net proceeds and the bond's face value F.

To illustrate, let us suppose that an issue of 9%, 25-year bonds is sold to investors at 98.5 percent of par value; the issue cost is one percent of par value; and the corporate tax rate is 50 percent. For any \$1,000 bond, then,

$$k_i = \frac{(0.09 \times \$1{,}000 + \$^{10}/_{25} + \$^{15}/_{25})(1 - .5)}{(\$1{,}000 + \$985 - \$10)/2} = 4.61\%$$

This figure is the effective rate of interest on the bonds to the company. Eq. (18-1) places the exact cost of the bonds at 4.62 percent.

Given the issue cost, the effective rate of interest varies inversely with the selling price of the bond. Moreover, given the effective rate of interest, the coupon rate can be adjusted, in theory at least, so that the bond will sell at par. Traditionally, however, coupons are in multiples of one eighth of one percent, which may explain why many bonds are offered to the public at prices slightly above or below par.

The above calculations assume that the coupon interest rate r is a fixed value. If, however, r varies with the market interest rate, as in the case of floating rate bonds, Eq. (18-1) is still applicable if we interpret r in each period as the management's expected interest rate in each period. In this

---

[2] The computer program in Figure B-3 of Appendix B can be used to solve for k_i.

case, the resulting k_i would, of course, also be an expected value. Since Eq. (18-2) assumes constancy of r, it should not be used.

Effects of Call Option and Redemption Provisions

Eq. (18-1) is not directly applicable to callable bonds because of the possibility that the entire issue may be refunded at a lower interest rate. To determine the effect of the call option on interest cost, the financial executive must first specify his target refunding date and calculate the break-even refunding rate of interest (see next section). If future interest rate exceeds this break-even rate, the bonds will not be refunded and Eq. (18-1) gives the correct effective cost. If future interest rate falls below this break-even rate, the bonds will be refunded, with a resulting lower effective cost. In practice, the financial executive, not being omniscient, can only forecast a probability distribution of future interest rates. There is then a different effective cost for each interest rate in the probability distribution. The effective cost of a callable bond, therefore, is best calculated as the expected value of a probability distribution. The difference between this expected value and the effective cost of a noncallable bond measures the value of the call option to the company.

But even if refunding at a lower interest rate is prohibited by contract, Eq. (18-1) must still be modified if the bonds are retired in installments. If sinking-fund or serial bonds are sold at par, Eq. (18-1) gives the correct value for k_i; but if the bonds are sold below or above par, (18-1) will distort the value of k_i. Instead of considering the formal proof of this statement, we shall explain the logic intuitively by reference to the term $(F - P)/n$ in Eq. (18-2).[3] Given the premium or discount at which a bond is sold, the annual amortization $(F - P)/n$ depends on the life of the bond. Both sinking funds and serial redemption, by shortening effective life, thus reducing n, increase the absolute value of this term and shift the true value of k_i above or below the value given by (18-1), depending on whether $F - P$ is positive or negative. By contrast, (18-1) is accurate for a bond sold at par because there is then no discount or premium to amortize; early retirement has no effect on the value of k_i.

THE ECONOMICS OF REFUNDING

Theory

Bonds are said to be refunded when they are redeemed with funds from the sale of new bonds. If the market interest rate is well below the coupon

[3] For formal proof, see Frank C. Jen and James E. Wert, "Imputed Yields of a Sinking Fund Bond and the Term Structure of Interest Rates," *Journal of Finance* 21 (December, 1966), pp. 700–706.

rate, a firm may find it profitable to refund its debt before maturity. Refunding entails an initial cash investment made up of the call premium, the cost of issuing the new bonds, and the overlapping interest. (For safety, new bonds are usually sold a month before the old are redeemed; hence, the month of overlapping interest.) The benefits of refunding accrue over time as reduced interest payments.

Four tax provisions affect the cash flows associated with refunding: both call premiums and overlapping interest expenses are deductible totally in the year of refunding; any unamortized premium (discount) on the old bonds is taxable (deductible) totally in the year of refunding; any unamortized issue cost of the old bonds is deductible totally in the year of refunding; and both the issue cost and premium (discount) of the new bonds must be amortized over the entire life of the new bonds. If refunding is to be profitable, the after-tax benefits must be great enough to assure that the implied rate of return on the refunding will exceed an appropriate hurdle rate.

To avoid ambiguity, let us express the total cost of refunding J and the annual benefit d in symbols:

$$J = \underbrace{gF(1-\tau)}_{\text{After-tax call premium}} + \underbrace{C_2}_{\text{Issue cost}} + \underbrace{r_2(1-\tau)F/12}_{\text{After-tax overlapping interest}} - \underbrace{C_1\tau}_{\text{Tax effect of unamortized issue cost}} \tag{18-3}$$

$$d = \underbrace{(r_1 - r_2)(1-\tau)F}_{\text{After-tax savings in interest expense}} + \underbrace{\tau(C_2 - C_1)/n}_{\text{Tax effect of change in issue cost}} \tag{18-4}$$

where F = the total face value of the old bonds
g = the redemption premium (as a percentage of face value)
C_1 = the unamortized costs of issuing the old bonds
C_2 = the total costs of issuing the new bonds
r_1 = the interest rate on the old bonds
r_2 = the interest rate on the new bonds
τ = the marginal tax rate
n = the life of the new bonds, which we shall assume is equal to the remaining life of the old bonds.

It is assumed here that both the new and old bonds are sold at par. Given J and d, we can determine the internal rate of return r^* of the refunding by finding the discount rate that equates J to the present value of its future benefits:

$$J = \frac{d}{(1+r^*)^1} + \frac{d}{(1+r^*)^2} + \cdots + \frac{d}{(1+r^*)^n} \tag{18-5}$$

Refunding will be profitable as long as r^* exceeds an appropriate hurdle rate k. Since refunding is a riskless investment, k is usually the after-tax interest rate on the new bonds. A higher hurdle rate may be justified, however, for a firm operating under capital rationing.

Application

Fifty million dollars worth of 8.5%, 25-year bonds are sold at par with an issue cost of one percent of par. Five years later, the market rate of interest drops to 7 percent, and management considers refunding the old bonds with a new 20-year issue. Four fifths of the original issue cost of \$500,000 remains to be amortized; the corporate tax rate is the usual 50 percent; the call premium is 6.8 percent. The financial executive must decide whether or not refunding will be profitable enough to meet a required rate k of 3.5 percent.

The following computation is an application of the analytical model presented above:

Cash outlay (J)	
After-tax call premium (6.8% × \$50M × .5)	\$1,700,000
Cost of issuing new bonds (1% × \$50M)	500,000
After-tax overlapping interest	
(7% × \$50M × 1/12 × .5)	145,833
Tax impact of unamortized issue cost	
(− \$400,000 × .5)	−200,000
	\$2,145,833
Annual savings (d)	
After-tax interest savings	
(1.5% × \$50M × .5)	\$375,000
Tax impact of change in annual issue cost	
(\$5,000 × .5)	2,500
	\$377,500

When we calculate J, we should note that the issue cost of the new bond generates no immediate tax saving because the cost must be amortized over the life of the bonds. When we calculate d, we must recognize that the new bonds generate a tax deduction of \$25,000 in annual issue cost but that the old deduction of \$20,000 per year is lost because the entire unamortized issue cost of the old bonds must be deducted in the year of refunding.

Putting the values of J and d in Eq. (18–5) gives us the following expression:

$$\$2,145,833 = \frac{\$377,500}{(1+r^*)^1} + \frac{\$377,500}{(1+r^*)^2} + \cdots + \frac{\$377,500}{(1+r^*)^{20}}$$

The value of r^* is 16.8 percent, which clearly exceeds the required rate of 3.5 percent, and thus, the company should refinance the bonds. Moreover, by setting k at the required rate, we can solve Eq. (18-5) for d and use Equation (18-4) to find the value of r_2 that will make the refunding break even. In our example, the break-even value of r_2 is 7.9 percent.

Finally, although refunding is profitable now, the financial executive must also decide when best to refund. If the interest rate drops further, postponing refunding may result in even greater interest savings. On the other hand, if future interest rates rise, the company may lose the opportunity to refund altogether. The optimal time to refund, therefore, depends on the executive's forecast of future interest rate movements.[4]

CONVERTIBLE BONDS

The Nature of Convertible Bonds

A convertible bond is a hybrid security in that it is both a debt and an option on the firm's common stock. Whereas a stock-purchase warrant is an independent instrument, a conversion option is related to a bond contract. The fusion of the two parts creates an instrument combining the appreciation potential of stock with the safety of a bond. If the price of the underlying stock rises, the conversion option will cause the price of the convertible bond to rise as well. If the price of the stock stays level or falls, the bondholder is protected because the company has agreed to regard his instrument as a debt as long as he does not exercise his conversion option.

The corporation, of course, derives its own benefits from the safety feature, since it makes the bonds more marketable. Convertible bonds have special appeal to those investors who desire an intermediate position between common stock and straight bonds. Moreover, these bonds are attractive to financial institutions which are constrained by law in the amount of common stock they may hold. Issuing convertible bonds enables a corporation to expand the market for its securities and to reduce the overall cost of its capital.

A convertible bond, being a debt, specifies the principal amount owed, the coupon rate of interest, the call prices, the annual sinking fund if any, the final maturity date, and the terms of the conversion provision. Uniroyal's 5½%, 25-year convertible subordinated debentures, due in 1996, provide us with sample data for conversion terms:

1. *Conversion price*—Each $25.375 of the principal amount of a Uniroyal bond may be exchanged for one share of Uniroyal common stock. The stock option is fused with the debt obligation since the

[4] See Edward J. Elton and Martin J. Gruber, "Dynamic Programming Applications in Finance," *Journal of Finance* 26 (May, 1971), pp. 473–505.

conversion price is payable in bonds. Although the conversion price is usually fixed, as in this case, it occasionally increases over the life of the bond.

2. *Conversion ratio*—The number of shares into which a bond is convertible varies uniquely and inversely with the conversion price. If each Uniroyal bond has a face value of $1,000, then each bond will buy 39.4 shares (1,000 ÷ 25.375). This is the conversion ratio.
3. *Conversion period*—Uniroyal is typical in permitting conversion during the entire life of the bond. In some cases, however, a company may limit the conversion period by postponing the initial conversion date or by terminating the conversion period before the bond maturity date.

Although conversion is the option of the bondholder, the corporation may, under certain conditions, advance the timing of conversion by exercising its call option. When a convertible bond is called, the bondholder may either turn in his bond in exchange for the call price or exchange his bond for stock. The market value of the stock received is the *conversion value* of the bond. If the conversion value is less than the call price, the bondholder will presumably redeem his bonds for cash. Redemption allows the corporation to save interest, to remove restrictive covenants, to return unneeded funds, or to prevent later conversion. If the conversion value is more than the call price, the bondholders will presumably convert their called bonds into stock. In this situation, the corporation may call its bonds in order to force immediate conversion.

Reasons for Use

Researchers have conducted questionnaire surveys of financial executives to find out specifically why corporations issue convertible bonds. Although answers vary, two general reasons prevail. First, convertible bonds are used to raise common equity on a delayed-action basis. One company sold debentures convertible into common stock at a conversion price of $45; direct sale of common stock would have depressed market price, netting the company only $35 per share. From management's viewpoint, the firm was in effect selling its shares for $45 instead of $35. Second, the conversion feature is used to enhance the marketability of the company's debt and thus reduce its cost. A firm's capital structure may make straight-debt financing either impossible or too costly. By offering a conversion option as a sweetener, the firm can raise debt capital at a lower interest rate and in larger amounts than otherwise. And the bondholders, especially if they anticipate early conversion, may feel less need for stringent protective covenants than in straight-debt contracts.

These findings reveal the proper framework for analyzing convertible bonds as a financing device. If, for example, the bonds are used as indirect equity financing, the alternative is the immediate direct sale of common stock. The bonds are the more attractive device because they permit the firm to sell equity (even though contingently) to investors willing to pay a higher-than-current price in return for built-in safety. If the conversion option is used to sweeten senior debt, the alternative is to sell straight debt now and an equity issue later. The use of the option implies that the firm would rather sell its stock indirectly now than directly later. The value of the option is what compensates the bondholder for the concessions he makes in the debt portion of the contract.

Even though convertibles enable a firm to sell common stock at higher future prices, many companies still sell common stock directly at lower current prices because future stock prices are difficult to predict. A firm issuing convertibles runs the risk that its stock price may not rise enough to make conversion profitable to the bondholders. If unfavorable market conditions keep a firm from forcing conversion even after some time, the issue is said to be "overhanging." It is possible that the market will reverse, enabling forced conversion. But meanwhile the overhanging convertibles tend to depress stock price, making direct sale of common stock costly. One chemical company, for example, sold an issue of convertible bonds in 1965. The issue was still outstanding in 1975 because share price never rose above the conversion price. Some firms prefer to avoid the risk of an overhanging issue and the resulting loss in financial flexibility by selling common stock directly.

Valuation and Design of Convertible Bonds

A Valuation Model. Let us suppose that Laserex, Inc., offers an issue of 6.0%, 20-year bonds, exchangeable for common stock at a conversion price of $50; Laserex's common stock is currently selling at $42 per share. The market interest on nonconvertible bonds of similar investment quality is 8 percent. The investor must appraise the bonds to decide how much he is willing to spend for them.

There are four value concepts which are relevant in appraising any convertible bond issue:

1. *Conversion value,* or *stock value,* is the total market value of the common stock into which the bond is convertible. This value equals the conversion ratio multiplied by the market price of the common stock. Assuming each bond has a face value of $1,000, Laserex's conversion value is $840 (= 20 × $42) per bond at the time of issue.

2. *Bond value* is the market value of the convertible bond evaluated as a straight bond (i.e., as if there were no conversion provision). If straight bonds comparable to Laserex's are selling at prices that yield an 8 percent return, bond tables show that investors should pay no more than 80.2 percent of par value for Laserex's bonds.
3. *Theoretical,* or *floor,* value is the conversion value or bond value, whichever is larger. The theoretical value of a Laserex convertible at the time of issue is $840.
4. *Market premium* is the amount by which the actual market price exceeds theoretical value. Thus, Laserex's bonds, if issued at par, would carry a market premium of $160 per bond.

The coupon interest rate on the Laserex convertibles is one fourth below the market rate. An investor will not purchase such a bond at par unless he expects the price of the Laserex shares to rise enough during his planning horizon to reward him for his sacrifice of current interest income. He realizes too that if the share price rises above conversion price, the firm could force conversion by calling the bonds. A called bond would reduce the investor's potential capital gain. Moreover, in reading the *Wall Street Journal,* the investor observes that in most forced conversions the conversion value is 20 to 60 percent above par. The outlook for the Laserex share price makes the investor think that forced conversion is most likely at the end of year 5. The investor thus takes five years as his planning horizon and forecasts probabilistically the Laserex share price at the end of that horizon, as summarized in the first two columns of Table 18-2.

Table 18-2 also shows the probability distribution of the terminal value of the convertible bond (at the end of year 5). If Laserex's stock sells for $75 per share, the firm will call the bonds. Since the stock value of the bond exceeds its redemption price, the bondholder will convert his bonds, receiving a terminal value of $1,500. Similarly, if share price is $62.50, the terminal value is $1,250. But if share price is $45, the conversion value is

Table 18-2 Terminal Value of Laserex's Convertible Bond

Probability	Market Price of Common Stock	Bond Value of Convertible	Stock Value of Convertible	Terminal Value of Convertible
.30	$75.00	*	$1,500	$1,500
.35	62.50	*	1,250	1,250
.20	45.00	*	900	1,000
.10	25.00	$827	†	880
.05	10.00	827	†	827

* Bond value lower than stock value.
† Stock value lower than bond value.

\$900—below par. The bonds will therefore not be called, and the terminal value will be given by the market price of the bond. The bondholder forecasts a market price of \$1,000, implying that the market will pay a premium of \$100 over theoretical value—partly because of the potential for appreciation and partly because of the built-in safety. If share price is \$25, the conversion value is less than the bond value of \$827, which now becomes the theoretical price (\$827 is the selling price of a 6%, 15-year straight bond when market interest is 8 percent). The investor forecasts a terminal value of \$880, implying a premium of \$53. Finally, if share price is \$10, the prospect of capital gains is so remote that there is no premium. The convertible now sells as a straight bond with a terminal value of \$827.

In summary, the investor expects to receive \$60 in interest each year for 5 years and then a terminal payment whose value is given by the probability distribution in Table 18-2. Using as a discount rate his required return of, say, 8 percent per annum, we obtain \$1,065 as the expected present value of the cash flows associated with the Laserex convertible bonds. The investor will probably consider the bonds attractively priced if they are offered at par.

The Design of Convertible Bonds. The key variables are coupon rate of interest and conversion price. To design a contract, the financial executive must know how changes in these variables will affect the market price of the bond. Our valuation model will be useful in this analysis.

Figure 18-1 depicts for Laserex convertible bonds the relationship between bond value, conversion value, and market value. Vertically, line

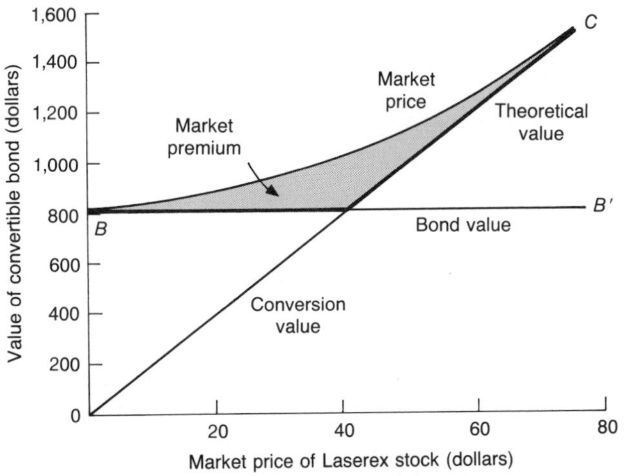

Figure 18-1 Valuation of Laserex Convertible Bonds

OC expresses the conversion value of each bond as a function of the current market price of Laserex's shares. (The slope of *OC* equals the conversion ratio.) Line *BB′* measures bond value—in this case, $802 at the time of issue. The heavily inked sections of lines *BB′* and *OC* express the theoretical value of each bond as a function of current share price. The market-price curve lies entirely above the corresponding theoretical prices. The vertical distance between theoretical value and market price gives the market premium. The premium is smallest at the ends of the share-price spectrum: when share price is low, the prospect of conversion is so remote that convertibles sell almost as straight bonds; when share price is high, the threat of forced conversion makes investors reluctant to pay substantial premiums.

Laserex convertible bonds have a coupon interest rate of 6 percent and a conversion price of $50. The financial executive should know what other combinations of interest rate and conversion price would yield the same market valuation. What change in conversion price, for example, would be necessary to compensate for a reduction in coupon rate of interest? We know that a low coupon rate reduces the support provided by bond value so that an investor will expect a smaller terminal value; moreover, the increased downside risk may make the investor demand a higher overall rate of return. Each of these changes makes the entire market-price curve shift downward. This effect could be offset by a reduction of conversion price, depicted graphically by a counter-clockwise rotation of line *OC*. The lower conversion price will increase the probability of conversion as well as the size of possible gain from conversion.

Suppose that, by experimenting with the valuation model, the Laserex financial executive has found that the bonds would sell at par with any of three combinations of coupon interest rate and conversion price. The task of optimal design, then, is to decide which combination will result in the lowest cost of capital. To do so, he needs a theory for measuring the cost of convertible-bond financing, which we shall now take up.

The Cost of Financing

Before he can determine the cost of convertible-bond financing, the financial executive must know how soon the corporation expects the bonds to be converted and the probable stock value at the time of conversion. He must also know whether the bonds are being issued in lieu of immediate stock financing or in anticipation of future stock financing.

Suppose that Laserex would like to sell common stock now but, since the current stock price is too low, is instead selling at par 6 percent convertible bonds. The firm expects, with a probability of .8, to force conversion at the end of year 5, at which time the shares are forecast to be selling at $62.50, or 25 percent above the $50 conversion price. The company sees a .2 probability that its stock will continue to be weak, causing the issue to overhang indefinitely.

Three additional facts will enable us to proceed to the calculation: the current market price of Laserex stock is \$42, the rate of return required by the stockholders is 14 percent, and the marginal tax rate on corporate income is 50 percent.

Ignoring selling expenses, the firm receives par value for the 6%, 20-year convertible bonds. There is a .2 probability that the bonds will not be converted, in which case the effective after-tax rate of interest will be only 3 percent for the next 20 years. But an overhanging convertible severely restricts a company's ability to raise more capital; the loss of financing flexibility, though not easily quantifiable, is a real cost. On the other hand, there is a probability of .8 that the bonds will be converted. In that case, Laserex will pay 3 percent interest for five years, after which the debt will be replaced by common stock. The cost k_e of this equity capital is calculated according to formulas already derived in Chapter 8:

Stock sold to existing stockholders
$$k_e = y \tag{18-6}$$

Stock sold to new stockholders
$$k_e = y \frac{P}{P'} \tag{18-7}$$

where y is the stockholders' required rate of return, P is the current market price of the common stock, and P' is the price at which the new shares are sold.

For the Laserex issue, y is 14 percent; P' is \$50 (the conversion price); and, since the convertibles are issued in lieu of immediate stock financing, P is \$42, the current share price. With these data, Eqs. (18-6) and (18-7) yield 14 percent and 11.8 percent, respectively, as the values of k_e. If we assume that the new shares are purchased equally by existing and new stockholders, and that the number of new shares is small relative to existing shares, the cost of common equity is midway between the two values: 12.9 percent.

In other words, there is a .2 probability that the cost to Laserex of the convertible bonds will be only 3 percent for the next 20 years. This also means that the company will be unable to attain its desired debt-to-equity ratio and will lose financial flexibility. There is a .8 probability that the bonds will be converted, in which case the company has an inexpensive source of debt capital for 5 years and can then convert this into equity at a lower cost than equity would entail now (12.9% vs. 14%).

Now let us change one of our assumptions: Laserex already has sufficient equity capital and is issuing the bonds in anticipation of future sales of common stock. Both P and P' in Eq. (18–7) must now be assigned their respective values at the time of conversion. Laserex forecasts that its share price will increase by some 50 percent over the next five years, so that P will be \$60. The company receives \$1,000 for each bond now, implying a share price of \$50 if and when the bond is converted. Let us say that \$50 has a future value to the firm of \$66 at the end of year 5, so that P' is \$66. Applying Eq. (18–7), we find that the cost for shares sold to outsiders is now 12.7 percent, or .9 percent higher than before. If all new shares are purchased by existing stockholders, the cost is still 14 percent. If the shares are purchased equally by outsiders and existing stockholders, the cost of equity has an intermediate value of 13.4 percent.

The above example presents a method for calculating the cost of convertible bond financing. This cost is seen to vary with the future outlook for the company's shares, the financing alternatives available to the company, and the percentage of new shares sold to outsiders. By comparing the cost of capital, the financial executive is able to design the best combination of coupon interest rate and conversion price for his convertible bonds.

BOND-WARRANT ISSUES

A few years ago, the American Telephone and Telegraph Company sold a bond-warrant issue with a market value of nearly \$1.57 billion, removing the stigma by which bond-warrant issues have traditionally been associated with firms not strong enough to issue convertibles. Since the AT&T issue, B. F. Goodrich Company, LCA Corporation, and Beehive Medical Electronics, among others, have used this method of financing.

The Nature of Bond-Warrant Issues

A warrant is an option, exercisable by the holder, to purchase for cash a specified number of shares of the company's stock at a specified exercise price over a specified period of time. A bond-warrant issue is a marketing device whereby a firm offers bonds and warrants in units combining the two types of securities in a fixed ratio.

In the B. F. Goodrich 1972 issue, for example, each warrant entitles the holder to buy one share of Goodrich common stock at an exercise price of \$30 until August 15, 1979, when the warrant expires. The exercise price of the Goodrich warrants is constant over a 7-year economic life, but exercise prices sometimes "step up" (i.e., increase) over time. Sutro Mortgage Investment Trust, for example, have issued warrants with "step-up" exercise prices. Occasionally, no expiration date is assigned, in which case they are referred to as perpetual warrants. Warrants are not callable at the option of the firm; but the bond part of the issue, being a debenture, may be.

At the time of issue, each Goodrich warrant commands one common share. If Goodrich were to split its stock two for one or to issue a 100 percent stock dividend, the value of a common share would be halved. A warrant holder paying $35 for one diluted share would therefore not be receiving the value to which he is entitled. Accordingly, the issue contains an anti-dilution provision, permitting the warrant holder to receive more than one share for the exercise price. Since warrant holders are not stockholders, they have neither dividend nor voting rights. Since they have no pre-emptive rights either, an anti-dilution provision is important to protect them against rights offerings of common stock at less than market price. A reverse stock split would, of course, reduce the number of shares purchasable for the exercise price. Many warrants consequently do not entitle the holder to exactly one share. Nevertheless, at the time of issue, a one-to-one ratio is typical and will henceforth be assumed.

Although the Goodrich issue must be purchased in units of bonds and warrants combined, the investor may later sell his debenture and his warrants separately. Such warrants are said to be detachable. A nondetachable warrant may not be sold apart from its debt instrument, although, naturally, once a nondetachable warrant has been exercised, the bond sells as pure debt.

Reasons for Use

Corporations issue bond-warrants for the same reasons as convertibles: to sell common stock above the current market price and to borrow money below the current rate. Why, then, do some firms use convertible bonds and others bond-warrant issues? One researcher found that financial executives are influenced by one or more of seven factors:[5]

1. *Marketability*—Convertible bonds are more familiar to the investing public and therefore generally easier to sell. Some investors, however, may prefer bond-warrant issues because of their separability after purchase. Investment fads also play a role.
2. *Cost*—Financial executives using each instrument claim that their method is the cheaper. This obvious impossibility reflects the difficulty of measuring cost of capital, changing fads in the securities market, and differences in the financial conditions of the issuing companies.
3. *Control over the exercise of option*—When convertible bonds are callable, the possibility of forced conversion gives the company

[5] Joe Lavely, "Choosing Between Convertible Bond and Bond-Warrant Issues," mimeographed paper, undated.

some control over the exercise of the option. Warrants, however, are generally noncallable. The exercise of a warrant may be encouraged only by stepped-up exercise prices or a short economic life, but such terms must be in the original contract.

4. *Control over potential dilution*—Given the size of a convertible-bond issue, the potential dilution is determined by the conversion price. A firm has less freedom to vary conversion price than to vary the number of warrants attached to a bond issue.
5. *Effect on reported EPS*—In determining the issue price of the bonds in a bond-warrant issue, standard accounting procedure calls for the value of the warrants to be deducted from total proceeds. The usual result is a bond discount, the amortization of which tends to depress the firm's reported *EPS*. In convertibles, there is no need to separate the value of the stock option from that of the bond itself.
6. *Cash-flow effects*—Some executives surveyed mentioned that the exercise of warrants brings in additional cash, while the conversion of bonds does not. It should be noted, however, that when a bond is converted, the debt is automatically extinguished; but when a warrant is exercised, the accompanying debt remains outstanding.
7. *Tax considerations in acquisitions*—In a merger, the selling stockholders may prefer receiving convertible bonds over bond-warrants because convertibles permit a longer and larger deferment of tax payments.

Valuation of Warrants[6]

The value of a bond-warrant unit is the sum of the values of the bond, which we have already discussed, and the warrant. The maximum price of a warrant cannot exceed the market price of the associated stock, since the warrant holder must pay additional cash to purchase the stock. And the minimum price will not fall below the amount by which the market price of the stock exceeds the exercise price, since arbitrage will quickly eliminate that possibility. (If the exercise price exceeds market price, the minimum price of the warrant is zero, not negative.)

Figure 18-2 delineates the limiting values of the price of a warrant. The price W of a warrant and the price P of the stock are measured along the vertical and horizontal axes, respectively. The 45° line, denoted as OM, traces the maximum values of W corresponding to all possible stock prices

---

[6] The following discussion is based heavily on the valuation model in Edward O. Thorp and Sheen T. Kassouf, *Beat the Market* (New York: Random House, 1967).

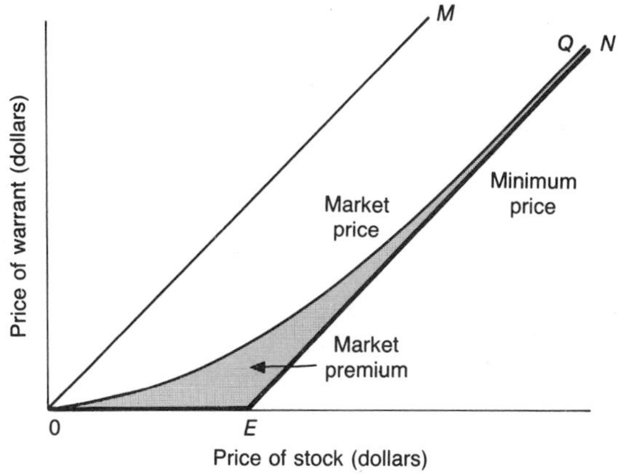

Figure 18-2 Valuation of Stock-Purchase Warrants

P. The minimum values of *W* for stock prices below the exercise price *E* are given by heavy line *OE*, while the minimum values for prices above *E* are given by heavy line *EN*, which parallels line *OM*. The minimum value of a warrant is analogous to the theoretical value of a convertible bond.

The market price of a warrant will fall on a curve, such as *OQ*, lying between the maximum and minimum value lines. The excess of market price over minimum price is the market premium. Given current stock price, the minimum value of a warrant is easy to determine, but the market premium is not. A market premium exists for three reasons. First, investors expect stock prices to rise. Second, if stock price does rise, a warrant yields the same profit as ownership, while requiring a smaller investment. And third, if stock price should fall, the maximum possible loss on a warrant is less than the corresponding loss for ownership. These reasons imply three determinants of premium size: the remaining life of the warrant, the probability distribution of future stock price, and the ratio of current stock price to exercise price. If a warrant is near expiration, future stock price is irrelevant and the warrant sells at its theoretical minimum price. Otherwise, the longer the remaining life of the warrant, the larger the premium.

The premium also varies directly with both the expected value and the volatility of stock price, since both augment possible profit. Finally, Figure 18-2 shows that a premium is small when current stock price is substantially below exercise price, because the investors will be pessimistic. The premium is also small when current stock price is very high relative to exercise price, because purchasing the warrant would require nearly as large an investment as purchasing a share: the greater investment both increases risk of loss and reduces the opportunity for financial leverage.

The Cost of Financing

We shall illustrate the cost of bond-warrant financing with the Goodrich example. Ignoring flotation expenses, Goodrich receives $1,000 for each unit of a 7%, 25-year debenture which has a principal amount of $1,000 plus 20 warrants. Each warrant has a lifetime of seven years and entitles the holder to one Goodrich share at an exercise price of $30. At the time of the issue, Goodrich common stock is selling at $27.

Suppose that, after forecasting its own future, Goodrich decides that there is a .2 probability that the warrants will expire without being exercised. In that case, the company will, in effect, sell its 7 percent bonds at par; and the effective cost of the debt will be 3.5 percent after tax for the life of the bonds. In addition, during the 7-year life of the warrants, the overhang will hamper the firm's ability to raise new equity. But there is a probability of .8 that the warrants will be exercised. In that case, the cost of debt will be the same, but we must now also calculate the cost of common equity to be issued at the end of year 7.

We shall assume first that Goodrich issues the bond-warrant units in lieu of immediate stock financing. The value of P is clearly $27, the current market price of Goodrich stock. But what is P', the actual price Goodrich receives? The company receives $1,000 of cash for each bond which has 20 warrants attached to it. Of the $1,000 bond, $600 can be retired with funds from the sale of stock if and when the warrants are exercised, so that the transaction can be viewed as $400 in debt and $600 in presale of common stock at $30 per share. So, P' equals $30. Let us say that the stockholders' required rate of return is 14 percent, which, according to Eq. (18-6), is the cost of common stock sold to existing stockholders. Eq. (18-7) will give us the cost of shares sold to outsiders. Applying Eq. (18-7), we find that the cost of common stock is 12.6 percent. If new shares are sold partly to outsiders and partly to current stockholders, we can find the cost of common equity by taking an average of the two limiting values.

Now let us change our assumption: Goodrich already has sufficient equity capital and is issuing the bond-warrant units in anticipation of future sales of common stock, Both P and P' in Eqs. (18-6) and (18-7) must now be assigned their respective values at the time the warrants are exercised. Suppose that Goodrich forecasts that its share price will be $35 and that the $30 received now will have a future value of $40 at the end of year 7. Thus, P equals $35 and P' equals $40. Applying Eq. (18-7), we find that the cost of common stock sold to outsiders will be 12.3 percent. Otherwise, the analysis remains the same as before.

Finally, the similarity between bond-warrant and convertible-bond financing should be emphasized. Both devices provide a company with an inexpensive source of debt capital and the prospect of future equity financing at a lower cost than present equity. The risk in the use of these devices is that the price of company stock may not rise high enough to effect the planned future sale of stock. In that case, the company's capital structure will be nonoptimal, with attendent loss of financial flexibility.

EXCHANGEABLE BONDS

The Nature of Exchangeable Bonds

Some companies sell bonds exchangeable for shares of other companies. Dart Industries, for example, has an outstanding issue of $4\frac{1}{2}\%$, 25-year subordinated debentures exchangeable for the common stock of Minnesota Mining and Manufacturing Company (3M). The Pittston Company has a similar issue exchangeable for shares of Brink's, Inc.

The contractual features of an exchangeable bond are similar to those of a convertible bond. The indenture specifies the exchange price, which is the value placed on the underlying stock for purposes of exchange. The exchange price is usually about 20 percent above the current market price of the stock. The Dart debentures were issued with an exchange price of $93 on the 3M shares, even though the actual market price was only $78. The indenture also contains an escrow agreement, under which the firm promises to turn over to an escrow agent enough shares of the stock to provide for the exchange of all bonds issued. The company, however, retains voting and dividend rights on shares that have not yet been exchanged. The exchange right usually lasts the life of the bond, though management may terminate it by exercising its call option if the exchange value of a bond exceeds call price (exchangeable bonds, like convertibles, are always callable).

The probabilistic model used to explain the valuation of convertibles applies equally to exchangeables. The investors must still consider the coupon rate of interest, the maturity of the bond, the terms of the exchange provision, his forecast of the future price of the underlying stock, and the likelihood of an early redemption call. There is, however, one important difference: tax treatment. When conversion takes place, the investor need not recognize any immediate gain (or loss) for federal income-tax purposes; but when exchange takes place, gain (or loss) must be recognized immediately. Convertible bonds are therefore in this respect more attractive to investors.

Reasons for Use

Let us suppose that a company has decided to sell its stock holdings in another firm for cash. If the holding is large, the company will have to accept a discount in selling price. Moreover, if there is a large capital gain, there may also be a large immediate tax bill. But if, instead, the company floats an issue of exchangeable bonds, the indirect sale brings a higher price and a tax postponement. The disadvantage is that the sale of stock is not final but contingent upon future market developments: investors will exchange their bonds only if the market price of the shares rises above the exchange price.

Dart Industries provides a good example of the circumstances that make an exchangeable-bond issue logical. In 1970, Dart sold its Riker Laboratories subsidiary to 3M and acquired about 1.5 million shares (before the two-for-one split) of 3M. Much of the stock was sold immediately, but by mid-1972 Dart still held about 900,000 post-split shares. A share then selling for $78 had cost Dart only $43, so direct sale would have resulted in a large immediate tax bill. Dart therefore decided to sell its remaining 3M shares indirectly. The firm sold $60 million worth of $4\frac{1}{2}$%, 25-year bonds exchangeable into 3M shares at $93 per share. To provide for future exchange, 645,000 shares of 3M stock were put in escrow—Dart meanwhile retaining for all unexchanged shares the right to vote *and* the right to receive the $1.85-per-share dividend. Even though Dart received cash for the bonds, it was thus enabled to postpone the recognition of capital gain on the 3M shares until the time of exchange. As a top Dart executive put it, "This way, we can get actually more than the market value [of the shares], defer our capital gains taxes and continue to get the dividends. We are maximizing our earnings from the 3M holdings."[7]

REVIEW QUESTIONS

1. Define the following terms. What features do the bonds within each group share? How do they differ?
   a. mortgage bonds, collateral trust bonds, equipment trust certificates
   b. debentures, subordinated debentures
   c. sinking-fund bonds, serial bonds
   d. convertible bonds, bond-warrant issues, exchangeable bonds.
2. The following questions deal with the essential terms found in bond contracts:
   a. What is a call option in a bond contract? Why is a call option valuable to the issuer and detrimental to the investor?
   b. Investors generally desire a sinking-fund position in a bond contract. Is this attitude inconsistent with their reluctance to grant a call option?
   c. Why do the holders of warrants and of convertible bonds need the protection an an anti-dilution provision?
   d. What is an acceleration clause? What would bring such a clause into effect?

[7] "How to Raise Money at Bargain-Basement Rates," *Business Week* (July 15, 1972), p. 66.

e. How could an after-acquired clause in a closed-end mortgage paralyze a firm's financing?

3. Describe the way railroads finance the purchase of their rolling stock under the Philadelphia Plan. What legal, economic, and financial aspects of the plan make equipment trust certificates a relatively safe investment for investors?

4. Standard Oil (Indiana) is one of the first companies to issue notes with a floating interest rate and variable maturity. The coupon rate varies with the U.S. Treasury bill rate. The maturity is 15 years, but the notes are redeemable at par two years after issue and every six months thereafter at the option of the holders. Discuss the liquidity and cost implications of this type of debt financing for a typical industrial firm.

5. The indenture of a certain bond issue gives the holder of each bond the option of purchasing 20 shares of the company's stock at a price of $25 per share; payment for the stock must be made in cash. Is this a convertible bond? If not, what is it? What change would be necessary to make it a convertible bond?

6. Eight months after initial offering, the McDonald's Corporation called all $25 million of its 4.5 percent convertible debentures (due in 24 years) for redemption at 104.5 percent of principal amount plus accrued interest. Each bond was convertible at a price of $70.50. At the time of the call, McDonald's stock was selling for about $95; the going interest rate on A bonds was about 7.7 percent. Why would a company call its 4.5 percent bonds when the market rate of interest was more than 3 percent higher?

7. At about the same time as the McDonald's transaction, the National General Corporation offered to repurchase up to $50 million of the principal amount of its 4 percent convertible subordinated sinking-fund debentures, due in 21 years, at $750 for each $1,000 of principal. How does this transaction differ from McDonald's? What financing motives underlie the offer? Are these motives the same as McDonald's?

8. In the choice between convertible bonds and bond-warrant issues, what might influence the issuer to favor one instrument over the other? What were the major findings of Lavely's survey of financial executives?

9. One of the major reasons for issuing convertible bonds is the relatively low cost of equity capital raised in this way. Why, then, is common stock ever sold directly?

10. What are the risks of issuing exchangeable bonds? What conditions would make such an issue especially advantageous?

PROBLEMS

1. The Fischer Company sold a $25 million issue of 9%, 25-year bonds at a public-offering price of 100 percent. The cost of issue was one percent of par value. Assuming no principal repayment before maturity, what is the effective rate of interest of the bonds? First find the exact rate, using Eq. (18-1); then find the approximate rate, using Eq. (18-2).

2. Five years ago, an electric utility sold at par an issue of 10 percent bonds with an original maturity of 25 years. The cost of issuing new bonds is equal to the cost of issuing the old bonds, which was one percent of par. Assuming a 7 percent call premium, a 50 percent tax rate, a maturity of 20 years for the new

bonds, and a 5 percent required rate of return, determine the break-even refunding interest.

3. When McDonald's called its convertible bonds for redemption (see Review Question 6 for details), the bonds had 24 years remaining. Suppose that immediately prior to the call, the stock was selling at $95 and the going rate of interest was 8 percent. What would the theoretical value of the bond have been? Would the actual market price of the bond have been higher or lower than its theoretical value? Would the call have affected the market price? By what percentage can the market price of the stock drop before the bondholder finds it more profitable to redeem his bonds than to convert them?

4. Suppose that Starr, Inc., has a capitalization consisting of 10,000 shares of common stock, $5,000 of 8 percent preferred stock, and $30,000 of 5 percent convertible bonds exchangeable into common stock at the conversion price of $30. Assuming that the operating income is $25,000 and the marginal tax on income is 50 percent, calculate the *EPS* before and after all the bonds were converted into stock. What is the probable effect of this bond conversion on stock price? Assuming an operating income of $15,000 and the same tax rate, repeat the above analysis.

5. Three years ago, ABC sold at par $10 million of 9%, 20-year noncallable subordinated debentures. If the going rate of interest today were 7 percent, what would be the market price of a bond? What is the possible interest saving to the company if it repurchases its bonds in the open market with new money raised now at the going 7 percent rate of interest? Make your own assumptions concerning underwriting commission, printing costs, legal fees, etc.

6. Advanced Radiation Technology (ART) is contemplating raising $20 million by selling either convertible bonds or bonds with warrants. The convertibles would have a coupon interest rate of 6.5 percent, a maturity of 20 years, and a conversion ratio of 50. The bond in a bond-warrant unit would have the same interest rate and maturity; each bond would have 50 detachable 5-year warrants, each entitling the holder to purchase one share of common stock at $20 up to expiration. Each issue would net par for ART. Assume that the company's current stock price is $16 and that investors' required rates of return on the company's straight debt and common stock are 9.0 percent and 14.0 percent, respectively. Management estimates a .85 probability that its future share price will be high enough to induce either conversion of bonds or exchange of warrants. For simplicity, management assumes that if bond conversion or warrant exercise takes place, it will occur at the end of year 5, when the stock price is expected to be $24. There is a probability of .15 that conversion or warrant exercise will not take place. Calculate the cost of financing for each instrument. Which alternative would you recommend, and why?

7. Suppose that at the end of year 5, the following liabilities and equity accounts appear on ART's balance sheet:

Noninterest-bearing debt	$ 5,000,000
6.5 percent bonds	20,000,000
7.0 percent preferred stock	4,000,000
Common stock ($1 par value)	1,000,000
Retained earnings	15,000,000
	$45,000,000

If convertible bonds were sold, how would conversion affect these accounts? If bond-warrant units were sold, how would the exercise of warrants affect the accounts?

8. Citicorp (the parent company of First National City Bank) sold an issue of 15-year floating rate notes, with interest rate for each 6-month period set at 1 percent above the current Treasury bill rate. These notes could not be redeemed at the option of the issuer for ten years, but were redeemable by the holder at half-year intervals beginning two years after their issue. The minimum purchase was $5,000. From the viewpoint of the bank issuer, how would one calculate the stability and the cost of this form of financing in comparison with savings deposits?

REFERENCES

BAUMOL, WILLIAM J., BURTON G. MALKIEL, and RICHARD E. QUANDT, "The Valuation of Convertible Securities," *Quarterly Journal of Economics* 80 (February, 1966), pp. 48–59.

BIERMAN, HAROLD, JR., "The Cost of Warrants," *Journal of Financial and Quantitative Analysis* 8 (June, 1973), pp. 499–503.

BREALEY, RICHARD A., *Security Prices in a Competitive Market* (Cambridge: The M.I.T. Press, 1971), Chs. 16–17.

BRIGHAM, EUGENE F., "An Analysis of Convertible Debentures," *Journal of Finance* 21 (March, 1966), pp. 47–54.

CHEN, ANDREW H. Y., "A Model of Warrant Pricing in a Dynamic Model," *Journal of Finance* 25 (December, 1970), pp. 1041–1059.

ELTON, EDWIN J., and MARTIN J. GRUBER, "Dynamic Programming Applications in Finance," *Journal of Finance* 26 (May, 1971), pp. 473–506.

HORRIGAN, JAMES O., "Some Hypotheses on the Valuation of Stock Warrants," *Journal of Business Finance and Accounting* 1 (Summer, 1974), pp. 239–247.

"How to Borrow at Bargain-Basement Rates," *Business Week* (July 15, 1972), p. 66.

JEN, FRANK C., and JAMES E. WERT, "The Deferred Call Provision and Corporate Bond Yields," *Journal of Financial and Quantitative Analysis* 3 (June, 1968), pp. 157–169.

JEN, FRANK C., and JAMES E. WERT, "Imputed Yields of a Sinking Fund Bond and the Term Structure of Interest Rates," *Journal of Finance* 21 (December, 1966), pp. 697–713.

JENNINGS, EDWARD H., "An Estimate of Convertible Bond Premiums," *Journal of Financial and Quantitative Analysis* 9 (January, 1974), pp. 33–56.

KALYMON, BASIL A., "A New Approach to the Bond Refunding Problems," in Samuel Eilon and Terrence R. Fowkes, eds., *Applications of Management Science in Banking and Finance* (Epping, Essex: Gower Press, 1972), Ch. 13.

KRAUS, ALAN, "The Bond Refunding Decision in an Efficient Market," *Journal of Financial and Quantitative Analysis* 8 (December, 1973), pp. 793–806.

LAVELY, JOE, "Choosing Between Convertible Bonds and Bond-Warrant Issues," mimeographed paper, undated.

RUSH, DAVID F., and RONALD W. MELICHER, "An Empirical Examination of Factors Which Influence Warrant Prices," *Journal of Finance* 29 (December, 1974), pp. 1449–1466.

Salomon Brothers. *Equipment Trust Certificates* (New York: 1974).

THORP, EDWARD O., and SHEEN T. KASSOUF, *Beat the Market* (New York: Random House, 1967).

VON FURSTENBERG, GEORGE M., "The Equilibrium Spread Between Variable Rates and Fixed Rates on Long-Term Financing Instruments," *Journal of Financial and Quantitative Analysis* 8 (December, 1973), pp. 807–819.

WALTER, JAMES E., and AGUSTIN V. QUE, "The Valuation of Convertible Bonds," *Journal of Finance* 28 (June, 1973), pp. 713–732.

WEIL, ROMAN L., JR., JOEL E. SEGALL, and DAVID GREEN, JR., "Premiums on Convertible Bonds," *Journal of Finance* 23 (June, 1968), pp. 445–463.

19 Preferred Stock Financing

Corporations have increased their reliance on preferred stock financing in recent years. Of all securities sold by corporations for cash, preferred stock recently constituted almost 10 percent, nearly three times the average percentage for the 1960's.[1] Public utilities are by far the largest issuer of preferred stock, straight or convertible. Cash-issue figures, however, tend to understate the true importance of preferred stock financing, since convertible preferreds, accounting for about two fifths of all preferreds,[2] are commonly issued not to raise cash, but in exchange for assets and other securities.

This chapter will deal with the nature of preferred stock, typical contractual features, the cost of preferred stock financing, the role of straight preferred stock in financing public utilities, and the role of convertible preferred stock in financing mergers and acquisitions.

THE FINANCING INSTRUMENT

The Nature of Preferred Stock

Preferred stock is often considered a hybrid security because its features are intermediate between those of bonds and common stock. Preferred stock resembles bonds in three ways: (1) holders of each have prior

[1] *Federal Reserve Bulletin,* various issues.

[2] George E. Pinches, "Financing with Convertible Preferred Stock, 1960–1967," *Journal of Finance* 25 (March, 1970), pp. 53–63.

claim over common stockholders to the company's earnings and assets; (2) holders of each generally have no vote in electing directors; and (3) the returns on each are fixed by contract and do not vary with earnings. The fixity of its dividends makes preferred stock a form of leverage capital. The proper use of preferred stock is therefore subject to the same general principles that govern the optimal use of bonds (see Chapters 13 and 14).

Preferred stock resembles common stock in that both represent ownership in a company. Since dividend payments are not obligatory, the failure to pay preferred dividends is not an act of default. Passing a preferred dividend may depress the price of the firm's common stock, weaken the company's ability to raise new money, and cause other financial embarrassments; but it will not precipitate bankruptcy, as defaulting on interest payments might. Preferred stock thus gives a corporation a less risky type of leverage financing than bonds provide. On the other hand, since preferred dividends, unlike bond interests, are not tax deductible, the direct cost of preferred stock financing is considerably higher than that of bond financing. There are, however, as we shall see, special circumstances under which, when indirect costs are taken into account, the substitution of preferred stock for bonds may yield a higher value for the firm.

Contractual Features

A corporation's authority to issue preferred stock is stated explicitly in its articles of incorporation. When the articles authorize only one class of stock, all shares are in effect common stock, with equal rights to dividends, assets, and voting privileges. When the articles authorize more than one class of stock, some shares may be granted dividend and/or liquidation preference; these shares are "preferred."

Dividend Preference. The claim on dividends of preferred stockholders is more certain than that of common stockholders. Consumers Power Company, for example, describes dividend preference in this way: "The holders of the Preferred Stock of each series are entitled to receive cumulative dividends, payable when and as declared by the Board of Directors, at the rates determined for the respective series, *before* any dividends may be declared or paid on the Common Stock" [italics mine].[3] But although preferred stocks have dividend priority, they also have fixed dividends. Each share of, say, $9.00 preferred stock is entitled to $9.00 – but no more – in dividends. This limitation on annual dividends means that the share is a nonparticipating preferred stock. Some contracts give preferred stockholders the right to participate with common stockholders in the distribution of dividends beyond the fixed rate; but such participating preferred stocks are rare.

[3] Consumers Power Company, *Prospectus,* October 30, 1973, p. 22.

Priority also makes preferred dividends fixed in another noncontractual sense. Consumers Power Company, for example, has paid cash dividends on its common stock uninterruptedly since 1913. To many financial executives, a continuous dividend record is a major corporate goal. If a company is to maintain an unbroken record of common dividends, then preferred dividends must become virtually a fixed annual payment.

Dividend Accumulations. If a preferred dividend is passed, one might wonder whether or not the amount has to be made up before a common dividend may be paid. The answer depends on whether the preferred stock is cumulative or noncumulative. Let us say that the XYZ Company has $40,000 of 9 percent preferred stock outstanding and that it has the following record of earnings and preferred dividends for years 1 through 3:

Year	Earnings	Preferred Dividends
1	0	0
2	$20,000	0
3	30,000	$30,000

Dividend omissions are $36,000, $36,000, and $6,000 in years 1, 2, and 3, respectively. If the preferred stock is cumulative, the passed dividends ($78,000) are carried as arrearages which must be paid to preferred stockholders before common dividends may be resumed. If the preferred stock is noncumulative, the passed dividends are permanently forfeited. (The only exception is in New Jersey, where the courts interpret the noncumulative feature to be cumulative to the extent earned but not paid. Since XYZ earned $20,000 in year 2 but paid no dividends, New Jersey law would require that the $20,000 arrearage be extinguished before common dividends are resumed.)

The weak investment position of noncumulative preferred stock makes it difficult to sell, so that preferred stock is generally cumulative. Most of the few noncumulative stocks outstanding originated with corporate reorganization, when circumstances forced the bondholders of insolvent companies to accept noncumulative preferred stock in exchange for their senior obligations.

After a company has passed dividends for many years and has accumulated a substantial arrearage, economic forces may improve so that the firm may suddenly recover. Perhaps the firm does not have enough cash to pay off the total arrearage, but would like to extinguish the arrearage as a step toward resuming regular dividend payments. A common strategy is to offer preferred stockholders new securities in exchange for their claims to past dividends. At one time, for example, ASG Industries, Inc., had 143,000 shares of its preferred stock outstanding, on which dividends were in arrear 47 quarterly payments, totaling $14.687 per share.[4] Rather than pay cash, the firm offered the preferred stockholders three shares of common stock in exchange for one share of preferred stock and the dividend arrearages on it. Since the company was beginning to show a profit after years of losses, the elimination of dividend arrearages would permit the resumption of common dividends. The prospect of cash dividends prompted the preferred stockholders to vote in favor of the exchange.

Liquidation Preference. The typical preferred-stock contract includes not only dividend preference but also asset preference. Consumers Power Company has this clause in its contract:

> Upon voluntary or involuntary liquidation, the holders of the Preferred Stock of each series, without preference between series, are entitled to receive the amount determined to be payable on the shares of such series (which, in the case of the New Preferred Stock, is $100 per share on involuntary liquidation and an amount per share on voluntary liquidation equal to the price to public set forth on the cover of this Prospectus, plus accrued dividends in each case) before any distribution of assets may be made to the holders of the Common Stock.[5]

It may seem that the prior right to recover full par value provides considerable protection for preferred stockholders. But, in practice, preferred stockholders rarely have the power to force liquidation, so that corporations are liquidated only as a last resort. By that time, the claims of creditors are likely to exceed realizable assets, making both preferred and common stock worthless. Nevertheless, security investors generally consider preferred stock to be of higher quality if it is fortified by an asset-preference clause.

Voting Rights. Most preferred stocks have no general voting power. The exceptions are stocks issued by companies chartered in states which do not permit nonvoting stocks, in which case preferred stocks do have general voting power, including the right to vote in the election of directors. But even with general voting rights, effective control by preferred stockholders is difficult to achieve because of the greater number of common shares. Preferred stockholders must therefore rely on contingency voting power, which gives them the right to vote under specified conditions, and on veto power, which gives them the right to prohibit certain corporate actions if management has not obtained their prior approval. Contingency voting power is most frequently triggered by the firm's passing preferred dividends

---

[4] *Wall Street Journal,* January 15, 1973, p. 11.

[5] Consumers Power Company, *op. cit.,* p. 23.

for a specified number of time periods. If Consumers Power Company were to pass four quarterly preferred dividends, "the Preferred Stock of all series would have the right, voting as a single class, to elect a majority of the directors of the Company and the Common Stock, voting as a class, would have the right to elect the remaining directors."[6]

The veto power of preferred stockholders usually applies to (1) the authorization of an issue of stock ranking equally with or prior to the existing preferred stock, (2) charter amendments affecting the rights of existing stockholders, (3) the sale of corporate assets, (4) the assumption of new debt exceeding a set critical amount, and (5) mergers and acquisitions. At Consumers Power Company, charter amendments and the issue of equal or prior stock must be approved by two thirds of the votes of outstanding preferred shares; sales of assets, issue of new debt exceeding limit, and mergers and acquisitions must be approved by a simple majority.

Protective Provisions. A preferred stockholder knows that even though his investment position may be sound when he acquires his shares, he needs protection against subsequent corporate actions that may weaken his position. In addition to granting contingency voting power and veto power, the preferred-stock contract usually prohibits the company from paying cash dividends on common stock if the dividends will cause the firm to violate stipulated financial tests. In the case of Consumers Power, these tests examine the effect of the contemplated payment on the size of retained earnings accumulated, on the ratio of retained earnings to preferred stock outstanding, and on the percentage of common equity in the total capitalization. (Other possible tests might evaluate the size of a firm's net current assets or the ratio of such assets to total assets.) If, despite their protective provisions, Consumers Power preferred stockholders find their dividends interrupted, they have the right to elect a majority of the board of directors as soon as four quarterly dividends have been missed. Such transfer of control is itself a kind of protective provision.

Other Provisions. Like bonds, preferred stock may be either convertible or nonconvertible, callable or noncallable, with or without sinking fund. Two innovations in the design of preferred stock are a mutually redeemable feature and an accelerated sinking-fund pattern. The former refers to an arrangement whereby after a relatively short initial period (usually 2 or 3 years) the shares may be redeemed at the option of either party. The latter provides for the complete amortization of the issue within as few as ten years. Both of these features serve to make preferred stock more attractive to investors in a tight capital market.

---

[6] Consumers Power Company, *op. cit.*, p. 22.

THE DIVIDEND COST OF PREFERRED STOCK

Investors' Required Rate of Return

Preferred stock is more risky than bonds, so it is natural to assume that preferred stockholders would require a higher rate of return than bondholders. Figure 19-1 shows the relationship between the market yield on preferred stock and that on bonds since 1950. During the early 1950's, the yield on high-grade preferred stock was, in fact, from 1 to $1\frac{1}{4}$ percent higher than that on high-grade corporate bonds. The differential steadily narrowed, however, so that by the mid-1960's the yield on preferred stock actually dropped below the yield on bonds, where it remained until 1974. Then, as a result of investors' increased desire for quality issues, preferred yield again rose above the yield on bonds.

Two factors may account for the reversal of the expected yield relationship between bonds and preferred stock during the period 1966–1973. First, interest income is fully taxable, whereas only 15 percent of the dividend income of corporate investors (fire and casualty insurance companies, life insurance companies, etc.) is taxable. Corporate investors therefore have a strong tax incentive to invest in preferred stock instead of bonds. A steady growth of these investors has created a long-term, high-level demand for preferred stock. Second, since bond interest is tax deductible for the firm but preferred dividends are not, the direct cost of preferred stock is roughly twice that of bonds. This tax incentive makes most corporations favor debt over preferred stock financing (although, as we shall see, there are situations

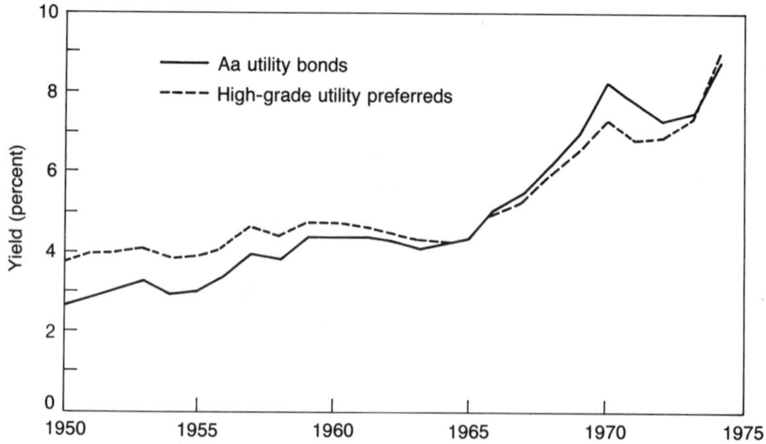

Source: Moody's Investors Service.

Figure 19-1 Bond vs. Preferred Stock Yields

in which preferred stock would improve a firm's capital structure). This combination of high demand and limited supply, both a result of tax incentives, accounted for the drop in the preferred-stock yield below the corresponding bond yield.

A Formula for Effective Dividend Rate

Tax treatment is not the only difference between bonds and preferred stock. Preferred stock has no maturity date; bonds do. When preferred stock is sold at a price other than par, the effective dividend rate is different from the contractual dividend rate. The following formula calculates the effective dividend rate k_p of a straight preferred stock by equating the present value of future dividend payments to the net price of the preferred stock received by the company:

$$P - C = \frac{Fd}{1 + k_p} + \frac{Fd}{(1 + k_p)^2} + \cdots \qquad (19\text{-}1)$$

where P is the price of the preferred stock to the public, C is the issue cost, d is the contractual dividend rate, and F is the face value of the stock. The right-hand side of Eq. (19-1) is a geometric series whose sum is equal to Fd/k_p, so that

$$k_p = \frac{Fd}{P - C} \qquad (19\text{-}2)$$

In other words, to calculate the effective dividend rate, one need only divide the annual dividend by the net price of the stock. Thus, if a 9 percent \$100-par preferred stock is sold at a net price of \$101.80, the effective annual cost to the company is 8.84 percent (= \$9.00/\$101.80).

The nondeductibility of preferred dividends places preferred stock at a distinct disadvantage compared with bond financing. At a tax rate of 50 percent, funds raised through preferred stock costing 8.84 percent must earn 17.68 percent before taxes merely to keep the per-share earnings on common stock from falling. Moreover, given the preferred-dividend rate, the break-even return varies directly with the tax rate. But since interest is tax deductible, funds raised through bond financing costing 8.84 percent need earn only 8.84 percent before taxes to break even. This cost comparison does not mean that a corporation should always favor bonds over preferred stock, since it considers only the direct costs of each type of financing. Determining which type is cheaper requires a comparison of both direct and indirect costs. Even though the direct cost of preferred stock is higher than that of bonds, the circumstances of a particular firm may mean that the addition of preferred stock will result in a lower overall cost of capital than the addition of bonds. If preferred stock financing increases the total valuation of the firm more than bond financing does, then preferred stock is clearly more desirable than bonds despite its higher direct cost.

Effect of Special Factors

Equation (19-2) gives the effective dividend rate of a straight preferred stock, assuming that the stock has a perpetual life. In practice, however, nearly all preferred-stock contracts include a call provision, enabling the issuer to refund its preferred stock if and when the market dividend rate falls to a level that makes refunding profitable. The possibility of recall tends to reduce the expected dividend rate below the value given by Eq. (19-2). The expected dividend rate can be calculated in the same way we calculated the expected interest rate on a callable bond.

Equation (19-2) must also be modified if the preferred shares are retired in installments through a sinking fund. If sinking-fund preferred stocks are sold at par, Eq. (19-2) gives the correct value of k_p. But if the stock is sold above or below par, the formula will overstate or understate the value of k_p, with the degree of overstatement or understatement varying directly with the size of the sinking-fund operation.

LEVERAGE FINANCING WITH PREFERRED STOCK

Corporations issue straight preferred stock to gain profitable leverage, whereas they issue convertible preferred stock primarily to pay for mergers and acquisitions. Let us first show that straight preferred stock may enhance a firm's total value more than either common stock or bond financing.

Effect on Valuation: Theory

Statement of the Problem. A new firm expects that its annual net operating income will be $\bar{X}$ perpetually. This figure assumes continual replacement of existing assets, but no net investments, so that the firm's earnings on common stock (i.e., residual earnings) equal its adjusted earnings as defined in Chapter 2. The firm's assets are partly contributed by the present owners as payment for their stocks and partly purchased at a price of $M + N$ dollars. The financial executive must decide how to raise the cash to pay for the assets.

Table 19-1 summarizes the three financing alternatives. Under Alternative 1, which carries intermediate risk, there is M dollars in bonds and N dollars in preferred stock, and the present owners receive n shares of common stock as evidence of their proprietary interest. The financial executive forecasts that the investors' required returns on the three classes of securi-

Table 19-1 Three Financing Alternatives

Financing Alternative	1	2	3
Capital structure			
Bonds ($)	M	$M+N$	M
Preferred stock ($)	N	0	0
Common stock (shares)	n	n	$n+\Delta n$
Investors' required rates of return			
Bonds (%)	k_i	k_i'	k_i''
Preferred stock (%)	k_p	k_p'	k_p''
Common stock (%)	k_e	k_e'	k_e''

ties will be k_i, k_p, and k_e, respectively. Under Alternative 2, which carries the highest risk, there is $(M + N)$ dollars in bonds, no preferred stock, and n shares of common stock for the present owners. The investors' required rates of return will be k_i', k_p', and k_e', respectively. To compensate for the higher risk, these rates are higher than the others, so that $k_i' > k_i$, $k_p' > k_p$, and $k_e' > k_e$. Under Alternative 3, which carries the lowest risk, there is M dollars in bonds, no preferred stock, and $n + \Delta n$ shares of common stock: n shares to go to the present owners and Δn shares to be sold to new stockholders. The value of Δn is such that, at the going stock price, the company receives N dollars, an amount that exactly compensates for the absence of preferred stock. The investors' required rates of return will be k_i'', k_p'', and k_e'', respectively. Since common stock financing entails the smallest risk, its rates are the lowest, so that $k_i'' < k_i$, $k_p'' < k_p$, and $k_e'' < k_e$. The financial executive needs to know the conditions under which preferred stock financing will result in a higher valuation for the firm than either of the other two alternatives.

Valuation Formulas. The next step is to derive the firm's valuation under each financing alternative. Under Alternative 1, the company has M dollars in bonds, on which it must pay k_iM dollars in interest, and N dollars in preferred stock, on which it must pay k_pN dollars in dividends. We shall designate k_iM dollars and k_pN dollars by I and Z, respectively. I is tax deductible; Z is not. With a net operating income of $\overline{X}$, the firm's earnings on common stock, E, are given by the formula

$$(\overline{X} - I)(1 - \tau) - Z$$

where τ is the tax rate on corporate income. Capitalizing E at k_e gives the value of existing common equity under Alternative 1. The total value V of the firm is accordingly given by the expression:

$$V = \underset{\text{Bonds}}{M} + \underset{\substack{\text{Preferred}\\ \text{stock}}}{N} + \underset{\substack{\text{Common}\\ \text{stock}}}{\frac{(\bar{X} - I)(1 - \tau) - Z}{k_e}} \tag{19-3}$$

where the three terms on the right-hand side are, respectively, the values of bonds, of preferred stock, and of common stock.

Under Alternative 2, the company has $(M + N)$ dollars in bonds, on which it must pay $k_i'(M + N)$ dollars in interest, and no preferred stock. Since the net operating income would still be $\bar{X}$, the earnings on common stock, E', equals

$$(\bar{X} - I')(1 - \tau)$$

where I' stands for $k_i'(M + N)$. Capitalizing E' at k_e' gives the value of the existing common equity under Alternative 2. The corresponding value V' of the firm is given by the expression

$$V' = \underset{\text{Bonds}}{(M + N)} + \underset{\text{Common stock}}{\frac{(\bar{X} - I')(1 - \tau)}{k_e'}} \tag{19-4}$$

where the two terms on the right-hand side are, respectively, the values of bonds and of common stock. The difference between Alternatives 1 and 2 may be viewed as the replacement of N dollars in bonds by an equal amount in preferred stock. Since the total amount of leverage capital remains unchanged, the replacement enhances the value of the shares held by common stockholders only if it increases the total value of the firm—that is, only if V is greater than V'.

Finally, under Alternative 3, the company has M dollars in bonds, on which it must pay $k_i''M$ dollars in interest. The net operating income is still $\bar{X}$, so the firm's earnings on common stock, E'', equal

$$(\bar{X} - I'')(1 - \tau)$$

where I'' stands for $k_i''M$. Capitalizing E'' at k_e'' gives the value of common equity, including the new issue. Adding the value of the bonds, we get the valuation V'' of the firm:

$$V'' = \underset{\text{Bonds}}{M} + \underset{\substack{\text{Common stock}\\ \text{(new and old)}}}{\frac{(\bar{X} - I'')(1 - \tau)}{k_e''}} \tag{19-5}$$

In this case, there is only M dollars of leverage capital, but the old stockholders no longer own the entire residual equity, since N dollars of it belongs to the new stockholders who provided the funds that compensate for the lack of preferred stock. For the existing stockholders, the difference between Alternatives 1 and 3 may be viewed as the replacement of N dollars in new common stock by the issue of an equal amount of preferred stock. Whether the N dollars is provided by preferred stock or by new common stock, the value of the shares of the existing common stockholders equals the total value of the firm less $(M + N)$ dollars. Replacing common stock with preferred stock therefore benefits the existing common stockholders only if the total value of the firm increases—that is, only if V is greater than V''.

Comparing the Alternatives. A firm should employ preferred stock financing only if it is superior to both common stock and bond financing. When the financial executive compares preferred stock financing with bond financing (Alternative 1 with Alternative 2) from the viewpoint of existing common stockholders, he finds that replacing bonds with preferred stock reduces interest payments and increases preferred dividends. The after-tax savings in interest is $(I' - I)(1 - \tau)$. The increase in preferred dividends Z is not tax deductible; Z is therefore paid with after-tax dollars. Preferred stock financing thus increases residual earnings on common stock only if

$$(I' - I)(1 - \tau) > Z \tag{19-6}$$

that is, only if the after-tax savings in interest exceeds the dividends on preferred stock.

An increase in residual earnings does not, of course, mean that the market price of common equity will rise, since market price depends also on the rate at which residual earnings are capitalized. If, however, Inequality (19-6) holds, the rate of capitalization will decline for two reasons: (1) because of the distinction between debt and equity, the replacement of bonds with preferred stock reduces the risk of insolvency; and (2) Inequality (19-6) insures that preferred financing imposes a smaller fixed charge on the firm than bond financing. This reduction in fixed charges tends to make residual earnings less volatile than they are under bond financing. Since the quality of residual earnings is improved, investors may be expected to capitalize earnings at a lower required rate of return.

Inequality (19-6) is most likely to be satisfied if security investors consider the present level of a firm's indebtedness excessive, in which case replacing bonds with preferred stock can lead to a significant reduction in bond interest rate. The company, of course, will realize a direct interest savings on bonds replaced even if the interest rate does not fall; but if the rate does fall, the firm will also realize an indirect savings on the bonds that are not replaced. At a rate of 50 percent, the direct after-tax interest savings are approximately one half the associated increase in preferred dividends. For Inequality (19-6) to hold, the indirect interest savings must therefore be at least slightly more than the direct interest savings. This condition is most likely to be met in public utilities and finance companies, which, because of their policies of fully utilizing their debt capacity, are often confronted with sharply rising marginal costs of borrowing. When Inequality (19-6) holds, preferred stock should replace bond financing since the shift will increase the total value of the firm.

Having examined the relative merits of preferred stock and bond financing, the financial executive must next compare preferred stock with common stock financing. Replacing common stock with preferred stock lowers the quality of residual earnings and thus raises the capitalization rate. The quality of residual earnings is lowered because (1) preferred dividends have priority over common dividends, and (2) preferred dividends increase the volatility of residual earnings. Under Alternative 3, the company issues Δn shares of common stock, with a market value of N dollars. Since the new stockholders require a return of k_e'', the cost of the new money to existing stockholders is $k_e''N$ dollars in annual earnings. Under Alternative 1, the company issues N dollars in preferred stock, on which it pays $Z(= k_pN)$ dollars in annual dividends. Moreover, the bondholders will demand a higher rate of interest on their funds, raising after-tax interest by $(I - I'')(1 - \tau)$. Preferred stock financing therefore increases the earnings to existing stockholders only if

$$Z + (I - I'')(1 - \tau) < k_e''N \qquad (19\text{-}7)$$

that is, only if the preferred dividends plus the associated increase in after-tax interest expenses are less than the earnings that the company must offer to entice new common stockholders to commit their funds.

Compared with the common stock alternative, preferred stock financing will enhance the value of existing common stock only if the earnings on existing common shares are increased proportionately more than the capitalization rate. The left-hand side of Inequality (19-7) must thus be substantially smaller than the right-hand side.

Let us suppose that a company needs x million dollars to finance an expansion program. The rate of retention is not sufficiently high, and so the program must be financed externally. The firm is already overburdened with debt; additional debt financing would jeopardize the firm's credit rating. The market price of the company's common stock is severely depressed relative to earnings. To raise the new money through common stock, the firm would have to give new stockholders an inordinately large share of company earnings. The cost of preferred stock may also be high, but perhaps not high enough to preclude a moderate issue. This is the typical situation that prompts a financial executive to choose preferred stock over either common stock or bonds.

Effect on Valuation: Application

A Numerical Illustration. To illustrate our analysis, let us consider the hypothetical Badger, Inc., with given physical assets, which are expected to generate an annual net operating income of $200,000. Part of the firm's assets came from present owners in payment for stock. The rest was purchased at a price of $1.10 million. The firm must now decide how to raise the cash to meet this payment. The choice is between Plans P, B, and C, capital structures which differ in their relative reliance on preferred stock, bonds, or common stock (see Table 19–2).

Plan P calls for the issue of $1 million in bonds and $100,000 in preferred stock, and for the present owners to receive 100,000 common shares as evidence of proprietary interest. The investors' required rates of return on the three classes of securities are expected to be 8.5 percent, 8 percent, and 14 percent, respectively. Plan B calls for the issue of $1.10 million in bonds, no preferred stock, and 100,000 shares of common stock (to the present owners). Since Plan B is more risky than Plan P, the required rates of return on the bonds and common stock are expected to be 9.5 percent and 15 percent, respectively. Plan C, like Plan P, calls for the issue of $1 million in bonds; but unlike Plan P, Plan C includes no preferred stock. The difference is made up by selling $100,000 worth of common stock to outside investors (in addition to the 100,000 shares issued to existing stockholders). Since Plan C is the safest, the required rates of return on bonds and

Table 19-2 The Financing Plans of Badger, Inc.

	Plan P	Plan B	Plan C
Capital structure			
Bonds ($)	1,000,000	1,100,000	1,000,000
Preferred stock ($)	100,000	0	0
Common stock (shares)	100,000	100,000	130,700*
Investors' required return			
Bonds (%)	8.5	9.5	8.25
Preferred stock (%)	8.0	—	—
Common stock (%)	14.0	15.0	13.8
Total value of firm ($)	1,453,371	1,418,333	1,425,725

* At $3.26 per share, the sale of 30,700 shares produces $100,000.

common stock are expected to be only 8.25 percent and 13.8 percent, respectively.

If we apply Eq. (19-4), we find that under Plan B the firm has a value of $1,418,333:

$$V' = \$1{,}100{,}000 + \frac{(\$200{,}000 + \$104{,}500)(.5)}{.15}$$

$$= \underset{\text{Bonds}}{\$1{,}100{,}000} + \underset{\text{Common stock}}{\$318{,}333} = \underset{\text{Total value}}{\$1{,}418{,}333}$$

(We assume throughout a corporate tax rate of 50 percent.) With $1.1 million in bonds, the interest is 9.5 percent, or $104,500. If $100,000 in bonds is replaced by an equal amount of preferred stock, the interest will be only 8.5 percent, or $85,000. The after-tax interest saving of $9,750 is greater than the $8,000 in dividends on the new preferred stock, and so Inequality (19-6) is satisfied. Preferred stock financing therefore will enhance the value of the firm. In fact, according to Eq. (19-3), the firm has a value under Plan P of $1,453,371:

$$V = \$1{,}000{,}000 + \$100{,}000 + \frac{(\$200{,}000 - \$85{,}000)(.5) - \$8{,}000}{.14}$$

$$= \underset{\text{Bonds}}{\$1{,}000{,}000} + \underset{\text{Preferred stock}}{\$100{,}000} + \underset{\text{Common stock}}{\$353{,}371} = \underset{\text{Total value}}{\$1{,}453{,}371}$$

To justify Plan P, however, the financial executive must also be able to demonstrate the superiority of preferred stock over common stock financing. If the $100,000 in bonds is replaced by common instead of preferred stock, the interest rate on the remaining $1 million in bonds will be 8.25 percent instead of 8.5 percent. In dollars, this amounts to a $1,250 after-tax savings. Adding this $1,250 to the $8,000 in preferred dividends, we get a total of $9,250, which is the amount that preferred stock financing will cost existing stockholders in reduced earnings. This cost is nevertheless smaller than that of issuing $100,000 worth of common stock under Plan C. With the new stockholders requiring a 13.8 percent return, the common stock issue will cost existing common stockholders $13,800 in reduced earnings. The existing common stockholders therefore will enjoy $4,550 more in earnings under preferred stock financing than under common stock financing. In this case, the $4,550 advantage is more than large enough to offset the higher capitalization rate associated with preferred stock financing. The value of the firm is therefore higher under Plan P than under Plan C. Applying Eq. (19-5), we find that under the common stock alternative the firm has a value of only $1,425,725:

$$V'' = \$1{,}000{,}000 + \frac{(\$200{,}000 - \$82{,}500)(.5)}{.138}$$

$$= \underset{\text{Bonds}}{\$1{,}000{,}000} + \underset{\text{Common stock}}{\$425{,}725} = \underset{\text{Total value}}{\$1{,}425{,}725}$$

Of the $425,725 in common equity, $100,000 belongs to the new stockholders, so that only $325,725 belongs to the old stockholders. This $325,725 is $7,392 larger than the corresponding equity value under Plan B (bonds) but $27,646 less than the value under Plan P (preferred stock).

Badger, Inc., should include $100,000 in preferred stock in its capital structure since the value of the firm is highest under this alternative. The Badger example depicts the situation of a heavily indebted firm whose common stock is selling at a relatively low price. With a higher stock price, a common stock issue might have been the best alternative. The above data could also be altered to apply to an under-leveraged firm whose value would increase if debt were substituted for equity. By experimenting with different data, one can use the model to simulate a variety of situations that confront financial executives. Some situations favor bonds, others favor preferred stock, and still others favor common stock. Polaroid and Campbell Soup, for example, find all-common capital structures best suited to their needs, while the Baltimore Gas and Electric Company and Commonwealth Edison both use a combination of bonds, preferred stock, and common stock. No absolute ranking of the three kinds of securities is possible. The characteristics of the individual firm, together with conditions in the market place, determine the relative cost of each type of financing. Relative costs, in turn, determine what combination of types is optimal.

A Case Study. Let us examine the circumstances and reasoning that might lead a large utility company to divide a $100 million issue equally between bonds and preferred stock. You may think of Figure 19-2 as an actual report prepared for the company's vice president of finance by a member of his department.

The reader may find it instructive to compare Mr. Jones' recommendations and reasons with Badger's. The reader may also wish to consider possible reasons for Mr. Jones' not mentioning share-value maximization, consideration of control, or risk of insolvency. It may be relevant to remember that the firm is a public utility.

Northland Utility Company

August 7, 19__

MEMORANDUM

To: Fred Case, Vice President of Finance

From: John Jones, Assistant Treasurer

I. Financing Needs and Assumptions

In order to pay off our heavy short-term indebtedness, we must raise $100,-000,000. In reviewing the financing alternatives open to us, I have quantified projections and narrowed choices on the basis of four assumptions:

1. There is a critical need to protect the firm's Aa bond rating.
2. Convertibles should not be issued at this time because of the large number of common shares reserved and because of the depressed current market price of common stock.
3. No conversions into common stock should occur during the rest of this year or next year.
4. At least $30,000,000 in rate relief will be approved, effective October 1 of this year.

II. The Financing Alternatives

Option 1—$100,000,000 bond issue. This option would provide the firm with funds at a relatively low cost and would improve earnings per share by 4¢ (at the end of next year) more than Options 2 and 3. It would, however, leave little flexibility in our capital structure, which would be 55 percent debt. Interest coverage would be approximately 20 basis points lower than under Options 2 and 3. The rate of return on the rate base would increase slightly more than under Options 2 and 3; this may be worth considering, especially if we determine that another application for a rate increase is necessary in the near future. It seems probable that our bond rating will be reduced if our interest coverage is not improved.

Option 2—$50,000,000 in bonds and $50,000,000 in preferred stock. This option has the advantages of maintaining capital-structure flexibility and interest coverage. But these advantages are partially offset by increased cash payouts resulting from the nondeductibility of dividends. Earnings per share are the same under Option 2 as they would be under Option 3 if common stock were substituted for preferred stock.

Figure 19-2 Company Memorandum on Financing Alternatives

Option 3—$50,000,000 in bonds and $50,000,000 in common stock. This option is similar to Option 2 in its flexibility advantages and cash payout disadvantage. There is, however, the additional disadvantage of adverse stockholder reaction to a common stock issue so soon after a prior issue, particularly since the current market price is depressed. Both Options 2 and 3 have the advantage of giving the firm some flexibility in eliminating or changing the size of either the equity or the debt portion of the issue at a later date in case significant price changes develop in the securities market.

III. Recommendations

Option 2, combining preferred stock and bonds, seems most desirable in light of the bond-rating problems under Option 1 and the adverse effect on common stockholders under Option 3. A preferred stock issue of $50,000,000 should sell well and will fit conveniently into our capital structure.

Attachments [not reproduced here]

Table A—Effects of Financing Alternatives on Capital Structure, Times Charges Earned and Earnings per Share

Table B—Effects of Financing Alternatives on Rate of Return on Rate Base

Table C—Data on Companies Whose Bond Ratings Were Recently Reduced by Moody's from Aa to A

Table D—Effects of Financing Alternatives on Cash Payout

Figure 19-2 *(continued)*

MERGER FINANCING WITH PREFERRED STOCK

Whereas straight preferred stock is primarily an instrument of leverage financing, convertible preferred stock is primarily a vehicle for financing mergers and acquisitions. According to one study, 87 percent of all convertible preferred stock issued was for mergers and acquisitions, leaving only 5 percent as direct exchange of securities and only 8 percent for raising cash.[7] In this section, we shall consider the reasons that make convertible preferred stock an attractive financing instrument for both the selling and the buying stockholders in a merger.

Tax Deferment

Perhaps the most important reason for financing mergers with convertible preferreds is the tax implication for the stockholders of the acquired

[7] Pinches, *op. cit.*, p. 55.

company. Since there is usually a capital gain, the selling stockholders will welcome any deferment in paying taxes on that gain. According to the Internal Revenue Code, if the stockholders of the acquired company receive stock (preferred or common) in the surviving company, the transaction is treated as a "tax-free" exchange, meaning that the selling stockholders need pay no taxes on their gains until they dispose of the stock received. If, on the other hand, selling stockholders receive payment in cash or bonds, capital gains tax must be paid immediately.

The buying stockholders also benefit: because of the tax deferment, selling stockholders are often willing to accept a lower price for their company than if they received cash or bonds and could not defer taxes.

A Safer Security

The tax deferment explains why mergers are often financed with stocks instead of bonds or cash, but it does not account for the preference of preferred over common stock. Selling stockholders find convertible preferred stock attractive because of its built-in safety features. Since preferred stock, whether convertible or not, has priority status, preferred dividends are more stable than common dividends. In addition, convertible preferred stocks provide greater downside protection than common stocks in a declining market. If selling stockholders receive common stock of the acquiring company and the price of the stock later falls, the selling stockholders suffer the full brunt of the fall. But if they receive convertible preferred stock, their loss in a declining market is limited since the fixed dividends specified in the preferred-stock contract establish a floor value for the stock. The buying company too benefits since by offering convertible preferred stock, an acquiring company is often able to buy a firm at a lower price than would be possible if common stock were offered.

Tailor-Made Dividends

An acquiring company may choose to employ convertible preferred stock in preference to common stock partly because of the flexibility in setting dividend rates. Let us imagine that Austin, Inc., is acquiring Baker, Inc., via a simple mutual exchange of common stock. Austin has 1 million shares of stock outstanding, on which it currently earns $2 million annually, for an *EPS* of $2. Austin's common stock sells at $40 per share; its price-earnings ratio is therefore 20 (see Table 19-3). Baker also has 1 million shares outstanding, on which it currently earns $1 million, or an *EPS* of $1. Since Baker's stock sells at $10, its price-earnings ratio is 10. As a fast growing company, Austin distributes only 20 percent of its current earnings (i.e., 40 cents per share) in dividends. Baker, on the other hand, as a slow growing firm, distributes 70 percent of its current earnings (70 cents per share) in dividends.

Table 19-3 Merger Financing: Common Stock Versus Convertible Preferred Stock*

	Premerger Financial Data		Postmerger (Common Stock Financing)		Postmerger (Conv. Preferred Financing)	
	Austin	Baker	Austin	Baker	Austin	Baker
Number of shares outstanding (in 1000's)	1,000 (C)	1,000 (C)	1,000 (C)	250 (C)	1,000 (C)	250 (CP)
Dividends per share	40¢	70¢	48¢	48¢	48¢	$2.80
Earnings per share†	$2	$1	$2.40	$2.40	$2.40	–
Total dividends (in 1000's)	$400	$700	$480	$120	$480	$700
Total earnings (in 1000's)	$2,000	$1,000	$2,400	$600	$2,300	–
Market price per share††	$40	$10	$43.20	$43.20	$43.20	$43.20
Total value of shares (in 1000's)	$40,000	$10,000	$43,200	$10,800	$43,200	$10,800
Dividend payout ratio	20%	70%	20%	20%	20%	–
Price-earnings ratio	20	10	18	18	18	–

* Common stock is abbreviated as C, and convertible preferred stock as CP.

† For convertible preferred financing, *EPS* is calculated on a *pro-forma* basis which reflects the dilution which would occur if the preferred stock were all converted into common stock.

†† The share price of a convertible preferred stock is taken to be the value of the common stock into which each preferred share is convertible.

If the two stocks are exchanged at the ratio of their respective market prices, one Baker share equals one quarter Austin share (see Table 19-3). Since the price-earnings ratios of the two firms are not the same, the exchange will redistribute the combined earnings in favor of Austin, which has the higher price-earnings ratio. Once the exchange is completed, there will thus be 1.25 million Austin-Baker shares, with a combined earnings of $3 million, or an *EPS* of $2.40. Since the original Austin stockholders still have 1 million shares, their current earnings increase from $2 million to $2.4 million; meanwhile, the original Baker stockholders now have only 250,000 shares, and their current earnings decrease from $1 million to $600,000. The quality of the combined earnings will lie between those of Austin and of Baker; Austin-Baker will therefore have a price-earnings ratio between 10 and 20. The actual ratio will depend on the investors' reaction to the merger. The weighted average of Austin's and Baker's price-earnings ratios, using their original earnings as weights, is $16\frac{2}{3}$. If the new price-earnings ratio is equal to or greater than $16\frac{2}{3}$, both Austin and Baker stockholders will find the value of their holdings increased after the merger. In Table 19-3, which assumes a post-merger price-earnings ratio of 18, the holdings of Austin stockholders increase from $40 million to $43.2 million; those of Baker stockholders increase from $10 million to $10.8 million. We have been assuming that the merger produces no synergistic effects on earnings. If, because of synergy, Austin-Baker earnings are greater than the sum of Austin's and Baker's earnings taken separately, the increase in share values will be even greater.

Before the merger, Baker stockholders received $700,000 in dividends annually. After the merger, if Austin-Baker follows a 20 percent payout policy (i.e., 48 cents per share), the dividends to Baker stockholders will be only $120,000. Although the merger increases the value of their holdings, some Baker stockholders may still dislike the idea of the merger since it will reduce their current income. The current income of Baker stockholders may be raised in three ways: (1) Austin-Baker can raise its dividend-payout ratio on common stock, although that may not be the optimal policy in light of the growth prospects of the company; (2) Austin can offer Baker a more favorable exchange ratio, but Austin stockholders may object to giving up more value than they receive; or (3) Austin can pay for the merger by issuing convertible preferred stock. For 1 million shares of Baker common stock, Austin can offer 250,000 shares of $50-par 5.6 percent preferred stock, convertible into Austin-Baker common stock on a share-for-share basis (see Table 19-3). This enables Austin-Baker to pay the Baker stockholders $700,000 in annual dividends without altering the payout ratio on Austin-Baker common stock. And, because of the conversion factor, the Baker stockholders still have an option on 250,000 shares of Austin-Baker common stock, the same number of shares they would have received in a common-for-common exchange. Baker stockholders may in fact favor convertible preferred stock because preferred dividends have priority and because the fixed dividend rate establishes an investment value that acts as a floor independent of the market price of the associated common stock.

Accounting Considerations

Accounting conventions also play a role in the decision whether to finance a merger with convertible preferred or with common stock. When Company A acquires Company B, A can value B's assets on its own books in two ways: the purchase method or the pooling-of-interests method. Under the purchase method, A records B's assets at fair market value. If the market value is higher than B's book value, future operations of A will be charged expenses higher than those that B used to charge; A will therefore show a smaller accounting profit on the acquired assets than B would have. Under the pooling-of-interests method, A records B's assets at B's book value, even if A paid a higher price. The assumption is that since no new business has been created, there is no need to change asset valuation. The acquiring firm generally prefers the pooling-of-interests method because it enables the company to report larger earnings.

A series of publications of the Accounting Principles Board (APB) gives the accounting profession's opinion of the pooling-of-interests method.[8] In 1965, the Board accepted convertible preferred stock financing as a means of effecting pooling-of-interests under certain conditions. The conditions are met only if the convertible preferred stock is voting stock, is redeemable only after convertibility becomes effective, and carries no significant sinking-fund provisions. In 1970, however, fearful that accounting methods might provide an artificial stimulus to merger activity, the APB issued Opinion No. 16, *Business Combinations,* to clarify and tighten its criteria for the use of purchase and pooling accounting methods in mergers. Mergers financed with convertible preferred stock no longer qualify for the pooling-of-interests method. To qualify for pooling, the acquiring company must now issue only common stock in exchange for virtually all the common stock of the acquired firm. This changes tends to favor the use of common stock in merger financing.

The relative attractiveness of convertible preferred and of common stock is also affected by the accounting definition of *EPS*. In the Austin-Baker merger, we calculated *EPS* on a *pro forma* basis which reflects the dilution that would occur if the preferred stock were converted into common stock. This practice conforms with APB Opinion No. 15, *Earnings Per Share,* which requires any firm with a complex capital structure to report its *EPS* on a fully diluted basis. Before Opinion No. 15 was issued, in 1969, companies were required to consider conversions in calculating *EPS* only if conversion would result in material dilution of *EPS*. Many firms therefore financed mergers with convertible preferred stock because it enabled them to avoid reporting an immediate dilution in *EPS*. Opinion No. 15 has eliminated this advantage.

REVIEW QUESTIONS

1. Preferred stock is considered a hybrid security because some of its features resemble those of bonds while others resemble the features of common stock. What are the key features of preferred stock? How do these features affect the determination of a firm's optimal capital structure?
2. Describe the typical protective covenants of a preferred-stock contract. Why do preferred stockholders require special protective convenants even though they already have dividend and asset preferences?
3. What financial and nonfinancial factors might account for the different relative proportions of preferred stock in the long-term capitalization of firms in the

[8] For a useful summary, see David F. Hawkins, *Corporate Financial Reporting: Text and Cases* (Homewood: Richard D. Irwin, Inc., 1971), Ch. 18.

following industries: public utilities, sales and consumer finance, and aircraft manufacturing?

4. The financial executive of an electronics firm says that a company should consider preferred stock financing only after it has decided not to issue common stock—in other words, only when the choice is limited to preferred stock or bonds. But the financial executive of an electric utility says that a company should consider preferred stock financing after it has decided against debt—in other words, when the choice is between preferred and common. Are these two lines of reasoning contradictory? If so, which is correct? If not, how do you resolve the apparent contradiction?

5. Suppose that Leabo, Inc., has 10,000 shares of $100-par 5 percent cumulative participating preferred stock outstanding, giving the holders a prior dividend claim of $5 per share as well as the right to share equally with the common stockholders in any dividends exceeding $5 per share. The firm is now considering making an offer to exchange 1.2 shares of common stock for each share of the cumulative participating preferred stock. What would be the advantages and disadvantages to the existing common stockholders of such an exchange? State your assumptions regarding the company's future earnings prospects and dividend policy.

6. When we discussed the replacement of bonds with preferred stock, we noted that if the after-tax interest savings exceeds the preferred dividends, then the rate at which investors capitalize residual earnings must fall. What economic reasons lie behind the phenomenon? If the preferred stock replaced common stock, and if we know that the change will increase residual earnings, why is there still no assurance that the value of the common stock will rise?

7. Suppose that the tax law is changed to make dividend payments on preferred stock a deductible expense and to make dividend income fully taxable for corporate recipients, how would that alter the appeal of preferred stock for different groups of investors and for different groups of corporate issuers? How would this change affect the yield differential between preferred stock and bonds?

8. In the text, we described an ASG recapitalization plan under which three shares of common stock, then selling at about $13 per share, were issued in exchange for each preferred share and its $14.69 dividend arrearages. What were the merits of this exchange offer from the viewpoint of the company? from the viewpoint of the preferred stockholders? If you were a preferred stockholder, would you have voted for or against the recapitalization plan?

9. When United Aircraft acquired Essex International in 1974, United paid for the acquisition by exchanging 3.54 million shares of its $8.00 convertible preferred stock and .55 million shares of its $2.84 convertible preferred stock for all outstanding shares of Essex common and preferred stocks. A few weeks after the merger, United made a public offer to repurchase up to 1.1 million shares of the $8.00 preferred for a total of about $93 million. Explain why United chose this roundabout method of issuing stock and later repurchasing it, instead of paying cash in the first place. Also, why would United choose to finance its acquisition with convertible preferred stock instead of with a straight common-for-common exchange? (Note: United Aircraft has since changed its name to United Technologies.)

10. How have the changes in rules governing merger accounting and *EPS* reporting affected the attractiveness of convertible preferred stock as a vehicle for financing mergers?

PROBLEMS

1. Pollay Industries, a conglomerate undertaking a divestiture program, has just sold a group of investors the entire assets of the Pollay Consumer Finance Company (PCFC). The $1,185,564 purchase price, paid in cash, was reached by adding up the book values of the individual assets:

Cash assets	$ 37,654
Notes and receivables (net of reserves)	1,114,552
Other current assets	12,713
	$1,164,919
Fixed assets (net)	20,645
	$1,185,564

The investing group wants to design a capital structure that will maximize PCFC's market value. Past operating records indicate that PCFC may be expected to generate earnings before interest and taxes (*EBIT*) of $150,000 per year. Three capital structures are being considered:

A. $1,000,000 in bonds, $100,000 in preferred stock, and 200,000 shares of common stock; investors' required returns would be 9 percent, 8.5 percent, and 15 percent, respectively.

B. $1,100,000 in bonds, no preferred stock, and 200,000 shares of common stock; investors' required returns would be 10 percent and 16 percent, respectively.

C. $1,000,000 in bonds, no preferred stock, and 200,000 shares of common stock; investors' required returns would be 8.5 percent and 14.5 percent, respectively.

Project the firm's income statement for each of the three capital structures, and calculate the coverage ratios of the company's bonds and preferred stock (if any). Which plan yields the highest value for the firm? How is this value divided between the different classes of securities?

2. On the basis of the data in Table 19-2, Badger, Inc., found that including $100,000 of preferred stock in its capital structure maximized the value of the firm. If the investors' required rates of return were those listed below, what would the optimal capital structure be?

	Plan P	Plan B	Plan C
Bonds	8 1/2%	9%	8 1/4%
Preferred stock	9	—	—
Common stock	14 1/4	14 1/2	13 4/5

In solving the problem, adopt the long-run viewpoint: when the company's borrowing rate changes, the new rate will apply to the total debt outstanding, not just to the amount borrowed most recently. The same applies to preferred stock financing.

3. Let Π_a = the price-earnings ratio of Appleton, Inc.
Π_b = the price-earnings ratio of Bassett, Inc.
Suppose that Appleton has acquired Bassett through an exchange of common stock according to the ratio of their respective market prices. Illustrate with a numerical example that, if $\Pi_a > \Pi_b$, then the exchange increases Appleton's earnings but decreases Bassett's.

4. In the Austin-Baker merger discussed in this chapter, we assumed that under the common-stock financing alternative the stocks would be exchanged at the ratio of their respective market prices. Suppose, however, that Austin paid Baker a 20 percent premium. How much of the total Austin-Baker earnings would accrue to the old Austin stockholders after the merger? How high can the earnings-capitalization rate rise after the merger if the merger is still to result in an increase in the value of stock held by Austin shareholders? How would your answer be affected if (a) because of synergy, Austin-Baker earnings are 10 percent higher than the combined pre-merger earnings of Austin and Baker? (b) using convertible preferred instead of common stock, Austin could purchase Baker at a premium of 10 percent instead of 20 percent over market value?

5. The acquisition of Essex International by United Aircraft (now United Technologies) involved these basic terms: (a) each share of Essex common stock was exchanged for one fifth of a share of United \$8.00 preferred stock; (b) each share of Essex \$2.84 preferred was exchanged for one share of United \$2.84 preferred; (c) each share of United \$2.84 preferred was convertible into two fifths share of United \$8.00 preferred; and (d) each share of the \$8.00 preferred was convertible into 2.22 shares of United common stock.

   At the time of the merger negotiation (in 1974), the prices of the United and Essex common stocks were \$25½ and \$14¼, respectively. Comparative *EPS* and *DPS* data for the two firms are presented below:

	1970	1971	1972	1973
United Common Stock				
EPS	\$3.76	−\$3.62	\$4.17	\$4.92
DPS	1.80	1.80	1.80	1.80
Essex Common Stock				
EPS	1.22	1.64	2.01	2.20
DPS	0.60	0.60	0.60	0.65
Essex Preferred Stock				
DPS	2.84	2.84	2.84	2.84

   Analyze the terms of the merger in the light of these data. Why was convertible preferred stock used?

REFERENCES

BILDERSEE, JOHN S., "Some Aspects of the Performance of Non-Convertible Preferred Stocks," *Journal of Finance* 28 (December, 1973), pp. 1187–1201.

COHEN, JEROME B., EDWARD D. ZINBARG, and ARTHUR ZEIKEL, *Investment Analysis and Portfolio Management* (Homewood: Richard D. Irwin, Inc., 1973), Chs. 9–10.

ELSAID, HUSSEIN H., "Non-Convertible Preferred Stock as a Financing Instrument 1950–1965: Comment," *Journal of Finance* 24 (December, 1969), pp. 939–941.

FISHER, DONALD E., and GLENN A. WILT, JR., "Non-Convertible Preferred Stock as a Financing Instrument 1950–1965," *Journal of Finance* 23 (September, 1968), pp. 611–624.

HAWKINS, DAVID F., *Corporate Financial Reporting: Text and Cases* (Homewood: Richard D. Irwin, Inc., 1971), Chs. 11 and 18.

MELICHER, RONALD W., "Financing with Convertible Preferred Stock: Comment," *Journal of Finance* 26 (March, 1971), pp. 144–147.

PINCHES, GEORGE E., "Financing with Convertible Preferred Stock, 1960–1967," *Journal of Finance* 25 (March, 1970), pp. 53–63.

PINCHES, GEORGE E., "Financing with Convertible Preferred Stock, 1960–1967: Reply," *Journal of Finance* 26 (March, 1971), pp. 150–151.

Salomon Brothers, *Preferred Stock Guide,* 1974 Edition (New York: 1974).

SPRECHER, C. RONALD, "A Note on Financing Mergers with Convertible Preferred Stock," *Journal of Finance* 26 (June, 1971), pp. 683–685.

STEVENSON, RICHARD A., "Retirement of Non-Callable Preferred Stock," *Journal of Finance* 25 (December, 1970), pp. 1143–1152.

WEYGANDT, JERRY J., "A Comment on Financing with Convertible Preferred Stock, 1960–1967," *Journal of Finance* 26 (March, 1971), pp. 148–149.

Part Seven

Intermediate- and Short-Term Financing

20 Term Credit and Leasing

A firm's capital structure must employ not only the optimal overall debt-to-equity ratio, but also the optimal distribution of maturities among the company's sources of capital. We have already dealt, in Chapters 17 through 19, with instruments of long-term capital: stocks (which, by nature, have no maturity) and long-term bonds with initial maturities of more than 10 years. The financial executive should also understand debt instruments of intermediate (1 to 10 years) and short-term (less than 1 year) maturities. In this chapter, we shall take up four forms of intermediate credit: term loans, revolving credit, installment loans, and financial leases.

THE TERM LOAN

Nature and Uses

A term loan is any business loan with an initial maturity of more than a year. In this chapter, we shall focus on loans with maturities of one to ten years. Since banks are the chief lenders in this category, we shall concentrate on bank practices.[1] Insurance companies also make term loans but tend to prefer longer maturities.

Firms in nearly all industries use term loans for a variety of needs. Here are some examples: (1) a tobacco company increases its permanent

[1] The following discussion of bank lending practices is based in part on my personal interviews with lending officers at several large commercial banks.

working capital; (2) a merchandising firm buys shares of a firm whose control it is trying to wrest from the current management; (3) an oil company buys drilling equipment; (4) a public utility pays for the costs of a generating plant during construction; (5) a conglomerate acquires another firm; and (6) a car rental company buys a fleet of automobiles.

Loan Agreement

A term-loan contract details the amount of the loan, the rate of interest, the repayment schedule, prepayment provisions, commitment fee, compensating balance requirements, and collateral security.

Amount of Loan. A national bank may legally lend no more than 10 percent of its capital and surplus to any one firm, and a state bank is subject to similar restrictions. Apart from this legal limit, the actual amount of the loan depends on the bank's assessment of the borrowing firm's ability to repay the loan.

Rate of Interest. The interest rate is generally quoted on the basis of "prime plus." The prime rate is the rate of interest that a bank charges its customers with top credit standing and with good deposit relationships with the bank. Lesser customers are charged the prime rate plus a premium the size of which varies with the borrower's credit risk, its deposit experience with the bank, the amount of the loan, and the state of the current credit market. Since the prime interest rate fluctuates with open-market interest rates, the cost of term loans, even to prime borrowers, varies over time.

Repayment Schedule. Banks generally consider seven or eight years the maximum maturity limit for term loans; the average maturity is three to five years. Most term loans are amortized, some fully at maturity, others only partly, leaving a lump-sum payment at maturity to be refinanced by perhaps an insurance company. The repayment schedule may call for annual, semi-annual, quarterly, or monthly payments; the size of the payments may be equal, increasing, or decreasing. There is considerable room to negotiate a suitable repayment schedule.

Prepayment Provision. Most banks permit prepayment of loans before maturity. Whether or not there is a penalty depends on the source of the funds used for the prepayment: there is no penalty if the funds are generated internally by the borrowing firm; but there is a penalty if the funds come from external nonbank sources at a lower cost of capital to the firm than the original loan.

Commitment Fee. A bank usually charges no commitment fee on a term loan if it expects the funds to be "taken down" within a short time.

If, however, the firm does not expect to borrow the funds for three or four months after the loan agreement is signed, the bank may charge a commitment fee. A fee somewhere between .5 and 1 percent (on an annual basis) of the unused portion of the loan is common.

Compensating Balance. In addition to interest payment, the borrowing firm must compensate the bank for its loan by maintaining a certain minimum deposit. A requirement of "ten and five" designates a compensating balance of 10 percent of the loan during the commitment period and an additional 5 percent while the firm is actually borrowing. If this requirement necessitates a balance beyond that which the firm would normally maintain for operating purposes, its effects must be taken into account in computing the effective cost of the term loan.

Pledge of Assets. Although banks granting loan credit are primarily concerned with a firm's earning capacity, they sometimes require the pledge of specific assets as added protection. This practice is more common in loans to small companies than in loans to large firms. The most commonly pledged assets are land and buildings, machinery and equipment, and stocks and bonds.

Amortization Schedule

Almost all term loans are amortized: that is, the principal is repaid throughout the life of the loan in monthly, quarterly, semi-annual, or annual installments. Full amortization repays the total obligation by maturity; partial amortization leaves a balloon payment due at maturity. An amortization schedule can be constructed to show the division of each payment into interest and principal. Such a table enables the borrower to determine at any time the amount of the loan still outstanding. Let us consider two typical amortization schedules.

Example 1. Let us first consider a loan which is fully amortized by a series of equal annual payments beginning at the end of the first year. L is the size of the initial loan, r is the rate of interest, and n is the maturity in years. We may now determine what size annual payment A will be needed to amortize the loan fully by maturity. The lender will recover the principal plus a return of r if A satisfies the condition:

$$L = \frac{A}{(1+r)} + \frac{A}{(1+r)^2} + \ldots + \frac{A}{(1+r)^n}$$

Solving for A, we find that

$$A = \frac{L}{a_{\overline{n|}\,r}} \qquad (20\text{-}1)$$

Table 20-1 Amortization of a Term Loan

End of Year	Annual Payment	Interest on Loan	Principal Repayment	Amount of Loan Outstanding
		A. Full, Immediate Amortization		
0	–	–	–	$40,000.00
1	$10,551.90	$4,000.00	$6,551.90	33,448.10
2	10,551.90	3,344.81	7,207.09	26,241.01
3	10,551.90	2,624.10	7,927.80	18,313.21
4	10,551.90	1,831.32	8,720.58	9,592.63
5	10,551.90	959.27	9,592.63	0.00
		B. Partial, Delayed Amortization		
0	–	–	–	$40,000.00
1	$ 0.00	$4,000.00	$ 0.00	44,000.00
2	9,571.30	4,400.00	5,171.30	38,828.70
3	9,571.30	3,882.87	5,688.43	33,140.27
4	9,571.30	3,314.03	6,257.27	26,883.00
5	29,571.30	2,688.30	26,883.00	0.00

where $a_{\overline{n}|r}$ is the present value of an annuity of $1 per year for n years at an interest rate of r. Thus, if $L = \$40{,}000$, $n = 5$, and $r = 10$ percent, then $A = \$10{,}551.90$. The amortization schedule in Part A of Table 20-1 shows that an annual payment of $10,551.90 will in fact fully amortize a 10 percent $40,000 loan in 5 years.

Example 2. We now consider a partially amortized loan with a skip-payment schedule permitting the omission of payments during the initial years of the loan. L is the size of the initial loan, r is the rate of interest, n is the maturity in years, and m is the number of years elapsed before the first payment. We may now determine the annual payment necessary to amortize the loan partially so that a balance of B will remain at maturity. The lender will recover the principal plus the required return r if A satisfies the condition

$$L = \frac{A}{(1+r)^m} + \frac{A}{(1+r)^{m+1}} + \cdots + \frac{A}{(1+r)^n} + \frac{B}{(1+r)^n}$$

Solving for A, we find that

$$A = \left[L - \frac{B}{(1+r)^n}\right] \Big/ (a_{\overline{n}|r} - a_{\overline{m-1}|r}) \tag{20-2}$$

Thus, if $L = \$40{,}000$, $n = 5$, $m = 2$, $r = 10\%$, and $B = \$20{,}000$, then $A = \$9{,}571.30$. Part B of Table 20-1 shows the amortization schedule for such a transaction.

Both examples assume annual payments of equal size, but unequal annual reductions of principal. It is possible, however, to reduce the principal by an equal amount each year. In that case, if the rate of interest is fixed, the annual interest and hence the annual payment decreases systematically. If, however, the interest rate varies with the prime rate, equal principal reduction results in irregular-sized payments.

The Effective Rate of Interest

The interest rate in the preceding examples is actually the nominal rate of interest and does not take into account the tax deductibility of interest or the bank's compensating balance requirement. Most banks require that a borrower's average deposit balance be at least equal to a certain percentage of the credit line. If the borrower normally maintains a lower average deposit, he must borrow beyond his true needs to meet the bank's requirement. This excess borrowing naturally increases the effective cost of money to the firm.

Let us say a firm needs Q dollars in order to buy equipment, but that it must borrow a larger amount L in order to keep a compensating balance of c percent of L on deposit at the bank. Let us also assume that the firm normally maintains an average deposit of M dollars, which is less than the required balance of cL dollars. Thus, $(cL - M)$ is the portion of the loan needed to raise the deposit level at the bank to its required level. If the firm needs Q dollars, it must negotiate a gross loan of L dollars such that[2]

$$\underset{\text{Gross loan}}{L} - \underset{\text{Compensating balance}}{(cL - M)} = \underset{\text{Net loan}}{Q} \tag{20-3}$$

It follows that $L = \dfrac{Q - M}{1 - c}$; and if r is the nominal interest rate and τ is the marginal tax rate, the after-tax interest rate k_i is given by the expression

$$k_i = \frac{(Q - M)(1 - \tau)}{(1 - c)Q}\, r \tag{20-4}$$

The relationship between the nominal and effective interest rates depends on the size of the firm's voluntary deposit balance M relative to

[2] Cf. Kenneth E. Reich and Dennis C. Neff, *Customer Profitability Analysis: A Tool for Improving Bank Profits* (Park Ridge: Bank Administration Institute, 1972), Appendix 1; see also William E. Gibson, "Compensating Balance Requirements," *National Banking Review* 2 (March, 1965), pp. 387–395.

the bank's compensatory balance requirement cL. We can show this relationship by substituting (20-3) into (20-4) to obtain

$$k_i = \frac{L(1-\tau)}{L(1-c)+M}\, r \tag{20-5}$$

Since it is unlikely that the bank requirement will be less than the borrower's voluntary balance, two cases remain. If the bank requirement is the same as the firm's voluntary balance (i.e., $cL = M$), then (20-5) implies $k_i = (1-\tau)r$. Second, if the bank requirement exceeds the voluntary balance (i.e., $cL > M$), then (20-5) implies $k_i > (1-\tau)r$. The after-tax effective interest rate is therefore either equal to or greater than the after-tax nominal rate, depending on whether the bank's compensating balance requirement is equal to or greater than the borrower's voluntary deposit balance.

To illustrate, let us suppose that a firm needs \$40,000 to pay for equipment. The firm pays taxes at the rate of 50 percent. It normally maintains a deposit balance of \$4,000 at a bank whose nominal interest rate on loans is 10 percent. Since this bank's compensating balance requirement is 10 percent of the loan, a \$4,000 deposit will support a loan of \$40,000. The company may therefore borrow exactly the amount it needs, so that the after-tax nominal rate of interest—5 percent—is also the effective rate of interest.

If, however, the firm keeps a voluntary deposit balance of only \$2,000, it must borrow \$42,222.22 in order to have \$40,000 to spend. Although the firm's deposit is only \$2,000 less than we assumed above, the gross loan would have to increase by \$2,222.22 in order to compensate for the original deficiency of \$2,000 and in order to satisfy the 10 percent requirement for the extra loan itself. As Eq. (20-4) shows, the after-tax effective rate of interest in this case is 5.27 percent:

$$k_i = \frac{(40{,}000 - 2{,}000)(.5)}{(1 - .1)(40{,}000)} \times 10\% = 5.27\%$$

Two other factors may also increase the cost of borrowing. First, if there is a substantial delay before a negotiated loan is utilized, a commitment fee may be required for the idle period. We shall postpone our discussion of these fees until the next section, since they are most commonly associated with revolving credit. Second, small, financially weak companies must sometimes provide additional incentives to lenders, often in the form of stock-purchase warrants or conversion options. We considered these incentive devices in Chapter 18.

REVOLVING CREDIT AND INSTALLMENT FINANCING

Revolving Credit

Nature and Uses. Revolving credit is a form of intermediate-term financing unique to commercial banks. Unlike a single-transaction term loan, revolving credit is an ongoing arrangement that permits repeated borrowing and repayment so long as the total indebtedness at any time does not exceed a predetermined limit. Such flexibility is valuable to a firm that foresees a future need for credit but is unsure of the timing and extent of the need. For example, a firm planning to acquire some new equipment and to trade in some old equipment may not be able to predict exactly the number of pieces to be traded in or acquired. Or a firm needing increased inventories and receivables financing to meet rising sales may not know if the sales growth will be permanent or temporary. Such firms may find term loans too rigid, since the amount, duration, and repayment schedule must be agreed upon initially. But revolving credit permits flexibility in the face of uncertain permanent needs. Once the needs have crystallized, the revolving credit may be replaced by a term loan or another form of long-term credit. Many loan agreements, in fact, known as "convertible revolvers," specifically give the borrower the option of converting the revolving credit into regular term loans on or before the date of maturity.

Like a term loan, revolving credit is evidenced by a loan agreement signed by both parties. Some points are shared by both types of agreement. Interest rates for both are quoted on a prime-plus basis; the interest rate is usually the same for the two types of loan. Banks require compensating balances on both kinds of loan. And both loans have maturities of one year or more, although the maturity of revolving credit is usually shorter than that of a term loan.

There are, however, certain differences. Many term loans, especially those to small borrowers, are secured; but since revolving credit is generally restricted to large borrowers to begin with, these loans are usually unsecured. Whereas term loans are generally amortized, with periodic payments scheduled in advance, revolving credit requires no payback until maturity. Thus, if a revolving credit is for three years, money borrowed under the agreement need not be repaid until the end of the 3-year period. And finally, whereas a commitment fee is charged on a term loan only when there is a significant interval before takedown, commitment fees are universally required for revolving credit. When money is tight, the fee may be as high as 1 percent per annum on the unused portion of the credit line.

Effective Rate of Interest. The calculation of the effective rate of interest on revolving credit is complicated by two facts: the borrower may go into and out of debt, and the bank invariably imposes a commitment fee on any unused credit. Let us suppose that under revolving credit the ABC Company can borrow a maximum of $1.2 million at a nominal interest rate of 8 percent. We shall focus on the first year, assuming that it is representative. The firm forecasts that, with different probabilities, it will be out of debt for one fourth or one half of the year. It forecasts also that, during the part of the year that it is in debt, its needs will be, with certain probabilities, $600,000, $800,000, or $1 million. Table 20-2 provides the probability distribution for the firm's forecasts.

The bank requires a compensating balance of 15 percent of the $1.2 million credit line, whereas the firm's voluntary deposit balance is only $75,000. Temporary surplus funds beyond the required compensating balance are normally invested in marketable securities at a net return (after expenses) of only 5 percent. The bank also requires a 1 percent commitment fee on the average daily unused portion of the credit line. The income of the firm is subject to a marginal tax of 50 percent.

There are six possible combinations of the amount and the duration of the firm's cash needs. Table 20-3 shows the calculation of the effective rate of interest for one of these combinations: $600,000 for half a year. During the half year the firm is in debt, it must borrow $705,000: $600,000 to meet actual cash needs and $105,000 to raise its deposit balance to the bank's requirement. The interest on the two parts of the loan is $24,000 and $4,200, respectively. In addition, there is a $2,475 commitment fee on the unused portion of the credit line. During the half of the year that the firm is out of debt, it must continue to maintain the compensating balance. At an opportunity cost of 5 percent, the involuntary $105,000 of deposit costs the firm $2,625 in foregone interest. The commitment fee for this part of the year is $6,000. For the entire year, then, interest and commitment fees total $39,300, or $19,650 after taxes. Dividing the last figure by the average net borrowing of $300,000 for the year gives the effective cost of the firm's revolving credit: 6.55 percent per annum.

Effective interest rates can be similarly calculated for the other five combinations. Taking a weighted average of the six rates, we find the ex-

Table 20-2 Joint Probability Distribution of Amount and Duration of Cash Needs

	Duration	
Amount	6 Months	9 Months
$ 600,000	.20	.25
800,000	.25	.10
1,000,000	.10	.10

Table 20-3 The Effective Interest Rate of a Revolving Credit

Interest and commitment fee		
Half year in debt		
Interest on net loan	($600,000)(.08)(.5)	$ 24,000
Interest on borrowed compensating balance	($105,000)(.08)(.5)	4,200
Commitment fee	($495,000)(.01)(.5)	2,475
Half year free of debt		
Interest on involuntary compensating balance	($105,000)(.05)(.5)	2,625
Commitment fee	($1,200,000)(.01)(.5)	6,000
Total cost (before-tax)		$ 39,300
Average net borrowing per year		$300,000
Effective interest rate (after-tax)	($19,650)/($300,000)	6.55%

pected after-tax cost of the revolving credit—in this case, 5.67 percent. This effective rate is less than the effective rate of interest for a $1.2 million term loan at 8 percent. Even though any portion of borrowed term-loan funds that turned out to be surplus could be reinvested, the net return on the surplus would be only 5 percent—3 percent less than the nominal interest rate. Under revolving credit, however, a firm with surplus funds may simply reduce the amount of its borrowing, thereby paying only a 1 percent commitment fee—a smaller penalty than the 3 percent net loss under a term loan. The after-tax cost for a term loan to our sample company, in fact, would be 6.85 percent.

Installment Financing

Nature and Uses.[3] Many businesses use industrial installment loans to spread the cost of equipment purchases over an extended period of time. These credit contracts typically have long maturities, although rarely as long as the life of the equipment.

It was natural that finance companies were the first to supply industrial installment credit as they had been engaged in consumer installment financing since the 1920's. Banks, on the other hand, were initially reluctant to engage in direct installment financing, primarily because of the social stigma then attached to installment credit. They did, however, supply much of the capital used in such financing by finance companies. By the 1930's, however,

[3] For a more extensive analysis, see Robert L. Krause, "Financing Industrial Time Sales," in Monroe R. Lazere, ed., *Commercial Financing* (New York: The Ronald Press Company, 1968), Ch. 7.

especially after the Depression, banks had such large reserves and so few demands for business loans that they were forced to become active in consumer installment financing. Experience in this field generally wore down the aversion to installment financing. This, coupled with the discovery that such financing was highly profitable, led banks to enter the field of installment credit for industry as well as for consumers.

Business assets purchased on installment credit now include every conceivable type of equipment: vending machines, printing equipment, machine tools, dental and surgical equipment, and trucks and bulldozers. Lenders involved in equipment financing sometimes extend credit directly to the user of the equipment, but a conditional sales agreement between the seller, the purchaser, and the lender is more common. The purchaser gives the seller a cash down payment and an interest-bearing installment note for the balance. The seller then converts the note into cash by discounting it with a bank or finance company.[4] The conditional sales agreement stipulates that the purchaser will not receive legal title to the equipment until he has fulfilled his contractual agreement. Meanwhile, of course, he has use of the equipment and is responsible for related property taxes, insurance, and maintenance. If the purchaser defaults, the lender immediately recovers the unpaid balance from the seller, who may repossess the equipment for resale. If the proceeds from the sale do not cover the unpaid balance, the purchaser is responsible for the difference. There is one exception to this procedure: if the lender purchases the note from the seller "without recourse," the lender himself must repossess the equipment.

Because installment credit is costly to administer, it tends to bear a higher interest rate than term loans or revolving credit. Firms buying equipment on installment credit are usually, therefore, small firms ineligible for the other types of credit, and are generally greater credit risks. This risk, in turn, reinforces the interest differential between installment credit and other loans.

Effective Rate of Interest. Ordinarily, the interest on a loan for any period is computed on the outstanding balance during that period; but installment credit lenders calculate interest according to the add-on method in which interest is computed on the entire initial loan balance. Thus, if L is the initial loan balance, r is the add-on interest rate, n is the loan maturity in years, and m indicates the number of payments each year, then the total interest, the face value of the installment note, and the size of each payment are given by these formulas:

---

[4] Finance companies that serve consumers are known as sales finance or consumer finance companies; those that serve businesses are known as commercial finance companies. Here we are dealing with commercial finance companies.

Total interest	Lrn
Face value of note	$L(1 + rn)$
Size of each payment	$L(1 + rn)/nm$

Each payment includes not only interest, but also the amortization of the principal, figured on a straight-line basis. When the frequency of payments is high, the net borrowing is only about one half of the initial loan balance. Since the interest is based on the full initial balance, the before-tax effective rate of interest is approximately double the nominal rate stipulated in the contract.

Let us suppose that a firm pays 15 percent down on \$50,000 worth of equipment and borrows the remaining \$42,500 from a finance company. The initial loan balance plus the interest are to be paid in 36 monthly installments. If the add-on rate is 12 percent, the total interest will be \$15,300 (= \$42,500 × .12 × 3). The borrowing firm must therefore sign an installment note with a face value of \$57,800 (= \$42,500 + \$15,300), calling for 36 monthly payments of \$1,605.56 each. The effective interest rate is given by the discount rate that equates the present value of the entire series of payments with the initial loan balance. This discount rate is approximately twice the nominal add-on rate of 12 percent. The after-tax cost of this loan is therefore about 12 percent annually.

THE FINANCIAL LEASE

Leasing has been used in real estate financing for centuries, and was extended to equipment financing after World War II. Today, nearly any asset may be leased: airplane hangars, retail stores, computers, road-building equipment, railroad cars, printing presses, nuclear fuel cores, offshore drilling platforms—even dairy cattle. The major lessors are banks, insurance companies, leasing companies, pension funds, charitable foundations, educational institutions, and individual investors.

The Leasing Alternative

The Nature of Leases. A lease is a contract whereby the lessor (owner) grants the lessee (user) the use of an asset in return for a promise to pay a series of rentals over the leasing period. By separating use from ownership, a lease enables a firm to enjoy the services of an asset without incurring the large initial cost of purchase. There are two kinds of lease: financial and operating. A financial lease has a relatively long term, is not cancellable by the lessee, and provides for full payout: i.e., the payments are large enough to permit the lessor to recover his entire capital investment plus his required rate of return. An operating lease has a relatively short term, is cancellable by the lessee, and provides less than full payout. The lessor thus assumes the risk that after the initial term, the asset may not be resold or re-leased at a price high enough to cover his investment plus required rate of return. An operating lease is thus essentially a device by which the lessee may shift the risk of ownership, especially of assets subject to rapid obsolescence, to lessors specializing in assuming such risks. Financial leases, since they provide full payout, impose no ownership risk on the lessor, although he does incur credit risks. Being a financing device, such leases place the responsibility for taxes, maintenance, and insurance on the lessee. Our concern here is with this type of lease.

Why Lease? Since a financial lease binds the lessee firm to a series of payments, it is similar to a debt contract. Whether or not it is advisable to lease can be determined only by comparing the consequences of leasing with those of the nearest alternative: purchasing the asset with borrowed funds. We shall assume that a firm has already decided to invest in an asset and has decided against equity financing. The remaining choice is thus between debt financing and leasing. At least seven reasons, singly or in combination, may prompt a firm to lease:

1. *Unavailability of debt financing.* Small and medium-sized firms frequently do not qualify for long-term debt financing. Moreover, for many of them, leasing is the only form of intermediate-term credit that is generally available.
2. *100 percent financing.* Financially weak companies often find that straight-debt lenders require large down payments, and so they receive less than the full value of the equipment. These same companies may be able to obtain more financing through leasing.
3. *Longer maturity.* Whereas the maturity of a term loan usually depends on the lender's general policy, the term of a lease is based on the life of the equipment.
4. *Off-balance-sheet financing.* A lease, like debt, imposes a fixed charge on a firm; but the lease does not appear on the balance sheet except as a footnote. Insofar as credit analysts slight footnotes, leasing enables a firm to increase its total credit pool. New accounting rules, however, may require firms to show lease obligations as a liability.
5. *Less restrictive covenants.* The covenants in lease agreements are usually less restrictive than those in term-loan agreements.
6. *Internal decision process.* In some firms, the manager of a division may authorize leasing but only corporate management may authorize purchase.

7. *Lower effective cost of money.* The cost of leasing depends on the nominal lease rate, maturity, taxes, and residual value. In some situations, leasing is less expensive than borrowing.

The Lease Agreement

In a typical transaction, the lessee tells the lessor what equipment he needs; the lessor then purchases the equipment and leases it to the lessee for a fee (see Figure 20-1). A written document then sets forth the essential aspects of the lease agreement.

Amount of Financing. Since the lessee makes no down payment, the lessor nominally finances the entire purchase price of the equipment. Some leases, however, require that the lessee make the first and last rental payments in advance. These payments reduce the net amount of financing to less than 100 percent of the purchase price.

Payment Schedule. The lessee is quoted a payment schedule stating not the percentage cost of money but the dollar amount of each rental payment. The number and size of these payments depend on the lessor's required rate of return, which in turn varies with the lessee's credit risk, type of equipment, the term of the lease, money market conditions, and the size of the transaction. The time pattern of rental payments is generally negotiable.

Term. Since payment size varies inversely with term, the lessee may prefer a long maturity. The lessor, on the other hand, may prefer a short maturity to minimize risk. The crucial factor in term, however, is the economic life of the leased property.

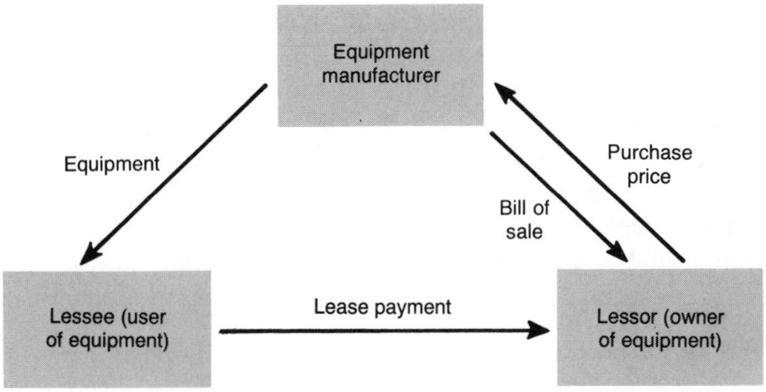

Figure 20-1 A Financial Lease

Disposition of Equipment at Expiration. Since the lessor is the actual owner of the equipment, he has the right to stipulate where, when, and how it is to be returned to him. Usually, the lessee has the option to purchase the equipment at fair market value or to renew his lease at fair market rental. If purchase price or renewal rental were not based on fair market value, the IRS could rule the transaction a conditional sale for tax purposes.

Settlement Value for Casualty Occurrence. Every lease agreement contains a casualty-value schedule specifying the amount, for any given time, that the lessee must pay the lessor if the equipment is totally destroyed. The same schedule serves as a basis for negotiating settlement value if the lessee wishes to trade in or abandon the equipment. In that case, since the lessee receives a benefit and since the tax implications for the lessor are unfavorable, the lessor will require a larger payment as compensation for lease termination.

Investment Tax Credit. A special provision in the present tax law states that a lessor may pass on his investment tax credit (ITC) to the lessee. The lease agreement specifies whether or not this election is made.

The Lease Amortization Schedule

The amortization schedule of a term loan shows the division of each payment into interest and principal and thus indicates the amount of the loan still outstanding at any given time. An analogous amortization schedule can be constructed for a lease to show how much of each payment is for capital recovery and how much is for imputed return; the lessor may thus see how much of his investment is still outstanding at any given time. The calculation is complicated, of course, by the fact that the lessor's cash inflow includes not only rental payments but also the tax savings provided by depreciation and ITC (if any).

Suppose that the Hagenford Leasing Company has agreed to purchase a $1,000 piece of equipment to lease to the Purple Shoe Company for 8 years.[5] The rental schedule calls for eight annual payments of $161.12 each, with the first payment due at the beginning of the leasing period.[6] To construct the amortization schedule, we must first determine the imputed yield on the lessor's investment. We shall assume that the lessor retains a 7 percent investment tax credit, uses the double-declining-balance method of depreciation, and is subject to a combined federal and state corporate income tax of 58 percent. Table 20-4 shows the derivation of the lessor's cash

[5] The data for this example are from the files of an actual leasing company; the names of the lessor and the lessee have been altered.

[6] All calculations pertaining to this example have been computerized, using the program in Figure B-6 of Appendix B.

Table 20-4 Lessor's Cash Inflows (+) and Outflows (−)

End of Year	Rental Income (1)	Depreciation (2)	Income Tax Payment or Saving (3)	Capital Outlay (4)	Net Flow (1) + (3) + (4)
0	$161.12	$ 0.00	−$23.45*	−$1,000.00	−$862.32
1	161.12	250.00	51.55	–	212.67
2	161.12	187.50	15.30	–	176.42
3	161.12	140.63	−11.88	–	149.24
4	161.12	105.47	−32.27	–	128.85
5	161.12	79.10	−47.57	–	113.55
6	161.12	59.33	−59.03	–	102.09
7	161.12	44.49	−67.64	–	93.48
8	0.00	133.48	77.42	–	77.42

* The ITC, 7%, is received immediately so that the net tax effect in year 0 = $70 − $161.12 × .58.

flows. At the end of year 0 (i.e., at the beginning of the leasing period), the lessor pays $1,000 for the equipment, receives $161.12 in rental, and pays $23.45 in taxes, for a net outflow of $862.32. At the end of year 1, he again receives $161.12 in rental, but he depreciates his equipment by $250, reducing his taxable income by $88.88. He thus has a tax savings of $51.55 and a net cash inflow of $212.67. It should be observed that accelerated depreciation accounts for the large cash inflow in year 1 and smaller inflows in later years.

The cash flows imply an *IRR* of 5.66 percent on the lessor's investment. Since the cash flows are after tax, this rate is equivalent to a before-tax return of 13.47 percent for a taxpayer in the 58 percent bracket. Hence, to the lessor, the lease is equal in profitability to a 13.47 percent term loan. The 5.66 percent after-tax rate is the implied return used to construct the lease amortization schedule in Table 20-5. Hagenford invested a net of $862.32 at the beginning of the lease period. He has an inflow of $212.67 at the end of

Table 20-5 Amortization of a Lease

End of Year	Net Flow	Imputed Interest	Recovery of Principal	Outstanding Balance	Casualty Payment
0	−$862.32	–	–	$862.32	$1,000.00
1	212.67	$48.78	$163.89	698.43	955.00
2	176.42	39.51	136.91	561.52	887.91
3	149.24	31.76	117.48	444.04	802.40
4	128.85	25.12	103.73	340.31	645.52
5	113.55	19.25	94.30	246.01	530.22
6	102.09	13.92	88.17	157.84	346.68
7	93.48	8.93	84.55	73.28	206.80
8	77.42	4.15	73.28	0.00	0.00

year 1; since the imputed return is 5.66 percent, \$48.78 of this inflow represents interest income and the remaining \$163.89 represents recovery of principal, reducing the outstanding principal to \$698.43. At the end of year 2, the inflow is \$176.42, of which \$39.51 is interest income and \$136.91 is principal recovery, reducing the outstanding principal to \$561.52. Proceeding similarly, we see that net inflows are sufficient to recover the initial investment of \$862.32 plus an after-tax return of 5.66 percent.

The outstanding lease principal is related, but not identical, to the casualty settlement value. The difference is that a lessor receiving a casualty payment must pay income tax on the portion of the payment in excess of the book value of the asset destroyed. In addition, he must repay the original ITC benefit to the government, in inverse proportion to the time the equipment has been in use. In order for the lessor to recover his capital in full, the casualty payment must exceed the value of the outstanding lease principal by the amount of the net tax. At the end of year 1, for example, Hagenford has taken \$250 in depreciation; the equipment has a book value of \$750; the \$70 of ITC must be repaid in full; and the outstanding principal (*before* second rental payment) is \$911.10 (= \$862.32 × 1.0566). Hence, the casualty payment X must be such that

$$\underbrace{X}_{\text{Casualty payment}} - \underbrace{(X - \$750)(.58)}_{\text{Tax on gain}} - \underbrace{\$70}_{\text{Repayment of ITC}} + \underbrace{\$250(.58)}_{\text{Tax benefit of depreciation}} = \underbrace{\$911.10}_{\text{Lease principal}}$$

Solving this equation, we find that X equals \$955. Casualty payments are computed in a similar way for other years.

The Cost of Money to the Lessee

The lessee is legally obligated to make the rental payments for the full term of the lease (barring casualty). Given the lease payment schedule, the lessee may compute a nominal lease rate by finding the discount rate that equates the present value of his payments to the cost of the equipment. This discount rate is comparable to the nominal rate of interest in straight debt financing. Thus, Purple Shoe's lease carries a nominal rate of 8 percent:

$$\$1{,}000 = \frac{\$161.12}{(1+.08)^0} + \frac{\$161.12}{(1+.08)^1} + \cdots + \frac{\$161.12}{(1+.08)^7}$$

This 8 percent figure, however, ignores the effects of income tax. Since a rental payment is entirely deductible, each dollar of rental payment costs a firm in the 50 percent tax bracket only 50 cents in cash outflow. In most cases, therefore, a firm actually pays less in total after-tax rentals than the net financing it obtains under the lease. This does not, of course, mean that the effective cost of leasing is lower than that of borrowing. The firm obtains the deductibility of its rental payments only by forfeiting the depreciation that it could have charged against income had it bought the equipment with borrowed funds.

In deriving the cash flows of leasing vs. borrowing, the tax trade-off between lease payment and depreciation may be taken into account in either of two ways. For each alternative – lease and debt – the net cash flow may be calculated by deducting the associated tax savings. Or the differential tax impact may be calculated by subtracting the tax savings of one alternative from those of the other, then adjusting the cash flows. Since the first method is simpler, we shall use it in the next section as we analyze the decision to lease or borrow.

THE LEASE-OR-BORROW DECISION

Analytical Framework

The relative costs of leasing and borrowing are affected by the differential impact of the two methods on the firm's tax position. One must also consider whether or not the leased property has a positive salvage value at the end of the lease (see Table 20-6). If the firm leases, each rental payment is a deductible expense. The lessor is entitled to depreciation and ITC, unless the ITC is passed on to the lessee. The lessor is also entitled to any salvage value at expiration. If the firm borrows enough capital to purchase the equipment, the interest is deductible; and the firm, as owner, is entitled to depreciation, ITC, and salvage value.

Table 20-6 Differences Between Leasing and Borrowing

Leasing	Lessee entitled to:	Lessor entitled to:
	Rental payment deduction	Depreciation deduction ITC benefit Salvage value
Borrowing	Borrower entitled to:	Lender entitled to:
	Depreciation deduction Interest deduction ITC benefit Salvage value	No deductions

An Illustration

The Purple Shoe Company leases a $1,000 piece of equipment for 8 years at an annual rental of $161.12. To compare the cost of this lease with borrowing, we assume that the company could have borrowed the necessary funds at 11 percent, a rate intermediate between the nominal lease rate and the before-tax lease yield. Since the first lease payment is due at the outset, the lease financing is in effect reduced to 83.88 percent of the cost of the equipment. To make the borrowing situation comparable to the lease, we shall assume a required down payment of 16.12 percent. The loan will be repaid in 7 annual installments of $178.05, the first due at the end of year 1. Depreciation is still calculated by the double-declining-balance method over an 8-year period; salvage value is still assumed to be zero at the end of year 8. The lessor receives the ITC under leasing, but Purple Shoe receives this benefit under borrowing. The company is in a 50 percent income-tax bracket.

Since the alternatives are mutually exclusive, the decision whether to lease or to borrow must take into account the rate at which any cash savings can be reinvested. We shall set this rate at 5.5 percent, the firm's after-tax borrowing rate. Whichever alternative is chosen, the full savings are virtually certain, so that a low rate of return is sufficient to justify the choice.

As in choosing between various depreciation methods in Chapter 9, we shall compare the alternatives here in terms of the future values of their net cash flows. Since the decision to lease or borrow will not affect the rate at which the market capitalizes the firm's earnings, a larger future value implies a larger present value as well. The future-value criterion enables us to avoid the *NPV* formula, which assumes equality between the market capitalization rate and the firm's reinvestment rate—an assumption which may not always hold.

To determine the effective cost of leasing, we begin with the lease payment schedule (see Part A of Table 20-7). From this we subtract the tax savings arising from rental deductions and derive a net cash flow series. Compounding these flows at 5.5 percent, we get a total cost of $825.24 (future value). To determine the effective cost of borrowing, we start with the down payment and the loan repayment schedule (see Part B of Table 20-7). From this we subtract the tax savings arising from the 7 percent ITC and the interest and depreciation deductions, and derive another net cash flow series. Compounding these flows at 5.5 percent, we get a total cost of $789.45 (future value). Leasing is therefore $35.79 more expensive (in future value) than borrowing.

The result illustrates a general principle for profitable firms. If leasing and borrowing provide the same amount of net financing and if the borrowing rate is only moderately higher than the nominal lease rate, then leasing will probably be more costly than borrowing. In choosing leasing over borrowing, the firm is in effect trading off interest and accelerated depreci-

Table 20-7 Purple Shoe Company: Leasing vs. Borrowing

A. Cost of Leasing

End of Year	Lease Payment	Tax Savings	Net Cash Flow	Future Value of Net Cash Flow
0	$161.12	$80.56	$80.56	$123.63
1	161.12	80.56	80.56	117.19
2	161.12	80.56	80.56	110.08
3	161.12	80.56	80.56	105.29
4	161.12	80.56	80.56	99.80
5	161.12	80.56	80.56	94.60
6	161.12	80.56	80.56	89.66
7	161.12	80.56	80.56	84.99
8	0.00	0.00	0.00	0.00
			Total Future Value	$825.24

B. Cost of Borrowing

End of Year	Down Payment	Loan Repayment	Interest	Deprecia-tion	Tax Savings	Net Cash Flow	Future Value of Net Cash Flow
0	$161.12	$ 0.00	$ 0.00	$ 0.00	$ 70.00	$ 91.12	$139.84
1	0.00	178.05	92.29	250.00	171.15	6.90	10.04
2	0.00	178.05	82.86	187.50	135.18	42.87	59.11
3	0.00	178.05	72.39	140.63	106.51	71.54	93.50
4	0.00	178.05	60.76	105.47	83.12	94.93	117.61
5	0.00	178.05	47.86	79.10	63.48	114.57	134.53
6	0.00	178.05	33.54	59.33	46.44	131.61	146.49
7	0.00	178.05	17.64	44.49	31.07	146.98	155.07
8	0.00	0.00	0.00	133.48	66.74	−66.74	−66.74
				Total Future Value			$789.45

ation for rental payments, but interest and depreciation generally provide a greater tax shield. Residual value, if any, also tends to favor borrowing.

The above example assumes, however, that Purple Shoe uses the ITC to reduce its immediate tax bill by $70. Purple Shoe may not be paying sufficient taxes to take full advantage of its ITC. Without the $70 of immediate tax credit, the cost of borrowing will increase to $896.87 (future value), making it $71.63 more costly than leasing. Moreover, if Purple Shoe is operating at a loss, it will be unable to benefit even from the deductibility of interest and depreciation. In that case, leasing enables the firm to "sell" its depreciation and ITC as tax shields to a profitable lessor that can benefit from them. If this arrangement prompts the lessor to make sizeable reductions in lease payments, leasing can be more advantageous than borrowing.

We should note, however, that when a firm tries to "sell" its depreciation and ITC, not all lessors are equal in their ability to benefit from them.

In fact, one bank recently had an overabundance of depreciation and ITC and had to shift from accelerated to straight-line depreciation in order to prevent a negative taxable income. The firm should shop around for a lessor who can best use the ITC and depreciation deductions and thus offer the best leasing terms.

A Final Note

We have seen how tax savings can play a key role in making leasing viable. These savings, of course, can be realized only if the contract qualify as a lease for tax purposes. The IRS regards the following features as characteristic of a true lease:

1. The leased property has a reasonable economic life remaining at the end of the lease term.
2. The lessee does not have a renewal option except at competitive rentals.
3. The lessee does not have a purchase option except at fair market value.

If these conditions (especially the last two) are not met, the IRS may rule the contract a loan transaction and tax accordingly.

In addition to tax savings, some lessors try to reduce the cost of leasing even more by introducing financial leverage directly into a lease. Two benefits, as we mentioned in Chapter 6, result from this leverage: the lessor acquires a greater tax shelter per dollar of investment; and, to the extent that borrowing costs are lower than the overall return from a lease, the return on the lessor's equity is increased. Some lessees in fact insist that the lessor incorporate debt in structuring the lease and may even specify the maximum interest rate which the lessor is allowed to pay on the debt. The resulting higher return to the lessor enables him to reduce rental payments so that both lessor and lessee benefit. The lessee judges a lease in terms of the number and size of payments he has to make. Given the payment schedule, the lessee can then compare the relative costs of borrowing and leasing in the same way as with a nonleveraged lease.

REVIEW QUESTIONS

1. What is a term loan? How does it differ from revolving credit? When and why would a firm choose a term loan over revolving credit? revolving credit over a term loan?
2. Commercial banks use a compensating balance to raise the true interest rate on loans above the nominal rate. At one time, Bankers Trust Company ad-

vertised no-balance loans with a true rate $2\frac{3}{4}$ percent above the rate it paid on its own certificates of deposits, plus a risk premium when necessary. What are the advantages and disadvantages of this explicitness in pricing bank loans —from the viewpoint of the bank? from the viewpoint of the borrower?

3. Why is the effective cost of installment financing nearly double the nominal rate of interest? Explain the add-on method of computing interest.

4. When a railroad finances its purchases with equipment trust certificates, a trust is set up to take title to the equipment and to lease it to the railroad, with the certificate holders as beneficiaries. Why does the IRS not view this kind of lease as a true lease?

5. Purple Shoe found that it could lease shoe equipment at a future value cost of \$825.24, which is 1.045 times the future value cost of \$789.45 associated with borrowing (see Table 20-7). Since the firm's borrowing interest rate is 11 percent, is it correct to say that the cost of leasing is 1.045 times 11 percent, or 11.5 percent?

6. Which financial variables determine the relative costs of leasing and borrowing? Explain the exact way in which each variable affects cost. Is leasing always cheaper than borrowing? or borrowing than leasing? What combination of factors makes one method less costly than the other?

7. Describe the financial arrangement in a leveraged lease. How may a firm use leverage to obtain funds more cheaply?

8. Describe the financial arrangement in a tax-shelter lease. How may a firm "sell" its ITC and depreciation to obtain funds more cheaply?

9. The following announcement appeared in a financial newspaper: Bankers Trust Company leased \$15 million of data-processing equipment from the American Road Equity Corporation (equity investor) and the NRG Incorporated (agent for senior lender). Why would Bankers Trust choose to lease the equipment from an outside company rather than from its own leasing department?

10. The SIG 400 Corporation designs, makes, and markets medium- and high-speed computer terminals which are leased, not sold. Instead of leasing directly, SIG 400 has a subsidiary, SIG 400 Leasing Inc., which purchases the terminals from the parent company and then leases them to users. What are the advantages of this indirect arrangement?

PROBLEMS

1. The Orange Tree Company needs \$100,000 in cash. Its tax rate is 50 percent. A bank will lend money to Orange Tree at 9 percent, plus a 20 percent compensating balance. The firm normally maintains a voluntary balance of \$8,000. How much must the company borrow to meet the bank's requirements? What will the effective cost of money be? Answer the same questions assuming that the firm's normal voluntary balance is only \$4,000.

2. Crafton Brothers, Inc., bought a \$70,500 piece of equipment, paying 10 percent down, with the balance to be paid over 36 months at an add-on interest rate of 9 percent. Calculate the total interest, the face value of the installment note, and the size of monthly payments. What is the effective cost of money?

3. After studying the method used in Table 20-3 to determine the effective rate of interest (k_i) of a revolving credit, work out an algebraic formula which will express clearly the procedure for determining this rate of interest.
4. Derive a corresponding formula for k_i for a term loan, taking into account the basic differences between a term loan and revolving credit.
5. Use the procedure from Table 20-3 to verify the before-tax effective interest rates of revolving credit and of term loans to ABC under each of six amount-duration combinations:

Amount-Duration	Revolving Credit	Term Loan
$1,000,000–1/2 year	10.66%	12.41%
1,000,000–3/4 year	9.51	9.94
800,000–1/2 year	11.58	14.26
800,000–3/4 year	10.13	11.17
600,000–1/2 year	13.10	17.35
600,000–3/4 year	11.18	13.23

6. Make the following changes in the data given for the Purple Shoe lease: assume that the nominal lease rate is 9 percent and that the firm's borrowing interest rate is 13 percent. Re-compute the lessor's cash flows, the lease amortization schedule, and the relative costs of leasing and borrowing.
7. Redo Problem 6 using the computer program in Figure B-6 of Appendix B.
8. Make the following changes in the original data given for the Purple Shoe lease: assume that the firm forecasts that at the end of year 8 the equipment will have a residual value with a certainty equivalent of 10 percent of the original cost. Re-compute the relative costs of leasing and borrowing.

REFERENCES

"Accounting Board Proposes New Rules in Controversial Area of Lease Reporting," *Wall Street Journal,* August 29, 1975, p. 13.

BERGER, PAUL D., and WILLIAM K. HARPER, "Determination of An Optimal Revolving Credit Agreement," *Journal of Financial and Quantitative Analysis* 8 (June, 1973), pp. 491–497.

"Changes in Bank Lending Practices, 1973," *Federal Reserve Bulletin* 60 (April, 1974), pp. 263–267.

CROSSE, HOWARD D., and GEORGE H. HEMPEL, *Management Policies for Commercial Banks* (Englewood Cliffs: Prentice-Hall, Inc., 1973), Chs. 10 and 11.

GIBSON, WILLIAM E., "Compensating Balance Requirements," *National Banking Review* 2 (March, 1965), pp. 387–395.

GORDON, MYRON J., "A General Solution to the Buy or Lease Decision: A Pedagogical Note," *Journal of Finance* 29 (March, 1974), pp. 245–250.

HAYES, DOUGLAS A., *Bank Lending Policies* (Ann Arbor: Bureau of Business Research, The University of Michigan, 1971), Chs. 5, 6, and 7.

JOHNSON, ROBERT W., and WILBUR G. LEWELLEN, "Analysis of the Lease or Buy Decision," *Journal of Finance* 27 (September, 1972), pp. 815–823.

KRAUSE, ROBERT L., "Financing Industrial Time Sales," in Monroe R. Lazere, ed., *Commercial Financing* (New York: The Ronald Press Company, 1968), Ch. 7.

MCGUGAN, VINCENT J., and RICHARD E. CAVES, "Integration and Competition in the Equipment Leasing Industry," *Journal of Business* 47 (July, 1974), pp. 382–396.

MURRAY, THOMAS J., "The Big Splash in Pooled Leasing," *Dun's* 100 (December, 1972), pp. 51–52, 134.

REICH, KENNETH E., and DENNIS C. NEFF, *Customer Profitability Analysis: A Tool for Improving Bank Profits* (Park Ridge: Bank Administration Institute, 1972).

"Survey of Finance Companies, 1970," *Federal Reserve Bulletin* 58 (November, 1972), pp. 958–972.

VANDERWICKEN, PETER, "The Powerful Logic of the Leasing Boom," *Fortune* 83 (November, 1973), pp. 132–136; 190–194.

WEISS, STEVEN J., and VINCENT JOHN MCGUGAN, "The Equipment Leasing Industry and the Emerging Role of Banking Organizations," in Federal Reserve Bank of Boston, *New England Economic Review* (November–December, 1973), pp. 3–30.

WELLS FARGO BANK, *Commercial Lending* (San Francisco: Wells Fargo Bank, 1975).

WIAR, ROBERT C., "Economic Implications of Multiple Rates of Return in the Leveraged Lease Context," *Journal of Finance* 28 (December, 1973), pp. 1275–1286.

21 Short-Term Debt Financing

Short-term financing is debt capital with a maturity of one year or less. Since this type of financing is used primarily to finance working capital, it is more commonly used by trading and manufacturing companies than by transportation, real estate, and public utility companies. The major forms of short-term debt are trade credit, line of credit, accounts receivable loans (including factoring), inventory loans, and commercial paper. A line of credit is available only to firms with strong credit ratings, and commercial paper is accessible only to the strongest of these. The other forms, however, are available to all firms.

TRADE CREDIT

When a business makes a purchase from another company, the selling firm often demands no immediate cash payment. The selling term "2/10, net 30," for example, means that the buyer gets a cash discount of 2 percent if he pays cash by the tenth day after the date of invoice; otherwise, the full amount is due 30 days after the date of invoice. In Chapter 13, we referred to this free credit during the 10-day period as spontaneous credit, since its value rises and falls with the volume of the firm's purchases from its suppliers. The buyer should always use this free credit to full advantage. If the buyer does not pay until the end of the 30-day period, he has in effect obtained an unsecured 20-day loan equal to the invoice price less the 2 percent discount. The interest on this trade credit is measured by the discount foregone. In Chapter 12, we analyzed the policy decisions confronting the seller granting trade credit; here, our point of view is that of the firm buying on credit.

Assuming that trade credit is available, should a firm use it? Its advantages are availability and flexibility. Because the credit is the by-product of a sale, the seller may apply a less strict standard for credit approval than a regular lending institution would apply. Trade credit is therefore used by some firms because regular lenders would not grant them credit. Another attraction is the flexibility in the size of trade credit in accordance with the firm's financing needs. Flexibility stems, also, from trade credit's being unsecured borrowing, whereas other loans may require collateral. Trade credit does, however, have one overwhelming disadvantage: its cost. This schedule gives the annual interest rates corresponding to several trade-credit terms:

Credit Term	Rate of Interest	Credit Term	Rate of Interest
1.5/10, net 20	54.8%	2/10, net 20	73.0%
1.5/10, net 30	27.4	2/10, net 30	36.5
1.5/10, net 40	18.3	2/10, net 40	24.3

The rates are high even on an after-tax basis. This high cost of trade credit means that a firm should take the cash discount whenever possible.

THE LINE OF CREDIT

A line of credit is an informal short-term arrangement whereby a bank grants a firm the privilege of repeated borrowing as long as the outstanding debt never exceeds a specified amount.[1] Since this type of credit minimizes bank supervision and eliminates the need for collateral, a line of credit is usually granted only to firms with high credit standing. But even a firm that does not fully qualify for a line of credit may be granted a transaction loan. Such a loan is made for a specific time period and requires separate negotiations each time the borrower takes out a loan. A series of transaction loans may be used to approximate borrowings under a line of credit.

The Loan Agreement

Enforceability. A line of credit is established when a firm receives a letter from its banker stating his willingness to enter into such an arrangement. The letter is only an informal agreement, not a contract. In theory, therefore, the firm has no enforceable legal claim if the bank is unable to

[1] The following discussion of bank lending practices is based in part on my personal interviews of lending officers at several large commercial banks.

honor its commitment. In practice, however, a firm may safely assume that its line will be honored.

Maximum Credit. A bank may lend no more than 10 percent of its capital and surplus to a single customer. The actual line, usually less than this amount, is determined by the bank's assessment of the maximum loan that the firm can comfortably repay. This assessment is based on financial statement analysis which stresses the amount and turnover of working capital, the purpose of the loan, repayment plan, and the quality of management.

Interest Rate. Prime rate is the interest rate that banks charge on short-term loans to firms with first-class credit ratings and adequate deposit balances. Less qualified firms pay the prime rate plus a premium, the size of which varies with the risk of the loan and the deposit balance the borrowing firm maintains at the bank. Interest is paid only on the amount actually borrowed; and there is no commitment fee on the unused portion of the line of credit.

Compensating Balance. Many banks require only that the average balance during the year meet the compensating balance requirement. Thus, a firm, by keeping deposits above the required level during the time it is free of debt, may let its deposits fall below that level during the actual borrowing period. In the past, because the prime rate changed infrequently, bankers adjusted the compensating balances to meet the actual cost of borrowing when credit conditions changed. Now, however, since the prime rate "floats" with short-term money rates, we may expect the bankers to de-emphasize compensating balances.

Expiration Date. A line of credit is usually negotiated for a one-year period, subject to renewal at expiration. Although the bank will not renege on its line commitment, it may terminate or adjust the line on renewal. Such a decision may be prompted by a tightening of general credit conditions or by a deterioration in the borrower's financial condition.

Seasonal Clean-ups. Since line of credit is short-term financing, the bank expects the borrower to "clean up" his indebtedness during the year. The frequency and length of clean-up periods are subject to negotiation to fit the normal cash-flow pattern of the firm. A firm in agriculture may thus have one seasonal clean-up, while a firm in manufacturing may have several clean-ups.

Restrictive Covenants. Beyond those already discussed, banks usually impose no further conditions on strong companies. A weak firm, however, may be restricted as to dividend payments, working capital position, and so on. Restrictive covenants on a line of credit are not yet typical but are increasing in frequency.

The Effective Rate of Interest

Since a line of credit is essentially revolving credit, the procedure in Table 20-3 for calculating the effective cost of revolving credit is applicable here as well. The only difference is the absence of a commitment fee under a line of credit. The analysis in Table 20-3 assumes that the firm meets the bank's compensating balance requirement exactly and constantly during the entire loan period. Now, however, we shall assume that a firm meets this requirement only on the average.

The XYZ Company's credit line permits it to borrow up to $50,000 to finance its seasonal bulge in working capital from October through December. The nominal interest rate is 10 percent; the compensating balance is 15 percent of the line, or $7,500; the firm's voluntary deposit balance is $2,000; and the net return (after expenses) on short-term investments is 7 percent. The firm takes out a 90-day loan of $50,000 on October 1, using the money for purchases in four installments: $20,000 on October 1, and $10,000 on October 10, October 20, and October 30. This gradual disbursement of cash leaves an average deposit balance of $20,000 during October. The goods purchased are resold on credit during November for a total of $60,000, of which $10,000 is received on December 1, December 10, and December 20, respectively, and $30,000 on December 31. This gradual build-up of cash before the loan repayment gives the firm an average deposit of $20,000 during December. These large deposits during October and December help the firm to meet the required average deposit of $7,500: during the other ten months, the firm needs an average deposit of only $5,000—i.e., only $3,000 more than its voluntary $2,000 balance.

This information enables us to calculate the total cost of the loan as follows:

Interest payment on 90-day loan ($50,000 × .10 × 3/12)	$1,250.00
Interest foregone on excess of compensating balance over voluntary balance ($3,000 × .07 × 10/12)	175.00
Total cost	$1,425.00

A $50,000 loan for 90 days is equivalent to an average loan of $12,500 for the entire year. The 10 percent loan thus carries an effective interest rate of 11.4 percent (= 1,425/12,500) per annum. Assuming a 50 percent tax rate, the after-tax cost is half that figure, or 5.70 percent.

ACCOUNTS RECEIVABLE LOANS

Firms with credit conditions too weak to qualify for unsecured credit may obtain short-term loans by pledging their accounts receivable. This form of financing is supplied not only by commercial banks, but also by commercial finance companies and factors (e.g., C.I.T. Financial Corporation, Walter E. Heller and Company, James Talcott, Inc., and United Factors). In general, commercial banks have more strict credit standards than either commercial finance companies or factors.

The Loan Agreement

There are three major areas of negotiation in financing receivables: percent of advance, maximum line amount, and rate of interest.

Percent of Advance. A firm's accounts receivable may be viewed as a pool, augmented by new credit sales and reduced by the collection of old accounts. The percentage of the pool that a lender is willing to advance varies with the borrower's general financial strength, the credit ratings of the account debtors, the age and size distribution of accounts, the firm's bad-debt experience, and its collection efficiency. Most commercial banks are willing to advance from 60 to 80 percent of the value of accounts receivable, while finance companies may advance up to 90 percent.

Maximum Line Amount. Commercial banks limit not only the percentage, but also the maximum dollar amount that a firm may borrow against its accounts receivable. This limit is usually based on an average of recently outstanding accounts receivable. Commercial finance companies, more liberal, impose no dollar limit: a firm may borrow as long as it has acceptable uncollateralized accounts receivable.

Rate of Interest. In receivable financing, a firm pays interest only on the money actually borrowed, only while it is in use, and on a daily-use basis. The interest rate for receivable loans is high because such loans require no compensating balance and are expensive to administer. The interest rate guidelines in Table 21-1 were in effect at a major commercial bank when its prime rate was 10 percent. Since commercial finance companies accept more risks than banks, they charge interest rates 3 to 5 percent higher.

Other Aspects. Accounts receivable loans involve no compensating balance since the lending institutions set the rate of interest on these loans sufficiently high to include all necessary returns. Loans are usually negotiated for one year at a time, and have no annual clean-up requirements.

Table 21-1 Bank Interest Rate on Accounts Receivable Loans

Average Daily Unpaid Balance	Rate of Interest	Average Daily Unpaid Balance	Rate of Interest
Under $ 50,000	14%	$250,000 to $ 500,000	12 1/4%
$ 50,000 to 100,000	13 1/2	500,000 to 750,000	11 3/4
100,000 to 250,000	13	750,000 to 1,000,000	11 1/4

Borrowing Procedure

Receivables are generally assigned as collateral under a continuing (or floating) lien, without a dominion requirement. The borrower signs a security agreement assigning to the lender all present and future accounts receivable. Cash collections on pledged receivables are credited directly to the borrower's loan account. In the case of a dominion requirement, all cash collections are first deposited in a control account and then released to the customer loan account only when new collateral has been pledged. With no dominion requirement, the borrower can withdraw funds without first replenishing the amount of collateral. This arrangement offers less protection to the lender, but is generally preferable since it is easier and cheaper to administer than one with the dominion clause.

Once the security agreement has been signed, the firm submits to the lending institution a complete list of its accounts receivable, classified by age. The lender deletes accounts ineligible as collateral: e.g., accounts more than 60 days past due, U.S. government accounts, and foreign accounts. The lender then makes, say, an 80 percent advance against the eligible accounts. As the firm generates new accounts receivable by making sales, it continues to assign its receivables to the lender; and as the firm receives payments, it turns the payments over to the lender in kind. Since the payments are deposited directly in the borrower's loan account, the borrower can, by comparing his outstanding loan with his collateral balance, easily determine his unused borrowing capacity.

At the end of each month, the lender prepares a statement showing the firm's daily loan balance and interest expense, based on the average loan balance for the month. Since there is neither a compensating balance requirement nor a commitment fee, the nominal rate of interest and the effective rate are the same.

Receivable Loans vs. Line of Credit

A Numerical Example. The nominal rate of interest is considerably higher on accounts receivable loans than on an unsecured line of credit. However, to assess relative costs correctly, we must recognize that, whereas a line of credit commits a firm to a fixed amount for a full 60- or

Table 21-2 Receivable Loan vs. Unsecured Line of Credit*
(in thousands of dollars)

	June			July		
Day	Receivable Loan (1)	Unsecured Borrowing (2)	Surplus Funds (3)	Receivable Loan (4)	Unsecured Borrowing (5)	Surplus Funds (6)
1	$36	$60	$24	$28	$60	$32
4	32	60	28	36	60	24
7	28	60	32	44	60	16
10	24	60	36	52	60	8
13	20	60	40	60	60	0
16	20	60	40	60	60	0
19	20	60	40	60	60	0
21	20	60	40	60	60	0
24	20	60	40	60	60	0
27	20	60	40	60	60	0
Average	$24	$60	$36	$52	$60	$ 8

*To simplify, we assume that the firm transacts its business every fourth day.

90-day period each time it borrows, receivable loans rise and fall with daily credit sales and collections. Thus, the firm may confine its borrowing to its actual needs. Moreover, receivable loans involve no compensating balance. When these differences are taken into account, receivable loans may be less expensive than lines of credit, particularly if needs vary greatly with time.

As an example, let us suppose that, under a receivable loan agreement, the ABC Company expects its daily loan balances during June and July to follow the pattern described in Columns 1 and 4 of Table 21-2.[2] The average balances for the two months are $24,000 and $52,000, respectively. At an interest rate of 15 percent, the financing cost for the two months totals $950:

$$\text{Cost of receivable financing} = (\$24{,}000 + \$52{,}000) \times \frac{.15}{12} = \$950$$

Let us suppose that ABC has the alternative of taking out an unsecured loan of $60,000 (to enable the firm to meet its peak loan demand in July) for two months at an interest rate of 10 percent (a rate high enough to eliminate the need for a compensating balance). Except during the days of peak demand, the $60,000 loan will result in surplus funds, averaging $36,000 in June and $8,000 in July (see Columns 3 and 6). The surplus funds could be

[2] This example is similar to Monroe R. Lazere's illustration in his *Commercial Financing* (New York: The Ronald Press Company, 1968), pp. 38–39.

invested in Treasury bills at a gross return of, say, 7 percent; but managing the portfolio of Treasury bills would cost, say, $400 per month. This managing cost would exceed the return, and the funds should instead be left idle. The unsecured loan would thus cost the firm $1,000 in interest:

$$\text{Cost of unsecured financing} = \$60{,}000 \times \frac{.10}{6} = \$1{,}000$$

In this case, even at a nominal rate of 15 percent, accounts receivable financing is less expensive than a 10 percent unsecured line of credit.

The volume of financing can significantly affect the relative attractiveness of accounts receivable loans. Let us, for example, multiply by ten the figures for receivable loan balance and unsecured borrowing in Table 21-2. Loan rates, Treasury bill rate, and the fixed cost of managing Treasury bills all remain as before. Our change increases the cost of receivable financing proportionately from $950 to $9,500:

$$\text{Cost of receivable financing} = (\$240{,}000 + \$520{,}000) \times \frac{.15}{12} = \$9{,}500$$

But the cost of unsecured financing increases from $1,000 to only $8,233.33. The larger volume of surplus funds now makes it worthwhile to invest the surplus, accounting for the less-than-proportionate increase in cost:

$$\begin{aligned}\text{Cost of unsecured financing} &= \left(\$600{,}000 \times \frac{.10}{6}\right) - \left(\$440{,}000 \times \frac{.07}{12} - \$800\right) \\ &= \$8{,}233.33\end{aligned}$$

In this case, accounts receivable financing is now more expensive than an unsecured line of credit.

A General Criterion. To generalize our findings, let us define a set of symbols:

n = the minimum maturity in days for an unsecured loan
R_j = receivable loan balance on day j
$\overline{R}_j$ = average value of R_j over an n-day period
L = size of unsecured loan (equal to the maximum value of R_j)
S_j = surplus funds on day j (equal to $L - R_j$)
$\overline{S}_j$ = average value of S_j over an n-day period
r = annual interest rate on receivable loan
r' = annual interest rate on unsecured loan

g = annual interest rate on short-term investments
M = annual cost of managing the short-term investment portfolio (a constant)

A receivable loan for n days will cost the firm the following amount in interest:

$$\bar{R}_j \times r \times \frac{n}{360} \tag{22-1}$$

An unsecured loan of size L for n days will cost (after deducting the net income derived from investing any surplus funds):

$$\left(L \times r' \times \frac{n}{360}\right) - \left(\bar{S}_j \times g \times \frac{n}{360} - \frac{Mn}{360}\right) \tag{22-2}$$

A receivable loan is thus less costly than an unsecured loan if the interest on the latter exceeds the interest on the former by more than the net income derived from investing the temporary surplus funds resulting from the unsecured loan.

While the cost of a receivable loan increases proportionately with the amount of the loan, the cost of an unsecured loan increases less than proportionately because of the constant term $Mn/360$. Other things being equal, then, large firms are more likely than small firms to find unsecured loans less costly than receivable loans. In any case, of course, few small firms qualify for unsecured loans. The preference of large firms, which do qualify, for unsecured loans is reflected in the fact that few accounts receivable loans, even at major banks, have average daily balances exceeding two hundred and fifty thousand dollars.

FACTORING OF ACCOUNTS RECEIVABLE

Instead of borrowing against its receivables, a firm may sell them to raise cash. This is called factoring, because the financial institutions that buy the receivables are known as factors. Originally used primarily by textile mills, factoring has spread to a wide range of industries: furniture, electronics, lumber, floor coverings, and toys. Until the mid-1960's, the factoring industry consisted mainly of small firms and a few large corporations. Since 1965, however, when the Comptroller of Currency designated factoring a suitable area of bank expansion, most of the small factors have been bought out by banks seeking quick entry into the market.[3] Bank participa-

[3] "Factors Borrow a Touch of Class," *Business Week* (March 6, 1971), pp. 88–89.

tion has made factoring a more respectable business, removing much of the stigma that used to be attached to it.

The Factoring Agreement

Maturity vs. Advance Factoring. In any kind of factoring, the factor buys the accounts receivable outright and assumes all credit risk.[4] In maturity factoring, the factor pays the firm a few days (usually ten) after the average maturity date of the previous month's invoices; and in advance factoring, the factor pays the firm as soon as it is assigned the invoices. In maturity factoring, the factor checks the customers' credit, carries out the ledgering and collection of accounts, and assumes the bad-debt risk. In advance factoring, the factor not only performs these services, but also provides the firm with a short-term cash advance.

Customer Notification. The customers of a firm factoring its accounts receivable are notified and instructed to mail their payments directly to the factor. The advantage of notification is that the customers will probably pay their bills more promptly; the disadvantage is that some customers may see factoring as a sign of financial weakness, though the stigma is steadily decreasing. In any case, notification is generally mandatory, not negotiable.

Cost of Factoring. Cost varies with services rendered. In maturity factoring, the commission is usually from 1.5 to 2 percent of the sales factored; the exact percentage depends on the dollar volume of sales, the character and quality of customers, the terms of sales, and the average size of the invoices. The standard contract gives the factor ten days to clear checks and to follow up on slow payments. This period, in effect, raises the commission above the nominal rate to the extent that the 10-day period is greater than the time necessary for payment.

In advance factoring, the firm must pay not only the commission but also interest on the cash advanced. The nominal rates charged by factors are comparable to those charged by commercial finance companies. Since interest is figured on a daily-use basis and since there is no compensating balance requirement or commitment fee, the effective rate of interest is the same as the nominal rate.

Other Aspects. Since the factoring house is not a bank and accepts no deposits, there are obviously no compensating balance requirements in this type of transaction. Contracts are usually negotiated for one year, are renewable, and involve no annual clean-up.

---

[4] Our discussion of factoring is based on Irwin Naitove, *Modern Factoring* (New York: American Management Association, 1969), and on descriptive literature issued by Walter E. Heller and Company, a commercial finance company which also engages in factoring.

Factoring Procedure

A firm does not need the factor's approval of every order it fills. Usually, the firm submits the names of its present and prospective customers, noting their credit needs. After checking their credit, the factor specifies the maximum amount of credit risk that it will assume for each customer. When the firm fills an order, it sends the customer the original invoice together with notification that the invoice is assigned to a factor. The factor receives a copy of the invoice, the shipping document, and an assignment schedule. When the factor receives payment, he credits the firm's account.

In maturity financing, the factor pays the firm for the month's sales on the adjusted average maturity date: first, the number of days to maturity of each invoice is determined; and then a weighted average of these "days to maturity" is taken, using the dollar values of the invoices as weights. The resulting average maturity date plus the number of days allowed to clear checks and follow up on slow payments gives the adjusted average due date for the month's sales.

In advance factoring, the firm receives cash payment for the month's sales at the end of each month. Since this payment involves a loan, the firm is charged not only a factoring commission but also interest for the number of days by which the payment precedes the adjusted average due date.

The Decision to Factor

Maturity factoring is advisable only when it is less costly than an in-house credit department. Small firms generally find factoring more economical than large firms, since the savings associated with factoring vary inversely with the volume of a firm's credit sales.

Suppose the commission that the Smalley Carpet Company pays for maturity factoring is given in this schedule:

Annual Credit Sales	Commission (% of Sales)
Under $750,000	$2\frac{1}{4}$
$ 750,000 to 1,000,000	2
1,000,000 to 2,500,000	$1\frac{3}{4}$
2,500,000 to 4,000,000	$1\frac{1}{2}$
4,000,000 and over	$1\frac{1}{4}$

If the firm operated its own credit department, it would incur a combination of fixed, semi-fixed, and variable costs:

Salary of credit manager	$15,000 per year
Salary of assistants	$10,000/first $1 million of sales + $2,500/each additional $1 million
Bad-debt losses	$\frac{1}{5}$ of 1 percent of sales

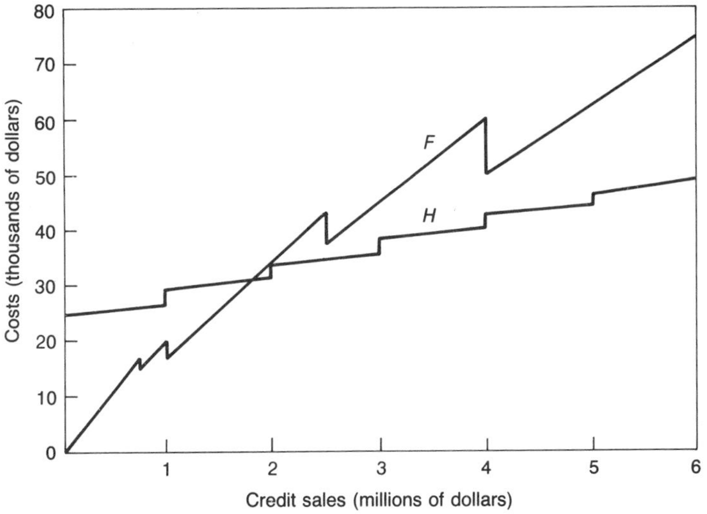

Figure 21-1 The Factoring Decision

In Figure 21-1, cost functions F and H show the respective costs of maturity factoring and an in-house credit department, expressed as functions of Smalley's sales. Since function F intersects function H from below at a sales volume of about $1.7 million, the firm will find factoring economical only if its sales volume is below this level.

In advance factoring, the firm gets a short-term cash advance. Borrowing from a factor may cost even more than borrowing from a commercial finance company. But the availability of credit may be the deciding consideration, since many firms that factor are small, weak companies unable to obtain other types of credit. A firm's balance sheet will show a higher current ratio if the firm factors than if it borrows against its accounts receivable. If this aspect can be assigned a dollar value, it can easily be incorporated into a financial analysis. Otherwise, this intangible should be balanced against the result of the cost and availability analysis.

INVENTORY FINANCING

Banks and finance companies generally prefer accounts receivable over inventories as loan collateral because of their greater liquidity. There are, however, businesses whose working capital requirements stem primarily from the need to carry large inventories during each operating cycle. A firm (e.g., a tomato cannery or a sawmill) whose production is seasonally concentrated but whose sales are not, or a firm (e.g., a toy maker or a dress manufacturer) whose sales are seasonally concentrated but whose production is not, will probably pledge both inventories and receivables as collateral against their short-term borrowings.

The Loan Agreement

Percent of Advance. The percentage advanced in an inventory loan depends on both the strength of the borrower and the quality of the collateral. An important consideration is the value the inventory would bring if it had to be liquidated. Finished products and basic raw materials command a high advance percentage because they are in marketable form. Work in progress has the lowest value as collateral because it generally needs further processing to be marketable. Most banks use these guidelines in setting the percentage of advance: finished goods, 70 percent; raw materials, 60 to 65 percent; work in progress, 45 to 50 percent. These percentages are based on cost or market value, whichever is lower.

Line Amount. An inventory loan may be set up as a revolving credit line so that the loan balance will rise and fall with the level of inventory. Or the loan may be set up as a pay-down loan, in which the initial loan balance is continuously reduced by scheduled repayments. In either case, the maximum amount of the loan depends on the strength of the borrower and the quality of the collateral. Firms borrowing against their inventories often borrow at the same time against their accounts receivable. The lender may set a maximum line amount limiting the combined borrowings.

Rate of Interest. Interest rates are lower on inventory loans than on receivable loans because the cost of administration is lower. Nevertheless, interest rates are higher on inventory loans than on unsecured lines of credit. A typical bank uses the rate guidelines in Table 21-3 for inventory loans, given a prime rate of 10 percent. Like receivable loans, inventory loans require no compensating balance. Interest is figured on the basis of the average daily balance, so that the effective rate is the same as the nominal rate. In securing inventory loans, a firm must pay a warehousing fee in addition to the interest. As with receivable loans, finance companies have more liberal standards than do banks, but interest rates are also higher.

Table 21-3 Bank Interest Rate on Inventory Loans

Average Daily Unpaid Balance	Rate of Interest	Average Daily Unpaid Balance	Rate of Interest
Under $100,000	11 1/2%	$500,000 to $ 750,000	10 1/2%
$100,000 to 250,000	11	$750,000 to 1,000,000	10 1/4
$250,000 to 500,000	10 3/4	Over 1,000,000	10 1/4

Borrowing Procedure

Inventories may be pledged either through public warehousing or through a security agreement. Under the former method, a firm puts its inventory in storage with a public warehouseman in return for a warehouse receipt. The firm then assigns the receipt to the lender, giving the bank or finance company title to the inventory. If the borrower prefers to have his inventory remain on his premises, a field warehouse may be set up by cordoning off a section of the premises, which is then put under the control of an independent warehouseman.[5] Because of the high cost, however, warehousing receipts are used only in fairly large inventory loans.

Under a security agreement, the borrower signs a document giving the lender title to the inventory in much the same way that accounts receivable are assigned. No third party is involved: the borrower retains physical possession of the collateral. When the borrower sells the collateralized goods, the lender's lien is converted into a lien on the sales proceeds. Consequently, when a firm borrows against its receivables, the lender usually requires a lien on all of the inventories to insure that there are no prior liens on the receivables.

As the inventory is used or sold, the firm must repay the lender correspondingly to reduce the loan balance. With a loan advance of 50 percent of cost, for example, every $100 of inventory removed from collateral calls for a $50 reduction of the loan balance. Generally, the firm simply negotiates a combination inventory-receivable loan so that, when inventory is converted to receivables, the receivables automatically yield a cash advance enabling the firm to pay off its inventory loan. Since the percentage advance is higher on accounts receivable than on inventories, and since receivables are valued at selling price, whereas inventory is valued at cost, a firm's cash position improves materially as its inventory loans are converted into receivable loans.

COMMERCIAL PAPER FINANCING

Nature and Scope

Commercial paper may be viewed either as a short-term investment medium or as a short-term financing instrument. Here, we take the latter viewpoint. Many large, well-financed companies sell their own promissory

[5] Independent control is necessary to verify the authenticity of inventory when warehouse receipts are used as collateral. In the famous salad oil scandal, lack of independent control enabled a food processing company to borrow millions of dollars against receipts supposedly backed by soybean oil but in fact only by water. For an account of this episode, see Norman C. Miller, *The Great Salad Oil Swindle* (New York: Coward McCann, Inc., 1965).

notes, or commercial paper, to raise cash. Like bank lines of credit, commercial paper is unsecured; but whereas bank lines result from personal negotiation between bank and borrower, commercial paper is sold to investors through the impersonal channels of the securities market. Since commercial paper is unsecured, the borrower avoids the costs and complexities of pledging specific assets. The issuance of commercial paper is, thus, effectively limited to financially strong companies. Commercial paper has traditionally been issued by companies in the finance, food, and tobacco industries and is now also issued by firms in many other industries: chemical, electronics, public utilities, transportation, rubber, banking, and insurance. Now, 600 to 700 firms issue commercial paper.

The maturities of commercial paper are usually between 4 and 6 months, but may range from a few days to 270. The 270-day limit derives from the Securities Act of 1933, which exempts commercial paper from registration requirements only if its maturity does not exceed this limit. The denominations are determined by the preferences of the investors, who are, typically, banks, mutual funds, corporations, insurance companies, and pension funds. Denominations frequently range from $100,000 to several millions.

As of June 30, 1975, the total amount of commercial paper outstanding was $48.9 billion, compared with $484.5 billion in outstanding bank loans of all maturities. In theory, a corporation could use commercial paper for all of its short-term borrowing; but in practice, as Nevins D. Baxter has found, commercial paper issued by industrial companies generally accounts for less than half of these companies' short-term borrowing.[6]

Selling Commercial Paper

Commercial paper may be sold either through investment dealers or by direct placement. In the dealer market, a very few investment houses (e.g., Goldman, Sachs & Co.; The First Boston Corporation; A. G. Becker & Co.) handle most of the business. A corporation selling commercial paper proceeds in this way:[7]

(1) The company negotiates with its bank(s) for additional credit lines to serve as liquidity back-up. It is an unwritten market requirement that all commercial paper be backed by bank credit lines.

(2) The firm applies to an agency such as Moody's or Standard and Poor for a commercial paper rating. Many institutional investors confine their commercial paper purchases to those with prime ratings.

---

[6] Nevins D. Baxter, *The Commercial Paper Market* (Boston: The Bankers Publishing Company, 1966), p. 61.

[7] For more detailed explanations, see The First Boston Corporation, *Commercial Paper* (New York: The First Boston Corporation, 1974), and Moody's Investors Service, "Commercial Paper: The Market & Moody's Role," a 3-page mimeographed statement issued in 1973.

(3) The firm negotiates with the dealer over selling commission (usually between 1/8 and 1/4 of one percent).

(4) The firm can now raise money the day it is needed simply by calling the dealer to inform him of its needs.

Direct placement, because it requires a permanent sales staff, is a practical way to sell commercial paper only if the firm needs several hundred million dollars continuously. The few firms, primarily finance companies, that sell directly are extremely large issuers of commercial paper; consequently, although the number of direct issues is small, the dollar volume is actually twice that of the paper sold through dealers.

Commercial Paper vs. Bank Borrowing

A firm strong enough to borrow by issuing commercial paper is also strong enough to obtain an unsecured loan from a commercial bank. Of the five factors to be considered in deciding whether to issue paper or borrow from a bank, three favor the former and two the latter.

Direct Interest Savings. The interest rate on commercial paper is generally lower than the bank prime rate. Moreover, banks require higher compensating balances against actual loans than against back-up credit lines. On the other hand, commercial paper is sold on a discount basis with the interest deducted at the outset. Figure 21-2 shows the effective rates of interest on

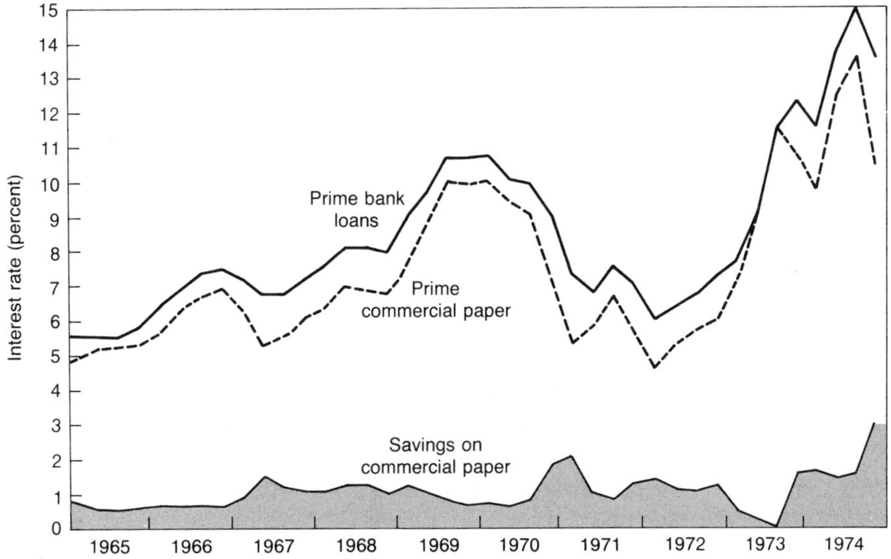

Source: The First Boston Corporation.

Figure 21-2 Effective Interest Rates: Bank Loans vs. Commercial Paper

prime bank loans and prime commercial paper for the period from 1965 through 1974. Except for the third quarter of 1973, commercial paper has been consistently less costly, with savings ranging from .21 percent to 3.00 percent.

Indirect Financial Benefits. Investor familiarity with a company's commercial paper may enable the firm to sell its stocks and bonds on more favorable terms than would be otherwise possible. In addition, having access to the open market enhances a firm's bargaining position with banks.

Availability of Credit. As mentioned before, a bank may lend no more than 10 percent of its capital and surplus to any single customer. Some giant corporations (e.g., General Motors Acceptance Corporation, and C.I.T. Financial Corporation) have such large short-term borrowing needs that, even after borrowing from hundreds of major banks, they must issue commercial paper to acquire additional funds.

Impersonality of the Open Market. The impersonality of the open market works against commercial paper. In times of tight money, a bank will try to meet the financial needs of its regular borrowers. The commercial paper lender, however, with no customer loyalty to worry about, will not hesitate to withdraw his funds at any time. Thus, when the Penn Central Transportation Company, with $85 million in commercial paper outstanding, filed for reorganization under federal bankruptcy laws in 1970, the demand for commercial paper plummeted. Both Chrysler Financial and Commercial Credit found it suddenly impossible to renew the millions of dollars of commercial paper they had outstanding. A crisis was averted only because they were able to obtain additional bank funds.[8]

Impairment of Relation to Bank. If a firm shifts from bank borrowing to commercial paper every time it sees a fractional interest advantage, its bank may become less willing to assist in times of financial need. For the sake of good will, many commercial paper issuers consistently divide their borrowings between commercial paper and bank loans.

LINEAR PROGRAMMING AND SHORT-TERM FINANCING

Some short-term lenders charge a high rate of interest but are willing to accept short maturities, while others charge a low rate of interest but require longer borrowing periods. Given a firm's short-term cash budget, the

---

[8] John Thackray gives a vivid report on the developments in the commercial paper market that followed Penn Central's action. See his article, "Where Does Commercial Paper Stand?" *Corporate Financing* 2 (September–October, 1970), pp. 22–26, and 62–66.

financial executive must design a financing plan that will make the greatest possible use of low-cost borrowing at the same time that it achieves the best possible synchronization of its cash flows. Linear programming is a useful tool for solving this type of problems.

Fancycraft, Inc.

Financing Requirements. Fancycraft, Inc., is the greeting-card business that we used in Chapter 10 to illustrate the technique of cash budgeting. We shall now add the following assumption to define Fancycraft's short-term financing problem. We assume that the company has an initial operating cash balance of $58,000 and follows a policy of maintaining a month-end balance equal to the operating cash drain for the following month, though never less than the minimum balance of $30,000. This information enables us to derive from the cash budget the firm's financing needs during its 12-month planning horizon (see Table 21-4).[9] Note that during eight of the twelve months, the firm has a cumulative deficit, peaking in October at $270,000.

Sources of Financing. We assume that Fancycraft can meet its anticipated cash drains through any of three financing alternatives: line of credit, commercial paper, or installment financing. In the first case, with a line of credit, the firm may borrow a maximum of $140,000 at 13.2 percent per annum. To simplify, we shall assume that the amount borrowed at the beginning of one month is repaid with interest at the beginning of the next month. We shall assume also that at 13.2 percent interest the bank requires no compensating balance.

Table 21-4 Fancycraft's Financing Requirements for the Next Twelve Months* (in thousands of dollars)

Month	Requirement	Cumulative Requirement	Month	Requirement	Cumulative Requirement
January	−150	−150	July	− 50	− 71
February	152	2	August	− 13	− 84
March	73	75	September	−156	−240
April	− 30	45	October	− 30	−270
May	126	171	November	62	−208
June	−192	− 21	December	7	−201

* Negative figures denote cash requirements that need to be financed.

[9] We shall interpret "month" flexibly to mean a basic unit of time, in this case a period of 15 days, so that the 12-month budget actually covers only 180 days, and a year includes 24 months.

In the second case, by issuing 3-month commercial paper, Fancycraft can borrow a maximum of $120,000 at 10.8 percent per annum. Although interest charges are actually payable at the outset, we shall assume them to be payable monthly. Because of the 3-month maturity, the amount borrowed in any month cannot be repaid until three months later. Surplus funds are invested at the beginning of each month in short-term securities at 10 percent per annum.

The third alternative is installment financing. Fancycraft's cash budget shows that the firm plans to buy a $100,000 plate in January. The manufacturer has offered to finance the plate with a 6-month installment loan. If Fancycraft borrows $Z(\leq \$100{,}000)$ dollars, there will be 6 monthly payments, beginning February 1, of $\$1.018Z/6$. The implicit interest rate is 14.4 percent per annum. A second plate, to be bought in June, could be financed the same way.

A Linear-Programming Model

Fancycraft's financing decision can be formulated as a problem in linear programming. To facilitate understanding, however, we shall present the program in an abbreviated nonmathematical form. The financing solution must observe the following set of constraints:

1. Constraint on bank credit. Fancycraft can have no more than $140,000 in bank loans in any given month.
2. Constraint on commercial paper. Fancycraft can have no more than $120,000 in commercial paper outstanding in any given month.
3. Constraint on installment financing. No installment loan can exceed $100,000, the price of the equipment to be purchased. Fancycraft can obtain this type of credit only in January and June.
4. Constraint on cash budget. In any month, the cumulative borrowing from all sources, less interest and principal repayments, plus interest income, must equal or exceed the firm's cumulative cash requirement.

In addition, given these constraints, the objective is to devise a short-term financing plan that will minimize total interest cost.

The complete mathematical model involves finding the optimal values of 26 variables subject to 38 constraints. Readers interested in this full model should consult the reference cited below.[10]

[10] For the full model, see my *Quantitative Analysis of Financial Decisions* (New York: The Macmillan Company, 1969), Ch. 11.

The Optimal Solution

The linear program we have generally described is too complex to solve manually, but a computer can solve it in a few seconds. Table 21-5 presents the optimal solution, showing how much should be borrowed from each source at what time and the extent to which surplus funds are available for reinvestment in short-term securities.

In order to meet the $150,000 cash deficit in January, Fancycraft should optimally borrow $120,000 in the commercial paper market and $30,000 from a commercial bank. In February, $705 of the $152,000 budgetary surplus is needed for interest expenses; $30,000 is needed to repay the bank loan; the balance of $121,295 is invested in short-term securities. In March, the firm has a budgetary surplus of $73,000, interest receipts of $505, and interest payments of $540, leaving a net inflow of $72,965. Since the commercial paper is not due until April 1, the $72,965 is invested in short-term securities, bringing the total holdings to $194,260. In April, there is a budgetary deficit of $30,000, interest receipts of $810, and interest payments of $540, for a net outflow of $29,730. To meet the outflow and to retire the $120,000 of commercial paper, Fancycraft must sell $149,730 worth of short-term securities, reducing its holdings to $44,530. And so on for the remaining months. We should note in passing that even though Fancycraft does not purchase its plates on installment in January, the optimal solution calls for $34,570 in installment financing in June.

We need now to turn to the economic logic underlying the optimal solution. Bank credit, we have said, costs .55 percent per month, while commercial paper costs .45 percent. Commercial paper thus saves a firm $10 per month for every $10,000 of borrowing. Commercial paper, of course, commits the firm to a 3-month loan; and any reinvested surplus will yield only .42 percent per month (or $42 per $10,000). This $42 in monthly interest income is, however, only $3 less than the monthly interest expense on $10,000 of commercial paper. It is therefore sound to use commercial paper even if financing needs are only for one month, while a bank loan should be considered only when the limit on commercial paper has been reached.

The .60 percent monthly cost of installment credit makes it the most expensive of the alternatives. The optimal solution calls for Fancycraft to use installment financing in June, only because the firm will have a maximum cumulative budgetary deficit of $270,000 in October. Given the limits on bank borrowing and commercial paper, Fancycraft would be unable to meet its peak deficit without installment credit.

The optimal financing plan costs Fancycraft a net total of only $5,050 in interest for the 12-month period. This solution assumes that the interest advantage of commercial paper over bank loans was substantial, the penalty for holding surplus funds was minimal, and installment credit was the least

Table 21-5 The Optimal Pattern of Financing for Fancycraft, Inc.*
(in thousands of dollars)

	Bank Credit			Commercial Paper			Installment Credit			Short-Term Securities		
Month	New Borrowing	Repayment of Principal	Amount Outstanding	New Borrowing	Repayment of Principal	Amount Outstanding	New Borrowing	Repayment of Principal	Amount Outstanding	Purchases	Sales	Amount Held
Jan.	30.00		30.00	120.00		120.00						
Feb.		30.00				120.00				121.30		121.30
Mar.						120.00				72.97		194.26
Apr.					120.00						149.72	44.54
May										126.19		170.73
June							34.57				156.72	14.01
July				120.00		120.00		5.76	28.81	64.19		78.20
Aug.						120.00		5.76	23.05		19.08	59.12
Sept.	103.03		103.03			120.00		5.76	17.28		59.12	
Oct.	140.00	103.03	140.00	120.00	120.00	120.00		5.76	11.52			
Nov.	85.18	140.00	85.18			120.00		5.76	5.76			
Dec.	85.04	85.18	85.04			120.00		5.76				

* Figures have been rounded; blank cells indicate values of zero.

flexible as well as the most costly alternative. These assumptions make the logic behind the optimal solution simple and straightforward. With different assumptions, the optimal solution may not be so obvious. In particular, if the cost advantage of commercial paper over bank loans were not so great, the optimal choice might well hinge on the duration of the cash need to be financed.

REVIEW QUESTIONS

1. Get quotations from banks, finance companies, factors, and commercial paper dealers on the cost of lines of credit, inventory loans, receivable loans, and installment loans. For each type of financing, explain how to calculate the effective cost of money from the nominal rates or commissions quoted.
2. How does each of these factors affect the relative costs of bank lines of credit and receivable loans:
   a. the ratio of the borrower's peak demand to the average loan demand during the borrowing period?
   b. the cost of managing surplus cash?
   c. the bank's compensating balance requirement?
   d. the size of the loan?
3. If you apply for an accounts receivable loan, what financial and nonfinancial information will the lender seek from you? How will this information influence the lender's decision whether or not to give you the loan and what rate of interest to charge? Answer the same questions for an inventory loan. Why might a lender grant an accounts-receivable loan and yet demand a lien on all your inventories as well?
4. Is a lender likely to prefer accounts receivable or inventory as collateral? Will the lender charge a higher interest rate on an accounts receivable loan or on an inventory loan? Would he be willing to grant a higher percentage loan on receivables or on inventory? Explain the reasons for your answers.
5. Explain the difference between maturity factoring and advance factoring. What services does the factor perform for the company under each type of factoring? The standard factoring contract gives the factor ten days to clear checks and to follow up on slow payments. Is this allowance actually an extra factoring commission or an extra interest charge? Which view does one take in calculating the effective cost of factoring? Why?
6. Explain the nature, the advantages, and the disadvantages of financing with commercial paper. Which aspects account for Nevins D. Baxter's finding that commercial paper issued by industrial corporations generally accounts for less than half of these firms' short-term borrowings?
7. Figure 21-2 gives a 10-year comparison of the relative costs of bank loans and commercial paper. Use the National Bureau of Economic Research's reference dates to identify the years of recession and the years of prosperity. Is the size of interest savings on commercial paper greater in the years of recession or of prosperity? If there is a clear pattern, use your understanding of the functioning of the money market to explain why the pattern is as it is.

8. One might guess intuitively that a larger proportion of all loans is made at the prime rate during periods of easy money than during periods of tight money. But a survey conducted by the Federal Reserve reveals just the opposite. Since this phenomenon seems at first glance to contradict common sense, how do you account for it?

9. Fancycraft is confronted with this set of interest rates: line of credit 12.0%; commercial paper 10.0%; installment credit 11.7%; and short-term investments 8.8%. Without using linear programming, design a financing plan to meet Fancycraft's budgetary needs while minimizing interest costs. Use the format of Table 21-5 to present your plan. What is the economic logic under your plan?

10. Analyze the working capital of each of these firms: a tomato canner, an electric utility, a ship builder, a toy manufacturer, a finance company, an automobile manufacturer, and a publisher. Give particular attention to the nature and size of the firm's working capital, the length of the working-capital period, and the way this period is divided among production, selling, and collection. Note any seasonality. How would the various differences in working capital and turnover be reflected in the method and timing of short-term financing?

PROBLEMS

1. Imagine that you are a customer of each of the following industries, which sell their products on the terms indicated. Calculate the effective cost of credit for each set of terms.
   - Bearings 5/10, net 30.
   - Worsted fabrics 7/10, 60 extra.
   - Automotive supplies 5/10th prox., net 30 ("10th prox." means that the cash discount may be taken if the bill is paid before the 10th of the following month).
   - Luggage 2/10, net 30, E.O.M. ("E.O.M." means that for determining the discount period and the free credit period, the invoice date is taken to be the end of the month).

2. D. Jones, Inc., a pharmaceuticals manufacturer, has been borrowing against its receivables from a finance company for several years. Jones is wondering if it might be cheaper to finance its receivables by establishing an unsecured line of credit with a commercial bank. In checking the records of a typical two-month period, Jones finds that his daily receivable loan balances were as follows:

Day*	Month 1	Month 2
1	$ 4,000	$ 5,000
6	6,000	7,000
11	5,000	14,000
16	9,000	7,000
21	8,000	9,000
26	12,000	6,000

* The firm transacts its business only on every fifth day.

Under receivable financing, the finance company charges 13.5 percent interest on the daily unpaid balance. With an unsecured loan, the bank would require Jones to take out a 60-day loan equal to his maximum need each time he borrows. The bank's interest rate would be 10 percent, with no compensating requirement. Jones calculates that, under a bank loan, he can invest any surplus funds in certificates of deposit at a return of 8 percent; but there will be a fixed cost of $100 per month for managing the portfolio. Which financing alternative will cost Jones less? By how much? Repeat the problem multiplying the daily receivable balances by ten.

3. Hillary Electronics, Inc., has had since its inception its own staff for making credit checks on its customers and for ledgering and collecting receivables. The firm was recently approached by Zee Factors, Limited, which offered to buy Hillary's receivables according to this schedule of commissions:

Annual Credit Sales	Commission (% of Sales)
$ 0 to $249,999	5.0%
250,000 to 499,999	4.5
500,000 to 749,999	4.3
750,000 to 999,999	4.0
1,000,000 and over	3.8

Zee would assume all credit functions and absorb all credit losses. Hillary's records show the following costs for operating its own credit department:

Salary of credit manager	$15,000 per year
Salary of assistants	$4,000 for the first quarter million dollars of sales plus $3,000 for each additional quarter million
Bad-debt losses	.5 percent of sales

Use a graph to determine the break-even sales volume at which the factoring commission would equal the cost of an internal credit operation. How would the factoring decision be influenced by the expected growth of sales? the availability or unavailability of bank credit?

4. Hillary had the following credit sales during May:

Invoice Date	Credit Term	Amount
5/2	Net 45	$600
5/9	Net 45	400
5/10	Net 45	700
5/27	Net 30	500
5/29	Net 30	800

Under maturity factoring, on what date of what month would Hillary receive cash payment for the May sales? How much will the firm pay in commission? Under advance factoring, if Hillary receives cash payment at the end of each month, how much cash will the firm receive at the end of May? Assume that the factor charges 13 percent per annum in interest and that he is allowed 10 days to clear checks and to follow up on slow payments.

5. When we re-solved the linear program for Fancycraft using the interest rates given in Review Question 9, we obtained the optimal values summarized in Table 21-6. Construct a table similar to Table 21-5 to show that the new optimal solution actually meets the firm's cash requirements for each month in the planning period. Compare the linear-programming solution with your intuitive solution to Question 9. How much does the linear program reduce the total interest cost over the 12-month period?

Table 21-6 The Optimal Pattern of Financing for Fancycraft, Inc.*

Source of Financing	Timing	Amount
Bank loan	January	$140,000
	September	106,780
	October	140,000
	November	85,000
	December	140,000
Commercial paper	January	10,000
	July	61,130
	September	55,270
	October	64,730
Installment loan	June	34,280

* Total interest cost = $4,700.

REFERENCES

BAXTER, NEVINS D., *The Commercial Paper Market* (Boston: The Bankers Publishing Company, 1966).

"Business Financing by Business Finance Companies," *Federal Reserve Bulletin* 54 (October, 1968), pp. 815–827.

"Changes in Bank Lending Practices, 1973," *Federal Reserve Bulletin* 60 (April, 1974), pp. 263–267.

CROSSE, HOWARD D., and GEORGE H. HEMPEL, *Management Policies for Commercial Banks* (Englewood Cliffs: Prentice-Hall, Inc., 1973), Chs. 10 and 11.

"Factors Borrow a Touch of Class," *Business Week* (March 6, 1971), pp. 88–89.

First Boston Corporation, *Commercial Paper* (New York: The First Boston Corporation, 1974).

HARRIS, DUANE G., "Some Evidence on Differential Lending Practices at Commercial Banks," *Journal of Finance* 28 (December, 1973), pp. 1303–1311.

HAYES, DOUGLAS A., *Bank Lending Policies* (Ann Arbor: Bureau of Business Research, The University of Michigan, 1971), Chs. 5, 6, and 7.

HERBST, ANTHONY F., "Some Empirical Evidence on the Determinants of Trade Credit at the Industry Level of Aggregation," *Journal of Financial and Quantitative Analysis* 9 (June, 1974), pp. 377–394.

LAZERE, MONROE R., ed., *Commercial Financing* (New York: The Ronald Press Company, 1968).

MAO, JAMES C. T., *Quantitative Analysis of Financial Decisions* (New York: The Macmillan Company, 1969), Ch. 11.

MERRIS, RANDALL C., "The Prime Rate," in Federal Reserve Bank of Chicago, *Business Conditions* (April, 1975), pp. 3–12.

MILLER, NORMAN C., *The Great Salad Oil Swindle* (New York: Coward McCann, Inc., 1965).

Moody's Investors Service, "Commercial Paper: The Market & Moody's Role," a mimeographed statement issued in 1973.

NAITOVE, IRWIN, *Modern Factoring* (New York: American Management Association, 1969).

PAPPAS, JAMES L., and GEORGE P. HUBER, "Probabilistic Short-Term Financial Planning," *Financial Management* 2 (Autumn, 1973), pp. 36–44.

POGUE, GERALD A., and RALPH N. BUSSARD, "A Linear Programming Model for Short Term Planning Under Uncertainty," *Sloan Management Review* 13 (Spring, 1972), pp. 69–98.

STONE, BERNELL K., "Cash Planning and Credit-Line Determination With a Financial Statement Simulator: A Case Report on Short-Term Financial Planning," *Journal of Financial and Quantitative Analysis* 8 (December, 1973), pp. 711–729.

SUMMERS, BRUCE, J., "Loan Commitments to Business in United States Banking History," in Federal Reserve Bank of Richmond, *Economic Review* 61 (September–October, 1975), pp. 15–23.

THACKRAY, JOHN, "Where Does Commercial Paper Stand?" *Corporate Financing* 2 (September–October, 1970), pp. 22–26, 62–66.

Part Eight

Corporate Restructuring

22 Mergers and Acquisitions

"Norton Simon Inc. Plans to Buy Max Factor in $480 Million Swap" —"LTV to Acquire Jones & Laughlin Steel, the Nation's Sixth Largest Steelmaker"—"Kentucky Fried Chicken Corporation Agrees to Merge with Heublein Inc."—"Mobil Considers Bid for $500 Million of Marcor Stock." These financial headlines describe firms choosing to grow through external means. A firm can grow either internally, by accumulating specific assets, or externally, by combining with other businesses. There is a distinction between two forms of combinations—in some, one firm absorbs another; in others, two firms create a third. The former are technically known as mergers (or acquisitions) and the latter as consolidations. This distinction, however, is generally without economic significance, so we shall refer to all combinations simply as mergers. In all cases, moreover, there is one firm which retains control, and in this chapter we shall consider mergers primarily from the viewpoint of this "acquiring" firm.

WHY COMPANIES MERGE

External vs. Internal Growth

Instead of acquiring another business, a firm could duplicate that business by expanding internally. Merger, however, eliminates start-up time. Let us suppose, for instance, that a manufacturer of photocopying equipment wants to enter the electronic computer field. If the firm chooses to develop internally the requisite technology and marketing capability, it may be years before the investment reaches fruition. But if the firm acquires an existing computer company, the investment may begin to generate profits much more quickly. External growth may have the further advantage of bringing to the acquiring firm resources (such as managerial talent, patents, and marketing capability) that would be difficult to duplicate. Moreover, merger eliminates some of the potential competition by preserving the existing market structure instead of adding another firm to the field. Although increased competition may be desirable socially, it inevitably dilutes the profit potential of all manufacturers in the industry.

Supply Price vs. Demand Price

Conditions for Merger. A merger can occur only if the selling firm's minimum supply (or asking) price is less than the buying firm's maximum demand (or bid) price.[1] Assuming that both seller and buyer are well informed about the business to be traded, one may wonder how the supply and demand prices could be far enough apart to make the merger profitable from both points of view. To see how a merger can benefit both firms, let us define the following terms for the acquiring firm (A), the target firm (T), and the combined firm (C):

$Y_m(\text{A})$ = Expected adjusted earnings of A in time period m if no merger takes place (as envisaged by A's stockholders)
$Y_m(\text{T})$ = Expected adjusted earnings of T in time period m if no merger takes place (as envisaged by T's stockholders)
$Y_m(\text{C})$ = Expected adjusted earnings of C in time period m after merger is completed (as envisaged by A's pre-merger stockholders)
k_a = Rate at which $Y_m(\text{A})$ would be discounted by A's stockholders if no merger takes place
k_t = Rate at which $Y_m(\text{T})$ would be discounted by T's stockholders if no merger takes place
k_c = Rate at which $Y_m(\text{C})$ would be discounted by C's stockholders (as envisaged by A's pre-merger stockholders).

The supply and demand prices are thus given, respectively, by these expressions:

$$V_s = \frac{Y_1(\text{T})}{(1+k_t)} + \frac{Y_2(\text{T})}{(1+k_t)^2} + \frac{Y_3(\text{T})}{(1+k_t)^3} + \cdots \quad (22\text{-}1)$$

$$V_d = \left[\frac{Y_1(\text{C})}{(1+k_c)} + \frac{Y_2(\text{C})}{(1+k_c)^2} + \cdots\right] - \left[\frac{Y_1(\text{A})}{(1+k_a)} + \frac{Y_2(\text{A})}{(1+k_a)^2} + \cdots\right] \quad (22\text{-}2)$$

---

[1] For a similar analysis, see Dennis C. Mueller, "A Theory of Conglomerate Mergers," *Quarterly Journal of Economics* 83 (November, 1969), pp. 643–659.

A merger of A and T can be consummated only if T's supply price V_s is less than A's demand price V_d.

How Mergers Create Value. In a merger, the acquiring firm generally expects the acquired firm to contribute more to the combined earnings than it had earned when operating alone. Thus, if A earned \$3 before the merger and T earned \$2, A would expect the combined earnings of post-merger firm C to exceed \$5. There are four reasons for this "$3 + 2 > 5$" phenomenon, which is known as synergy. First, since V_d and V_s are based on future earnings, it is possible for A to see latent potential in T which T itself may be unaware of. Second, the merger may permit funds to be raised externally at a lower cost than the combined costs to the separate firms. Third, there are possible tax savings if one firm has a loss which the other firm can use to reduce its taxable income. Finally, operating economies resulting from merger should enable C's earnings to exceed the combined earnings of A and T. A well-conceived merger may, for example, smooth out irregular production patterns, thus reducing production costs. There may also be savings in administrative overhead and distribution costs.

The extent to which operating economies may be realized depends on the nature of the merger: horizontal, vertical, or conglomerate. In a horizontal merger, the combining firms were previously competitors: Proctor and Gamble, for example, acquired Clorox Chemical Company (which it later divested), a bleach manufacturer. This type of merger generates the greatest opportunities for real savings. In a vertical merger, the combining companies previously had a supplier-customer relationship: for example, Georgia Pacific Corporation acquired a paper mill in order to have a ready market for its wood pulp. Operating economies are limited in this sort of merger but nonetheless possible. In a conglomerate merger, the combining firms had no previous relationship: for example, Brown and Williamson, a tobacco company, acquired the totally dissimilar Gimbel Brothers department-store chain. In this case, operating economies are obviously less likely.

The values of V_d and V_s depend not only on expected earnings but also on the stockholders' required rates of return. The demand price may thus diverge from the supply price even if a merger is expected to produce no operating economies. Firm A might be a large public company acquiring a small private company T. T's owner may wish to sell because he fears competition or other inherent risks, because he wishes to insure continuity, because he wants to anticipate death and estate taxes, or for other personal reasons. His motives may prompt him to use a high discount rate to appraise the expected earnings of T, resulting in a low supply price. Firm A, on the other hand, can evaluate T solely on its business merit. A's management may see the same risk in T but will be better able to assume the risk, which it can reduce through diversification. This difference may justify A's appraisal of T's expected earnings at a lower discount rate, thus yielding a demand price higher than T's supply price. The differential permits a merger that is profitable to both sides.

We have been assuming that companies merge in order to maximize stockholders' wealth. But this is not always the case. In many corporations, management is oriented toward growth and is thus more concerned with expansion than with wealth. This orientation is encouraged by the executives' compensation system and reflects personal ambitions as well. Management may therefore be willing to offer a higher demand price than the stockholders would offer. A similar situation may also occur on the seller's side. If T's management fears a takeover by an unfriendly interest, it may try to promote a merger with a friendly company even at a selling price below the shareholders' minimum. Mergers taking place under either of these conditions do not benefit the stockholders.

GAINING CONTROL OF THE TARGET COMPANY

In attempting to gain control of a target company, the acquiring firm must consider four factors: antitrust legislation; negotiation vs. takeover bids; legal modes of merger; and single vs. multi-corporate structures.

Antitrust Legislation

Section 7 of the Clayton Act prohibits any merger, the effect of which "may be substantially to lessen competition, or to tend to create a monopoly." At one time, for example, Proctor and Gamble, the leading seller of detergents, soaps, and household cleansers, acquired the Clorox Chemical Company, the leading seller of liquid bleach. After the Federal Trade Commission (FTC) filed suit to divest, the Supreme Court ruled that the merger was illegal because it discouraged both actual and potential competition. Proctor and Gamble then sold 15 percent of interest in Clorox to the public and exchanged the remaining 85 percent with its stockholders for Proctor and Gamble common shares.

Negotiation vs. Takeover Bids

Negotiation. Firm A may approach T either through negotiation or through a takeover bid. If the former method is chosen, A's management negotiates with T's to reach a mutually satisfactory price. A's management needs to know the present and future tax liabilities that will result from the merger, the effect of the merger on A's financial statements, and the securities laws that must be complied with. T's management has similar tax, accounting, and legal concerns. Since a merger does not always require a vote of the stockholders of the acquiring firm, the demand price set by A's management may exceed the maximum price that A's stockholders would be willing to pay. But the formal approval of the stockholders of the selling company is always necessary, so that in theory T's supply price cannot be lower than T's shareholders' minimum selling price. In practice, however, T's management can use persuasion and proxy power to induce T's stockholders to accept an offer which they would normally reject. T's management would not then be acting in the best interests of T's stockholders, as in fact they sometimes do not. From A's viewpoint, negotiation is advantageous because, once an agreement has been reached, A can rely on T to use persuasion and proxy power to promote the merger.

Takeover Bids. If A anticipates a rebuff by T's management, or even if it has already been rebuffed, it can still gain control of T by appealing directly to T's stockholders. Such a takeover bid may be made either as a cash-tender offer or as a registered-exchange offer. The Newell Companies, Inc., for example, acquired EZ Paintr through a cash tender offer after being turned down in attempted negotiations. Newell offered $15 per share (about $2 above market price) for 250,000 of EZ's one million shares then outstanding. Before the offer was made, Newell already owned or controlled approximately 25 percent of EZ's shares. Through the tender offer, Newell was able to buy an additional 318,385 shares, creating a comfortable margin beyond the 50 percent needed for control.

Not all cash tender offers, of course, succeed. In order to avoid being taken over, the management of the target company may try to dissuade its stockholders from selling their shares, or they may dilute the acquiring company's control by issuing new shares, or they may even, with proper grounds, bring legal action against the would-be acquirer. Gulf and Western Industries, for example, tried to gain control of The Great Atlantic & Pacific Tea Company but was stopped by A & P's court actions.

In a registered-exchange offer, the acquiring firm offers the stockholders of the target firm securities rather than cash for shares in the target company. Since the offer is public, the securities must be registered with the SEC, making this method less effective than a cash tender offer. Registration requires detailed financial disclosures and a waiting period, giving the target firm's management time to mount a counter-offensive. Although a tender offer also involves some financial disclosure, it can be implemented quickly enough to surprise the target firm's management.

Legal Forms of Merger

To implement a merger, the acquiring firm may employ one of three legal forms: statutory merger or consolidation; acquisition of assets; or acquisition of stock.[2]

[2] Earl W. Kintner writes clearly on the relative merits of these three forms of mergers in his *Primer on the Law of Mergers* (New York: The Macmillan Company, 1973), Ch. 3; see also Charles A. Scharf, *Acquisitions, Mergers, Sales and Takeovers* (Englewood Cliffs: Prentice-Hall, Inc., 1971), Ch. 1.

Statutory Merger or Consolidation. A statutory merger or consolidation is a combination of two or more companies in conformity with state corporation laws. There are several standard requirements:

1. Approval by the board of directors of each company.
2. Approval by a set percentage of the stockholders of each company.
3. A merger agreement to be filed with state authorities.
4. Provision for dissenting stockholders to sell back their shares at a fair price.

In a merger, the acquiring firm completely absorbs the target company. In a consolidation, the two firms combine to form a new company. As we noted earlier, since the distinction is without economic significance, we may refer to both types of transactions as mergers.

One advantage of a statutory merger is the ease with which the acquiring company can gain control of the target firm's assets: no specific title transfers need be filed. Moreover, the acquiring company is permitted to use a wide range of securities to pay the target company, without jeopardizing the merger's tax-free status. A statutory merger may be disadvantageous, however, if the acquiring firm is interested only in a portion of the target company—a single division or even a single product line. In addition, the acquiring firm is exposed to any undisclosed or contingent liabilities of the target company.

Asset Acquisition. In asset acquisition, the acquiring company purchases all or some of the assets of the target company, but does not assume the latter's liabilities. The acquiring firm has the added advantage of being able to restrict its purchases to particular divisions or product lines. The purchase price becomes the new tax basis of the assets; and any tax arising from depreciation recapture is levied on the seller. One disadvantage is that asset acquisition requires the filing of specific transfer documents, which can be costly and complex if a variety of assets is involved.

Stock Acquisition. In stock acquisition, the acquiring firm purchases all or some of the stock of the target firm. Since only stock is purchased, there is no complex documentation process of asset transfer. Moreover, the acquiring firm does not assume the target company's liabilities. On the other hand, stockholders who refuse to sell constitute an uncertain minority which may limit the actions of the acquiring firm. (In statutory combinations, dissenting stockholders are bought out; in asset acquisitions, dissenting stockholders have no recourse.) A further drawback to stock acquisition is that the acquiring firm is liable for any tax arising from depreciation recapture if and when the target firm is liquidated.

The Use of a Holding Company

Stock acquisition raises an additional question: is it better to operate the different units of a business as a single unified corporation or as separate corporations under a holding company? A holding company is a firm that controls one or more other companies through the ownership of voting stock.

Advantages of a Holding Company. A holding company with a multi-corporate structure has several advantages.[3] First, since the effective stock control of a subsidiary may require as little as 20 percent of the voting stock, a holding company may control assets worth several times the value of its own capital. Second, since the subsidiary company retains its own name, any bad publicity it receives will be less damaging than otherwise to the other members of the affiliated group. Third, since subsidiary companies are separate legal entities, other members of the group are free of each firm's liabilities. The holding company can thus insulate its corporate core from extreme risk. A fourth advantage is the greater incentive for management performance since separate companies involve more precisely defined areas of responsibility and more flexible compensation and benefits for individual achievement. Finally, a multi-corporate structure is of advantage in circumventing government regulations. A bank may thus create a so-called one-bank holding company in order to engage, through the company's other subsidiaries, in activities not legally permitted to a bank.

Disadvantages of a Holding Company. The greatest disadvantage of a multi-corporate structure is the possible double taxation to which intercorporate dividends are liable. If acquiring firm A owns more than 80 percent of all the stock of subsidiary T, tax law permits the filing of a consolidated return, so that dividends received by A from T are excluded from any taxation. But if A owns less than 80 percent of T, the firms must file separate returns and pay separate taxes. Since 15 percent of any dividends A receives from T are taxable, and if A's marginal tax rate is 50 percent, the effective rate of double taxation on intercorporate dividends is 7.5 percent.

Another disadvantage is the risk of excessive debt financing when a holding company "pyramids" a firm's investment. Pyramiding occurs when A controls T with, for example, a 20 percent investment, and T in turn controls Z with a 20 percent investment. In this case, A in effect controls Z with 4 cents of investment for every dollar of assets owned and operated by Z. The danger is that the top holding company may attempt to reduce its equity investment even more by introducing debt at each level. When the system includes several levels, the total debt may become excessive, even

---

[3] For a fuller discussion, see Robert S. Holzman, "The Uses of a Multiple Corporation," in William S. Mishkin, ed., *Techniques in Corporate Reorganization* (New York: Presidents Publishing House, Inc., 1972), Ch. 18.

though the debt-to-equity ratio appears acceptable at each level. This leverage means that any fluctuation in earnings at the operating level will be transmitted upward in geometric proportion, making the top holding company especially vulnerable to a general business recession. It was such a misuse of the holding company structure that enabled Samuel Insull to control with each dollar of investment at the top as much as $2,000 in assets owned by electric utility operating companies at the bottom of the pyramid. The collapse of the Insull empire in 1932 gave impetus to the passage of the Public Utility Holding Company Act of 1935, which now limits the degree of pyramiding in electric and gas utility companies.

TAX AND SECURITIES LAWS AFFECTING MERGERS

Tax Considerations

Every merger involves tax considerations which affect the price that the buyer is willing to pay and the seller to accept. The subject is complex, but a few issues are basic.[4]

Tax Objectives. The most basic tax decision facing both seller and buyer is whether to structure a merger as a taxable or a "tax-free" transaction. When the selling company transfers its assets to the acquiring firm, the selling price may be either higher or lower than book value. Ordinarily, any gain would be immediately taxable and any loss immediately deductible. When, however, assets are transferred as a result of merger, the seller may postpone the tax consequences if the merger is structured as a tax-free "reorganization." (Here we are using reorganization as a concept in tax law, as distinct from its usage in bankruptcy proceedings.) If securities received in exchange qualify for tax postponement, the tax need not be paid until the securities are sold. Most taxpayers would naturally prefer to have taxes postponed, but to have deductions immediately realized. Therefore, if the selling price is above book value, the seller will prefer a tax-free structure; whereas if the selling price is below book value, he will prefer a taxable structure.

The buyer's tax objective is generally the reverse of the seller's. We must remember that if the transaction is tax-free, the buyer's tax base is the same as the seller's, and that if the transaction is taxable, the buyer's tax base will be the actual price paid for the acquired assets. Hence, if the merger price is lower than the seller's tax base or book value, the buyer will prefer a tax-free transaction so that he can compute depreciation on the

---

[4] A useful reference is Douglas A. Kahn, *Basic Corporate Taxation* (Ann Arbor: The Institute of Continuing Legal Education, 1973), Ch. 4; see also Scharf, *op. cit.*, Chs. 10 and 11.

basis of the seller's high book value, thus reducing his taxable income. Conversely, if the merger price is higher than book value, the buyer will prefer a taxable transaction so that he may equate his new tax base to the actual merger price, which will result in larger depreciation and smaller taxable income.

Tax-Free Acquisitions. Three types of transactions are legally defined as tax-free acquisitions:

1. Statutory mergers or consolidations (Type "A" reorganizations).
2. Stock-for-stock exchanges in which the acquiring company, by issuing only voting stock, gains control of at least 80 percent of the voting stock of the acquired company (Type "B" reorganizations).
3. Stock-for-asset exchanges in which the acquiring company, by issuing only voting stock, receives virtually all assets of the acquired company (Type "C" reorganizations).

A merger must also meet three judicial tests in order to qualify as tax-free: the business-purpose test; the continuity-of-interest test; and the step-transaction test. The first of these stipulates a business reason for the merger. The other two insure that a sale will not be camouflaged as a merger in order to gain tax-free status. If, for example, Firm A acquires Firm T in a statutory merger by paying T's stockholders a nominal number of A shares and a large cash balance, the transaction fails the continuity-of-interest test because T's shareholders do not receive equity in the new company equal to at least half the value of their old stock. The stockholders of the acquired company may receive cash or bonds up to 50 percent of their old stock's value without losing tax-free status, but such compensation is itself taxable. The step-transaction test covers the type of situation in which A pays cash for a portion of T's stock and then formally merges with T, paying with stock equal in value to 50 percent of T's remaining stock. The IRS will view the two steps as a single transaction, denying tax-free status to the merger. All three types of acquisitions are, of course, subject to these tests.

In a Type B merger (stock-for-stock), the method of payment often includes an "earn-out" clause, whereby the purchase price is contingent on the future earnings of the acquired company. Such an arrangement lessens the buyer's risk of overpaying and enhances the seller's ability to obtain a high purchase price. As long as there is a business reason for the earn-out clause, the clause does not affect tax-free status.

Tax Effect on Conglomerate Financing. Since conglomerates prefer debt financing, their acquisitions are typically taxable. Debt financing permits the reduction of the amount of stock issued, thus minimizing *EPS* dilution. Moreover, interest on debt is tax deductible. A conglomerate can satisfy the seller's wish for a tax-free transaction by using the installment method, enabling the seller to distribute his tax payments over a period of time. A merger qualifies as an installment sale if the initial payments (exclusive of evidences of debt) are no more than 30 percent of the sale price. The Tax Reform Act of 1969 limits, however, the type of debt qualifying for exclusion, making debt financing more difficult for conglomerates. Because the government wishes to limit such financing, the Act also restricts the annual deductible interest on merger indebtedness to $5,000,000.

Securities Laws

Because securities laws are complex, we shall discuss here only the most relevant aspects: those concerning the registration of securities offered in a merger proposal and their subsequent resale by the recipient stockholders.

Registration Requirements. Securities offered as payment in a merger proposal must now be registered with the SEC before they can be issued. For many years, however, SEC Rule 133 stated that the offering of such securities constituted neither a sale nor an offer to sell and so was not subject to registration requirements. This "no-sale" theory assumed that mergers were corporate acts, not the investment decisions of individual stockholders. But even before rescinding Rule 133, the no-sale theory was qualified in that the SEC applied it only to the initial issuance of the securities in a merger, not to public re-offerings after the merger. In 1973, SEC replaced Rule 133 with Rule 145, which classifies the offer of securities in a merger proposal as an offer to sell, therefore requiring registration.

Resale of Securities. SEC restrictions on the resale of securities acquired in a merger apply only to controlling stockholders, not to small stockholders. The controlling stockholders are, of course, free to offer publicly their entire holdings if they register their securities. But they may sell without registration only if the sale satisfies certain requirements of Rule 144:

1. The person making the resale must have owned the securities for at least two years.
2. For unlisted securities, the amount sold during any 6-month period must not exceed one percent of the class of securities outstanding; for listed securities, the amount must not exceed one percent of the class outstanding *or* the weekly trading volume for the preceding four weeks, whichever is smaller.
3. The sale must be made through a broker who neither solicits customers nor receives more than the normal brokerage commission.

4. The public must have access to certain information (balance sheet, income statement, etc.) about the issuer.

Rule 144 governs the resale of both securities acquired by private placement and securities held by controlling stockholders. The resale of privately placed securities must conform not only to the requirements listed above but also to certain additional strictures.

ACCOUNTING RULES AFFECTING MERGERS

Accounting Issues

The acquiring firm must determine the value at which new assets are to be entered on the books: historical cost (seller's book value) or market price (actual price paid). Accountants distinguish between outright purchase, in which the market price should be the basis for valuation, and pooling of interests, in which historical cost should be the basis.[5]

A purchase transaction takes place when the buyer pays for the acquired assets with cash or debt; the assets are then recorded at actual price. Since the actual price is often higher than book value, the buyer must assign the excess valuation in some distribution among the new assets. In a taxable transaction, the buyer may prefer to assign most of the excess value to depreciable assets (e.g., plant and equipment) so that he can benefit from future tax deductions. The seller, on the other hand, may prefer to assign most of the value to nondepreciable assets (e.g., land and goodwill) so that he can minimize depreciation recapture, which is taxable at the ordinary income-tax rate. The seller must pay tax on any gain on nondepreciable items but only at the capital-gains rate.

In a pooling-of-interests transaction, the buyer pays for the acquired assets with stock. Until 1970, management could choose either pooling-of-interests or purchase accounting for such a transaction. But in 1970 APB Opinion 16 revised the Accounting Principles Board's conditions and stipulated that a transaction meeting those conditions must use pooling-of-interests accounting; all others must use purchase accounting.

Pooling-of-Interests vs. Purchase Accounting

A hypothetical example adapted from Norton Simon's acquisition of Max Factor & Co. will illustrate the difference between accounting methods. Let us assume that on January 1 of the current year Company N issued 11 million shares of common stock in exchange for all 10 million shares of Company M's outstanding common stock. At the time, each company's

[5] See *Opinions of the Accounting Principles Board, No. 16* (New York: The American Institute of Certified Public Accountants, 1970).

Table 22-1 Company M, Balance Sheet, January 1, Current Year (in millions of dollars)

Assets		Liabilities and Stockholders' Equity	
Cash and marketable securities	$ 25	Short-term liabilities	$ 40
Accounts receivable	60	Long-term bonds	0
Inventories	50	Common stock	50
Plant and equipment	45	Surplus	90
Total	$180	Total	$180

stock was selling at a market price of $40 per share, so that N paid $440 million in stock for M's equity. After the merger, N dissolved M and took over its assets and liabilities. Since M had $40 million in outstanding debt, N paid in effect $480 million for M's assets. Table 22-1 shows M's pre-merger balance sheet; Column 1 in Table 22-2 shows that of N.

If the merger qualifies as a pooling of interests, Company N must record the acquired assets at Company M's old book value (see Column 2, Table 22-2). The balance sheet of the post-merger Company NM is obtained simply by combining the balance sheets of the two merging companies (see Column 4, Table 22-2). Even though the exchange is based on a $480 million valuation of M's assets, the acquisition is recorded at the old book value of $180 million.

Table 22-2 Pooling-of-Interests vs. Purchase Accounting (in millions of dollars)

	Company N	Company M		Company NM	
		Pooling	Purchase	Pooling	Purchase
	(1)	(2)	(3)	(4)	(5)
Cash and marketable securities	$200	$ 25	$ 25	$ 225	$ 225
Accounts receivable	300	60	60	360	360
Inventories	150	50	100	200	250
Plant and equipment	250	45	145	295	395
Goodwill	–	–	150	–	150
Total	$900	$180	$480	$1,080	$1,380
Short-term liabilities	$220	$ 40	$ 40	$ 260	$ 260
Long-term bonds	250	0	0	250	250
Common stock	100	50	50	150	150
Surplus	330	90	390	420	720
Total	$900	$180	$480	$1,080	$1,380

If, however, the merger does not qualify as a pooling of interests, the acquired assets will be recorded according to the purchase method at the actual purchase price of $480 million. Since this amount is greater than the book value by $300 million, the excess must be assigned to the various assets; any amount left over is designated goodwill. Column 3 in Table 22-2 shows a possible distribution of excess value. Company NM's post-merger balance sheet again represents the total assets, liabilities, and equities of the two firms (see Column 5, Table 22-2).[6]

Under a pooling of interests, Company NM's post-merger assets are valued at $1.08 billion; under purchase accounting, at $1.38 billion. The lower value under pooling implies lower future depreciation and other expenses, implying in turn that NM will report artificially inflated per-share earnings.[7] If NM believes that investors will accept the inflated *EPS* at face value, it will expect its stock price to be higher under pooling than under purchase accounting. This, then, is the central appeal of pooling of interests.

Since purchase accounting results in a higher asset value, it also results in higher depreciation, lower reported earnings, and therefore lower taxes. The tax benefit may at first appear to override the potential benefit of higher reported earnings. It is, however, the taxable or tax-free status of a merger, rather than the accounting method, which determines whether or not a firm is permitted to step up the tax basis of its assets. Although ordinarily there is considerable overlapping of the conditions for tax-free status and those for pooling of interests, it is quite possible to structure a taxable merger such that it will qualify for pooling of interests.

Conditions for Pooling

There are four major conditions which must be met for pooling-of-interests accounting:

1. The merger must involve a combination of previously autonomous and independent companies, neither of which has recently been a subsidiary or a division of another company.
2. The acquiring company may issue only common stock in exchange for 90 percent or more of the voting common stock of the target company.
3. The acquiring company may not, prior to a merger, buy back its own stock in order to use it to acquire another company, nor may

---

[6] For the sake of simplicity, we have assumed that the shares issued by N have a total par value equal to that of the shares of M being retired. Otherwise, an adjusting entry would be necessary to account for any difference.

[7] It is this accounting quirk, which endows stock with the power to inflate reported earnings, that prompts financial writers to call stock used in acquisition "funny money."

it agree to buy back later the common stock with which it has transacted a merger.

4. The acquiring company must not plan to dispose of a significant part of the acquired assets within two years after the merger unless it is necessary for the ordinary conduct of business or for the elimination of duplicate facilities or excess capacity.

FINANCIAL EVALUATION OF MERGERS

Once an acquiring company has determined its target firm's minimum selling price, it must then place its own value on the target company in order to decide whether or not to proceed with the planned merger. Capital-budgeting theory enables us to derive a set of merger-acceptance criteria which shows the fallacy of judging an acquisition solely on the basis of its immediate effect on the *EPS* of the acquiring company.

Merger as an Investment Decision

Basic Acceptance Criteria. Acquiring a business is similar to buying a piece of equipment or building a plant, insofar as each is an investment in earning assets. The capital-budgeting framework for evaluating plant and equipment is therefore also applicable to mergers and acquisitions. In general, an investment is worthwhile if its cost is less than the present value of its future benefits. A merger, specifically, is worthwhile only if the price paid is less than the present value of future benefits attributable solely to the target firm.

Let us suppose that Company A contemplates acquiring all of Company T's shares by paying either in cash, straight debt, or straight preferred stock. After the merger, all of T's assets and liabilities will be taken over by the combined Company C. To derive the acceptance criteria, we define the key financial variables of the two combining firms:

$Y_1(\mathrm{A})$ = Current adjusted earnings (i.e., dividends) accruing to the common stockholders of A if no merger takes place

$Y_1(\mathrm{T})$ = Current adjusted earnings accruing to common stockholders of T if no merger takes place

$Y_1(\mathrm{C})$ = Current adjusted earnings accruing to common stockholders of C if merger takes place

g_a = Constant annual growth rate of A's pre-merger earnings stream

g_t = Constant annual growth rate of T's pre-merger earnings stream

g_c = Constant annual growth rate of C's post-merger earnings stream

k_a = Investors' required rate of return on A's pre-merger earnings stream
k_t = Investors' required rate of return on T's pre-merger earnings stream
k_c = Investors' required rate of return on C's post-merger earnings stream
S = Seller's minimum supply price for T's shares.

Since adjusted earnings are the equivalent of cash dividends, we shall refer to them as such below, to avoid confusion with earnings per income statement. We assume that the amount reinvested by A makes A's dividends grow at an annual rate of g_a and that, if the merger takes place, the reinvestment will make the combined dividends of C grow at an annual rate of g_c. Applying the dividend-capitalization formula, we derive the respective total market values for shares of A and of C:

$$\frac{Y_1(\mathrm{A})}{k_a - g_a} \text{ and } \frac{Y_1(\mathrm{C})}{k_c - g_c}$$

A merger is therefore profitable to A's stockholders only if

$$\underbrace{\frac{Y_1(\mathrm{C})}{k_c - g_c}}_{\substack{\text{Value of} \\ \text{C shares}}} - \underbrace{\frac{Y_1(\mathrm{A})}{k_a - g_a}}_{\substack{\text{Value of} \\ \text{A shares}}} > 0 \qquad (22\text{-}3)$$

i.e., only if a merger increases the value of the shares held by A's stockholders. Note that, in this inequality, $Y_1(\mathrm{C})$ varies inversely with the price paid for T's shares, which in turn varies directly with S. Hence, although S does not appear in (22–3), S nonetheless influences a merger's profitability.

The above criterion applies only when payment is made in a form that does not dilute the ownership interest of A's stockholders. In a common-stock-for-common-stock exchange, by contrast, A pays for T by issuing a certain number of common shares; after the merger, therefore, A's original stockholders do not own 100 percent of the new company. To take account of this complication, we define n_a as the number of A shares outstanding before the merger and Δn_a as the number of shares issued by A in exchange for the shares of T. After the merger, there are thus $n_a + \Delta n_a$ shares of A (now Company C), $n_a/(n_a + \Delta n_a)$ of which are owned by A's original stockholders and $\Delta n_a/(n_a + \Delta n_a)$ of which are owned by the original T stockholders. A merger will be profitable to A's stockholders only if

$$\underbrace{\frac{Y_1(\mathrm{C})}{k_c - g_c}\left(1 - \frac{\Delta n_a}{n_a + \Delta n_a}\right)}_{\substack{\text{Value of C's shares} \\ \text{owned by A's stock-} \\ \text{holders}}} - \underbrace{\frac{Y_1(\mathrm{A})}{k_a - g_a}}_{\substack{\text{Value of A's} \\ \text{shares without} \\ \text{merger}}} > 0 \qquad (22\text{-}4)$$

where $Y_1(C)$ and k_c are as defined before, but have different values because of the changed method of financing. Condition (22-4) is similar to (22-3) in that each criterion states, in effect, that A should acquire T only if a merger will increase the value of the shares held by A's old stockholders.

When these formulas are applied, the post-merger growth rate g_c is not necessarily the weighted average of the pre-merger growth rates of the separate companies. Depending on whether the merger produces economies or diseconomies of scale, g_c may be either higher or lower than the weighted average. Similarly, depending on whether the merger increases or decreases risk, the new capitalization rate k_c may be either higher or lower, respectively, than the weighted average of the pre-merger capitalization rates. Finally, when an acquisition is paid for with convertible securities, A must provide for the possibility that the future price of C's common stock may not rise sufficiently to bring about conversion. If conversion does not take place, (22-3) is the appropriate formula for judging the merger's profitability; if conversion does take place, (22-4) is appropriate. Since any future conversion is only probable, the assessment of such a merger's profitability is also only probable.

A Numerical Example. We shall suppose that Allen, Inc., a maker of digital watches, contemplates the acquisition of Thomas, Inc., a maker of sleeping bags, by an exchange of common stock. The first column of Table 22-3 gives the symbols for the key financial variables of these companies; the next two columns give the respective values of the variables in the absence of a merger. Each Allen share currently generates \$2 in earnings and pays \$1.28 in dividends. Since investors expect Allen dividends to grow at 6 percent and since they require a return of 10 percent, each Allen share sells at a market price of \$32 (= \$1.28/[.10 − .06]), or 16 times its current earnings. Each Thomas share currently generates \$2.50 in earnings and pays \$1.00 in dividends. Since investors expect Thomas dividends to grow at 10 percent and since they require a return of 15 percent, each Thomas share sells at a market price of \$20 (= \$1.00/[.15 − .10]), or 8 times its current earnings. There are 5 million Allen shares outstanding with a total market value of \$160 million and 400,000 Thomas shares outstanding with a total market value of \$8 million. To effect a merger, Thomas stockholders have agreed to accept, in exchange for all their common stock, 250,000 shares of newly issued Allen common stock, which also have a total market value of \$8 million. It is understood that the combined company will adopt a 60 percent dividend-payout ratio.

After the merger, Allen-Thomas will have combined earnings of \$11 million, of which \$6.6 million will be paid out in dividends. There will be a total of 5.25 million shares, so that per-share earnings will be \$2.10 and per-share dividends will be \$1.26. Taking into account its reinvestment policy and the possible effect of synergy, Allen's management expects

Table 22-3 Comparative Financial Data of Allen, Inc., and Thomas, Inc.

	Symbols	Before Merger		Allen-Thomas After Merger*
		Allen	Thomas	
Total earnings	nE	$10,000,000	$1,000,000	$11,000,000
Total dividends (Y)	nD	$ 6,400,000	$ 400,000	$ 6,600,000
Growth rate	g	6%	10%	6.8%
Capitalization rate	k	10%	15%	10.3%
Number of shares	n	5,000,000	400,000	5,250,000
Earnings per share	E	$2	$2.50	$2.10
Dividends per share	D	$1.28	$1.00	$1.26
Price per share	P	$32	$20	$35.92
Price-earnings ratio	Π	16	8	17.1

*The results are calculated using four decimal places. Because of rounding, the numbers may appear not to agree.

post-merger dividends to grow at a rate of 6.8 percent. This rate is somewhat higher than the weighted average growth rate of 6.4 percent, using the separate companies' earnings as weights. Allen's management expects investors in the shares of the combined company to require a return of 10.3 percent, implying a post-merger share price of about $35.92 (= $1.26/[.103 − .068]). A capitalization rate of 10.3 percent implies that investors view Allen-Thomas as slightly more risky than the pre-merger Allen firm. Since the merger increases share price by about $3.92, acquisition is profitable to Allen stockholders, whose 5 million shares increase in market value by $19,591,800 after the merger. Merger is also profitable to Thomas stockholders, who gain $979,600 as a result.

Inequality (22-4) confirms the profitability of the proposed merger to Allen's stockholders. The new Allen-Thomas shares have a total value of $188,571,400:

$$\frac{Y_1(C)}{k_c - g_c} = \frac{\$6{,}600{,}000}{.103 - .068} = \$188{,}571{,}400$$

Of this amount, $8,979,600, or 4.76 percent, represents the value of the shares issued to the old Thomas stockholders:

$$\left(\frac{250{,}000}{5{,}250{,}000}\right)(\$188{,}571{,}400) = \$8{,}979{,}600$$

Hence, after the merger, the holdings of Allen's original stockholders have a value of $179,591,800, which is $19,591,800 higher than the value of the old Allen shares.

Even though the merger raises Allen's per-share earnings from \$2.00 to \$2.10, we should not infer that an immediate rise in per-share earnings is a condition for profitable merger. The value of any share is determined jointly by its earnings, payout ratio, expected growth rate, and market capitalization rate. Since a merger affects all four of these variables, the acquiring firm may benefit even if its immediate *EPS* declines. Conversely, the firm may suffer even if its immediate *EPS* rises.

To illustrate this, let us retain the pre-merger data for Allen but change the corresponding data for Thomas. We shall now assume that Thomas' investors require a return of only 12.5 percent, so that Thomas' stock sells at a market price of \$40 per share. The new figures imply a price-earnings ratio of 16 (the same as Allen's) and a total market value of \$16 million for Thomas' 400,000 outstanding shares. We shall also assume that Thomas' stockholders demand a 20 percent premium. Allen must thus issue 600,000 shares in exchange for Thomas' 400,000 shares. The exchange will make Allen's *EPS* fall from \$2.00 to \$1.96. This merger is even more profitable to Thomas than a merger under previous terms; but more to the point, it is also profitable to Allen's stockholders, though not so profitable as the previously postulated merger.

The converse proposition may be verified by retaining the pre-merger data for both Allen and Thomas, and by applying a high capitalization rate of, say, 11.3 percent to the post-merger dividend stream of Allen-Thomas. In this case, the price of Allen-Thomas shares is only \$27.94; and, in spite of the increase in *EPS* from \$2.00 to \$2.10, the original stockholders of Allen will suffer a loss totaling \$20.3 million.

The EPS Game

Our example shows that it is fallacious for an acquiring firm to evaluate a merger solely in terms of its immediate effect on *EPS*. And yet in the "*EPS* game" of the 1960's, many conglomerates sought nothing more than instant earnings from their acquisition candidates. The game was based on a simple theorem for combining earnings: if A acquires T through a common stock exchange in which the shares exchanged have equal total market value, then A's *EPS* must rise or fall depending on whether A's price-earnings ratio was higher or lower than T's.

It is easy to derive this theorem. Pre-merger A has n_a shares of common stock outstanding; each share earns E_a dollars and sells for P_a dollars. T has n_t shares outstanding; each earns E_t dollars and sells for P_t dollars. In exchange for all of T's stock, A will issue Δn_a shares of its own stock, so that

$$\underbrace{(\Delta n_a) P_a}_{\text{Value of A shares issued}} = \underbrace{n_t P_t}_{\text{Value of T shares}} \tag{22-5}$$

If E'_a is the EPS of A's stock after the merger, then

$$E'_a = \frac{E_a n_a + E_t n_t}{n_a + \Delta n_a} \tag{22-6}$$

Substituting (22-5) into (22-6) and rearranging the terms, we find the ratio of the post-merger EPS to the pre-merger EPS of A's stock:

$$\frac{E'_a}{E_a} = \frac{E_a n_a + E_t n_t}{E_a n_a + \frac{\Pi_t}{\Pi_a} E_t n_t} \tag{22-7}$$

where Π_t and Π_a are the price-earnings ratios of T's and A's shares, respectively. Clearly, if $\Pi_a > \Pi_t$, then $\frac{E'_a}{E_a} > 1$, which means that merger will increase A's EPS. Conversely, if $\Pi_a < \Pi_t$, then $\frac{E'_a}{E_a} < 1$, which means that merger will decrease A's EPS.

We now have the means to explain the EPS game. The first step is the creation of an instant increase in EPS through acquisition. The above theorem explains why in the 1960's many conglomerates restricted their acquisitions to firms with low price-earnings ratios. But the acquired company may lack growth potential, so that the second step is to convince the investing public that the acquisition has had no adverse effect on the growth potential of the conglomerate. In the 1960's, this was not difficult because, as Andrew Tobias noted, the investors "wanted to believe."[8] (Tobias was a vice president of the National Student Marketing Corporation, a glamor company of that era.) If the investors are gullible enough, they may even see the contrived growth as a basis for raising the price-earnings ratio of the conglomerate stock. When NSMC was at its peak, its stock sold at a price-earnings ratio of about 100. The mere combination of two firms could thus create a higher market valuation. The basic strategy of the EPS game was to purchase the earnings of target companies at a low price-earnings ratio and then to resell them at a higher ratio.

If a firm could buy growth companies during their formative periods at low price-earnings ratios, the EPS game could conceivably go on for a long time. Most firms that sell at a low price-earnings ratio, however, do so because they lack growth potential. It is this lack of internal growth that forces the conglomerate into a program of continual acquisition. The example in Table 22-4 shows that the acquisition pace necessary to protect a contrived growth image by external means cannot, in practice, be sustained.

---

[8] Andrew Tobias, *The Funny Money Game* (Chicago: Playboy Press, 1971), p. 64.

Table 22-4 Pace of Acquisition Needed to Sustain Constant 11% Growth in *EPS*

Year	Earnings of Acquiring Company	Earnings of Acquired Company
1	$ 10,000	$ 2,500
2	12,500	3,125
3	15,625	3,906
4	19,531	4,883
5	24,414	6,104
6	30,518	20,345
7	50,863	33,908
8	84,771	56,514
9	141,285	94,190
10	235,475	156,983

In this example, Company A acquires earnings of other companies by exchanging common stock of equal value.[9] During the first five years, A's common stock has a price-earnings ratio two times that of the acquired companies; during the next five years, the ratio drops to 1.33 times that of the acquired companies. Suppose now that in the first year A has $10,000 in earnings and acquires T, with its earnings of $2,500; the result is an 11 percent increase in *EPS* for A. To sustain this rate of growth in the second year, A must acquire companies with earnings of $3,125; and so forth. By the tenth year, A would have to acquire companies with earnings totaling $156,983 in order to maintain its growth rate. A constant 11 percent growth rate would force A to acquire earnings totaling $383,500 over the course of ten years—more than 38 times A's original size! Dolly Madison Industries, Inc., one of the 1960's glamor companies, was able to set a fast pace for a few years but could not sustain it indefinitely. Finding itself overextended, the company was forced to reorganize under federal bankruptcy laws.

SPINOFFS AND SEGMENTAL FINANCING

Let us posit a firm operating several different lines of business, either as divisions of a single company or as subsidiaries of a holding company. The firm must decide whether or not it is advisable to separate these businesses from the main company in order to create a public market for the securities of the individual firms. Spinoffs and segmental financing are the

---

[9] The data in Table 22-4 are computed using the formula $\rho = \frac{\alpha(1-\beta)}{1+\alpha\beta}$, where ρ = A's percentage increase in *EPS;* α = the ratio of acquired firm T's total earnings to A's; and β = the price-earnings ratio actually paid for firm T divided by A's price-earnings ratio. For the derivation of this formula, see Uwe E. Reinhardt, *Mergers and Consolidations: A Corporate-Finance Approach* (Morristown: General Learning Press, 1972), pp. 19–20.

two main techniques for separating a division from its parent company. They are in effect the opposite of mergers and are generally prompted by forces opposite to those which encourage merger.

Spinoffs

Method. In a spinoff, a company distributes to the public its ownership interest in a segment of its business (a segment, that is, which was previously operated either as a division or as a subsidiary). The stock may either be given free to the company's stockholders, sold to the stockholders through subscription rights, or sold to the general public. In all three cases, a new public market is created. A spinoff may be total or partial: either all or some of the stock may be distributed. Examples of spinoffs include those of Wilson and Company from LTV, the Baskin-Robbins Ice Cream Corporation from United Brands Company, Olinkraft, Inc., from Olin Corporation, and Avis, Inc., from ITT.

Reasons. The benefits of a multi-corporate structure include the isolation of risk, the protection of the corporate image, and a greater incentive for management. These benefits apply also to spinoffs, although the goal of a spinoff is not merely to establish a multi-corporate structure. The major advantage of a spinoff is the possible increase in the market valuation of a division or subsidiary. In a classic example, LTV acquired Wilson and Company, a meat-packing firm with pharmaceutical and sporting-goods divisions. LTV separated these divisions from the meat packer and spun them off as Wilson Pharmaceutical, Wilson Sporting Goods, and the parent Wilson and Company. Although LTV spun off only 20 percent of each firm, the higher valuations placed on the companies by investors netted LTV more than half the price of the original Wilson and Company.

When the securities are sold, rather than given free to stockholders, spinoff may also be advantageous as a method of raising money. In a period of tight money, spinoff may be cheaper than any other financing alternative. In addition to financial advantages, spinoff may be motivated by legal considerations. Antitrust action, for example, compelled ITT to divest itself of the Avis car rental company.

Segmental Financing

Method. Segmental financing is the transfer of a part of a company's assets to a wholly-owned subsidiary so that the subsidiary, rather than the parent company, may borrow against the assets. Whereas spinoff creates a separate market for the common stock of a subsidiary, segmental financing creates a separate market for the debt instruments of the subsidiary. The subsidiary may be either a newly created captive finance company or newly created captive leasing company. The General Motors Acceptance Corporation, for example, is a wholly-owned or "captive" company engaged primarily in the installment financing of GM automobiles and trucks. GMAC is not a division of GM but rather a wholly-owned subsidiary with a separate capacity to borrow in both the long- and the short-term capital markets. Similarly, a computer manufacturer may create a captive leasing company to help the parent company finance the heavy investment in leased computers. Since a captive finance company has the same benefits as a captive leasing company, a discussion of one will suffice for both.

To preserve its separate borrowing status, the subsidiary, even though wholly-owned, will not be consolidated with the parent company in any financial reporting. General Motors thus combines its investment in GMAC with other nonconsolidated subsidiaries and records the total in a single line on its balance sheet. GM has a debt-to-equity ratio of roughly .6 to 1, while GMAC has a ratio of approximately 12.7 to 1. If GMAC were consolidated with GM, the latter's balance sheet would have reported a much higher debt-to-equity ratio. Because of segmental financing, debt which appears on the balance sheet of GM's finance subsidiary does not appear directly on its own.

Reasons. The market value of a manufacturing company with a financing operation may be higher if that operation is organized as a wholly-owned subsidiary than if it were operated as a division of the manufacturing company. This possibility stems from the greater borrowing capacity of a separate finance operation. Many lenders will lend more money per dollar of equity—and will lend it at a lower rate of interest—against installment paper held by a finance company than they will lend against the same assets held by a parent concern, which is often a manufacturer. Lenders seem to rely more on the borrower's industrial classification than on its actual operations.

Some financial writers disagree that a manufacturer can increase its overall borrowing capacity by segmental financing. Wilbur G. Lewellen, for example, argues for the opposite effect: if a manufacturer keeps its financial operation as a division, he argues, the pooling of cash surpluses and deficits will better enable the company to weather financial setbacks.[10] He goes on to claim that if the assets of the finance operation are formally segregated, even in a wholly-owned subsidiary, legal barriers interfere with the free transfer of funds. While the parent company's creditors still have full access to the net assets of the subsidiary, the subsidiary's creditors have no such access to the assets of the parent company. This insulation of the parent company protects the creditors as a group less than a manufacturing concern without segmental financing. Lewellen thus concludes that lenders will charge more

---

[10] Wilbur G. Lewellen, "Finance Subsidiaries and Corporate Borrowing Capacity," *Financial Management* 1 (Spring, 1972), pp. 21–31.

and lend less to companies under segmental financing. Such a conclusion is, in fact, in conflict with the analysis which prompts many manufacturing companies to set up finance subsidiaries.

Lewellen's analysis assumes a perfect market in which all lenders are fully informed and behave perfectly rationally. Such an assumption may not be realistic, however, because of the cost and difficulty of gathering and interpreting credit information. Though financial institutions are better equipped than individual investors for it, credit analysis is far from being a science. Because information is costly, credit analysis is always based on incomplete data; and lacking omniscience, loan officers tend to base their decisions on established conventions and rules of thumb. In view of these imperfections in the actual capital market, the creation of finance subsidiaries by manufacturing concerns may well be economically justified.

REVIEW QUESTIONS

1. In any merger, the range of negotiations is limited by the buyer's maximum demand price and the seller's minimum supply price. Assuming that both parties are well informed as to the earning capacity of the target company, why do the maximum demand price and the minimum supply price not coincide?
2. Distinguish between a statutory merger, an asset acquisition, and a stock acquisition. What are the advantages and disadvantages of each method from the standpoint of the acquiring firm?
3. To what extent are "tax-free" mergers really tax-free? When is tax-free status desirable from the acquiring firm's viewpoint? from the acquired firm's? Which three types of mergers may qualify as tax-free? What three judicial tests must be satisfied for a merger to receive tax-free status?
4. Explain the "no-sale" theory of merger. What role has it played in securities law? Why was this theory discarded? What SEC rules have replaced it?
5. Pooling-of-interests accounting has been described as the effective treatment of a merger as a purchase retroactive to the date of the original organization of the acquired company. If this is true, could purchase accounting be similarly described as the effective treatment of a merger as a pooling of interests from the date of acquisition?
6. Eagles Hat Company has acquired all the stock of Laserex, Inc. Eagles may either operate Laserex as a division or set it up as wholly-owned subsidiary. Discuss the advantages and disadvantages to Eagles of each method.
7. Explain how the *EPS* game was played by many conglomerate companies in the 1960's. What was the outcome? Was it inevitable?
8. Define spinoffs and segmental financing and discuss their similarities and differences. For each method of "un-merging," specify the reasons and illustrate with recent examples.
9. The Canada Development Company made a tender offer to acquire 10 million shares of Texasgulf, Inc., at $29 per share. The Texasgulf shares closed on the New York Stock Exchange that day at 26\frac{1}{8}$ and then began to decline. A

week after the offer was made, Texasgulf shares were trading at $25. Why would the stock trade at $25 even though CDC was ready to buy it for $29?

10. In *The Funny Money Game,* Andrew Tobias gives an interesting account of his experience as an officer of the National Student Marketing Corporation in the 1960's. Speculate on the financing instrument Tobias calls funny money used in making acquisitions. Why does he give this label to this instrument?

PROBLEMS

1. Imagine two earnings streams, A and B, each totaling $10,000 in year 1. Stream A grows at an annual rate of 10 percent; stream B, at 20 percent. Project the probable annual growth rate for combined stream A + B: will the growth rate be closer to 10 percent, 15 percent, or 20 percent in year 10? Year 20? Year 30?

2. Suppose that we have set up an electric utility system in which operating company C is controlled by holding company B, which is in turn controlled by holding company A. The accounts below describe the asset composition and capital structure of each company:

Holding Co. A

Stock of B	$16.0	9% Bonds	$8.0
		8% Preferred stock	4.8
		Common stock	3.2
Total	$16.0	Total	$16.0

Holding Co. B

Stock of C	$400	9% Bonds	$200
		8% Preferred stock	120
		Common stock	80
Total	$400	Total	$400

Operating Subsidiary C

Operating assets	$10,000	9% Bonds	$ 5,000
		8% Preferred stock	3,000
		Common stock	2,000
Total	$10,000	Total	$10,000

If *EBIT* is 13 percent of C's assets, what is the return on book value of the equity for C, B, and A? For purposes of calculation, assume that corporate income is taxed at 50 percent, that B and C make dividend payouts of 100 percent, and that only 15 percent of intercorporate dividends are taxable income for the recipient corporation.

3. Using data based substantially on Ingersoll-Rand's acquisition of Schlage Lock Company, let us suppose that on July 1 of year 1 Ingersoll-Rand issued 965,148 shares of common stock in exchange for all (784,672 shares) of Schlage's common stock. At the time, Ingersoll-Rand stock was selling at about $87; Schlage, at about $90. The pre-merger balance sheets of both firms are given below. Prepare the post-merger combined balance sheet under pooling-of-interests accounting; under purchase accounting.

Ingersoll-Rand and Schlage, Balance Sheets, June 30, Year 1 (in thousands of dollars)

	I-R	S		I-R	S
Current assets			Current debt	$ 349,236	$10,590
Cash	$ 50,449	$ 1,934	Long-term debt	127,972	563
Accounts receivable	251,963	9,915	Other liabilities	2,546	531
Inventories	452,754	26,487	Owners' Equity		
Prepaid expenses	—	499	Preferred stock	6,445	—
			Common stock		
Investments	9,299	—	I-R: ($2 par value; 15,404, 640 shares)	30,809	
Fixed assets					
Building and equipment	382,576	35,663	S: ($3.33 par value; 787,647 shares)		2,625*
Depreciation reserve	(164,474)	(18,280)	Capital surplus	34,626	19,085
Land	10,876	1,323	Earned surplus	472,943	25,499
Other assets	14,417	1,620	Less: treasury shares	(16,717)	(92)
Total	$1,007,860	$59,161	Total	$1,007,860	$59,161

* Include 2,975 shares held in treasury.

4. Company P is contemplating the acquisition of Company S through an exchange of common stock. The table below summarizes the values of the key financial variables of the two firms before the merger:

	Company P	Company S
Total earnings	$2,000,000	$1,000,000
Payout ratio	50%	70%
Growth rate	8%	7%
Dividend-capitalization rate	13%	15%
Number of shares	400,000	200,000

   a. At what price will each firm's stock sell? If the merger involves an exchange of equal market values, how many P shares must be issued in exchange for all of S's shares? How will the exchange affect P's *EPS?* Why?

   b. After the exchange, P dissolves S, taking over all assets and liabilities. P continues its 50 percent payout ratio. Because of synergy, its growth rate rises to 8.5 percent; but because of increased risk, its dividend-capitalization rate also increases, from 13 percent to 13.5 percent. Does the merger enhance the total market value of the two firms? If so, by how much? How is the gain divided among the stockholders of the two companies?

5. If A acquires T through a common-stock exchange in which the shares exchanged have equal total market value, then A's *EPS* will rise or fall depending on whether A's price-earnings ratio is higher or lower, respectively, than T's. Prove this theorem.

6. Table 22-4 shows the pace of acquisition needed to sustain a constant growth rate in *EPS*. Using the formula below, verify the data in the table:

$$\rho = \frac{\alpha(1-\beta)}{1+\alpha\beta}$$

where ρ = A's percentage increase in *EPS;*
α = the ratio of acquired firm T's total earnings to A's; and
β = the price-earnings ratio actually paid for firm T divided by A's price-earnings ratio.

REFERENCES

AUSTIN, DOUGLAS V., "Tender Offers Revisited: 1968–1972 Comparisons with the Past and Future Trends," *Mergers and Acquisitions* 8 (Fall, 1973), pp. 16–29.

BUCKLEY, ADRIAN, "A Review of Acquisition Valuation Models—a Comment," *Journal of Business Finance and Accounting* 2 (Spring, 1975), pp. 147–151.

FRANKS, J. R., R. MILES, and J. BAGWELL, "A Review of Acquisition Valuation Models," *Journal of Business Finance and Accounting* 1 (Spring, 1974), pp. 35–53.

FREUND, JAMES C., *Anatomy of a Merger* (New York: Law Journal Press, 1975).

GOLDBERG, STUART CHARLES, *SEC Regulation of Corporate Insiders* (New York: Newcourt Publishing House Ltd., 1973), Ch. 4.

GUNTHER, SAMUEL P., "Financial Reporting for Mergers and Acquisitions: Current Problems with Pooling and Purchasing," *Mergers and Acquisitions* 8 (Winter, 1974), pp. 8–23.

HALPERN, PAUL J., "Empirical Estimates of the Amount and Distribution of Gains to Companies in Mergers," *Journal of Business* 46 (October, 1973), pp. 554–575.

KAHN, DOUGLAS A., *Basic Corporate Taxation* (Ann Arbor: The Institute of Continuing Legal Education, 1973), Ch. 4.

KINTNER, EARL W., *Primer on the Law of Mergers* (New York: The Macmillan Company, 1973).

LEWELLEN, WILBUR G., "Finance Subsidiaries and Corporate Borrowing Capacity," *Financial Management* 1 (Spring, 1972), pp. 21–31.

MELICHER, RONALD W., and DAVID F. RUSH, "Evidence on the Acquisition-Related Performance of Conglomerate Firms," *Journal of Finance* 29 (March, 1974), pp. 141–149.

MISHKIN, WILLIAM S., ed., *Techniques in Corporate Reorganization* (New York: Presidents Publishing House, Inc., 1972).

MUELLER, DENNIS C., "A Theory of Conglomerate Mergers," *Quarterly Journal of Economics* 83 (November, 1969), pp. 643–659.

NIELSEN, JAMES F., and RONALD W. MELICHER, "A Financial Analysis of Acquisition and Merger Premiums," *Journal of Financial and Quantitative Analysis* 8 (March, 1973), pp. 139–148.

Opinions of the Accounting Principles Board, No. 16 (New York: The American Institute of Certified Public Accountants, 1970).

REINHARDT, UWE E., *Mergers and Consolidations: A Corporate-Finance Approach* (Morristown: General Learning Press, 1972).

SCHARF, CHARLES A., *Acquisitions, Mergers, Sales and Takeovers* (Englewood Cliffs: Prentice-Hall, Inc., 1971).

TOBIAS, ANDREW, *The Funny Money Game* (Chicago: Playboy Press, 1971).

WINSLOW, JOHN F., *Conglomerates Unlimited* (Bloomington: Indiana University Press, 1973).

23 Recapitalization and Reorganization

Recapitalization and reorganization are financial processes whereby a firm recasts its capital structure. Recapitalization is a voluntary procedure, undertaken to enhance the value of a firm's common equity; reorganization is an involuntary act, forced upon a company by actual or imminent default on its contractual obligations. Recapitalization helps a firm to improve its capital structure; reorganization, to avoid dissolution and forced liquidation. In this chapter, although we shall look at certain legal procedures and concepts, the focus will be on financial principles.

DEFINITIONS AND EXAMPLES

Definitions

Recapitalization and reorganization are both financial measures aimed at readjusting the capital structure of a single company or group of affiliated companies—that is, altering the amount, income, priority, or ownership of outstanding stocks and bonds. (Mergers do not fall within either of these categories, since they alter the capital structure of two or more independent companies.) The two procedures differ both in purpose and in the degree to which capital structure is changed. In general, recapitalization is undertaken by healthy firms wishing to improve capital structure, or by weak firms hoping to avoid financial embarrassment. Reorganization, on the other hand, is undertaken by companies already in financial distress, seeking concessions from their creditors so that they may rehabilitate themselves and preserve their status as ongoing concerns.

A recapitalization plan may be very simple or quite complex. At its simplest, it may involve no more than a change in the denomination in which the company issues its shares. Recapitalization may also involve exchanges of securities on terms which are quite complex. Reorganization is a more radical process, typically calling for greater changes and frequently involving court action. When there are few creditors, the concessions in a reorganization plan can often be negotiated privately, out of court. But when there are many creditors, court action is necessary to protect the faltering business from being broken up by dissenting creditors. The judicial process contains safeguards to ensure the financial feasibility of the plan, as well as its fairness and equitability. Because reorganization affects the rights of all classes of investors in a firm, it is more complex than recapitalization, which may involve the rights of only selected classes. Reorganization thus tends also to be more time-consuming than recapitalization.

Typical Examples

Although the financial executive hopes never to face reorganization, he will probably engineer many recapitalizations, even for a financially strong firm, in the course of routine management. Several conditions are likely to make such action desirable:

1. A firm's profits may have driven the market price of its shares above the level management considers desirable. The solution is often a stock split or a stock dividend.
2. A plan to simplify its capital structure may prompt a firm to eliminate its convertible securities. Under certain conditions, the objective may be achieved through "forced conversion."
3. The passage of time shortens the average maturity of a firm's outstanding debt. If debt is a prominent source of financing, the firm must periodically refund its debt simply to maintain its original debt level.
4. New investments, or other developments, may necessitate an increase or a decrease in the firm's debt-to-equity ratio. The company may wish to exchange new debt for outstanding stock, or new stock for outstanding debt.
5. When money is easily accessible, opportunities may arise to refund existing debt at a reduced interest rate.
6. A firm may wish to reduce its taxes by substituting debt for preferred stock.

In addition, a company that is weak, but not in actual default, may also find recapitalization advisable in some cases. The following list gives common situations where such recapitalizations are carried out by various means:

1. A firm with an excessive debt burden may offer to exchange new stock for outstanding debt.
2. A firm may ask its creditors to agree to a reduction in interest rate, an extension of maturity, or even outright forgiveness for (usually only a portion of) outstanding debt.
3. A company unable to meet its preferred dividends may ask preferred stockholders to exchange their shares for common stock and, if the preferred stock is in arrears, to accept the arrearage in common stock instead of cash.

A firm in actual or imminent default on its obligations has only two alternatives: forced liquidation or reorganization. Both creditors and stockholders generally prefer to avoid forced liquidation since it results in the destruction of the firm's going-concern value. Reorganization is, in essence, a program of rehabilitation in which creditors agree to modify their claims so that the firm may continue. In private negotiations, the most common creditor concessions are extensions of maturities, and compositions (scaling down of debts). Both extensions and compositions may also be effected in court, under Chapter XI of the Federal Bankruptcy Act, provided that the reorganization does not alter the rights of secured creditors. If these creditors are affected, Chapter X of the Act applies to industrial corporations and public utilities. Railroads previously reorganized under Section 77 of the Act, but since 1948 use the simpler procedure set forth in Section 20b of the Federal Transportation Act.

DECISION CRITERIA

Recapitalization

The objective of recapitalization is the maximization of the wealth of the continuing stockholders—i.e., those who hold stock both before and after the recapitalization. If recapitalization involves only debt and preferred stock, then all post-recapitalization common stockholders are continuing stockholders. But if the procedure involves common equity, new shares may be issued or old shares re-acquired. A company may issue new common stock in exchange for existing debt or preferred stock, or vice versa. (We are not considering stock splits and stock dividends here since they were already discussed in Chapter 15.) If new shares are issued, the number of common stockholders will increase; and in this case, management should be guided only by the welfare of those who held stock before the recapitalization. If old shares are re-acquired, some existing common stockholders may be eliminated if they find it advantageous to terminate ownership; but once again, management should be concerned only with those stockholders who choose to retain an interest in the firm. In either case, then, management's first responsibility is to the continuing stockholders.

By definition, continuing stockholders own the same number of shares before and after recapitalization. Recapitalization will, then, increase wealth if it enhances the market price of the firm's shares. Let us suppose, for example, that the XYZ Company generates total adjusted earnings of Y_1, Y_2, and $Y_3 \ldots$ in years 1, 2, and 3, . . . , respectively. If n common shares are outstanding, the market price P of each share will be given by the formula:

$$P = \frac{1}{n}\left[\frac{Y_1}{(1+k)^1} + \frac{Y_2}{(1+k)^2} + \frac{Y_3}{(1+k)^3} + \cdots\right] \qquad (23\text{-}1)$$

where k is the stockholders' required rate of return. Recapitalization will result, let us say, in total adjusted earnings of Y_1', Y_2', Y_3', . . . ; the number of common shares will be $n + \Delta n$, where Δn may be greater than, equal to, or less than zero. If the stockholders' required rate of return is now k', the post-recapitalization market price P' of each share will be

$$P' = \frac{1}{n+\Delta n}\left[\frac{Y_1'}{(1+k')^1} + \frac{Y_2'}{(1+k')^2} + \frac{Y_3'}{(1+k')^3} + \cdots\right] \qquad (23\text{-}2)$$

Recapitalization, then, will enhance the wealth of the continuing stockholders if and only if $P' > P$.

If adjusted earnings are constant from year to year, then $P = Y/nk$ and $P' = Y'/(n + \Delta n)k$, where Y and Y' are, respectively, the constant yearly earnings before and after recapitalization. In this special case, $P' > P$ implies

$$\frac{Y'/(n+\Delta n)}{Y/n} > \frac{k'}{k} \qquad (23\text{-}3)$$

Since recapitalization will probably affect the investors' required rate of return, the profitability of the undertaking cannot be judged simply in terms of the change in adjusted earnings per share; recapitalization will increase share value only if per-share adjusted earnings increase relatively more than the discount rate at which they are evaluated.

Condition (23-3) is based on a short-run analysis in which capital is relatively immobile because most funds are supplied under long-term contracts and have both fixed rates of return and fixed dates of maturity. Such an analysis is, of course, limited in scope. If a firm wishes to replace part of its existing equity with new debt, Inequality (23-3) evaluates such replacement only in terms of its effect on the market value of common stock, but ignores any effects on other existing securities. In the long run, however, all forms of capital are completely mobile, so that a firm must pay the full price to attract and retain every dollar from any source. If a company tries to exploit the short-term immobility of existing capital, it will find it more difficult to raise capital in the long run.

A long-term approach is therefore necessary to ensure that any benefits to common stockholders arising from recapitalization are permanent, not transitory. If the common stock of XYZ is temporarily underpriced in the market, the company may use the opportunity to launch a substantial share repurchase, using proceeds from the sale of new bonds. This transaction may, however, push the debt-to-equity ratio beyond the long-term optimal level. If the firm takes prompt action to adjust this ratio, short-run benefits from the share repurchase might be made permanent. But if the company ignores the excessive debt, it may later have to refund its debt at an excessively high interest rate to compensate creditors for increased risk. This increased interest may reduce residual earnings to common stockholders to a level low enough to counteract any short-term benefits from the original share repurchase.

Short-run and long-run objectives are not, of course, always in conflict. But when they are, a policy guided solely by the long-run objective will probably be too conservative, while a short-run policy will probably be foolhardy. The best policy is the middle course in which the firm is alert to short-run opportunities while cognizant of long-run implications.

Reorganization

The objective of reorganization is to rescue a firm from dissolution and forced liquidation so that it may have a chance to rehabilitate itself. Even this objective may be subsumed under share-value maximization, since reorganization is preferable to liquidation only if continued operation will lead to greater value. Reorganization is thus subject to the same decision criteria as recapitalization. There is, however, one important difference: if recapitalization increases the total market value of a firm, the full benefit accrues to the common stockholders; but if reorganization preserves a firm's going-concern value, only part of the benefit accrues to the common stockholders. The key to successful reorganization is scaling down the fixed claims of creditors, who will understandably demand corresponding sacrifices by the firm's stockholders. Moreover, under Chapter X of the Federal

Bankruptcy Act, the court will not permit stockholders to participate in reorganization if the value of the reorganized firm falls short of the total claims of creditors.

Chapter X of the Bankruptcy Act also has a feasibility test, requiring that the capital structure of a reorganized firm be commensurate with the firm's earning capacity. Once the new structure is conceived, a new corporation is usually formed to purchase the old firm's assets and to issue new securities. The distribution of value among the various classes of original investors is determined by the terms on which the new securities are exchanged for old. The interests of shareholders and of creditors inevitably conflict, since one group can acquire value only at the expense of the other. The actual division of value will depend on the relative bargaining strengths and on the bargaining skills of the representatives of the two groups. When judicial process is necessary, the court's notion of "fair and equitable" distribution will also come into play.

RECAPITALIZATION INVOLVING COMMON STOCK

In common stock recapitalization, a firm issues new securities in exchange for all or part of its existing common stock. We have already seen such recapitalization practices as changes in par value, stock splits, and stock dividends. We shall now consider offers to exchange straight debt for common stock and to exchange convertible debt for common stock.

Fuqua Industries[1]

The Exchange Offer. Fuqua Industries, Inc., is a diversified firm whose principal operations are in leisure-time products and services. Because the general stock market in 1973 was depressed, Fuqua shares were trading at slightly less than $10, in comparison with $28 in the second quarter of the preceding year. Viewing its stock as undervalued, the company offered to issue a new class of 9½%, 25-year subordinated debentures in exchange for up to 2 million shares of Fuqua common stock. Under the terms of the offer, Fuqua was to exchange $15 in principal amount of its new debentures for each share of common stock.

Analysis. The effect of this recapitalization on the price of Fuqua shares depends on the effect of the exchange on per-share earnings and

[1] All factual information for the following cases of recapitalization comes from company offering circulars, but interpretative statements are my own. An offering circular generally contains the company's own estimate of how its recapitalization will affect its accounting earnings, which will be the basis of our analyses. Since adjusted earnings and accounting earnings are closely correlated, the use of accounting earnings will not materially alter our conclusions.

earnings-capitalization rate (see footnote 1). Given a net operating income (*EBIT*) of *X*, Fuqua's per-share earnings *E* before the exchange were

$$E = \frac{(X - \$9{,}490{,}000)(1 - .5)}{9{,}424{,}236} \qquad (23\text{-}4)$$

Annual interest is \$9,490,000; the tax rate is 50 percent; and the number of common shares plus common equivalent shares is 9,424,236. At full acceptance of the exchange offer, per-share earnings *E*′ after the exchange would be

$$E' = \frac{(X - \$12{,}340{,}000)(1 - .5)}{7{,}424{,}236} \qquad (23\text{-}5)$$

Figure 23-1 shows that the break-even net operating income is \$22,919,600; with any income below this figure, per-share earnings would be reduced. Since Fuqua's net operating income was nearly \$45 million, the firm could reasonably expect a favorable effect on per-share earnings. At a net operating income of \$45 million, as Table 23-1 shows, *EPS* was \$1.88 before the exchange and \$2.20 after, an increase of 17 percent.

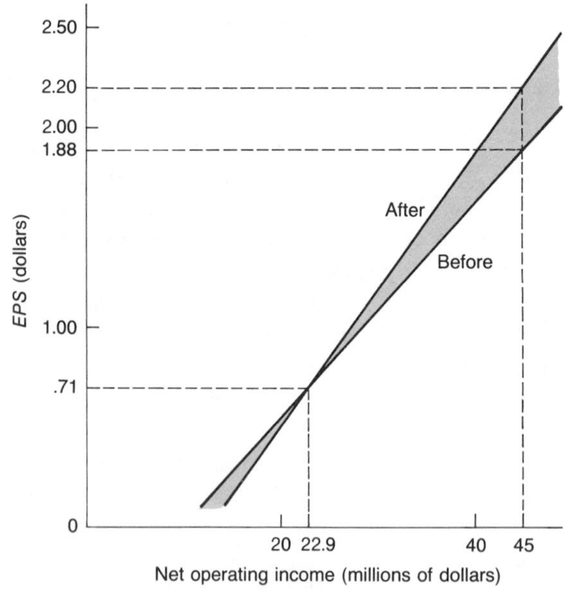

Figure 23-1 Break-Even Analysis of Fuqua's Exchange Offer

Table 23-1 Effect of Exchange on Fuqua's *EPS*

	Before Exchange	After 100% Exchange
Net operating income*	$45,000,000	$45,000,000
Interest	9,490,000	12,340,000
Taxable income	$35,510,000	$32,660,000
Taxes	17,755,000	16,330,000
Net income	$17,755,000	$16,330,000
Number of common and common equivalent shares	9,424,236	7,424,236
Earnings per share	$1.88	$2.20

* Assumed.

The impact on the earnings-capitalization rate depends on the effect of the exchange on the variability of earnings and on the firm's risk of insolvency. Earnings variability is measured by the index $X/(X - I)$, where X is net operating income and I is interest expense. The exchange increases interest expense from $9,490,000 to $12,340,000. At an assumed net operating income of $45 million, the increase raises the variability index from 1.27 to 1.38. In other words, when net operating income rises by 1.0 percent, the corresponding variation in residual earnings increases from 1.27 percent to 1.38 percent.

The simplest measure of the risk of insolvency is the interest coverage ratio. In this case, the ratio decreases from 4.74 to 3.65 after the exchange. Recapitalization thus not only increases the variability of earnings but also weakens the firm's solvency ratio. Fuqua should therefore expect the exchange to have an unfavorable effect on its earnings-capitalization rate.

The exchange, then, gives rise to conflicting forces. On the one hand, it increases earnings per share; on the other, it raises the discount rate at which earnings are capitalized. There is no deductive way to determine which is the stronger. Fuqua must, however, have expected the increase in *EPS* to be relatively greater than the increase in capitalization rate: otherwise, it would not have offered the exchange.

Bell Industries

The Exchange Offer. Bell Industries is a diversified company that makes and distributes products for the recreational, residential, electronics, and computer markets. Except for a small loss in 1971, the firm has been consistently profitable since 1966, with earnings per share ranging from $0.26 to $0.48. In 1973, the company was earning $0.36 per share and had just paid its first cash dividend of $0.08 per share. But because share prices in general were depressed, the firm's stock price had fallen from a 1968 high of $\$20^3/_4$ to a low of $\$2^1/_4$. Bell felt that its shares were underpriced and offered to exchange convertible debt (instead of the straight debt Fuqua offered) for its common stock. Under the terms of the offer, Bell would exchange its new 7%, 25-year convertible subordinated debentures for up to 1.7 million shares of its common stock at a rate of $4 of principal amount for each share. The debentures would be convertible into common stock at $8 per share.

Analysis. When the computations applied to Fuqua's exchange are applied to Bell's, assuming 100 percent exchange, we find that the break-even net operating income is $2.021 million. Since the firm's net operating income was nearly $4 million, Bell could reasonably expect a favorable effect on earnings per share. Table 23-2 shows that the company could report per-share earnings of $0.48 after the exchange, in comparison with $0.35 before. But the effect of the exchange on both the earnings-variability index and the interest coverage ratio would be negative, the former rising from 1.22 to 1.43, the latter falling from 5.44 to 3.30. The exchange would therefore make investors capitalize Bell's earnings at a higher rate than previously. Bell presumably expected this increase to be more than offset by the rise in per-share earnings.

Our analysis does not, however, take into account the convertibility of the 7 percent debentures. In this case, the great difference between the conversion price and the current price of Bell shares will delay conversion; but, as long as the firm is profitable, conversion is a possibility. If the debentures are converted at $8 per share, only half of the original 1.7 million exchanged shares will have to be reissued. Recapitalization would thus reduce the firm's net common shares by 850,000—the difference between the number of shares received in exchange and the number reissued upon con-

Table 23-2 Effect of Exchange on Bell's *EPS*

	Before Exchange	After 100% Exchange
Net operating income*	$4,000,000	$4,000,000
Interest	735,000	1,211,000
Taxable income	$3,265,000	$2,789,000
Taxes	1,632,500	1,394,500
Net income	$1,632,500	$1,394,500
Number of common and common equivalent shares	4,594,000	2,894,000
Earnings per share	$0.35	$0.48

* Assumed.

version. Fewer outstanding shares mean, of course, higher earnings per share. Moreover, since the debt would be extinguished upon conversion, the earnings-capitalization rate would then fall back to the pre-exchange level.

Bell may have made its bonds convertible to improve the chances of a successful exchange. In fact, only 209,000 shares were actually tendered, and Bell decided to cancel the exchange altogether. The price of the shares continued depressed, and a plan for a reverse stock split was instituted in 1974. This, however, did not receive the necessary stockholders' approval. In 1975, the company made a new proposal to exchange debentures for common stock, this time on terms more favorable to the stockholders.

RECAPITALIZATION INVOLVING CONVERTIBLE SECURITIES

In Chapter 18, we examined forced conversion of convertible securities. Here we shall consider two other types of recapitalization involving convertibles: the exchange of new convertible debentures for old convertible debentures, and the exchange of straight preferred stock plus common stock for old convertible preferred stock.

Fibreboard Corporation

The Exchange Offer. The Fibreboard Corporation is a leading manufacturer and distributor of forest products, including paperboard, packaging, lumber, and plywood. In this recapitalization, Fibreboard had $19.5 million outstanding in 4¾%, 20-year debentures, convertible into common stock at $31¼ per share. Since the common stock was selling at only $17⅛, conversion was not imminent. The company offered to exchange $750 in principal amount of new 6¾%, 25-year convertible debentures for each $1,000 of the old debentures; the new debentures were to be convertible into common stock at $18½ per share. The exchange was successfully completed in 1974.

Analysis. The key point of this recapitalization is the reduction in conversion price. The old debentures were issued near par in 1968, when Fibreboard's borrowing rate was relatively low and its stock price relatively high. Since then, with a tightening bond market and generally falling stock prices, the firm's borrowing rate had risen and its stock price fallen, so that its old debentures were selling at a discounted price of $66 per $100 of principal amount. Such a large discount made it unlikely that the company would be able to force conversion in the near future. The overhanging debentures probably hampered Fibreboard's ability to raise additional funds in the capital market.

Fibreboard's aim, it seems, was to eliminate the overhang by inducing the holders of the debentures to exchange their bonds for a new issue with a substantially reduced conversion price. It was necessary that the terms of the exchange benefit the common stockholders as well as the debenture holders. Working back from the figures, we may reasonably infer that the company employed the following guidelines for the exchange: (1) the new conversion price was to be only slightly higher than the current market price of the common stock, and (2) the old debenture holders were to be offered new securities with a market value 5 percent higher and interest income 7 percent higher than their old debentures. Common stock was selling at \$17⅛, so the conversion price was set at \$18½. Each old \$1,000 bond was selling at \$660; a 5 percent gain indicated a market value of \$693. For each old bond, Fibreboard thus offered \$750 principal amount of the new bonds. Because these new bonds were convertible into 40.54 (= \$750 ÷ \$18½) shares of common stock, they had a minimum market value of \$694 (= 40.54 × \$17⅛) at the time of the exchange. Note also that each old bond was earning \$47.50 in annual interest; a 7 percent increase indicated \$51 in annual interest. The new interest rate of 6¾ percent yielded about \$51 annually on \$750 of principal.

Each old bond was convertible into exactly 32 shares of common stock; each new bond, into 40.54 shares. The exchange therefore increased the potential for earnings dilution. Thus, according to Fibreboard, for the first half of 1973, *EPS* before extraordinary items on a fully diluted basis was \$1.72.[2] By adjusting for 100 percent exchange, this figure was reduced to only \$1.66.

Recapitalization may, however, create indirect benefits for Fibreboard. By reducing the outstanding debt, the exchange can improve the firm's debt-to-equity ratio. This improvement, along with the elimination of convertible overhang, will enable the firm to raise money more cheaply in the future. And the improvement in capital structure may prompt investors to capitalize the company's earnings at a lower rate than previously. These indirect benefits may more than offset the dilution potential and may thus have a favorable long-run effect on the firm's share price.

Leasco Corporation

The Exchange Offer. Leasco Corporation is a diversified concern that writes insurance, leases business equipment, and offers consulting and computer software services. In 1973, 3,580,757 shares of Series B Preferred Stock were outstanding, each share carrying a cumulative preferential dividend of \$2.20 per annum and convertible at any time into 1.53 shares of

[2] Fully diluted earnings per share are computed on the assumption that all outstanding dilutive convertible securities were converted *and* that all warrants and options were exercised.

Table 23-3 Effect of Exchange on Leasco's EPS*

	Before Exchange	After 100% Exchange	Before Exchange	After 100% Exchange
Income before preferred dividends**	$40,000,000	$40,000,000	$50,000,000	$50,000,000
Preferred dividends	0	9,309,968	0	9,309,968
Net income	$40,000,000	$30,690,032	$50,000,000	$40,690,032
Number of common and common equivalent shares	16,337,000	12,656,000	16,337,000	12,656,000
Earnings per share	$2.45	$2.42	$3.06	$3.22

* In calculating *EPS* before the exchange, no preferred dividends are deducted because it is assumed that all preferred shares have been converted into common stock. After the exchange, however, the new preferred shares are nonconvertible, so the preferred dividends must be deducted in arriving at net income.

** Assumed.

common stock. The market price of common stock was about $10, so that each preferred share had a stock value of about $15.30. Nonetheless, since the market price of the preferred stock was about $26, conversion seemed remote. The preferred shares were overhanging. Leasco was required by contract to retire systematically all Series B Preferred at $55 per share between 1988 and 1993. Instead, Leasco offered in 1973 to exchange one share of Series C Preferred and half share of common stock for each share of Series B Preferred. The Series C Preferred, carrying a cumulative preferred dividend of $2.60 per annum, were to be nonconvertible. All Series C Preferred shares were to be retired between 1988 and 1993 at the reduced redemption price of $26 per share.

Analysis. The purpose of this recapitalization, it seems, was to preempt the conversion of Series B Preferred Stock in a way that would minimize earnings dilution. Three aspects of the exchange offer are worth noting: (1) The number of new common shares to be issued was only about one third of the number of shares into which Series B was originally convertible. (2) For each preferred share exchanged, the investor lost $29 in redemption value. Assuming redemption in 18 years, the present value of this loss at a discount rate of 10 percent was about $5.20, which approximated the market value of the half share of common stock included in the exchange package. (3) A higher dividend rate on the new preferred stock was to be the key incentive to exchange.

Table 23-3 shows the effect of this exchange on earnings per common and common equivalent share. If Leasco has an income of $40 million before preferred dividends, its net income before exchange will be also $40 million. Net income after exchange will be only $30,690,032. The exchange will also decrease the number of common and common equivalent shares from 16,337,000 to 12,656,000, so that complete exchange will lower *EPS* slightly from $2.45 to $2.42. But, if income before preferred dividends is higher, say, $50 million, the exchange will increase *EPS* from $3.06 to $3.22. Since Leasco can reasonably expect an income considerably higher than $40 million, it can also reasonably expect a favorable impact on *EPS*. Moreover, the elimination of the convertible overhang will enhance Leasco's new financing capacity. The improvement in capital structure may also prompt investors to capitalize Leasco's earnings at a reduced discount rate. These indirect benefits reinforce the direct effect on *EPS*, so that the long-run effect on Leasco's common shares is clearly favorable.

RECAPITALIZATION INVOLVING NONCONVERTIBLE SECURITIES

We have already mentioned some companies' decisions to eliminate preferred stock from their capital structures for tax reasons, and a company's (ASG) decision to recapitalize its preferred stock and dividend arrearages. In this section, we shall consider two other situations: exchange of common stock for the preferred stock of a subsidiary, and a major restructuring of debt obligations by means of persuasion of bondholders.

Westvaco Corporation

Westvaco Corporation is a major producer of paper and paperboard, and United States Envelope Company (USE) is the largest producer of envelopes in the country. Prior to 1973, although Westvaco owned 58 percent of USE, the two companies filed separate tax returns because a minimum of 80 percent ownership is required before a parent company may legally consolidate its taxable income with that of its subsidiary. Separate returns meant that 15 percent of the dividends which Westvaco received from USE were subject to the corporate income tax. To avoid paying this tax, in 1973 Westvaco offered to exchange its common stock for all the remaining stocks of USE in the following ratios: (a) .85 of a share of Westvaco common for each share of USE common, and (b) .50 of a share of Westvaco common for each share of USE preferred.

In its prospectus, Westvaco explains how it arrived at the exchange ratios for the USE stocks. In looking at the explanation relating to the USE preferred stock, we see that each preferred share entitled the holder to receive cumulative preferred dividends at the rate of 70 cents per annum. The dividend rate on the Westvaco common stock was $1.10 per annum, so that the equivalent in Westvaco common stock of one share of USE preferred received 15 cents less in dividends after the exchange. Westvaco emphasized, however, that it placed relatively greater weight on the higher market price of its common stock and the different earnings and dividend outlooks of the two companies. The prices of Westvaco common and USE preferred were $34.75 and $16.75, respectively, so that the exchange increased the value of a preferred stockholder's holding by about 4 percent. Moreover, Westvaco in the last ten years had increased its common dividends seven times, raising the annual rate from 60 cents per share to $1.10. (In fact, in the year following the exchange, there was an eighth increase from $1.10 per share to $1.40.) Although Westvaco does not mention it, the exchange also gave the USE stockholders greater liquidity, since the Westvaco shares have a more active market than did USE shares.

The exchange offer was successful, enabling Westvaco to raise its ownership in USE to about 95 percent. As a result, on every $1 million of dividends which Westvaco receives from USE, Westvaco will save approximately $75,000 in taxes—the savings it sought in the recapitalization.

Bio-Medical Sciences, Inc.

Bio-Medical Sciences, Inc., founded in 1967 primarily as a manufacturer of a revolutionary single-use thermometer, announced in September 1974 that they had terminated an agreement with Johnson and Johnson to market its products. The following month the SEC suspended trading in the company's shares because of financial uncertainties, and many bondholders demanded repayment from a $10 million fund held in escrow from the original sale of $25 million worth of convertible debentures.

Subsequently, the company announced an agreement with Akzo N.V. (Holland) and Akzona, Inc., under which the two firms were granted licenses to make and market Bio-Medical products. This agreement, however, was conditional on Bio-Medical's being able to restructure its outstanding debt. To effect this debt restructuring, Bio-Medical offered its convertible bondholders three alternatives: (1) immediate conversion of the debentures into common stock, (2) waiver of interest through 1976 accompanied by a reduction in conversion price, and (3) deferral of interest till 1977 with no change in conversion terms. (Although the debentures were theoretically convertible, the prospect of conversion was so remote that we may view these bonds as straight bonds.) This restructuring was successfully accomplished in early 1975, enabling the company to implement its licensing agreement with Akzo and Akzona.

The company's debenture holders no doubt agreed to these proposals because they realized that the worth of their claims depended on the long-term viability of the company. Bio-Medical did not default on its obligations, and for that reason the company's measures are classified here as an example of corporate recapitalization.

NONJUDICIAL REORGANIZATION

If a company defaults on its debt obligations, either the company itself or a group of the company's creditors may petition the court to declare the firm bankrupt. All creditors are then restrained. The bankrupt company and its creditors may choose either to liquidate or to rehabilitate (i.e., to reorganize) its faltering business. Since liquidation is a last resort and costly to all parties, we shall focus on reorganization: first, on simple nonjudicial adjustments suitable to private or semi-private corporations with few creditors; then, in the next section, on complex judicial reorganization appropriate to public corporations with many creditors.

Extensions and Compositions[3]

A firm unable to meet its maturing obligations is said to be "technically" insolvent. The business may be basically sound financially but temporarily short of cash. The shortage may be due to excessive inventory build-up, which could have been avoided, or to a wildcat strike, which could not. In any case, if the problem is short-term and correctable, the firm needs only an extension: a creditors' agreement to extend credit for the period needed for adequate rehabilitation.

Technical insolvency may be accompanied by various degrees of "insolvency in the sense of bankruptcy." A firm is said to be insolvent in this sense if the total of its liabilities exceeds the fair market value of its assets. A company may have managed its working capital efficiently and still sustain yearly losses. If the losses result partly from a permanent decline in the demand for the firm's products and partly from excessive debt, an extension would only postpone the final reckoning; the continuing losses would, in fact, make the firm less liquid each day. Such a company needs a composition: a contract between the firm and its creditors, whereby the creditors release the firm from debt and the firm settles its debts at a prescribed percentage of face value. Composition thus permits an insolvent company to scale down its debts to a level relatively commensurate with its long-term earning capacity.

Procedure

Creditors are more likely to agree to an extension or a composition if they are convinced that the debtor firm is honest and that the causes of insolvency are temporary and remediable. An extension is arranged through a trust agreement between the firm and an adjustor representing the creditors.

---

[3] For a more thorough discussion, see Paul M. Van Arsdell, *Corporation Finance* (New York: The Ronald Press Company, 1968), Ch. 49.

The agreement may permit the firm to continue operations, supervised by the adjustor, or it may put the firm under the adjustor's direct control until debt obligations are fully met. In composition, the debtor presents his compromise offer to his creditors, usually collectively. In this case, too, a trust may be established to effect some control over the firm's operations until obligations are satisfied.

The success of both nonjudicial extensions and compositions depends on cooperation and goodwill, since the terms are binding only upon creditors who choose to sign. A creditor who refuses to sign can force the firm into liquidation. Major creditors who favor compromise must often, therefore, pay off dissenters who might jeopardize the success of the agreement. Since it is impossible to force settlement on uncooperative creditors, nonjudicial reorganization is suited primarily to small firms with few creditors.

JUDICIAL REORGANIZATION

The Constitution of the United States authorizes the Congress to pass uniform laws governing bankruptcy. Federal legislation originally provided only for liquidation, not for rehabilitation. But in 1933, Section 77 of the Bankruptcy Act covered the reorganization of interstate railroads; and in 1934, Section 77B was added to cover the rehabilitation of other corporations. In 1938, Section 77B was replaced by Chapter X of the Chandler Act, and Chapter XI of this Act also provides for milder extension and composition remedies. We will consider Chapter XI first, since it is simpler than Chapter X proceedings.

Chapter XI Arrangements

Chapter XI of the Chandler Act deals with the arrangements for either an extension or a composition of a firm's unsecured debt.[4] Judicial process, unlike voluntary agreement, is binding on all creditors. A company operating under Chapter XI thus has court protection against lawsuits while it systematically pays off its indebtedness. Many corporations have resorted to protection under Chapter XI: Mammoth Mart, Inc.; W. T. Grant Co.; and Meister Bräu, Inc., among others.

Procedure. Chapter XI arrangement includes four essential steps:
(1) Proceedings may be initiated only voluntarily, by a debtor petition which must include the debtor's proposed terms.

---

[4] For a more thorough discussion, see Van Arsdell, *op. cit.*, pp. 1541–1548; and Harry G. Henn, *Law of Corporations* (St. Paul: West Publishing Company, 1970), pp. 823–826.

(2) If the court approves the petition, it acquires immediate jurisdiction over the firm's assets, although the firm may usually continue to operate under court authority. No lawsuits against the debtor are permitted.

(3) The judge sets a date for creditors to meet to demonstrate their claims and to hear arguments for or against the debtor's proposed arrangements. Before the meeting, the judge must distribute copies of the arrangement and a summary of the firm's assets and liabilities.

(4) If all creditors accept the plan, the court must confirm it. If creditors representing a majority both in number of creditors and in amounts of claim approve the proposal but others dissent, the court may still confirm the plan as long as it is "in the best interests of the creditors and is feasible."

Legal Aspects. Insolvent firms often prefer the arrangements outlined in Chapter XI of the Chandler Act to those in Chapter X because the former permits management to continue operation; Chapter X requires that the company be controlled by a court-appointed trustee. But the debtor does not always have a choice. If secured creditors are involved, for example, Chapter X is mandatory. And even under other circumstances, a petition under Chapter XI may be rejected if the judge deems Chapter X reorganization more appropriate. The decision is based on the "needs to be served." A judge believing that managerial reorganization is as essential as debt readjustment will prefer the safeguards – a disinterested court-appointed trustee and the benefits of SEC advisory function – provided only under Chapter X.

The court will confirm an arrangement only if it is "in the best interests of the creditors" and is "feasible" (in 1952 these terms replaced the "fair and equitable, and feasible" requirement); i.e., only if the arrangement will realize more value than liquidation and only if the debtor is likely to be able to carry out and maintain rehabilitation. Once confirmed, all creditors are bound by the agreement, and all unsecured debt is cancelled unless provided for in the arrangement.

Chapter X Reorganization

Chapter X of the Chandler Act provides for the rehabilitation of all insolvent corporations except interstate railroads.[5] Unlike Chapter XI, Chapter X may affect both secured and unsecured debt.

Procedure. Chapter X provides more safeguards and greater relief than Chapter XI.

---

[5] Van Arsdell is excellent on the practical and legal aspects of Chapter X reorganization. See *op. cit.*, pp. 1532–1541, 1551–1581. See also Henn, *op. cit.*, pp. 826–834.

(1) Proceedings may be initiated either voluntarily, by debtor petition, or involuntarily, by creditor petition.

(2) If the petition is approved, the judge sets a date by which creditors and stockholders must file and prove their claims.

(3) If the firm's liabilities exceed $250,000, the court appoints a disinterested trustee to take title of the company's property and to manage it in a way that will preserve the firm's going-concern value. No suits against the debtor are permitted.

(4) The trustee must formulate a reorganization plan, indicating the effects of the proposal on the income, control, and priority of claims of all classes of creditors and stockholders. The plan must also identify and state the qualifications of the persons who will be directors or officers of the firm after reorganization.

(5) At a hearing of the trustee's proposal, any creditor or stockholder may make objections or propose amendments. If the company's liabilities exceed $3 million, the SEC advises on the fairness, equity, and feasibility of the plan.

(6) After the judge grants tentative approval, the plan is sent to creditors and stockholders. If the plan is to be approved, two thirds (in dollar amounts) of each class of creditors must vote favorably; if the firm is still solvent in the bankruptcy sense, a majority of stockholders must also vote acceptance.

(7) After a vote of acceptance and the final approval of the judge, the firm distributes its new securities according to the plan.

Legal Aspects. The law requires that a reorganization plan be "fair and equitable, and feasible." "Feasible" in this sense means that the reorganized firm must have a sound capital structure, a cash flow great enough to meet the new fixed obligations, and earnings sufficient to support the value of all new securities. "Fair and equitable" means that the plan must conform to the rule of absolute priority: when there are several classes of creditors and stockholders, the claims of the class with highest priority must be met in full before those of junior classes may be met even partially. Thus, if a firm owes $1 million in senior debt and $1 million in junior debt, but its reorganized value is only $1.5 million, the senior creditors will receive their full $1 million, the junior creditors only $500,000, and the stockholders nothing.

Although the rule of absolute priority is simple, its application may be difficult. Does value refer to market value or book value? going-concern value or liquidation value? long-run or short-run value? Correct valuation is imperative since it determines which classes of creditors or stockholders are entitled to participate in the reorganization. The Supreme Court has declared that reorganization value is to be calculated by capitalizing future earnings; but since future earnings cannot be forecast with certainty, valuation necessarily reflects human judgment.[6] But even after reorganization value has been determined, a problem remains: distribution. The original company may have had several classes of debt with various priorities, but the feasibility of reorganization may require a simplified capital structure with only one class of debt, with uniform priority. The new capital structure thus conflicts with the rule of absolute priority. The Supreme Court has ruled that priorities may be rearranged as long as former senior creditors receive full compensation for foregoing their priority status. The next case study illustrates this ruling.

THE REORGANIZATION OF SFO HELICOPTER AIRLINES: A CASE STUDY

Background

The reorganization of San Francisco and Oakland Helicopter Airlines, completed in 1974, illustrates corporate rehabilitation under Chapter X of the Bankruptcy Act.[7] SFO began business in 1961, providing scheduled passenger helicopter service between various points in the San Francisco Bay Area. In 9 out of its first 10 years, the company sustained sizeable operating losses. In 1968, SFO acquired the Larkin Specialty Manufacturing Company, a maker of metal products, for $269,000 in cash and securities. Larkin turned out to be unprofitable and was later liquidated for slightly more than $100,000. Operating losses and the acquisition of Larkin drained SFO's liquid resources so much that by July 1970 SFO had current assets of only $1,108,150, consisting of $214,180 in cash and $893,970 in receivables and inventory. At the same time, SFO's liabilities were $5,970,160, which was partly secured by liens on the firm's three helicopters. Unable to meet its debt payments and fearing that secured creditors might seize its helicopters, SFO petitioned on July 31, 1970 for reorganization under Chapter X of the Bankruptcy Act. The court approved the petition the same day and appointed two well-known San Francisco attorneys as trustees.

After blocking the bank's attempt to seize SFO's cash, the trustees determined the feasibility of SFO's continuation. They eliminated unprofitable routes, reduced overhead, and developed new business; but SFO continued to lose money. In 1972, however, the firm showed a profit when its passenger business increased and its new nonpassenger business began to

---

[6] *Consolidated Rock Products Co. vs. DuBois*, 312 U.S. 510, 526 (1941).

[7] Information pertaining to this case is based on *In the Matter of San Francisco & Oakland Helicopter Airlines, Inc.*, United States District Court for the Northern District of California, No. B-70-5175 (April, 1973).

pay off. Encouraged, the trustees submitted their plan to reorganize SFO as a going concern.

Reorganization Plan

The central aspects of the March 1973 reorganization plan were the valuation placed on SFO and the recommendations for distribution of this value among creditors and stockholders. The trustees made the following forecast of SFO's earnings (*EBIAT*):

Year	EBIAT	Year	EBIAT
1974	$171,751	1976	$254,080
1975	195,462	1977	290,718

On the basis of the $228,000 average *EBIAT* for 1974–77 and the price-earnings ratio of 13, the trustees concluded that SFO had a going-concern value of $2,964,000. Since the projected liabilities as of June 30, 1973 (the anticipated date for consummating the plan) were $4,900,000, SFO was deemed insolvent in the sense of bankruptcy. The plan therefore excluded stockholders from participation in reorganization.

The plan also included details on the proposed redistribution of the reorganization value among creditors and stockholders. Table 23-4 summarizes the trustee's projection of SFO's balance sheet before reorganization, cash payments and recapitalization under the plan, and the balance sheet after reorganization. The plan included a cash payment of $323,000 for priority claims and taxes, leaving $4,910,735 in liabilities to be recapitalized. Thirty percent of this last amount was secured and 70 percent unsecured (see Table 23-5). The debt would be recapitalized thus:

1. The Bank of America, with a first lien on two helicopters, would receive a 7 percent note in the principal amount of about $107,000, payable in 18 equal monthly installments.
2. Nishi Nippon Airlines Co., Ltd., the conditional vendor of one helicopter, would receive the balance due of $246,000 in 24 monthly installments of $9,000 each, with any remaining balance due to be paid 25 months after consummation of the plan.
3. TWA, with a second lien on the two helicopters pledged to the Bank of America, would have a claim of $1,099,000 at consummation. TWA agreed to convert $500,000 of this amount into 125,000 shares of new Class A stock in the reorganized firm. The remaining $599,000 would be paid in 60 equal monthly installments at 8 percent interest.

4. Unsecured creditors, with a total claim of $3,459,000, would receive a total of 603,025 shares of Class B stock in the reorganized firm on a prorated basis.
5. Class A shares, as a class, would be entitled to elect two of the reorganized firm's nine directors. If liquidation were necessary, Class A shares would receive $4 each, a total of $500,000, before any distribution to Class B. Class B shares would receive a second preference of $4 each, and any surplus would be distributed pro rata to both classes. No other distinctions would exist between A and B shares.

Table 23-4 SFO, Inc., Projected Balance Sheets Before and After Reorganization (in thousands of dollars)

Assets	Before Plan	Cash Payments	Recapitalization	After Plan
Cash	$ 604	$(323)		$ 281
Receivables (net)	483			483
Inventory	322			322
Current assets	$1,409	$(323)		$1,086
Property and equipment (net)	1,930			1,930
Other investments	13			13
Deferred items	48			48
Total assets	$3,400	$(323)		$3,077
Liabilities and Equity				
Accounts payable	$ 25			$ 25
Accrued liabilities	136			136
Priority claims	24	$ (24)		–
Taxes–pre-bankruptcy	119	(119)		–
Estimated allowances	180	(180)		–
	$ 484	$(323)		$ 161
Bank of America	107			107
Nishi Nippon Airways	246			246
TWA	1,098		$ (500)	598
$7^3/_4$% debentures	2,413		(2,413)	–
Other general claims	1,046		(1,046)	–
Liabilities	$5,394		$(3,959)	$1,112
Common stock	2,506		(2,506)	–
Earned deficit	(4,500)		4,500	–
New equity			1,965	1,965
Total liabilities and equity	$3,400	$(323)	$ 0	$3,077

Table 23-5 Security Status of Major Creditors of SFO

Secured:		
Bank of America	$ 107,259	
Nishi Nippon	245,749	
TWA	1,098,690	$1,451,695
Unsecured:		
$7\frac{3}{4}$% debentures	$2,412,799	
Other general claims	1,046,241	3,459,000
		$4,910,735

SEC Comments

In its advisory report to the judge, the SEC endorsed the plan as feasible as well as fair and equitable. The Commission observed that the trusteeship had demonstrated the viability of SFO as a going concern. It pointed particularly to the steady growth of passenger business and to the diversification provided by the firm's new cargo business. The SEC also noted the conversion into stock of $500,000 of TWA's secured claim, enabling SFO to begin anew with a sound capital structure. Before reorganization, SFO had had a negative equity; after reorganization, its equity equalled 64 percent of its total assets at cost:

	Before Plan	After Plan
Equity	−$1,994,000	+$1,965,000
Equity/Assets	−59%	+64%

Cash projections convinced the SEC that the reorganized company would be able to service its new reduced fixed obligations in the normal course of events. The plan was thus deemed feasible.

In considering fairness, the SEC accepted the trustees' figure of approximately $3 million as the going-concern value of SFO. Since the firm's liabilities exceeded this sum, the Commission considered it fair to exclude stockholders from participation in reorganization. In regard to creditors, the central issue was the conversion of part of TWA's claim into 125,000 Class A shares. Since the Class A shares gave TWA liquidation priority as well as the right to elect 22 percent of the directors, the SEC determined that these shares constituted fair compensation for the loss of senior creditor priority.

Even though the SEC did not raise the question, perhaps we should ask why TWA, with liens on two helicopters, was willing to abandon its senior priority. The answer may bear on the fairness accorded to TWA. First, SFO lands first and departs last from one of TWA's gates at the San

Francisco International Airport. TWA may well have wished this beneficial arrangement to continue. Second, since TWA is itself an airline, it may have wished to avoid forcing another line out of business.

In its only reference to unsecured creditors, the SEC held that there can be "no doubt that the plan is fair and equitable. . . ." Presumably because this conclusion seemed obvious, no supporting analysis was given.

Results

The court approved the trustees' plan of reorganization on April 9, 1973; creditors were given two months to vote approval or disapproval. All of the secured creditors voted approval, as did more than 70 percent of the unsecured creditors—more than the two thirds needed for approval. On June 26, 1973, the court confirmed the plan. At this time, the new securities were issued and operation control was passed from the trustees to the new board of directors. The responsibilities of the trustees ended in 1974 when several lawsuits involving the old SFO were finally settled.

REVIEW QUESTIONS

1. Recapitalization and reorganization have been defined as the recasting of a firm's existing capital structure. Are the criteria for the decisions similar to or different from the criteria for designing the capital structure of a new firm?
2. Fuqua Industries' circular describing its offer to exchange its 9.5%, 25-year debentures for its own stock contains this reasoning: "Fuqua's management believes that Fuqua Common Stock is undervalued at the present time and that its purchase of such stock at current prices for a consideration consisting of debt securities will benefit Fuqua and its stockholders." Why would a stockholder consider selling his stock if it is presently undervalued? Can both the company and the selling stockholders gain by the exchange?
3. ABC Industries is offering to purchase 20,000 of its common shares for cash. Is this an investment decision, a recapitalization decision, a dividend decision, or all three? Explain.
4. An ABC stockholder is inclined to accept the repurchase offer. Why might he postpone his final decision until shortly before the offer expires? What could ABC do to induce stockholders to accept the offer early?
5. Look up an example of recent recapitalization involving common stock; preferred stock; bonds; convertible securities. Briefly give the background of each company, and summarize the exchange offer. What did each firm hope to accomplish through recapitalization?
6. In the Fibreboard recapitalization, each $1,000 of principal amount in old bonds convertible into 32 common shares was exchanged for $750 in new bonds convertible into 40.54 shares. Could Fibreboard have achieved its objective simply by reducing the conversion price of the old bonds from $31¼ to about $25?

7. In response to Bio-Medical's offer, the holders of over $8 million of convertible debentures accepted the offer to exchange their bonds for common stock. Why, in spite of their legal right, were these bondholders willing to trade their position as creditors for a position as stockholders?

8. Bell Industries cancelled its offer because only 209,000 shares were tendered, whereas the firm was prepared to accept 1,700,000. Fuqua Industries' offer, on the other hand, was reasonably successful: the firm was willing to accept up to 2 million shares, and 1.2 million were tendered. Investigate the circumstances behind the two offers; try to account for the different results in terms of your findings.

9. XYZ is in imminent default on its fixed obligations and is considering either judicial or nonjudicial reorganization. Which factors should XYZ consider in determining whether to seek nonjudicial extension or composition, a Chapter XI arrangement, or Chapter X reorganization?

10. What is the rule of absolute priority? Does it permit any rearrangement in the priority status of the various classes of claimants? If so, under what conditions? In SFO's reorganization, was priority status altered? Under what justification? Why was there no violation of the fairness-and-equity test required of all Chapter X reorganization plans?

PROBLEMS

1. In the text, we analyzed Fuqua's exchange offer, assuming 100 percent acceptance. Recalculate Fuqua's after-exchange *EPS*, after-exchange interest coverage ratio, and index of variability, assuming that only 1.2 million shares were tendered, instead of the target maximum of 2 million shares. Will the new calculations affect the break-even *EBIT?* If so, recalculate that figure.

2. Analyze the price behavior of Fuqua common stock relative to the Dow-Jones average of 30 industrials for the period since the exchange. By how much has the exchange benefited Fuqua's continuing stockholders? If you cannot tell, what additional information do you need?

3. Recalculate the effect of Bell Industries' exchange offer on *EPS*, earnings-variability index, and interest coverage ratio, assuming 50 percent exchange. Assume also that the firm has 4,594,000 shares, including common stock equivalents, before the exchange.

4. What formula would you use to calculate the break-even income before preferred dividends for the Leasco exchange offer? In what way does this formula differ from the one we used to calculate the break-even *EBIT* for the Fuqua exchange offer?

5. In Question 5, you were asked to look up examples of recapitalization. For one of your examples, calculate the break-even *EBIT* and the effect of the exchange on *EPS*. How will the exchange affect the earnings-capitalization rate? the share price?

6. The XYZ Company has 1 million outstanding shares of preferred stock, each share carrying a cumulative preferential dividend of $1.00 per annum and convertible into .6 share of common stock. The market price of the preferred is $10 per share; that of common stock, $2.50. The company offers to exchange

$13 in principal amount of a new 10%, 25-year subordinated debentures for each share of old preferred. Before exchange, XYZ's income statement read:

Net operating income	$14,000,000
Interest	7,000,000
Taxable income	$ 7,000,000
Income taxes	3,500,000
Net income	$ 3,500,000

Calculate the effects of the exchange offer on *EPS*, earnings-variability index, and interest coverage ratio. Assume that, before the exchange, preferred dividends total $1 million annually and that common stock and common stock equivalents total 7 million shares.

7. In commenting on the fairness of the trustee's plan for reorganizing SFO Helicopter Airlines, the SEC stated that there can be "no doubt that the plan is fair and equitable to the unsecured creditors." Do you agree? Why or why not? Show all calculations.

REFERENCES

ALTMAN, EDWARD I., *Corporate Bankruptcy in America* (Lexington: Heath Lexington Books, 1971).

ANG, JAMES S., "The Two Faces of Bond Refunding," *Journal of Finance* 30 (June, 1975), pp. 869–874.

BECKMAN, THEODORE N., and RONALD S. FOSTER, *Credits and Collections* (New York: McGraw-Hill Book Company, 1969), Chs. 27 and 28.

EDMISTER, ROBERT O., "An Empirical Test of Financial Ratio Analysis for Small Business Failure Prediction," *Journal of Financial and Quantitative Analysis* 7 (March, 1972), pp. 1477–1493.

FRANK, WERNER G., and JERRY J. WEYGANDT, "A Prediction Model for Convertible Debentures," *Journal of Accounting Research* 9 (Spring, 1971), pp. 116–126.

GORDON, MYRON J., "Towards a Theory of Financial Distress," *Journal of Finance* 26 (May, 1971), pp. 347–356.

HENN, HARRY G., *Law of Corporations* (St. Paul: West Publishing Company, 1970), Ch. 10.

In the Matter of San Francisco & Oakland Helicopter Airlines, Inc., United States District Court for the Northern District of California, No. B-70–5175 (April, 1973).

MILLER, ROGER W., "Convertible Exchange Offers – Everyone Can Win," *Financial Executive* 42 (February, 1974), pp. 25–31, 69.

NADER, FORSETT SEELYE, "Px for the Sick Corporation," *Mergers and Acquisitions* 7 (Fall, 1972), pp. 21–31.

VAN ARSDELL, PAUL M. *Corporation Finance* (New York: The Ronald Press Company, 1968), Chs. 48–53.

Appendices

A: Present and Future Value Tables

(Tables A-1 to A-4)

B: Financial Computing Programs

(Figures B-1 to B-6)

Table A-1 Present Value of $1

Year	2%	4%	6%	8%	10%	12%	14%	16%	18%	20%
1	0.980	0.962	0.943	0.926	0.909	0.893	0.877	0.862	0.847	0.833
2	0.961	0.925	0.890	0.857	0.826	0.797	0.769	0.743	0.718	0.694
3	0.942	0.889	0.840	0.794	0.751	0.712	0.675	0.641	0.609	0.579
4	0.924	0.855	0.792	0.735	0.683	0.636	0.592	0.552	0.516	0.482
5	0.906	0.822	0.747	0.681	0.621	0.567	0.519	0.476	0.437	0.402
6	0.888	0.790	0.705	0.630	0.564	0.507	0.456	0.410	0.370	0.335
7	0.871	0.760	0.665	0.583	0.513	0.452	0.400	0.354	0.314	0.279
8	0.853	0.731	0.627	0.540	0.467	0.404	0.351	0.305	0.266	0.233
9	0.837	0.703	0.592	0.500	0.424	0.361	0.308	0.263	0.225	0.194
10	0.820	0.676	0.558	0.463	0.386	0.322	0.270	0.227	0.191	0.162
11	0.804	0.650	0.527	0.429	0.350	0.287	0.237	0.195	0.162	0.135
12	0.788	0.625	0.497	0.397	0.319	0.257	0.208	0.168	0.137	0.112
13	0.773	0.601	0.469	0.368	0.290	0.229	0.182	0.145	0.116	0.093
14	0.758	0.577	0.442	0.340	0.263	0.205	0.160	0.125	0.099	0.078
15	0.743	0.555	0.417	0.315	0.239	0.183	0.140	0.108	0.084	0.065
16	0.728	0.534	0.394	0.292	0.218	0.163	0.123	0.093	0.071	0.054
17	0.714	0.513	0.371	0.270	0.198	0.146	0.108	0.080	0.060	0.045
18	0.700	0.494	0.350	0.250	0.180	0.130	0.095	0.069	0.051	0.038
19	0.686	0.475	0.331	0.232	0.164	0.116	0.083	0.060	0.043	0.031
20	0.673	0.456	0.312	0.215	0.149	0.104	0.073	0.051	0.037	0.026
21	0.660	0.439	0.294	0.199	0.135	0.093	0.064	0.044	0.031	0.022
22	0.647	0.422	0.278	0.184	0.123	0.083	0.056	0.038	0.026	0.018
23	0.634	0.406	0.262	0.170	0.112	0.074	0.049	0.033	0.022	0.015
24	0.622	0.390	0.247	0.158	0.102	0.066	0.043	0.028	0.019	0.013
25	0.610	0.375	0.233	0.146	0.092	0.059	0.038	0.024	0.016	0.010

Year	22%	24%	26%	28%	30%	32%	34%	36%	38%	40%
1	0.820	0.806	0.794	0.781	0.769	0.758	0.746	0.735	0.725	0.714
2	0.672	0.650	0.630	0.610	0.592	0.574	0.557	0.541	0.525	0.510
3	0.551	0.524	0.500	0.477	0.455	0.435	0.416	0.398	0.381	0.364
4	0.451	0.423	0.397	0.373	0.350	0.329	0.310	0.292	0.276	0.260
5	0.370	0.341	0.315	0.291	0.269	0.250	0.231	0.215	0.200	0.186
6	0.303	0.275	0.250	0.227	0.207	0.189	0.173	0.158	0.145	0.133
7	0.249	0.222	0.198	0.178	0.159	0.143	0.129	0.116	0.105	0.095
8	0.204	0.179	0.157	0.139	0.123	0.108	0.096	0.085	0.076	0.068
9	0.167	0.144	0.125	0.108	0.094	0.082	0.072	0.063	0.055	0.048
10	0.137	0.116	0.099	0.085	0.073	0.062	0.054	0.046	0.040	0.035
11	0.112	0.094	0.079	0.066	0.056	0.047	0.040	0.034	0.029	0.025
12	0.092	0.076	0.062	0.052	0.043	0.036	0.030	0.025	0.021	0.018
13	0.075	0.061	0.050	0.040	0.033	0.027	0.022	0.018	0.015	0.013
14	0.062	0.049	0.039	0.032	0.025	0.021	0.017	0.014	0.011	0.009
15	0.051	0.040	0.031	0.025	0.020	0.016	0.012	0.010	0.008	0.006
16	0.042	0.032	0.025	0.019	0.015	0.012	0.009	0.007	0.006	0.005
17	0.034	0.026	0.020	0.015	0.012	0.009	0.007	0.005	0.004	0.003
18	0.028	0.021	0.016	0.012	0.009	0.007	0.005	0.004	0.003	0.002
19	0.023	0.017	0.012	0.009	0.007	0.005	0.004	0.003	0.002	0.002
20	0.019	0.014	0.010	0.007	0.005	0.004	0.003	0.002	0.002	0.001
21	0.015	0.011	0.008	0.006	0.004	0.003	0.002	0.002	0.001	0.001
22	0.013	0.009	0.006	0.004	0.003	0.002	0.002	0.001	0.001	0.001
23	0.010	0.007	0.005	0.003	0.002	0.002	0.001	0.001	0.001	0.000
24	0.008	0.006	0.004	0.003	0.002	0.001	0.001	0.001	0.000	0.000
25	0.007	0.005	0.003	0.002	0.001	0.001	0.001	0.000	0.000	0.000

Table A-2 Present Value of an Annuity of $1

Year	2%	4%	6%	8%	10%	12%	14%	16%	18%	20%
1	0.980	0.962	0.943	0.926	0.909	0.893	0.877	0.862	0.847	0.833
2	1.942	1.886	1.833	1.783	1.736	1.690	1.647	1.605	1.566	1.528
3	2.884	2.775	2.673	2.577	2.487	2.402	2.322	2.246	2.174	2.106
4	3.808	3.630	3.465	3.312	3.170	3.037	2.914	2.798	2.690	2.589
5	4.713	4.452	4.212	3.993	3.791	3.605	3.433	3.274	3.127	2.991
6	5.601	5.242	4.917	4.623	4.355	4.111	3.889	3.685	3.498	3.326
7	6.472	6.002	5.582	5.206	4.868	4.564	4.288	4.039	3.812	3.605
8	7.325	6.733	6.210	5.747	5.335	4.968	4.639	4.344	4.078	3.837
9	8.162	7.435	6.802	6.247	5.759	5.328	4.946	4.607	4.303	4.031
10	8.982	8.111	7.360	6.710	6.145	5.650	5.216	4.833	4.494	4.192
11	9.787	8.760	7.887	7.139	6.495	5.938	5.453	5.029	4.656	4.327
12	10.575	9.385	8.384	7.536	6.814	6.194	5.660	5.197	4.793	4.439
13	11.348	9.986	8.853	7.904	7.103	6.424	5.842	5.342	4.910	4.533
14	12.106	10.563	9.295	8.244	7.367	6.628	6.002	5.468	5.008	4.611
15	12.849	11.118	9.712	8.559	7.606	6.811	6.142	5.575	5.092	4.675
16	13.577	11.652	10.106	8.851	7.824	6.974	6.265	5.668	5.162	4.730
17	14.292	12.166	10.477	9.122	8.022	7.120	6.373	5.749	5.222	4.775
18	14.992	12.659	10.828	9.372	8.201	7.250	6.467	5.818	5.273	4.812
19	15.678	13.134	11.158	9.604	8.365	7.366	6.550	5.877	5.316	4.843
20	16.351	13.590	11.470	9.818	8.514	7.469	6.623	5.929	5.353	4.870
21	17.011	14.029	11.764	10.017	8.649	7.562	6.687	5.973	5.384	4.891
22	17.658	14.451	12.042	10.201	8.772	7.645	6.743	6.011	5.410	4.909
23	18.292	14.857	12.303	10.371	8.883	7.718	6.792	6.044	5.432	4.925
24	18.914	15.247	12.550	10.529	8.985	7.784	6.835	6.073	5.451	4.937
25	19.523	15.622	12.783	10.675	9.077	7.843	6.873	6.097	5.467	4.948

Year	22%	24%	26%	28%	30%	32%	34%	36%	38%	40%
1	0.820	0.806	0.794	0.781	0.769	0.758	0.746	0.735	0.725	0.714
2	1.492	1.457	1.424	1.392	1.361	1.331	1.303	1.276	1.250	1.224
3	2.042	1.981	1.923	1.868	1.816	1.766	1.719	1.673	1.630	1.589
4	2.494	2.404	2.320	2.241	2.166	2.096	2.029	1.966	1.906	1.849
5	2.864	2.745	2.635	2.532	2.436	2.345	2.260	2.181	2.106	2.035
6	3.167	3.020	2.885	2.759	2.643	2.534	2.433	2.339	2.251	2.168
7	3.416	3.242	3.083	2.937	2.802	2.677	2.562	2.455	2.355	2.263
8	3.619	3.421	3.241	3.076	2.925	2.786	2.658	2.540	2.432	2.331
9	3.786	3.566	3.366	3.184	3.019	2.868	2.730	2.603	2.487	2.379
10	3.923	3.682	3.465	3.269	3.092	2.930	2.784	2.649	2.527	2.414
11	4.035	3.776	3.543	3.335	3.147	2.978	2.824	2.683	2.555	2.438
12	4.127	3.851	3.606	3.387	3.190	3.013	2.853	2.708	2.576	2.456
13	4.203	3.912	3.656	3.427	3.223	3.040	2.876	2.727	2.592	2.469
14	4.265	3.962	3.695	3.459	3.249	3.061	2.892	2.740	2.603	2.478
15	4.315	4.001	3.726	3.483	3.268	3.076	2.905	2.750	2.611	2.484
16	4.357	4.033	3.751	3.503	3.283	3.088	2.914	2.757	2.616	2.489
17	4.391	4.059	3.771	3.518	3.295	3.097	2.921	2.763	2.621	2.492
18	4.419	4.080	3.786	3.529	3.304	3.104	2.926	2.767	2.624	2.494
19	4.442	4.097	3.799	3.539	3.311	3.109	2.930	2.770	2.626	2.496
20	4.460	4.110	3.808	3.546	3.316	3.113	2.933	2.772	2.627	2.497
21	4.476	4.121	3.816	3.551	3.320	3.116	2.935	2.773	2.629	2.498
22	4.488	4.130	3.822	3.556	3.323	3.118	2.936	2.775	2.629	2.498
23	4.499	4.137	3.827	3.559	3.325	3.120	2.938	2.775	2.630	2.499
24	4.507	4.143	3.831	3.562	3.327	3.121	2.939	2.776	2.630	2.499
25	4.514	4.147	3.834	3.564	3.329	3.122	2.939	2.777	2.631	2.499

Table A-3 Future Value of $1

Year	2%	4%	6%	8%	10%	12%	14%	16%
1	1.020	1.040	1.060	1.080	1.100	1.120	1.140	1.160
2	1.040	1.082	1.124	1.166	1.210	1.254	1.300	1.346
3	1.061	1.125	1.191	1.260	1.331	1.405	1.482	1.561
4	1.082	1.170	1.262	1.360	1.464	1.574	1.689	1.811
5	1.104	1.217	1.338	1.469	1.611	1.762	1.925	2.100
6	1.126	1.265	1.419	1.587	1.772	1.974	2.195	2.436
7	1.149	1.316	1.504	1.714	1.949	2.211	2.502	2.826
8	1.172	1.369	1.594	1.851	2.144	2.476	2.853	3.278
9	1.195	1.423	1.689	1.999	2.358	2.773	3.252	3.803
10	1.219	1.480	1.791	2.159	2.594	3.106	3.707	4.411
11	1.243	1.539	1.898	2.332	2.853	3.479	4.226	5.117
12	1.268	1.601	2.012	2.518	3.138	3.896	4.818	5.936
13	1.294	1.665	2.133	2.720	3.452	4.363	5.492	6.886
14	1.319	1.732	2.261	2.937	3.797	4.887	6.261	7.988
15	1.346	1.801	2.397	3.172	4.177	5.474	7.138	9.266
16	1.373	1.873	2.540	3.426	4.595	6.130	8.137	10.748
17	1.400	1.948	2.693	3.700	5.054	6.866	9.276	12.468
18	1.428	2.026	2.854	3.996	5.560	7.690	10.575	14.462
19	1.457	2.107	3.026	4.316	6.116	8.613	12.056	16.776
20	1.486	2.191	3.207	4.661	6.727	9.646	13.743	19.461
21	1.516	2.279	3.400	5.034	7.400	10.804	15.667	22.574
22	1.546	2.370	3.603	5.437	8.140	12.100	17.861	26.186
23	1.577	2.465	3.820	5.871	8.954	13.552	20.361	30.376
24	1.608	2.563	4.049	6.341	9.850	15.179	23.212	35.236
25	1.641	2.666	4.292	6.848	10.835	17.000	26.462	40.874

Year	18%	20%	22%	24%	26%	28%	30%	32%
1	1.180	1.200	1.220	1.240	1.260	1.280	1.300	1.320
2	1.392	1.440	1.488	1.538	1.588	1.638	1.690	1.742
3	1.643	1.728	1.816	1.907	2.000	2.097	2.197	2.300
4	1.939	2.074	2.215	2.364	2.520	2.684	2.856	3.036
5	2.288	2.488	2.703	2.932	3.176	3.436	3.713	4.007
6	2.700	2.986	3.297	3.635	4.001	4.398	4.827	5.290
7	3.185	3.583	4.023	4.508	5.042	5.629	6.275	6.983
8	3.759	4.300	4.908	5.589	6.353	7.206	8.157	9.217
9	4.435	5.160	5.987	6.931	8.004	9.223	10.604	12.166
10	5.234	6.192	7.305	8.594	10.086	11.806	13.786	16.060
11	6.176	7.430	8.912	10.657	12.708	15.112	17.921	21.199
12	7.288	8.916	10.872	13.215	16.012	19.343	23.298	27.982
13	8.599	10.699	13.264	16.386	20.175	24.759	30.287	36.937
14	10.147	12.839	16.182	20.319	25.421	31.691	39.373	48.757
15	11.974	15.407	19.742	25.196	32.030	40.565	51.185	64.359
16	14.129	18.488	24.085	31.242	40.358	51.923	66.541	84.953
17	16.672	22.186	29.384	38.741	50.850	66.461	86.503	112.139
18	19.673	26.623	35.849	48.038	64.072	85.070	112.454	148.023
19	23.214	31.948	43.735	59.568	80.730	108.890	146.190	195.390
20	27.393	38.337	53.357	73.864	101.720	139.379	190.047	257.915
21	32.323	46.005	65.096	91.591	128.167	178.405	247.061	340.448
22	38.142	55.206	79.417	113.573	161.490	228.359	321.180	449.391
23	45.007	66.247	96.888	140.831	203.478	292.299	417.533	593.196
24	53.108	79.497	118.203	174.630	256.382	374.142	542.793	783.018
25	62.668	95.396	144.208	216.541	323.041	478.902	705.631	1033.58

Table A-4 Future Value of an Annuity of $1

Year	2%	4%	6%	8%	10%	12%	14%	16%
1	1.000	1.000	1.000	1.000	1.000	1.000	1.000	1.000
2	2.020	2.040	2.060	2.080	2.100	2.120	2.140	2.160
3	3.060	3.122	3.184	3.246	3.310	3.374	3.440	3.506
4	4.121	4.246	4.375	4.506	4.641	4.779	4.921	5.066
5	5.204	5.416	5.637	5.867	6.105	6.353	6.610	6.877
6	6.308	6.633	6.975	7.336	7.716	8.115	8.535	8.977
7	7.434	7.898	8.394	8.923	9.487	10.089	10.730	11.414
8	8.583	9.214	9.897	10.637	11.436	12.300	13.233	14.240
9	9.754	10.583	11.491	12.488	13.579	14.776	16.085	17.518
10	10.949	12.006	13.181	14.487	15.937	17.549	19.337	21.321
11	12.168	13.486	14.971	16.645	18.531	20.655	23.044	25.733
12	13.412	15.026	16.870	18.977	21.384	24.133	27.271	30.850
13	14.680	16.627	18.882	21.495	24.522	28.029	32.088	36.786
14	15.973	18.292	21.015	24.215	27.975	32.393	37.581	43.672
15	17.293	20.024	23.276	27.152	31.772	37.280	43.842	51.659
16	18.639	21.824	25.672	30.324	35.949	42.753	50.980	60.925
17	20.011	23.697	28.212	33.750	40.544	48.884	59.117	71.673
18	21.412	25.645	30.905	37.450	45.599	55.750	68.393	84.141
19	22.840	27.671	33.759	41.446	51.158	63.440	78.968	98.603
20	24.297	29.778	36.785	45.762	57.274	72.052	91.024	115.379
21	25.783	31.969	39.992	50.423	64.002	81.699	104.767	134.840
22	27.298	34.248	43.392	55.457	71.402	92.502	120.434	157.414
23	28.844	36.618	46.995	60.893	79.542	104.603	138.295	183.601
24	30.421	39.083	50.815	66.765	88.496	118.155	158.656	213.977
25	32.029	41.646	54.864	73.106	98.346	133.334	181.868	249.213

Year	18%	20%	22%	24%	26%	28%	30%	32%
1	1.000	1.000	1.000	1.000	1.000	1.000	1.000	1.000
2	2.180	2.200	2.220	2.240	2.260	2.280	2.300	2.320
3	3.572	3.640	3.708	3.778	3.848	3.918	3.990	4.062
4	5.215	5.368	5.524	5.684	5.848	6.016	6.187	6.362
5	7.154	7.442	7.740	8.048	8.368	8.700	9.043	9.398
6	9.442	9.930	10.442	10.980	11.544	12.136	12.756	13.406
7	12.141	12.916	13.740	14.615	15.546	16.534	17.583	18.696
8	15.327	16.499	17.762	19.123	20.588	22.163	23.858	25.678
9	19.086	20.799	22.670	24.712	26.940	29.369	32.015	34.895
10	23.521	25.959	28.657	31.643	34.945	38.592	42.619	47.062
11	28.755	32.150	35.962	40.238	45.030	50.398	56.405	63.121
12	34.931	39.580	44.873	50.895	57.738	65.510	74.326	84.320
13	42.218	48.496	55.745	64.110	73.750	84.853	97.624	112.303
14	50.818	59.196	69.009	80.496	93.925	109.611	127.911	149.239
15	60.965	72.035	85.191	100.815	119.345	141.302	167.285	197.996
16	72.938	87.442	104.934	126.010	151.375	181.867	218.470	262.354
17	87.067	105.930	129.019	157.253	191.733	233.790	285.011	347.308
18	103.739	128.116	158.403	195.994	242.583	300.251	371.514	459.447
19	123.412	154.739	194.251	244.032	306.654	385.321	483.968	607.469
20	146.626	186.687	237.987	303.599	387.384	494.211	630.158	802.859
21	174.019	225.025	291.343	377.463	489.104	633.590	820.205	1060.77
22	206.342	271.030	356.439	469.054	617.270	811.995	1067.26	1401.22
23	244.484	326.236	435.855	582.627	778.760	1040.35	1388.44	1850.61
24	289.490	392.483	532.743	723.458	982.237	1332.65	1805.98	2443.81
25	342.599	471.979	650.946	898.087	1238.62	1706.79	2348.77	3226.82

Figure B-1 Financial Statement Forecasts

```
C     FINANCIAL STATEMENT FORECASTS
C
C     A           PERCENTAGE OF CREDIT SALES
C     P           SELLING PRICE PER PRODUCT UNIT
C     B           RAW MATERIALS COST PER DOLLAR OF SALES
C     G           DIRECT LABOR COST PER DOLLAR OF SALES
C     T           INCOME TAX RATE
C     D           DEPRECIATION PERCENTAGE
C     DIV         DIVIDEND PER SHARE OF COMMON STOCK
C     SAG         SELLING, ADMINISTRATIVE, AND GENERAL EXPENSES
C     CMS         CASH AND MARKETABLE SECURITIES
C     ACR         ACCOUNTS RECEIVABLE
C     INV         INVENTORIES, AT THE LOWER OF COST OR MARKET
C     ACD         ACCUMULATED DEPRECIATION
C     STB         SHORT-TERM BANK LOAN
C     ACP         ACCOUNTS PAYABLE
C     FIT         FEDERAL INCOME TAX
C     LTD         LONG-TERM DEBT
C     CST         COMMON STOCK
C     CAS         CAPITAL SURPLUS
C     RER         RETAINED EARNINGS
C     IPU         FINISHED GOODS INVENTORY (IN UNITS, AT QUARTER'S END)
C     PAE         PLANT AND EQUIPMENT
C     SHR         NUMBER OF COMMON STOCK SHARES
C     POW         POWER BILL
C     HTL         HEAT AND LIGHT BILL
C     REM         REPAIRS AND MAINTENANCE
C     INS         INSURANCE PREMIUM
C     IDL         INDIRECT LABOR COST
C     DATE1       DAY AND YEAR
C     DATE2       DAY AND YEAR
C     QUARTR      QUARTER OF THE YEAR
C     SAL         SALES IN PHYSICAL UNITS
C     LTR         LONG-TERM DEBT REPAYMENT
C     STR         SHORT-TERM DEBT REPAYMENT
C     NVT         INVESTMENTS
C     INT         INTEREST EXPENSE
C     TCA         TOTAL CURRENT ASSETS
C     TCL         TOTAL CURRENT LIABILITIES
C     SEQ         STOCKHOLDER'S EQUITY
C     TLE         TOTAL LIABILITIES AND EQUITY
C     ACD         ACCUMULATED DEPRECIATION
C     REV         SALES REVENUE
C     PPU         PRODUCTION IN UNITS
C     VRM         VALUE OF RAW MATERIALS
C     VDL         VALUE OF DIRECT LABOR
C     FME         TOTAL MANUFACTURING EXPENSES
C     TCP         TOTAL COST OF PRODUCTION
C     AUC         UNIT COST OF PRODUCTION
C     CGS         COST OF GOODS SOLD
C     NET         NET PROFIT
C     TDV         TOTAL DIVIDEND
C     OME         MANUFACTURING EXPENSES (EXCLUDING DEPRECIATION)
C     CSL         CASH SALES
C     CAB         TOTAL CASH AVAILABLE
C     TCD         TOTAL CASH DISBURSEMENTS
C     NTF         NET FINANCING
C     ECB         ENDING CASH BALANCE
C     BOR         TOTAL BORROWING (SHORT- AND LONG-TERM)
C     REP         TOTAL DEBT REPAYMENTS (SHORT- AND LONG-TERM)
C     IFLAG       INDICATOR OF INITIAL BALANCE SHEET PRINTOUT (0 OR 1)
C
      IMPLICIT REAL*8(A-Z)
      DIMENSION DATE1(4),DATE2(4),QUARTR(2)
      DATA END/'      '/
      IFLAG=0.0D0
      READ(5,100)A,P,B,G,T,D,SAG,CMSL,ACRL,INVL,ACDL,STBL,ACPL,FITL,
     1LTDL,CSTL,CASL,RERL,IPUL,PAEL,SHR,POW,HTL,REM,INS,IDL
  100 FORMAT(8F10.0)
      READ(5,101)DATE1(1),DATE1(2),DATE1(3),DATE1(4)
  102 READ(5,101)DATE2(1),DATE2(2),DATE2(3),DATE2(4)
```

```
      IF(DATE2(1).EQ.END)GO TO 120
      READ(5,101)QUARTR(1),QUARTR(2)
  101 FORMAT(4A8)
      READ(5,100)SAL,SALN,LTB,LTBN,STB,STBN,LTR,STR,NVT,NVTN,DIV,INT
      TCAL=CMSL+ACRL+INVL
      PLDL=PAEL-ACDL
      TASL=TCAL+PLDL
      TCLL=STBL+ACPL+FITL
      SEQL=CSTL+CASL+RERL
      TLEL=TCLL+LTDL+SEQL
      IF(IFLAG.EQ.1.0D0)GO TO 104
      WRITE(6,105)DATE1(1),DATE1(2),DATE1(3),DATE1(4)
  105 FORMAT(1H1,//,40X,'EL CAMELO CORPORATION',/,43X,'BALANCE SHEET',
     1/,42X,4A8,//)
      WRITE(6,106)CMSL,STBL,ACRL,ACPL,INVL,FITL,TCAL,TCLL,PAEL,LTDL,
     1ACDL,PLDL,TASL,CSTL,CASL,RERL,SEQL,TLEL
  104 CONTINUE
      PAEL=PAEL+NVT
      DEP=PAEL*D
      ACDL=ACDL+DEP
      PLDL=PAEL-ACDL
      REV=SAL*P
      IPU=.5*SALN
      PPU=IPU+.5*SAL
      VRM=PPU*B*P
      VDL=PPU*G*P
      FME=POW+HTL+REM+DEP+INS+IDL
      TCP=VRM+ VDL+FME
      AUC=TCP/PPU
      INV=IPU*AUC
      CGS=TCP+INVL-INV
      NET=(REV-CGS-SAG-INT)*(1-T)
      TDV=SHR*DIV
      RER=NET-TDV
      OME=FME-DEP
      TOT1=TCP+INVL
      TOT2=REV-CGS
      TOT3=TOT2-SAG
      TOT4=TOT3-INT
      FIT=TOT4*T
      IF(FIT.LT.0.0)FIT =0.0
      CSL=(1-A)*REV
      CAB=CMSL+ACRL+CSL
      TCD=ACPL+VDL+OME+SAG+INT +FITL+TDV+NVT
      NTF=LTB+STB-LTR-STR
      ECB=CAB-TCD+NTF
      ACR=REV*A
      TCA=ECB+ACR+INV
      TAS=TCA+PLDL
      STBL=STBL-STR+STB
      TCL=STBL+VRM+FIT
      RERL=RERL+RER
      SEQ=CSTL+CASL+RERL
      LTDL=LTDL-LTR+LTB
      TLE=TCL+LTDL+SEQ
      BOR=STB+LTB
      REP=STR+LTR
      WRITE(6,108)QUARTR(1), QUARTR(2)
  108 FORMAT(1H1,//,34X,'EL CAMELO CORPORATION',/,32X,'COST OF GOODS SOL
     1D BUDGET'/37X,4A8,////)
      WRITE(6,109)VRM,VDL,DEP,OME,TCP,PPU,AUC,INVL,TOT1,INV,CGS
      WRITE(6,110)QUARTR(1),QUARTR(2)
  110 FORMAT(1H1,34X,'EL CAMELO CORPORATION',/,32X,'PROFIT AND LOSS STAT
     1EMENT'/37X,4A8,////)
      WRITE(6,111)REV,CGS,TOT2,SAG,TOT3,INT,TOT4,FIT,NET,TDV,RER
      WRITE(6,112)QUARTR(1),QUARTR(2)
  112 FORMAT(1H1,//,34X,'EL CAMELO CORPORATION',/,38X,
     1'CASH BUDGET',/,37X,4A8,///)
      WRITE(6,113)CMSL,ACRL,CSL,CAB,ACPL,VDL,OME,SAG,INT,FITL,TDV,
     1NVT,TCD,BOR,REP,NTF,ECB
  113 FORMAT(///,' BEGINNING BALANCE',14X,F14.2,//,
```

Figure B-1 (*continued*)

```
   1' BUDGETED RECEIPTS',/,3X,'COLLECTION OF'/3X'ACCOUNTS RECEIVABLE',
   D10X,F14.2,/,3X,'CASH SALES',19X,F14.2,/,32X,14(1H-),/,3X,
   A'TOTAL', 24X,F14.2,/,32X,14(1H-),//,' BUDGETED DISBURSEMENTS',//,
   V3X,'ACCOUNTS PAYABLE',13X,F14.2,
   I/,3X,'DIRECT LABOR',17X,F14.2,
   D/,3X,'MANUFACTURING EXPENSES',/,
   E3X,'(EXCLUDING DEPRECIATION)',5X,F14.2,/,3X,'SELLING, ADMINISTRATI
   .ON', /,3X,'AND GENERAL EXPENSES',9X,F14.2,/,3X,'INTEREST',21X,
   IF14.2,/,3X,'FEDERAL INCOME TAX',11X,
   NF14.2,/,3X,'DIVIDENDS',20X,F14.2,/,3X,'PLANT EXPANSION',14X,F14.2,
   H/,32X,14(1H-),/,3X,'TOTAL',24X,F14.2/32X,14(1H-),//,' FINANCING',
   O/,3X,'BORROWING',20X,F14.2,/,3X,'REPAYMENTS',19X,F14.2,/,32X,14(1H
   F-),/,3X,'NET FINANCING',16X,F14.2,/,32X,14(1H-),//' ENDING CASH BA
   ELANCE',12X,F14.2)
    CMSL=ECB
    ACRL=ACR
    INVL=INV
    TCAL=TCA
    ACPL=VRM
    TASL=TAS
    FITL=FIT
    TCLL=TCL
    SEQL=SEQ
    TLEL=TLE
    WRITE(6,105)DATE2(1),DATE2(2),DATE2(3),DATE2(4)
    WRITE(6,106)CMSL,STBL,ACRL,ACPL,INVL,FITL,TCAL,TCLL,PAEL,LTDL,
   1ACDL,PLDL,TASL,CSTL,CASL,RERL,SEQL,TLEL
    IFLAG=1.0D0
    GO TO 102
106 FORMAT(4X,'CURRENT ASSETS:',48X,'CURRENT LIABILITIES:',
   1//,2X,'CASH AND MARKETABLE SECURITIES',17X,'$',F14.2,1X,
   2'SHORT TERM BANK LOAN',19X,'$',F14.2,//,2X,'ACCOUNTS RECEIVABLE',
   329X,F14.2,1X,'ACCOUNTS PAYABLE',24X,F14.2,//,2X,'INVENTORIES',
   437X,F14.2,1X,'FEDERAL INCOME TAXES',20X,F14.2,/,50X,14(1H-),
   541X,14(1H-),/10X,'TOTAL CURRENT ASSETS',20X,F14.2,5X,
   6'TOTAL CURRENT LIABILITIES',11X,F14.2,//,2X,'PLANT AND EQUIPMENT',
   713X,F14.2,17X'LONG TERM DEBT',26X,F14.2,//,2X,
   8  'LESS ACCUMULATED DEPRECIATION',3X,F14.2,2X,F14.2,1X,
   9'STOCKHOLDER EQUITY:',
   1/,34X,14(1H-),2X,14(1H-),/,10X,'TOTAL ASSETS',28X,F14.2,5X,
   1'COMMON STOCK',8X,F14.2,//,69X,'CAPITAL SURPLUS',5X,F14.2,//,69X,
   2'RETAINED EARNING',4X,F14.2,2X,F14.2,/,
   389X,14(1H-),2X,14(1H-),/,65X,
   4'TOTAL LIABILITIES AND EQUITY'12X,F14.2,////)
109 FORMAT(10X,'RAW MATERIAL COSTS',22X,F14.2,//,10X,'DIRECT LABOR',
   128X,F14.2,//,10X,'DEPRECIATION', 28X,F14.2,//,10X,
   2'OTHER MANUFACTURING EXPENSES',12X,F14.2,/,50X,14(1H-),/,14X,
   3'TOTAL COST OF PRODUCTION',12X,F14.2,//,14X,'(UNITS PRODUCED)',
   419X,'(',F14.2,')',//,14X,'(UNIT COST OF PRODUCTION)',
   510X,'(',F14.2,')'//10X'ADD BEGINNING INVENTORY',17X,F14.2/50X,
   614(1H-),/,50X,F14.2,/ ,10X,'LESS ENDING INVENTORY',19X,F14.2,/,
   750X,14(1H-),/,14X,'COST OF GOODS SOLD',18X,F14.2,////)
111  FORMAT(10X,'NET SALES',21X,F14.2,//,10X,'COST OF GOODS SOLD',
   112X,F14.2,/,40X,14(1H-),/,40X,F14.2,/, 10X,
   2'SELLING,ADMINISTRATIVE,',/,10X,'AND GENERAL EXPENSES',10X,F14.2,
   3/,40X,14(1H-),/,40X,F14.2,//,10X,'INTEREST EXPENSES',13X,F14.2,/,
   440X,14(1H-)/40X,F14.2,//,10X,'FEDERAL INCOME TAX',12X,F14.2,/,
   540X,14(1H-),/,10X,'NET PROFIT',20X,F14.2,/,40X,14(1H-),/,
   640X,14(1H-),//,10X,'DIVIDEND',22X,F14.2,/,40X,14(1H-),/,10X,
   7'TRANSFER TO EARNED'12X,F14.2,/,10X,'SURPLUS',////)
120 STOP
    END
```

Figure B-2 Simulation of the Risk of Insolvency

```
C      SIMULATION OF THE RISK OF INSOLVENCY
C
C      XN           LENGTH OF RECESSION PERIOD
C      XSALES       ARRAY CONTAINING DAILY CREDIT SALES
C      XDELTA       ARRAY CONTAINING CHANGE IN LENGTH OF CCLLECTION PERIOC
C      NTIMES       NUMBER OF SIMULATIONS
C      ISEED        INITIAL VALUE FOR RANDOM NUMBER GENERATCR
C      OVER         NUMBER OF SIMULATIONS WITH POSITIVE ENDING CASH BALANCE
C      UNDER        NUMBER OF SIMULATIONS WITH NEGATIVE ENDING CASH BALANCE
C      PROB         ARRAY CONTAINING JOINT PROBABILITIES OF XSALES AND XDELTA
C      ACCPR        ARRAY CONTAINING ACCUMULATED PROBABILITY DISTRIBUTION
C      B            GROSS MARGIN PERCENTAGE
C      D            OUTSTANDING DEBT
C      C            COLLECTION OF RECEIVABLES DURING RECESSION
C      V            VARIABLE CASH EXPENSES DURING RECESSICN (EXCLUDING TAXES)
C      F            TOTAL FIXED EXPENSES DURING RECESSION
C      XI           TOTAL INTEREST EXPENSES DURING RECESSION
C      T            TOTAL TAX PAYMENT DURING RECESSION
C      K            CASH BALANCE AT END OF RECESSION
C      CASH1        CASH BALANCE AT START OF RECESSION
C      CASH2        SUM OF K VALUES FOR ENTIRE SIMULATICN
C      AVCASH       AVERAGE VALUE OF K FOR ENTIRE SIMULATION
C
      DIMENSION PROB(16),ACCPR(17),XSALES(16),XDELTA(16)
      DATA XSALES/5.,5.,5.,5.,4.8,4.8,4.8,4.8,4.3,4.3,4.3,4.3,4.1,4.1,
     14.1,4.1/
      DATA XDELTA/10.,20.,30.,40.,10.,20.,30.,40.,10.,20.,30.,40.,10.,
     120.,30.,40./
      REAL K
      NTIMES=100
      XTIMES=NTIMES
      ISEED=1743
      READ(5,100) (PROB(I),I=1,16)
  100 FORMAT(4F10.4)
      WRITE(6,101)
  101 FORMAT(//,' JOINT PROBABILITY MATRIX: ',//)
      WRITE(6,102) (PROB(I),I=1,16)
  102 FORMAT(4(1X,F10.4))
      ACCPR(1)=0.0
      DO 103 I=1,16
  103 ACCPR(I+1)=ACCPR(I)+PROB(I)
  104 READ(5,100)XN, B, D
      IF(XN.EQ.0.0) GO TO 105
      OVER=0.0
      UNDER=0.0
      CASH2=0.0
      WRITE(6,106)XN, B, D
  106 FORMAT(//,1X,'XN = ',F10.2,3X,'XB=   ',F10.2,3X,'XD = ',F10.2)
      DO 107 LL=1,NTIMES
      XX=UNIRAN(ISEED)
      DO 108 J=1,16
      IF(ACCPR(J).LT.XX.AND.XX.LE.ACCPR(J+1))GO TO 109
  108 CONTINUE
  109 SALES=XSALES(J)
      DELTA=XDELTA(J)
      CASH1=40.
      C=165.+SALES*(XN-30.-DELTA)
      V=(1.-B)*SALES*XN
      F=1.888*XN
      XI=D*.08*XN/360.
      T=.5*(SALES*XN*B-F-.3125*XN-XI)
      IF(T.LT.0.0)T=0.0
      K=CASH1+C-V-F-XI-T
      IF(K.GT.0.0)OVER=OVER+1.0
      IF(K.LE.0.0)UNDER=UNDER+1.
      CASH2=CASH2+K
  107 CONTINUE
      AVCASH=CASH2/XTIMES
      WRITE(6,110)
  110 FORMAT(  /' PERCENT SOLVENT',5X'PERCENT INSOLVENT',5X,'AVERAGE CA
     1SH',/)
```

Figure B-2 (*continued*)

```
      OVER=OVER*100./XTIMES
      UNDER=UNDER*100./XTIMES
      WRITE(6,111)OVER,UNDER,AVCASH
  111 FORMAT(2X,F14.3,9X,F14.3,5X,F14.2)
      GO TO 104
  105 STOP
      END
      REAL FUNCTION UNIRAN(KSEED)
      KSEED=KSEED*1220703125
      IF(KSEED) 1,2,2
    1 KSEED=KSEED+2147483647+1
    2 TEMP=KSEED
      UNIRAN=TEMP*.4656613E-9
      RETURN
      END
```

Figure B-3 Rate-of-Return Calculations

```
C     RATE-OF-RETURN CALCULATIONS
C
C     NGRPS       NUMBER OF PROJECTS TO BE ANALYZED
C     N           DURATION OF PROJECT (IN PERIODS)
C     N1          N1 = N + 1
C     A           ARRAY CONTAINING EACH PERIOD'S CASH FLOW
C     SN          PROJECT BALANCES FOR A SIMPLE INVESTMENT
C     SNX         PROJECT BALANCES FOR A NONSIMPLE, MIXED INVESTMENT
C     SNK         PROJECT BALANCES FOR A MIXED INVESTMENT
C     R           INTERNAL RATE OF RETURN (PURE CASE);
C                 RETURN ON INVESTED CAPITAL (MIXED CASE)
C     XK          COST OF CAPITAL
C     XINC        INCREMENTAL CHANGE IN R TO FIND EXACT SOLUTION BY
C                 TRIAL-AND-ERROR METHOD
      INTEGER D
      DIMENSION A(30),SNX(30),SNK(30)
      LOGICAL L,LL
      READ (5,10) NGRPS
   10 FORMAT(I3)
      DO 1000 ILOOP=1,NGRPS
      WRITE(6,20)
   20 FORMAT(1H1)
      READ(5,10) N
      N1=N+1
      READ(5,30) (A(I),I=1,N1)
   30 FORMAT(4F20.10)
      WRITE(6,40) N
   40 FORMAT(1X,'N = ',I3//)
      WRITE(6,50)
   50 FORMAT(1X,'CASH FLOW FOR EACH OF N PERIODS'/)
      WRITE(6,70) A(1)
      WRITE(6,60) (A(I),I=2,N1)
   60 FORMAT(1X,5(5X,F12.3)/)
      XINC=.2
      L=.FALSE.
   70 FORMAT(6X,F12.3/)
      DO 100 D=2,N1
      IF (A(D).LT.0.0) GO TO 300
  100 CONTINUE
      R=-XINC
  105 CONTINUE
  110 CONTINUE
      R=R+XINC
  115 SN=A(N1)
      Z=1.0
      DO 120 I=2,N1
      J=N1-I+1
      Z=Z*(1.+R)
  120 SN=SN+A(J)*Z
      IF (SN.LE.0.0) GO TO 150
```

Figure B-3 (*continued*)

```
      IF (.NOT.L) GO TO 250
      TEM=XINC/(ABS(R+XINC))
      IF (TEM.LT..002) GO TO 150
      XINC=XINC/2.
      GO TO 250
150   IF (SN.GE.0.0) GO TO 220
      IF (R.LE.0.0) GO TO 200
      XINC=XINC/2.
200   R=R-XINC
      L=.TRUE.
      GO TO 115
220   WRITE(6,225) R
225   FORMAT(//,3X,'IRR = ',F7.4)
      GO TO 1000
250   CONTINUE
      TE4=XINC/(ABS(R+XINC))
      IF (TE4.GE..002) GO TO 110
      GO TO 270
260   FORMAT(//,3X,'IRR IS GREATER THAN',F7.4,' BUT MAXIMUM INCREMENTA',
     $'L VALUE IS ONLY ',F10.6//'      FOR PRACTICAL PURPOSES IRR IS E',
     $'QUAL TO ',F7.4)
270   WRITE(6,260) R,XINC,R
      GO TO 1000
300   LL=.FALSE.
      R=0.
320   SNX(1)=A(1)
      DO 400 J=2,N
      J1=J-1
      SNX(J)=SNX(J1)*(1.+R)+A(J)
      IF (SNX(J).LE.0.0) GO TO 400
      IF (.NOT.LL) GO TO 350
      XINC=XINC/2.
350   R=R+XINC
      GO TO 320
400   CONTINUE
      IF (R.EQ.0.0) GO TO 450
      TEN2=XINC/(ABS(R+XINC))
      IF (TEN2.LT..002) GO TO 450
      XINC=XINC/2.
      R=R-XINC
      LL=.TRUE.
      GO TO 320
450   CONTINUE
      WRITE(6,460) R
460   FORMAT(//,3X,'RMIN = ',F7.4)
      SNX(N1)=SNX(N)*(1.+R)+A(N1)
      IF (SNX(N1).GE.0.0) GO TO 950
      WRITE(6,20)
      WRITE(6,500)
500   FORMAT(1X,'COST OF CAPITAL',10X,'RETURN ON INVESTED CAPITAL'/)
      XK=-.0025
      LWRT=4
      LCT=0
      DO 900 K=1,4001
      XK=XK+.0025
      R=0.0
      XINC=.2
      L=.FALSE.
550   SNK(1)=A(1)
      DO 600 M=2,N1
      SNK(M)=SNK(M-1)*(1.+R)+A(M)
      IF (SNK(M-1).GT.0.0) SNK(M)=SNK(M-1)*(1.+XK)+A(M)
600   CONTINUE
      IF (XINC.LT.1.0E-7) SNK(N1)=0.0
      IF (SNK(N1).LE.0.0) GO TO 750
      IF (.NOT.L) GO TO 700
      XX=ABS(R+XINC)
      IF (XX.EQ.0.0) TEM3=10.
      IF (TEM3.EQ.10.) GO TO 650
      TEM3=XINC/(ABS(R+XINC))
650   CONTINUE
```

Figure B-3 *(continued)*

```
      IF (TEM3.LT..002) GO TO 750
      XINC=XINC/2.
  700 R=R+XINC
      GO TO 550
  750 CONTINUE
      IF (SNK(N1).GE.0.0) GO TO 850
      IF (R.LE.0.0) GO TO 800
      XINC=XINC/2.
  800 R=R-XINC
      L=.TRUE.
      GO TO 550
  850 CONTINUE
      IF (K.EQ.4001) GO TO 865
      IF (LCT.EQ.0) GO TO 865
      LCT=LCT+1
      IF (LCT.LE.LWRT) GO TO 900
      LCT=0
  865 LCT=LCT+1
      WRITE(6,870) XK,R
  203 FORMAT (5X,I5)
  870 FORMAT(2X,F12.6,21X,F12.6)
      IF (K.EQ.401) GO TO 1000
  900 CONTINUE
  950 XINC=.2
      GO TO 105
 1000 CONTINUE
      STOP
      END
```

Figure B-4 **Capital Budgeting with Divestment Option**

```
C     CAPITAL BUDGETING WITH DIVESTMENT OPTION
C
C     A0          CASH FLOW AT TIME 0
C     A1          CASH FLOW AT TIME 1
C     A2          CASH FLOW AT TIME 2
C     A3          CASH FLOW AT TIME 3
C     NPV         NET PRESENT VALUE OF PROJECT
C     AV          EXPECTED VALUE OF NPV
C     VAR         VARIANCE OF NPV
C     SDVNPV      STANDARD DEVIATION OF NPV
C     AVA1        EXPECTED VALUE OF A1
C     AVA2        EXPECTED VALUE OF A2
C     AVA3        EXPECTED VALUE OF A3
C     VARA1       VARIANCE OF A1
C     VARA2       VARIANCE OF A2
C     VARA3       VARIANCE OF A3
C     COVA12      COVARIANCE OF A1, A2
C     COVA13      COVARIANCE OF A1, A3
C     COVA23      COVARIANCE OF A2, A3
C     K           RATE OF DISCOUNT
C
      REAL K,NPV
      K=.07
      A0=-11000.
      SUM=0.0
      SUM2=0.0
      SUMA1=0.0
      SUMA2=0.0
      SUMA3=0.0
      SUM2A1=0.0
      SUM2A2=0.0
      SUM2A3=0.0
      SUMA12=0.0
      SUMA13=0.0
      SUMA23=0.0
      DO 10 I=1,27
```

Figure B-4 (*continued*)

```
      READ(5,100) A1, A2, A3
  100 FORMAT(3F10.2)
      NPV=A0 + A1/(1.+K) + A2/((1.+K)**2.) + A3/((1.+K)**3.)
      SUM=NPV+SUM
      SUM2=NPV*NPV+SUM2
      SUMA1=SUMA1+A1
      SUMA2=SUMA2+A2
      SUMA3=SUMA3+A3
      SUM2A1=SUM2A1+A1*A1
      SUM2A2=SUM2A2+A2*A2
      SUM2A3=SUM2A3+A3*A3
      SUMA12=SUMA12+A1*A2
      SUMA13=SUMA13+A1*A3
      SUMA23=SUMA23+A2*A3
   10 WRITE(6,300) A0, A1, A2, A3, NPV
      AV=SUM/27.
      VAR=SUM2/27.-AV*AV
      SDVNPV=SQRT(VAR)
      WRITE(6,400) AV,VAR,SDVNPV
  400 FORMAT(' E(NPV) =', F10.4,3X,'VAR(NPV) = ',F14.4,3X,'STDV(NPV) =',
     1F14.2)
  300 FORMAT(5(2X,F10.2))
      AVA1=SUMA1/27.
      AVA2=SUMA2/27.
      AVA3=SUMA3/27.
      VARA1=SUM2A1/27.-AVA1*AVA1
      VARA2=SUM2A2/27.-AVA2*AVA2
      VARA3=SUM2A3/27.-AVA3*AVA3
      COVA12=SUMA12/27.-AVA1*AVA2
      COVA13=SUMA13/27.-AVA1*AVA3
      COVA23=SUMA23/27.-AVA2*AVA3
      WRITE(6,202)
  202 FORMAT('      E(A1)          E(A2)          E(A3)        VAR(A1)        VAR
     1(A2)       VAR(A3)       COV(A1,A2)     COV(A1,A2)    COV(A2,A3)',/)
      WRITE(6,201) AVA1,AVA2,AVA3,VARA1,VARA2,VARA3,COVA12,COVA13,COVA23
  201 FORMAT(9(1X,F12.2))
      STOP
      END
```

Figure B-5 Cash Budgeting and Sensitivity Analysis

```
C       CASH BUDGETING AND SENSITIVITY ANALYSIS
C
C       FSALES(I)    FSALES(1),FSALES(2), AND FSALES(3) = THE SALES
C                    FOR THE LAST THREE MONTHS OF THE PREVIOUS YEAR
C                    FSALES(I+3) = 'BASIC' FORECAST OF SALES FOR
C                    MONTH I OF THE COMING YEAR
C       AFACT(J)     THE PERCENTAGE BY WHICH THE FORECAST VALUES IN
C                    FSALES ARE TO BE RAISED OR LOWERED
C       SALES(I)     REVISED SALES FORECAST, EQUAL TO BASIC FORECAST PLUS
C                    OR MINUS AFACT PERCENTAGES
C       PRML         PAYMENT FOR MATERIALS (PERCENTAGE OF CURRENT SALES)
C       PLCO         PAYMENT FOR LABOR AND CASH OVERHEAD (PERCENTAGE OF
C                    SALES 3 MONTHS HENCE)
C       SAE          SELLING AND ADMINISTRATIVE EXPENSES
C       ASAE(I)      SELLING AND ADMINISTRATIVE EXPENSES FOR MONTH I
C                    (EQUAL TO SAE IN THE FIRST MONTH OF EACH QUARTER;
C                    ZERO OTHERWISE)
C       DVT          DIVIDENDS AND TAXES
C       ADVT(I)      DIVIDENDS AND TAXES FOR MONTH I (EQUAL TO DVT IN
C                    THE THIRD MONTH OF EACH QUARTER; ZERO OTHERWISE)
C       SKF          SINKING FUND
C       ASKF(I)      SINKING FUND IN MONTH I (EQUAL TO SKF IN
C                    JANUARY AND JULY; ZERO OTHERWISE)
C       PLT          PLATES
C       APLT(I)      PAYMENT FOR PLATES IN MONTH I (EQUAL TO PLT IN
C                    JANUARY AND JUNE; ZERO OTHERWISE)
C       TSD(I)       TOTAL CASH SURPLUS OR DEFICIT IN MONTH I
```

Figure B-5 ***(continued)***

```
C      CSD(I)       CUMULATIVE CASH SURPLUS OR DEFICIT FOR MONTHS
C                   UP TO AND INCLUDING MONTH I
C
       DIMENSION FSALES(18),SALES(18),RML(12),ALCO(12),ASAE(12),ADVT(12),
      1ASKF(12),APLT(12),TSD(12),CSD(12),AFACT(4),ADJUST(9)
       READ(5,30) FSALES
    30 FORMAT(2X,9F8.1)
       READ(5,30) PRML,PLCO,SAE,DVT,SKF,PLT
       READ (5,30) AFACT
       M=1
       ADJUST(1)=1.0
       DO 1 I=1,4
       IF(ABS(AFACT(I)).LT..001)GO TO 1
       ADJUST(M+1)=1.0+AFACT(I)/100.0
       ADJUST(M+2)=1.0-AFACT(I)/100.0
       M=M+2
     1 SALES(I)=FSALES(I)
       DO 8 K=1,M
       DO 2 I=4,18
     2 SALES(I)=FSALES(I)*ADJUST(K)
       WRITE(6,40)
    40 FORMAT(55X,'CASH BUDGET',//)
       IF (K.GT.1)WRITE(6,41)ADJUST(K)
    41 FORMAT(30X,'IN THIS BUDGET THE ORIGINAL FORECASTS HAVE BEEN ',
      1     'MULTIPLIED BY A FACTOR OF ',F5.2,//)
       WRITE(6,42)
    42 FORMAT(2X,'LINE'4X,'ITEM',13X,'JAN    FEB    MAR    APR    MAY',
      1  '   JUNE   JULY   AUG   SEPT    OCT    NOV    DEC',//)
       WRITE(6,44) (SALES(I),I=1,12)
    44 FORMAT(4X,'1  COLLECTION',7X,12F7.1)
       DO 3 I=1,12
     3 RML(I)=.01*PRML*SALES(I+3)
       WRITE(6,46) RML
    46 FORMAT(4X,'2  MATERIALS',8X,12F7.1)
       DO 4 I=1,12
     4 ALCO(I)=.01*PLCO*SALES(I+6)
       WRITE(6,47) ALCO
    47 FORMAT(4X,'3  LABOR & CASH OVHD',12F7.1)
       DO 5 I=1,12
       ASAE(I)=0.0
       ADVT(I)=0.0
       ASKF(I)=0.0
     5 APLT(I)=0.0
       DO 6 I=1,4
       J=3*I-2
       ASAE(J)=SAE
       J=3*I
     6 ADVT(J)=DVT
       ASKF(1)=SKF
       ASKF(7)=SKF
       APLT(1)=PLT
       APLT(6)=PLT
       WRITE(6,48) ASAE
    48 FORMAT(4X,'4  SELLING & ADM EXP',12F7.1)
       WRITE(6,49) ADVT
    49 FORMAT(4X'5  DIV & TAXES',6X,12F7.1)
       WRITE(6,50) ASKF
    50 FORMAT(4X,'6  SINKING FUND',5X,12F7.1)
       WRITE(6,51) APLT
    51 FORMAT(4X,'7  PLATES ',10X,12F7.1,//)
       SUM=0.0
       DO 7 I=1,12
       TSD(I)=  SALES(I)-RML(I)-ALCO(I)-ASAE(I)-ADVT(I)-ASKF(I)-APLT(I)
       SUM=SUM+TSD(I)
     7 CSD(I)=SUM
       WRITE(6,52)TSD
    52 FORMAT(3X,' 8  TOTAL SURPLUS     ',12F7.1,//)
       WRITE(6,53)CSD
    53 FORMAT(3X,' 9  CUM SURPLUS       ',12F7.1,///)
       WRITE(6,54) (SALES(I),I=13,15)
    54 FORMAT(2X,'SALES FOR THE LAST THREE MONTHS OF THE ',
      1  'YEAR WERE TAKEN TO BE ',3F7.1)
```

Figure B-5 *(continued)*

```
      WRITE(6,55) (SALES(I),I=16,18)
   55 FORMAT(2X,'SALES FOR THE FIRST THREE MONTHS OF THE FOLLOWING ',
     1 'YEAR WERE TAKEN TO BE ',3F7.1)
      WRITE(6,56)PRML
   56 FORMAT(2X,'PAYMENT FOR MATERIALS IS ',F5.1,' PER CENT OF ',
     1 'PRESENT SALES')
    8 WRITE(6,57)PLCO
   57 FORMAT(2X,'LABOR AND CASH OVERHEAD IS ',F5.1,' PER CENT OF ',
     1   'SALES THREE MONTHS AHEAD',////)
      STOP
      END
```

Figure B-6 Leasing vs. Borrowing

```
C       LEASING VERSUS BORROWING
C       (THIS PROGRAM ALSO GENERATES THE CASH FLOWS TO LESSOR AND
C       A LEASE AMORTIZATION SCHEDULE AS A PART OF ITS OUTPUT.)
C
C       N           LEASE PERIOD
C       CAPOUT      EQUIPMENT COST
C       R           NOMINAL LEASE RATE
C       T           LESSOR'S TAX RATE
C       T2          LESSEE'S TAX RATE
C       ITC         INVESTMENT TAX CREDIT
C       A           ANNUAL LEASE PAYMENT (FIRST PAYMENT AT TIME 0)
C       RENTIN      ANNUAL RENTAL RECEIPT
C       DEP         DEPRECIATION
C       TAX         INCOME TAX PAYMENTS OR SAVINGS
C       OUTLAY      EQUIPMENT COST
C       FLOW        CASH FLOWS TO LESSOR
C       RR          AFTER-TAX YIELD TO LESSOR
C       BTYTL       BEFORE-TAX YIELD TO LESSOR
C       SUMDEP      ACCUMULATED DEPRECIATION
C       OUTBAL      OUTSTANDING LEASE BALANCE
C       PUTINT      IMPUTED INTEREST IN LEASE AMORTIZATION
C       REC         RECOVERY OF PRINCIPAL IN LEASE AMORTIZATION
C       INT         INTEREST IN LOAN AMORTIZATION
C       PRM         PRINCIPAL REPAYMENT IN LOAN AMORTIZATION
C       TS          TAX SAVINGS TO LESSEE UNDER LEASING ALTERNATIVE
C       TS2         TAX SAVINGS TO OWNER UNDER BORROWING ALTERNATIVE
C       CF          NET CASH OUTFLOWS OF LESSEE (LEASING ALTERNATIVE)
C       FV          FUTURE VALUE OF CF
C       LOAN        LOAN UNDER BORROWING ALTERNATIVE (= CAPOUT - A)
C       B           ANNUAL PAYMENT ON LOAN
C       L           OUTSTANDING LOAN BALANCE
C       FLOW2       NET CASH OUTFLOWS OF OWNER (BORROWING ALTERNATIVE)
C       FV2         FUTURE VALUE OF FLOW2
C       SUM         TOTAL FUTURE VALUE
C
        DIMENSION RENTIN(100),DEP(100),TAX(100),OUTLAY(100),FLOW(100)
        DIMENSION PUTINT(100),REC(100),OUTBAL(100),CASBAL(100)
        DIMENSION INT(100),PRM(100),L(100),TS2(100),FLOW2(100)
        DIMENSION FV2(100)
        REAL ITC,INT,K,L,LOAN
        READ(5,100)N,CAPOUT,R,T,ITC,K,T2
    100 FORMAT(I10,6F10.2)
        NN=N-1
        SUM=0.0
        DO 10 I=1,NN
     10 SUM=SUM+1.0/((1.+R)**I)
        A=CAPOUT/(1.+SUM)
        XN =N
        N1=N+1
        RENTIN(N1)=0.0
        DEP(1)=0.0
        DEP(2)=CAPOUT*2./XN
        SUMDEP=0.0
        TAX(1)=ITC*CAPOUT-A*T
```

Figure B-6 (*continued*)

```
      OUTLAY(1)=-CAPOUT
      DO 20 I=1,N1
      IF(I.NE.N1)RENTIN(I)=A
      IF(I.GT.2.AND.I.NE.N1)DEP(I)=(1.-2./XN)*DEP(I-1)
      IF(I.NE.N1)SUMDEP=SUMDEP+DEP(I)
      IF(I.EQ.N1)DEP(I)=CAPOUT-SUMDEP
      IF(I.NE.1)TAX(I)=(DEP(I)-RENTIN(I))*T
      IF(I.NE.1)OUTLAY(I)=0.0
   20 FLOW(I) = RENTIN(I) + TAX(I) + OUTLAY(I)
      WRITE(6,200)
  200 FORMAT(//,' END OF YEAR',2X,'RENTAL INCOME',2X,'DEPRECIATION',2X,
     1'INCOME TAX',2X,'CAPITAL OUTLAY',2X,'NET FLOW',//)
      DO 30 I=1,N1
      J=I-1
   30 WRITE(6,300)J,RENTIN(I),DEP(I),TAX(I),OUTLAY(I),FLOW(I)
  300 FORMAT(4X,I4,6X,F10.2,6X,F10.2,3X,F10.2,4X,F10.2,4X,F10.2)
      CALL IRR(FLOW,N,RR)
      BTYTL=RR/(1.-T)
      WRITE(6,400)RR,BTYTL
  400 FORMAT(//,' YIELD TO LESSOR AFTER TAX = ',F8.5,//,' BEFORE TAX YIE
     1LD TO LESSOR = ',F8.5,//)
      OUTBAL(1)=-FLOW(1)
      SUMDEP=0.0
      DO 40 I=2,N1
      SUMDEP=SUMDEP+DEP(I)
      PUTINT(I)=RR*OUTBAL(I-1)
      REC(I)=FLOW(I)-PUTINT(I)
   40 OUTBAL(I)=OUTBAL(I-1)-REC(I)
      WRITE(6,500)
  500 FORMAT(//,' END OF YEAR',3X,'NET FLOW',3X,'IMPUTED INTEREST',2X,'R
     1ECOVERY OF PRINCIPAL',2X,'OUTSTANDING BALANCE')
      J=0
      WRITE(6,600)J,FLOW(1),OUTBAL(1)
      DO 50 I=2,N1
      J=I-1
   50 WRITE(6,700)J,FLOW(I),PUTINT(I),REC(I),OUTBAL(I)
  600 FORMAT(4X,I4,4X,F10.2,47X,F10.2)
  700 FORMAT(4X,I4,4X,F10.2,5X,F10.2,10X,F10.2,12X,F10.2)
      SUM=0.0
      WRITE(6,900)
  900 FORMAT(////,' END OF YEAR',2X,'LEASE PAYMENT',2X,'TAX SAVINGS',2X,
     1'NET CASH FLOW',2X,'FUTURE VALUE')
      DO 60 I=1,N
      J=I-1
      TS=A*T2
      CF=A-TS
      FV=CF*((1.+(1.-T2)*K)**(N-I+1))
      SUM=SUM+FV
   60 WRITE(6,800)J,A,TS,CF,FV
  800 FORMAT(4X,I4,6X,F10.2,5X,F10.2,1X,F10.2,5X,F10.2)
      WRITE(6,1000)SUM
 1000 FORMAT(//' TOTAL FUTURE VALUE = ',F10.2,//////////)
      SUM=0.0
      DO 70 I=1,NN
   70 SUM=SUM + 1./((1.+K)**I)
      LOAN=CAPOUT-A
      B=LOAN/SUM
      INT(1)=0.0
      INT(2)=K*LOAN
      INT(N1)=0.0
      PRM(2)=B-INT(2)
      L(2)=LOAN-PRM(2)
      DO 80 I=3,N
      INT(I)=L(I-1)*K
      PRM(I)=B-INT(I)
   80 L(I)=L(I-1)-PRM(I)
      TS2(1)=ITC*CAPOUT
      DO 90 I=2,N1
   90 TS2(I)=(INT(I)+DEP(I))*T2
      FLOW2(1)=A - TS2(1)
      DO 110 I=2,N
```

Figure B-6 *(continued)*

```
 110  FLOW2(I)=B-TS2(I)
      FLOW2(N1)=-TS2(N1)
      SUM=0.0
      DO 120 I=1,N1
      FV2(I)=FLOW2(I)*((1.+K*(1.-T2))**(N-I+1))
 120  SUM=SUM+FV2(I)
      WRITE(6,1100)
1100   FORMAT(///,' END OF YEAR',2X,'DOWN PAYMENT',2X,'LOAN REPAYMENT',
     12X,' INTEREST',2X,'DEPRECIATION',2X,'TAX SAVINGS',2X,'NET CASH FLO
     2W',2X,'FUTURE VALUE',//)
      XB=B
      XA=A
      DO 130 I=1,N1
      IF(I.EQ.1.OR.I.EQ.N1)XB=0.0
      IF(I.GT.1)XA=0.0
      J=I-1
      WRITE(6,1200) J,XA,XB,INT(I),DEP(I),TS2(I),FLOW2(I),FV2(I)
 130  XB=B
1200  FORMAT(4X,I4,7X,F10.2,2X,F10.2,1X,F10.2,3X,F10.2,3X,F10.2,3X,F10.2
     1,3X,F10.2)
      WRITE(6,1300) SUM
1300  FORMAT(//,' TOTAL FUTURE VALUE= ',F10.2,//)
      STOP
      END
      SUBROUTINE IRR(A,N,R)
      DIMENSION A(1)
      LOGICAL L
      N1=N+1
      XINC=.2
      L=.FALSE.
  70  FORMAT(6X,F12.3/)
      R=-XINC
 105  CONTINUE
 110  CONTINUE
      R=R+XINC
 115  SN=A(N1)
      Z=1.0
      DO 120 I=2,N1
      J=N1-I+1
      Z=Z*(1.+R)
 120  SN=SN+A(J)*Z
      IF (SN.LE.0.0) GO TO 150
      IF (.NOT.L) GO TO 250
      TEMP=ABS(R+XINC)
      IF(TEMP.EQ.0.0) GO TO 300
      TEM=XINC/(ABS(R+XINC))
      IF (TEM.LT..002) GO TO 150
 300  CONTINUE
      XINC=XINC/2.
      GO TO 250
 150  IF (SN.GE.0.0) GO TO 220
      IF (R.LE.0.0) GO TO 200
      XINC=XINC/2.
 200  R=R-XINC
      L=.TRUE.
      GO TO 115
 220  CONTINUE
      GO TO 1000
 250  CONTINUE
      TEMP=ABS(R+XINC)
      IF(TEMP.EQ.0.0) GO TO 110
      TE4=XINC/(ABS(R+XINC))
      IF (TE4.GE..002) GO TO 110
1000  RETURN
      END
```

Index